Family Systems

within

Educational Contexts

Understanding At-Risk
and Special-Needs Students

Rosemary Lambie
Virginia Commonwealth University

Love Publishing Company
Denver, Colorado 80237

Chapter 1, from "The Phi Delta Kappan study of students at risk" by J. Frymier & B. Gansneder, *Phi Delta Kappan, 71,* 142–146. Copyright 1989 by Phi Delta Kapan. Reprinted by permission of John Wiley & Sons, Inc.

Chapter 1, from "Needed: A Whole-Curriculum Approach" by Kenneth P. Komoski, *Educational Leadership, 47* (5), 72–78. Reprinted with permission from ASCD.

Chapter 5, from "Between Two Worlds: Cultural Discontinuity in the Dropout of Native American Youth" by M. W. Garrett, *The School Counselor, 42* (3), 186–195. Copyright 1995 by the American School Counselor Association. Reprinted by permission.

Chapter 5, from *Bread and Spirit: Therapy with the New Poor* by Harry J. Aponte. Copyright 1994 by Harry J. Aponte. Reprinted by permission of W. W. Norton & Company, Inc.

Chapter 6, from *The Vulnerable Child,* (pages 49, 63, 181, 183) by Richard Weissbourd. Copyright 1996 by Richard Weissbourd. Reprinted by permission of Addison Wesley Longman.

Chapter 7, from *The Adoptive Family as a Healing Resource for the Sexually Abused Child: A Training Manual,* (1990, page 3) by D. H. Minshew & C. Hooper. Reprinted by special permission of the Child Welfare League of America.

Chapter 7, from *The Violence of Men: New Techniques for Working with Abusive Families* by C. Madanes, J. P. Keim, & D. Smelser . Copyright 1995 by Jossey Bass Inc. Publishers. Reprinted by permission.

Chapter 7, from Strategies to Address Violence in the Lives of high-risk Youth by D. A. Wolfe, C. Wekerle, D. Reitzel, & R. Gough in E. Peled, P.G. Jaffe, & J. Edleson (Eds.), *Ending the cycle of violence: Community responses to children of battered women* (pp 255–274). Copyright 1995 by Sage Publications. Reprinted by permission of Sage Publications.

Chapter 8, from *Practicing Family Therapy in Diverse Settings* by M. Berger. Copyright 1984 by Jossey Bass Inc. Publishers. Reprinted by permission.

Chapter 8, from "Parental Perspectives on Attention Deficit/Hyperactivity Disorder: How School Counselors Can Help" by T. Kottman, R. Robert, & D. Baker, *The School Counselor, 43* (2), 142–150. Copyright 1995 by the American School Counselor Association. Reprinted by permission.

Chapter 9, from *The Prophet* by Kahlil Gibran. Copyright 1923 by Kahlil Gibran and renewed 1951 by Administrators CTA of Kahlil Gibran Estate and Mary G. Gibran. Reprinted by permission of Alfred A. Knopf, Inc.

Chapter 9, from *Communication of Social Support: Messages, interactions, relationships, and community* by B. R. Burleson, T. L. Albrecht, & I. G. Sarason. Copyright 1994 by Sage Publications. Reprinted by permission of Sage Publications.

Chapter 10, from Integrating Specialized Curricula by D. M. Switlick in D. F. Bradley, M. E. King-Sears, & D. M. Terrier-Switlick (Eds*.), Teaching Students in Inclusive Settings: From Theory to Practice* (pp 252–282). Copyright 1997 by Allyn & Bacon. Reprinted by permission.

Chapter 11, from *A Resource Handbook for Satir Concepts* by J. Schwab. Copyright 1990 by Science & Behavior Books. Reprinted by permission of J. Schwab and Science & Behavior Books.

Chapter 12, from "Making Homework at Home: The Parent's Perspective" by P. J. Kay, M. Fitzgerald, C. Paradee, and A. Mellencamp, 1994, *Journal of Learning Disabilities, 27* (9), 550–561. Copyright 1994 by PRO-ED, Inc. Reprinted by permission.

Chapter 13, from *Principles of Problem Formation and Problem Resolution* by Paul Watzlawick, John Weakland, and Richar Fisch. Copyright 1974 by W. W. Norton & Company, Inc. Reprinted by permission of W. W. Norton & Company, Inc.

Chapter 14, from The Process of Reorganization by S. A. Roy in H. G. Garner (Ed.), *Teamwork Models and Experience in Education.* Copyright 1995 by Allyn & Bacon. Reprinted by permission.

Chapter 15, from *Satir, Step by Step* by V. Satir & M. Baldwin. Copyright 1983 by Science & Behavior Books. Reprinted by permission of V. Satir, M. Baldwin, and Science & Behavior Books.

Published by Love Publishing Company
Denver, Colorado 80237

Copyright © 2000 Love Publishing Company
Printed in the United States of America
ISBN 0-89108-265-4
Library of Congress Catalog Card Number 98–67860

Preface

When I came to the field of family systems after years of being a teacher in the field of special and general education, I had reached the conclusion that special-needs and at-risk children and youth came from families with substantial challenges and that, when those challenges were faced, the pupils would make greater gains. In 1982–1983, I attended monthly seminars in the Washington, DC, area led by Drs. Murray Bowen and Michael Kerr of the Georgetown Family Center. During that year, I also attended a 3-day workshop conducted by Virginia Satir. In the summer of 1983, I attended one of Satir's month-long institutes in Crested Butte, Colorado. It was then that I realized the field of family systems had much to offer to professionals who worked with families of special-needs and at-risk children.

During the next several years, I completed my licensure requirements and became a licensed professional counselor. Since 1991, I have been the executive director of the Behavioral Intervention Program, at Virginia Commonwealth University, which provides services to individuals with disabilities as well as their families, schools, and service providers. Our in-home, in situ services are provided to a diverse population, most of whom are minorities who live in situations that place them at risk.

In the fall of 1983, I began the first of 6 pivotal years of training in family systems at the Family Institute of Virginia. "The Person and Practice of the Therapist," a supervisory group, co-led by Harry Aponte and Joan Winter, met for 2 days a month during each academic year. What I learned from this family systems training group about my own family-of-origin—one that included a chronically physically ill parent, a child with a severe learning disability, and a child with other special needs—taught me a great deal. The knowledge I acquired on family systems has made a great difference in my life and in the lives of the many at-risk and special-needs children and youth with whom I have worked.

The co-author of the first edition of this text, clinical psychologist Debbie Daniels-Mohring, also belonged to the family systems training group mentioned above. She has a doctoral degree in psychology and majors in family therapy and child clinical studies. Her influence continues to be felt within the second edition of this textbook; however, due to the time constraints of a busy clinical practice, she chose not to be involved in this revision. My hope is that our blending of experiences will continue to make a difference for school professionals reading the second edition of this text.

Why This Book Was Written

The first edition of this text was conceived by two authors who grew up in families with children who had disabilities. Both acquired a deeper level of understanding about their respective family experiences by studying family systems approaches. Both also felt a deep commitment to sharing their insights and understandings as well as methodology with school professionals and those who train them.

The first edition of this book stemmed from a collaborative training effort conducted by Dr. Daniels-Mohring and myself on a state-funded training grant. The positive response of the audience to that training in family systems resulted in our decision to write the original text. I committed to write an expanded, enlarged second edition to reflect changes in the fields of education and family systems. All chapters were extensively updated to reflect current thinking. A new chapter was added and one chapter was divided into two chapters because the field had burgeoned over time. This second edition contains expanded appendices, with a new one devoted exclusively to books for children and youth. The number of books listed for professionals and family members has been quadrupled. Virginia Commonwealth University graduate assistants Jennifer Grossnickle, Tabitha Hogge, and Holly Kagan and I made every effort to include a few words on as many books as possible listed in the appendices. We updated and expanded Appendix D, which lists resources for families and professionals, and we included the web sites or e-mail addresses for all resources having them. We contacted every resource listed in the first edition for updated information.

With the ever-changing nature of families in our society, I also wanted to expand on information in the text itself concerning changing family demographics and challenging home life situations. To that end, I added a chapter on resilient children and youth and the community as resource. We can learn much about how to improve the lives of at-risk and special-needs children and youth by knowing what contributes to their resilience. Thus, the emphasis of this second edition has been expanded to go beyond students with disabilities to include students with any kind of special need and their families as well as their social networks. As we increasingly face natural disasters, violence, and trauma in the world around us, it becomes more and more critical for school professionals to know how to become a healing influence with these students and their families rather than silent onlookers lacking the skill or Weltanschauung that can make a difference in their lives.

Acknowledgments

D r. Debbie Daniels-Mohring's influence continues to be felt in this second edition. I am appreciative of our collaboration and joint venture in writing the first edition.

I know there are angels on earth, because they helped me with this second edition. The archangel was Dr. Sherry Sandkam. Her diligence to detail in editing greatly increased the readability of this book. She also kept me stable during the difficult last weeks of revisions. I respect both her dedication to our field and the service she provided in this writing effort. Dr. John Seyfarth, my department chair, was supportive of my writing and provided necessary resources that allowed this work to come to completion, including editing a chapter on his personal time. Drs. Fred Orelove and Howard Garner also provided timely and important support during the final phase. Many thanks to Therese Eaton and Chris Mohring for their assistance with the editing. Mehdi Mansouri developed figures and tables that are readable and helpful when reading the text. Lisa Grinde, Tabitha Hogge, Jennifer Grossnickle, and Holly Kagan, four outstanding graduate assistants, helped me with library research, resources, and computer work as well as with copying and carrying books. Dr. Cathy Cauley was my cheerleader at VCU and she revived my spirits when needed. Chris Martin reflected with me about the book and provided meaningful insights that improved the content, edited chapters that relate to his work, and played with my infant daughter, Mariah, so I could have more time to write. I am grateful not only for that but also for his cheerful, supportive nature during the press to the finish line.

Also loving Mariah while I wrote were Kathy Benham, Jan Brandt, Patsy Hemp, Greta Gill, Suzee Leone, Linda Luck, Debbie Daniels-Mohring, Donna Moore, Maria Philips, Mindy Pignato, Lynda Richardson, Laura Robertson, Sherry Sandkam, Ellen Shaffer, and Wrenn Thompson. I have learned that *It takes a village to write a book* also! I am struck by the amazing beauty of those who have stood by me as well as helped me in this endeavor. My father's Scottish heritage makes it difficult for me to turn to others for help. It is something I have had to do, and I am deeply grateful to all who have been supportive. Beyond that, I realize that what I am writing about is true—that neighbors, friends, relatives, and strangers help us make it through life and that we are part of a community that makes life more meaningful and enjoyable as well as less stressful. Never have I been so aware of grace in community as in this past year. In this process of writing with an infant and turning to others for help and support, I realized that "when I train my eye to look in the right direction, I see great beauty." I thank all those people who formed a network of support surrounding me with love, encouragement, and raw hard work. I am richly blessed and humbled.

Again, Stan Love, has been most encouraging and patient. I am deeply appreciative of his support and input. His gentle nature makes writing much less stressful. Stepping in during the final stages, Tom Love has shown himself to be as considerate and respectful as his father. Beverly Rokes, copy editor at Love Publishing, has been a rare gift turning this manuscript into a textbook with high fidelity and readability. My thanks.

My family of origin and extended family have been my greatest teachers about family systems. Being the sibling of a child with a severe learning disability and the daughter of a father with severe, chronic physical illnesses have provided me with many opportunities for growth and affected my choice of careers. My large extended family on farms in Michigan has also taught me much about family as resource. They have shared life's joys and stood beside me through the trials and tribulations of family and life. Helen Miles, my fifth-grade teacher and my mother's best friend during my childhood, affected my view of life and family at a critical time in my childhood, and I continue to be appreciative of her influence. My adopted daughter, Mariah Rose, has brought the value of family systems into clear focus. She has given new meaning to family and enriched my life, now as part of a nuclear family, thus making the experience of writing this second edition even more meaningful and powerful.

Murray Bowen's theory of family systems has greatly affected my personal and professional life. In 1979 reading his work started me on my journey to understanding family systems concepts and approaches. The unexpected side benefit that has changed my life is that I now have a deep sense of connection to my extended family. That alone was worth the journey.

Virginia Satir died in 1988. I deeply appreciate the continued influence she has on my life. A lesson she taught me is that anything a human being has done can be understood and that any person can learn new ways of living with family, friends, and society. She did not judge people, and the tolerance she had for what many people quite understandably see as intolerable is a fitting tribute to a woman who had the capacity to surrender, forgive, and believe in the possibility for healing. I often heard her say, "Heal the family and you heal the planet."

Harry Aponte and Joan Winter provided 6 valuable years of family systems training.

Molly Dellinger-Wray, Kim Spears, Paul Rupf, Joel Diambra, Laura Robertson, and Emily Wilson have allowed me to supervise their work with families, schools, and service providers, enabling me to remain in contact with the everyday challenges faced by individuals with special needs. Their dedication to this population has been a privilege to witness.

I acknowledge Kathy Snowden, quintessential therapist, for holding up a light in the dark recesses of family life so that I might grow stronger and find the truth that frees creative spirit.

RAL

Dedication

- To Mariah Rose Lambie, light of my life and my greatest blessing

- To Sherry Sandkam, fairy godmother and midwife for this book

- To Debbie Daniels-Mohring, co-author of the first edition of this textbook and friend

- To the Virginia Commonwealth University students who have opened their hearts and minds to me, trusting me on their journey, thus providing for a gratifying professional life filled with awe and meaning

- To the pupils I have taught and their families, especially the Hallins in Denver, Colorado

- To my mother and father, my brothers, Tom and George; my sister-in-law Karen; my nephew Patrick and his mother Carla; and especially my extended family in Michigan who continue to support and care for us

- To the *family of man* and all who have faced significant family and life challenges

- To the *family* that has influenced my life in meaningful ways, celebrating with me the joys of life and standing by me through its challenges: Kathy Benham; Chris Clark; Cathy Cauley; Vic Dempsey; Joel, Trish, Nathan, and Nicole Diambra; Howard and Ann Garner; Greta, Joe, Sarah, and Joey Gill; Tom, Sandy, and Theresa Hale; Patsy Hemp; Carol Herod; Katty Inge; Jean and Wes Wilkinson;

Erik, Jannie, Stina, and Mickel Laursen; Suzee Leone; Linda, Allen, Allen, Travis, Molly, and Mason Luck; Chris Martin; Debbie and Kelsey Daniels-Mohring and Chris Mohring; Donna and Mike Moore; Fred Orelove; Maria Philips; Lynda Richardson; Laura, Michael, and Miles Robertson; Sherry Sandkam; Carol Scearce; John and Suzie Seyfarth; Ellen, Gordon, Jacob, and Joshua Shaffer; Kathy Snowden; Eve Soldinger; Elisabeth Talbot Stewart; Charlene Wilton; and Tim Wright . . . bless you all

- To Paul Kessler and his family, whose influence on my family life has been profound

- To Mariah's birth mother and all birth parents with the courage and heart to allow their children to be adopted—there is no greater gift in our world

Contents

TABLES

FIGURES

To protect the identities of families,
names and significant data
have been changed in the case examples
within this text.

Part I
Description of
Family Systems

Introduction

The purpose of this book is to provide practical information about the field of family systems. It is written primarily for school professionals who work with students who are at risk or who have special needs. Because the field of family systems is not well known, this book can also provide a basic foundation of family systems concepts for professors who train educators as well as those who provide in-service training.

At-risk students are those who are characterized as "likely to fail at school or fail at life" (Frymier, 1992, p. 1). Because the number of at-risk students is increasing (Frymier & Gansneder, 1989), adequate education and training for professionals who deal with at-risk students is critical. The same is true for those professionals who deal with children with special needs. Children with special needs are defined as those who have been labeled and found to be eligible for special education or related services. Currently, federal law refers to "a child with a disability." (Individuals with Disabilities Education Act reauthorized in 1997).

This book provides specific, substantial information for both the general educator and the special educator, as well as those who train both. In addition, it provides information that will be useful to all of the other people—parents and professionals—with whom the general and special educator collaborate, as well as their professors and trainers. Specifically, administrators, psychologists, social workers, counselors, and their professors and trainers will find a background of information and family systems approaches that will improve their professional work as well as the lives of the children and youth whom they serve. Appendix A is essential reading for university professors as well as in-service trainers.

Family systems theories and approaches provide techniques that can be used with children, youth, and adults. Specific problems are viewed within the context of an individual's life experiences and relationships (Haley, 1987). Based on the assumption that changes in one part of an individual's life reverberate in all other areas of that person's experience, interventionists deem all aspects of the person's experience to be inseparable parts of a whole. Research is clear, for example, that students of low socioeconomic status fall behind academically during the summer when their parents influence their learning most (K. L. Alexander & Entwisle, 1996; Slavin, Madden, Dolan, & Wasik, 1996).

A family systems perspective is especially appropriate for professionals who have responsibility for the care and instruction of children and youth, because the experiences of children and youth are determined and shaped by adults, especially their parents (Peeks, 1993). A family systems model would not call for remediating a student's performance in school or improving a student's adjustment without attention to the child's interactions with family members and other individuals.

It is not necessary to know family systems theory to understand this book. If you are well versed in individual psychology and the currently prevalent explanation for behavioral and emotional problems, you may find that this book provides you with new and different ways of looking at your background. You will not need to discard your current beliefs and opinions when reading this text, but you will likely add another dimension to your thinking, one that is systemic in nature. Systemic approaches consider the interconnectedness and interrelatedness of all the parts of a whole. From the family systems perspective, the interrelationships of all the members of a family are considered when dealing with any one member, in our case a student who is at risk or who has special needs.

When you have finished reading this book, you will have been exposed to a good deal of information on a variety of family systems concepts and methods, which will prepare you to interact in systemic ways with at-risk and special-needs students and their families. Although reading this text will not make you an instant expert in the field of family systems, it will provide you with a variety of strategies and methods that you can apply in your interactions with this population.

The purpose of this first chapter is to introduce you to systemic thinking as it relates to at-risk and special-needs students and their families. To provide a context for understanding systemic thinking, the chapter begins with a definition of family. Next, a background on the fields of psychology and counseling as they relate to the field of family studies is provided, and an elaboration is made on the definition of the latter. For professionals unfamiliar with at-risk and special-needs students, a brief background is given. Holistic perspectives, from which all professionals work when focusing on families of at-risk and special-needs students, are then mentioned. An overview of the remainder of the book follows, and the chapter concludes with extension activities that may be self-selected by readers and/or assigned by professors and trainers.

FAMILY

From 1981 to 1989 nearly 6 million people from Asia, Africa, Europe, and Latin America became U.S. citizens, adding to America's ethnic diversity. During that time, formidable economic and social pressures resulted in increasing *structural* diversity among these families (Entwisle, 1994). The different rates of structural change have resulted in a magnification of subcultural differences. Since 1950, major changes in the family have occurred, most of which are nonnuclear in nature. These changes in the family have led to changes in how professionals view families. Changes in family structure, responding to economic and social forces, have led to different patterns from one period of history to another. Doris Entwisle (1994) has provided a chapter well worth reading on fluid family structure titled "Subcultural Diversity in American Families."

Family can be defined in a number of ways. Some people take a narrow view of mother, father, and children. Others broaden the view to include all those living in the home. Still others are very restrictive and, to the exclusion of adopted children, include only blood relations. Dan Quayle, vice-president under George Bush, started an uproar about the definition of family with his comments on the then popular sitcom "Murphy Brown." The main character, a single mother, was having a baby alone, and Quayle's disparaging remarks on her family situation resulted in a conversation across America. From my experience, his comments polarized people rather than bringing them together in acceptance of differences. Nevertheless, the family became a topic of widespread discussion.

A widely respected book edited by McGoldrick, Giordano, and Pearce (1996) on ethnicity and family therapy focuses on how people from different ethnic backgrounds relate to family. Some ethnic groups define family narrowly; other families are almost tribal in nature. Rather than judge the viability of a family that is different from yours, it might help to see the gifts that each ethnic background brings. When I read the first edition of the McGoldrick et al. text (McGoldrick, Pearce, & Giordano, 1982), I realized how many years I had been interacting with families without having basic information that would have created a richer, more meaningful, and constructive experience. In particular, I had worked with many African-American children and families, though while living and teaching in Colorado I had rich, diverse experiences with other subcultures as well. Upon reading the book on ethnicity, I realized how much I had been able to glean on my own and how much I would have benefitted from foreknowledge. From my reading of their text I gained a deeper understanding of, and respect for, the gifts of each ethnic heritage.

My belief is that family should be defined in the broadest possible sense, with the parents or caregivers in the family defining it for themselves. If a family defines its members as everyone who lives in the house, then that is the definition that should be accepted. If Jennifer says she has two mommies, then she has two mommies. The only caveat is legal in nature. A child cannot be taken from a school unless the primary caregiver/parent who has legal custody has given written permission. If a single mother says her mother can attend a "parent conference," I recommend that you welcome the grandmother and that you encourage the mother to attend as well.

FAMILY STUDIES BACKGROUND

Before the 1950s, the fields of psychology and counseling were focused on the diagnosis and treatment of the individual. Psychological and behavioral problems were viewed as originating from some underlying tension or conflict within the mind and experience of the individual. Treatment involved psychotherapy sessions during which the counselor and the patient tried to discover the root of the problem through discussion and association. In addition, the individual might have been given medication designed to diminish depression or anxiety or to help change personal behavior.

In the middle of the 20th century, the field of family studies began to take shape (Corey, 1996). Sociologists, psychologists, educators, physicians, and counselors began to think of the individual in relationship to other people, including friends, colleagues, and family members.

M. P. Nichols and R. C. Schwartz (1995) indicated that during the initial years of the development of family studies, "families with schizophrenic members proved to be an especially fertile area for research because their strange patterns of interaction were so dramatic and striking" (p. 19). The first data generated regarding families were descriptive in nature (Berardo, 1980). Professionals who worked with psychiatric patients began to observe and write about their patients' involvement with and reactions to their families. Professionals from various fields of mental health, primarily in hospital settings, began to notice that patients who were "cured" in the hospital and then sent home would begin to exhibit their symptoms again. Educators who developed elaborate behavioral programs for use in the home discovered that what worked in the classroom did not necessarily work in the family setting. For those who worked with these patients and students, the question became, "Why do things change when the family becomes involved in therapy?"

Since the mid-1950s, professionals in the field of family studies have witnessed the generation of numerous answers to this question. The early description of family process was followed by experimentation and theory construction. Family interaction has been videotaped and analyzed by sophisticated computer programs. Family theories have proliferated to the point that an article by Holman and Burr published in 1980 listed at least 18 different approaches. Clearly, it is beyond the scope of this book to attempt to discuss the content and impact of each of these theories. The three theories having the most impact on the field of family studies seem to be interactionist theory, exchange theory, and systems theory. This text addresses systems theory only.

FAMILY SYSTEMS

Systems theory has been the basis for the development of most of the family treatment approaches that have been created and applied since the 1960s. The generalizations that have arisen from systems theory are useful for understanding not only the family but also other systems such as the school, community, and workplace. Of the conceptual models of family therapy that have developed out of this theoretical base, I have chosen to present four in this book: the communication model of Virginia Satir, the transgenerational model of Murray Bowen, the structural conceptual model, and the strategic conceptual model. Each of these family systems models includes an approach to treatment that has proven effective with families experiencing problems. I present these in particular because of their potential impact on students who are at risk or who have special needs. As M. P. Nichols and R. C. Schwartz (1995) wrote:

> Certain problems are especially likely to benefit from a family approach, among
> them problems with children (who must, regardless of what happens in therapy,
> return home to the influence of their parents), complaints about a marriage or other

> intimate relationship, family feuds, and symptoms that develop in an individual
> around the time of a major family transition. (p. 4)

Thus the family systems field intersects with school professionals working with at-risk and special-needs students (Fine & Carlson, 1992). Though this book is not about training school professionals to conduct family systems therapy, professionals will benefit from an understanding of these models and how the concepts can inform their practice.

Appendix A contains an overview of the communication, transgenerational, structural, and strategic models from the field of family systems. You can understand this text without reading Appendix A, but reading it will add to your understanding and enjoyment of the text. If you are interested in this background, I recommend that you read Appendix A before reading Chapter 2.

Again, the basic principle underlying family systems theory is that *no individual can be understood without looking at how he or she fits into the whole of the family*. When trying to understand a family system, one must consider not only the individuals within the family but also how they interact and how their histories have unfolded. A student who looks distracted or lethargic in the classroom might be viewed differently if the teacher knew that his parents were going through a divorce or that her parents had just had another child.

A second family systems principle is that *families need both rules for structure and rules for change*. Rules for structure organize the day-to-day functioning of the family. Rules for change allow for adaptability to new circumstances. For example, all newly married couples have to come to agreement about how to run their household in terms of cooking, cleaning, and paying bills. When children are born, or if one or both spouses become highly involved in their careers, the tasks assigned to one or both of the individuals may need to be changed. If the couple is not able to renegotiate these responsibilities, the marriage will become more and more unhappy and divorce may become a possibility. The children of these parents will be at risk for failure in life and at school.

A third principle of importance is that *interaction of the family with the school, community, extended family, and friends is essential to the life of the nuclear family*. All of these external systems need not be included in the most intimate details of family life; however, family members should interact with some people outside of the nuclear family. Families that remain reclusive and hostile toward outsiders tend to be dysfunctional in nature, and their children are at risk for failure.

For understanding this book, it may be helpful to know something about how family systems produce symptoms in a family member. All families become unbalanced at times and react to stress with nonproductive interactions. Many people describe this process as a "pushed my button" phenomenon. Once a particular topic is broached, or once a particular action is taken, each family member can then predict how every other family member will react. It is as if everyone is watching a very familiar one-act play, but they cannot seem to change their lines to change the outcome.

In healthy families, there comes a point when someone does change his or her lines, and the nonproductive cycle is broken. In dysfunctional families, these cycles continue to repeat over and over for months or years at a time until a crisis ensues. It is at this point that a family member develops symptoms that provide a stabilizing force for the family stress. Just as the old saying goes that people pull together in times of crisis, the family tends to pull together around the member with symptoms, who is usually a child, and avoids making any real changes in the family patterns that caused the initial crisis. This pulling together around the problem member might make it look, to observers, as though the family has changed its dysfunctional patterns and is functioning better. The essence of the system, however, has not changed; the dysfunctional process will simply resurface in another way.

A deeper understanding of these general ideas by school professionals, which I hope to foster through the content of this book, can form the foundation for knowing when, how, and why to apply these principles to families of students who are at risk or who have special needs. The connection between family experiences and at-risk as well as special-needs students takes on a new meaning when viewed from a family systems perspective.

AT-RISK AND SPECIAL-NEEDS STUDENTS

The focus of this text is on at-risk and special-needs students and their families in both elementary and secondary classrooms. For those who have not had experience with at-risk and special-needs students, a brief background on both types of individuals is now provided.

At-Risk Students

Professionals have written and hypothesized about at-risk students for some time. The following chronological descriptions trace the prevalent views about this population since the 1980s.

Frymier and Gansneder (1989) described at-risk students as those who are likely to fail either in school or in life. They pointed out that:

> "At-riskness" is a function of what bad things happen to a child, how severe they are, how often they happen, and what else happens in the child's immediate environment. For example, a pregnant 14-year-old is at risk. But a pregnant 14-year-old who uses drugs is even more at risk. And a pregnant 14-year-old who uses drugs, has been retained in grade, has missed 30 days of school, and has a low sense of self-esteem is still more seriously at risk.
>
> Moreover, being at risk is not solely a phenomenon of adolescence. Children of all ages are at risk. A 6-year-old whose parents are in the throes of a divorce and who is doing poorly in school is at risk. A 17-year-old whose grades are good but who is deeply depressed because she just lost her boyfriend is also at risk. A 10-year-old whose brother dropped out of school a year ago and whose father just lost his job is certainly at risk. (p. 142)

Slavin and Madden (1989) suggested that "a practical criterion for identifying students at risk is eligibility for Chapter 1, special education, or other remedial services under today's standards" (p. 4). Using 45 factors that research had linked to being at risk, Frymier and Gansneder (1989) found that between 25% and 35% of the students in their study were seriously at risk. Ralph (1989) indicated that at-risk behaviors were not growing worse but that professionals were simply identifying more students who were at risk.

Cuban (1989) offered a new explanation for at-risk students. He departed from the notion that these students are the cause of their own poor performance or that their families do not prepare them for school and do not provide proper support. His alternative view is that schools fail to meet the needs of these children

> because the culture of the school ignores or degrades their family and community backgrounds. Middle-class teachers, reflecting the school's values, single out for criticism differences in children's behavior and values. . . .
>
> The structure of the school is not flexible enough to accommodate the diverse abilities and interests of a heterogeneous student body. Programs are seldom adapted to children's individual differences. Instead, schools seek uniformity, and departures from the norm in achievement and behavior are defined as problems. (p. 781)

Slavin and Madden (1989) agreed with this view. They indicated that it was the incapacity of the school to meet the needs of each pupil, rather than the incapacity of the learner, that caused failure. They saw at-risk students as those in danger of failing to complete their education with adequate skills. They included as risk factors low achievement, retention in grade, behavior problems, poor attendance, low socioeconomic status, and attending school with a large number of poor students.

Liontos (1991) indicated that the term "at-risk" had become a cliche used as a description and a prediction. As educators, when we think of at-risk students, we often focus on school and academic failure, dropouts and the educationally disadvantaged, and underachievement. Liontos, however, saw the term as one that described personal, educational, and societal ills. According to Jens and Gordon (1991), the concept of risk only recently entered the field of education and is misunderstood by many. Risk implies the potential for negative outcome, but it also points to the possibility that a negative outcome can be avoided. Resiliency is the term used when the negative outcome is avoided, as discussed in Chapter 9 of this text.

Westfall and Pisapia (1994) grouped factors indicated in the literature as characteristic of at-risk students into three areas: social/family background, personal problems, and school. Factors relating to social/family background included sibling/parent dropout, low socioeconomic status with poor nutrition, damage to dignity, inadequate housing, English used as a second language, dysfunctional family system including a lack of structure and stability, abuse (substance, physical), single-parent home; lack of commitment to schools, and communication problems between home and school.

Factors relating to personal problems included having an external locus of control, learned helplessness and accepting failure, attempts at suicide, substance abuse as well as health problems, poor self-esteem, teen pregnancy, being in trouble with the law, learning disabilities, having few goals and an inability to envision options, hopelessness around the future, and having a distinct lack of coping skills.

Factors relating to school included behavioral disturbances such as acting out, absenteeism, authority problems and a sense of alienation toward school authority, failing school (particularly in the early years), suspension/expulsion, failing courses, dissatisfaction with school, having few counseling opportunities, inadequate mental health, social, and physical health services in the school, and hostile school climate for students who do not fit in. These authors also reported characteristics of at-risk students who were successful in school. This textbook focuses on resilient at-risk students in Chapter 9.

Fortunately, there are many programs for at-risk students. Brendtro, Brokenleg, and Van Bockern (1990) wrote a thoughtful book about the reclaiming of youth who are at risk. They viewed this reclamation process as our hope for the future. Slavin et al. (1996) described a successful multidimensional program for students at risk for failure that included a parent component.

Although this text does not focus on the academic programs developed for students who are at risk, it does discuss means for understanding and working with the families of these students. With an understanding of the families of at-risk students, school professionals can address the needs of at-risk students before problems become unmanageable. In this way, the orientation of this text intersects in a meaningful way with this population. As can be seen by the literature cited previously, there is much overlap of family and school in working with at-risk students.

Students With Special Needs

Like others before him, Skrtic (1991) suggested that schools contribute to the problem of students who fail. In his thought-provoking examination of schools, he focused in particular on the schools' impact on students who are or have traditionally been placed in special education classes—that is, those students labeled as having special needs.

In discussing students with special needs, this text focuses on those with physical disabilities and chronic illness, behavior disorders, learning disabilities, and mental retardation. It does not discuss working with families of individuals with severe disabilities. The background information dealing with family systems concepts, however, can be generalized to all families. Therefore, professionals who work with individuals with severe disabilities will find much in this text that pertains to their situations.

HOLISTIC APPROACH

A holistic approach is one that examines all of the various aspects of the whole that is under consideration. Holistic education focuses not only on the academic curriculum, but also on all of the other relevant aspects of education. Thus, working with families would be one aspect of holistic education.

Furthermore, the particular approach that family systems contributes to at-risk and special-needs students, like holistic approaches, is systemic in nature. A holistic approach is, by definition, systemically oriented. It focuses on the interrelatedness and interconnectedness of all aspects of its subject, be it holistic education, holistic medicine, holistic health, or any other related subject.

Margaret Mead once stated, "There is hope, I believe, in seeing the human adventure as a whole and in the shared trust that knowledge about mankind sought in reverence for life can bring life." It is this reverence for life that supports my interest in working with families, a crucial part of the life of the child. As Komoski (1990) stated:

> As the idea of holism opens new ways of approaching science, the environment, and our health, educators are beginning to advocate holistic approaches to teaching and learning. This trend signals a growing appreciation of the interconnectedness of things and recognition of the truth of the adage, "the whole is greater than the sum of its parts." (p. 72)

Holistic approaches (Hendrick, 1984; Reinsmith, 1989; Sonnier, 1985) to education reflect a rebalancing of practice that departs from the behaviorist/reductionist view. Most of the writing on holistic education focuses on systemically balanced curriculum or whole curriculum; however, Byers (1992), in the journal *Holistic Education Review,* further recommended addressing the topic of spirituality in the classroom. This text also goes beyond the mainstream in proposing that working with families using family systems concepts and methods is a logical extension of holistic education.

Holistic education provides a context for increasing the breadth and depth of your interactions with at-risk and special-needs students and their family members. When you look at schools with the perspective of holistic education, your responsibility increases for involvement with families, especially those targeted in this book.

OVERVIEW

Part I, which includes Chapters 1 through 4, provides a description of family systems. Chapter 1 has related background information on family systems as well as a rationale for writing about family systems and schools. Chapters 2 through 4 discuss theoretical concepts that are necessary for an understanding of family systems and include suggestions for educators dealing with at-risk and special-needs students.

Chapter 2 describes the family life cycle to provide an understanding of how changes in the life cycle of the family affect at-risk and special-needs students. Interventions are suggested for helping families to be aware of life cycle shifts and stresses and to know how to deal with them. From my experience, most human-service professionals are quite familiar with the individual life cycle from the perspective of Erikson (1963), with his emphasis on phases from birth through death, or Sheehy (1976, 1995), with her description of passages in adult life, yet they are not aware of the family life cycle literature.

Chapter 3 supplies professionals with ways of looking at roles and communication within families from a family systems perspective. Ways in which family interaction patterns can be out of order and techniques for changing dysfunctional interaction patterns are also covered.

Chapter 4 helps school professionals understand how the history of a family can affect the day-to-day functioning of students. Family values, unresolved issues, and patterns of relating that change the experience of the child in the family are described. This chapter also includes information on genograms, or family maps, a tool that encapsulates a great deal of information about the family onto one chart the school professional can use repeatedly to refresh his or her memory regarding family facts and processes.

Part II, which includes Chapters 5 through 9, focuses on students who are at risk or who have special needs, as well as resilient students. Chapter 5 contains information about socioeconomic and ethnic differences as they relate to at-risk students. Differences in values, patterns of relating, and cognitive strategies that may result from cultural upbringing are described. Concrete suggestions for becoming more personally aware and sensitive to the differing backgrounds of these families are provided. Also described are specific ways for school professionals to make a positive impact in this area.

Chapter 6 focuses on at-risk students from nontraditional families. Families who have experienced divorce, single-parent families, blended families, and adoptive families are covered. A companion to the at-risk focus of Chapter 6 is Chapter 7, which focuses on at-risk students from dysfunctional family systems. The family may be addictive or abusive. The aim of Chapter 7 is to reveal how educators can best help students from dysfunctional families. Suggestions are presented for providing information that can be shared with students and their families to help them deal with the situations described in both Chapters 6 and 7.

Chapter 8 relates to the dysfunctional families of students with special needs. The focus in this chapter is on physical disabilities and chronic illness, behavior/social disorders, learning disabilities, and mental retardation. Typical family patterns are identified, and suggestions are provided for interventions.

Chapter 9 is a new chapter to this edition that focuses on resilient children. From reading the preceding three chapters you will realize the many challenges faced by at-risk and special-needs children and youth. Some of these children are resilient. A goal of our schools should be to increase the numbers of students who are resilient. To that end, the initial focus of Chapter 9 is on collaborating with internal and external resources as well as sharing information with family members. The latter is not always an easy process, and family members may misconstrue the intention of professionals. Helping the professional avoid alienation and increase involvement and trust is a major objective of this subsection. I also focus on resourcing as it relates to the family, their friends, and the school community, as well as resources external to those mentioned already. My view of families is that they need resources on a temporary basis only and that they themselves possess rich and diverse resources.

Chapters 2 through 9 each include ideas about how specific issues, such as family history, sociocultural context, and environmental factors, impact family life and thus impact student adjustment. In addition, each of these chapters contains examples of how educators can use a family systems approach in helping students and provides a case example to allow you to reflect on the concepts presented as they relate to one family in particular. Each example includes a child in school and focuses on how school professionals, as well as other service providers, interact with the family. Initially, background information on the case is provided, and then questions are suggested for the reader to answer before seeing the answers to those questions. These questions will allow the reader to relate the content of the chapters to a particular case. My hope is that this opportunity will present a bridge between reading this text and focusing on the families of at-risk and special-needs students in your communities.

New to this edition are the extension activities at the end of each chapter in Parts I and II. These exercises will help readers relate systems concepts to their lives, as well as to the lives of others. Some are training-related activities, and others are for the individual to pursue alone.

Part III discusses particular applications of family systems approaches to education, with the focus being at-risk and special-needs students and their families. Human-services professionals from many fields will find this information useful. Teachers and administrators, social workers, clinical psychologists, counselors, school psychologists, nurses, and physicians will all find these chapters of value when interacting with families who have children who are at risk or who have special needs. Those who train these professionals in a pre-service or in-service capacity will find that Part III provides depth to their foundational backgrounds.

Although the first chapter in Part III focuses on family involvement with school teams in the traditional sense, the other four chapters are devoted to more detailed applications of the family systems concepts within school contexts. Those four chapters contain considerable information distilled from concepts from the field of family systems as well as already existing applications from the field of family systems.

As mentioned, Chapter 10 relates to family involvement with school teams. It focuses on such topics as different approaches to working on teams, who is included on educational teams, and how teams evolve over time. The aspects of planning and implementing team process that are presented will allow the reader to formulate ideas that can be used in specific situations. Means of avoiding problems and facing challenges are also presented. The chapter concludes with information on the linking of families and schools.

Chapter 11 covers both family conferences as they relate to at-risk and special-needs children and the process of working to alleviate student problems before the student is considered for referral for special education. Family systems concepts permeate the discussion of both topics.

Chapter 12 concerns working with family members to design and implement family-focused interventions (FFIs). Woven throughout the chapter are references to the family systems concepts described in Part I. Aspects of intervening with families and working with them in the development and implementation of individualized education programs (IEPs) are highlighted.

Chapter 13 extends concepts of family systems to such previously uncharted waters as academic curriculum and instruction. Techniques popular in the field of family systems are described for application in the classroom. This chapter also focuses on educational support and counseling groups in schools, as well as systemic thinking that bridges the disciplines serving schools and communities.

The last chapter in Part III provides information that will strengthen possibilities for implementation of the systemic approaches proposed in this text. My hope is that professionals will be able to prevent barriers from developing, and, if not, to at least be able to lessen the impact of those barriers. A major portion of Chapter 14 focuses on aspects of change, providing a systems view of the stages of growth and change. Implementing family systems concepts in schools will require a planned change process, and the model presented speaks to that effort.

Part IV contains a comprehensive case study. It also contains the appendices, references, and index. In my view, the most important part of this text for understanding the family systems perspective is contained in Appendix A. It provides the conceptual frameworks that undergird the branch of family therapy known as family systems. An understanding of these frameworks is essential, since, after nearly 50 years, the field of family therapy has yet to develop a single, comprehensive, integrated theory. Appendix A focuses on those strands of family systems that are covered in this text. There are others beyond the scope of this book. I have selected those strands that have been most useful to me as an individual and as a professional in the field of education.

A good portion of Appendix A deals with Murray Bowen's contributions to the family systems field. Murray Bowen has provided the only background that I consider to be a theory in this field. An understanding of his key concepts has deeply enriched my ability to work with families. Virginia Satir's view and methods are also discussed in detail, since they lend themselves so well to working within schools. I have known innumerable high school students across the country who, when exposed to her work, found it wholly meaningful to their lives. The information on structural and strategic family therapy in Appendix A of the first edition of this text was written by Debbie Daniels-Mohring. For this edition I have added to those sections by translating even more of the key concepts for educators.

Appendices B and C are reading lists that are useful in educational arenas. The readings concern at-risk and special-needs students. Appendix B lists books that adults can read to help them understand at-risk and special-needs children and youth and their families. Professors, trainers, school personnel, and family members will find this listing helpful. Appendix C lists readings for children and youth. Both of these appendices are divided by topic area. My graduate assistants, Tabitha Hogge, Jennifer Grossnickle, and Holly Kagan, and I have included a few words describing as many of these books as possible so that you can more easily find what you need. We also suggest that if you have access to the Internet, you search the "bookstore" site known as Amazon [www.Amazon.com].

The books identified in Appendix C will be worthwhile resources for sensitizing others to the concerns of families with at-risk children or children with disabilities. They will also be useful when working with those families and children or youth themselves. Mullins (1983) wrote a chapter on the use of bibliotherapy in counseling families who have a child with special needs. She quoted an inscription over a library in ancient Thebes that read, "The Healing Place of the Soul." I agree that, in reading, we heal. As a sibling of an individual with a serious learning disability, I have read many books that have helped me understand and heal. Mullins, too, provided a useful list of selected readings. Christenbury, Beale, and Patch (1996) wrote about interactive bibliocounseling for adolescents and provided annotated citations of books divided by topic area. Theirs is a particularly useful resource for teachers and parents of adolescents. An article on bibliotherapy for children with special needs by McCarty and Chalmers (1997) includes an annotated bibliography for students of all ages. Orr et al. (1997) also provided an annotated bibliography for exploring developmental disabilities.

Appendix D includes an extensive list of resources professors, trainers, school professionals, and families may find useful. It is arranged by topic and provides current addresses and phone numbers of many agencies, organizations, and associations. It also includes many Internet sites that professors, trainers, school professionals, and family members might want to consult about particular resources.

I am enthusiastic about the possibilities this text presents. I invite you to learn more about your own family as you read this book. On many occasions, I recommend that you try out methods, such as mapping your family life with a genogram. I believe that the better you understand your family-of-origin and your nuclear family, the better you can apply family systems concepts in relation to students who are at risk or who have special needs. Self- knowledge is a basis for knowledge of others.

Information that is not applied through example or practice is seldom used and generally forgotten. Therefore, this second edition includes extension activities for Parts I and II with which readers can explore the concepts presented. They include recommended areas for reflection, journal assignments, discussion topics for outside class, and in-class exploratory activities and topics for those who are reading this text as part of a university or in-service course. University professors and in-service trainers will find it useful to explore these activities before using them in class, perhaps even using the suggestions with informal brown-bag lunches with peers prior to using them in class. Such exploration should allow the professor or in-service trainer to expand his or her knowledge base prior to leading class discussions and activities, thus preventing or minimizing problems that might arise. The following extension activities should be completed before reading further.

EXTENSION ACTIVITIES

Reflection: Now that you have read the introductory chapter, think about what you expect to learn from this book.

Journal: Begin a traditional "KWL" process by first listing what you *know* about family systems and then what you *want to know* about family systems. After reading the whole text, you can complete the process by writing what you *learned.* Save your entry for comparison later. You may want to keep a running log of 5 or 10 key concepts from each chapter.

OR

In-Class/Training Discussion: Leader instruction: Lead a discussion on "know" and "want to know." Write the comments offered on chart paper, and save the chart for the end of the course/training for comparison with what was learned.

Reading: Read Appendix A before moving on to Chapter 2. It presents a foundation of knowledge that will allow a richer understanding of family systems. It covers several different conceptual frameworks that undergird unique family systems models. It is essential reading for instructors and trainers and very useful for all others.

Survey/Question: Survey the chapters in Part I by skimming the topics one chapter at a time. After reading the topic headings for a chapter, write down three questions that come to mind. Do not censor your questions. Review your list as you prepare to read each chapter in Part I.

In-Class/Training Small-Group Discussion: Discuss some of the questions that came to mind while surveying the chapters in Part I.

Later In-class/Training Large-Group Discussion: [Select a few adjectives from the following question to use for the whole group discussion, and add any adjectives of your own.] What do you think you will find to be the most [intriguing, meaningful, disturbing, scary, unnerving, conflict-inducing, conflict-resolving, exciting, uninteresting, stabilizing, value-engendering, and quality-enhancing] topic in the chapters of Part I?

In-Class/Training Discussion: [If only a portion of the class/group has had professional experiences, have the professionals sit in a center circle with everyone else surrounding them in an outer circle listening while the professionals discuss the following.]

Relate experiences you have had with families of students who are at risk by elaborating on challenges met as well as lessons learned. AND/OR relate experiences you have had with families of students with special needs by elaborating on challenges met as well as lessons learned.

[If both topics are covered:] In your experience, how are these two kinds of families similar and different from one another?

Family Life Cycle

To understand how a student functions in the classroom, the school professional must have a knowledge of the child's family life cycle. This chapter presents one perspective on the development of the family and describes how particular issues affect family development during the child's life. By knowing something about the impact of the family's development on the child, the school professional can place classroom behaviors in an understandable context. It is not possible for school professionals to know in-depth information about the family of each student, but it is helpful to know more about some students in particular.

One of the primary tasks faced by our educational systems is to promote healthy development. The family life cycle concept provides an opportunity to extend this task to the promotion of the healthy family as well. Knowledge of the principles of the family life cycle can assist professionals who meet with family members, both formally and informally, as well as in phone contacts or through written communication. Healthy family development can then be promoted, initially through providing families with general life cycle information and then through information gathering and sharing about individual family's experiences. Basic life cycle information provided to families through both written means and verbal interactions can help families to place their own development and struggles in a larger, systemic context.

This chapter presents background information followed by a section providing specific information about how the normal family life cycle operates. Subsections are included on plateaus, transitions, and tasks and changes typically faced within each life cycle stage. The next section focuses on family life cycle challenges and covers stressors, sociocultural and transgenerational impact, and pile-up. The section on families with special needs describes typical situations within each life cycle stage as they relate to different disability categories. It also provides information on alternative life cycles to the intact-family life cycle, such as remarriage. The discussion then turns to coping strategies for families and limitations to the family life cycle perspective. As with all of the remaining chapters, a case example and extension activities are presented to allow readers to deepen their understanding of, appreciation for, and ability to benefit from the information presented in the chapter.

BACKGROUND

The development of the child as an individual has been studied extensively from a number of different perspectives. Piaget (1952) wrote about changes in cognition that occur as the child grows. Motor development was cataloged by Gesell, Ilg, and Ames (1974). Freud, Jung, Adler, and other personality theorists have emphasized the importance of various periods in the psychological development of the child (C. S. Hall & Lindzey, 1978). Erik Erikson's (1963) theory of the tasks of ego development was the first to introduce the concept that psychological challenges continue into adulthood. The book *Passages* by Gail Sheehy (1976), which was based on the work of Gould (1970), addressed the struggles and changes faced by adults as they age. Sheehy's 1995 book, *New Passages,* addresses the stages of individual adult development. Although each of these theories acknowledges the influence of relationships upon personality development, the primary focus is on the individual, *from the inside,* and the changes and struggles that occur during different periods of development.

Socialization, however, also occurs. Socialization implies growth from *outside* of the individual (L'Abate, 1994b). The influence of external agents on personality development is assumed with socialization. Early writers in the field of psychology saw these external agents as culture or society. According to L'Abate (1994b), only in the past 20 years have references been found in the literature to the family as an influential factor in human development. The context in which we live and the relational aspects of our lives continue to be minimized by writers in the field of psychology. Our society, that is individualistic in nature, and our psychology reflects a deeply entrenched orientation toward individual explanations for behavior. From my point of view, a systemic lens enriches our understanding of human behavior and can lead to the expansion of human potential. Both internal and external influences are important in human development.

> "From a developmental perspective the transition to a transactional, multirelational, and multidirectional paradigm allowed us to see that development takes place within a context, and that the most immediate, influential context throughout the life span, *is* the family" (p. 4).

Social constructionism goes beyond the developmental perspective by pointing to the postmodern world in which truth and reality are seen as conceptualizations or points of view bound by both context and history. The focus of social constructionism is on the ways we make meaning in any social relationship, including family life (Gergen, 1991).

In 1948, at the Conference on Family Life in Washington, sociologists Evelyn Duvall and Reuben Hill presented a framework for focusing on development from the perspective of family that combined Burgess's (1926, 1969) concept of a developing unit with Havinghurst's (1948, 1952) and Erikson's (1963) lifelong developmental task concept. Duvall and Hill's framework for characteristic tasks of family life encompassed eight stages, beginning with the formation of the family by marriage. Duvall's book, first published in 1957 and now, following her death, in its fifth edition (1977), marked the beginning of a shift in focus from the individual to the family as the primary unit for the study of development.

Other theorists (B. Carter & McGoldrick, 1989b; L'Abate, 1994a; W. C. Nichols, 1996) have followed Duvall and Hill's lead, proposing models to describe predictable events and stages that occur in the development of families. These stages are collectively termed the *family life cycle*. W. C. Nichols (1996) stated, "The family life cycle is concerned with the developmental tasks of the family itself as it deals with the needs of the adult members and the development needs of the offspring" (p. 57). E. B. Rosenberg (1992) has presented an "adoption life cycle" that describes the developmental tasks of birth parents, adoptive parents, and the child who is adopted. Hajal and Rosenberg (1991) also have written on the family life cycle in adoptive families. Others (Carney & Gamel-McCormick, 1996; Turnbull & Turnbull, 1996) have focused on the life cycle of families with children with special needs. Baber and Allen (1992) have provided guidance for families with different structures.

L'Abate (1994b) noted that

> development occurs along a variety of routes. Here, a *delta* model, much like the estuary of a large river, seems to embody the view that most individuals in most families go straight ahead, normatively following the mainstream, major flow of the river; whereas some go sideways and get lost in the marshes of life; others who go sideways come back to the mainstream; some stop altogether; some recoup; and some never recover along the path from birth to death (Caspi, Elder, & Herbener, 1990; J. M. White, 1991).
>
> No trajectory is like another trajectory. Yet in the midst of all this variety, some similarities can be found. One can safely predict that most members of the same family will follow different life cycle patterns (Kreppner & Lerner, 1989; Rossi & Rossi, 1990). What similarities, if any, can we find among these differences? (p. 4)

There is danger, I believe, in seeing life only through the lens of the individual. Context and relationship are critical to understanding students who are at risk or who have special needs. Imagine having a new student in your classroom who has a behavioral problem. You know nothing more about her than that she just moved into your school area. By learning something about her family life cycle, you will more likely accept her, separating the behavior from the individual. You'll then be able to focus on the unacceptable behavior, which will be more understandable under the circumstances and which will preserve your acceptance of the child. Thus, this chapter focuses on the family life cycle, which takes context and relationship into consideration and provides an important base of information for school professionals who work with students who are at risk or who have special needs.

At each stage in the family's life cycle, a particular nodal event occurs that ushers in the next phase of development. Theorists have developed many ways of thinking about the developmental phases. Carter and McGoldrick (B. Carter & McGoldrick, 1989; E. A. Carter & McGoldrick, 1980) proposed a six-stage family life cycle model that included single adulthood prior to marriage. Turnbull and Turnbull (1996) developed a model consisting of four stages (birth and early childhood, childhood, adolescence, and adulthood). For purposes of exploration later in this text, the Carter and McGoldrick model (B. Carter & McGoldrick, 1989b; E. A. Carter & McGoldrick, 1980) has been adapted by dividing their third stage, families with young children, into the following two stages: young children 0–5 years old and elementary aged children 6–12 years old. This adapted version still has six stages, but the revised stages more easily translate to the structure of schools in America.

The family life cycle is a particularly useful concept for diagnosis in the family systems perspective known as *strategic family therapy* (see Appendix A), which looks at the family's stage of development as an important factor in understanding the etiology of symptoms in family members. According to this model, family members are prone to developing symptoms at transition points in the family life cycle. When the family system is unable to adjust its interactions to accommodate changes in the life cycle, the family becomes "stuck" at a particular stage and cannot move on in its development. Interactions within the family become more and more inflexible and nonproductive until one or more members of the family become symptomatic (Haley, 1980).

NORMAL FAMILY LIFE CYCLE

This section describes specifics on how the family life cycle operates. The challenges and tasks required of the family at each stage of the life cycle are delineated. Clearly, family life cycle patterns change over time. Myriad factors contribute to changing patterns, including differences in the role of women in society, our assumptions about what is "normal" and what is considered "family," as well as ethnic and cultural variability. For purposes of simplicity however, this section focuses on one family life cycle model, the Intact Middle-Class American Family Life Cycle Model developed by B. Carter and M. McGoldrick (1989b) and adapted, as noted previously, for use in this text are as follows:

Stage 1: The Newly Married Couple

Stage 2: Families With Young Children (ages 0–5 years)

Stage 3: Families With Elementary Aged Children (ages 6–12 years)

Stage 4: Families With Adolescents (ages 13–19 years)

Stage 5: Families Launching Children (ages 20 and over)

Stage 6: Families in Later Life

This model has been chosen despite the fact that it is "more or less mythological, though statistically accurate, relating in part to existing patterns and in part to the ideal standards of the past against which more families compare themselves" (B. Carter & McGoldrick, 1989b, p. 12).

In this family life cycle model, the family's and the oldest child's development parallel one another. For the most part, developmental changes required of the family are determined by the age of the oldest child because that child is the first catalyst for new demands upon the family. The diagnosis of a child with special needs, however, can affect this pattern (Imber-Black, 1989). So too can divorce and remarriage, as well as chronic illness, death and serious illness, alcohol problems, accidents, and the discovery of extramarital affairs (B. Carter & McGoldrick, 1989; L'Abate, 1994a; W. C. Nichols, 1996). Further, as indicated by chapters in the edited text of B. Carter and M. McGoldrick (1989a) devoted to the family life cycle of "poor black families" (Hines, 1989) and "lower income and professional families with a comparison of structure and life cycle processes" (Fulmer, 1989), socioeconomic status can affect the pattern.

The focus of the school professional is clearly on Stages 2 through 4 of the model, from the birth of children through the rearing of adolescents. Stage 2 is particularly relevant for schools in relation to children with special needs (early childhood education). With the increasing literature available about the importance of the first 3 years of life for later growth and development, it is reasonable to predict that schools will soon become more involved with families at Stage 2 in an attempt to prevent at-risk status later. Editorials currently abound about the natural marriage of schools and parents for training families with infants. The need for training parents to provide experiences that stimulate learning during the first 3 years of their children's lives is a particular concern. IDEA (the Individuals With Disabilities Education Act), known as Public Law 105-17, was reauthorized in 1997 with four sections, one of which is entitled "Infants and Toddlers With Disabilities." One of the seven authorities listed under Part D of the Act is Parent Training and Information Services (Part D, Chapter 2, Sec. 682-684). Part D funds support three activities: Parent Training and Information Centers, Community Parent Resource Centers, and Technical Assistance for Parent Training and Information Centers. This emphasis on parent training likely will result in an increased need for professionals to be knowledgeable about family life cycle stages.

Within each stage of the family life cycle, plateaus, transitions, and tasks and challenges occur. These are described in the following sections.

Plateaus

Each stage of the family life cycle includes a "plateau period" and a "transitional period" (E. A. Carter & McGoldrick, 1980). Plateaus are periods of relative stability when the family operates predictably within roles and functions. For example, a young married couple who have worked out the initial difficulties of living together and have settled into a lifestyle pattern are experiencing a plateau period. During plateau periods the forces of homeostasis (see Appendix A, "Strategic Family Therapy") or sameness are in operation. School professionals are unlikely to find student problems related to the family life cycle during plateau periods. Reminiscing about your childhood will help you recall periods of stability in your family of origin. If your nuclear family is experiencing a time of stability that reflects a plateau period in your childhood, the experience may remind you of similar times when you were growing up.

Transitions

Transitional periods occur when a life event occurs that demands changes in the structure or function of the family. Carter and McGoldrick listed (B. Carter & McGoldrick, 1989b; E. A. Carter & McGoldrick, 1980) eight normative events that usher in new life cycle stages: marriage, the birth of a child, a child entering school, a child entering adolescence, a child launched into adulthood, the birth of a grandchild, retirement, and transition to old age. Events that occur "on time," or at expected points in the life cycle, are less stressful than events that occur earlier or later than expected (Jameson & Alexander, 1994; F. Walsh, 1982). For example, an unplanned teenage pregnancy will be more emotionally stressful than a planned pregnancy for a couple who have been married for some time. The early, unexpected death of a spouse will be more stressful and require more family changes than the death of a spouse at an older age.

In addition to events that usher in new life cycle stages, other events may occur that change the normal cycle of the family and precipitate a transition period. These nonnormative events include, but are not limited to, miscarriage, marital separation and divorce, illness, disability, death, relocation, changes in socioeconomic status, and catastrophes that result in dislocation of the family unit. When these events occur, not only must the individuals within the family deal with their own reactions to the loss or change in circumstances (F. Walsh & McGoldrick, 1991), but the family as a whole must change communication patterns, roles, and functions to deal successfully with the change (Cusinato, 1994; Patterson, 1985).

Transition periods are often marked by anxiety, uncertainty, and a sense of loss (B. Carter & McGoldrick, 1989b; Olson, 1988; Olson et al., 1983). Flexibility and adaptability, described in Appendix A, are needed during transition periods. Change events can be a stimulus either for successful adaptation and growth or for dysfunction (Cusinato, 1994; F. Walsh, 1983). Clinical or behavioral problems are particularly likely to appear at transition points in the family life cycle if the basic structure and roles of family members are not reorganized (B. Carter & McGoldrick, 1989b; Cusinato, 1994; Hadley, Jacob, Miliones, Caplan, & Spitz, 1974; Haley, 1980; F. Walsh, 1982).

Tasks and Changes

As with individual development, specific developmental tasks are required at each stage of the life cycle for the family. In addition, each stage of the family life cycle requires a change in the family goal orientation and direction. Successful completion of tasks at early stages builds a foundation for successful completion of later stages. Like a child who must learn to stand before learning to walk, the family must learn to negotiate the tasks of raising children before it can successfully launch children into adulthood. Failure to complete the tasks of early stages may lead to difficulties with later ones.

The primary themes and developmental tasks required at each stage are as follows.

Stage 1: The Newly Married Couple

Primary theme—Attachment (Bardill, 1997; Kantor, 1983)

Primary tasks—Realignment of relationships with friends and family to include spouse and spouse's family; commitment to marriage; commonality of goals and directions for the future

An example of this realignment is the decision about where the couple will spend holidays— with her family or his? The successful resolution of this question is a good indicator that the individuals have made the transition to viewing themselves as part of a couple.

Individuals who marry without successfully resolving issues in their own families of origin (see Chapter 4) are more likely to experience marital difficulties and adjustment problems (Bardill, 1997; Fogarty, 1976). In fact, in a classic study by Lidz, Cornelison, Fleck, and Terry (1957a) of families with schizophrenic children, the authors found that in five out of eight marriages in their study, the focus of the spouse's loyalty remained in the parental home rather than in the current nuclear family. These individuals had never successfully transitioned from the role of child in their own families to the role of partner in a marital system.

Stage 2: Families With Young Children

Primary theme—Industry, developing strategies for getting things done (Kantor, 1983)

Primary parental functions—Nurturing, protecting, and caring for the infant; providing behavioral model and appropriate limit setting (Cusinato, 1994)

Primary tasks—Realignment of marital system to include a child; changes in the sexual relationship of the couple; coping with lack of privacy; development of parenting style; realignment of relationships with extended family and friends to include presence of a child and requirements of parenting

Bardill (1997) indicated and Rollins and Galligan (1978) found that the companionship between spouses decreased with the arrival of an infant. The presence of dependent children in the home placed new demands on time, energy, and the financial resources of the couple, and many couples reported a decrease in marital satisfaction. Couples who had successfully negotiated the changes brought on by an infant in the home reported that children brought them closer together, giving them a shared task and a common goal.

One example of how this process occurs comes from a study (Pedersen, 1983) of fathers' involvement with their infants. This study found that the father's role was influenced by his involvement with the birth process. If fathers were involved in anticipation of the birth, in planning for the child's space in the home, and in the actual birth, they were more likely to feel a commitment to and involvement with the new baby. Pedersen described the father's primary role as an emotional support for the mother. He found that the more support the mother felt from her spouse, the more she worked to include him in her relationship with the baby, and the more direct interaction occurred between the father and the infant.

Stage 3: Families With Elementary Aged Children

Primary themes—Affiliation and inclusion, allowing others to be brought within the family boundaries; consolidating the accomplishments of family members (Kantor, 1983)

Primary parental functions—Sensitivity to the growth needs of the child; providing opportunities for the child to develop independence; letting the child go and grow; vicarious enjoyment from the child's experiences (Cusinato, 1994)

Primary tasks—Involvement with peer network; establishing sibling roles; division of family responsibilities

At this stage, parents must begin to accept the personality of the child and the ways in which this personality is expressed both within and outside the home (Barnhill & Longo, 1978). Interactions concerning the school, extracurricular activities, and families of peers must be negotiated.

The need for parental rules is most clear during this child-rearing stage. Rules provide the structure and identity for family life. In a successful training program developed by McFadden and Doub (1983) to teach parents to cope with family life cycle changes, the following guidelines for parents regarding the responsibility for making family rules are presented in the first session:

1. Make rules.
2. Stay in charge.
3. Stick together.
4. Make room to play with your children.
5. Change with the times. (p. 143)

These guidelines put in simple form the need for guidance, cohesion, and adaptability in families experiencing transitions.

For some parents, the need to share authority when their child begins school is a difficult transitional demand. Parents are accustomed to making all of the decisions about their child's well-being and may be reluctant to adhere to guidelines that are proposed by a teacher. For such parents, the teacher would do well to keep in mind his or her knowledge of the life cycle and help the parents make the transition into the child-rearing stage by sharing authority and asking for input. If the teacher's attempts to elicit parental cooperation continue to fail, there may be more severe family dysfunction. Two of the classic signs of abusive and neglectful families are extreme family secrecy and a lack of inclusion of people outside the nuclear family.

Stage 4: Families With Adolescents

Primary theme—Decentralization; loosening boundaries

Primary parental functions—Providing assistance in establishing identity; tolerating generation gap (Cusinato, 1994)

Primary tasks—Managing the child's increasing independence; refocusing on midlife career and marital issues; increasing flexibility of roles

This stage of the family life cycle has become particularly difficult in contemporary society. As Quinn, Newfield, and Protinsky (1985) argued:

> The accelerated pace of physiological growth (of children) . . . has stretched the stage we have come to define sociologically as adolescence. . . . We have not come to a consensus on how to determine its [adolescence] onset or termination. This uncertainty obscures guideposts for defining roles and status of family members and, subsequently, family interactional patterns. (p. 102)

Often, in families, the physical maturity of children is mistaken for emotional maturity. It is the difficult job of parents during this stage to develop appropriate and flexible rules for their adolescents, allowing enough room for them to experiment with independence. Parents who are extremely involved with their children often have problems with their own identities and tend to perceive adolescent rebellion as a personal affront. In addition, for the married couple, watching their children's sexual development may bring up their own unresolved sexual issues from previous stages.

A good strategy for the school professional during this stage is to try to help parents have a sense of humor about their child's attempts at rebellion. Just knowing that struggles for independence are normal and necessary at this stage and that they need not be taken personally can be a relief to parents who are trying to achieve a balance between control and letting go. An adolescent's constantly messy room may not seem so important to the parent when seen in the light of alternative forms of rebellion such as gang membership and drug abuse.

Stage 5: Families Launching Children

Primary themes—Differentiation; detachment (Kantor, 1983)

Primary parental functions—Supporting independence; accepting adult-to-adult relationship; encouraging, reassuring, and appreciating (Cusinato, 1994)

Primary tasks—Negotiating to become a couple again; renegotiating roles with adult children; realignment to include in-laws of children who marry

During this stage, women who have stayed at home with their children have more time and energy to develop themselves in personal areas. Women who have made a deep commitment to motherhood may experience feelings of purposelessness or lack of meaning (Bardill, 1997; Hesse-Biber & Williamson, 1984). At this point, both the parents and their children are adults and, in some ways, social equals. Thus, family members must change communication patterns to include the possibility for equality and differences of opinion among members of two generations (Hess & Waring, 1978).

Stage 6: Families in Later Life

Primary themes—Letting go, dissolving ties (Kantor, 1983)

Primary parental functions—allowing role reversals to occur, with adult child assuming more responsibility (Cusinato, 1994)

Primary tasks—Redefinition of roles between aging spouses; dealing with the death of friends and family

Retirement and advancing years may mean a loss of income, loss of occupational status, large blocks of time at home, and loss of roles (Aldous, 1978; Bardill, 1997). Senior citizens may experience the loss of their homes and communities, their physical well-being, or their mental capacity (E. M. Brody, 1974). When one spouse dies, the surviving spouse must reformulate a personal identity as widow or widower and renegotiate relationships with children and extended family. If older parents are ill or disabled, children must negotiate care-giving tasks involving caring for their parents (Bardill, 1997; Montgomery, Gonyea, & Hooyman, 1985).

Research by Spark and Brody (1970) showed that, contrary to popular belief, older parents are not usually abandoned by their children. In fact, three fourths of the senior citizens Spark and Brody interviewed lived within 30 minutes of at least one child, and more than four-fifths had seen an adult child in the previous week. Spark and Brody argued for the inclusion of grandparents in family therapy to help with the resolution of multigenerational dysfunctional family patterns. This phenomenon has become known as the *sandwich generation* (Bardill, 1997) and speaks volumes to the caring for older parents by adult children.

Thus far, the focus of this chapter has been on the progression of the normal life cycle, with a framework presented for the developmental demands and changes required at each of the six life cycle stages. Equally important is an understanding of the problems that can arise to make progression through the life cycle more difficult for the family.

FAMILY LIFE CYCLE CHALLENGES

Families experience each stage of the life cycle with varying degrees of success. The degree of flexibility and adaptability of the family contributes to how successfully the child develops in all realms. The past history of the family, the timing of life events, and the extent of family stressors are all important in determining how the family will adapt to life cycle difficulties. Awareness of challenges faced by a student will help the school professional better prevent difficulties as well as respond to those that surface and affect the school life of the student.

Stressors

All of us are accustomed to facing stress in life. The family is no different from the individual in that there are stressors faced by the family as a unit. Some stressors are naturally occurring and predictable in all families as they make transitions; others are related specifically to particular families, such as recurring transgenerational patterns.

According to Jameson and Alexander (1994):

> A developmental trajectory deviating from the norm results when the stressors exceed a system's capacity to cope. Of particular interest is identification of the way in which an event or process alters "normal" developmental trajectories. The mediating/intervening systems may function as a sort of wall of defense, or immune system, when operating well, diffusing, deflecting, or encapsulating stressors and focusing adaptation. When a system or subsystem (family or individual) does not work, it can add stress to the individuals or to the system itself. The stressor may ultimately overcome normal family processes. (p. 402)

In a study of the predictable stressors that must be faced at each life cycle stage, Olson and colleagues (1983) asked 1,140 families across the life cycle about significant stressors they experienced. The authors found that the following factors were the most problematic stressors reported at each stage:

Stage 1—The Newly Married Couple: Work-family (balancing changes with extended family, dealing with in-laws, and developing dual career goals)

Stage 2—Families With Young Children: Financial strains (coping with the added financial burden of young children, buying a family home, making decisions about both spouses' careers and the cost of child-care options)

Stage 3—Families With Elementary Aged Children: Intra-family strains (dealing with the added stress of involvement with the school, extracurricular activities, and families of children's peer group)

Stage 4—Families With Adolescents: Financial strains (handling the financial demands of feeding, clothing, and entertaining adolescents)

Stage 5—Families Launching Children: Financial strains (dealing with paying for college, weddings, or helping children begin their own nuclear families)

Stage 6—Families in Later Life: Financial strains (planning for the loss of income following retirement, paying medical bills, health care costs)

The inability to handle significant stress is one factor that can arrest or slow down life cycle progression. Although each life cycle stage brings a primary stressor, there are many other stresses at each stage. Focusing on the six stages of the family life cycle and thinking back to your family of origin can help you identify with this aspect of the family life cycle.

Sociocultural and Transgenerational Impact

Other factors that can influence the family's response to a normative event are the *socio-cultural context* and the *family's past experience* over many generations. The significance of a particular life event, the normative timing of its occurrence, and the rituals that mark it vary with different cultures and ethnic groups.

Bowen's (1985) transgenerational theory, briefly discussed in Chapter 3 and elaborated on in Appendix A, focuses on the significance that particular life cycle events have over many generations. For example, if a young couple is having their first child at the same time that a grandparent is dying, the birth and death will be woven together emotionally and symbolically. When the couple has another child, the feelings of joy and loss from the first event will most likely recur at the second birth. If the couple does not make the connection about how birth and death were linked in time at the birth of their first child, they may be confused about their mixed feelings about the second birth. They may feel guilty that their feelings of anticipation and happiness are mixed with fear and sadness.

There will always be some unresolved issues and conflicts at one or many of the stages of the life cycle. A potential problem occurs when, as Barnhill and Longo (1978) described,

> the family must continue to move on if it is to meet the new challenges ahead. The conflicts can then become sealed over, though vulnerable points can be left behind. It is possible then to conceive that under a later situation of stress . . . the family can regress to previous levels of functioning. . . . Old unresolved conflicts . . . can become uncovered and alive again. Thus, as if it is not enough for the family to deal with one difficulty, an old conflict is reawakened, together with the old unsuccessful patterns of coping with the stress. (p. 471)

With this comment in mind, it is clear that professionals need to look not only at the current difficulty that a family is experiencing but also at what old issues possibly are being reenacted by the family. There might be a legacy of problems from previous generations that occurred at this particular stage of the family life cycle. In many families, myths and stories surrounding births, deaths, and other life events are passed down from generation to generation. These myths can and do influence family members on unconscious and conscious levels. For example, in many Southern families, little boys receive their first hunting gun as a rite of passage. The gift of the gun takes on a meaning and intensity born of generations of men sharing the ritual of their first hunt together. What happens in these families when a boy with a disability reaches the typical age to receive his gun? Many issues and feelings will need to be considered before a decision is made about this boy's rite of passage. The school professional who takes into account this type of family culture and legacy will better understand when this boy becomes depressed or confused about his identity. If this boy begins to play with make-believe weapons in the classroom or begins to act aggressively, the teacher can have a much greater impact if he or she is aware of the cultural importance of this transition point in the student's life.

Pile-Up

Another important issue in predicting family responses to life cycle adjustments is the concept of *pile-up* (H. I. McCubbin & Patterson, 1982). A large number of changes within a brief period of time will contribute to disrupting the family unit and may make life cycle adjustments more problematic. If the family resources are already depleted from dealing with other changes, the family may be less well-equipped to adapt to future changes.

As one at-risk adolescent girl commented to her counselor, "First, my brother graduated in June, so he's looking for a job. Then my father changed jobs in August, and we had to move. My mom hates our new neighborhood. Who cares what I'm going through?"

Three different areas in which major life cycle problems can be generated have been presented. First are predictable significant *stressors* that are faced at each stage, including financial strains, family strains, career demands, and extended family demands. Second are *cultural demands* from former generations paired with *family myths* that arise due to the timing of life cycle events and the significance that an event takes on for the family at future stages. Last are the problems that arise because of the *pile-up* of numerous stressors within a short period. For the school professional who understands the dynamics of the family life cycle, students' behavior problems can be viewed and managed within a context of possible extended family difficulties.

FAMILIES WITH SPECIAL NEEDS

The diagnosis of a child with intellectual, emotional, sensory, or physical disabilities is a significant life stressor that will affect the future development of the family at all levels (Hurtig, 1994). At each life cycle stage, as the demands upon the family change, the family must again accept the child's disability (Wikler, 1981). A number of researchers have discussed the significant issues and challenges that must be faced by families with children who have special needs (Blacher, 1984; Carney & Gamel-McCormick, 1996; Combrinck-Graham, 1983; Cullen, MacLeod, Williams, & Williams, 1991; Hajal & Rosenberg, 1991; Hanline, 1991; Leigh, 1987; LePere, 1988; McGrath & Grant, 1993; Patterson & McCubbin, 1983; Prosen, Toews, & Martin, 1981; C. L. Rich, Warsradt, Nemiroff, Fowler, & Young, 1991; Shapiro, 1983; Stutman, 1984; Thorin & Irvin, 1992; Turnbull & Turnbull, 1996). The challenges at each stage are summarized in the following sections. As you read these sections, think about how these issues may be reflected in the classroom behaviors of students with special needs, as well as their siblings.

Stage 1: The Newly Married Couple

Siblings of children with special needs must address particular issues when they prepare for marriage and for forming their own nuclear families. Will the disabled sibling be involved in the wedding ceremony? How will the new in-laws and extended family be introduced to the exceptionality? Is the sibling's disability genetically transmitted? If so, what impact will that have on the couple's future plans regarding their own family? What genetic counseling is in order? Is there a difference of opinion regarding abortion? Openly talking about these potentially thorny problems before the marriage can help reduce stress later as well as assist in avoiding inherent pitfalls. There will be fewer surprises if everything is talked about openly. Seeing a counselor or psychotherapist to help discuss these kinds of matters will be helpful for some couples. Trying to negotiate these waters alone can add undue stress to already stressful times.

In the case of remarriage, it is important to discuss the special needs of children either partner may bring to the marriage. It is critical that each person's view of the situation be fully discussed so that the children do not suffer. Blended families present a particular challenge, and when a child with special needs is part of the new mixture, it is important to talk over the issues faced so that there are fewer surprises. This open communication can also help reduce the likelihood of re-divorce in the newly formed family. A number of professionals (Heavey, Shenk, & Christensen, 1994; McGoldrick & Carter, 1989; W. C. Nichols, 1996) have written on the formation of the remarried family and the challenges affecting the family members.

Stage 2: Families With Young Children

Most children with special needs are not diagnosed at birth, and even for those who are, the question of degree of disability often is unresolved for years. Writing about the family with a child having a disability, Seligman (1991a) reported stress factors associated with five developmental stages that were identified in 1984 by Olson, McCubbin, Barnes, Larsen, Muxen, and Wilson. During Stage 2, stress factors of families with children having disabilities include obtaining an accurate diagnosis, making emotional adjustments, and informing other family members.

The parents of a child diagnosed at birth or during the preschool years will be trying to understand the exceptionality, and some will be coping with the loss of their "dream child" (F. H. Brown, 1989; Carney & Gamel-McCormick, 1996; Featherstone, 1980). Stage 2 is a particularly vulnerable time for most couples, even when their child is born normal. When a child is born with problems, there may be an interruption of the bonding and attachment between mother and infant because of long separations at birth (Sobsey, 1994). The parents who have dreamed of holding and feeding their baby may be faced with an infant who is maintained in an incubator or respirator with various sorts of tubes attached and who cannot be held or nursed.

For some parents, the diagnosis of their infant as having a disability brings on a period of depression and mourning and the mourning process is complicated by the fact that the child is not really dead—only the image of the dreamed for child is dead (Blacher, 1984; Carney & Gamel-McCormick, 1996; Howard, 1978; Turnbull & Turnbull, 1996; Wikler, Wasow, & Hatfield, 1981). Postpartum depression in the mother may be significant and prolonged, and the mother's depression and anxiety can affect her attachment to the baby. Schell (1981) indicated that the failure of the mother to become involved in the normal nurturing rituals with her developing child, such as gazing, cooing, and smiling, may make the disabled infant particularly at risk for abuse. Sobsey (1994) touched on the issues of attachment at the birth of a child with disabilities in his comprehensive exploration of abuse and violence in the lives of people with disabilities. Clearly it is possible that the lack of bonding can result in a higher risk for abuse later in life.

Trout (1983) wrote that grieving for a lost child is complicated by the demands of caring for the needs of a new baby. Caring for an infant is tiring and stressful, even under the best of circumstances (Carney & Gamel-McCormick, 1996). The emotional and financial strain of a child with special needs is even more extensive. Quality medical care and specialized day care may be required. Finding a baby-sitter for a few hours' respite may be a monumental task. From her interview of 31 families with infants with disabilities, Beckman (1983) found that the most significant stress the families reported was the additional care-giving demands the children required. Cullen et al., (1991) found that mothers of young children who have mental retardation are in need of greater support. Only half of the families in the study had child care available for respite. The researchers found that mothers' concerns were focused mostly on current needs, whereas the major concerns of spouses, as reported by the mothers, was on what was lost, such as time, rest, and play time. In the face of added demands, parents may feel resentful and angry and yet have nowhere to express these feelings. In fact, parents may feel guilty about their anger if they view it as directed at the child, a helpless infant, rather than at the demands placed upon them as parents.

Some writers have focused on alternative experiences of having a child born with a disability. For example, Hanline (1991) indicated:

> In fact, a growing body of knowledge suggests that the presence of a family member with a disability may contribute to the strengthening of the entire family unit, as well as contribute positively to the quality of life of individual members of the family. In addition, current perspectives of families question the appropriateness of applying the concept of grief to all families and of assuming that all families adapt to the birth of a child with disabilities by progressing through various "stages" of adaptation, culminating in a stage of "acceptance." (p. 53)

An emergent model for family therapy in the 1990s, based on the work of Australian Michael White, proposes that even greater shifts be encouraged in family members' views of problems. The shift provides a way to move outside of the subjugation accompanying the oppression of a world view of being controlled by what is perceived as the "problem." Still worse would be assuming responsibility for creating the "problem." As noted in M. P. Nichols and R. C. Schwartz (1995):

> White isn't interested in what causes problems, but he is interested in the evolving effects of problems on families over time. His belief is that people with problems often develop what he calls "problem-saturated descriptions" of their lives: The negative events in their lives and negative aspects of their personalities are constantly in the foreground, making them feel powerless and, consequently, easy prey of problems. As family members try and fail to solve their problems, this story of failure comes to dominate the family. (p. 463)

At one time, interventions that were seen as helpful at the early state of diagnosis of having a child with a disability included listening and offering emotional support for parents, providing information about resources in the community, and activating family and external support systems (Dunlap & Hollinsworth, 1977). If we are to follow the emerging models of the 1990s, such as that of Michael White, helping professionals will focus on "re-storying," assisting family members to separate from the preceding problem-saturated stories and to externalize their problems. This intervention will help family members realize that the problem was their relationship with a "problem" and will thus allow them to separate themselves from what they had seen as the problem and to construct a new story. The new story will allow them to be in control of their lives and to recast old notions. It becomes incumbent upon school professionals to help families see life in a new way, to focus on possibilities, and to recognize the control they have over their lives. In Chapter 9 of this text, the view of the family as a resource is covered.

Stage 3: Families With Elementary Aged Children

The majority of children with special needs who have not been recognized at birth will be diagnosed during Stage 3. During this stage, the diagnostic process will probably involve the school system in some manner. It is imperative that the interactions that occur between school personnel and these families be a support to the families, rather than an added stress. The more knowledgeable school personnel are about the child's disability and the family's life cycle stage, the more positive potential there is in the diagnostic process.

Seligman (1991a) reiterated the following stress factors associated with Stage 3 (originally identified by Olson et al., 1984) for families with children with special needs: clarifying personal views regarding placement of their child (inclusion versus self-contained or resource rooms); dealing with reactions to the child by the child's peer group; and arranging for both child care and after-school activities. School personnel who are aware of these stressors can make suggestions that are helpful to the family members of students with special needs. They can describe advantages and disadvantages of the different delivery models and can introduce family members to others who have been in the system for a while and who have the wisdom of experience to share.

School personnel also need to help parents and siblings learn how to talk to the child's nondisabled peers. By doing so, they give the family members permission to speak with the child's peers as well as the language with which to talk to elementary age children. Sometimes parents do not realize that the probing questions children ask do not require technical answers and can easily be handled with simple responses. Many different school personnel can assist in this learning process; it does not always have to fall on the teacher to provide this support. Often, support groups exist in which family members can discuss as well as role-play talking with the child's nondisabled peers.

In some communities, parent groups have taken responsibility for developing resource lists for child care as well as extracurricular activities for children with disabilities. The school counselor is another good resource to help families network in the community. In addition, local universities often have lists of students who are studying in the field of special education who welcome the experience of baby-sitting or working with children with disabilities.

Dyson and Fewell (1985) compared 15 families with children with disabilities to 15 families with children of the same age who had not been diagnosed with problems. They found, predictably, that the families with children with disabilities reported greater overall levels of stress and that the experience of stress increased with the severity of the child's condition. Stress in these families seemed to stem from four primary sources: characteristics of the child, such as basic personality style and personal response to the diagnosis; degree of physical incapacitation of the child; parental pessimism about the child's health and future; and severity of the disabling condition. The researchers found that parents who reported the highest levels of social support were most able to enjoy their parenting role despite their child's difficulties.

The Dyson and Fewell (1985) study points to several important factors in family adjustment during this life cycle stage. First, families need to have basic information about their child's special needs. The longer and more difficult the diagnostic process, the greater the potential for negative effects on the family's stability. Once the child's difficulties have been established and understood, the family can begin the process of acceptance. Support groups are invaluable resources in helping families move toward acceptance.

Second, parents need to be educated about appropriate services and school placement. The better informed the parents are, the more likely they are to become actively involved in the child's school placement and contribute to his or her positive adjustment. If parents are confused about their child's needs or have misperceptions about the limitations imposed by a particular disability, they may try to shield their child from challenges and may actually become overinvolved in school placement decisions, to the detriment of the student. A sign that parents have not adequately made the transition to the child-rearing life cycle stage (Stage 3) and have not incorporated the themes of affiliation and inclusion is their expression of a "we versus they" mentality that pits the family against the school.

The following scenario provides an example of the failure to transition. The couple described was seeking help from a psychologist to identify an appropriate placement for their 11-year-old daughter.

> Sheronda, now in the fourth grade, had been identified with behavior problems in kindergarten. She was originally tested at 5 years old and had an IQ in the borderline range of mental retardation. The parents did not feel that their concerns were heard by the school system, and they were unable to accept the mental retardation diagnosis. When the girl entered first grade, placement in a classroom for Educable Mental Retardation was recommended. The parents refused to agree to this setting for their daughter, so she was placed in a regular classroom with resource help.
>
> In spite of the test results that were used in the original diagnosis, during their initial meeting with the psychologist, the parents insisted that their daughter was suffering from attention deficit disorder and learning disabilities that had never been adequately evaluated or treated. They felt that the school system had never, in 5 years, listened to their experiences with the girl in the home. They were requesting that the psychologist assist them in pursuing a court case against the school system for failure to provide adequate services for their daughter.

The psychologist reviewed 6 years of evaluations and found that the girl was, indeed, functioning at the borderline mentally retarded range of intelligence. However, she also exhibited many behavioral symptoms of hyperactivity, attentional difficulties, and areas of intellectual functioning that were within the average range. In addition, she was significantly depressed because of her continued failure experiences at school and her perceived lack of acceptance by her parents.

In this case, the parents' failure to feel heard, to receive adequate explanations about their daughter's functioning, and to accept their daughter's dysfunctions and mourn the loss of their "perfect child" had caused the family to be stuck at Stage 2 of the family life cycle. The family had never adequately transitioned into Stage 3 with its focus on child-rearing; they had not yet involved themselves in a coalition with the school system and in helping Sheronda develop appropriate friends and activities for herself.

During Stage 3, one of the major struggles for families with children with special needs is balancing the functional and emotional tasks of a family. Parents must establish routines to take care of the specialized needs of the child with the disability while also managing the needs of the remainder of the family. An area of family functioning that is often neglected in the face of the functional demands of caring for a child with special needs is family recreation and relaxation (Shapiro, 1983).

Gallagher, Cross, and Scharfman (1981) found that the major stress reported by families following the diagnosis of a child with chronic illness was the alteration of the family's social and recreational life. The study revealed that the presence of a strong personal support network between spouses and with family friends made the biggest difference in the families' coping abilities. When families felt that their friends understood their child's disability, did not stigmatize the family, and offered their support with carpooling, babysitting, and recreational activities, their stress was reduced.

Stage 4: Families With Adolescents

When adolescents without disabilities successfully complete Stage 4, they emerge from this period with adequate self-esteem, a comfortable body image, an established identity, and emotional independence. Virtually all adolescents experience adjustment problems during this stage. The presence of a chronic illness, emotional or intellectual limitations, or the struggles of a learning disability cannot help but exacerbate those problems. For all families with adolescents, added to the stresses of the youth's adjustment are the struggles of the family to loosen boundaries and promote independence. Given the variability of the adolescent's special circumstances, it is clear that this life-cycle stage will be most difficult.

Seligman (1991a) reported the following stressors (originally identified by Olson et al., 1984) for families with adolescents with special needs: adjusting to the chronic nature of the disability; dealing with issues related to sexuality, peer isolation, and rejection; and making plans for transition from work to school. As in Stage 3, school personnel can help families alleviate these stressors.

During Stage 4, all adolescents begin to know their limitations and compare themselves to their peers (Patterson, 1985). The formation of a personal identity should include the reality of the individual's strengths and weaknesses. Of course, this realization will affect self-esteem. Taking personal risks, assertively dealing with peers, confronting challenges, and increasing independence are more difficult if the adolescent is starting from a base of low self-esteem or a negative identity.

In addition to the difficulties of emotional adjustments, many adolescents with special needs face issues of physical adjustment. Adolescents and parents must deal with the changes brought about by the onset of puberty and emerging sexuality. Parents who have been responsible for their child's physical well-being must now decide how much physical care to relinquish to the adolescent (Patterson & McCubbin, 1983). If no concessions are made to the adolescent's increasing needs for privacy and autonomy, the adolescent may take control by not complying with medical treatment (Blumberg, Lewis, & Susman, 1984). Refusal to monitor blood sugars and overeating are common rebellion behaviors for adolescents with diabetes. Many adolescents with cerebral palsy or spina bifida stop following their catheterization procedures. Anorexia and bulimia occur in many adolescents, including adolescents who seemed perfectly normal before this period. For all of these behaviors, the common theme is a lack of feelings of autonomy and control on the part of the adolescent.

Finally, the adolescent life cycle stage brings with it the challenges of planning for the vocational development of the student with special needs. Questions that must be answered include: How much does the disability affect the student's intellectual potential? Are there motivational, emotional, and financial factors that must be considered? What are the student's physical limitations? What are the student's desires and dreams for the future? The task of the family and the school system is to help the student set realistic goals that do not underestimate or overestimate individual potential. In developing vocational goals, it is important to keep in mind the adolescent's need for feelings of control and autonomy. Within particular limitations imposed by school rules and the student's abilities, the student should be given as many choices as possible regarding future plans.

For adolescents, both with and without special needs, and their parents, the struggle between independence and dependence is heightened during this stage. The parents must try to be supportive and available while at the same time allowing for privacy and autonomy when the adolescent is ready. Adolescents may vacillate between resenting their parents' overprotection and needing their support. If some balance and resolution are not achieved, problems in communication and relationships may occur.

Zetlin (1985) studied the families of 25 adolescents with mild retardation over an 18-month period. He divided family styles into supportive, dependent, and conflict-ridden. He found that members of the supportive group were least likely to experience serious behavioral disturbances during adolescence. When there was a disturbance, it was usually one of emotional confusion rather than one of an antisocial or rebellious nature. Those adolescents who were involved in conflict-laden relationships with their parents were most likely to act out and exhibit antisocial behavior, including theft, inappropriate sexual behavior, and delinquent or violent behavior. In addition, 75% of the dependent group displayed behaviors reflecting emotional disturbance, including withdrawal, alcohol or drug use, and self-abusive or suicidal behavior. Clearly, the relationships between parents and adolescents that were characterized as supportive but not dependent in nature were most likely to reduce adolescent dysfunction.

Along these same lines, Nihira, Mink, and Meyers (1985) found that the home environment was the most significant contributor to children's development of various social, educational, and behavioral skills from their longitudinal study of 148 families having an adolescent diagnosed as a slow learner and 151 families having an adolescent diagnosed as Trainable Mentally Retarded (Nihira, Meyers, & Mink, 1983). Specifically, the factors of harmony in the family and cohesive, quality parenting had a strong effect on a wide range of adjustment behaviors. Again, family relationships that were nonconflicting and supportive without being smothering were the best indicators of positive adjustment in the adolescent.

Education professionals are in a unique position to be able to provide information about adolescent struggles to families in a nonthreatening way. Parent information seminars can be held during high school enrollment. PTA meetings or discussions can be geared toward adolescent developmental issues and family relationships. If parents are informed, they are more likely to know what to expect from their adolescents and to be able to respond with appropriate guidance and support.

Stage 5: Families Launching Children

Seligman (1991a, p. 35) related Olson et al.'s (1984) listing of stressors in this phase of launching children as "recognizing and adjusting to the family's continuing responsibility, deciding on appropriate residential placement, and dealing with the paucity of socialization opportunities for the disabled family member."

From data collected from 19 families having a young adult with a severe developmental disability, Thorn and Irvin (1992) found residential concerns to be prominent predictors of overall stress for both family members and the young adults with mental retardation. The most stressful concern of the family members was related to residential placements. Specifically, the availability, quality, and interactions with providers were the foci of the stress.

Parents and social agencies must help the young adult find a job or enroll in an appropriate vocational program. Transition programs abound, and many job coaches are funded by public funds. Depending upon the abilities of the person with the disability, he or she might need help finding an appropriate adult residence and learning how to manage financial resources. Socialization opportunities outside the family are particularly important at this stage.

Clearly, each stage of the family life cycle brings particular challenges to the family of a child or youth with special needs. Hanline (1991) indicated that professionals need to respect the individuality of family members as they adapt to having a child with a disability. Each person will respond to and cope with disabilities differently, and not all parents will "progress through the same predetermined stages as they adapt to having a child with disabilities" (Hanline, 1991, p. 56). Thus, it is important to focus on the unique aspect of each family. Hanline also indicated that families may need continued support during transitions and critical events, as these may be challenging and difficult even though they occur many years after the diagnosis of the disability. As she stated:

> The professional's role is to assist parents by identifying actual and potential problem areas, helping parents to carry out the tasks posed by the transition or critical event, and encouraging parents to learn skills and utilize supports that can be applied to all transitions and critical events. (p. 57)

Hanline also recommended that professionals help family members make use of informal supports (e.g., babysitting, shopping, and carpooling) on which they can rely during times of transition. Helping family members use these supports increases their autonomy, competence, and esteem.

COPING STRATEGIES FOR FAMILIES

In addition to being aware of the challenges families face, it is important to be aware of how families can be helped to cope with these stressors and the adjustments they require. In this section, research concerning coping strategies for families experiencing life cycle stressors is discussed, as well as an educational program that has been successful in addressing the needs of families under stress.

Characteristics of Coping

Figley and McCubbin (1983) identified a number of general positive characteristics that predict a family's ability to cope with life stresses. They are as relevant today as when they were identified. These characteristics are being able to determine the cause of the stress; thinking systemically rather than individually; focusing on solutions instead of casting blame; tolerating differences in the family; openly demonstrating affection; using effective communication; showing a high level of family cohesion; demonstrating role flexibility; tapping resources internal and external to the family; and being free from violence and substance abuse. These characteristics can provide a useful diagnostic checklist for the educator involved with families of children with special needs. Whenever possible, educational programs geared toward helping families develop these characteristics should be provided. In addition, individual families may be helped to develop their own unique adaptive capacities (Reiss & Oliveri, 1980). Of course, if there is evidence of physical violence or substance abuse, the family should be referred to an appropriate treatment facility. For further discussion of violence and chemical dependency in families, see Chapter 7.

In general, functional family coping patterns appear to arise from adequate information about and understanding of the stress; supportive versus conflicting relationships within the family; and adequate social network support. From their study of 500 families with a child with a chronic illness Patterson and McCubbin (1983) found three predominant functional coping patterns: The families preserved a sense of optimism and were cooperative; experienced support from others, maintained their feelings of self-worth, and were emotionally stable; and had gained an understanding of the chronic problem from interactions with peers and consulting with the medical establishment.

Coping Workshops

McFadden and Doub (1983) developed a series of workshops for family survival and coping that can be easily adapted for parent groups within a school setting. They begin the workshop series with a set of rules for survival during hard times. The rules encourage members to recognize when they are having a hard time; to stick together during the hard times; to slow down; and to get external help when they perceive their family is stuck.

These rules express in basic terms some of the coping characteristics cited earlier. The professional who is planning a family group may wish to develop, with the families, a personalized set of coping "rules."

LIMITATIONS OF THE FAMILY LIFE CYCLE PERSPECTIVE

Since the first edition of this textbook was written, a number of professionals (Breulin, Schwartz, & Kune-Karrer, 1992; L'Abate, 1994b; W. C. Nichols, 1996) have pointed to the inherent limitations of the developmental family life cycle perspective. Often cited is the limitation of a static perspective that cannot take into consideration the many ways family structure presents itself in our culture. Indeed, many professionals in the field of psychology and family studies consider the usefulness of the concept of the family life cycle to be declining. Breulin et al. (1992) presented an alternative in their book, *Metaframeworks,* that attends to five levels: biological, individual, subsystemic, familial, and societal. Their orientation focuses on microtransitions and the negotiation of those changes through oscillation rather than on the typical definite and discrete stages of the family life cycle literature. However, the alternatives to the life cycle perspective have their limitations as well. As W. C. Nichols (1996) stated:

> My own speculation is that one reason some family therapists lost their interest in the family life cycle may have been an overemphasis on the transitions between stages and on the production of pathology in relation to failures or difficulties in effecting those between-state transitions. The other side of the overemphasis on transitions and the related spawning of pathology appears to have been an underemphasis on the significance of normal "inside-the-stages" developmental tasks. (p. 65)

Regardless of its real or implied limitations, the family life cycle can provide valuable information for use by school professionals. Simply knowing about the family life cycle perspective can help educators better understand and therefore relate to students and their families. Empathy should be evoked more easily, and explaining the family life cycle to family members can help them gain a perspective that normalizes the humps and bumps of transitions as well as allows them to look forward to the predictable plateaus. If school problems can be diagnosed within the context of family development, interventions are more likely to be successful.

SUMMARY

Much of traditional psychological thought focuses on issues of development, primarily from an individual perspective. The family life cycle is a logical extension of this tradition into a family systems context.

The family life cycle provides a framework for the developmental aspect of systems theory and, as such, provides the school professional with the same tools that theories of psychosexual, cognitive, moral, or emotional development do for the individual student. The life cycle model serves to identify patterns of normal development for the entire family and provides a basis for judgment about dysfunction when developmental difficulties are encountered.

CASE EXAMPLE

Nancy, age 13, was brought to the attention of the school counselor by her maternal grandmother. She was eligible for placement in a special education classroom for children diagnosed with educable mental retardation. She had been receiving special education services since she was 3 years old and had adjusted well until the past 2 years. Her parents, who were stationed with the military in Germany, were requesting that Nancy begin living with her grandmother. Their expressed reason was that Nancy could receive better special education and recreational services in the States than in Germany. They felt that inadequate resources were provided for special-needs students of Nancy's age in the American school in Germany. The grandmother was asking the school for their recommendations about Nancy's living situation and possible placement options.

The psychologist took a thorough family history and discovered the following time line: Nancy was diagnosed with borderline mental retardation when she was 3 years old. The family began receiving early intervention services from their local school system, and the parents seemed to adjust well to Nancy's diagnosis and special needs. The maternal grandparents, who lived nearby, were actively involved in Nancy's care and adjustment.

Four years later, Nancy's family moved to Germany following her father's military transfer. Nancy continued to receive special education services through the American school. Up to this point, the parents reported that both they and Nancy seemed to make the necessary adjustments with few problems.

While the family was living in Germany, the mother was not required to work outside of the home. For the first time in Nancy's life, her mother was available when she got home from school. Things were going so well for the family that when Nancy was 9 years old, her parents had another child, a son. This birth was planned and was anticipated by the family with excitement. Again, the parents reported that the family seemed to make a sound adjustment to having an infant in the home. Their daughter expressed love for her brother and often helped with basic care such as bottle feeding. The parents viewed Nancy as compliant and good-natured about the changes in the family. Now in the third grade, Nancy was actively involved in school and peer activities.

During the following year, the mother's father was diagnosed with cancer. Over the next 2 years, the mother made four extended trips to the United States to help with her father's care and with decisions regarding his treatment. Each time, the mother took her infant son with her but left Nancy in Germany to attend school. Nancy was very close to her grandfather, but when he died during her sixth-grade year, she was unable to attend the funeral and never got to say goodbye.

It was during this period that Nancy began to show changes in mood. Her parents reported that she was unhappy about her mother's frequent absences from home. Because of her mother's trips, Nancy was placed in an after-school day care center where she stayed until her father got off from work each evening. Nancy's behavior became demanding; she was at times openly defiant of her parents' wishes. Nancy, now 12, refused to clean her room or do basic household chores that had been hers since she was 6 years old. Her school performance deteriorated, and she spent more and more time isolated in her room. When her mother was at home, Nancy reacted to her in an angry and sullen manner. Her father finally stated that he could not handle Nancy alone and work his full-time job. The next time Nancy's mother went to the States to settle her father's estate, she brought Nancy with her. They stayed with Nancy's maternal grandmother. After a week, Nancy's mother asked if Nancy could remain with her grandmother. It was at this point that the grandmother sought help from the school counselor.

Questions and Comments

1. *Which life cycle stages and stressors were Nancy's family able to negotiate success-fully? What factors and dynamics supported positive adjustment?*

    This couple appears to have made the transition through Stage 1 (Newly Married Couple), Stage 2 (Families With Young Children), and Stage 3 (Families With Elementary Aged Children) of the family life cycle with adequate adjustment. Even the diagnosis of their daughter with mental retardation at age 3 and the family's move to Germany did not appear to cause this family significant problems. The couple had the support of extended family and community services.

    They seemed to be able to share parenting roles while both had careers. When the mother stopped working outside the home, the family made this adjustment as well. In fact, the couple made a purposeful decision to reenter the stage of families with young children when the mother's time was more free. Even after the birth of the son, the family continued to adapt and reestablish a plateau period. They included Nancy in the birth process and allowed her to help with the initial caretaking of their infant son.

2. *At what stage did Nancy's family become "stuck"? What were the contributing factors and dynamics identified as precipitating the disruption of the family life cycle?*

    It was not until the family reached Stage 4 (Families With Adolescents) that the failure to adapt and reorganize roles was evident. The concept of pile-up is clearly demonstrated in this family. Parental and marital decisions about the family had been made based on the plan that the family would live in Germany, the mother would be able to stay at home with her children, and the family would have a period of relative stability. This stability was threatened, however, by events outside of the family's control. Within a short period after the baby's birth, the mother's father was diagnosed with cancer. Not only did she have her own family to manage, but she was also responsible for helping with her father's care. This change left her husband trying to manage his own job as well as Nancy and their home.

When the grandfather died, the mother was the only member of Nancy's family who was able to attend the funeral and experience the grief with her extended family network. The family did not give Nancy an opportunity to work through her own grief. In fact, the death of her grandfather was not even discussed to any great degree. The parents were unsure how well Nancy could understand the concept of death, and much of their energy was directed toward reinvolving the mother in family life and raising an infant.

Nancy's reaching adolescence appears to be the final factor in the pile-up of transitional demands and stresses that sent this family into crisis. The daughter's noncompliant behaviors and sullen attitude were her expression of the distress that the entire family was experiencing, as well as a predictable response to her growing sense of independence and the struggles that adolescence brings. The parents felt so overwhelmed by the changes they saw in Nancy that their solution was to place her outside of the home altogether.

3.   *What interventions could be used to help the family move on in the family life cycle?*

Intervention for this family involved a number of different paths. First, the family was given information about the family life cycle, and their pile-up was acknowledged. Nancy's development as an adolescent was discussed, and the mother was given information about the struggles faced by other families with an adolescent with special needs. The mother was invited to attend a support group for parents with children with special needs. She attended a meeting and was able to discuss the changes in her daughter with other parents who had experienced similar difficulties.

Second, the family was helped through the grief process that had slowed down their ability to make an adequate transition. The mother was advised to talk to her daughter about the loss of her grandfather and to give her as much information as she wanted about her grandfather's illness, death, and funeral. In fact, the family made a visit to the grandfather's grave site so that the Nancy could say her goodbyes and have a concrete way to experience the meaning of death.

Finally, the parents were advised to not leave Nancy with her grandmother. Nancy was able to tell her mother that she did not want to be left behind. She cried and expressed how much she had missed her mother over the past 2 years. With help from the school counselor, Nancy was able to communicate some of her turmoil and confusion about becoming an adolescent. Nancy's mother was convinced that leaving Nancy in the United States at this time would be interpreted by Nancy as the ultimate rejection.

The mother also was advised about special education services that she could receive through the military in Germany. She was able to see that if, in a few years, Nancy was not happy with the situation in Germany, she could always choose to return to the States. By this time, however, the grandmother would have had time to adjust to her own loss, and Nancy would have had time to reconnect with her family.

The counselor also advised that the parents begin to spend individual time with their daughter and time alone as a couple. The family had developed a lifestyle, when they were together, of always going everywhere and doing everything with both children. As Nancy's developmental needs were significantly different from those of her younger brother, she needed some individual attention and activities that were geared to her age level. The parents needed some time together so that some of their stress could be alleviated and so they could solidify their relationship as a couple.

With information, the parents realized that even though their daughter was 13 years in age, she was functioning at a much younger level because of her intellectual limitations coupled with the family's unresolved grief and failure to make transitional adjustments. The parents were then able to provide more support and work with Nancy in controlling her moods and noncompliant behaviors. When the parents were able to view their daughter's rebellious behaviors within the context of the family stress, they were more willing to help her through this transition.

EXTENSION ACTIVITIES

Reflection: Select an age when you were in elementary school, and then later in secondary school, and focus on your family and the life cycle of your family at both of those life cycle stages (i.e., Families With Elementary Aged Children and Families With Adolescents).

Journal: How do you see the primary theme of both these life cycle stages affecting your family, and in what ways were the primary tasks accomplished or poorly handled? To what do you attribute any difficulties that your family of origin faced in either or both life cycle stages?

Reflection: When you were growing up, at what time(s) do you recall your family of origin facing pile-up. What was going on in your family during those times?

Journal: In what ways did your family cope with pile-up? Was the pile-up related to transition times or other factors? If other factors, what were they, and how have you come to understand them? If you are part of a nuclear family (i.e., if you have children), in what ways have you learned to cope effectively when facing pile-up? What meaning did you learn to bring to those stressful experiences, both then and now?

Discussion: If you are part of a nuclear family discuss what life cycle stage your family is currently in with a member of the class group or someone else. What do you see as the primary theme and primary tasks of this stage in relation to your nuclear family? In what ways do your nuclear family's experiences reflect those of your family of origin (or that of your partner, if you have one) when your family of origin was in the same family life cycle stage?

Discussion: If you have held a professional position in which you have interacted or are interacting with families, select a family with which you are quite familiar, and, while maintaining the anonymity of the family, discuss what you have observed about life cycle stages in this family. Use what you have learned about the six stages in reading this chapter.

In-Class/Training Exploration Leader Instruction: Have a member of the class/session who has worked with families of at-risk or special-needs students describe one of those families through the lens of the family life cycle. After others listen to the story, have them tell how they see the family.

In-Class/Training Discussion Starter: How can knowledge of the family life cycle of students help professionals in schools improve school and family relations?

In-Class/Training Discussion Starter: How can you, as a school professional, help students bring meaning to stressful experiences? What value does ascribing meaning have in our lives? [Read Victor Frankl's *Man's Search for Meaning.*]

Family Interaction Patterns

This chapter introduces the family systems theory known as *structural family therapy*. The structural concepts related to closeness and distance between family members and to roles, functions, and distribution of power within the family are explained. A case example that illustrates these structural concepts and their usefulness for the school professional in understanding how and why families communicate in particular ways follows, and extension activities complete the chapter.

INTRODUCTION

A key concept in viewing students' school difficulties within a family systems approach is that the individual's behavior is not solely dependent upon what is going on in that person's head. Rather, the behavior is maintained by a complex set of interactions that occur with regularity and can be predicted by observing the family system over time (M. P. Nichols & Schwartz, 1995). This basic systemic premise is evidenced in the work of Salvadore Minuchin, a pediatrician turned psychiatrist, and his co-workers (Minuchin, Montalvo, Guerney, Rosman, & Schumer, 1967), who developed the treatment approach known as structural family therapy.

Early in the development of the structural model, Minuchin (1974) noted that the primary job of the family is to "enhance the psychosocial growth of each member" (p. 51). To accomplish that task, the family must operate with some predictability and stability. For instance, children should be able to forecast that each time they misbehave they will receive a similar response from their parents. In addition, the family must also be able to respond to changing circumstances with some flexibility. When prolonged stress occurs, if the family is not capable of changing roles and communication patterns, family conflict and dysfunctional behavior will result. Minuchin and Nichols (1993) presented case studies in their book *Family Healing* that painted pictures of common types of family dysfunction. Colapinto (1991) indicated that family dysfunction stems from both stress and failure of the family to realign to cope with the stress. Writing about family therapy, Minuchin (1992) said, "It is a process in which therapist and family members, working together, search for and enact an alternative reality that expands the possibilities for the family and its members" (p. 14).

In structural family therapy, the role of the helper is to help families adapt to changing circumstances through changes in the structure of the family. According to this theory, family members have prescribed roles and functions that set up a pattern of behaviors within the family. The trained observer can identify these patterns by watching how the family interacts. The student is only one member of this complex family network. If students' behaviors are to be understood, they must be observed in the context of their families' patterns of relating.

Minuchin and his colleagues have observed and worked with thousands of families over the past 30 years. Through their observations, they have identified patterns of relating that occur frequently in families. They developed the terms boundaries, subsystems, and hierarchy to describe those patterns. In the structural family approach, problems of an individual are viewed as a result of dysfunctional family structure in one of these three areas. These dysfunctional family patterns will eventually result in the manifestation of behavioral, emotional, or physical symptoms in a family member, usually a child.

Intensive Structural Therapy, described by Fishman (1993), involves:

> working with the contemporary context, the people who are key parts of the identified patient's present social environment and the social forces they represent. The social context that impinges on the nuclear family can, and usually does, include people and forces well beyond the family's bounds. To address fully the needs of the modern family, one must work to transform these outside social forces as well as the forces within the family. (p. 13)

For more information regarding the theoretical principles underlying structural family therapy, see Appendix A.

BOUNDARIES

In observing family structure, one aspect of importance to structural family therapists is the pattern of distance and closeness between family members (M. P. Nichols & Schwartz, 1995). In other words, how emotionally connected are family members? How openly do they communicate with one another? How well is individuality tolerated in the family? This dimension of closeness and distance is defined through boundaries, the rules that determine "who participates and how" in the system (Minuchin, 1974, p. 53).

If a system is functioning well, boundaries are clear and semipermeable. Indications of clear boundaries within a school would be that the teacher is responsible for evaluating and managing the student within the classroom, and the school psychologist is responsible for evaluating the student and meeting with families at the request of the teacher. Indications of semipermeable boundaries would be that the psychologist might observe the student within the classroom and ask for the teacher's feedback, or the teacher might meet with the family and the psychologist to discuss a particular student's behavior.

Assuming that both professionals are adequately skilled, if the system is operating in a functional manner, the teacher appreciates the psychologist's presence in the classroom and the psychologist values the teacher's presence at the family meeting, both professionals feel that they are joining resources for a student's well-being. If the two professionals are communicating openly, respecting each other's domains and contributions, and working for a common outcome, then the boundaries in this system are clearly defined.

Boundaries are described as dysfunctional if they are either blurred or too rigidly defined. At the extremes of distance and closeness are *disengaged* and *enmeshed* systems. Figure 3.1 provides a visual representation of this continuum.

Families with a pattern of relating that falls at either extreme of the continuum are at risk for having a member who exhibits physical or emotional symptoms. Children tend to be at high risk for reacting to family stress and dysfunctional family patterns.

Disengaged

At one extreme of the continuum are families or systems in which boundaries are inappropriately rigid and there is excessive distance between people. According to W. C. Nichols (1996),

> the disengaging patterns of family process are characterized by a remarkable absence of affective intensity in family attachments. Relationships throughout the family subsystems are marked by emotional distance, lack of sensitivity to individual needs, and a high frequency of independent activities. (p. 197)

Communication between members is limited, and collaboration within the home or with the school is difficult. Nuances of behavior tend to go unnoticed in a disengaged system, and thus children may go to extremes of behavior such as temper tantrums, fire-setting, suicidal threats, or stealing to get attention. Members of a disengaged system report feeling as

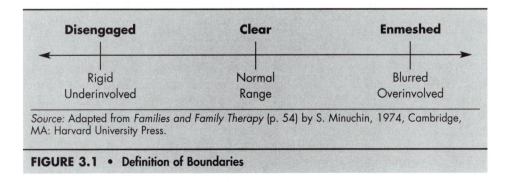

Source: Adapted from *Families and Family Therapy* (p. 54) by S. Minuchin, 1974, Cambridge, MA: Harvard University Press.

FIGURE 3.1 • Definition of Boundaries

if they are required to make decisions or handle problems alone. W. C. Nichols (1996) indicated that family members from disengaged systems are likely to become independent and autonomous much earlier than members of families with clear or enmeshed boundaries, but the cost of the emotional loss and limiting affective ties is large.

Family Systems

Students who come from highly disengaged families are more likely to exhibit behavior problems or problems of externalizing versus internalizing. If appropriate intervention is not given, these students are at risk for becoming involved with legal or court systems in the future. Acting-out behaviors such as speaking with a loud voice, acting as the class clown, stealing from other students, cursing, and acting belligerent are all possible indications of inappropriate distance and rigidity in the family.

The school professional can observe disengagement by watching the responses and interactions of family members. Do people in the family sit far apart from one another? Do the children have to repeat themselves to be heard? When the teacher calls a parent or sends a note home, does it take a long time for the parent to respond? Another aspect of disengagement to watch for is inattention to expressions of feeling on the part of family members. Do family members have to escalate their behavior to receive attention for their feelings?

Other aspects of family life may also reflect disengagement. For example, does the family have regular meals together? Are there regular activities in which the whole family participates, such as church, vacations, or sports events? Are the parents involved in PTA activities? Do they attend their children's school activities when invited? Failure of the family to be involved in these types of activities may be an example of disengagement and should be noted by the school professional.

Corey (1996) shared an extreme story of disengagement in a family. A teacher had noticed that one of her students had been absent for days and called home to no avail. She finally called the police. When they went to the home to investigate, they found that the parents had not even noticed that their sixth-grade son had not been home in 3 days. Both physical and emotional cutoff were evident in this extreme case of disengagement.

When disengagement is observed, school professionals can view students' behaviors in a different context and adjust their manner of dealing with the families. A note sent home to a family that is disengaged may need to be stated more forcefully with the subject matter highlighted as a potential crisis if the teacher is to gain a response. If an initial note or phone call does not elicit parental concern, the teacher may want to ask the principal or assistant principal to sign the next notice in an attempt to signal its importance to disengaged parents.

It is also important for teachers to note any feelings they have that the children of disengaged families are more resistant to their direction than other children. A child's lack of responsiveness may, in fact, be a function of the family pattern. In the same vein, a teacher's efforts to provide approval and nurturance may be initially rejected by the child from a disengaged family.

Professionals have a tendency to define disengaged families as "bad" or abusive. Keeping in mind the principles of how and why a system operates as it does is a helpful check against being judgmental. Often disengagement is a systemic response to extensive conflict, long-term family stress, or overtaxing of emotional resources. The distancing is an attempt by the family system to gain a balance and to continue to function in the face of these forces. In fact, once these families do notice that something is wrong, the school professional may observe high levels of conflict and verbal reactivity. It is often fear of out-of-control conflict (Colapinto, 1982) or fear of enmeshment (Feldman, 1992) that leads to the initial disengagement process.

The families of a child with special needs often have a long history of involvement with special educators, health care providers, or social services. At a particular point, disengagement may be observed between parent and child. However, the distance may be a reactive response to years or months of overinvolvement or overtaxing of the parents in the service of their child. In these instances, understanding the historical context may be useful in understanding and changing the disengagement process.

Family Systems Example

Kevin, an 8-year-old deaf boy, was identified by his third-grade speech and hearing teacher as experiencing a family systems problem when he was absent for three consecutive weeks. The teacher had called Kevin's mother, a single parent, after a week's absence and had left a message of concern on her telephone answering machine. When Kevin did not return to school after another week, the teacher contacted his mother at work and was told that Kevin had just gotten over a bad case of the flu, was being nursed back to health by his grandmother, and would return to school the next week. After a third week of absence, the teacher asked the school counselor if she would contact the mother and invite her to the school for a meeting. Both professionals hypothesized disengagement on the part of this mother due to her failure to respond to two teacher requests about her son's absences. In addition, because this mother was a single parent, they believed that she might be overwhelmed with the demands of parenting and thus relieved by Kevin's being allowed to stay with her mother.

School Systems

Disengagement can also be observed in school environments. If school professionals feel that they each have their own domain within the building, and if there is little collaboration between instruction, counseling, and administration, disengagement likely exists within the system. Steps toward resolving the disengagement may include identifying the fear or conflict that has led to the rigidly defined distance, increasing understanding of the different roles and functions within the school, and conducting team-building and collaboration exercises.

Enmeshed

At the opposite end of the continuum are families or systems in which boundaries are blurred and there is excessive closeness between people. In enmeshed systems, autonomy and independence are difficult to achieve. There is a lack of privacy, and individual differences are not well tolerated. Members of an enmeshed system may report feeling smothered or overprotected. A comment made about enmeshed families is that if one person is cut, the rest of the family bleeds (Aponte & Hoffman, 1973). W. C. Nichols (1996) discussed the identifiable emotional intensity that members of enmeshed families experience related to attachment, frequency of interactions, and reciprocal dependency. At times, family members speak on behalf of one another. Nichols cautioned professionals to not confuse enmeshment with emotional closeness or intimacy.

Enmeshment is often evident in families with psychosomatic conditions such as diabetes and asthma. According to I. Goldenberg and H. Goldenberg (1991), psychosomatic families are

> overprotective, inhibiting the child from developing a sense of independence, competence, or interest in activities outside the safety of the family. The physiologically vulnerable child, in turn, feels great responsibility for protecting the family. The manifestation of symptoms typically occurs when stress overloads the family's already dysfunctional coping mechanisms. Thus the symptoms are regarded as having a regulating effect on the family system, the sick child acting as a family conflict defuser by diverting family attention away from more basic, but less easily resolved, family conflicts. (p. 167)

Family Systems

Students who come from highly enmeshed families are more likely to exhibit emotional problems or problems of internalizing than to act out or externalize their difficulties. Without early intervention, these children are at risk for future need for mental health services or psychiatric hospitalization. Child and adolescent behaviors such as sadness and withdrawal, identity problems, and poor social skills may be evidence of an enmeshed family environment. In some families, the children act like parents and the parents have ineffective control. In enmeshed families, a child's acting-out behaviors, such as having temper tantrums or threatening to run away, are usually in response to limit setting where in the past limits have been blurred or nonexistent. This is in contrast to disengaged families, where lack of involvement precipitates acting-out behaviors. Typically, family members from enmeshed systems put an overly high value on cohesion of the family and relinquish autonomy—leaving less time to explore and master problems in wider systems.

Questions that may indicate if a family is enmeshed include: Do family members sit too closely together or inappropriately touch? Do younger children exhibit clingy behavior or acute distress at separation? Do people in this family interrupt one another or speak for each other? For example, if Johnny is asked how he feels about something, does his mother respond, "Johnny feels _____" as if she feels for him? If someone expresses a disagreement, is he or she ignored or talked over?

If the school professional observes signs of a family being enmeshed, he or she should heed certain cautions. In contrast to the disengaged system, in enmeshed families reactivity and emotionalism are the standard. A note sent home about a student's behavior to a family that is enmeshed may result in frantic phone calls or visits from the parents. Criticism of one family member, such as the student, may be perceived as a personal affront to other family members as well and may elicit a defensive reaction. In dealing with the enmeshed family, understatement should be the rule. Rather than needing to "loan" reactivity, the professional dealing with enmeshed systems needs to maintain a calm and nonreactive stance.

· The teacher may find children from enmeshed families to be more clingy and attention-seeking. These students may have difficulty with self-direction and may request frequent teacher assistance. The families may create problems with their children by hindering the mature development of behavior and interfering with their children's problem solving process (M. P. Nichols & Schwartz, 1995). These children may ask the teacher inappropriate personal questions or make requests for his or her time that are outside the regular school structure. In such instances, it is important for the teacher to view the student's behavior within a personal context. In an overinvolved family culture, these behaviors are seen as appropriate.

As with the disengaged family, it is vital for the school professional to recognize that family enmeshment is a result of systemic forces in operation. The need for intense closeness and family loyalty is often a homeostatic response designed to avoid extreme levels of anxiety (Colapinto, 1982; I. Goldenberg & H. Goldenberg, 1991; M. P. Nichols & Schwartz, 1995). Again, the family usually becomes enmeshed in response to chronic family stress or unfulfilled and unresolved emotional needs.

Particularly in families with a child with special needs, parents are fearful of allowing too much independence (Foster, 1986; E. Lusthaus & C. Lusthaus, 1993). They may feel that someone who has not "walked in their shoes" cannot understand or comment upon their parenting or attachment to their child. In these situations, recommendations for a family support group may be beneficial. Even enmeshed parents will often validate the opinions of other parents who have had similar experiences with their children. Keeping this context in mind may help the school professional to maintain personal boundaries in a clearer fashion when dealing with enmeshed systems.

Family Systems Example

Ranu, a 16-year-old girl with Down syndrome, had begun requesting frequent passes to leave her second period reading class. She complained of dizziness and headaches and asked to go to the school clinic. When this pattern was repeated five times in 2 weeks, Ranu's teacher discussed the problem with her co-workers and was informed that Ranu had been meeting a male student in the hall during these alleged trips to the clinic. The teacher refused to write another pass and sent a note home regarding this problem. The following day, Ranu's parents brought her to school and went to the principal's office, requesting a meeting. The reading teacher went to the meeting prepared to face the forces of an enmeshed system.

School Systems

The enmeshed school environment is easily recognized by its degree of involvement. It is characterized by excessive togetherness. Decisions regarding school policy are often laborious because of the need to involve everyone in a consensus, whether or not they will be affected by the particular decision. In these systems the agenda at staff meetings is frequently unfinished because of the emphasis on expression of feelings over accomplishment of tasks. If a staff member chooses to leave the school and take another job, his or her behavior is often viewed as disloyal.

Steps to resolving an enmeshed school system may include clarification of functions and goals for each member, instituting an incentive program for innovative ideas and accomplishment of goals, and focusing on solutions that minimize disagreement rather than require complete agreement from all staff.

Summary

Families and systems can usually be characterized as functioning, on the whole, somewhere along the boundary continuum between disengaged and enmeshed. This terminology is used to describe the overall emotional climate of the system and a preferred transactional style. At dysfunctional extremes, the terms enmeshed and disengaged describe the usual patterns of functioning within the family. However, in most families there are examples of both disengaged and enmeshed boundaries. A parent might be overinvolved or enmeshed in interactions with a child with special needs to the exclusion of other children in the family. A highly enmeshed pattern between mother and children may leave the father feeling excluded, and he may disengage in response. A father who is highly involved in his work and excludes his family may find his wife overinvolved with parenting in an effort to combat her loneliness. This dysfunctional pattern, consisting of an overinvolved mother and a disengaged father, is often found in families having a child with special needs. For further discussion and details regarding this pattern, see Chapter 8.

The school professional may benefit from information regarding the overall family style of boundary management. Knowledge of family boundaries is important for understanding such dimensions of children's behavior as emotional reactivity and degree of need for attention and for understanding parental responses to the identification of problems in a child. Opening the door to communication with an enmeshed family may require appealing to the emotionalism in the family system. A request made to an enmeshed family may begin with, "Since I know how much you love and worry about Cindy, I'm asking you . . ." The same request of a disengaged family might begin, "Although I'm aware of how busy you are, I'm asking you . . ." The school professionals' ability to communicate in a way that parallels the family's boundary style may be a key factor in developing a relationship with the family that supports problem solving and an effective partnership between parents and the school system.

SUBSYSTEMS

In structural family therapy the primary building blocks of family structure are the subsystems within the family. The traditional nuclear family consists of four subsystems (Minuchin, 1974):

- Spousal subsystem

- Parental subsystem
- Sibling subsystem
- Extrafamilial subsystem

Each subsystem has roles and functions that are common to all families. For example, every family has some person or persons who are identified as executives or decision makers for the family, that is, the parental subsystem. Other aspects of subsystem functioning are uniquely defined by each family. For example, in single-parent families there is no spousal subsystem. As another example, the extrafamilial subsystem may include biological family or friends and neighbors.

In an intact nuclear family, the marital partners constitute two different subsystems. As husband and wife, they compose the marital or spousal subsystem. As mother and father, they are the parental subsystem. These two subsystems have different but often intertwined functions. If there are communication problems between spouses, their functioning as parents will be affected.

Spousal Subsystem

The primary tasks of the spousal subsystem are providing for the functional needs of the family and providing for the individual emotional and sexual needs of husband and wife. As discussed in Chapter 2, the successful resolution of the first stage of the family life cycle, the formation of the marital system, is the framework upon which the entire future life of the family is built. Thus, the initial task of the spousal subsystem is to establish a sense of commitment and mutual trust (J. L. Framo, 1981; M. P. Nichols & Schwartz, 1995).

In our modern age, there are many variations of the intact, nuclear family pattern. Because of these variations, the definition of the spousal subsystem may need to be expanded to address the functioning of particular families. For example, in most single-parent families, there is no spousal subsystem. The functions of the spousal subsystem may be carried out by one parent and a significant dating or live-in relationship. In these instances, the reasons for the lack of a legal commitment and the impact upon the family must be considered. The basic premise that the emotional well-being of parents, revolving around their primary relationship, affects their functioning within the family still holds true.

Functional Support

Once the issue of commitment is resolved, the couple must work together to build a future for themselves. Basic skills in negotiating and division of labor must be developed. For healthy family functioning, the marital couple should divide chores and communicate about and resolve problems in order to evolve an interdependent relationship, as well as to accomplish the tasks of daily life. Early in their marriage, spouses must make many decisions about how household tasks will be divided, who will make money and how much they will make, how money will be allocated, how leisure time will be spent. The positive resolution of these questions comes from open, honest communication and mutual respect.

Emotional Support

Equally important is the role that the spousal subsystem plays in providing for the basic emotional needs of the marital couple (Reimers & Street, 1993). It is this emotional foundation that determines psychologically healthy patterns of interaction within the family and with other systems. Friedrich (1979), from a study of mothers of children with special needs, found that reported marital satisfaction of the couple was the most accurate predictor of successful coping and family adjustment to the child's special needs. In a follow-up study of 158 families with a child with mental retardation, marital satisfaction was found to be the best predictor of positive overall family relations (Friedrich, Wilturner, & Cohen, 1985). Quoting recent research, Turnbull and Turnbull (1996) concurred, stating, "Thus it appears that a strong marriage makes a difference in overall family well-being" (p. 100).

The happiness and stability of the primary relationship between the couple contribute heavily to the individual self-esteem, motivation, and mood of the husband and wife. Particularly in modern U.S. society, where extended family has become subordinate to the nuclear family, the spousal relationship may be the couple's primary source of intimacy and sense of connectedness in the world. With a basic sense of connection as the foundation for the spousal relationship, many life problems may be faced more flexibly and productively.

Families With Special Needs

Marital stability is often threatened by the demands of a child with special needs (Featherstone, 1980). Parents who are trying to make time for their own careers, the needs of their other children, and functional household tasks may take time away from their relationship as a couple to meet these various demands. Love (1973) reported that separation and divorce in families with a child with special needs are three times as high as in the rest of the population. From their interviews with 48 couples with a child with an exceptionality and 42 couples with children without a disability, Wright, Matlock, and Matlock (1985) reported that "parents of the handicapped . . . were six times as likely as parents of the non-handicapped to indicate that their children caused marital problems" (p. 38).

There are, however, many couples with a child with disabilities whose marriages are intact and satisfying. Longo and Bond (1984) noted that 10 studies from 1959 to 1981 reported no differences between the level of marital adjustment, parental friction, or incidence of divorce in couples having children with chronic illnesses and control couples. The primary characteristics that appear to relate to healthy marital response in these cases are strong, supportive spousal relationships prior to the diagnosis of the child and the individual personality strength of the spouses (Abbott & Meridith, 1986).

Questions that school professionals can ask themselves when diagnosing the functioning of the spousal subsystem include: When was the last time the couple went out on a "date" together? How do they make decisions? When conflicts arise, how are they resolved? Does the couple have common interests and friends? Do they have a process for problem solving? Is communication open, direct, and honest?

Parental Subsystem

The tasks of the parental or executive subsystem are primarily oriented around nurturing and teaching or disciplining children. In the intact nuclear family, this subsystem consists of a biological or adoptive mother and father. In a divorce situation, the roles of the parental subsystem may be fulfilled by a single parent, by a parent and a grandparent, or by a parent and a stepparent. When the parental subsystem is not composed of mother and father, the emotional issues involved in parenting become more complex.

Nurturing Function

For many parents of children with special needs, the nurturing and protecting functions of the parental subsystem are particularly complicated. As was discussed in Chapter 2, the feelings of shock, guilt, and grief that are associated with the diagnosis of a child with disabilities may initially interfere with the parents' ability to bond with their infant adequately (Darling, 1991a; Trout, 1983). As the child develops, parents will go through many stages of adjustment and many ambivalent feelings about the child; however, their adaptive capacity results in most parents forming strong attachments to their infant (Darling, 1991a).

In the midst of these conflicting feelings, these parents, like parents of children without disabilities, must make decisions about how much or how little freedom to allow their children while at the same time insuring their safety. Lack of clarity about the child's developmental progress may make parental decisions surrounding independence even more difficult.

Disciplining Function

An issue of primary importance in all families with children is the agreement between parents about discipline. If parents divide roles rather than share them, children learn how to negotiate around their parents rather than learning to internalize values and responsibilities. For example, a typical pattern in dysfunctional families is for one parent to be viewed by the children as a "softie" and the other parent to be seen as "abusive." In most cases, the abusive parent believes he or she needs to be a strong disciplinarian to combat the partner's permissiveness. The soft parent believes he or she needs to pamper the children to make up for the abusiveness of the other parent. The parenting subsystem has reached a homeostatic balance; however, the basic tasks of teaching and disciplining children are not being adequately fulfilled.

In the family with special needs, this parental "splitting" is often unknowingly intensified by those offering supportive services. If the mother is the parent who attends all meetings, takes all telephone calls, and schedules all appointments involving her child with special needs, she may have a different understanding of her child than her husband has. Particularly in cases where the child's disability is not physically evident, lack of understanding on the part of one parent may lead to different disciplining styles.

For the school professional, a first step in joining with parents is to acknowledge their conflicting feelings and struggles. A second step may be to provide information about child development in general and specifically about the child's particular level of functioning. Finally, the school may serve as a resource for information on parenting classes or support groups that can help alleviate some of the stress of parenting. For further discussion of resources, see Chapter 9 and Appendix D of this book.

Sibling Subsystem

The primary tasks of the sibling subsystem are the socialization and development of the children in the family (Powell & Gallagher, 1993). As the most long-lasting and influential relationship, the sibling relationship ebbs and flows in intensity over time and has a life cycle of its own. With younger children, companionship is an everyday experience and sharing toys, rooms, and parents helps young children develop social skills and a base for other relationships. As adolescents, siblings often rely on one another for advice and as confidants. As adults, they provide one another with support and encouragement, and as aunts and uncles, they experience new family roles and provide a network of support and love for their siblings' children. Some siblings maintain the same degree of intensity as they had when they were children for their entire lives.

The sibling subsystem provides an identification network in which values are formed, negotiations with parents are carried out, and perceptions of the outside world are supported or clarified (Bank & Kahn, 1982; Kahn & Lewis, 1988). In addition, cross-cultural studies have characterized the sibling group as an important in vivo testing ground for the transmission of cultural norms, roles, and functions (C. L. Johnson, 1982; Weisner, 1982). Beginning at a very young age, sibling interactions can teach sharing, negotiation, assertiveness, and empathy.

Having a Sibling With Special Needs

In families with a child with special needs, the siblings must adjust to decreased parental time and energy (Meyer & Vadasy, 1994; Powell & Gallagher, 1993). Whereas in most families the parents tend to distribute their emotional resources somewhat evenly across siblings, in families with one child who is experiencing special problems, that child will often receive the lion's share of parental focus. At times, siblings may feel competitive and angry with the brother or sister who has a disability and then may feel guilty about these feelings (Meyer & Vadasy, 1994; Powell & Gallagher, 1993). They may also experience a form of "survivor's guilt" about being healthy when their sibling has problems (Meyer & Vadasy, 1994; Powell & Gallagher, 1993). Siblings may feel they can't express their emotions to their parents, for fear of causing more stress (Koch, 1985).

Finally, some children incorporate having a sibling with special needs into a negative self-concept of their own (Meyer & Vadasy, 1994). They may feel that because their sibling has a disability, they are damaged as well. However, Dyson and Fewell (1989) found that self-concept was no different for young children who did and did not have a sibling with a disability.

Awareness   It is important that siblings have information about their brother's or sister's special needs that is understandable to them. Parents are often reluctant to discuss specifics about their child's problems for fear that they will distress their other children. Through overidentification, siblings may worry that they will "catch" the problem themselves (Meyer & Vadasy, 1994). Siblings seem more likely to have these worries if the disability is mild and not physically evident. They may be afraid to tell their friends that this difficulty has occurred in their family for fear of being ostracized. They may then withdraw from the sibling with problems and from their peer network, adding to the family's sense of isolation. As indicated in a study by McHale, Sloan, and Simeonsson (1986), who interviewed 60 siblings of children with special needs, when siblings have a better understanding of the child's condition, the sibling relationships tend to be more positive. The same need for information is true of parents (Powell & Gallagher, 1993).

Responsibility   Siblings may be asked to take on more personal responsibility than usual when there is a child with special needs in the home. The oldest female sibling in these families is at particular risk for *parentification* (W. C. Nichols, 1996; Powell & Gallagher, 1993). Mothers who are overwhelmed with caretaking tasks for their diagnosed child may ask, either covertly or overtly, that their oldest daughters take over more parenting functions. These girls are then at risk for not having their own emotional needs met and for developing problems in later life.

Abilities   As children develop, they may have concerns about surpassing an older sibling with special needs who is functioning at a younger age (Meyer & Vadasy, 1994; Vadasy, Fewell, Meyer, & Schell, 1984). The younger child may feel guilty about surpassing his or her older sibling even though that sibling is diagnosed with special problems. Younger children may try to hide their abilities or may refuse to take part in activities in which they will likely excel.

Educators should be particularly alert to motivational problems in students with a sibling who has special needs, as the process of parentification or feelings of guilt may be operating. A discussion with the sibling and the parents about the issues of survivor guilt and the struggles of having a sibling with a disability may provide the information and support that is needed to readjust the family structure.

Positive Aspects   Although siblings of children with special needs are at risk for various types of problems, the extent of these problems seems to depend, most significantly, on the adjustment of others in the home, especially the parents (Ferrari, 1984). Given adequate coping skills, open communication, and an environment of mutual support, there are some positive aspects of having a sibling with special needs. Siblings tend to have a greater understanding of and tolerance for differences in people and may become advocates for individuals with special needs (Grossman, 1972; Meyer & Vadasy, 1994). Siblings of children with emotional problems frequently show an orientation toward idealism and humanitarian interests. Often siblings, particularly females, will choose careers that are influenced by the disability (Cleveland & Miller, 1977; Powell & Gallagher, 1993).

Groups for Siblings of Children With Special Needs

The school professional may be in a unique position to provide services to the siblings of children with special needs. Daniels-Mohring, co-author of the first edition of this text, led sibling groups at a self-contained special education setting. The school served children with special needs between the ages of 4 and 16. In this setting, one evening a week was designated as Parent Night. Teachers and counseling staff were available during this evening to meet with families for counseling, updates on students' progress, problem-solving sessions, and goal-developing sessions. During one quarter, a 4-week sibling group was offered. Meeting on Parent Night, this group contained eight siblings of children in the school. Activities included group discussion, sharing of information, and role-playing of difficult situations encountered by the siblings. Role-plays were videotaped, and at the conclusion of the group, the members elected to invite their parents to view their videotapes. After parents were able to see their children acting out some of their concerns and problems about their siblings, a lively and open discussion followed. Evidently, the group met a need that had previously gone unnoticed.

Meyer and Vadasy (1994) developed a handbook for sibling workshops entitled *Sibshops: Workshops for Siblings of Children With Special Needs*. The workshops described developed from their experiences with 8- to 13-year-old siblings of children with special needs at the University of Washington. They are held on Saturday mornings for 2 to 3 hours or on 2-day overnight camping trips and include both an informational and a recreational component. Some informational activities suggested in the handbook include discussion groups using problem-focused activities; panel discussions involving adult siblings or parents of children with special needs who are willing to share their experiences; and presentations by a speech therapist, physical therapist, special education teacher, or other professionals about their experiences with students having special needs. The handbook also includes an extensive reading list of suggested fiction and nonfiction books for siblings of individuals with disabilities. For further information about implementing a sibling workshop, this handbook is highly recommended.

Extrafamilial Subsystem

In addition to the subsystems already discussed, family systems have an extrafamilial aspect. Not truly a subsystem of the nuclear family, the extrafamilial interactions represent those parts of the family system that interface with the outside world.

Extrafamilial contacts provide assistance and exchange of resources, a source of social and recreational activities, and emotional support (Turnbull & Turnbull, 1996). Support for family and cultural values is also supplied by the extrafamilial subsystem. Within each of the other family subsystems, particular issues and functions affect or are affected by extrafamilial interactions.

Interaction With the Spousal Subsystem

One task in the formation of the spousal subsystem is for the couple to make decisions about interactions with the extended family. If one spouse continues to be involved with his or her family of origin to the exclusion of the other spouse, problems in the spousal subsystem will result. Likewise, if a spouse is overinvolved with his or her friendship network, the level of intimacy within the spousal subsystem may be affected. In special-needs families, if only one spouse participates in special functions or support groups regarding the child, marital distance may result.

Interaction With the Parental Subsystem

For the parental subsystem, day care providers, baby-sitters, school professionals, and extended family and friends are all extrafamilial contacts. These persons interact with parents to make decisions regarding their children's care. They provide support and assistance to parents and may also serve as role models for appropriate parenting skills (Kazak & Wilcox, 1984). The parental subsystem must be functioning cohesively and clearly to allow these extended network interactions to operate positively. Otherwise, there may be mixed messages between the parents about which role models to follow in parenting. Again, in a family with special needs, if one parent is attending special parenting classes or listening to the advice of school professionals to the exclusion of the other parent, conflict in the disciplining function may result.

Interaction With the Sibling Subsystem

The sibling subsystem also has extensive extrafamilial involvement. The family must negotiate around school activities with peers, sports teams, extracurricular activities, and daily peer interactions. How many times do parents say, "It's not my child's fault; it's the crowd he[she] runs around with"?

The role of peer relationships in children's adjustment and socialization has been clearly demonstrated (Abramovitch & Strayer, 1977; K. H. Rubin, 1985; Sluckin & Smith, 1977). If children have positive peer relationships, they will bring these skills home to share with their sibling network. Likewise, if children feel rejected or isolated from their peers, the resulting self-image problems and poor social skills will become a part of their sibling interactions. In families with special needs, the acceptance of peers is particularly important to both the child with the disability and to the siblings.

Extrafamilial Subsystem Dysfunction

Dysfunction in the extrafamilial subsystem occurs when the family is either too inclusive or too exclusive about network involvement. If family members have very enmeshed and diffuse boundaries, they may not be able to make family decisions without input from the extrafamilial subsystem. At the opposite extreme, if family members have very rigid or disengaged boundaries, they may isolate themselves from any social supports.

Questions that school professionals may ask themselves to diagnose extrafamilial functioning include: Do the children ever have peers over to spend the night or go to friends' homes to spend the night? Are the children involved in any extracurricular activities? Is the family active in a church community? Are grandparents regularly involved with the family? Do the parents have their own friends?

If it is clear that the extrafamilial subsystem is not fulfilling the family's needs, the school professional may want to make suggestions about Boy or Girl Scouts, sports teams, Special Olympics, specialized summer camps, or other activities that are geared to the needs of the particular student. More specific suggestions about networking resources may be found in Chapter 9 and in Appendix D of this book.

Families With Special Needs

Families with a child with special needs often feel isolated from their extrafamilial subsystem (Kazak, 1987). The parents may feel they have few sources of support. The extended families may go through their own mourning process when a child is born with a disability. As Gabel and Kotsch (1981) argued, "Grandparents who are angry, grief stricken, or who deny the child's handicap may become an additional burden to parents" (p. 32).

Kazak and Wilcox (1984) compared families with a child with spina bifida with matched control families and found that the friendship networks of the parents in the former group were smaller in size than were those in the latter group. The authors hypothesized that not only might friends withdraw support because of their lack of knowledge about the child's illness and their feelings of fear or inadequacy about providing help, but the parents might also be less receptive to support because of their own fears and anxieties. Particularly with children who require specialized physical attention, parents may be afraid that their friends or family will not know how to adequately respond to the child's needs. In addition, they may feel that asking for help with their child will place too great a burden on their friends.

Another potential difficulty of families with a child with special needs stems from the required interactions with outside services. Often these families must have frequent meetings with physicians, counselors, teachers, physical therapists, and other professionals to maintain their child's functioning. The majority of these services focus on the child rather than the family (Foster, Berger, & McLean, 1981). Parents often feel overwhelmed with demands from these extrafamilial systems rather than feeling a sense of support in their struggle.

The extrafamilial aspects of the family system are particularly important to school professionals. The most functional view of the family will include the school professional as part of the family's extrafamilial subsystem. When teachers or counselors view themselves as being joined to the family system in meaningful and positive ways, interactions that affect the system will follow. This framework lends itself to cooperation between school and family rather than to defensiveness and alienation.

HIERARCHY

Minuchin used the term *hierarchy* to describe the distribution of power in families (Minuchin, 1974), or the power relationships between the members of a subsystem. Hierarchy has three aspects: power, order, and balance. Power relates to who has the power. In a healthy family, the parents have the power. Order relates to the pecking order of wielding power. When the parents are not there and the oldest child, followed by the next-oldest child, and so on, clearly has the power, the family would be viewed as functional. If, however, the youngest rules the roost, then there is a serious hierarchical dysfunction. Balance refers to shared power. When both parents share in decision-making there is balance, and the parental dyad would be viewed as functional. As children grow older, a healthy system includes them in the decision making process about those areas of life that pertain to them, such as where to take the family vacation.

The member or members at the top of the hierarchy are those who have the most relational power within the system. In an adequately functioning family system, parents and children have different levels of authority that are accepted and respected. Likewise, in a school system, the principal has the final authority and accepts ultimate responsibility for management decisions.

There may be different levels of hierarchy within a system. Parents may share authority, but at times one or the other parent may be in charge. Parents may delegate authority to a teenage sibling or a grandparent. In such cases, the functioning of the subsystem would be affected by *order*. Sibling subsystems that have children of different ages tend to have a clear sibling hierarchy. Older siblings normally serve the dominant role in interactions with their younger siblings (Dunn & Kendrick, 1982). A hierarchy dysfunction would exist if that order were not followed in a family unless an obvious factor, such as the oldest sibling having mental retardation, were involved.

School systems have different levels of hierarchy. Teachers are the ultimate authority in their classrooms. Team leaders may be at the top of the hierarchy with regard to decisions made by their team. Counseling departments may have one person designated as the director of guidance. Finally, there may be a principal and an assistant principal who lead the decision-making process (somewhat like a parental subsystem).

Dysfunctional Hierarchy

When the hierarchy in a family or system is unclear, as with a weak parental subsystem, turmoil and chaos result. In highly stressed families, this lack of management may be evident in many areas. Children may come to school wearing dirty or torn clothing. Messages to the home may be left unanswered and papers unsigned.

At times the hierarchy in a family or system is clear but inappropriately reversed, with children having as much or more power than their parents or teachers. In families where one child's demands take priority over the needs of the rest of the family members, a hierarchy problem is evident. When a child regularly functions in a parental role and assumes an inordinate level of responsibility for his or her age, hierarchy dysfunction is operating in the system. This type of dysfunction is called inversion of the hierarchy.

Cross-Generational Coalition

One type of hierarchy shift is called a cross-generational coalition. Minuchin (1974) defined a coalition as an inflexible alignment between two or more family members against another family member. When the alignment occurs between a parent and a child or a grandparent and a child, the alignment is crossing generational boundaries.

In families, cross-generational coalitions are seen when a child is drawn into an alliance with one parent against the other. These coalitions typically occur when spouses are disengaged from one another. The child may be expected to assume excessive responsibilities, may be the confidant for a parent, or may be asked to compensate for the absent spouse by providing emotional support.

In schools, a cross-generational coalition occurs when, for example, a student is in an alliance with his or her parents against a teacher or a school counselor is in alliance with a student against the student's parents or teachers. In either case, hierarchical and generational boundaries have been crossed inappropriately.

Detouring

A hierarchy dysfunction often seen in enmeshed systems is called detouring (Minuchin, Rosman, & Baker, 1978) or scapegoating (Boszormenyi-Nagy & Spark, 1973). Within families, this pattern is seen when parents detour their energy away from potential spousal conflict or distance to focus together on a particular child. Detouring may take the form of parents uniting to protect a vulnerable child, as in the case of a child with intellectual deficits or chronic illness, or uniting to blame a child as the cause of family problems, as with the acting-out adolescent. In either case, the family focus is exclusively on the identified child. This child then has the hierarchically inappropriate power to control family interactions by his or her behavior. Boundaries are blurred, with the ultimate result being the temporary avoidance of marital conflict that might destroy the family.

Detouring may be observed within a school system in situations in which multiple staff members are involved with a particular student. When decision making about a particular student causes emotions to run high, this may be an indication that conflict between staff is being detoured through the student. An example of this process might be as follows:

> A teacher and an assistant principal disagree about the management of a particular student. The teacher feels blamed by the assistant principal. She and many of her colleagues think that the assistant principal does not provide adequate support for them when they intervene in management problems in the classroom. The next time this student acts out, the teacher sends him directly to the assistant principal's office. The administrator gives the student 2 days in after-school detention under the teacher's supervision. The teacher, who disagrees with this consequence and has other commitments after school, fails to enforce the detention. The student is caught in a detouring of conflict between the teacher and the assistant principal.

Sibling Hierarchy Dysfunction

Daniels-Mohring (1986) conducted an observational study comparing the interactions of pairs of siblings in which the older sibling had been diagnosed with psychiatric problems with the interactions of same-age control sibling pairs in which the older child had not been diagnosed with psychiatric problems. She found that the older siblings who were diagnosed as emotionally disturbed lost some of their relational power within the sibling subsystem. This loss of role disrupted the typical hierarchy organization of sibling interactions in which the older sibling is in a dominant position. Not only did the emotionally disturbed youngsters have to cope with problems of identity in dealing with their peer networks, but they also had to adapt to the loss of power within their own family systems.

To diagnose hierarchy dysfunction, the school professional might ask the following types of questions: Do parents defend the student even when the student's behavior is obviously inappropriate? Are parents inconsistent with discipline—for example, threatening to ground the adolescent and not following through? Does one parent act more like "one of the kids" than as an authority figure? Does the student talk back to the parents, exhibiting lack of respect? When parents begin to disagree, does the conversation shift to focus on the student's behavior?

Hierarchy dysfunctions are, in general, very common in families and systems. Often the people involved are unaware of the hierarchy reversals in their interactions. The school professional who observes a hierarchy problem may be able to affect the system simply by neutrally commenting on the process. Some helpful comments might be: "I understand Billy's concerns about serving detention, but I think it's important that we present a united front to him to avoid confusion" or "Hey, Leanne, do you always talk to your mom that way? It surprises me because you're usually so respectful in class." Observational comments such as these may be sufficient to help the parent reflect on his or her behavior and take action to reestablish appropriate hierarchy.

INVOLVING SCHOOL PERSONNEL IN THE TRANSFORMATION OF THE FAMILY SYSTEM

Fishman (1993) devoted a chapter of his book, *Intensive Structural Therapy: Treating Families in Their Social Context,* to the context of schools. In the chapter, he focused on how therapists can involve school personnel in empowering the family and presented the following basic principles to be followed by professionals, which focused on the capabilities of the family:

- Ensure that the therapist, not the school, determines the agenda for the therapy.
- Explore the parents' attitudes toward school and school authorities.
- Assume that the child is strong and that the problem is one the family can handle.
- Search for conflicting loyalties and hidden agendas.
- Encourage an attitude of shared responsibility and involvement between the family and the school.
- Clarify boundaries and roles.
- Establish an alliance between parents and school. (pp.180–184)

According to Fishman, involving school personnel in therapy is invaluable in aiding the transformation of the total family system. His model of choice is collaboration with roles clearly defined. He gave a sad example of a student, typical of many in that he had more loyalty to the school than to the family, who ended up killing another student with a knife. Fishman indicated that peers can be closer to an individual than other family members and can be important, powerful forces in a therapeutic endeavor, particularly with adolescents. Because poor peer relationships during middle childhood have been found to be predictive of emotional and social dysfunction in later years, as well as of drug use and antisocial behavior, Fishman advocates that schools be a powerful force in bringing about transformation. He wrote,

> Our work with schools is more important than ever, and perhaps more sensitive now, when budgets and, frequently, tempers are already stretched to the limits. As the economy is rapidly changing and there are fewer jobs for the undereducated, success in school becomes all the more essential. (p. 193)

Fishman also related the changing infrastructure of society to the changing infrastructure of the family, and pointed to the decreasing taxpayer dollars available, especially for the poorer school systems, thus the importance of success in school because fewer jobs will be available for the less educated.

SUMMARY

This chapter presented the basic theory of structural family therapy. The school professional who has a clear understanding of these structural characteristics will more easily view the student's behavior as part of a family pattern. The three major areas in which observations can be made regarding the family transactional patterns described are boundaries, subsystems, and hierarchy. Boundaries indicate the quality of distance and closeness within a family. The four subsystems are the subgroups of the family system that provide the building blocks of family interaction. Diagnosis of family interaction patterns must include some assessment of how well each subsystem is sustaining its roles and functions. The concept of hierarchy/power describes the distribution of power and decision making within a system. Once family interaction patterns have been assessed, the student's behavior can be viewed within the context of his or her family structure and transactional style. Armed with an understanding of these contextual variables, the school professional can better promote individual students' academic and emotional development. In Appendix A, at the end of the description of Structural Family Therapy, an ecostructural assessment process is described.

CASE EXAMPLE

Charles W., a 9-year-old boy, was referred to the evaluation team due to his poor school performance during this semester. Charles was currently placed in a third-grade classroom and received resource help in reading and math due to severe learning disabilities. Recently, he had begun acting out by refusing to dress for physical education. Soon after, he began to dawdle during class assignments, frequently commenting that he could not understand the work. The teacher consulted with the school psychologist and confirmed that the work she was giving Charles was within his capacity. After an initial note home regarding this problem, Charles's mother, Mrs. W., had contacted the teacher by telephone each week to check on Charles's progress. Despite the fact that the teacher was sending Charles's assignments home, Charles was falling further and further behind in his studies.

Mrs. W. reported that Charles would get up every morning complaining of a stomach-ache. She would coax him out of bed even though he looked a little pale and had dark circles under his eyes and would send him to school. Mrs. W., who did not work outside of the home, picked Charles up from school each day. She reported that since the teacher's initial report regarding Charles's missed assignments, she spent every afternoon helping Charles with his homework even after her other two children, ages 12 and 15, returned home from school.

When asked how Mr. W. felt about Charles's performance problems, Mrs. W. replied that he was angry and upset. She stated that Mr. W. worked long hours and had no idea of how Charles really felt or whether or not he was completing homework. By the time her husband returned home in the evening, Charles was usually preparing for bed. In fact, Mrs. W. volunteered, her husband had never understood Charles's problems. Ever since Charles was diagnosed as having a learning disability, her husband had been negative and withdrawn in his interactions with Charles. According to Mrs. W., her husband had expectations for Charles that were beyond his capabilities, and he tended to blame her for the fact that Charles was not achieving.

Questions and Comments

1. *From the information provided, what is your hypothesis about the structural characteristics of this family (i.e., boundaries, hierarchy, alignments)? What data support this hypothesis?*

   The referral team hypothesized that there was an unresolved conflict between father and mother, at least regarding Charles and probably more extensively. Distance between the father and Charles was indicated by the mother's report that the father was "negative and withdrawn" in his interactions with Charles and that by the time the father returned from work, Charles was usually preparing for bed. Apparently, Charles and his father had limited interactions. In general, the father was *disengaged* from the family system and the mother and Charles were overinvolved in their relationship. *Enmeshment* was indicated by the mother's "coaxing" Charles out of bed, her extreme concern about his physical appearance, her picking him up after school each day, her weekly phone calls to the teacher, and her daily help with his homework. The parents' marital conflict seemed to be *detoured* onto Charles, indicated by the fact that despite his mother's extensive "help," Charles was still unable to perform at school. Apparently the mother was not willing to make appropriate demands on Charles. This behavior can be viewed as a reaction to what she considered inappropriate and negative demands made by the father. According to the available information, the other two children were functioning adequately and did not seem to be the focus of parental conflict.

2. *If the family dysfunction were to be resolved, what would the probable family structure look like?*

   The ideal structure for this family would include the mother and father as equals in the family *hierarchy*. They would make *joint decisions* regarding their child's school problems and support one another in carrying out plans for helping their child. The adolescent child would be higher in the sibling hierarchy than either of the two younger children. All *boundaries* between subsystems would be appropriate and *flexible,* as indicated by open communication, the expression of individual identities, and clear roles and functions within the family.

3. *What types of intervention strategies might be appropriate for working with this family?*

To work toward a functional family structure, the referral team would want to make certain that the father was involved in any meetings or future communication regarding Charles. Both parents might be brought in to review Charles's records and clarify his functioning level, to decrease the possibility of misunderstanding about Charles's abilities. Further, to interrupt the enmeshment between Charles and his mother, the team might suggest that Charles be required to complete his assignments during school hours or stay after school for study hall. Another suggestion might be that Charles's adolescent sibling help him with minor homework assignments in order to build some cohesion in the sibling subsystem. Finally, the team might suggest that Charles be allowed to ride the bus home from school to increase his peer interactions and level of independence.

EXTENSION ACTIVITIES

Reflection: Thinking back to your childhood and family of origin, reflect on how you would describe your family in terms of subsystems, boundaries, and hierarchy. Was there a marital subsystem, or did you grow up in a single-parent family during all or part of your childhood? If there was a parental subsystem during all or part of the time, how would you describe it in terms related to the structural hypothesis (e.g., enmeshed, disengaged, or semipermeable boundaries; emphasis on balanced or shared decision making)? Unless you were an only child, describe the sibling subsystem in your family of origin. How did the siblings follow or fail to follow expected behaviors (e.g., oldest being responsible, middle being the glue, and youngest being playful). Would you describe the boundaries of the sibling subsystem as enmeshed, disengaged, or semipermeable, and what behavioral descriptions can you think of to substantiate that belief? Recall the influence of the extrafamilial subsystem and determine its significance and impact on the life of your family of origin.

Journal: What have you learned about your family of origin that can help you with a nuclear family? How has your mode of operation, learned within family-of-origin structures, been generalized to your school and/or work relationships? What meaning or significance do you attach to the strengths and challenges of your family of origin relative to structural concepts?

Observation: Watch a few television sitcoms. After each one reflect on a structural hypothesis in terms of subsystems (marital, parental, sibling, extrafamilial), boundaries (enmeshed, disengaged, semipermeable), hierarchy (power, order, balance), and alignments/coalitions (positive, negative, and neutral).

Journal: Write about what you noted in watching the sitcoms. If you watch sitcoms regularly, do you see any pattern to the type of shows you watch? If so, what is it that you might find attractive about the shows you watch? Is there something to be learned in these shows that can help you understand your family and/or that of others? *In-Class/Training Discussion:* Focus on the sitcoms people saw and the patterns that emerged. How would you describe the human nature that you observed? Why do people enjoy watching sitcoms?

Discussion: Discuss the importance of knowing about the structural concepts described in this chapter in relation to your family of origin. How can knowing about structural concepts help you as a school professional? What could you do to share this knowledge with others in a school setting? How might you network with professionals in the community external to your school about what you have learned from reading this chapter?

In-Class/Training Exploration: Consider a particular family about whom you can provide substantial information. Provide everyone in the group with basic information about the family. Then, as a class, attempt to construct a structural hypothesis using the information provided in the ecostructural assessment section in Appendix A. The family may be from a school or the external community. The important part of this exercise is to practice putting pieces of the puzzle together and to become accustomed to dealing with the concepts; less important is being accurate in the hypothesizing. [An alternative exercise is for several group members or the leader to write up information from a student's life and distribute it to all class members for use as a common base for group hypothesizing.]

In-Class/Training Discussion: How can knowledge of structural concepts inform school professionals and improve their work with at-risk and special-needs students? How can school professionals find answers to the more private or difficult questions that allow actual structural hypotheses to be drawn? What ethical considerations come into play when school professionals become involved with structural concepts as they relate to students and their families and communities?

Historical Factors

This chapter gives a framework for viewing students' problems within a historical context. Its focal point is a theory of family process developed by Murray Bowen that utilizes historical factors. (See Appendix A for more in-depth coverage of this theory.) For the educator, the framework of family history can provide information about motivational factors, toxic issues, and family scripts from many generations. Together or individually, these factors can influence students' reactions and performance within the school environment.

INTRODUCTION

To the same extent that historical information about human growth and development is important in understanding the individual, the family's history plays an important role in understanding family systems. It is intuitively appealing to believe that what we are and how we behave today maintains some continuity with a history that extends back several generations. This chapter focuses on the theory of Murray Bowen (1966, 1978, 1985), who emphasized the historical aspects of systems theories. His theory expands the consideration of behavior not only from the individual to the system, but also from the present to the past.

A number of specific concepts from Bowen's work address the notion that personal family history is important in the formation of a person's identity and life choices. The concept of *differentiation* addresses the theme of individuality and self-integration. *Emotional transmission* describes the forces by which family prejudices, rules of behavior, and patterns of relating are relayed through several generations. The concept of *birth order* deals with how factors within the sibling subsystem affect personality development and relational patterns throughout a family's history. *Triangulation* refers to the process by which historical patterns of relationships are played out in the present. In addition to covering these topics, the chapter describes and provides examples of genograms, a technique for mapping family history. A case example provided at the end of the chapter, which illustrates the use of historical factors in understanding a student's educational difficulties, helps translate the many concepts introduced in the chapter. The extension activities that close the chapter encourage deeper exploration into historical factors and family systems.

DIFFERENTIATION

The concept of differentiation is the core around which Bowen's theory was built (M. P. Nichols & Schwartz, 1995). Differentiation is the process by which one becomes increasingly less emotionally dependent upon the family and more able to make independent choices and decisions. This process involves the ability to keep intellectual and emotional systems separate (Bowen, 1985).

For example, suppose you were bitten by a dog at a young age, and you are now deathly afraid, almost phobic, of dogs. If you see a dog and you automatically run out into a busy street to avoid being chased, your actions are being controlled by your emotional system. If, however, you can see a dog and ask yourself, "How dangerous is this dog? Is it a miniature poodle or a great dane? Is it housed within a fence or on a chain?" Before you decide whether or not to run, your emotions are being mediated by your intellectual system. When your emotional system is mediated by your intellectual system, your capacity for making choices is increased (Kerr & Bowen, 1988).

Corey (1996) wrote, "In family systems theory, the key to being a healthy person encompasses both a sense of belonging to one's family and a sense of separateness and individuality" (p. 371). Differentiating a self in a family of origin is a lifelong process.

Levels of Differentiation

Individual levels of differentiation may show up in a number of factors. The following descriptions are intended as a framework to help school professionals increase their understanding. I do not suggest that determining levels of differentiation is realistic for those working within the educational system. It is not possible for educators to know enough about individual students or their family members to determine a level of differentiation. Hence, this information on levels of differentiation is best thought of as a guide. Bowen made it clear that until individuals are on their own financially they cannot be differentiated; thus, children cannot be expected to have achieved a high level of differentiation. Nevertheless, I have found Bowen's description of levels of differentiation helpful when dealing with students and their families and, at times, colleagues.

Higher Levels of Differentiation

People who are well differentiated can make choices about personal behavior based on information as well as feelings (Guerin & Chabot, 1992). These individuals are not overly dependent in their relationships; they can cooperate and negotiate with others in patterns that may differ from their family experiences. Their behavior is based on a set of personal values and principles that have been derived from their experience and moral development. According to Roberto (1992), they have "goal direction, clear values and beliefs, flexibility, security, autonomy, conflict tolerance, and neurotic-level symptoms under stress" (p. 12). Furthermore, they have a more defined *basic self* and less *pseudoself,* or less fusion, when in close relationships and focus more on goal-directed activities. They typically evaluate themselves realistically and can be in intimate relationships without anxiety.

Clearly, higher levels of differentiation are not possible until adulthood. Bowen (1985) believed that no one living in his or her parents' home can be operating at a high level of differentiation. However, he also proposed that we tend to achieve a level of differentiation that is the same or lower than that of our parents, unless we attempt some purposeful intervention to change this pattern. In other words, "like begets like" in terms of differentiation. Therefore, students' predisposition for a general level of differentiation can be viewed in light of their parents' emotional patterns.

Midrange Levels of Differentiation

People functioning in the midrange have "definite beliefs and values on important life issues, but still tend to be overfocused on the opinions of others" (Roberto, 1992, p. 12). Some of their decisions are driven by emotional reactivity. They are concerned that others who are important to them will disapprove of their choices, and they adapt in order to please the other person. Kerr (1988) noted, "They are sensitized to emotional disharmony, to the opinions of others, and to creating a good impression. They are apt students of facial expressions, gestures, tone of voice, and actions that may mean approval or disapproval" (p. 43). They can react wildly to praise or criticism, being elated or dashed depending on whether they've received approval or disapproval. Rather than focusing on self-determined goals, they seek love and approval. At work, their sense of success is driven by the approval of their superiors rather than by their own values.

Lower Levels of Differentiation

There are several signs of low levels of differentiation (Roberto, 1992). People with low levels of differentiation are excessively influenced by others and dependent upon or reactive to their opinions. They have difficulty keeping their emotions in balance, and they often deny feelings or outbursts that are out of proportion to external events. They have poorly defined boundaries between self and others. They tend to feel responsible for others or to blame them; they have an inability to see themselves clearly in relation to others. People with low levels of differentiation may feel a need for intense closeness to combat loneliness or a need for much distance to relieve fear of fusion with another. Their principles and values are based on emotional reactions or family prejudices rather than on a well thought-out personal identity (Bowen, 1985).

Relational Patterns and Differentiation

Bowen (1985) suggested that we tend to form relationships with, and marry, persons at our same or a similar level of differentiation. For those with a low level of differentiation, there is a connection between level of differentiation and codependency. As defined by Beattie (1987), a codependent individual has allowed another person's behavior to affect him or her to the degree that the codependent person is obsessed with controlling the dependent person's behavior. E. Kaufman and P. Kaufmann (1992), focusing on the alcoholic family, stated,

> Proof of the codependent's own adequacy becomes based on his or her abilities to keep the alcoholic sober. In other words, alcoholic and codependent world views are absolutely consistent. Alcoholics think other people make them drink, and codependents think they should be able to make the alcoholic not drink. The same unrealistic efforts to gain self-esteem by controlling the uncontrollable are often modeled by both parents in an alcoholic family. (p. 214)

In codependent relationships, both partners fit into the low level of differentiation. Highly reactive emotional forces control the relationship. Partners describe feeling tied to the relationship even when it causes them pain. Physical or emotional symptoms in one member of the couple develop when the level of stress is too high for the relationship to manage given the attending low level of personal differentiation.

Degree of differentiation also impacts individuals' effectiveness in work or organizational settings (Weinberg & Mauksch, 1991). The ability to maintain appropriate task focus, to adopt suitable organizational roles with peers, superiors, and subordinates, and to sustain productivity may be closely related to one's level of differentiation. Thus, understanding general levels of differentiation can be helpful in work relationships.

Assessment of Differentiation

The degree of differentiation in a family or work system may be assessed by testing the emotional reactivity in that system. To try this out, take some stance about what you believe or who you are that is different from that of others in the system and observe the response. If others respond with their own "I" positions, differentiation is high. If they try to engage you in arguments, differentiation is presumably lower.

In family interviews, level of differentiation may be assessed by how well individuals can express a feeling or thought without eliciting emotional reactivity from other family members. Can one person cry or express anger and be comforted or confronted by the rest of the family without everyone else dissolving into tears or displaying explosive temper? In the special-needs family, can family members show empathy and understanding for the child with a disability without feeling as if they were responsible for the disability or feeling guilt at being nondisabled? In at-risk families, do the family members see themselves as victims and blame others for their situation? Do they turn these feelings inward, displaying the accompanying low self-esteem, and become frozen and unable to act?

A convenient way to assess one's own level of differentiation is to determine the degree to which returning to one's parent's home elicits feelings that were familiar and uncomfortable during childhood and adolescence. An indication of your personal level of differentiation can be found in how quickly you revert to feeling like a child rather than an adult in your family or how quickly you revert to old patterns of relating with family members. Parents who come to a school conference and act like children instead of adults may have slipped back into a familiar relationship pattern learned in childhood.

As mentioned earlier, differentiation represents the core construct in the Bowen (1985) model. It is a process that extends throughout the life span, with the individual moving from the total dependence of infancy toward increasing independence and self-integration. To a great extent differentiation represented, for Bowen, the struggle for emotional development in the face of the forces of family history. As such, it represents a major determinant of quality of life in relationships. While differentiation is a concept specific to the Bowen model, it integrates well with other major lines of thought in family systems theory.

Applications

For school professionals, the concept of differentiation may be meaningful in terms of evaluating both student behavior and organizational dynamics within the school. In the earlier grades, students who exhibit clingy behavior, excessive dependence on teacher direction, and less well-developed peer relationships likely come from families in which the level of differentiation is low. In adolescence, low levels of family differentiation may be expressed by intolerance for others, personally loaded rebellious behavior such as name calling, and limited acceptance of changes in schedule, routine, or expectations. It may also be expressed through chemical dependency, teenage pregnancy, and rigid thinking.

A tendency toward lower levels of differentiation is frequently seen in families with a child with special needs. Chronic stress and chronic anxiety strain even a healthy family's adaptive capabilities. When coping with the functional and emotional needs of a child with a disability, personal emotional issues may take control over reason and thought. Thus, even when correct information is being given to the parents of a child with special needs, their capacity to use the information to effectively change their behavior may be limited by their anxiety and low levels of differentiation of self.

Children who are at risk often come from families who are functioning at lower levels of differentiation. Like families having a child with special needs, these families face chronic stress and anxiety that make constructive coping difficult. The disorganization evident in at-risk families is a sign of stressors that make higher levels of differentiation less frequent.

In schools, colleagues and administrators who exhibit a flexible approach to management of students, instructional methods, and system policy most likely have higher levels of personal differentiation. These educators are able to understand and relate to a variety of perspectives, to consider multiple factors in decision making, and to engage in healthy and productive collaboration.

EMOTIONAL TRANSMISSION

In addition to believing that the members of each family tend to have similar levels of differentiation, Bowen contended that each family also has its own set of issues that bring intense emotional reactions. For some families, tension focuses around gender role issues with rules about what women should do or how men should behave. For others, the issue of religion, having children, or achievement is deeply rooted in family myths and values. As discussed in Chapter 2, family myth and secrets are often attached to a particular stage of the family life cycle. The passing of these issues from generation to generation and the patterns of relating over generations of family life are known as emotional transmission.

Transmission of Family Issues

The process of emotional transmission of particular issues within a family can be seen in how students react to peers from different cultures or backgrounds. Satir and Baldwin (1983) described families as being either open or closed in structure. Open family systems allow for change, depending upon the family's life cycle stage as well as the emotional and relational context. People from open family systems learn values and morals that do not embody extreme prejudices or judgments about others. Acceptance of self and others is the theme transmitted through the life of families characterized as open. The emotional transmission of unconscious and unresolved issues is low in these families.

In contrast, closed family systems are distinguished by their level of rigidity and negativity. These families are based on control, dominance, and conformity. Children in closed families develop low levels of self-esteem that are indicated by their judgmental attitude toward others. Prejudicial values are transmitted in closed systems across many generations. The emotional transmission of unresolved issues, family secrets, and inappropriate myths is greater in closed families.

Assessment

To discover which prejudices and family issues have been emotionally transmitted in your family, ask yourself the following questions: What topics did your parents never talk about? What can't your children or students talk to you about? What things about your life would surprise or shock your parents or colleagues? What is a statement that is guaranteed to induce guilt or shame in you? Where did this statement originate?

In terms of the classroom, values clarification exercises will often uncover issues or prejudices that have been emotionally transmitted in your students. A simple exercise such as the following may help identify family issues.

> How would you complete the following sentences? Women are . . . Men are . . . A wife is . . . A husband is . . . A mother is . . . A father is . . . How would your parents complete these sentences? How are the two sets of answers different?

Often the experience of being asked to identify and discuss one's own values will help break the cycle of transmission.

Family Patterns of Emotional Transmission

According to Bowen theory, emotional transmission is also responsible for patterns of family relating over generations (Jacobson & Gurman, 1995; Roberto, 1992). As he developed his theory, Bowen classified family relational patterns as being either cohesive or explosive in nature (Guerin, 1976).

Cohesive Families

Cohesive family systems have extended families that usually cluster together in a somewhat limited geographic area. Frequent telephone calling, visiting, and shared communication occur in these families. Nuclear and extended family members are taken into account in making various family decisions such as where the family will live, take vacations, and attend church or school.

At the extreme, cohesive families can be highly intrusive systems that do not allow for personal differentiation or privacy. The pattern observed in dysfunctional cohesive families parallels the enmeshed family pattern described in Chapter 3. Typically, in dysfunctional cohesive families, there is extensive leakage, or emotional transmission of anxiety, from the extended family into the nuclear family.

Explosive Families

Explosive family systems are characterized by extensive fragmentation (Guerin, 1976). The family roots are in one geographic location, and in fewer than two generations the extended family has scattered over a wide area. In this type of family system there are often very few ongoing relationships between members. The nuclear family is on its own, without much support from the extended family. Family contacts tend to be ritualized and predictable, such as holidays or family reunions. Family members do not generally share their everyday lives with one another or really know one another at an intimate level.

This type of multigenerational pattern may leave the special-needs family without extended family resources for helping with the functional and emotional demands of a child with a disability. Therefore, the stress experienced by the nuclear family may be increased. For families that are historically explosive in nature, the provision of outside support services is especially important to the family's well-being. Support is focused on in Chapter 9.

At the most severe level of the explosive family system, the extended family may become fragmented in response to a dramatic family event that leaves members "not speaking" to one another over many years or even generations. This type of avoidance is known as an emotional cutoff. Explosive families that are dysfunctional parallel disengaged families, as seen in the structural model described in Chapter 3 and Appendix A.

Although the level of contact in highly explosive families is minimal, the level of differentiation is extremely low. A couple who has moved to another area to take the "geographic cure" from their family may be as poorly differentiated as a couple who lives next door to their in-laws and sees them every day. In both cases, if the decisions about living arrangements are made in reaction to issues stemming from the family of origin, the level of emotional reactivity to the nuclear family is high. The emotional transmission of family anxiety results in the couple's living decisions being made to reduce that anxiety. In one case, anxiety is relieved by closeness; in the other, by avoidance.

E. H. Friedman (1986) discussed how emotional transmission can be important through multiple generations, giving this example related to "individuals who have been catapulted out of their families to achieve."

> The "standard bearer" usually is the oldest male, or the only male, or anyone, male or female, who has replaced a significant progenitor two or even three generations back. Such individuals have great difficulty giving emotion or time to their marriage or their children. . . . Success has the compelling drive of ghosts behind it. They have too much to do in the short span of a lifetime. In addition, failure is more significant because it is not only themselves or even their own generation that they will have failed (pp. 420–421).

The process of emotional transmission can be seen in the behavior of many different types of students. Often overachievers are students who feel compelled to make up for some failure or unhappiness in their parents' lives or for the disability of another sibling (Seligman, 1983b, 1991c). They may be pushed by the expectations of their parents or grandparents beyond their level of ability. The aggressive student may come from a physically abusive or aggressive family. Parents who abuse their children or one another are likely to have grown up in an abusive environment themselves (Ammerman & Hersen, 1990b; Meier & Sloan, 1984; Peled, Jaffe, & Edleson, 1995). Depression is also a symptom that is often transmitted through many generations of family life. Severe depression, unexpressed anger that is turned inward, results from a context where the expression of anger is not tolerated. In these families people believe that displays of anger will cause a crisis to ensue or that someone will be extremely hurt by the anger. This pattern of fear around anger typically has many generations of unexpressed and unresolved feelings behind it.

Realization of the forces of emotional transmission may help the school professional to remain nonjudgmental about certain prejudices, values, or ways of relating that are evidenced by students and their families. When these issues are seen as multigenerational in origin rather than personal, more objectivity and easier problem resolution are possible.

BIRTH ORDER

One of the factors that is often considered when looking at historical patterns in families is sibling position. Much of the literature regarding siblings has focused on the actual temporal order in which siblings are born. Theories of personality related to ordinal sibling position were developed by Freud and Adler in the early 1900s. Since the 1970s, however, the trend has been to focus on the psychological position of the sibling, or his or her birth order. In defining sibling status, birth order includes the consideration of not only temporal birth order but also family crises, death of a sibling, sibling spacing, family size, and the gender of the siblings.

Personality Factors

On the basis of observations, Adler (1959) characterized firstborn siblings as dependable, conforming, and believing in rule and responsibility. He also hypothesized that firstborns, as adults, tend to have a feeling of natural power. Later borns, according to Adler, tend to be more active, aggressive, and nonconforming. Youngest children were described as having a tendency toward dependency and passivity.

Dethronement

Adler (1959) developed a number of different theoretical constructs to explain the process of sibling identification. One is the concept of dethronement, which is a process affecting firstborns following the birth of a sibling (Schvaneveldt & Ihinger, 1979). The process is one in which the child who has been the sole recipient of parental caretaking in the past must lose a certain status within the family and feels rejection. This feeling explains the firstborn's need to conform and excel in an effort to regain the throne, or the family status.

Enthronement

Another construct that has been derived from Adlerian theory is that of enthronement (Shulman & Mosak, 1977), which describes the relationships of youngest children in the family. Enthronement is the process whereby parental forces operate to savor the final child and tend to be somewhat smothering. Youngest children are never forced to experience dethronement, nor do they need to be competitive in order to gain a special family role. However, they may depend upon the power of the baby role to provide their major sense of identification and esteem, resulting in a passive and dependent personality.

Deidentification

The final construct derived from Adler is that of deidentification (Niels, 1980), which is primarily used to describe the personality development of later-born children. This premise is that later borns observe areas where their older siblings are proficient and avoid competing in those areas. They choose areas of interest that are, typically, nonconforming and different from those of their older siblings.

Birth Order and Relationships

Building on the work of Adler, Toman (1993) developed a theoretical framework for the impact of siblings on personal identification and relationship patterns that takes into account temporal birth order as well as the gender of siblings. Toman maintained that siblings are important factors in the identification process through which children acquire a basic social/sexual sense of themselves and resulting patterns of relating to others. Based on clinical observations, Toman predicted relational patterns with same and opposite gender friends as well as choice of marriage partners and potential for marital success in terms of birth order and gender of siblings. His findings are discussed in the following sections.

Duplication Theorem

Toman (1993) proposed the duplication theorem, in which "other things being equal, new social relationships are more enduring and successful the more they resemble the earlier and earliest (intrafamilial) social relationships of the persons involved" (p. 78). According to this theorem, marital relationships are easiest when a partner is chosen whose sibling constellation pattern is complementary rather than conflicting with one's own in terms of sibling rank and gender.

For example, when an oldest brother of sisters marries a youngest sister of brothers the relationship is complementary. When an oldest brother of brothers marries an oldest sister of sisters, the relationship is conflicting in terms of sibling constellation. In conflicting relationships, the same sibling roles are held by both partners. Thus, they compete with each other rather than having personalities that complement one another or work together.

Other Sibling Factors

Within the concept of birth order, predictions about sibling personality must take into account other aspects of the family constellation as well as ordinal sibling position. Large families may have several sibling subgroups in which, depending upon the ages and spacing between children, there may be several children who function as oldest or only children (Toman, 1993). For example, in a two-child family in which there is at least a 7-year age difference between siblings, both children will be, functionally, only children.

The psychological effects of sibling status may also be mediated by age spacing between siblings. From a survey of 2,200 boys, Peterson and Kunz (1975) found that younger siblings were perceived most positively by their older brothers when the spacing between them was either less than 12 months or greater than 4 years.

The gender of sibling groups must also be taken into account in the concept of birth order. Female-dominated sibling groups tend to be oriented around language, accommodation, caretaking, and prosocial interactions (Abramovitch, Corter, & Lando, 1979; G. H. Brody & Stoneman, 1983). Male-dominated sibling groups are more physically active and challenging in nature (Abramovitch et al., 1979; Cicirelli, 1972; C. L. Johnson, 1982).

Finally, the presence of a sibling with a disability may change the expected birth-order effects in sibling groups. As discussed in Chapter 3, Daniels-Mohring (1986) found that an oldest sibling who has emotional disturbance tends to lose some personal power and rank in the expected sibling hierarchy. In families where the sibling with the disability is the oldest, a younger sibling may behave as the functional eldest child. No matter what the actual sibling position of the child with the disability, other siblings may be required to accept responsibility beyond their years if the physical or emotional demands of the child with special needs are extensive.

Breslau (1982) studied 237 siblings of children with congenital disabilities. She found that, for males, younger siblings of children with disabilities scored higher on psychological impairment than did older siblings of children with disabilities. This effect was particularly pronounced for those siblings who were fewer than 2 years younger than the child with the disability. For females, the effect was opposite, with older siblings evidencing more impairment than younger ones. Breslau concluded that, for girls, the role of oldest female tends to bring with it an increased sense of responsibility for the child with the disability that may bring on depressive/anxious feelings that are more intense than the general stress experienced by other siblings in the family. For males, the impact of being born into a family with an infant having a disability preceding them by fewer than 2 years tends to make them at risk for psychological impairment later in life.

Bowen Theory on Sibling Position

The Bowen perspective on sibling position functions as a bridge between the birth-order literature and the conceptualization of the family as an active system. Bowen (1985) proposed that knowledge of birth order gives one some guidelines within which to predict an individual's family role assignment. His framework examines the sibling position of people in past and present generations in an attempt to discover family patterns that may have arisen concerning the emotional value associated with a particular sibling position (M. P. Nichols & Schwartz, 1995). For example, if three generations of women are all oldest daughters, family expectations and roles will be passed on about how an oldest daughter should operate. The family pattern might be that oldest daughters take care of their parents and don't marry or leave home until they are well into adulthood. This pattern sets up a family script that may be acted out generation after generation outside of the conscious awareness of family members. The third or fourth generation oldest daughter may have to struggle with her own needs, her present social culture, and the unconscious demands of her family pattern. If she breaks out of the script and marries young or moves away from her parents to pursue a career, she may feel unexplained anxiety that stems from abandoning this standard.

Certain patterns of personality tend to go along with particular sibling positions. To discover the significance of sibling factors in the life of a student, one must take into account not only ordinal sibling position but also family size, spacing between siblings, and the gender of siblings. With this information, the school professional may be better able to understand students' personalities and interactions with peers.

TRIANGULATION

According to Bowen (1985), any two-person emotional system is inherently unstable. When two people become anxious about negotiating closeness and distance in their relationship, the anxiety is most easily resolved by bringing in a third person (Corey, 1996). This results in a lowering of anxiety between the twosome and creates an emotional triangle. Individuals who have higher levels of differentiation of self are more able to observe and control the patterns of relating within a triangle. Individuals with lower levels of differentiation of self tend to be reactive to tensions within the triangle.

Triangles

Bowen (1985) contended that the most stable relational systems are composed of three-person emotional configurations called triangles. Triangles are the building blocks of all systems, including families, work systems, and peer groups. Any emotional system is made up of a series of interlocking triangles.

For example, the student in Figure 4.1 was involved in three different but overlapping triangles when he was reprimanded for stealing lunch money from a peer. The peer reported the stealing to their teacher, who relayed the information to the student's mother. That evening, the student's mother and father considered the problem and decided about consequences for their son. In Figure 4.1, triangle 1 involves the student, his teacher, and the peer. Triangle 2 includes both parents and the student. The third triangle consists of the student, the teacher, and the mother.

Bowen used the term *triangulation* to describe the pattern of emotional reactions within a particular triangle. This pattern is fueled by emotional reactivity within the system (Roberto, 1992). The process of triangulation can stabilize anxiety and conflict between two people by the following forces:

> The twosome works to preserve the togetherness, lest one become uncomfortable
> and form a better togetherness elsewhere. The outsider seeks to form a togetherness
> with one of the twosome. . . . The emotional forces within the triangle are constantly
> in motion from moment to moment. (Bowen, 1976, p. 76)

In dysfunctional families, when emotional forces become highly anxiety-producing, patterns of relationships begin to repeat themselves and people eventually have fixed roles in relation to one another.

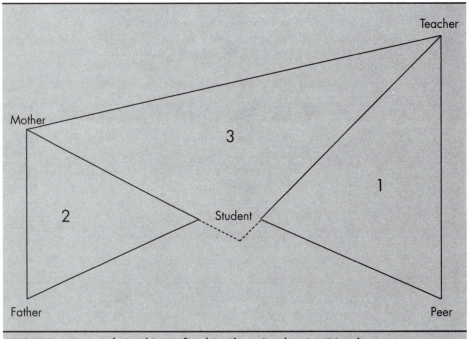

FIGURE 4.1 • Relationships Defined By Three Overlapping Triangles

Parent and Child

In the case of a child or adolescent, the typical triangulation process occurs between two parents and one child. Satir called this relationship the primary triad (Satir & Baldwin, 1983). She believed that this triad is the main determinant of the child's identity, self-esteem, and relational patterns. When there is marital discord in a family, the parent who is feeling most alienated may turn to the child for a feeling of emotional closeness (M. P. Nichols & Schwartz, 1995). This child may be favored for involvement with parents in the triangle due to the processes of family emotional transmission. For example, the child's place in a particular sibling position may be emotionally important to the parent(s), or his or her personality may remind the parents of themselves or one of their siblings, triggering identification issues (Kerr, 1988).

It is difficult to differentiate a self and develop a fluid sense of self when engaged in a triangled relationship across generational boundaries. Under periods of anxiety or family stress, the lack of differentiation is typically expressed by the appearance of behavioral or psychiatric symptoms in the most vulnerable member of the triangle, the child. The child who is triangulated is at risk for physical, emotional, or academic problems (Kerr, 1988; M. P. Nichols & Schwartz, 1995).

Remarriage

Another example of triangulation is found in second marriages where the couple initially connects by comparing the breakups of their former marriages and the abusiveness of their ex-spouses. The ability to focus on their former relationships may be the third leg of the triangle that keeps an optimum level of distance in the marital relationship. Chapter 6 addresses the issues of stepfamilies.

Families and Agencies

In times of family distress, the family system may triangulate with an outside force such as the school, social agencies, the court system, or the mental health system. If the emotional tension can then be blamed on that outside agency, the family may unite together to remain calm.

This process often occurs when school personnel are faced with evidence of family abuse. Unless steps are taken to avoid triangulation, as soon as the school confronts the family about the abuse or as soon as Social Services is contacted, the school professional or social worker may become the "bad guy" who is attempting to destroy an otherwise ostensibly happy family. The family then bonds together, and the outside agency serves the role of the third, distant leg of the triangle. To avoid being cast in this position, school professionals need to maintain their neutrality with these families and focus on keeping open communication among all parties involved in the allegations.

In addition, triangles may overlap, as discussed earlier, and problems in one system, such as the family, may create problems in another system, such as the school (E. H. Friedman, 1986). When dealing with a highly distressed family, if the school personnel suddenly find themselves arguing among the team or feeling high levels of anxiety, overlapping triangles may be in operation.

In the example of the student reprimanded for stealing (see Figure 4.1), three triangles were operating. If communication between parties is clear, if levels of differentiation are adequate, and if there are no unresolved or underlying issues between members of the triangles, the resolution of this problem may go smoothly. However, if the stealing issue becomes overshadowed by unresolved anxieties between people involved in the triangles, the forces of triangulation are operating and the stealing may be exacerbated rather than handled effectively. For example, if the mother believes that the teacher does not adequately manage her classroom, she may not discipline her son for his behavior. If the father believes that his son is a "mama's boy" and is angry at his wife for giving in to their son, he may explode at the boy or at his wife and reenact his wife's relationship with her abusive father rather than negotiating appropriate discipline. In each of these scenarios, the process of triangulation is in operation.

Schools can provide a stabilizing force when working with family systems personnel to help a student. Wendt and Ellenwood (1994), writing about conjoint systemic change in the family and school, clarified a number of means of collaborating. Case studies were provided to demonstrate how the process can work. Indeed, my own experience has shown that agencies and families can work together effectively to decrease triangulation and its negative impact on students and their families.

Detriangulation

Once you are involved in a triangle, how can you become disentangled? The first step is to know that the triangle exists. Second, it is important to not take sides in a conflicting situation. Third, you should not talk to another person in the triangle about a third person and should not listen when someone tries to discuss a third person with you. For example, if a student comes to you to complain about a teacher, a response that would promote detriangulation is, "I'm sorry you feel that way, but I think things will have a chance to get better only if you talk to that teacher. I'd be glad to help you set up a meeting with him."

Triangulation can also occur between colleagues in a system. If you notice that a co-worker tends to talk to you about other people, the easiest way out of the triangle is to ask that person something about himself or herself or to volunteer something about yourself or your values. These statements are geared toward increasing the connection between you and the colleague, thus decreasing the need for triangulation to manage the anxiety between the two of you. For further discussion of how the school professional can stay out of triangles, see Chapter 11.

Triangles or triadic relationships are not dysfunctional in themselves. In fact, they are the basic building blocks of any system (Jacobson & Gurman, 1995). When the intensity between two people becomes uncomfortable, bringing in a third person will diffuse the tension and allow the system to operate with less anxiety. It is only when the anxiety level within a two-person system cannot be managed that the process of triangulation comes into operation. In this process, relationships are indirect and issues are not resolved openly. The forces of constantly changing alliances keep the tension in the system alive.

GENOGRAMS

A technique used for mapping family history on a chart something like a family tree is called a family genogram. The genogram can help the professional and the family view symptoms within a much larger context. Though helpful, the social history, another technique for studying family history, typically involves many pages of written material without any standardized format. To use the information presented in a social history, school professionals must read the material, organize it in their minds, and assimilate it into their experience of the family. In contrast, the genogram organizes up to three generations of family data in a one-page visual representation (M. P. Nichols & Schwartz, 1995). It can help school professionals identify multigenerational patterns, family roles, sibling position, important triangles, and the time line of significant family events in a brief scan.

In diagramming a family on a genogram, certain symbols are used. Squares represent males and circles represent females. As much as possible, fathers are drawn on the left side and mothers on the right. Siblings are drawn oldest to youngest from left to right. Marriages and generations are connected by a series of horizontal and vertical lines. For example, the genogram for a two-parent family with two children, a son age 15 and a daughter age 11, appears in Figure 4.2. Other commonly used symbols are shown in Figure 4.3.

The hypothetical genogram shown in Figure 4.4 was "drawn" in 1997. It is provided to show you what a genogram looks like, not to identify patterns of dysfunction. It conveys the following information: John, age 45, and Elizabeth, age 42, were married for 15 years and had two children, John, Jr., age 13, and Marsha, age 10. In 1995, the couple was separated and subsequently divorced. John remarried immediately and is now expecting a child with his second wife, Selina, age 30. This is Selina's first marriage.

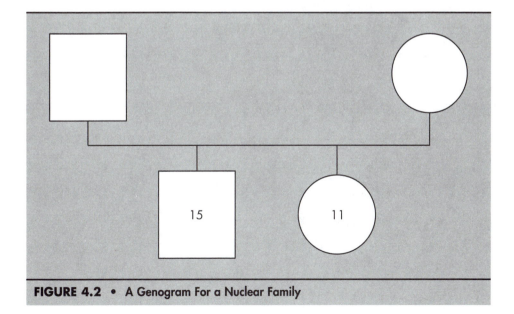

FIGURE 4.2 • A Genogram For a Nuclear Family

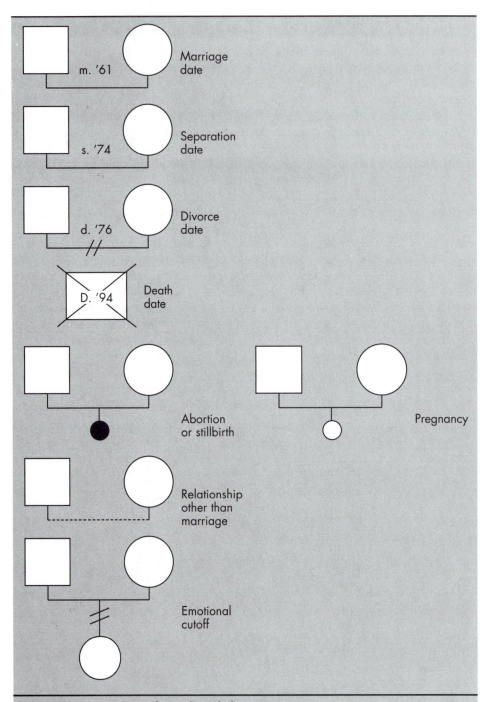

FIGURE 4.3 • Commonly Used Symbols in Genograms

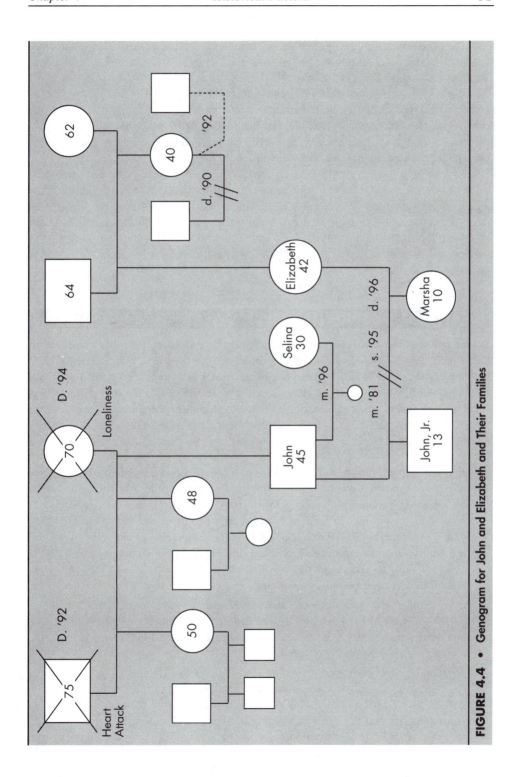

FIGURE 4.4 • Genogram for John and Elizabeth and Their Families

The genogram also conveys that John's parents are both deceased. They died within 2 years of one another, during the period from 1992 to 1994. John's father died of a heart attack and his mother died of "loneliness." They were ages 75 and 70, respectively, when they died. John is the youngest of three children and the only son. His two older sisters are 48 and 50 years old. They are both married and have children. Elizabeth's parents are both still living. Her father is 64 years old and her mother is 62 years old. Elizabeth has a younger sister, age 40, who has been divorced since 1990 but has been involved in a relationship for the past 5 years. She has no children.

As indicated in this example, much information can be communicated quickly by using genograms. A good way to begin practicing this technique is to draw your own family genogram. Once you become adept at drawing a basic genogram, you can begin to use the genogram to indicate major triangles, family roles, areas of significant conflict, emotional cutoffs, multigenerational patterns, and family nodal events. For the reader who is interested in a more in-depth study of the use of genograms see M. McGoldrick and R. Gerson (1989).

MEANS OF DIFFERENTIATING

Bowen believed that when one person in a family becomes free from the reactive emotional process, it is possible for a lowering of anxiety to filter down throughout the relationship system of the family (Guerin & Chabot, 1992). A therapist, by remaining free of the family's reactive emotional process, can assist in beginning this filtering down process. Potentially useful to school professionals is a description of the process Bowen recommended therapists engage in to be more capable of such work, which was described in Guerin and Chabot (1992).

1. *Know the facts about your family relationship system.* Bowen encouraged his trainees to construct comprehensive family diagrams in order to document the structural relationships among members of their family and to gather facts about the timing of important events such as deaths, births, and so forth, which he termed *nodal events*. He also taught the importance of including in the family diagram evidence of physical and emotional dysfunction, relationship conflicts, and emotional cut-offs, which he viewed as indicators of a family's level of emotional functioning

2. *Become a better observer of your family and learn to control your own emotional reactivity to these people.* Bowen charged therapists-in-training with this central task, which was to be accomplished on planned visits with key members from their family of origin.

3. *Detriangling self from emotional situations.* This part of the method entails developing an ability to stay nonreactive during periods of intense anxiety within one's own family system. To foster this process of "detriangling," Bowen encouraged therapists in training to visit their families of origin at times of predictably high tension, such as the serious illness or imminent

death of a key family member. During these visits the goal was to make contact with family members around an anxiety-ridden issue, to remain less emotionally reactive than other family members, and to not choose sides when competing influences and differences of opinions led to relationship conflict.

4. *Develop person-to-person relationships with as many family members as possible.* This instruction was aimed at both fostering detriangulation and encouraging the reestablishment of relationship connections where cutoffs or potential cutoffs had previously existed.

Professionals in schools may want to pursue growth opportunities such as these and meet in groups with a trained Bowen family therapist. Reading Appendix A may also be helpful in the process of learning to differentiate self.

SUMMARY

This chapter provided information from the Bowen (1985) theory concerning how historical factors may affect family and organizational dynamics. Levels of differentiation and means of assessing them were discussed so that school professionals can better understand their own interactions as well as individual levels of differentiation within the families of their students. The personality effects of sibling position and the powerful family role definitions that are assigned as a result of this factor were delineated. The forces of triangulation within the family system, within the school system, and across systems were addressed. Finally, family genograms were illustrated. Appendix A expands on Bowen theory, and additional concepts are elaborated in other chapters as well.

CASE EXAMPLE

Megan, a 17-year-old high school senior, comes from a family consisting of her parents, who are both 34 years old, and her two younger brothers, Allen, 12 years old, and Mark, 10 years old. Her parents have been married for 17 years. Her father is employed as a salesman, and her mother is a secretary.

Although Megan had always been an adequate student, her grades began to drop earlier this year, and she has had frequent absences. When the school counselor met with Megan to discuss these problems, Megan burst into tears and could not return to her classes for the remainder of the day. On more than one occasion, Megan had begun to cry during classes and asked to see her counselor. Most recently, Megan revealed that she and Chuck, her boyfriend of 4 years, were considering breaking up. She reported that Chuck had been spending more and more time with his friends and had told her that he needed his "space." Megan felt that she couldn't stand this rejection and needed to end the relationship with Chuck. Megan also reported feeling that her parents were putting excessive pressure on her about applying to colleges. She was too upset about her problems with Chuck to fill out her applications. With questioning, Megan admitted that she was fearful about rejection from college. She was not sure that her high school record was adequate in spite of her good grades.

Attempting to establish a historical framework for Megan's attitudes, the counselor asked her about her parents' adolescence. The following information was revealed.

Megan's mother, Anne, is the youngest of two siblings, with a sister 2 years older. When Anne was 4 years old, her parents were divorced, and her father married a much younger woman. He subsequently had three more children and did not keep in contact with Anne, her sister, or his ex-wife. Megan's grandmother was remarried 5 years later to an alcoholic. When Anne was 17 years old, she became pregnant with Megan. When Anne talked to her parents about her pregnancy, they kicked her out of the house. She then moved in with her boyfriend's (Megan's father's) family and got married.

Megan's father, Albert, Jr., is the oldest of four siblings, all male. His younger brothers are 3, 5, and 7 years younger than he. Albert's father is an attorney, and his mother is a housewife. They have been married to one another for 40 years. Albert was always an "A" student and a football star. His family had planned for him to attend college and become an attorney like his father, his namesake. When his high-school girlfriend became pregnant, his parents demanded that Albert "do the right thing" and marry her. They let him know that they were disappointed in him. Albert was forced to go to work after graduation and never returned to pursue his college degree.

Questions and Comments

1. *How would you draw a genogram for this family? Assume that it is 1998. [The reader can look at Figure 4.5 for feedback after drawing the genogram.]*

2. *Using factors from the family history and genogram, how can Megan's behaviors be explained in a historical context? A good strategy is to use the chapter subtitles in order to write your speculations.*

   Megan's dependence upon her boyfriend is the result of low levels of differentiation and the emotional transmission of the shame related to her mother's pregnancy out of wedlock. Megan is at risk for becoming pregnant herself as part of the family "script" concerning achievement and failure.

   There is a primary triangle between Megan and her parents in which Megan's future is scripted to atone for her parents' failures. Megan has triangulated Chuck in an attempt to defuse the anxiety between her and her parents. By focusing on her relationship with Chuck, she avoids dealing with her anxiety about college and possible failure.

3. *What interventions might be used to help detriangulate Megan?*

   The counselor could help Megan identify the process of triangulation in her family. She could give Megan information about colleges that are appropriate for her achievement level and assure Megan that her record is adequate for acceptance in college.

   During a meeting between Megan, her counselor, and her parents to discuss Megan's crying spells, Megan could be helped to bring up the issue of her parents'

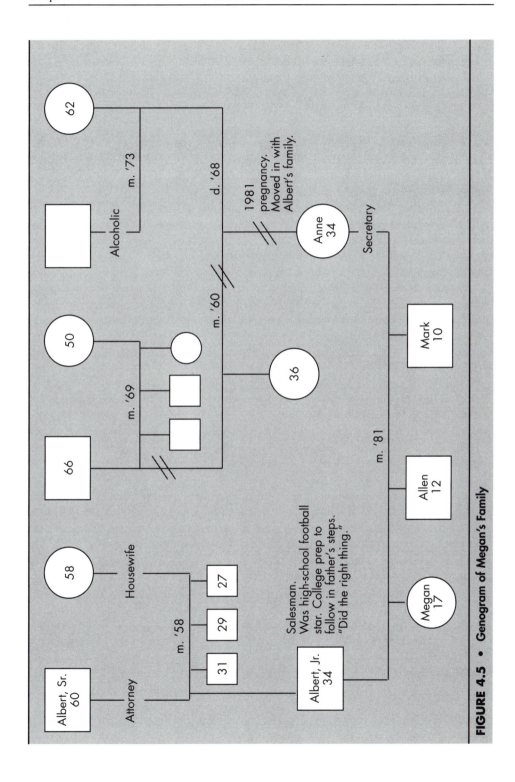

FIGURE 4.5 • Genogram of Megan's Family

pressure on her. The family history of Megan's birth and the emotional cutoffs in her parents' families of origin would be appropriate topics for discussion. Megan would then be liberated from the forces of unresolved loss in her parents' history and would be more likely to develop a higher level of differentiation and self-esteem.

EXTENSION ACTIVITIES

Reflection: Reflect on levels of differentiation in your family of origin as well as your nuclear family, if you are part of one.

Journal: How would you describe your family of origin in terms of emotional reactivity. To what degree does emotional reactivity make it difficult for the intellectual system to inform and guide decisions?

Journal: If you are married or in a partnership, how would you describe what you have observed (e.g., during holidays and other family gatherings) about your partner's family and their levels of differentiation? Remember that those at higher levels of differentiation do not judge others and accept differences! How would you compare and contrast your family of origin with that of your spouse or partner?

Journal: If you have children, consider the levels of differentiation of your nuclear family members. What challenges do you and your spouse or partner face in being models for your children?

Reflection: If you have held a job in the past, reflect on what kinds of experiences you faced at one job site in terms of the levels of differentiation present and how they impacted you.

Journal: What are some examples of higher and lower levels of differentiation that you have observed in a work site?

Constructing a Genogram: Using information presented in this chapter, map out the genogram of your family of origin. If you cannot go back two generations, find people in your family who will share stories with you so you can develop an accurate picture of your family of origin. Initially, just focus on filling in the factual information, then let the stories you remember hearing and the ones people repeat to you inform you of the interaction patterns that have passed down over generations.

Reflection: Think about your family of origin and nuclear family (if you have one) in terms of the family relational patterns being cohesive or explosive.

Journal: Assuming you have or will have children, in what ways would you like to see things change in terms of emotional transmission so that the next generation of your family is healthier?

In-Class/Training Discussion: The professional literature indicates that relationships are deeply affected by birth order. What examples have you noted related to birth order that substantiate examples provided in the text.

In-Class/Training Discussion: How have you seen triangles play out in family life or work circumstances. In terms of triangulation, have you noticed any repeating patterns in others or yourself?

OR

In-Class/Training Discussion: What triangles of prominence have occurred in your family of origin?

Constructing a Genogram: If you are part of a nuclear family, construct a genogram for your youngest child. Even if you are in a blended family or have grown children, you can still construct the genogram.

Journal: What human relationship patterns have passed down to your generation from other generations in your family of origin?

Part II
At-Risk,
Special-Needs,
and Resilient Students

At-Risk Students and Environmental Factors

This chapter begins by describing the impact of socioeconomic factors on children and the family. The next section, "Ethnic Differences," focuses first on the general life strategies of various ethnic groups, then on the cultural values of Hispanic, African, Asian, and Native Americans, and ends with a discussion of differences in cognitive styles prevalent in each ethnic group. The third section, on affirming diversity and promoting equity, describes activities and programs that can be used for achieving greater understanding of ethnic differences. A case example follows, illustrating how a school team might integrate environmental factors into its approach with a student of Hispanic and Native American backgrounds. The chapter concludes with a series of extension activities that can be used to help professionals deepen their understanding of the influence of ethnic differences on the lives of children.

INTRODUCTION

By being exposed to differing socioeconomic backgrounds and cultural influences, people can enhance their sensitivity to others (D. Johnson, 1997) and help to dispel stereotypes about families in a particular cultural category. Regardless of cultural background, families have more similarities than differences. They struggle with similar issues and demands throughout the life cycle and strive toward the same ends.

Ethnic background influences how families cope, express themselves, and interact with external systems such as schools. It is helpful for professionals to ask themselves, "Within this person's experience, is this behavior adaptive, normal, or pathological?" For example, when African-American, Hispanic, or Asian-American parents discipline their child, they expect the child to indicate acceptance by lowering his or her eyes. Making eye contact may be interpreted by a parent from these backgrounds as defiance. In contrast, parents from Anglo-Saxon backgrounds expect their children to maintain eye contact to indicate attentiveness when being disciplined. The Anglo child who lowers his or her eyes may be thought of as being passively resistant.

A meeting of the minds between family members and school professionals about the definitions of problematic behavior is essential. This type of understanding can often be facilitated when educators have knowledge of the family's socioeconomic status, history, and ethnic and cultural patterns. The purpose of this chapter is to help school professionals understand and respond appropriately to these influences.

SOCIOECONOMIC DIFFERENCES

The most powerful cultural determinant of how families interact with society is socioeconomic status (J. S. Coleman, 1987). This is particularly evident when comparing middle-income families with families coping with poverty. Many of the most common ethnic stereotypes derive more from the environmental influences of socioeconomic status than from ethnic background. For example, a middle-class African-American family has a lifestyle more similar to that of a middle-class white family than to the lifestyle of a poor African-American family, regardless of common African heritage. As Wilson (1982), a sociologist, argued, "Class has . . . become more important than race in determining black life chances in the modern industrial period" (p. 389).

Weissbourd (1996) related that "in 1993, 22 percent of all children under 18 lived in families with incomes below the federally established poverty line—which was then about $14,764 for a family of four" (p. 10). He also indicated that most poor children are poor on a temporary basis. In America, only 8% are poor for more than 6 years, and more than 30% experience poverty some time in their lives. About 17.5% of children who are poor live in ghettos. About 19% of children who are African American live in ghettos. Educators know that these children are at risk. Weissbourd suggested that we view these children as vulnerable but not create a self-fulfilling prophecy that dooms them to failure. He related that "over 75 percent of poor children ages 6–11 have never experienced significant developmental delays, or emotional troubles, or a learning disability in childhood" (p. 17).

DeVillar and Faltis (1994) related demographic data indicating disproportionately large birth and emigration rates among minority populations. The younger ages and increasing poverty of minority populations, they wrote, "compound the bleakness of their educational futures and add to the mounting pressure for institutional change" (p. 1).

Family Systems Factors

One of the first issues professionals meet when working with low-income families is facing the realities of how a poor environment affects the normal workings of family life. Aponte (1976a, 1994), who worked with poor families from inner-city Philadelphia, found that the structure of these families (see Chapter 3) was loose and undefined. He used the term "chaotic" to describe the lack of clear leadership, poorly defined boundaries, and unstable structure that he found when trying to help poor inner-city families. About his perceptions of the relationship between professional and family, he stated, "The socioeconomic difference creates a communication gap that complicates the task of mutual understanding" (1976b, p. 432). He wrote the following about the underorganization in the poor family:

> This brings us to a specific phenomenon that is, I believe, central to understanding what it means to do therapy with the poor—*underorganization.* Social destitution in the *absence of a strong sense of self and cohesive familial and social network* can injure the fundamental structure of the individual's psychological development, the formation of family, and the vitality of a community. Individuals may fully develop neither their intellectual and emotional capacity, nor the ability to form intimate and committed personal relationships, nor their potential to perform effectively in society. Families may fail to serve as stable, safe, nurturing nests for their members. People may not learn to live in community where they learn to depend upon one another. Life becomes difficult, painful, and even frightening. (Aponte, 1994, p. 15)

Aponte communicated that socioeconomic factors affect the most basic development of the family and its communication with the world. In 1994, discussing the poor in America, he wrote: "People certainly suffer deprivation, but I believe that at the core they suffer a poverty of *despair*. This is a poverty that robs people of their souls—of meaning, purpose, and hope" (p. 1). To be socioeconomically disadvantaged represents an extreme stressor on the integrity of the family system. Because the adjustment of students to the school environment is tied to the well-being of the family, when family stability is threatened by poverty, as with other stressors, students will suffer. Children from poor families are obviously at risk, and if a child with special needs is included in the family, the stress is multiplied.

Parent Factors

The stress of financial instability influences how parents feel about themselves as providers for and protectors of their children. How much stress the parents feel will influence their involvement with and availability to their children, their discipline style, and the value system that they teach their children.

Homelessness results in a major strain on children in schools. M. E. Walsh and M. A. Buckley (1994) noted that on any given night in the United States, between 60,000 and 100,000 children are homeless and that children make up 24% of the homeless population. Of the children who are homeless, 43% do not attend school and 30% are one grade or more behind their peers (J. A. Hall & Maza, 1990).

Numerous studies have shown that low-income mothers have the highest rate of depression of any demographic group (Eheart & Ciccone, 1982). Further, there is often no consistent, positive father figure in low-income families but rather a male "floater" (Fischgrund, Cohen, & Clarkson, 1987) or a father living in the home who is chronically out of work. If there is an unemployed father at home, he is often tyrannical in his authority and discipline. As Montalvo and Guitierrez (1983) wrote, "The more the man fails against competitive barriers of the American society, the more uncompromising and absolute his power must be at home" (p. 29).

A child growing up in a home with an extremely depressed parent or a parent who is experiencing role loss due to joblessness will bring the effects of these concerns with him or her to the classroom. The following case example of a child at risk illustrates this process:

> A 7-year-old who had been doing well in his first year of school suddenly began to be distracted in the classroom. He was not listening to the teacher's directions and had received numerous negative consequences over a 3-week period. After 3 weeks, when the teacher called home, she discovered that the father had been laid off from his job 1 month before. When asked, the boy volunteered that his father's job loss was a principal source of anxiety for him. He stated that he worried all the time about his family and money problems. The teacher began to make her school contacts directly with the father, who was now at home. She told the father of his son's concerns and asked that he provide some reassurance for the boy. She met with the father to devise a plan for getting his son's behavior back on track and for reinforcing the boy's behavior when he began to pay attention again.

With this plan, the teacher was able to give the father a new identity as a powerful figure for his son, regardless of his temporary joblessness. As demonstrated by this example, the parental roles in the home will often have an effect on what interventions will work with a particular student in the classroom and in the home environment.

It is also important that the school professional take into account parental needs and demands when planning family contacts. Looking at parental needs, Eheart and Ciccone (1982) studied 36 low-income mothers whose children were diagnosed with developmental delays. The authors found that the biggest problem reported by these mothers was the stress of meeting basic needs of their children such as feeding, cleanliness, and safety. What the mothers wanted most in terms of services was a support group where they could talk to other mothers who were having similar problems.

Maslow (1970) proposed that love and belonging as well as self-care needs cannot be addressed before basic physiological and safety needs are met. Within this context, talking with an impoverished mother about showing unconditional positive regard for her child or even about establishing a home behavioral program may be useless when she is trying to make sure she has electricity in the home. The mother may feel more inclined to talk with someone who will listen to her feelings and struggles than with someone who is trying to tell her how to handle her child differently. It is only after the mother feels heard and supported that she will respect suggestions about her disciplining.

The following story, relayed to me by my colleague Chris Mohring, illustrates how one school professional responded to a child-related school problem stemming from parental poverty.

> Charles was a 14-year-old placed in a special education program because he was a slow learner and demonstrated aggressive, out-of-control behavior. In the program

for 2 months, he had been experiencing failure and rejection by his peers. After some observation, the director found that Charles had personal hygiene problems. Charles's dirty clothes and body odor led his peers to taunt him, which, in turn, led to his aggressiveness and withdrawal. Engaging Charles in the classroom was futile. If pushed, he would explode and become verbally or physically abusive. The director talked to Charles and found that he was aware of his body odor. He had no running water at home and was able to take a bath only about once a week. At an age when he was increasingly sensitive to peer group social interactions, he was also aware of his lack of academic achievement and the inadequacy of his hygiene, leaving him with a profound sense of alienation. The director asked the parents' permission to have Charles shower in the gym before school each day. Charles began bathing every morning and the teasing diminished. He obviously felt better about himself, and he began to succeed in school.

In this case, the school professional understood the parents' poverty and the dilemma that it created for Charles and intervened to provide for one of Charles's basic needs.

Student Factors

School professionals must also be aware of the world view and self-image of economically disadvantaged students. Most children growing up in a poor environment experience prejudice on a daily basis. In addition, poverty has an impact upon where the family will live, because fewer and fewer living options are available when income is low or the family is dependent upon welfare programs. All of these factors influence the growth and development of children within the family and how they approach the demands of growing up, including the demands of the educational system (Garmezy, 1991).

Socioeconomically disadvantaged children have experienced so many unmet needs that they see little hope of ever changing their lives or fulfilling their dreams. They become frustrated over the lack of opportunities available to them and can become aggressive, violent, apathetic, and depressed (A. H. Smith, 1978). In addition, they are at risk for school failure.

Minuchin et al. (1967) studied 12 low-income families with delinquent boys between the ages of 8 and 12 who were living in a residential treatment center and 10 low-income families with children who were not delinquent. They found that the delinquent children viewed their home environments as impermanent and unpredictable and that they had learned to react to the present moment rather than to what might be in the future.

Minuchin et al. (1967) also observed that parental responses in the families with delinquent boys were random and unpredictable, hindering the children's ability to internalize rules and set limits for themselves. The emphasis in the delinquent families was on control of behavior rather than on guidance. Because the boys had no expectation of predictable rewards for their performance, their motivation was reduced and they did not learn to be proud of themselves for competence or achievement. Instead, these boys learned that gang involvement and hustling were the subsistence and survival strategies that meant competence in their culture (Coates, 1990).

By the time children who grow up in poverty reach adolescence and are able to think abstractly, they realize that the things they see in the media are not available to them and will not be theirs without years of hard work and a great deal of luck. The disillusionment that sets in is a source of stress in itself, and quick sources of gratification become even more appealing. In the study by Minuchin et al. (1967), many of the delinquent boys had been caught stealing or selling drugs as a way of quickly obtaining the money and status that they desired.

Abi-Nader (1991) wrote of her observations of a program entitled PLAN (Program: Learning According to Needs), which is specifically geared to address the feelings of powerlessness that many disadvantaged Hispanic high-school students face. The approach includes a mentor program in which Hispanic college students talk to high-school students about their experiences. The program also seeks to provide the high-school students with successful Hispanic role models. Finally, the curriculum includes frequent references to the future in positive terms, using phrases like "when you go to college" rather than "if you go to college." The outcome of this program is that 60 to 65% of the PLAN students ultimately attend college.

Conclusions

When dealing with socioeconomically disadvantaged families, the educator must consider family systems factors, parent factors, and student factors (Garmezy, 1991). For these families, the process of developing a conceptual style, a world view, and a motivational style begins long before the children enter the school system. By the time school professionals encounter families who are economically disadvantaged, the factors of frustration, apathy, and depression must be included in any realistic picture of the overall family system. These factors typically have immediate impact on the nature of the families' interactions with the educational system, and they do so with the potency of generations of importance.

Many school professionals have experienced the suspicion, mistrust, and reticence that seem to be common in the reactions of many poor families to school personnel. Professionals should not take these reactions personally. Instead, it is important for professionals to remember the historical and socioeconomic context that breeds this type of negativity and to strive to convince the parents that the common goal is the adjustment of their child or adolescent. Professionals can best serve the child by maintaining their personal boundaries (as described in Chapter 4) and by understanding the parents' initial response to school contact.

ETHNIC DIFFERENCES

This section focuses on the complex issue of ethnic differences and attempts to sensitize the reader to the diversity of ethnic traditions in our nation. U.S. Census Bureau statistics indicate that dramatic increases in nonwhites in the United States will lead to 30% of the population under age 18 being of African, Hispanic, Native, or Asian descent by the year 2000 (Ho, 1992). Thus, it is vitally important for school professionals to consider different cultural realities when working with families in educational contexts. Methods for doing so are described in this section. However, reading about cultural issues is inadequate to the task of understanding the richness that tradition brings to a family. School professionals must also develop personal sensitivities to and methods of exploring these issues with the families they encounter. Only through interaction and exchange with the families themselves can we be educated about our differences and similarities.

It is also important for school professionals to keep in mind that not all members of an ethnic group are alike in respect to life styles, values, or achievement. In a text on African-American families, Willie (1991) indicated that different and distinct lifestyles exist among African Americans from different class levels (affluent, working-class, poor) that relate to family composition, child-rearing, as well as community participation. The author found that affluent African-American parents were very active in their children's schools, the working-class mothers attended some school meetings, and the poor African Americans had little community involvement beyond church attendance.

Life Strategies

Cultural background affects every person's value system, style of responding to stress, way of defining self, and approach to life. For example, the way members of different cultures respond to emotional problems (their own and those of others in the culture) is based on the overall life strategy of the culture.

Middle-class Americans, particularly those from a British cultural background, tend to be independence-oriented and to develop a concept of self based on one's potential future. When emotional problems are encountered, they want to know how the person can be helped to function as an adult member of society. Much inner turmoil may precede any external expression of discomfort in British/Irish families, where emotional experience is taught to be contained within the individual (McGill & Pearce, 1996).

Japanese-American culture assigns shame to the emotionally distraught individual. Internal conflict is viewed as the lack of centeredness of the individual within society. This view stems from traditional Asian cultures, in which the general emotional strategy is one of role conformity, centeredness, and a balancing of life forces within familial and societal roles (Ho, 1992; Kuo, 1984). Asian Americans tend to keep family members with mental disorders in the home, unless they are acting out, and to underutilize mental health resources (Lee, 1996; Lin, Inui, Kleinman, & Womack, 1982).

In contrast, the Jewish-American culture tends to attribute emotional problems to external influences. This approach stems from an Eastern European and Middle Eastern life strategy that teaches the sharing of life. In this culture, life is with and from people, and problems are solved by sharing them. Individual expression is secondary to family and community.

Coming from this same cultural root, Iranians and Italian Americans tend to project emotional problems onto outside events or forces such as loss and social or religious prejudice rather than attributing them to internal processes. For the most part, however, in these two cultures, outsiders are not involved in family business. The family solves its own problems—family loyalty and solidarity are the first priority (Giordano & McGoldrick, 1996; Jalali, 1996).

In these cultures, disgrace to the family is the worst crime. Because of this credo, psychological problems are often ignored, disguised as physical complaints, or contained within the family for long periods of time before any outside intervention is sought. By the time help is pursued, many difficulties have become physical problems such as ulcers, anorexia, and bulimia.

A final example of differing ethnic approaches to psychological problems comes from the Native-American culture. Native Americans acknowledge culture-specific syndromes that are born out of a belief in spiritualism, harmony with nature, and reincarnation rather than acknowledging traditional forms of mental illness. Some of these syndromes include spirit intrusion, in which ghosts of past ancestors return to affect a person's behavior; soul loss, resulting from behavior that is against tribal law; and windigo psychosis, which is an extreme form of psychotic behavior that is connected with the seasons (Kelso & Attneave, 1981). The school professional who deals with Native American families will need to understand their cultural definitions of illness to be able to join with the family in defining a problem (Sutton & Broken Nose, 1996).

Cultural Values

Aponte (1994) wrote poignantly about culture and values:

> The poorest in America, either through slavery (African Americans), conquest (Native Americans), or colonization (Puerto Ricans), have lost much of their original cultures. These cultures once told them who they were and gave them values that helped structure their families and communities. With these cultures there also came purpose, whether in mythology or religion. They had reasons for living and loving that were independent of economic achievement.
>
> America's pragmatism and consumerism have since filled the space created by the loss of the original traditions and rituals of these cultures. The result has been tragic for minorities. (p. 2)

Aponte went on to describe the sad degeneration of these cultures and the willingness of their members to steal or even kill for clothes symbolizing status. Distanced from their heritage, they have attempted to replace their lost cultural values and traditions with American substitutes, such as consumerism. Aponte juxtaposed this situation with that of immigrants from Europe and Asia who, not subjugated, were accompanied into America with their heritage. "Their ghettos, even with poverty and discrimination, became nurseries that fostered identity, social role, personal values. They contended with American society from a core that affirmed who they were, what they were worth, and why they should strive" (p. 3).

Today, minority students are overrepresented in special education programs. Particularly at risk are Hispanic Americans, African Americans, and Asian Americans, who compose 21% of the overall population but are the most represented group in the special education population (Peschley, 1988). According to Hodgkinson (1990) Native Americans have the highest rate of school dropouts (35.5%) of all the ethnic groups in the United

States. Because of language and color barriers, these four groups are the least well assimilated in our present culture. By virtue of their minority status alone, many of these families feel isolated from educational institutions. This sense of isolation puts the children at risk for educational and behavioral problems. The following sections describe the general, traditional values of each of these four cultural groups. This discussion is not intended as an exhaustive picture of specific family and community values within these cultures but rather as a broad overview of old-world values that are a part of the legacy of each culture.

Hispanic Americans

This ethnic group includes many different specific cultural groups, such as Cuban Americans, Mexican Americans, Salvadoran Americans, mainland Puerto Ricans, and Latin Americans. The discussion in this section focuses on the commonalities of cultural values across the subgroups rather than on the specifics of any one subgroup. Ho (1992) indicated that the Hispanic-American population is "the fastest growing ethnic group in the country. If present trends continue, this group will someday replace Blacks as the nation's largest minority group" (p. 94). Over 60% of Americans from Hispanic backgrounds live in the states of California, Texas, and New York.

In general, traditional Hispanic values place importance on dependence, the theory of sacrifice, respect, machismo, and virginity (Garcia-Preto, 1996). Family members are viewed as interdependent, and no sacrifice is seen as too great for the family. It is the parents' job to sacrifice and give themselves up for the children. Children, in turn, are to show gratitude by submitting to the family rules. Although the mothers conduct the everyday running of the family, including discipline, they are seen as more passive than the fathers; their job is to teach respect for the father, who is the ultimate decision maker. Boys are to be aggressive and macho in the outside world but, in contrast, are to mind their mothers at home. Girls are viewed, traditionally, as helpless and needing protection (Adkins & Young, 1976; Garcia-Preto, 1996).

Ho (1992) identified unifying cultural concepts across the Hispanic-American subgroups. These include familism, or the importance of family and family obligation and of putting aside one's own needs for the betterment of the family; personalism, which relates to self-respect and dignity as well as to respect for others; a sense of hierarchy, which is related to socioeconomic status, the father being the head of the household, and the children obeying their parents and older siblings; spiritualism, which is seen as more important than material satisfaction and emphasizes linking directly with the spiritual realm; and fatalism, with an emphasis on transcendent qualities "such as justice, loyalty, or love" (p. 99).

These cultural values may be evidenced in several ways in the classroom. For one, Mexican Americans and Native Americans share the highest school dropout rate of all ethnic groups in this country (C. I. Bennett, 1990). In addition, adolescent Hispanic girls may seem, from a European-American perspective, to be overprotected and denied privileges that are appropriate in the Anglo culture. In contrast, when the teacher believes a Hispanic male child needs discipline, the parents may see the behavior as natural and driven by the male's inherent nature to be macho and somewhat out of control from the Anglo point of view. In these instances, an unspoken conflict arises between cultural value systems.

In a study of Puerto Rican families, Montalvo and Guitierrez (1983) found a large number of children experiencing elective mutism after entering preschool. These authors characterized the identified children as coming from families that had limited interaction with the outside world. The parents spoke Spanish at home and were often shy and fearful of the English-speaking culture. They communicated to their children that the outside world was a frightening place. Soon after these children entered preschool, many witnessed some type of teasing, perceived intimidation by an adult, or their parents acting intimidated by the school personnel. From that point on, the children, who could speak English, did not speak at school though they continued to speak Spanish at home. The teachers left the children alone about their mutism. They backed off and gave them more time to integrate into the English-speaking environment. Montalvo and Guitierrez found it to be more helpful for parents to be empowered to ask the school to make more demands, rather than fewer, upon their children. When parents were able to be more assertive with the school, their confidence in other areas increased and positive changes for the children followed.

Families with special needs.   Nazzaro (1981) presented a paradigm for general characteristics of children with disabilities from various ethnic groups. According to this classification, the primary problems encountered by professionals in diagnosing and working with Hispanic children with special needs are the pervasive difficulties posed by bilingualism.

When facing stress, Puerto Ricans will ask their family for help. The expectation is that someone in the family, particularly someone in a stable position, will help others who have a problem or crisis (Garcia-Preto, 1996). Thus, accessing social services becomes a last resort.

In a study of Puerto Rican parents with children having learning disabilities or mental retardation, Harry (1992) found that the parents discounted the labels placed on their children because of the different cultural meanings of disability and normalcy that they held. Harry recommended that professionals become sensitive to the values and norms of their students. She cautioned, however, that professionals must first "become aware of their own values, and of the fact that most human values are not universal but are generated by the needs of each culture" (p. 36).

Adkins and Young (1976) wrote of their experiences with an early intervention program for Hispanic children in El Paso, Texas. They found that many factors interfered with Hispanic families being able to obtain appropriate help for their children with disabilities. They noted a mistrust of medical institutions and a fear of medical procedures and testing that kept many children from obtaining adequate diagnosis of their difficulties. Even when a diagnosis was made, families often turned to religion, folklore, or superstition rather than to doctors or educators for advice on how to intervene with their child. The families also felt cultural pressure to take care of their own problems, including those associated with children who were not functioning normally, and a fear of losing face if a family member were to be found to have a disability. Finally, there was a cultural tendency toward overindulgence for children who are found to have a disability. These children were generally treated as dependent and incapable and had everything done for them. When professionals from outside the culture begin to recommend that families try to teach their child independence or self-help skills, they often are confronted by the force of this cultural stereotype.

African Americans

Like Hispanic cultures, the African-American culture includes a diverse group of people, such as Caribbean and African cultures and American southern and urban groups. The discussion in this section, like that for the Hispanic culture, should be taken as global rather than specific to a particular heritage. Ho (1992) related that 12% of the American population is African American. That percentage is expected to rise to 13.3% by the year 2000.

The following statistics may help provide an understanding of the African-American experience in America. Fischgrund et al. (1987) found that while 8 in 10 white children live in two-parent families, only 4 in 10 African-American children live in two-parent families. The African-American children lived in female-headed homes over 3.5 times as often as children from Caucasian backgrounds. Nearly 10% of the African-American children lived in homes that involved supervision by a welfare agency. For Caucasian children, the figure was approximately 2.5%. Further, the authors reported that African Americans earned 60% less than Caucasian families. They also found that nearly half of African-American children are considered poor, as contrasted with approximately 17% of Caucasian children.

The African principles of human connectedness and interdependence can be seen in present-day African-American cultures (Hale-Benson, 1982; Hines & Boyd-Franklin, 1996; Ho, 1992). Most African-American families are embedded in a complex kinship and social network. This network may include both blood relatives and close friends. The concept of an augmented family, one in which extended family or friends live in the home for various periods of time, is an integral part of the African-American culture. The humanistic values of cooperation and "we-ness" that are inherent in the augmented family arrangement are extensions of an African cultural base (Delaney, 1979; Hines & Boyd-Franklin, 1996). The kinship bonds that developed in this culture were also influenced by shared trauma and remain essential for coping with the oppression experienced in U.S. society (Staples, 1994).

Another characteristic of the African-American culture is role flexibility or adaptability (Hale-Benson, 1982; Hines & Boyd-Franklin, 1996; C. C. Mack, 1981). Various people within the family may interchange roles and functions without engendering a sense of instability in the family system. Thus, older children, grandparents, or neighbors—whoever is at hand—may provide child care, discipline, or household tasks at various times. The school professional may need to expand his or her definition of who is "family" or who is responsible for helping a student with problems in this cultural context.

A final consideration in the African-American culture is the importance of childbearing and child rearing as validation for women. Prior to the emancipation of the slaves, families were frequently separated, and African-American men and women were not allowed to legalize their marriages. Procreation was encouraged to increase the labor supply, and fertility in an African-American female was considered an asset. A woman's identity was tied to her role as a mother (Hines, 1990). A matriarchal society with multiple nurturing figures resulted (Pinkney, 1975). Child-rearing styles became authoritarian to encourage self-sufficiency and toughness in children, because the mothers knew that the children could be taken away from them at any time that they became useful. African-American women were viewed as all-sacrificing and frequently turned to religion to help themselves deal with the grief of constantly losing their children. It is upon this basis of physical disconnection that the present African-American experience was formed. School professionals need to increase their awareness of these multigenerational forces before attempting to intervene in the relationships among parents and children in this culture.

An example of how African-American cultural values extend to the school experience may be seen by many school professionals at the high-school level. Counselors and teachers have expressed frustration at the large number of African-American girls they work with who become pregnant early in adolescence and drop out of school in favor of taking on a parenting role. For many of these girls, the self-esteem that they feel in being a mother outweighs the motivation to continue their studies and work to achieve a career identity (Hale-Benson, 1982; Hines & Boyd-Franklin, 1996). Unfortunately, many of our social welfare programs have functioned to reinforce this dynamic. Even for African-American girls whose mothers are working at professional jobs and are career-oriented, the peer culture often perpetuates the sense that motherhood is the only identity of value. With an understanding of the multigenerational patterns that contribute to a primary maternal identity, educators may be able to help young people develop alternative role models and begin building self-esteem around competency early in the educational process.

Families with special needs.   Nazzaro (1981) identified two primary issues as affecting the diagnosis and treatment of African-American students with disabilities. First is the tendency of an Anglicized culture to diagnose African-American youth as conduct-disordered or juvenile delinquents when they have behavioral problems. Nazzaro argued that behavior viewed as antisocial in a disadvantaged African-American culture, which is often behavior used to achieve status, may go unnoticed when working within "the majority controlled system." Second, African-American students with learning disabilities are often misdiagnosed with mental retardation because of test biases and dialectic use of language.

D. Y. Ford and J. J. Harris (1995) found that person-environment transactions and related sociocultural influences were stronger predictors of underachievement among gifted African-American students than intellectual and academic factors. "Such factors as a positive self-concept, an understanding of racism, and the existence of support systems," they wrote, "are more predictive of African-American success than academic ability" (p. 198).

The entire October/November 1992 issue of the journal *Exceptional Children* was devoted to issues in the education of African-American youth in special education settings. The topics of the articles range from self-concept to early pregnancy of teens. Administrators may find it useful to distribute reprints of some of these articles at fall faculty meetings.

Asian (Pacific) Americans

This general cultural category includes the Chinese, Filipino, Korean, Vietnamese, and Japanese. Ho (1992) indicated that this population has doubled in America since 1970. As reported by Momeni (1984), Asian Americans have the lowest proportion of households headed by women, the lowest divorce rate, and the lowest childbirth rate of all ethnic groups in the United States.

The major socialization goals for Asian-American children reflect traditional values: a sense of collectivity and identification with the family, dependence on the family, obedience, and a sense of responsibility and obligation to the family (Lee, 1996; Serafica, 1990). These strong ties mean that often at least one grandparent is living in the family home. Ho (1992) listed the following important cultural values that operate among Asian Americans:

- filial piety and unquestioning loyalty toward parents;
- shame as a behavioral influence for reinforcing expectations of the family and for communicating proper behavior;
- self-discipline, modesty, humility, and stoicism in adversity, with an emphasis on the middle-position virtue of feeling neither haughty nor unworthy;
- focus on a sense of belonging and togetherness in contrast with the typical American search for perfectionism and individualism;
- awareness of social milieu and sensitivity to the opinions of others;
- fatalism, or detachment with resignation to fate's impact on one's life, bringing equanimity as well as a pragmatic orientation; and
- inconspicuousness stemming from fear of being picked out as an illegal immigrant or of being ostracized by the racist segment of American society.

Traditional Asian roles identify fathers as educators and disciplinarians and mothers as protective and nurturing. A wife is expected to have complete obedience to her husband. Loyalty and respect for one's parents and elders is of primary importance. Behaving well is valued more highly than self-expression (delCarmen, 1990; Lee, 1996).

The most stressful period of development for Asian Americans is adolescence, a period in which many of the traditional Eastern values are in direct contradiction to the Western American values of independence and self-sufficiency. Whereas creative ideas and questioning of values are encouraged in the U.S. educational system, Asian-American culture stresses loyalty and obedience. Whereas self-expression and self-disclosure are considered desirable in American society, expression in the Asian culture is implicit, nonverbal, and intuitive.

There is increasing evidence that more egalitarian views of male and female roles are being accepted in the Asian-American community (Lee, 1996). However, such a dramatic change in values may cause some role and marital strain in early generations of Asian immigrants. School professionals may see the effects of parental disagreement about gender roles being enacted in role confusion and anxiety in students, particularly adolescents who are struggling with their identity. The school professional needs to be aware of the possibility of this conflict and avoid triangulation into the primary struggle between the parents.

Families with special needs. One of the most frequently cited areas of concern regarding Asian Americans is their general underutilization of mental health services (Ho, 1992; Lee,

1996; Tashima, 1981). Although foreign-born Asians and Asian women married to American military men are at very high risk for adjustment problems, their reliance on mental health services tends to be limited. When they do receive mental health services, they tend to be diagnosed as schizoid, schizophrenic, or retarded due to the language barrier and their style of low emotional expressiveness. Frequently, however, the diagnosis is inappropriate. Therefore, children of these two populations may grow up in a household with a severely depressed or dysfunctional parent who is not receiving treatment or who is receiving inappropriate treatment. The children may show signs of moodiness, physical and cognitive lethargy, or withdrawal that come from their experience of modeling the behavior of a parent.

Typically, Asian Americans show strain through somatic complaints (Ho, 1992). In the holistic view of health adopted by Asian-American culture, physical complaints stigmatize the individual less than emotional problems do. Also, because self-disclosure and strong expressions of feeling are discouraged, physical complaints can be used to express personal and interpersonal problems. This internalization of problems makes school phobia more likely.

Nazzaro (1981) spoke to the impact of bilingualism on the diagnosis of Asian-American children, particularly in the areas of hearing, language arts, and learning disabilities. The passive learning style and the self-controlled emotional style of this culture often results in misdiagnosis. Both of these qualities may lead school professionals to view Asian-American children as cognitively slow, disinterested, or nonmotivated.

Native Americans

In the United States, over two million people from 500 tribes and 314 reservations identify with being of Native-American descent (U.S. Census Bureau, 1993). Although Native Americans make up only 1% of the U.S. population, Native Americans have been described as having "fifty percent of the diversity" existing in the country (Hodgkinson, 1990). Some have a great-grandparent who was Native American, others were born on a reservation. Some who claim Native-American descent have no identification with being Native American, having always lived in a city and having had no exposure to native customs or language. Many live in both worlds, balancing their two identities. Thus, speaking of Native Americans in general is difficult yet helpful for those unfamiliar with their rich heritage.

Among the tribes cultural identification varies widely. Each tribe holds a different world view. Tribes have dissimilar practices and customs as well as differences in family structure and views of spirituality. Those Native Americans connected with tribal traditions, have "a radically different view of themselves than the one created by the dominant culture. The importance of this should never be underestimated" (Sutton & Broken Nose, 1996, p. 35).

Whereas the dominant culture in the United States identifies siblings as brothers and sisters, in the Native American culture the extended family of cousins is referred to as brothers and sisters with the grandparents being the primary relationship. A grandaunt or granduncle would hold the same position as grandparent in providing training and discipline.

Parental roles are filled by the parents as well as by the parents' siblings (aunts and uncles). An in-law is not spoken of in Native-American culture; the person referred to as a daughter-in-law in the dominant culture's reference to daughter-in-law would be called a daughter in Native-American culture. Marriage thus erases distinctions between natural and inducted family members. Families become blended rather than joined by marriage.

Native Americans value the family solving problems together. They think in terms of "we" (Sutton & Broken Nose, 1996), as opposed to the competitive "I" of the dominant culture. Communal sharing is highly valued, and those who give much to others are held in the highest regard. Native Americans place great value on feeding, housing, clothing, and transporting visitors or travelers (Attneave, 1982).

Cautioning that the Native-American population is not a homogenous group, Garrett (1995) described Native-American values as consisting of "sharing, cooperation, noninterference, being, the group and extended family, harmony with nature, a time orientation toward living in the present, preference for explanation of natural phenomena according to the supernatural, and a deep respect for elders" (p. 188). Going on to describe the values of the dominant culture in the United States, Garrett showed that the two world views are diametrically opposed to one another:

> *Mainstream values* emphasize saving, domination, competition and aggression, doing, individualism and the nuclear family, mastery over nature, a time orientation toward living for the future, a preference for scientific explanations of everything, as well as clock-watching, winning as much as possible, and reverence of youth. (p. 188)

According to Garrett, in Native-American culture there is a focus on self-mastery and inner strength as well as on developing personal abilities in children. Ideals held in high regard include kindness, sharing, autonomy, and noninterference. Values are communicated by the elders through storytelling. Spiritual and humanistic qualities are emphasized, as is modesty.

Humor has also been described as important to the Native-American culture. Focusing on the use of humor in Native-American Indian cultures, Herring and Meggert (1994) wrote, "Indians use humor's ability to erase, cleanse, or change what was embarrassing, oppressive, sorrowful, or painful" (p. 68). After reviewing the influences of humor on the Native-American culture, the authors discuss specific strategies involving humor that counselors can use when working with Native-American children.

Coming from a history of victimization, Native Americans look for authenticity, respect, and concern for others when they meet with professionals (Sutton & Broken Nose, 1996). Respect is paramount for school professionals who work with students of Native-American descent.

Families with special needs.   Native Americans share with Mexican Americans the highest school dropout rate of all the ethnic groups in the United States. According to Hodgkinson (1990, cited in Garrett, 1995), the school dropout rate for Native-American students is 35.5%. Garrett, focusing on *cultural discontinuity,* placed the blame on a cultural clash with the dominant culture. Whereas Native-American culture stresses family, leadership, and noninterference, the dominant culture emphasizes achievement and monetary gain. Garrett provides many usable recommendations for school professionals for alleviating cultural discontinuity in the schools.

According to Saunders (1987), Native American children come to school ready to learn, yet by the end of fourth grade their achievement declines rapidly. This finding is in line with Garrett's explanation that changing family life quality and the pressure to succeed applied by educators conflict with Native-American cultural values that place family ties, intrinsic worth, and traditional beliefs first (Garrett, 1995).

Sexual abuse in a Native-American family is a thorny issue, since sex is not considered an acceptable topic for discussion. Child abuse prevention education requires prework to build trust (Willis, Dobrec, & Sipes, 1992).

The difficulty of working with Native-American adolescents who are attempting to differentiate from the family was highlighted by Topper (1992) in a case study. He viewed development of an independent adult identity as challenging in this culture because of the economic underdevelopment of the reservations, their restricted funds for support services, the culture clash already described, and fall out in social and medical areas stemming from all of these factors.

Alcohol and drug abuse are high among Native-American youth. Trimble (1992) likened the effect of this abuse to a second "trail of tears," noting that Native-American youth have a higher rate of abuse than any other minority. Discussing the difficulty of using traditional approaches to deal with problems of Native-American youth, Trimble recommended a cognitive-behavioral approach for drug abuse prevention and intervention. He described a group prevention-intervention program tailored to Native-American youth.

Cognitive Styles

Another consideration for school professionals is the influence of culture on cognitive style. For the past 30 years, studies have been conducted that attempt to discern the differences between the thinking of mainstream American cultural groups, such as Anglo-Americans, and that of minority groups, such as Hispanic, African, and Native Americans (J. A. Anderson, 1988; R. Cohen, 1969; Hale-Benson, 1982).

In general, the research indicates that two very different cognitive styles exist in mainstream and minority cultural groups. These styles have been referred to by various researchers as *field-independent* versus *field-dependent* (J. A. Anderson, 1988), analytic-cognitive versus relational (R. Cohen, 1969), and linear versus circular (Hale, 1981). Euro-Western or Anglo thought is characterized as field-independent, analytic-cognitive, and linear in nature, whereas Hispanic, African, and Native American thought tends to be field-dependent, relational, and circular in nature.

Historically, American public schools have tended to reward Euro-Western cognitive styles. Characteristics of this type of thought are:

- Task-oriented
- Standardized
- Objective

- Logical
- Scheduled
- Factual

- Meaning is absolute
- Mechanistic

- Individual mastery
- Deductive

In contrast, characteristics of minority thought include:

- Process-oriented
- Creative
- Subjective
- Meaning is contextual
- Humanistic

- Affective
- Flexible
- Group cooperation
- Inductive

School professionals must begin to adapt their teaching methods and curriculum to address these contrasting forms of thought (Reed, 1992).

For school professionals who wish to study the issue of cultural diversity in more depth, the seminal work on ethnic issues in families is an edited volume by McGoldrick et al. (1982). A revised edition (1996) includes discussion of many varied ethnic backgrounds and how knowledge of ethnicity can be useful to the professional in understanding family functioning. The authors describe how life-cycle and situational stressors, such as the diagnosis of a child with a disability, may put families into greater contact with the roots of their traditions and belief systems and challenge their identity, and they suggest cultural-specific intervention strategies that professionals may find useful.

AFFIRMING DIVERSITY AND PROMOTING EQUITY

Increasing understanding of ethnic differences is approached on two levels in this section. First, activities aimed at achieving a greater personal awareness and sensitivity to differing backgrounds and families are recommended. Second, specific programs that have been used to increase intercultural awareness and connection on the school and community level are described and suggestions are made to help educators be more culturally sensitive. At the end of the section the issue of promoting equity is focused upon briefly.

Personal Awareness

McGoldrick et al. (1996) proposed that "the most important part of ethnicity training involves . . . coming to understand (your) . . . own ethnic identity" (p. 22). Only by becoming aware of our own prejudices and values can we learn to open our minds to the values of other cultures. To heighten your understanding in this area, you may want to ask yourself the following questions, which were adapted from McGoldrick and Giordano (1996, p. 24):

1. How would you describe yourself ethnically and socioeconomically? Is your present socioeconomic position the same or different from that of your parents and grandparents?

2. Who in your family influenced your sense of ethnic identity? How did they teach you these values?

3. Which ethnic groups other than your own do you think you understand best and least?

4. Which characteristics of your own ethnic group do you like most and least?

5. Imagine that your socioeconomic level decreased drastically over the next year. What would change about your life?

By asking yourself questions such as these and discussing your answers with friends and colleagues, you may increase your awareness of your values, prejudices, and fears.

To increase personal awareness of other ethnic groups, the school professional will benefit from developing an attitude of problem solving in alliance with the family being counseled. When beginning contact with a family of differing cultural or socioeconomic background, a stance of respectful curiosity and openness to learn is helpful. The following techniques may prove useful:

1. *Self-disclosure and joining.* Introduce yourself as "Ms./Mr./Dr. _____. I'm your son's _____." Don't use the parents' first names unless they give you permission to do so. Tell the family an interesting story about your cultural background. "I grew up with a house full of kids and my husband is an only child. What a difference that makes."

2. *Family self-identification.* How do the family members see themselves? "Your last name is pretty unusual. Is it German or Swedish? Do you know anything about that background?"

3. *Clarification about questions.* Tell the family why you need to know the information you're asking; how it will be used. "Could you tell me something about the Mormon religion? I'm really not that familiar with it. I wonder how Mark might share some of your traditions with our class."

4. *Cultural heritage.* Ask questions about family rituals. "The holidays are coming up. How does your family celebrate?"

By expressing an interest in the family's beliefs and values, the professional begins the relationship with the family in a spirit of openness and acceptance. This beginning will provide the foundation for developing a problem-solving alliance with the parents, which is vital for helping their children adapt to the school environment.

Believing that ethnic pride is important to a healthy self-concept, B. A. Ford and C. Jones (1990) described a method used to promote cultural awareness within 9- to 12-year-old African-American students with developmental disabilities. The project involved 10 weeks of daily sessions, lasting from 30 to 45 minutes, from an ethnic feeling book. The students, their teacher, and the teacher educator who developed the ethnic feeling book were African Americans. Methods such as this can provide an ongoing means of promoting cultural awareness.

Institutional Sensitivity

As described earlier in this chapter, one of the difficulties with educating minorities in American public schools is the fact that our educational institutions have been formed from a base of Euro-Western thought and values (Trimble, 1992). Hale-Benson (1982) argued that to optimally address the needs of minority children, schools must make changes in their ideology, method, and content (p. 152). Ideologically, education must teach minorities how to struggle and survive. Methods need to include cognitive strategies that are more relational and creative than cognitive and structured.

Content needs to be ethnocentric in nature, that is, teaching the history, crafts, music, historical and political figures, and important events of various ethnic groups. An example of an ethnocentric curriculum can be found in a guide developed by Wendell and Leoni (1986) for the Virginia Department of Education. The guide includes general information about the cultural values of 19 ethnic groups and provides suggestions for ethnocentric lessons and activities for each cultural group. Your local education department may have developed a similar guide. For further sources providing useful information on cultural diversity see the listings of books for adults and children in Appendices B and C under the heading "Diversity."

To respond to the needs of various minorities, Cummins (1989) recommended that schools develop an intercultural orientation based on the values of inclusion, collaboration, interaction, and experiential learning rather than try to force minorities to conform to an Anglo orientation through the transmission of Anglo values. Some of the ways he and others have proposed to help schools create a climate that is welcoming to minority parents and reinforcing to students' identity follow (Cummins, 1989; Lynch & Stein, 1987):

1. Respect the various cultural groups in the school district by hanging signs in the main office that welcome people in the different languages of the community.

2. Recruit parents or other people from the community who can tutor students in different languages or provide a liaison between the school system and other parents. In some instances, these parents could be paid with money for teacher's aide positions or grant money allocated for this purpose.

3. Include greetings and information in the various languages in newsletters, parent handouts, and other official school communications. Make materials about school services available in the appropriate languages at local churches, community centers, markets, and other businesses frequented by families.

4. Display within the school pictures and objects representing the various cultures and religious groups of the student body.

5. Encourage students to write contributions in their native language or about their family culture for school newspapers and magazines.

6. Provide opportunities for students to study their culture in elective subjects and in extracurricular clubs. It is often eye-opening for students to become aware that, for example, Africa and China had extremely advanced cultures at a time when the British

(whom we typically study in history classes) were still living in dirty, flea-infested castles.

7. Encourage parents to help in the classroom, library, playground, and clubs so that all students have the opportunity to interact with people of different cultures.

8. Invite people from ethnic minority communities to act as resources and to speak to students in both formal and informal settings. These individuals can also be asked to provide in-service education to school personnel to sensitize the school staff to the values and beliefs of the families they serve.

Frequently, school professionals report that the services offered for parent involvement are underutilized. In an effort to discover the barriers to parent involvement in a socioeconomically disadvantaged neighborhood, Lynch and Stein (1987) conducted three studies, in which they interviewed a total of 434 families receiving special education services. The sample consisted of Hispanic, African-American, and Anglo families from a metropolitan school district in southern California. According to family reports, the main barriers to parent participation in school meetings were work, time conflicts, transportation problems, and child-care needs. When asked what could be changed to help parents get to the school, the parents who were interviewed suggested that the schools hold bilingual meetings, select times convenient for parents, provide transportation, provide advance notice of meetings, provide child care, inform them of the subjects that pertain to their children, and send personal notes or make calls about the meetings.

This study highlights the importance of sensitivity to the needs of parents. The types of services offered by the school and the times of school and parent meetings may need to be geared differently based on needs of each unique community. Boyd-Franklin (1989) indicated that it is important to train African-American parents for professional positions in the schools. They serve as role models as well as have considerable cultural material that will help the school.

Gorman and Balter (1997) reviewed the available quantitative research for culturally sensitive parent education programs that related to child rearing. They described in detail a number of programs for African-American and Hispanic families. They did not find efficacy studies for Native-American and Asian-American parents but did describe efforts to serve them. Reading this review will provide educators with important information about the parent training programs that have been used with culturally different parents.

McIntyre (1996) presented guidelines for the provision of appropriate services to culturally diverse students who have emotional or behavioral problems. These guidelines were developed by a task force on ethnic and multicultural concerns formed by the Council for Children With Behavior Disorders. McIntyre related that the guidelines do not make distinctions between races, cultures, sexual orientation, or generational status and that educational and therapeutic practices should not be prescribed on those bases. Instead, the guidelines call for multifaceted and complex practices in schools and treatment. He wrote, "We cannot support, condone, or excuse behaviors, even culturally based, if they undermine basic human rights and the more commonly held values of humankind" (p. 142). The following seven goals were delineated as a result of the task force effort: removing culturally different students from special programs if their behaviors are culturally based rather than emotional and/or behavioral in nature; providing respectful and culturally appropriate education and treatment to those who do not have emotional and/or behavior disorders but are culturally different; implementing assessment procedures that are culturally and linguistically competent; recruiting professionals who are culturally different; providing training in modifications of practice that focus on the characteristics of culturally different students who have emotional and/or behavioral disorders; creating a welcoming atmosphere in which culturally different students with emotional and/or behavioral disorders are valued, respected, and safe; and enhancing the cultural knowledge of professionals, students, and the public.

Sontag and Schacht (1994) investigated differences among ethnic groups concerning the perceptions parents have of their need for information and sources of information as well as the nature and preference of parental participation in early intervention for children with special needs. In regard to the effective diffusion of information to minority families, the researchers found differences within specific minority groups; elusive local networks for communication, each having different opinion leaders and communication channels; an interest in funding as well as technical assistance to help develop culturally relevant solutions; and suspicion and skepticism within the community toward those who come from the outside to help make changes. The researchers related that American Indian children receive a lower level of service than white children. Also, minority parents reported low level of involvement in early intervention activities with their children but wanted to increase their participation. These findings indicate that schools need to make a greater effort to include parents from ethnically and culturally diverse backgrounds in decision making.

Teacher and Counselor Applications

The literature also includes a number of strategies that individual teachers and counselors can use at the classroom or group level to increase cross-cultural awareness in their students. Schniedewind and Davidson's 1998 book *Open Minds to Equality: A Sourcebook of Learning Activities to Affirm Diversity and Promote Equity* includes different types of activities for upper elementary and middle school students that teachers can use to foster an understanding of cultural and racial differences. This book also includes resources and curriculum materials for teachers. I highly recommend that at least one copy be available in every elementary and middle school.

Hayes (1996) studied storytelling and its influences on first-grade students in a suburb of Chicago. She was looking at whether stories could increase interest in and positive feeling for people from different cultural backgrounds. She concluded that rich learning opportunities can be established in this manner. Phillips-Hershey and Ridley (1996) shared a model for increasing classroom acceptance of diversity in students with mental retardation. They recommended that the school counselor collaborate with general and special education teachers to provide "an integrative experience that incorporates the basic understanding of group processes and group developmental stages with planned neutral activities" (p. 291).

Isaacs and Duffus (1995) described a Scholars' Club used to increase achievement among high school minority students. Primarily an honor society, the club members also took part in community activities such as fashion shows, public speaking, peer tutoring, and mentoring. The researchers found that self-esteem was enhanced through such support experiences.

Moles (1993) reviewed the literature to provide suggestions for helping parents strengthen learning for their children. He suggested that low-income and minority families would benefit from a variety of family interactions including leisure reading; family conversations about current events or life in the family; home life activities, which would stimulate language development; and the demonstration of personal interest as well as intense involvement by parents in their child's development.

Garrett (1995) reiterated recommendations made by Little Soldier (1985) and Sanders (1987) for counteracting cultural discontinuity in schools leading to dropout among Native-American youth. The suggestions included increasing opportunities for visual and oral learning; using culturally relevant materials; respecting family-related and tribe-related absences; using Native-American elders as mentors; using peer tutoring to amplify the values of sharing and cooperation; encouraging intergroup rather than individual competition; emphasizing the present with short-term goals; and modeling appropriate behavior and skills.

Values clarification exercises can also be useful for dealing with value conflicts. To help Native-American students reach solutions to value conflicts that retain and strengthen their pride in their heritage and values, Garrett (1995) made the following recommendations to school counselors:

1. Encourage the youth to make choices and to take a look at specific choices as examples from everyday life.

2. Help the youth discover and examine available alternatives when faced with choices.

3. Help the youth weigh alternatives thoughtfully and reflect on the consequences of each.

4. Encourage the youth to consider what they prize and cherish (for example, by making a list or writing a short story together).

5. Give the youth opportunities to make public affirmations of the choices they have made (for example, through a role-play).

6. Encourage the youth to act, behave, and live in accordance with the choices they have made and to be able to justify their choices through appropriate communication.

7. Help the youth examine repeated behaviors and life patterns in relation to the choices they have made.

Also from the area of school counseling, M. E. Walsh and M. A. Buckley (1994) spoke to what homeless children have said they want from the adults who assist them. They do not want to be judged or labeled. They desire a trusting relationship that respects and honors confidentiality. Although they want to talk with others about their lives, they also want to choose when and where they talk. They want reassurance that they are not alone. "Finally, they express a great concern that others know that they, their families, and others in the shelter are 'nice people'" (p. 14).

Gustafson (1997) related how her sixth-grade class increased its ethnic awareness through their focus on a slain civil rights leader from their community, Edwin T. Pratt. The students learned much about civil rights, public speaking, writing grants, and public art. They created a memorial that was dedicated on the last day of school. Through this process all of the students grew in their appreciation of sacrifices made by those with the courage of their convictions. Such activities encourage students to act, rather than remain idle.

For teachers to be successful in multicultural schools, they need to relate curriculum content to the cultural background of their students. In an article in *Educational Leadership* Wlodkowski and Ginsberg (1995) outlined four conditions necessary for culturally responsive teaching and gave examples of norms under each of the four conditions. The conditions included establishing inclusion, developing positive attitudes, enhancing meaning, and engendering competence. The authors encouraged the use of holistic approaches for culturally different students that engage the students in the learning process. This article is helpful reading for all school professionals and those who train them.

Another article of particular interest written by M. Franklin (1992), describes culturally sensitive instructional practices for African-American students. The article focuses on using and accepting dialect in specific situations; presenting real-world tasks related to students' cultural background; including a people focus through small groups, an instructional approach that meets the preferred learning style of many African-American learners; using grouping patterns that allow African-American students to problem solve together and be allowed to go off-task on occasion; employing cooperative learning for content-related tasks; using peer–cross-age grouping to allow informal interactions; and using peer tutoring to foster relationship building.

Sexton, Lobman, Constans, Snyder, and Ernest (1997) reported on early interventionists' perspectives on their multicultural practices with African-American families having children with special needs. The professionals were positive about the multicultural aspects of their interactions with families. They also thought that there should be in-service training that focused on issues facing African American families. These same professionals were, however, less positive about administrative support for multicultural practices. They recommended that training be provided in multicultural issues and that administrators, as well as interventionists, attend the training. Sexton, et al. (1997) stated: "A portion of the training related to the use of positive behavioral supports with young children could consider how cultural values, beliefs, and preferences affect the acceptability of various behavioral techniques" (p. 326). They further recommended that parents from different perspectives speak to other families, interventionists, and administrators in training sessions.

Promoting Equity

Sociologist James Coleman (1987) indicated that families are finding it more difficult to provide a context for which schools are the complement. However, organizations such as church schools can make a significant positive impact on dropout rates. These organizations cross generations and provide children and youth with access to an adult community, promoting the development of social capital. He pointed to the need for the establishment of a new institution, stating, "It is a demand not for further classroom indoctrination, nor for any particular content, but a demand for child care: *all day; from birth to school age; after school, every day, till parents return home from work; and all summer*" (p. 38). He elaborated by noting that the new institutions must "induce the kinds of attitudes, effort, and conception of self that children and youth need to succeed in school and as adults" (p. 38).

Teacher and co-chair of the National Coalition of Education Activists Stan Karp (1997), reflecting on inequality and responding to others' views of educating for a democratic life, stated, "The core issue is inequality. Schools are being asked to compensate for structural inequities in our society that the economy has magnified in recent years" (p. 41). He went on to say that the structuring of schools leads to inequality from the inside, giving tracking as an example, and leads to inequality outside the school with schools merely reflecting divisions of race and class in the larger society.

SUMMARY

The most important factor in dealing with families of different ethnic and socioeconomic backgrounds is an openness and willingness on the part of the school professional to learn about family values and beliefs. The specific activities and strategies used to accomplish this goal will differ from community to community, from school to school, and from professional to professional.

CASE EXAMPLE

Jose is a 14-year-old boy diagnosed with attention deficit disorder (ADD). His mother is a Hispanic American; his father, who died in an accident when Jose was 5 years old, was of Cherokee descent. Jose's ADD was diagnosed in the second grade when he was having difficulty learning to read and paying attention in class. At that point, Jose's mother took parenting classes to learn strategies for dealing with a child having attentional problems. Jose had been enrolled in resource instruction for his reading problems. In addition, his teachers had been asked to seat Jose in the front of the room for increased structure and to provide him with positive reinforcement as often as possible to keep his motivation at a maximum. Jose had been prescribed Ritalin by a local psychiatrist and had received counseling for 6 months to help with the grieving process following his father's death. Jose took the medication until the sixth grade, when school personnel, his mother, and the psychiatrist all agreed that it should be discontinued. Jose's reading skills improved, and he was functioning at grade level without the medication up until the eighth grade.

During his eighth-grade year, Jose had become increasingly distractable. His teachers had tried sending notes home to his mother, keeping a weekly assignment sheet that was sent home on Fridays, and having Jose attend an after-school study hall. In spite of these efforts, Jose repeatedly failed to turn in assignments. During the first semester, he failed two classes as a result of receiving zeros from homework. Most recently, he had become verbally belligerent and threatening when his teachers tried to intervene.

After an episode involving a physical fight with another student, Jose's mother was asked to attend a meeting with Jose's teachers and school counselor. Jose's mother revealed that she also was having difficulties with Jose at home. He had begun to refuse to do basic chores, even though he had willingly helped in the past. He had frequent temper outbursts where he hit walls or threw books around in his room. She expressed concern about the crowd of friends with whom Jose was spending time. She considered them to be a "rough" group of primarily Hispanic boys who had a reputation for troublemaking and "machismo."

Jose's mother stated that she felt badly for Jose because of the lack of a father figure in his life. At 14, Jose was beginning to identify with the macho image and to believe that self-control and doing the right thing were not necessary. He had no appropriate male role models, as the mother had not remarried and none of her family lived close by. And, although Jose attended the Catholic church with his mother, he did not seem to relate to any of the men in the church.

Questions and Comments

1. *What intervention strategies could be used with this family? How could cultural issues be included in the interventions? [Prior to reading about the intervention used, consider strategies on your own, then see how they compare to that which follows.]*

    The team in this case developed a strategy for dealing with Jose's problems that included imposing positive and negative consequences for his behavior at school and at home as well as having the school counselor hold weekly meetings with Jose and his mother. It was agreed that the natural consequence for Jose's failure to turn in assignments would be for him to attend summer school or repeat the eighth grade. The team, including as many male staff members as could attend (to impress upon Jose the power of the message in a way that had meaning in his own macho culture), met with Jose to tell him of the program and remind him of the consequences. He, of course, resisted but began meeting with the counselor.

    The counselor began by asking Jose questions about his family. He refused to answer them and said he didn't want to talk about his family. Because his mother was present, the counselor asked her if she could give some family background. She was specifically asked questions about her Hispanic culture and her husband's Cherokee Indian heritage. While Jose listened, his mother described his father's beliefs about spiritualism and harmony with nature. She described his father as a very strong man but one who practiced emotional restraint and noncompetitiveness. Jose's mother admitted that she knew very little about her husband's religious beliefs. She said that he had talked about "healers" and spiritual healing, but she did not know details.

    Following this meeting, the counselor went to the library and checked out books on Native-American culture and beliefs. In future meetings, he read to Jose and his mother from these books. The mother asked questions about what was being read while Jose sat sullenly by, seeming not to listen. The counselor also told Jose and his mother that there were universities across the United States that pay for the tuition of individuals of Native-American heritage and commented that if Jose did well in school he would likely be able to attend one of the universities for free.

2.   *How might things change for Jose following the interventions that were described? What are some potential results? [First, reflect on expected changes and then read what actually occurred.]*

The first hint that the program was working came when Jose chose as his topic for an assigned paper for history class "The Plight of the American Indian." In his paper, he identified how the Indian culture had endured numerous hardships yet kept their pride and sense of community. He wrote about the cultural values of silence, nonreactivity, and balance with nature. His teacher was so impressed with the paper that she showed the class the video *Dances With Wolves,* which depicts the strength, creativity, and harmony of the Indian culture.

After this point, changes began to be evident in Jose's behavior. He became more self-controlled. He began to talk with his counselor about cognitive strategies for relaxing and remaining nonreactive when he was angry or upset. He allowed his counselor to help him establish a study structure for himself at home, to help him become "balanced" as the Indian culture proposes. Jose began to dress with more of an Indian or southwestern style and was heard talking to peers about himself as a Cherokee Indian.

As this example illustrates, the openness and creativity of the school professionals in dealing with Jose allowed him to be able to "save face" in his community by forming a new identity of strength born out of control and passive resistance. The school used the power of Jose's ethnic background to help him adapt to the demands of the classroom.

EXTENSION ACTIVITIES

Reading: Read children's and young adult literature that depicts the diversity within your school system. Ask the librarian for titles or refer to the titles listed in Appendix C under "Diversity."

Reflection or Journal on Reading: How has your reading about diversity affected you? Has it evoked any strong feelings? How could you use this literature with children or youth and their families?

Guest Speakers/Leader Instruction: Invite minorities from diverse backgrounds to speak to your class/group, either on a panel or individually. Be sure they know what you are looking for before they come. If possible, provide the speakers with questions from class/group members prior to their speaking engagement so that they can better judge the interests and knowledge of your group.

Participant Instruction: Divide into small groups and share your reactions, thoughts, and feelings about the speakers' message(s). Have any of your questions remained unanswered? How can you find answers to your remaining questions?

Readings/Discussions: Read or view a video about diversity. In your class/group, discuss your insights, the ideas you found enlightening, what touched your heart, what surprised you, what you did not like, what you disagreed with, and what questions remain.

Invited Speaker/Leader Instruction: Invite a diversity trainer to your class/session. Ask that the trainer involve the participants in activities that will allow them to gain greater understanding, respect, and empathy for those from diverse backgrounds. Ask the trainer to facilitate rather than lecture.

OR

Experiential Activities/Leader Instruction: Check out David Johnson's sixth edition of *Reaching Out: Interpersonal Effectiveness and Self-Actualization* and use some of his in-class activities to explore diversity.

Journal Swap/Leader Instruction: Have each person in your group/class read a different professional journal article on diversity. A good journal to consult is the *Journal of Multicultural Counseling & Development.*

Participant Instruction: In groups of four or five, share information from your articles, with each discussion taking about 15 minutes. Then pool your wisdom as a whole group/class by describing at least one of the following: any change you experienced in your heart as a result of what you read or heard, what information was new to you, which data were surprising, what ideas you think would be useful for schools or homes, what you found hard to believe, what you found disheartening.

At-Risk Students from Nontraditional Families

Historically, the primary model for the definition of family has been two parents and their biological children. Today, this definition no longer represents the norm. Samuels (1990) estimated that there were about nine million adopted children in the United States. Depner and Bray (1993) quoted statistics from the National Center for Health Statistics that indicate that half of all marriages end in divorce. Bogolub (1995) quoted statistics indicating that there is a slightly higher divorce rate for second marriages than for first marriages. These statistics reinforce earlier reports by Beal and Hochman (1991). Listening Incorporated, a web site on the Internet that focuses on helping step-families, reported that fewer than 11% of the families in the United States today fit the stereotype of the traditional American family. It also reported that 20% of all births in the United States are to single mothers, 54% of couples who divorce have children, 12 million children who are under age 18 live in divorced households and about 1 million are added to this count each year, and 25% of those children will, during their formative years, experience another divorce.

Weissbourd (1996) predicted that 60% of children born in the early 1990s will spend part of their childhood in a single-parent home. He also shared demographics on the comparison of this rate with those in the past, noting that, for example, the figure was about 33% in 1900 due to the death of a parent. He also reported that, in 1940, 1 in 10 children in America did not live with either parent, whereas that figure is 1 in 25 today.

This chapter discusses issues faced by children, parents, and educators in dealing with nontraditional family situations. It covers the impact of divorce, single parenting, and remarriage on children and their families. Then, issues related to adoption are addressed. Each section includes suggestions for support as well as interventions that can be made within the context of the school system. Referral options are mentioned, and the reader is encouraged to turn to Appendices B to D to locate alternative means of finding support for these families and their children. Principles for working with at-risk students are adopted from Weissbourd (1996). The chapter concludes with a case example that illustrates the effects of parental divorce on a fourth-grade girl's school adjustment and extension activities aimed at increasing understanding of the effects on nontraditional family situations on children and youth.

INTRODUCTION

In his book *The Vulnerable Child,* Weissbourd (1996) argued against apocalyptic images of the state of children and indicated that such images oversimplify the changes that children face today:

> Divorce and other modern trends need to be seen in terms of the kinds of interactions that imperil individual children and in light of the basic needs of every child. How do these trends affect whether children receive continuous, caring attention from a parent or guardian? How do these trends affect whether children are able to draw support from peers and community adults? How do they affect children's opportunities for accomplishment and recognition?
>
> Viewing children in terms of these basic needs reveals that most children are not simply better or worse off because of these trends; they are likely to be vulnerable in different ways. Those who make policies and those who work for children need both to understand these differences and to identify the family, school, and community circumstances that will help children stay in one piece when both their parents are working or when their families are torn apart. (pp. 48–49)

In *The Vulnerable Child* Weissbourd repeatedly made the point that children are not necessarily worse off because of poverty, divorce, or being illegitimate, but that they are vulnerable in different ways. He emphasized that children often experience more difficulties in families with high stress because of marital conflict than in nontraditional families. Further, he noted that we would have high rates of childhood problems even without divorce, citing as an example the school dropout rate, which is 10 percent for all children and 13 percent for those not from intact families. Thus, the task of educators is to discover ways to support our vulnerable children.

Weissbourd shares Dan Hertzel's view that school staff often worsen the situation for children in nontraditional families by not talking to them about their situation. He wrote, "'They want to know if teachers, too, will abandon them, and sometimes they may secretly hope that causing trouble will get their parents to come to a meeting together.' Yet teachers have little or no training in how to respond to this testing" (p. 59). Weissbourd also shares Hertzel's belief that teachers can far more easily talk about the death of a family member with a child than the divorce of the parents. From his research, he found no guiding rituals for school personnel for dealing with children of divorce. His research indicates that school professionals would benefit children by finding nonintrusive means of opening conversations with them about divorce. Empathy and responsiveness mean a great deal to children who experience divorce. Teachers can help by referring students who are experiencing distress with regard to divorce to a school counselor or social worker.

Sociologist James Coleman found that if children from single-parent homes are supported by community, educational, and religious networks they are no more likely to drop out of school than children from two-parent families. Thus, the schools can be a vital part of the web of support that promotes children's well-being. McLanahan and Sandefur (1994) argued that "growing up with only one biological parent frequently deprives children of important economic, parental, and community resources, and that these deprivations ultimately undermine their chances of future success" (p. 3). Weissbourd (1996) noted that the design of our major economic and social institutions does not support single-parent families. U.S. society is, in effect, not in sync with modern realities.

To better understand the experience of their student population, school professionals need to understand the psychological effects of different family configurations on the child. Table 6.1, from Visher and Visher (1991), highlights the major differences between the various family patterns that school professionals encounter.

As this table indicates, stepfamilies, first marriage families, single-parent families, adoptive families, and foster families have many common characteristics. However, all of these family configurations differ appreciably from the traditional nuclear family. The implications of these differences for the adjustment of students and their families are described in this chapter.

DIVORCED, SINGLE-PARENT, AND BLENDED/STEPFAMILIES

Children of Divorce

Divorce causes a period of disequilibrium in the lives of both children and parents in the separating family. For the child, this adjustment period lasts for at least 2 to 3 years and may last for up to 10 years (Wallerstein & Blakeslee, 1989). During this adjustment period, children are at risk for developing emotional and behavioral problems that will be displayed in school. The length and form of the adjustment process depend upon a number of factors, which are described in the following sections.

Keith and Finlay (1988) examined a white population and found that "parental divorce is associated with lower educational attainment" (p. 797). Certainly, parents influence the course of adjustment. According to Teyber (1994),

> Children's long-term reactions vary greatly, depending primarily on how the parents respond to the child during and after the separation. In particular, the amount of parental harmony or disharmony children experience after divorce will be the most important determinant of their long-term adjustment. In contrast, children's short-term reactions tend to be more uniform. (p. 10)

Initially and in the short term almost all children are very upset by parental divorce. Upon reflection, adults who experienced divorce as children refer to the initial stage as the

TABLE 6.1 • Comparison of American Family Patterns

Stepfamilies	First Marriage Families	Single-Parent Families	Adoptive Families	Foster Families
Loss of relationships (parent-child; grandparents) and loss of dreams for what family life would be	Typical life changes with shifts of space and people	Unless adoption by single parent, everyone experiences loss of important relationships, and dreams	Children may lose friends, schools, and community	Children lose family friends, community, environment
Everyone has a prior family history	Two adults with different family histories	Parent and child begin with similar family history	Different family histories for children and parents	Family history is different for children joining established family
Bonds between parent and child longer than with marital dyad			In stepchild adoption the parent-child bond is longer than couple	
Biological parent lives elsewhere		Unless status is due to death of a parent, biological parent(s) elsewhere	Biological parent(s) elsewhere	Biological parent(s) elsewhere
Many children live in two homes		Children may belong to two homes		Children may belong to two homes
Lack of legalized relationship of child and stepchild (i.e., not adopted)				No legal relationship between child and foster parent(s)

Source: Adapted from *How to Win as a Stepfamily* (2nd ed., p. 194) by E. B. Visher and J. S. Visher, 1991, New York: Brunner/Mazel.

most stressful in their lives. Initial shock and surprise are common even when conflict between the parents was obvious. Children do not want their parents to divorce despite the tension and unhappiness they have felt and witnessed. The announcement of parental divorce does not produce a feeling of relief unless physical violence has been observed. Typically, during the first year after divorce, children experience increased fear, depression, anger, and guilt; however, these abate in the second year.

Gender Factors

Overall, boys tend to have a more difficult and prolonged adjustment to divorce than girls (Teyber, 1994; Weissbourd, 1996). Boys also have more trouble than girls in the initial stage of separation (Teyber, 1994). Mothers are, most often, assigned as the custodial parent (Guidubaldi & Cleminshaw, 1985; Weissbourd, 1996). The boy's primary male role model, then, becomes a part-time parent.

According to Teyber (1994), major gender differences exist in children of divorce. Boys who have experienced parental divorce are more likely to fight with their mothers and be disobedient, whereas the same aged girls who have experienced parental divorce often have no problems getting along with their mothers. The aggressive and uncooperative behavior seen in boys at home extends to schools and is attributed to the fact that almost all of these children live with their mothers. The girls have maintained the parent with whom they have same-sex identification, whereas the boys, in 90% of the cases, have lost theirs. Thus, divorce is more problematic for boys than girls. Teyber noted that problems in daughters from divorced families "are more apt to emerge (1) in adolescence as they begin dating and exploring heterosexual relationships and (2) when they enter a stepfamily" (p. 13).

Downey and Powell (1993) looked at 35 psychosocial as well as educational outcome variables for children living with same-sex and opposite-sex single parents. They did not find evidence of any differences based on gender match. They recommended that custody settlements not be based on a same-sex argument.

Keith and Finlay (1988) found that daughters of parents who divorce face a higher probability of one day divorcing themselves. Sons have a lower probability of ever marrying, and if they are from a lower social class background, they have a higher probability of divorcing if they marry. All of the individuals in the study were white.

Age Factors

Younger children tend to experience divorce as cause for grief and sadness. Their feeling of loss may be prolonged because they know that the departed parent is not dead. Disruption in play and anger are common. Some preschool girls begin to act like little adults, being overly good and scolding peers, almost as though they were the parent or teacher. More frequent crying is demonstrated, and the children often become more demanding. Regression is not unusual when children are initially confronted by the divorce. A child who had stopped using a pacifier may want it back. Another may hit siblings, and another may want to be fed. Losing one parent in the home may result in fear that the other will also leave. Nightmares and bed-wetting, which relate to these fears, are not uncommon in preschoolers.

Children ages 6 to 8 often take parental divorce harder than children of other ages. Sadness is common, and crying episodes are frequent. The children's lives may be controlled by longing for the absent parent and conflicting feelings about what they perceive as abandonment and rejection. As a result, they often experience lower self-esteem and depression. It is not unusual to note a drop in academic performance, since concentration is affected by worrying.

For those 9 to 12, the primary feeling is anger. Parent(s) are usually the target of their anger, and the children may take sides with one parent and blame another. Discipline often becomes an issue, especially with boys. The children also feel sad, lonely, and powerless. Not wanting the divorce and being embroiled in anger, their school achievement may plummet. Many have trouble with peer relations and evidence physical complaints such as stomachaches.

Most adolescents adjust to divorce better than younger children, mainly because of their increasing independence and ability to distract themselves with their own lives. Feeling betrayed, some adolescents whose parents divorce are more likely to act out feelings of anger and embarrassment or to become embroiled in their own relationship conflicts with peers (Teyber, 1994). Dating relationships may take on more importance due to feelings of emotional neediness. At the extreme, sexual acting out may occur. Some adolescents become depressed, withdrawn, and lacking in ambition. Problems generally surface when they feel that they are being put in the middle of parental conflicts.

Parent Factors

Of course, divorce is hard on the parents, too. Adjustment for the parents takes 2 or 3 years, during which time the parents usually experience poor work performance, depression, health problems, sleep difficulties, and anxiety. Some turn to alcohol, drugs, or cigarettes to relieve the stress they are experiencing. Exaggerated guilt and blaming are common and important for parents to resolve when divorcing. In the context of an often critical society, it is important for school professionals to not increase the feelings of guilt these parents experience.

Stinson (1991) identified parental factors that have been related to more positive adjustment for children living with divorced parents. She stated, "positive relationships between the child and both the custodial and the non-custodial parent, particularly with the same-sex parent, as well as a positive relationship between the divorced parents themselves, positively affect child adjustment" (p. 13). Free access to the noncustodial parent has been shown to have a positive effect on adjustment of children to divorce (Ferreiro, 1990). Frequent visits by the noncustodial father also have a good effect on the relationship (Arditti & Keith, 1992).

Because of the stress they are experiencing from the divorce, some parents handle their parental responsibilities poorly. They may fight in front of the children and frighten them. At worst, they engage in yelling, throwing, breaking things, hitting one another, or even kidnapping their children. It is important for parents to realize that their children are badly damaged by such actions (Schwartz & Kaslow, 1997). Donnelly and Finkelhor (1992) found that parents who had high levels of disagreement with each other also had more disagreements with their children. They stressed the importance of divorcing parents keeping conflict to a minimum. The child's adjustment is heavily impacted by the amount of conflict parents experience.

It is important to share this type of information with parents through newsletters or support groups and to encourage them to find counseling if they have high levels of disagreement so that the tension does not transfer to their children. A nonjudgmental comment like the following can be effective: "Mrs. Smith, I know you don't want your children hurt by seeing your husband and you fighting. Maybe you could take the children to a neighbor's house when you need to meet with your husband and then get them when the two of you have finished your discussions." Also nonthreatening and likely to be heard would be: "We know that when parents fight they usually have more disruptive relationships with their children. I know several people who have benefited from counseling during the rough times of transition that all of us face from time to time. This might be just that time for you to reach out for some support."

Children's adjustment to divorce also may be hindered by their parents' need to lean on them for emotional support and to involve them in battles with the divorced spouse. A study of 40 adolescents conducted at the University of Georgia found that a high level of parental conflict had a detrimental effect on the academic and behavioral performance of adolescents, whether or not their parents were divorced. According to this study, if parents keep battling after a divorce, the effects on their adolescent children are worse than the effects experienced by children whose parents have stayed in a high-conflict marriage (S. Rich, 1986). Other writers (Schwartz & Kaslow, 1997; Weissbourd, 1996) have agreed with this finding.

Richards and Schmlege (1993, quoted in Bogolub, 1995) wrote, "Some custodial parents find childrearing during the postdivorce phase an impossible strain, rather than a challenge that can be mastered" (p. 183). Bogolub (1995) provided a number of reasons for postdivorce dysfunctional parenting that were related to chronic psychological struggles. Among the factors contributing to the dysfunction were "disorganization, fragility, impulse-ridden behavior, or excessive narcissism" (p. 184) on the part of the custodial parent. Bogolub indicated that for mothers experiencing these problems, dysfunctional parenting was less evident before the divorce because the spouse's financial support provided a buffer from overload. Bogolub also noted that social isolation can contribute to dysfunctional parenting after divorce and reported that it cuts across ethnic lines. Serious parenting problems often come from the parent's emotional disturbance, poverty, and inadequate social support.

Wallerstein and her colleagues (Wallerstein & Blakeslee, 1989; Wallerstein & Kelly, 1980) conducted a 10-year longitudinal study of 131 children from 60 divorcing families. Ten years after their parents' divorce, only one third of the children defined themselves as functioning well. Another one-third reported that they were clinically depressed and still had fantasies of reconciliation between their parents, even if one or both parents had remarried. Most of the depressed children and adolescents were still experiencing intense bitterness between their parents. The final third saw themselves as continuing to struggle with the implications of their parents' divorce in their relationships with siblings, peers, and parents. These authors found that the functioning of the custodial parent and the level of conflict between ex-spouses during the entire postseparation period are the primary determinants of the child's well-being.

Hawkins, Christiansen, Sargent, and Hill (1993) explored the differences in the developmental trajectories of mothers and fathers based on their involvement with their children. They found that men's growth and development were fostered by helping them "accept greater responsibility for nurturing children" (p. 546). Though not specifically concerned with divorce, their work points to the benefit for men of being involved with child care.

Acknowledging that the purpose of divorce is to get away from a bad situation and to start a new life, Wallerstein and Blakeslee (1989) cautioned that how adults build this new life will be of primary importance not only to themselves but also to their children. They wrote:

> Getting one's external life back on track, however, does not begin to resolve the profound internal changes that people experience in the wake of divorce. Children's fundamental attitudes about society and about themselves can be forever changed by divorce and by events experienced in the years afterward. (p. xii)

We know that the more stability children have in their lives the better they will cope with the divorce of their parents. These children need continuity, familiarity, and predictability, and schools can help provide these. Schools provide structure and routine as well as consistent discipline, all of which help children of divorce.

To better meet the needs of children of divorce who are at risk for various types of symptomatic behavior, school professionals must become aware of the struggles faced by the parents and their children. At a minimum, empathy is important in serving children of divorce and their families. Recognizing the phases the family will experience is also helpful, and knowing that things typically settle down in 2 to 3 years can help with patience and perspective.

Psychological Tasks for Children of Divorce

In 1983, Wallerstein outlined six psychological tasks for children in the process of adjusting to divorce. They are as relevant today as they were more than a decade ago. School professionals who are aware of the need for children to successfully negotiate these tasks can support their development by giving messages that reinforce their management of the tasks. The tasks are as follows:

1. Acknowledging that the marital separation is real.
2. Staying out of parental conflict and distress and resuming age-appropriate involvements.
3. Resolving feelings of loss.
4. Resolving feelings of anger and self-blame.
5. Accepting the permanence of the divorce and giving up reconciliation fantasies.
6. Achieving realistic hopes regarding their own future relationships.

When hearing a student talk about his or her parents' divorce, a school professional might be able to get a sense of whether the child is being pulled into the marital conflict. To a mature student, the school professional might say something like, "It sounds like your parents are not getting along very well. One thing I have done when someone puts me in the middle of a disagreement is to suggest they talk it out with the person they are not happy with." Alternatively, the educator might say, "When that happens it might help if you tell your mom it is easier on you if she doesn't tell you about her fights with your dad." After hearing a child blame himself or herself for the divorce, an educator might say, "You are not to blame for the problems your parents are having." The sensitive educator will take the experiences of the children in the class into account when making book selections for reading to the class. The following anecdote speaks to this.

> On the first day of class in a new school I let a child pick out a book for me to read. He had chosen one called *Daddy Is Home*. Chris was grieving for his divorced father's absence from home. He held that book in his arms nearly all day long. It did not register with me until later in the day that his parents were divorced. I wished I had removed the book from my shelf when I read the cumulative files.

Support, Prevention, and Intervention With Children of Divorce

Changes in the emotional life of children and the structure of families following divorce may lead to a confusing family picture for educators. When dealing with divorce, school professionals can benefit by holding to several basic principles:

1. Be aware of the potential impact of divorce upon your students; remember that disequilibrium for 2 to 3 years following divorce is typical.

2. Take into account the individual child and his or her coping mechanisms when trying to help children move through the psychological tasks necessary for adjustment.

3. Always attempt to reinforce parental hierarchy and keep both parents involved with their children as much as possible. Maintaining the parental subsystem even though the marital subsystem is dissolved is of primary importance in children's adjustment.

4. Have on file a list of referral sources, including therapists who specialize in divorce issues, support groups for separating and divorcing parents, books to read, and information about local chapters of Parents Without Partners.

Farmer and Galaris (1993) viewed support groups for children of divorce as an important means of ameliorating the negative impact of divorce on children. Their description of a model used in Philadelphia provides informative reading for school professionals. The type of group described was one to which school professionals could make referrals. Similarly, Rossiter (1988) described a six-session group therapy intervention program for preschool children whose parents were divorcing.

Pedro-Carroll and Alpert-Gillis (Youngstrom, 1990) used a school-based model of intervention for children of divorce for the 8 years preceding their publication of their model. Their model consists of support groups for children grades K through 6 and periodic meetings and support groups for parents. These authors found that about 80% of the students in their project were not told when their parents were planning to divorce. The children had many misconceptions about divorce and tended to feel that they could not ask their parents any questions concerning the divorce.

The school-based support groups the authors described were designed to clarify children's misconceptions about divorce and to teach these children how to express their feelings, develop self-esteem and internal coping skills, and get support from their friends and relatives. The goals of the parent groups were to teach parents about their children's heightened needs following divorce, to help them keep their children out of triangles with their ex-spouse, and to provide guidelines for maintaining stability and consistent limits with their children. School professionals may find it useful to adapt this model to their own setting to provide services for students whose parents are divorcing. School counselors are natural aids in the adjustment process.

Sprinthall, Hall, and Gerler (1992) described findings from an experimental study of a peer counseling program for middle-school and high-school students who were experiencing parental divorce. Students in the program began to express more positive feelings and comments, which was indicative of increasing self-esteem. The researchers' empirical measures confirmed the self-reports.

Parker (1994) described a workshop for students' parents who were going through divorce. Parents were encouraged to attend the workshop particularly during the transitional period of separation. The workshop was designed for counselors to provide support to parents. An unplanned outcome was that parents often developed support groups with others they met in the workshops.

In a book entitled *How to Help Your Child Overcome Your Divorce,* Benedek and Brown (1995) provided many useful suggestions for teachers. Because schools are secure and predictable, the authors viewed them as important anchors for children of divorced parents. The authors note that teachers can help in the children's adjustment by asking parents about the family's situation, about where the child lives, and about any problems the child may be having. The teacher can ask the parent(s) about their child's strengths in academic areas and build on those, thus helping bolster the child's self-esteem. When a student is experiencing academic problems, the teacher can let the parents know. It is much easier to deal with a new problem than with an ingrained one, and together the teacher and family can work to eliminate the problem. To enhance the children's self-esteem, the teacher can assign special responsibilities to them. For the same purpose, they can learn what the students' interests are and allow them to show their expertise to others. If a child seems distracted or upset, school professionals can provide extra attention and care. In addition, they can invite these children to become involved in extracurricular activities that match their interests and let parents know about late bus routes when available. When necessary, the teacher can provide phone progress reports to parents who do not live close to their child.

The authors also noted the importance of inviting both parents to teacher conferences. If both will not attend together, conferences with each can be held at different times. At the conferences, teachers can let parents know about any special programs or services the school or community provides for children from divorced families.

There are many good books about divorce that school professionals can recommend to parents. A number of these are listed in Appendix B. Should a school professional be told by a parent that he or she is thinking about divorce, he or she might want to recommend that the parent read the book *Healthy Divorce.* With a positive focus, this book coaches parents in ways to resolve differences and remain functional, thereby lessening the negative impact on their children.

Bernard (1989), in a chapter on school interventions related to divorce, listed the following issues that school personnel should consider when intervening on a family systems basis:

1. Working with the family system will be easier than working with the school system or with the child's entire ecosystem. This is because membership in the school system will interfere with one's role as a systemic therapist.

2. Because of the homeostatic quality of systems, there might be resistance when the counselor or psychologist takes on a new role in the school system, one that seems juxtaposed to how this person was perceived previously (Fine & Holt 1983).

3. A systemic orientation is a challenging one that takes a considerable amount of training and supervision. With programs in school counseling, school psychology, and social work increasing in their requirements, it is unlikely that the trainee will opt for this additional training, or that faculty in these programs will be able to offer it. Training as a family therapist is not yet appreciated by school districts or state departments of education. Therefore, incentives are low to receive additional training.

4. Even more central than item 3, most training programs in school counseling or school psychology adhere to theoretical positions that are linear. It must be questioned whether a functional melding of orientations and roles can be accomplished by one person. (p. 261)

These points are still valid today. I recommend Bernard's chapter as helpful reading for all school professionals and particularly for the counselor, psychologist, social worker, and principal.

Thus far, the focus of this section has been on intervention. Prevention strategies are equally, if not more, important. A school-based prevention strategy that educates adolescents about the challenges they will face in marriage and parenting can help increase the likelihood of children being born into functional homes. An emphasis on the difficulties of divorce and unwed parenthood is useful in an educational program for adolescents.

Single-Parent Families

It has been estimated, that on the average, women with custody of minor children experience a 73% decline in standard of living during the first year after a divorce (Wallerstein & Blakeslee, 1989). Dowd (1997) stated that "nearly 90 percent of children raised in single-parent families are raised by single mothers; half of those households are below the poverty line" (p. xiii). The children who are recipients of this decline in socioeconomic status see themselves as survivors of a tragedy. How they handle the change will depend mostly upon the adjustment of their custodial parent and the level of other stressors in their lives.

Reiterating Bureau of the Census data, Dowd noted that divorced or separated single parents constitute the largest group of single parents (60%), never-married single parents make up 30% of the single-parent population, and widowed single parents make up about 7%.

There may be some positive aspects to single-parent households (Bogolub, 1995). For instance, if the single parent can relish the independence and freedom in making decisions without having to confer with a partner, he or she can pass that attitude on to the children. Single-parent families tend to work most effectively when there is a sense of interdependence between parent and children without a blurring of the functioning of the parental subsystem (Bogolub, 1995; Teyber, 1994). Flexibility and adaptability on the part of the parent are critical in this adjustment process. It is also important that parents not begin dating too soon after their divorce. Both the parent and the children need time to adjust to the divorce and to establish a new family life together. The presence of a new partner or multiple partners will heighten feelings of loss and anger and prolong the adjustment process. Thus, a period of being part of a single-parent household is better for children and youth than moving too quickly into another relationship.

Disorganization/Time Management

Guidubaldi and Cleminshaw (1985) found that the biggest difference between married and divorced families was a general level of disorganization in single-parent situations. According to their study, even routine tasks and the basic scheduling of meals, bedtimes, and so forth, were more disorganized because of the role overload experienced by the single parent. Feiring and Lewis (1985) concurred with these findings. From a study of single-parent households headed by mothers, they concluded that the primary impact of divorce upon children results from the mother's lack of economic and emotional support. The mother's sense of well-being influences her parenting ability and thus her children.

Current writers in the field hold the same opinion (Schwartz & Kaslow, 1997; Weissbourd, 1996). Their focus, however, has been more on time management than disorganization as the problem.

McLanahan and Sandefur (1994) indicated that the mother's level of responsiveness to her children decreases when she is trying to work and provide for the family's functional needs, such as cooking, shopping, laundry, and cleaning, by herself. She also experiences a conflict between fulfilling her own needs for support and friendship and the demands of parenting. If keeping up with household tasks is overwhelming, where can she find the energy for dating or socializing? The single parent who has a child with a disability will feel an even greater sense of stress and role overload (Somers, 1987).

Hierarchy Dysfunction

One of the most common problems in single-parent families is a hierarchy imbalance. For many parents, dissolution of the marital subsystem implies dissolution of the parental subsystem as well. In these situations, the oldest or highest functioning child is often cast in the role of substitute parent (Bogolub, 1995). The parentified child may operate as the parent's confidant and be given inappropriate information about the divorce. He or she may also be assigned overwhelming responsibility for household tasks or for taking care of other children in the family (Schulman, 1984; Teyber, 1994). When the pressure of these responsibilities becomes too great, the parentified child will often begin to exhibit academic or behavioral problems. If the single parent, who is usually unaware of the source of the problems, then tries to exert influence as a disciplinarian, the child may respond with oppositional or disrespectful behavior. Often, this behavior is born out of the parent's inappropriate dependency upon the child.

Support and Intervention

Effective buffers to the long-term emotional stresses of divorce are adequate social supports for both children and single parents (Benedek & Brown, 1995). When Berman and Turk (1981) interviewed members of Parents Without Partners about their adjustment to divorce, the single parents reported that the most important determinant of their overall positive mood up to 15 years after their divorce was the presence of a social support system.

Benedek and Brown (1995) and Guidubaldi and Cleminshaw (1985) have also stressed the importance of support variables for the adjustment of the single parent. According to their studies, the availability of helpful relatives, including in-laws, the availability of friends and paid child-care assistance, and a positive relationship with one's ex-spouse are important factors in the well-being of single parents.

An in-service education program to sensitize educators to the risks faced by children in single-parent households is highly recommended as an educational strategy. School professionals can serve an important function by supporting the parental subsystem in these families. By holding to the belief that parents need to work together for their children, despite the dissolution of their marriage, school professionals will project an attitude of acceptance toward separating or divorced parents. Record keeping that identifies children from divorced homes and includes addresses and telephone numbers of both parents is basic to maintaining the parental system.

In cases of joint custody, schools need to make sure that both parents receive copies of important communications from the school, including invitations to parent-teacher conferences and school activities. In situations in which one parent has been assigned sole custody, his or her written permission is needed for the noncustodial parent to be included in these events. The educator needs to ask the custodial parent for permission to contact the other parent and must be prepared to give him or her reasons why the inclusion is important to the child's sense of well-being. When possible, educators must avoid supporting the dissolution of the parental subsystem by favoring one parent over the other.

As noted earlier, for most single parents, access to a support network is the most important factor in their adjustment (see Chapter 9). The school may contribute to the formation of a network by including single parents in homeroom, PTA, or other school activities with other parents who have been through similar circumstances. The school may also provide adult education programs and a resource library for single parents regarding adjustment to divorce or death of a spouse. When scheduling school activities, educators need to recognize the logistical problems of employed single parents. By providing baby-sitting services and an evening timetable of events, they will help to project an attitude of inclusion and acceptance toward single-parent families.

Speaking of children in single parent homes Weissbourd (1996) suggested:

> It is hard to exaggerate the importance of anchors in their lives—children and adults
> outside their families who are caring and attentive over time. Some communities and
> schools are now seeking to deepen and extend children's involvement with other
> children and adults. Many large high schools across the country are creating more
> personal environments—environments in which children spend the bulk of their day
> with the same group of teachers and students—by clustering teachers and students,
> for example, or by creating schools within schools or houses within schools. Multi-
> grade classrooms, where children stay with the same teacher for two or even three
> years, enable teachers to deepen their involvement with children. (p. 63)

Mentoring is another means of involving more adults in the lives of children. Mentors
should be instructed in ways to strengthen both the child and the child's family. It is important for mentors to not undermine the relationship the child has with family members.
Freedman (1993) recommended that children be surrounded by "mentor rich" environments with a variety of community adults and that they not become overly reliant upon
particular mentors.

As Weissbourd (1996) indicated, at a minimum school professionals "need to work to
eliminate tacit messages that single-parent families are deficient. Parent support programs
and other kinds of help in reducing isolation are also vital to the growing ranks of single
mothers" (p. 63). Like other researchers, he highly recommended that schools involve
noncustodial parents in their child's education—for example by inviting them to attend
parent-teacher conferences and school assemblies, by scheduling activities at night so
working parents can attend, and by sending them their child's report cards. Reachable
moments for fathers have been found to include the child's birth, entry into school, graduation, and physical illnesses. Schools are encouraged to use the latter three of these times
to help absent fathers form deeper connections with their children.

Blended/Stepfamilies

Between 1960 and 1990 the proportion of children in the United States living with their
two married, biological parents decreased from 83% to 58% (Popenoe, 1994). Although
approximately 66% of divorced women and 75% of divorced men in this country remarry
within 5 years of the dissolution of their marriages (Cherlin, 1992), the average remarriage
does not survive beyond the first 5 years (Bray & Berger, 1993), and the divorce rate
increases when children from previous marriages are involved. Even if remarriages do
endure, there is general consensus among researchers that the process of integration, consolidation, and emotional connection in these families takes from 3 to 5 years (J. H. Larson, Anderson, & Morgan, 1984; Visher & Visher, 1996; Whiteside, 1983). For couples
involved in a second marriage who married with the hope that everyone will live "happily
ever after," these figures may seem staggering. In working with blended families, school
professionals need to be aware of particular problem areas that tend to occur at different
stages in the remarriage process.

Premarriage

The first arena for problems occurs before the couple actually remarries. How the premarriage stage proceeds for everyone involved depends partially upon the age of the children at the time of the remarriage. Younger children may still be mourning the loss of their biological parent or may continue to have fantasies about the reconciliation of their natural parents (Benedek & Brown, 1995; Bogolub, 1995; L. J. Friedman, 1981). For the child who has served a parentified role in the single-parent household, the remarriage may represent, on the one hand, a relief from responsibility and, on the other hand, a threat to his or her position in the family (Weissbourd, 1996).

Adolescent children may have a particularly difficult time accepting the remarriage because of their own developmentally appropriate identity and sexuality concerns. For those who have just begun dating, watching their parent being "in love" and going through the rituals of courting may be embarrassing and threatening. Adolescents may also be particularly aware of the reactions of the other biological parent to the remarriage (M. D. Framo, 1981). If the ex-spouse has not resolved his or her relationship with the parent who is planning to remarry, the ex-spouse may experience again the sense of rejection and depression from the initial divorce. Adolescents, who are themselves struggling with the dynamics of heterosexual relationships, may become embroiled in a loyalty struggle (Visher & Visher, 1991).

Other potential problems in the premarriage stage derive from the way in which children learn about the impending remarriage. Ideally, the children will have had positive involvement with the new spouse and his or her children prior to the decision to remarry. As a couple, the partners should tell the children about their engagement. They should acknowledge the difficulty in their decision and the impact that the remarriage will have upon the children. They should also inform the children that although they love each other, they have no expectation of "instant love" between the children and the new spouse (Visher & Visher, 1996). From this point on, the biological parent should make him- or herself available to answer questions and listen to the feelings of the children.

Within the boundaries of the family hierarchy and the personal tastes of the couple, children should be given a role in planning and participating in the wedding ceremony and the new living arrangements. Here is an example of how one couple helped their children feel included in their remarriage:

> A couple were married after three years of dating, following each of their divorces. The woman had three children from her previous marriage and the man had two children. Their wedding ceremony consisted not only of the traditional wedding vows for the couple, but also of vows to join the two families in a commitment. Each parent initially recited part of the vows with his or her own children. At the end of the ceremony, all of the children and both parents recited a phrase together. For this couple, the symbolism of coming together was expressed through these rituals.

Initial Struggles

Once the remarriage has occurred, the families must begin the process of "blending." Difficulties during this stage may occur at the individual, subsystem, or family levels.

Individual.   At the individual level each person in the blended family has concerns about bonding with other family members. Steprelationships are new and untested. It is not a given that all members of the family will accept one another as they do within an intact family (Visher & Visher, 1991, 1996). In addition, each individual has personal issues related to the dissolution of the former marriage and family. Insecurity, low self-esteem, fear, and grief are all possible repercussions of the previous loss.

Subsystem.   At the subsystem level difficulties are experienced in the marital subsystem, the parental subsystem, and the sibling subsystem. With regard to the marital subsystem, the new couple has to nurture their attachment. All of the early marriage concerns discussed in Chapter 2 are replayed in this marriage. However, each person now has a history of failure to bring to the relationship (Visher & Visher, 1996). In addition, the life-cycle stages do not evolve in sequential order in the blended family. The couple must work through the early marriage stage at the same time that they are dealing with raising children or helping adolescents leave home.

In the parental subsystem issues of hierarchy and role definition must be faced. In blended families, there is a biological parent outside of the stepfamily unit and an adult of the same sex in the household. This configuration makes for confusion about who has membership in the parental subsystem. As one mother in a blended family stated:

> We discovered that we had too many actors for the traditional parts of mother and father, and we had to create some new roles for them. My husband has found a spot as an older friend and advisor to one of my sons. . . . After giving up . . . my accustomed role of nurturer, I have learned to be comfortable playing the part of counselor and house manager to my husband's children, leaving the mothering to their mother. (Barney, 1990, p. 146)

Quite often parents in blended families complain of hearing the phrase "He's not my father" or "She's not my mother" in response to disciplining. Discipline is a troublesome area in stepfamilies (Visher & Visher, 1996). Since the parent-child relationships precede the marital bond, when a difference in disciplining techniques and household rules arises, history often wins out over the couple working through the difference (Teyber, 1994; Visher & Visher, 1991). Benedek and Brown (1995) suggested that the stepfather will not be regarded by his stepchildren as an authority until he has earned their respect and trust. They recommended that "the mother should remain the children's prime disciplinarian while being clear with the children about the stepfather's authority and backing up his efforts" (p. 243). It is critical for the parents to establish and maintain a united front so that the children do not triangulate a parent. Disagreements between spouses are best discussed in private. If children feel that they are in charge of making family rules because their desires are more important than those of a spouse, a hierarchy dysfunction will develop.

Finally, the sibling subsystem in blended families is often divided into a number of subgroups, which can cause confusion and difficulties early on. Typically, there are siblings who live with this family, siblings who live with the other parent, stepsiblings who live with their other parent, and stepsiblings who live with this family. Sibling rivalry thus takes on a new and more complex meaning (M. D. Framo, 1981; Visher & Visher, 1991). The logistical problems that must be resolved early in the blending process, such as who sleeps in which bedroom, who gets the most time with each parent, how money is divided, what bedtimes and chores are, and so forth, frequently result in conflict between siblings and stepsiblings.

Family.   There are initial struggles that occur between the two families that are coming together as well. Members of the blended family come together from what may be two very different historical backgrounds. The rules and rituals of one family may be very different from those in the other family. Adding to the complexity, the children in a blended family often spend time with the family of their other biological parent. Behavior that is allowed at dad's house may not be tolerated at mom's house, and vice versa. Schedules, eating habits, religious beliefs, rituals, and bedtimes may all be different from one family to the other. Flexibility and tolerance for differences are important in minimizing struggles across families (Visher & Visher, 1991).

Long-Term Struggles

After 4 to 5 years, the blended family that remains together will usually have resolved its initial cohesion struggles. However, blended families experience unique problems and concerns throughout the life cycle. When children reach adolescence, identity and commitment issues often resurface. Stepparents who felt bonded with and accepted by their stepchildren may suddenly find themselves the "bad guy" once again. When normal adolescent power struggles surface, a parent may slip up and threaten the child with return to the other biological parent if the child doesn't "straighten up." Adolescents, in turn, may make threats to run away to their other parent when they aren't happy with the rules of their current family. It is vital that any changes of custody and living situation be made by parental consensus and not during an emotional battle. When parents calmly discuss these changes and come to the decision that it is in their adolescent's best interest to change homes, the parental hierarchy remains intact.

Finally, cohesion issues often resurface when the married couple have children of their own. Stepchildren who had adequately bonded to their new parent may feel that their place has been usurped by the baby in the family. As one 13-year-old girl stated, "My father told me that I would become second best with my mom and stepfather when the baby was born. It turns out that he was right. Why should they care about me when they have this cute little boy that belongs to both of them in the house?"

In terms of the classroom, teachers may notice that children who live in blended families go through periods of acceptance and periods of regression. It is important that school professionals take into account the long-term nature of the adjustment to divorce and remarriage when trying to understand the needs of children of divorce.

Successful Remarriages

Based on the research literature and clinical observations, Visher and Visher (1990) described six characteristics of successful remarried families. The first is that losses are mourned. Unrecognized losses and those not grieved tie up energy and contribute to difficulties in the present situation. Group support with others facing the same kinds of losses is helpful in mourning losses.

The second characteristic of successful stepfamilies is that their expectations are realistic. The family members know their family is different from the nuclear family they'd experienced and do not long for it to become an "ideal" nuclear family. Rather than trying to duplicate a nuclear family, they accept the realities of stepfamily life, such as a stepparent's parents not becoming like grandparents. Over time they develop an appreciation for diversity and respect themselves for their flexibility. Finally, they do not expect there to be instant love and realize that integration takes time. It is helpful for the family members to know what to expect, for example, to understand that it will take about 2 years for a stepparent to develop co-management status with his or her spouse and to understand that it generally takes 5 to 6 years for families who have older children to become comfortable as a stepfamily. This kind of basic information can be provided to parents by schools through newsletters and support groups.

Third, in successful remarriages there is a strong and unified couple. Successful remarriage requires spousal time together so that the marital subsystem is developed and enriched. Parents who had been previously married may worry about whether their remarriage will end in divorce. Thus, time together is essential for building trust. Children benefit from the model of a strong marital subsystem.

Fourth, constructive rituals are established. Positive shared memories and a sense of belonging engender good relationships and are supported by having a familiar way of doing things. Successful stepfamilies usually share their prior rituals and ceremonies as well as ways of going about their lives with one another. They then combine, retain, or develop new ways of being in life as a family. Successful stepfamilies are flexible as well as resourceful. They have worked out creative and innovative ways of dealing with transitions when siblings move from one household to another. They creatively share chores around the house.

Fifth, satisfactory steprelationships have formed. The stepparent has usually entered the family system slowly, working to develop his or her relationship with the children. A friendly relationship is a necessary prerequisite to becoming responsible for discipline of stepchildren. Together the parent and stepparent must demonstrate that they have made active decisions about each of their roles in relation to limit setting. Eventually the parents and children experience satisfaction in the new relationships.

Sixth, the separate households cooperate. The parents from both households build a "parenting coalition." The cooperative relationship that evolves benefits both the adults and children. The stepparents become part of the coalition, forming permeable boundaries from which the children come and go with ease. There is an absence of competition between parents and stepparents, and loyalty conflicts on the part of the children are curtailed.

School professionals may find it helpful to make a copy of Visher and Visher's article, from which these characteristics were drawn. Pointing these characteristics out in a newsletter or flyer is also helpful.

Support and Intervention

It is important for teachers to make note of children in their classrooms who live in blended families and to reinforce the parental subsystem whenever possible. In blended families, however, clarifying who is to be identified as part of the parental subsystem may be a complex task. When sending handouts home for "parents," teachers may want to include more than one copy for children in blended families so that students can define "parent" for themselves and distribute the handout as necessary.

Within the classroom, the exercises designed to help children become more accepting of people from diverse backgrounds and cultures (see Chapter 5) can be adapted and used to increase tolerance for stepsiblings or stepparents who come from a different family and thus have a different historical background. A helpful, easy classroom exercise is to ask students to discuss how their families celebrate certain holidays. For instance, for some families, Thanksgiving isn't Thanksgiving without a turkey and dressing. For others, a certain dessert or vegetable dish represents what it means to have Thanksgiving dinner. When students are exposed to different symbols from different peer families, they may be able to more easily negotiate the rituals and symbols in their own blending family systems.

Barney (1990) suggested that educators make an effort to normalize the concepts of stepfamily, adopted family, foster family, and other nontraditional family constellations. This may be accomplished through class discussions, students sharing their experiences in different types of families, or a curriculum that addresses the changing picture of the family. Numerous books are also available that normalize nontraditional family constellations (see Appendix C).

Information given by school counselors can help parents and adolescents normalize blended family status and can help parents strategize before situations occur. Just like a new parent reads everything about "what to expect in the next month" when their child is an infant or toddler, parents in blended families will benefit by knowing what they might expect along the way and how situations can be handled.

ADOPTIVE FAMILIES

The number of children living with adoptive parents in the United States is becoming increasingly large. Estimates indicate that there are as many as nine million adopted children under the age of 18 in the United States (Samuels, 1990). In 1992, the most recent year for which total adoption statistics are available, 127,441 children were adopted in the United States (National Adoption Information Clearinghouse [NAIC], 1996). Of those, 42% were stepparent or relative adoptions, 15.5% were adoptions of children from foster care systems, and 5% were adoptions of children from other countries. D. Mack (1997), citing figures from Connie Craig, wrote that "only 20,000 of the 119,000 adoptions in 1992 . . . were sponsored by public agencies" (p. 72). Mack went on to provide statistics on costs for foster care in the United States. She indicated that in 1990 approximately $5 billion of the $7.2 billion spent on child welfare went to foster care and that the number doubled to $10 billion in 1993. At the end of the fiscal year in 1994, 461,163 children were in foster care in the United States (NAIC, 1996).

The number of foreign adoptions continues to increase in the United States, bringing with it unique situations (Register, 1991). Some foreign adoptions have been from orphanages highlighted in the news for neglect. Children adopted from these orphanages will be at a disadvantage for life as a result of the cognitive stimulation as well as simple touch and basic nurturing they missed in their early years. Most children adopted from foreign countries by American parents, however, do not fit into that category.

Brodzinsky, Schechter, and Henig (1992) estimated that 1% to 2% of the U.S. population is adopted yet 5% of the children receiving out-patient psychotherapy have been adopted. They also noted that school systems identify between 6% and 9% of adopted students as having a perceptual, neurological, or emotional impairment. Given these figures, many teachers are being confronted with the unique concerns and adjustment problems of adopted children.

Brodzinsky (1990) also indicated that adopted children are at increased risk for developing psychological and academic problems, although he noted that this difference diminishes by the time they reach adolescence. He cited initial stresses in the adoptive family system as factors in this increased risk. Adoptive parents have often had to deal with the stress of confronting infertility and that of the adoption process itself (e.g., agency evaluation, waiting periods, cycles of hope and disappointment). Adopted children are usually born from unwanted pregnancies or family situations in which their presence taxed the family system beyond its available emotional and tangible resources. Children who have been offered for adoption may have developed a sense of insecurity, anger, guilt, and self-blame. Infants may suffer from problems with primary attachment if they did not experience a healthy bond with a primary caretaker.

Special-Needs Adoptions

Glidden (1994) reported that between 25% and 30% of domestic adoptions in America are special-needs adoptions and that the percentage is higher for foreign adoptions. She defined special-needs adoptions as those of children "who are older, are members of a minority, have disabilities, and/or need to be placed as a sibling group of more than two" (p. 198).

Interestingly, adoptions of children with special needs tend to be more successful than average. Samuels (1990) found that cross-race adoptions and adoptions of children with disabilities had higher than average success rates (about 75% being successful). R. J. Simon and H. Altstein (1992) came to the same conclusions from their study of 100 transracially adopted children. Glidden (1994) reached the same conclusion, suggesting that adoptions of children with disabilities are "resoundingly successful." Glidden (1989) noted a similar finding from her study of 42 families adopting children with mental retardation. A. Coyne and M. E. Brown (1985) found a failure rate of only 8.7% in families adopting children with developmental delays.

The success rate of these adoptions may be promoted by several factors. First, parents adopting children with special needs may be better informed and more considered in their decisions than other adoptive parents, and caseworkers who deal with special-needs adoptions usually orient their work toward matching the child with a family who can best provide for his or her needs. Second, these parents may hold more realistic expectations of the adoptive child, particularly with regard to potential problems, because they are informed and educated about the child's special needs prior to the decision to adopt. Finally, for these parents, seeking and using an external support network is often encouraged and legitimized.

Adoption Adjustment

Positive adjustment of a child to adoption is a complex process. Brodzinsky and colleagues (Brodzinsky, 1990; Brodzinsky et al., 1992) identified several stages in the adjustment process and showed how Erikson's psychosocial tasks of development relate to each stage. Those tasks, as well as issues adoptive parents face, for the stages of infancy through young adulthood are described in the following sections.

Infancy

In infancy, parents must resolve feelings related to infertility, develop appropriate role models for themselves, and develop realistic expectations of the child. They must manage anxieties and issues of social stigma (if such issues are present in their community). Finally, they must develop appropriate attachment to the child. The task for the adoptee in this stage is resolution of *Trust Versus Mistrust*. The infant is adjusting to the new home and developing secure attachments. Difficulty with this task is more evident when placement is delayed.

Preschool Years

For children during the preschool years, Erickson's developmental tasks are the resolution of *Autonomy versus Shame and Doubt* and the resolution of *Initiative versus Guilt*. As is typical of all children at this age, adoptees are learning about birth and reproduction. In cases of interracial or international adoption the child will become aware of differences in appearances. It is important that parents make the child aware of his or her adoptive status and create a climate in which questions can be raised and dealt with in comfort. Although experts have not always been in agreement about the best time for disclosure, most indicate that it is during the preschool stage (Hajal & Rosenberg, 1991). At this stage, the child's understanding of adoption is limited; most children are primarily aware of being "chosen."

Middle Childhood

Erikson's developmental task for children in the middle childhood years is the resolution of *Industry versus Inferiority*. For the adoptee, this task may be particularly difficult, since the child's increasing cognitive ability leads to the awareness that being "chosen" by one family implies being relinquished by another. This awareness may challenge the child's sense of security and belonging. As the adoptee begins to understand the implications of being adopted, he or she may start to ask questions about family origin and why his or her birth parent(s) chose adoption. Parents must be sensitive to the child's ambivalence and potential sense of rejection, which can be accompanied by grief and insecurity. An atmosphere of openness to the child's need to explore the issues of the adoption is extremely important. Disclosure of adoption to people outside of the family often occurs during this phase (Hajal & Rosenberg, 1991). Thus, children may need to face coping with physical differences that are noticeable as well as the stigma often associated with adoption. Educators can read books to children in elementary school to help normalize the adoption process. They can also suggest books for families related to the loss their child may feel. In addition, bibliotherapy can help parents respond positively to their child's struggle.

Adolescence

Erikson's task in adolescence is the resolution of *Identity versus Role Confusion*. The adoptee, like all other adolescents, must be assisted in dealing with biological issues and the usual adolescent concerns regarding identity. Those concerns, however, are made more complex by adoptive status. Adolescent adoptees will likely explore both the meaning and implications of being adopted. They will often connect adoption to their sense of identity. In interracial adoption, they will be dealing with racial identity and with physical differences from family members. During this stage the adoptive parents may need to assist the youth in learning about his or her birth parents or, at least, give their permission for this search to take place (Hajal & Rosenberg, 1991). Many adolescent adoptees will have to deal with the fantasy about the birth family being the perfect family and feelings stemming from such fantasizing. Whatever the adoption-related issues are, it is important for adolescents to deal with them so that their sense of self is fostered and they move toward identity rather than role confusion.

Young Adulthood

Erikson's task for this stage is the resolution of *Intimacy versus Isolation*. During this time the adoptee will likely go deeper into exploring the adoption and, if it was a closed adoption, may begin to search for his or her birth parent(s). The adoptee may be facing issues surrounding becoming a parent in the future in light of having been adopted. If the youth's genetic history is unknown, issues may also arise concerning having children in the future. Loss will continue to be a focus for adoptees at this stage. Issues of intimacy and the ability to form bonds with others will need to be addressed. Usually, a reaffirmation of the parental-adoptee bond occurs in this stage. According to Hajal and Rosenberg (1991), it is during this stage that the young adult "adopts" the parent(s).

Overall, the best predictor of the adoptee's social adjustment, according to Hoopes (1990), is the child's perception of belonging and stability in the adoptive family. Hoopes found that the parents' openness and comfort in discussing issues about adoption were closely related to the older adoptees' sense of identity and self-esteem.

The book by Brodzinsky et al. (1992), from which the discussion in this section was drawn, provides helpful information for professionals as well as parents. Helping a child successfully resolve one developmental task will increase the likelihood of resolution of the next developmental task (LePere, 1988).

LePere (1988) identified successful adoption factors, and Raynor (1980) identified factors that tend to interfere with successful postadoption family adjustment. According to these researchers, parents who see adoption as different from biological parenthood are more successful than those who reject the differences. Those who continually deal with adoption revelation are more successful. Other factors leading to successful adjustment are acceptance by the birth parents and the adoptive parents' sharing of information and assisting with a search. Adoptive parents who deal effectively with their infertility are more successful in their adoption. Parental prejudice and self-fulfilling prophecies tend to diminish the likelihood of successful adoption adjustment. Parents who hold images of the ideal child and attempt to mold their adopted child to their expectations tend to have greater difficulty. When parents have early doubts and do not adequately address them, adjustment is more problematic. Finally, trauma at first meeting and legal delays have been identified as negative factors.

Support and Intervention

When dealing with adoptive families, any action on the part of school professionals that enhances successful adoption is desirable. Much has been written on adoption (Bartholet, 1993; Brodzinsky, 1990; Brodzinsky et al., 1992; Hoffman-Riem, 1990; Liptak, 1993; Reitz & Watson, 1992; E. B. Rosenberg, 1992; R. J. Simon & Altstein, 1992), and reading about it is one way school professionals can educate themselves so they are more comfortable teaching and serving adopted children. Appendix B has a section on books for adults to read about adoption; professionals can choose from those books as well as recommend them to families. The text by R. J. Simon and H. Altstein (1992) focuses on adoption, race, and identity in transracial adoptions. The text by Reitz and Watson (1992) has a family systems base, thus correlating closely with the focus of this textbook.

One of the most beneficial activities educators can pursue is helping adoptive parents develop realistic expectations about their children. Often adoptees are the only child in the family. Parents may need information about child development and age-appropriate achievement or may be anxious about and reactive to minor concerns. Basic education in child development may help parents with these concerns. Offering parent training is another way to cover this territory.

Educators may also help parents by normalizing problems that arise. Adoptive parents might need assistance in guarding against the tendency to make biological or genetic interpretations of their child's behavior or academic achievement. The educator's ability to place observed behavior in an appropriate developmental context may be critical to helping these parents maintain their connection to, and sense of responsibility for, the child. Skills in reframing (see Chapter 13) are useful in this regard.

In addition, external network supports are important for the successful adjustment of adoptive families. The school may provide some social supports through its personnel, programs, and parent groups. School personnel should encourage the use of these resources as well as identify available resources external to the school and family. External resources may include community programs, agencies experienced with adoption concerns, web sites on the Internet, information sources, and educational materials (see Chapter 9 as well as Appendices B–D).

In the classroom, teachers with an awareness of the issues related to children who are adopted can adjust classroom activities to better meet the needs of these children. For example, if students are given an assignment to draw a family tree, teachers should be aware of the concerns this assignment may cause for adopted children. Questions should be dealt within a relaxed and open manner with attention to the individual child's needs.

Teachers should maintain open communication with parents and may be instrumental in helping parents identify stages, issues, and questions in the child's adjustment.

Finally, educators should be aware that adopted children are predisposed to emotional difficulties, particularly in the areas of trust, sensitivity to rejection, feelings of belonging and stability, and self-esteem. Misbehavior in these children may arise from their neediness and identity confusion. Nurturing is effective as an intervention strategy.

PRINCIPLES OF EFFECTIVE SCHOOLS AND TEACHERS

Children from divorced, single-parent, blended, and adoptive families are at risk for school failure and failure in life. Being at risk is not a certainty of failure, but it is indicative of the possibility of failure becoming a reality. Educators need to become a voice for children beyond the schools so that social policy and laws will support research-based solutions and prevention strategies.

It is also critical for professionals to find ways of intervening in schools and classrooms that lower the risk for failure and increase the possibility that these children and youth become resilient. In a chapter titled "Schools That Work," Weissbourd (1996) presented two tables listing principles of effective schools and teachers working with vulnerable children. The principles are pertinent for all of the populations written about in this chapter as well as those discussed in the next two chapters. Weissbourd's principles for effective schools were as follows:

1. Staff emphasize academics and pay careful attention to results, to academic achievements.
2. Staff have the capacity to respond to the emotional and social troubles and material needs of children.
3. Staff create a safe and orderly but not severe school environment.
4. Staff imbue high expectations for children in every aspect of school functioning.
5. Staff work with parents and children respectfully and collaboratively. When a child has a problem, staff examine the child's role, the family's role, and community's role, and the school's role.
6. Staff need to identify root problems and to turn negative interactions into cycles of success.
7. Staff give parents authority and a sense of belonging; they reach out to all parents and provide a variety of opportunities for parents to become involved in school.
8. Staff work to engage noncustodial parents and other adults of great importance to the child.
9. Administrators mine teachers' wisdom, seek to provide teachers the time, support, and resources they need to work with struggling students and continually promote teachers' learning and professional development.
10. Guidance counselors, school nurses, and other school staff are similarly supported, and school staff are enabled to support and strengthen one another.

11. Staff form effective partnerships with community services, businesses, and other community resources. These partnerships are designed to achieve specific goals that further children's academic achievements. (p. 181)

Weissbourd's principles for effective teachers working with vulnerable children included:

1. Effective teachers operationalize high expectations for every child and focus on academic results.
2. Effective teachers attribute failure to aspects of a child or classroom that can be positively influenced, rather than to intractable aspects of a child, family, or community.
3. Effective teachers provide every student with the elements from which real and durable self-esteem is built, including specific, tangible skills and achievements, progressively increased responsibilities, and opportunities to give to others.
4. Effective teachers view children as having complex constellations of strengths and weaknesses and communicate this understanding to parents.
5. Effective teachers work to develop children's adaptive capacities, their ability to manage disappointment and conflict.
6. Effective teachers pick up on the quiet troubles that undermine children in school, such as mild hunger or wearing the same clothes day after day and respond aggressively to these problems.
7. Effective teachers view the classroom and school as a complex culture and system and seek to understand the difficulties of a child in terms of the interactions between a particular child and a particular culture and system.
8. Effective teachers engage parents proactively and have the skills to work with parents when a child is in crisis.
9. Effective teachers are self-observing and are responsive to feedback and ideas from both other school staff and children—they see children as active partners in their education.
10. Effective teachers know when to respond to a child's problem themselves and when a child needs to see another professional who has specialized training.
11. Effective teachers innovate, take risks, and reshape their activities based on close attention to results. (p. 183)

If we follow these principles in schools and have educators read Weissbourd's book *The Vulnerable Child,* it is more likely that schools will strengthen both children who are vulnerable and their families.

CONCLUSIONS

For educators in the 21st century, the definition of normal family characteristics may be complex and confusing. In this chapter, some guidelines have been provided for understanding the adjustment process of the child and family in divorced, single-parent, remarried, and adopted family situations. Many of the factors that place children in these family situations at risk for emotional or behavioral problems have been identified. Just as families need to remain flexible in their adjustment process, so too must school professionals maintain a sense of flexibility and openness to understanding family dynamics in nontraditional family situations. As always, interest in and emotional connection with each family are the most important tools to understanding and working with families in educational contexts.

SUMMARY

The days of the nuclear, intact family as the primary family constellation have faded in the face of a host of pressures and issues encountered by the modern family. Children who are raised in nontraditional families are more the norm than the exception. For the school professional, awareness of the issues and dynamics of nontraditional family configurations is imperative. If children from alternative family situations, who are at risk for academic as well as emotional and behavioral problems, are identified early, many future problems may be prevented. Furthermore, it is important for educators to accept the realities of modern life and to help strengthen vulnerable children (Weissbourd, 1996) rather than focus on family life as an excuse for school problems.

CASE EXAMPLE

Hannah, a 10-year-old girl in the fourth grade, had begun to complain of frequent headaches and tiredness. Her complaints had resulted in her being excused from class almost daily. In addition, her school absences had increased in the previous 2 months and her grades, which had been average, had deteriorated.

After sending numerous written notices home, the teacher contacted Hannah's mother by telephone and requested a meeting with both parents. During this conversation, the mother informed the teacher that she was not sure whether Hannah's father would attend the meeting. She gave the teacher her husband's office number and suggested that she contact him there to inform him of the meeting.

The teacher contacted Hannah's father at the office, and he agreed to a meeting time. He also informed her that he and his wife had made a decision to divorce 3 months earlier but were still living in the same home, awaiting a settlement agreement. He tended to work late to avoid being in the same house with his wife for extended periods.

The parents both arrived for the meeting and listened, sullenly, while Hannah's teacher described her concerns. The parents stated that they had not told their children about their plans to divorce. However, they believed the children were aware of the divorce because they had overheard their parents arguing. The teacher then asked how the stress of the present arrangement was affecting each of the parents and their children.

Following the teacher's question, the parents began to blame each other for Hannah's problems. The mother stated that Hannah was upset because her father was never at home. The father felt that Hannah was responding to her mother's lethargy and crying spells.

It became clear to the teacher that the decision to divorce had been initiated by the father. When she inquired as to why the couple were still living in the same home, she was met with another round of accusations. The father claimed that if he left the home, his wife would "take me to the cleaners" by filing charges of desertion. The wife felt that her husband was staying in the home to "play a waiting game, hoping I will give up and let him off the hook."

Comments and Questions

1. *What interventions could be tried with these parents? [Develop strategies for meeting with the parents, the points you would cover, suggestions you would make, and resources you would recommend. Then read the following description. This exercise can be completed alone or in small or large groups.]*

   Initially, the teacher could point out that Hannah's difficulties were, most likely, a response to the family confusion and her own stress level. She could ask about any signs or symptoms of stress in the other children, ages 16 and 12.

   Once the teacher has elicited the parents' concern about their children, she could then give them information about the effects of parental divorce on children of different ages and about the necessity for providing as much stability and predictability as possible. She could suggest that the parents, together, openly discuss the plans for their divorce with the children and give them an explanation of why the living situation had remained as it was. She could also suggest that the parents each consult their attorneys to get a time frame for resolving the settlement issue so that the children could be given a general plan. She could stress to the parents that the worst possible outcome for the children would be to become embroiled in their parents' disputes and loyalty conflicts.

   The teacher could then talk about the possible concerns about divorce in children Hannah's age and could ask that each parent sit down with Hannah and reassure her that:

   - the divorce was not her fault;
   - her parents' separation did not mean they did not love her;
   - she would continue to have contact with both parents, even after the divorce;
   - she did not need to feel responsible for her parents' happiness—her parents would get the support they needed from their friends and family, rather than putting this pressure on their children;
   - both of her parents were available to Hannah if and when she wanted to discuss her feelings about the divorce, and she had permission to talk about it with her friends; and
   - it was important that Hannah attend school, be with her friends, study, and do the things that 10-year-olds do everyday.

   Finally, the teacher could offer the parents resources for reading about the effects of divorce on themselves and their children (see Appendices B and C). Reading *Healthy Divorce* by Everett and Everett (1994) would be a good place to start. The teacher could also provide information about postseparation support groups and a group for children of divorced parents in the area. The school counselor would likely have such a list available. A list of counselors in the area could also be offered. If the teacher were not comfortable covering this territory alone, the school principal, counselor, social worker, or psychologist might be willing to sit in on the conference.

EXTENSION ACTIVITIES

Reflection: In recent years, media attention has focused more and more on divorce, remarriage, single-parent households, and adoption. Consider situations you have known, heard of, or experienced that relate to nontraditional families. Recall these families and your reactions to their situation, including what you thought and how you felt at the time.

Journal: How has your increased knowledge about the topic of divorce, remarriage, adoption, and single-parent households impacted you personally and professionally? What remaining questions do you have about children affected by these situations?

In-Class/Training Panel Discussion: Leader instruction: Ask for students/group members to volunteer to serve on a panel and speak about their personal experiences related to being in one of the following categories: their parents divorced while they were still living at home; they are raised by a single parent for part of their childhood; they are a member of a blended family; or they are an adoptee. Invite each member of the panel to prepare a 5-minute talk about his or her background to be used as a springboard for the question-and-answer session. Those not on panel will write questions they would like answered on cards while the panel members are speaking. A moderator will facilitate the brief background sharing prior to introducing the question-and-answer session. The moderator will then collect all of the question cards and pose the questions to the panel members.

AND/OR

In-Class/Training Panel Discussion: Leader instruction: Ask for students/group members to volunteer to serve on a panel and speak about their personal experiences related to being in one of the following categories: they are a divorced parent, they were a single parent for part or all of their child(ren)'s youth, they are a parent in a blended family, they adopted a child. Invite each member of the panel to prepare a 5-minute talk about his or her background to be used as a springboard for the question and answer session. Those not on the panel will write questions they would like answered on cards while the panel members are speaking. A moderator will facilitate the brief background sharing prior to introducing the question-and-answer session. The moderator will then collect all of the question cards and pose the questions to the panel members.

In-Class/Training Expert Speakers: Leader instructions: In a small group or as a whole class/group activity work together to arrange for either one expert or a panel of experts to come to the class/session and address the divorce, single-parent, remarriage, and adoption areas covered in this chapter. You might want to arrange for a series of speakers, one of which could talk for a half hour at each class/session, or you might prefer to have several speakers come at once to cover diverse topics related to divorce and its impact on children, blended families and their challenges, single-parent households, and adoptive families. If you have trouble finding speakers, you can call the American Association for Marriage and Family Therapy at (800) 374-2638 to request names of licensed professionals in your area. Be sure to prepare the speaker(s) by discussing the audience characteristics including their range of experiences, whether remuneration is available, what you would like them to cover and how, whether other experts will be there, what the audience has read concerning the topic, how long their talk should be, and whether questions will be asked. By taking part in arranging this type of activity you will learn what is involved so that you will be able to replicate such activities in the future.

Invitational Principals' Panel Leader Instruction: In a small or large group, arrange for a panel of principals from elementary, middle, and high schools to speak to your class/session about the impact on schools of the special populations covered in this chapter. If possible, include principals who represent urban, suburban, and rural schools. Prior to their talks, provide the speakers with similar kinds of information as discussed for the panel on nontraditional families.

At-Risk Students From Dysfunctional Families

In addition to the structural changes covered in Chapter 6, the American family experienced a dramatic increase in dysfunction over time. There are at least 28 million children of alcoholics in the United States, with over 7 million being under the age of 18 (Nastasi & DeZolt, 1994). Statistics from the National Institute for Drug Abuse (NIDA), cited in Schaefer and DiGeronimo (1994), reveal that "more than 1.6 million children, aged 12 to 17, use illicit drugs. Moreover, just under five million alcohol users are children under age 17" (p. 167). Although prevalence estimates vary, approximately 2 million children in the United States are neglected or physically or sexually abused each year (Courtois, 1988; Snow, 1997). With all of these numbers on the rise (Barry & Collins, 1997), there is increased pressure on our schools to help children with adjustment problems and those who are at risk for future problems in school or society. Parents who are dealing with their own concerns may be less able or less likely to devote themselves to their children's adjustment.

This chapter provides descriptions of addictive family systems as well as of child maltreating and incestuous families. Professionals who come into contact with these types of dysfunction usually assign blame to a particular *problem* member of the family. The underlying principle of this entire book, and particularly of this chapter, is that dysfunction must be viewed as part of a system, not as a problem within an individual.

The chapter begins with a discussion of concerns faced by educators in dealing with students who have parent(s) addicted to alcohol and/or drugs. Next, concerns in dealing with students from neglectful, abusive, or violent families are discussed. In the last section, the focus shifts to incestuous families. Each section includes suggestions for prevention and strategies for schools. Appendices B through D provide additional useful information for helping families link with external sources of support and assistance. The chapter concludes with a case example that illustrates the effects of several areas covered in this chapter on a 14-year-old boy in middle school, followed by extension activities that provide suggestions for deepening one's knowledge about and experience with dysfunctional families.

ADDICTIVE FAMILIES

Since the 1960s, awareness of problems with drug and alcohol addiction has increased dramatically in the United States, and recently, the concerns of adults who were raised in alcoholic homes, known as adult children of alcoholics (ACOAs), have taken on the status of a social movement. Unfortunately, despite the increased consciousness and attention, addiction continues to be a leading social problem (D. J. Hanson, 1996). Large numbers of youth currently live in homes where one or both parents are addicted to drugs or alcohol. It is estimated that as many as 14 million adults in the United States have had problems with drinking (National Institute on Alcohol Abuse and Alcoholism, 1994). Educators, knowing or not knowing about their parents' addiction, encounter the children of these adults regularly.

This section briefly focuses on characteristics of addictive families and then turns to parental impact, child concerns, at-risk students, and prevention and intervention.

Characteristics of Addictive Families

Characteristics of children and families in which parents have addiction problems include the following: denial of the problem ("There's an elephant in the living room" and everyone pretends not to notice); rigid external boundaries, isolating the family from social supports; rigid internal boundaries, so that there is poor interpersonal communication and no expression of feelings; and unresolved family history or sudden or traumatic loss of a member (Ackerman, 1989; Brooks & Rice, 1997; E. Kaufman & Kaufmann, 1992; Nastasi & DeZolt, 1994; Saitoh, Steinglass, & Schuckit, 1992; Schlesinger & Horvberg, 1988; Treadway, 1987).

Educators who see these characteristics in students may suspect that the student comes from an addictive family. However, many of the characteristics are also applicable to other forms of dysfunction. It is important not to jump to conclusions, but simply to be aware. Talking with the school counselor or social worker about the student may be helpful.

Parental Impact

School personnel should be aware of the impact of parental addiction on the parental subsystem (Nastasi & DeZolt, 1994). For the chemically dependent parent, the ability to parent effectively is severely diminished. The individual's emotional availability to his or her spouse and children is limited, and depending on the severity of the addiction, many other aspects of the individual's functioning may be impaired.

The nonaddicted spouse has been viewed as an enabler who tolerates aberrant behavior to preserve the relationship and family (Brooks & Rice, 1997). Lacking a functional marital subsystem, the nonaddicted spouse often turns to older children for emotional support and assistance in coping with the demands of managing the family. These children become *parentified* (W. C. Nichols, 1996). The hierarchy in the family is disrupted, and the boundaries between the family and external systems are rigidified to preserve the family secret. Thus, family members are cut off both from external supports and from one another.

Child Concerns

For children, the chemically dependent family is characterized by inconsistency, conflict, and emotional stress (Brooks & Rice, 1997; Dulfano, 1992; Nastasi & DeZolt, 1994). In an article published in 1987 Treadway provided the following quote by a child living in an alcoholic home:

> I could always tell what kind of night it was going to be by how my father came in the door. I would listen for how he put the key in the lock. If he fumbled around and didn't get the key in, I would know it was going to be the kind of night that I would just make myself scarce. (p. 18)

As described by this child, these are families in which the addiction organizes the family system. A child in this kind of family feels that the adults upon whom he or she is supposed to trust and depend behave in unpredictable ways. The children learn to survive by becoming self-sufficient, by blocking out feelings, and by learning not to depend upon others. Even when the parent stops drinking, these family patterns and personality styles remain intact (Brooks & Rice, 1997; Dulfano, 1992).

In 1985, Wegscheider-Cruse identified patterns or adaptive roles, that children assume in order to survive in an addictive family. The terms she used—Hero, Lost Child, Scapegoat, and Mascot—have become standard reference terms in the professional and popular literature about addictive families. Nastasi and DeZolt (1994) charted the four roles, and Brooks and Rice (1997) gave examples of each. Glover (1994) focused solely on the hero in the alcoholic family and provided recommendations for school counselors. The following is a consolidation of descriptions from these four references:

Family Hero or Super Kid—Often the oldest child in the family. Overachiever, needs to control, can't fail. Successful in school, sports, community, clubs; brings recognition to family. Hides feelings of hurt, inadequacy, confusion, and guilt. Self-critical, poor self-esteem, sense of inadequacy, lonely. As an adult will probably become a workaholic and marry a dependent person.

Family Scapegoat—Often a middle or second child. Life centers around delinquency, abuses drugs/alcohol, defiant, always in trouble. Acts out to draw attention away from the alcoholic. Hides feelings of hurt, abandonment, anger, rejection. Feels lonely, guilty, low self-worth. As an adult will probably become an alcoholic or addict.

The Lost Child—Frequently the middle child in the family. Shy, withdrawn, a loner. Hides feelings of unimportance, abandonment, inadequacy. Has extended fantasy life. Tries not to add to burden of family. Seems independent. As an adult will probably be indecisive, nonassertive, depressed, isolated, and experience physical illnesses.

Mascot or Family Clown—Usually the youngest child. Life characterized by clowning and hyperactivity. Hides feelings of sadness, anxiety, fear, and insecurity. Fears losing contact with reality. As an adult will probably become a compulsive clown, won't be able to handle stress, will marry a hero, will have dependent relationships.

These personality patterns and roles often become so ingrained in the developing child that they are carried long into adulthood. The behavior patterns are evident not only at home but also in the classroom context.

Students at Risk

Knight (1994) identified the following behavioral patterns for children of parents who are substance abusers: absenteeism, neglected physical appearance, fluctuating academic performance, fatigue and lack of energy, psychological symptoms, people-pleasing behavior, conflict avoidance, problems controlling mood and behavior, attention problems, social isolation, parental concerns, and physical symptoms. She presented a long list of reasons for educators to not identify children of alcoholics in the schools. Instead, she highly recommended "that chemical dependency-related education and prevention efforts [be] directed to all children" (p. 282). She indicated that self-identification could be the best method of identifying these children, as anonymity and safety would be within the individual child's hands. She viewed partnerships between school, family, and community as key to the provision of support and resources necessary for children of alcoholics.

Placing these children at perhaps even greater risk than the behavioral patterns just described is the finding that the child of a chemically dependent parent is more likely than other children to become addicted later in life. Many adolescent children of addicted parents have been found to abuse alcohol or drugs themselves. A number of authors (Hanson, 1996; Marshall, 1992; Nastasi & DeZolt, 1994; Szapocznik & Kurtines, 1989) have focused on drug and alcohol abusing youth. Szapocznik and Kurtines (1989) focused on a family systems approach, known as Brief Strategic Family Therapy, as a strategy for helping families with a child who abuses drugs.

Alcoholism is clearly a genetic and biochemical, as well as a psychosocial, phenomenon. Vaillant (1995) reviewed a variety of studies on alcoholism in adults who had been adopted or cross-fostered children. One of these, a landmark study of adoptees in Denmark, found that children born to alcoholic parents and adopted into nonalcoholic homes at birth developed alcoholism in adulthood at a rate five times greater than that of children of nonalcoholic parents. A variety of subsequent studies reviewed by Vaillant confirmed this genetic link. Vaillant also discussed the differences between *familial* and *acquired* alcoholism. He indicated that familial alcoholism is "thought to have a poorer prognosis and to begin at an earlier age" (p. 69).

L. A. Bennett, S. J. Wolin, D. Reiss, and M. A. Teitelbaum (1987) interviewed 68 couples in which one spouse was a child of an alcoholic. They found that the following significant emotional and behavioral factors mitigated against becoming an alcoholic in adult life, even with a genetic history of alcoholism: the alcoholic family maintained family rituals, holidays, and family dinners while the child was growing up, despite the behavior of the alcoholic parent; the child related to people and activities outside of the alcoholic home; the young adult selected a spouse from a stable, nonalcoholic family and emotionally attached to this alternative family; and the couple anchored themselves in a network of nonalcoholic friends, established their own family rituals, and maintained limited involvement with the alcoholic family of origin. This study indicated that emotional and social supports can help to disentangle the child of an alcoholic from the multigenerational nature of this problem.

Because of the increased risk for children of substance abusers, Vail-Smith, Knight, and White (1995) stressed the importance of training school personnel, including counselors, on how best to help children of substance abusers. The counselors they interviewed saw elementary counselors as having a key role in providing education, support, and referral for these children. Thus, school counselors need to be adequately prepared for these roles.

Support, Prevention, and Intervention

When working with students who are children of addicted parents, the teacher can provide support and promote healing through, among other things, curricula focusing on the process of addiction, the expression of feelings, and identity formation (Bagnall, 1991; Bates & Wigtil, 1994; Hanson, 1996; Marshall, 1992; Nastasi & DeZolt, 1994). Providing information about local chapters of Alateen or local Children Of Alcoholics (C.O.A.) meetings is often helpful. The book *Alateen: Hope for Children of Alcoholics* has been beneficial for many teenagers.

Nastasi and DeZolt (1994), who viewed prevention as paramount, wrote of the importance of "creating school cultures that foster the development of social competence and personal efficacy of all children, with particular attention to the needs of COAs" (p. vii). Their ESCAPE model can be embedded within existing curricula. An older text that is still useful for educators is *Children of Alcoholics: A Guidebook for Educators, Therapists, and Parents* (Ackerman, 1983).

Often the nonaddicted spouse is aware of and uncomfortable with the family situation but feels unable to break out of the family rules to proceed toward change. School professionals can provide support to the nonaddicted spouse in accessing resources that can help change the system. Suggestions may include attending local Al-Anon meetings or support groups and recommending literature on the family dynamics of addiction (see Appendix B). As nonaddicted spouses become healthier, they may provide more support for their children and become more able to engage the addicted spouse in treatment. The book *How to Talk to Your Kids About Really Important Things: For Children Four to Twelve* (Schaefer & DiGeronimo, 1994) includes information on addiction as well as myriad other topics that parents and children face in life. The focus of the book is on straight talk and ending the deadening silence.

If the nonaddicted spouse can elicit help from a network of friends and family, the school professional might mention an intervention process (Brooks & Rice, 1997; Forman, 1987) in which the addict is confronted by his or her family, friends, and employer about the effects of the addiction and treatment recommendations are made. The intervention process is led by a counselor who specializes in substance abuse treatment. It is helpful for school professionals to have on hand a list of professionals in their area who are trained and experienced in conducting interventions.

For addicted adolescents—and their families—therapy has been shown to be useful. Family therapy focuses on the problem with a systems lens (Brooks & Rice, 1997; Dulfano, 1992; A. S. Friedman & Granick, 1990; Kaufmann, 1992; Todd & Selekman, 1990). To help school counselors in referring abusing and dependent youth and their families to therapy, schools should have available a listing of family-oriented therapists who practice in the vicinity. The names and phone numbers of certified therapists can be obtained through the American Association of Marriage and Family Therapy (800-374-2638). Another helpful resource is the social work school at a local university.

A good book for educators to recommend to parents of drug abusing youth is the revised edition of *Tough Love* (Neff, 1996). Another helpful book for parents of addicted teens is *Teenage Addicts Can Recover* (Marshall, 1992). This book moves from identification through aftercare of teens who received treatment for addiction.

Also, support groups for students who return to school after in-patient treatment are beneficial. Most treatment facilities provide such services, but individuals in rural areas may find that schools are a better source for providing such groups. Networking with churches and synagogues is another possibility, and almost every town in America has chapters of Anonymous groups that can be found in the local phone directory. The reader is referred to Appendix D for other resources school professionals may find helpful.

NEGLECTFUL, ABUSIVE, AND VIOLENT FAMILIES

Much has been written about the turbulence in recent years in U.S. society (see, for example, Ackerman & Graham, 1990; Ammerman & Hersen, 1990b, 1990c; 1991; Barth, Berrick, & Gilbert, 1994; A. Coleman, 1995; Finkelhor, 1987; Finkelhor, Hotaling, & Yllö, 1988; Fontana & Moolman, 1991; Gelles, 1996; Gelles & Loseke, 1993; Hampton, 1991; Justice & Justice, 1990; Madanes, Keim, & Smelser, 1995; Peled et al., 1995; Sobsey, 1994; Weissbourd, 1996; Whetsell-Mitchell, 1995; Willis, Holden, & Rosenberg, 1992; Wolfe, Wekerle, & Scott, 1997). Many authors have focused in particular upon maltreatment related to children and youth and their families. Some have focused on children with disabilities (Ammerman, Lubetsky, & Drudy, 1991; J. C. Levy & Lagos, 1994; Sobsey, 1994; Sobsey, Wells, Lucardie, & Mansell, 1995). Others have focused on ethnicity and maltreatment (Chen & True, 1994; Hammond & Yung, 1994; Hampton, 1991; H. M. Hill, Soriano, Chen, & LaFromboise, 1994; Soriano, 1994; Yung & Hammond, 1994). All forms of dysfunction in the family put children at risk for school failure and failure in life.

This following section describes neglect, abuse, and violence. The discussion is followed by sections on the roots of child maltreatment, characteristics of abusive families, risk factors, the impact of neglect and abuse on children and youth, and responding and reporting abuse. The chapter ends with a discussion on prevention and intervention within schools.

Maltreatment of Children in Dysfunctional Families

Neglect

While abuse and violence are more obvious forms of child maltreatment than neglect and have received more attention from professionals, the fact remains that neglect is more common (Gil, 1996; A. H. Green, 1991) and is quite debilitating to children. According to A. H. Green (1991), neglect can take the forms of "inadequate parenting, interruption of maternal care, affective and social deprivation, inappropriate or premature expectations of the child, parental detachment, indifference, overstimulation, and failure to anticipate or respond to the child's needs at specific changes of development" (p. 136). Ammerman and Hersen (1990a) differentiated between physical neglect and psychological neglect and pointed to the difficulty in defining neglect. Furthermore, they viewed psychological neglect and its damage as being more long lasting than physical injury.

Along the same lines, Willis, Dobrec, and Sipes (1992) stated that "the insidious nature of neglect and emotional maltreatment may have more far-reaching consequences on the child's development than physical maltreatment, since it imparts the message to the child that he or she is neither valued nor loved" (p. 283). Aber, Allen, Carlson, and Cicchetti (1989) noted that maltreatment affects a child's readiness to learn.

Parents of neglected children are often poor, alcoholic, or antisocial. Many experienced deprivation and neglect in their childhood (Vondra, 1990). Overwhelmed with life, they do not recognize their child's needs. They tend to have more children, be less often married, experience more stress, and have poorer relationships with their families than parents who are not neglectful of their children.

The term *latch-key children,* which became popular in the 1980s to describe a growing phenomenon of children arriving home after school for a period of time with no adult supervision, points to a current example of neglect. Schools began after-school programs partially in response to the lack of adult supervision facing many children when they left school at the end of the day. Community agencies and the churches also stepped up their efforts to provide supervision for America's children and youth after school hours. More insidious than that form of neglect is the neglect that comes from parents being too young or lacking the education to meet the needs of their offspring; parents being so overwhelmed with making ends meet that they do not meet their child's emotional needs; and parents being too narcissistic to spend quality time with their youngsters (Gil, 1996).

Children who experience severe neglect may have physical and developmental retardation, which is most noticeable in speech and language. These children also do not form healthy attachments with their caregivers. They suffer from failure to thrive and experience diminished initiative and enjoyment in play. Many neglected children are malnourished, dirty, and not adequately clothed. It is not unusual for neglected children to have poor impulse control and behavioral problems. Recent medical studies on orphans from wartorn countries, written about in news magazines, show areas of the brain that vividly demonstrate the results of neglect.

Intervention with neglecting parents should be focused on strengthening the family. Counselors can help strengthen the family by advising them on how to reduce their stress, providing concrete support, offering therapy and drugs for parents and children when necessary, using a family therapy approach, and presenting parenting education (A. H. Green, 1991). Schools are in an optimal position to help parents develop the skills necessary for effective parenting.

Abuse

Ammerman and Hersen (1990c) related that child abuse is divided into three categories: physical, psychological, and sexual abuse. Vondra (1990), following a review of the literature, reported an incidence rate for child abuse of 33% for parents similarly maltreated in childhood. She went on to say, "It is significant that these impoverished relations are typically reflected in their other intimate relationships as well" (p. 153). In *Too Old to Cry*, a book about teens who are abused, Ackerman and Graham (1990) related that 30% of reported cases of child abuse and neglect involve adolescents and the highest percent is for infants. They stated:

> By today's standards the three major elements to consider when distinguishing discipline from abuse are degree, duration, and intent of the punishment. A child who is slapped once, and no more, for breaking a dish may not be considered abused. However, a child who is smacked every day for not setting a table properly may be considered abused, especially if the child is injured by this discipline. (p. 8)

Hampton, Gelles, and Harrop (1991) found that the "rate of severe violence toward black children was double the rate toward white children in 1985 (p. 16)." They were unable to relate the lack of progress in reducing severe violence among African Americans to inadequate opportunities to enter programs for prevention or treatment. They pondered whether the disproportionately high rate of African-American children and youth experiencing severe violence resulted from changing cultural attitudes concerning the appropriate use of acts of violence on children.

Violence

Violence in U.S. homes is increasing at alarming rates. Peled et al. (1995), citing data from Straus, reported that as many as 10 million children in America are at risk for witnessing abuse of their mothers each year. Children who are witnesses to family violence may suffer from a variety of emotional, physical, cognitive, and spiritual wounds (M. S. Rosenberg & Gilberson, 1991). When children witness repeated violence in the home, they live as though they are continually bracing for the next verbal or physical assault they will see. They live in crisis. They do not feel secure or emotionally safe. Many suffer from posttraumatic stress disorder (PTSD).

As noted by Wolfe, Wekerle, Reitzel, and Gough (1995), they are also at risk for becoming perpetrators of abuse. Pointing to statistics that between three and four million American families experience a significant amount of violence that is aimed at women and/or children each year, they wrote:

> In addition to [the effect of] prior abuse experiences, the risk of becoming a victim or perpetrator of violence increases as a result of negative influences from peers

(condoning violence), the absence of compensatory factors (e.g., success at school; a healthy relationship with siblings and friends), and the relative lack of alternative sources of information, all of which serve to counteract existing biases, attitudes, and beliefs. (p. 256)

The authors provided strategies for addressing violence in high-risk youth. Because the type of dating adolescents experience will have an effect on their forming nonviolent relationships in later life, the authors focused on stereotypical male/female roles and the importance of intervention in the early teen years. They viewed programs for at-risk youth as ways to build strength, resilience, and coping skills that can reduce violent behavior in the future.

Relationship problems are frequent outgrowths of the trust issues inherent in abusive families. Marital discord and violence spill over into parent-child relationships. A mother may become emotionally unavailable because she is preoccupied with the battering that she is experiencing. Some battered parents turn to their children for support and affection. These children may become parentified and act like little adults. Still other battered parents vacillate between meting out punishment and ignoring the misbehavior of their children.

Wolfe et al.'s 1997 text, *Alternatives to Violence: Empowering Youth to Develop Healthy Relationships,* is an invaluable resource for school professionals. Among other foci, the book lists core ingredients of successful prevention programs. The authors also describe a curriculum aimed at helping youth handle power in a healthy manner.

Many children who witness violence on a regular basis have trouble coping with their memories of violence (Arroyo & Eth, 1995). Some children shift from feeling powerless to feeling powerful and able to control others. Many have trouble demonstrating emotions, and some experience either an excess or deficit of emotional sensitivity. These children live in a world of extremes and react to the world in dichotomies. Understanding these dynamics may help school professionals relate more effectively to children who witness violence in the home. Four chapters in the edited text by Peled et al. (1995) on violence in U.S. communities focus on prevention and education, with one chapter (by Gamache and Snapp) focusing on elementary schools and another (by Suderman, Jaffe, and Hastings) on secondary schools.

Roots of Child Maltreatment

Child neglect and abuse are transgenerational problems (Ackerman & Graham, 1990; A. Berger, 1985; Egeland, 1993; Hampton & Gelles, 1991; Vondra, 1990). In most, though not all, cases (J. Kaufman & Zigler, 1993), abusive parents and people who marry abusive spouses were themselves abused or neglected as children. Growing up in an abusive family system, they may have developed a belief that hitting is a legitimate form of discipline.

In addition, many adults who were abused have low self-esteem, unmet dependency needs, highly distorted and unrealistic expectations of themselves and their children, and problems with empathy (Gelles & Loseke, 1993; Vondra, 1990; Youngblade & Belsky, 1990). According to Vondra (1990), "Attachment issues can apparently predispose vulnerable parents to maltreat their own children, who then carry forward the socioemotional legacies of another generation of disturbed attachment relationships" (p. 153). Ammerman and Hersen (1990c) related that children who present behavioral problems have a higher likelihood of maltreatment but noted that this characteristic alone is not sufficient to result in abuse. Risk for maltreatment is increased greatly when preexisting elements, such as high stress, inability to cope, and accepting physical punishment as a way to discipline a child, also are present. Thus, school programs that provide parent training and/or behavioral intervention for families can likely help to lower the incidence of child abuse in society.

Egeland (1993), like Ammerman and Hersen and others, indicated that multiple etiologies of child maltreatment exist and that being abused does not automatically result in abuse against one's own child. Individuals who were abused simply are at greater risk for abusing than others.

Differences have been found in the prevalence of abuse in American homes for different races. For instance, the rate of severe violence by parents toward children was reported to be 114% greater in African American families than in families of Caucasians (Hampton & Gelles, 1991). Research is needed to clarify reasons for the vulnerability or resistance to maltreatment found in high incidence populations.

Gelles and Loseke (1993) and Hampton and Gelles (1991) noted that particular experiences seem to help insulate individuals who are at risk from falling into abusing patterns. Knowing and responding to this information will help professionals strengthen children and youth and their families and thereby will help vulnerable children to create productive and meaningful lives. The experiences included having found emotionally supportive individuals and involvement in psychotherapy.

In trying to understand the dynamics of abuse, it is helpful to draw a genogram of the families of both parents (see Chapter 4). Viewing the abuse in a transgenerational context may help the school professional stay clear of blaming and emotional reactivity, which are strong barriers to working effectively with these families.

Characteristics of Abusive Families

Abusive families tend to have the following characteristics (Ammerman & Hersen, 1991; A. Berger, 1985; R. J. Green, 1995; Martin, 1980; Oates, 1991; Otto & Smith, 1980; Weissbourd, 1996):

- Isolation from social supports
- High levels of environmental stress, such as financial and medical problems
- High levels of parental conflict
- Dominant/submissive pattern in the marital relationship
- Low levels of physical contact of any sort
- Inconsistent and overly punitive discipline
- Chaotic family structure

Risk Factors For Abuse or Neglect

Ackerman and Graham (1990) reported risk factors that can signal school professionals to suspected abuse or neglect and allow them to better judge the situation. They suggested that it is not the number of risk elements that occur within a family that is indicative of abuse or neglect but rather how the family copes with the situation. The risk factors include:

1. Parents who act indifferent, intolerant, or overanxious toward the child
2. An existing history of family violence
3. Socioeconomic problems such as unemployment
4. A child who had a premature birth or low birth weight
5. Parents who were themselves abused or neglected as children
6. A blended family including a stepparent or a parent cohabitee
7. A single or separated parent
8. A mother who was younger than 21 at the time the child was born
9. A history of mental illness, or drug or alcohol addiction
10. A child who as an infant was separated from the mother for greater than 24 hours post-delivery
11. A child who is mentally or physically handicapped
12. Children in the family spaced closer than 18 months
13. A child who was never breast-fed as an infant (p. 204–205)

In addition to listing risk factors these authors also provided a comprehensive description of suggestions for filing charges of abuse or neglect.

Impact of Abuse or Neglect on Children and Youth

The physical abuse of children and youth results in many deaths and injuries every year (Oates, 1991). Snow (1997) reported data that 1,299 confirmed child abuse and neglect fatalities occurred in the United States in 1993. Most of the deaths were linked with the economy and drug abuse. An equally important point to raise concerns the effect on children of the deprivation of their basic needs. Parents who physically abuse their children cannot meet their children's need for security, praise, and realization of worth. The children will live in fear and have poor self-esteem, trouble forming relationships, low trust levels, and behavioral problems. When these children grow up and have children, they will find it difficult to cope with child rearing.

Children who are raised in violent and abusive homes learn to relate along dimensions of aggression and submission rather than along lines of equality and negotiation. They learn to focus on the needs and moods of their parents rather than on themselves to avoid punishment. Students from abusive families may be aggressive toward their peers but overly fearful in response to a teacher reprimand. Symptoms of bed-wetting, nightmares, and psychosomatic complaints as well as developmental regressions, withdrawal, and aggression may be seen in young children who have been abused (Thaxton, 1985). These children may also feel extreme anxiety about any sort of failure; thus, they will hold themselves back from attempting new experiences or from struggling with challenging academic material. Adolescents from abusive or neglectful families do not know what a healthy family looks like (Ackerman & Graham, 1990). Maltreated males are more likely to be aggressive, whereas females tend to become self-destructive (Eckenrode, Powers, & Garbarino, 1997). Furthermore, researchers have found that the rate of reported abuse as children is much higher in juvenile delinquents than the general population (Maxwell & Widom, 1996).

A child with special needs sometimes induces feelings of resentment in parents who feel overwhelmed and needy. If the bond between parent and child is not strong, the child may be subjected to parental anger and frustration (Ammerman et al., 1991). The parent may not be clear about the child's areas of deficit and may perceive poor performance by the child as a power struggle rather than a developmental problem. The parent may then react with increased dominance, anger, and subsequent abuse (Council for Exceptional Children, 1979).

Researchers have found that children with disabilities are at greater risk for maltreatment than are children without disabilities (Ammerman, Van Hasselt, Hersen, McGonigle, & Lubetsky, 1989; Sobsey, 1994). Snow (1997) reported that children with disabilities are twice as likely to be abused as other children and that they are often the target for the anger of other family members. According to Ammerman et al. (1991), the processes that exist in families of children with disabilities that lead to increased risk for maltreatment include "(1) disruption in the formation of infant-caregiver attachment, (2) prolonged stress associated with raising some children with disabilities, and (3) increased vulnerability to maltreatment" (p. 210).

Sobsey (1994) presented an integrated ecological model of abuse in individuals with disabilities and identified factors related to the potential victim, potential offender, environment, and culture. He saw individuals with disabilities as being vulnerable because of learned helplessness and learned compliance. Those experiencing *learned helplessness* have learned that fighting back does no good; they do not think anything they can do or say will change the outcome. *Learned compliance* is related to being overly compliant. Unfortunately, compliance is often encouraged as a means of getting help from service providers. As Sobsey wrote,

> Although it is true that many of these individuals exhibit some form of unacceptable behavior, that behavior often results from desperate attempts to exercise the last remaining bit of control that they have over their own lives. The elimination of unacceptable behavior without teaching any positive alternative obliterates these last attempts at self-empowerment, leaving them in a state of learned helplessness and extremely vulnerable to all forms of abuse. (p. 165)

Responding to and Reporting Abuse

In cases of abuse, it is usually more functional, in terms of children's long-term adjustment, for professionals to work with an intact family than to try to separate the children from a dysfunctional parent (Kolko & Stauffer, 1991). Resolution of these problems comes from addressing the needs of the system, not from dissolution of the family. Focusing on blaming and ostracizing tends to consolidate the defenses of the family rather than to change the cycle of problems. In some cases, however, it is imperative that the children be removed from their families for a period of time and, on occasion, forever.

The school professional who becomes aware of abuse must take on the roles of both helper and enforcer. By law, any accusation or evidence of child abuse must be reported to child protective services. Ackerman and Graham (1990) presented comprehensive guidelines for reporting abuse. Professionals should follow the procedures of the system within which they work. Such procedures should be available in writing and read by all professionals in schools.

If written procedures are not available, the school professional should take the following approach to reporting cases of abuse. First, he or she should talk with the parents and tell them about the accusation or evidence. The school professional should then inform the parents that this information must be reported to child protective services. Indeed, many school policies require that parents be informed before a report is made. The school professional should give the parents the opportunity to make the call to child protective services. If the parents do not call, the professional is legally obligated to do so. If possible, the initial telephone contact with protective services should be made in the presence of the parents. By using this approach, the parents are given the opportunity to feel somewhat in control of the process. They will then be more likely to feel actively involved in the resolution of problems rather than becoming defensive and isolating themselves from helping professionals (Palazzoli, Boscolo, Cecchin, & Prata, 1980).

Prevention of and Intervention for Child Maltreatment

Daro (1990) described several prevention programs in use in North America. The research she reviewed indicates that prevention is far more effective than intervention. Focusing on individuals with disabilities, Sobsey (1994) indicated that,

> the contents of abuse prevention education for individuals with disabilities are basically the same as they are for all members of society. There are overlapping areas of curriculum. These include:
>
> 1. Personal safety skills training
> 2. Individual rights education
> 3. Assertiveness and self-esteem training
> 4. Communication skills training
> 5. Social skills training
> 6. Sex education
> 7. Self-defense training (p. 178)

Sobsey not only provided information that is useful for school professionals who work with students with disabilities, but he also provided information that is useful for all school professionals about building safer environments; recruitment, training, and leadership; and abuse prevention and intervention teams.

Following a review of the literature on abuse and neglect, Zuvarin and Starr (1991) also recommended prevention strategies because treatment for abusing families had not been found to be very successful. They recommended differences in prevention strategies by race and suggested that the target population include very low-income white mothers and teens from low-income African-American families. In particular, African-American teens would be targeted if they bore a first child prior to age 18, had a history of adverse family life without a close attachment to a primary caretaker, had few close interpersonal relationships, and experienced infrequent contact with their families.

Writing on preventing child sexual abuse, Hazzard (1990) reported evaluations of a number of elementary school programs. Although some programs for the prevention of child sexual abuse among children with disabilities do exist, Hazzard indicated that not much has been developed for these children despite the fact that they are at increased risk for sexual abuse.

D. J. Hansen, L. P. Conaway, and J. S. Christopher (1990) recommended strategies for treating children who have been abused including providing training in social skills development, relaxation approaches, anger control, and self-instruction. Schools can help students with these areas of development.

For school professionals, the first step in knowing how to help children from abusive family situations is understanding the problem of abuse. Attending workshops or lectures dealing with the issues of abuse and neglect may be useful. The Council for Exceptional Children developed a 10-session curriculum entitled "We Can Help" (Council for Exceptional Children, 1979) for training educators about the prevention and treatment of child abuse. This excellent training package, consisting of audiotapes, filmstrips, overhead transparencies, and resources, takes the educator through the identification, reporting, and treatment of abuse and neglect. A school system with this curriculum and identified trainers from the ranks of the school counselors or social workers can both help prevent neglect and abuse and intervene in sensitive and productive ways. This resource is available on microfilm through ERIC (Document No. ED 177 754). One may also be able to find it in libraries. Unfortunately, the Council for Exceptional Children no longer sells this product.

Parent training through Systematic Training for Effective Parenting (STEP) programs or other behavioral programs has also been found to be effective in decreasing physical abuse (Otto & Smith, 1980; Wahler, 1980). These training programs can easily be taught by school professionals. At a minimum, the school building or school funding can be donated for parenting groups that are facilitated by an outside resource person. The American Guidance Service (AGS) can be contacted for a brochure on STEP programs or to register for a STEP workshop by calling (800) 328-2560. AGS also has a web site (www.agsnet.com) and an e-mail address (agsmail@agsnet.com). Current programs include STEP—completely revised, STEP/Teen, and Early Childhood STEP. Each program includes videotapes, handbooks, and a facilitator's resource guide. Active Parenting, which can be contacted at (800) 825-0060 also has workshops that teachers can lead.

Garbarino and Eckenrode (1997a) suggested the use of applied behavioral analysis followed by helping parents to use nonviolent disciplinary techniques as a practical means of preventing abuse. School professionals can provide the necessary parent training.

Further, the school system can address the isolation of abusive families through parent support groups. Involving parents in positive outlets with their children may decrease negativity in the family system. School professionals who work to build a relationship with these parents may then be in a position to make a referral to a local chapter of Parents Anonymous or to outpatient counseling or psychotherapy.

A helpful resource for high schools is *The Youth Relationships Manual* by Wolfe et al. (1996), which provides a group approach for use with adolescents who have experienced abuse or neglect. The purpose is the prevention of violence against women and the development of healthy relationships. If the program is used, the youths' involvement must be voluntary. Designed for groups of between 8 and 15 males and females 14 to 16 years of age, the program involves 18 weekly, 2-hour sessions with an activity plan provided for each session. The manual provides adaptation suggestions for schools that want to adopt the program.

In an excellent, up-to-date book on a systems approach for dealing with abusive families, Gil (1996) contended that there is not one treatment model that is considered most effective. She indicated that the most frequent form of abuse is neglect, followed by physical abuse. School counselors, psychologists, and social workers would benefit particularly from her information on the education of parents.

Reading about abuse is also helpful for school professionals. *Violence and Disability: An Annotated Bibliography,* by Sobsey, Wells, Lucardie, & Mansell (1995), is useful for finding material to read or recommend. The texts cited are equally applicable for recommendation to incestuous families, a dysfunction covered in the next section of this text. An edited text by Willis, Holden, and Rosenberg (1992) entitled *Prevention of Child Maltreatment* also provides considerable information relevant to school professionals. This book, focused on prevention, includes chapters on neglect and sexual abuse. Justice and Justice (1990) suggested that high schools teach nurturing, ages and stages of child development, and child rearing and that they require their students to volunteer in day care or nursery schools. They proposed a 1-year course in child rearing that would be required of all students. In the course the students would not only have classroom work but would also experience firsthand some of the tasks faced by parents. They noted that evidence exists indicating that high-school students would want such child development and management training.

School professionals aware of the need to reduce stress on families of children with disabilities can organize educational opportunities as well as support groups for these parents. Problem solving skills training for parents of children with disabilities can help them organize their lives, thereby reducing problems that create stress. Stress management training, relaxation strategies, and recreation are also helpful adjuncts to an improved lifestyle. In addition, helping parents develop Positive Behavioral Support (PBS) plans can be useful. Described in Koegel, Koegel, and Dunlap (1996), PBS involves

> the broad enterprise of helping people develop and engage in adaptive, socially desirable behaviors and overcome patterns of destructive and stigmatizing responding. The term typically refers to assistance that is provided for people with developmental, cognitive, or emotional/behavioral disabilities; however, the principles and approaches have much greater generality. (p. xiii)

Kogel et al. provide concrete means of developing such support.

Fontana and Moolman (1991) provided five ways friends can help stressed-out parents let off steam:

1. Sympathetically listen to the parents talk about their life situation.
2. Empathize with the struggle they are experiencing and avoid showing disapproval through words or body language.
3. Offer to help the parents (e.g., shopping for them).
4. Baby-sit for the children so the parent(s) can get away for a while.
5. Learn about neighborhood resources, such as mother's groups, respite centers, and Parents Anonymous, and tell the parents about them (adapted from p. 272).

School professionals can include these guidelines in a newsletter that goes out to all parents. A creative way to reach beyond the school community, since 75% of adults do not have children in the home, is to ask supermarkets to display posters with these suggestions.

The National Committee for the Prevention of Child Abuse provided the following list of "Twelve Alternatives to Lashing Out At Your Child" that can be similarly sent out to the internal and external community. These alternatives include:

The next time everyday pressures build up to the point where you feel like lashing out—STOP! Try any of these simple alternatives. You'll feel better . . . and so will your child.

1. Take a deep breath . . . and another. Then remember you are the adult.
2. Close your eyes and imagine you're hearing what your child is about to hear.
3. Press your lips together and count to 10 . . . or better yet, to 20.
4. Put your child in a time-out chair. (Remember the rule: one time-out minute for each year of age.)
5. Put yourself in a time-out chair. Think about why you are angry: is it your child, or is your child simply a convenient target for your anger?
6. Phone a friend.
7. If someone can watch the children, go outside and take a walk.
8. Take a hot bath or splash cold water on your face.
9. Hug a pillow.
10. Turn on some music. Maybe even sing along.
11. Pick up a pencil and write down as many helpful words as you can think of. Save the list. (NCPCA, 1998)

INCESTUOUS FAMILIES, YOUTH WHO ABUSE, SEXUAL ABUSE

Sexual abuse of children occurs across social, economic, racial, and educational categories. It is estimated that in 80 to 90% of the cases, the offender is male (A. Coleman,

1995; Schaefer, Briesmeister, & Fitton, 1984; Whetsell-Mitchell, 1995). Although father-daughter incest is the most common form of sexual abuse, it has recently come to light that sexual abuse of male children is more common than previously thought, as is abuse by females. Furthermore, sexual abuse can occur with family members other than fathers, including cousins, uncles, grandfathers, and siblings. In about 10 to 15% of the cases, the abuser is a stranger (Whetsell-Mitchell, 1995). In 80% of cases, the perpetrator is a relative. Thus, in 15% of the cases, the abuser is a trusted adult such as a friend of the abused child's family, a neighbor, a scout leader, or a Sunday school teacher (Minshew & Hooper, 1990). Because the offender is a member of the family or known to the family, the abuse is often denied, forgotten, or kept secret. In many cases it is unreported.

J. A. Cohen and A. P. Mannarino (1991) clarified the different effect upon a child of incest versus sexual abuse by someone outside the family. In the case of incest, the child is usually engaged in a relationship with the abuser that also has its upside. And even though trust is violated, the child may not see it that way. Because of the child's emotional attachment to the perpetrator, he or she may find it hard to achieve resolution regarding the abuse. Survivors of extrafamilial abuse do not face these complications and conflicts.

Juvenile sex offense is another form of sexual abuse found in families. From a survey of adolescent sexual offenders Moody (1991, 1994) found that the average age of those abused was 6.4 years with a range from 2.5 months to 11 years.

Madanes et al. (1995) described a population of 81 juvenile sex offenders entering therapy between January 1987 and November 1992. Fifty percent were considered to have a learning disability, 26% had health problems, 13% experienced language disorders, and 25% had past records of school truancy or disruptive behavior. Thirty-three percent had a history of substance abuse, and 23% had a record of other delinquent acts. Lending support to the transgenerational theory of transmission, 40% indicated they had been sexually abused themselves, yet the authors believed that figure to be much higher. Interestingly, 53% were not related to the children they abused. The authors' description of the juvenile offenders, who ranged in age from 7 to 21, continued with a barrage of negative life experiences.

Systems Issues

Incest, like other forms of child abuse, is a transgenerational process. Offending parents have often been victimized as children either through rape or sexual, physical, or emotional abuse. They tend to have had relatively poor models for what it means to be a nurturing parent. A nonoffending spouse who was abused as a child may have unconsciously chosen to marry an offending spouse because of his or her own unresolved issues from the family of origin. It is this pattern that makes the process of incest a systemic, rather than an individual, problem (Kolko & Stauffer, 1991).

Recognizing that incest is transgenerational does not absolve the perpetrator from responsibility for his or her actions. As Madanes et al. (1995) indicated, it is important for professionals to hold people accountable for their actions.

Maddock and Larson (1995) focused on double binds in the incestuous family. They specified five double binds related to damage in the abused individual's ability to separate and move away from the family enmeshment: "independent identity and action are experienced as disloyal; setting boundaries is seen as act of defiance; individual identity requires compliance with others; survival is threatened both inside and outside the family; and self sacrifice may be the only effective way to gain love" (pp. 95–98). They also specified five double binds related to damage in the ability to connect: "people who love and trust each other are expected to hurt one another; setting boundaries with each other is an act of rejection; honesty and openness create pain, and empathy is to be exploited; being dependent is dangerous; and sexual feelings are associated with fear, hurt, anger, and power/control conflicts" (pp. 98–102). Excellent examples are provided for each of these 10 double binds. The authors contend that family members cannot resolve the double binds unless they restructure the beliefs that create them and are fundamental to continuation of the incest. This text is highly recommended to school professionals interested in learning more about incest and family systems.

Characteristics and Manifestations

Whetsell-Mitchell (1995) summarized the characteristics of families in which incest occurs. Boundaries inside the family are unclear and diffuse. There is a lack of privacy between family members. External boundaries are rigid. The family is isolated from outside contacts (Eckenrode et al., 1997). Children must remain cut off from the world to preserve the secret (Minuchin & Fishman, 1981). The victim is often parentified (W. C. Nichols, 1996; Whetsell-Mitchell, 1995) and used in an adult way to meet the needs of others. The family maintains an illusion of happiness. Conflict is avoided; family loyalty is paramount (Machotka, Pittman, & Flomenhaft, 1967; Maddock & Larson, 1995). Following a study in which they examined children's drawings to detect potential child sexual abuse, Sadowski and Loesch (1993) strongly recommended that a child's drawings should never be the sole basis for concluding that sexual abuse occurred.

Among the family indicators of incest cited by Whetsell-Mitchell (1995) were extreme dominance, restrictiveness, or protectiveness by mother or father; lack of family connections with the community or outside the family; family history of sexual abuse for either parent; alcohol or drug abuse by parents or children; violence in the home; absence of a parent due to chronic illness, divorce, or separation; and parents labeling their child as seductive.

Besharov (1990) provided examples of children's behaviors that may indicate the need to assess potential for sexual abuse. Specifically they looked for signs of sexual activity seen on the body of the child and for emotional manifestations that may point to sexual abuse. The latter included:

> Difficulty in walking or sitting. Unwillingness to disrobe in the presence of others, as when changing for a gym class. Excessive fear of being approached or touched by persons of the opposite sex. Fear of going home. Running away from home. Adolescent prostitution. Sexual behavior or references that are bizarre or unusual for the child's age. Sexual knowledge that is too sophisticated for the child's age. Seductiveness that is not age appropriate. Behavior that is withdrawn, infantile, or filled with fantasy (the child may even appear to be retarded). Attempted suicide.

> Dramatic changes in behavior or school performance. Unusual accumulations of money or candy. Indirect allusions: A sexually abused child may seek out a special friend or a teacher to confide in. These confidences may be vague and indirect, such as "I'm afraid to go home tonight," "I'd like to come and live with you," or "I want to live in a foster home." (p. 97)

Whetsell-Mitchell (1995) boiled down the physical signs to include "difficulties in walking and sitting; trauma to the genitals and rectum that could include bruises, bleeding, lacerations, pain and itching, or inflammation; pregnancy; and the presence of sperm in or on the body" (p. 21). All of these signals should cause concern among professionals and caring persons. School professionals who observe such behaviors should talk with the school counselor for further advice.

Personality Issues

Children who have been raised in an incestuous family system learn a number of undesirable lessons about life, such as: don't trust yourself or others; be loyal, keep secrets, and obey the family; put others' needs before your own; love means being hurt or used; don't ask for help; don't show hurt feelings; stay in control; and don't be a child (Calof, 1988; Whetsell-Mitchell, 1995). Because of the pressure to keep the family secret and remain loyal, children will often exhibit physical, behavioral, or emotional symptoms rather than talk about their concerns. For boys, stomachaches, encopresis, and fire-setting are typical symptoms that may arise from unresolved sexual abuse. For girls, withdrawal, fearfulness, and a tendency to sexualize relationships inappropriately may be symptomatic indicators. Any of these symptom patterns that are evident in the classroom, along with family dynamics of secrecy and isolation, are indicators that further attention may be warranted.

Disclosure

Historically, incest has been handled as a legal issue. Offenders are typically separated from their families, and criminal charges are brought against the individual. Often, even after a child has disclosed the sexual abuse, he or she will deny the initial report. Typically, these children have experienced overwhelming pressure from the family. When the investigation is begun, the child is usually blamed for the shame and the potential breakup of the family. The nonoffending parent will often reject the victim, accusing the child of lying, being seductive, or causing trouble. The motive to preserve the family is so great that even siblings who have themselves been victimized may reject the child who has told the truth. The child, then, not only suffers from the abuse but also from abandonment and isolation from the remainder of the family system. All of these dynamics are important to consider when reporting cases of physical and sexual abuse. Through his or her words and actions the school professional can be both a helper to the child and the family and an enforcer of state laws. Being a helper to the family does not mean that the professional should fail to report the abuse but that he or she should provide the necessary supports and attitude that will alleviate fallout from reports of suspected abuse.

Prevention and Intervention for Sexual Abuse/Incest

Controversy exists over whether prevention is appropriate or adequate for sexual abuse and incest (Gelles & Loseke, 1993). Certainly we want to prevent sexual abuse and incest, and school professionals can make a difference (Plummer, 1993) in helping to prevent sexual abuse. For a look at the controversy of child sexual abuse prevention programs, see Reppucci and Haugaard (1993).

Moody (1994) described a number of abuse prevention programs including available printed materials; interventions using drama, lecture or discussion, or audiovisual materials; teacher training models; and parental workshops. He recommended that programs for prevention include professionals, teachers, counselors, and parents and that experts be consulted before prevention programs are implemented. He found that prevention programs that reduce child vulnerability are more empowering than others and also addressed the issue of false reporting.

An investigation by James and DeVaney (1994) revealed that although a large majority of school counselor trainees and school counselors indicated they would report sexual abuse by a stepparent to the authorities as required by state law, only 41% of the trainees and 44% of the counselors indicated they would report suspected abuse by a teacher. The researchers suggested that the underreporting might occur because of concern that staff relations would be disrupted. That concern, the researchers posited, often supersedes counselor and trainee concerns for client welfare or state law. Like families who do not report abuse, school personnel may find that fear of recrimination and loyalties overrides their responsibility. The investigators recommended in-service training so that counselors would understand their "duty to report, proper reporting procedures, preplanning, and the necessity of consultation in all suspected child abuse cases" (pp. 261–262).

De Luca, Hazen, and Cutler (1993) examined the effectiveness of a group counseling program for girls who had endured intrafamilial sexual abuse. The program involved weekly 90-minute treatment sessions over a 10-week period. Self-report measures indicated that those involved in the program had increased self-esteem as well as decreased anxiety. Although no significant changes in loneliness were found, the value of group counseling for these girls was reinforced by the results of the study.

Incest is, for many professionals, one of the most emotionally loaded family dysfunctions. Most professionals have a strong tendency to blame the offender and move to protect the victim. While protection is important, the school professional can best adopt a healing attitude toward these families by recognizing that all of the family members are victims and are involved in a family system that is out of control. It is only through healing and regaining control in the family system that members of the family can move beyond the initial stages of identification into a healthy resolution of the problems. Sobsey et al.'s annotated bibliography of publications related to disabilities and violence (Sobsey et al., 1995) is an excellent resource that professionals can consult for further reading suggestions.

By law, the school professional must report any knowledge of incest to child protective services, and treatment by appropriate professionals must be initiated. Beyond the legal concerns, when a school professional is aware that a family is in treatment, he or she can be most helpful by dealing openly with the family, accepting the role of all family members in the problem, and providing individual support for the student who has been abused. One suggestion gleaned from the mental health field is to refer to those involved in incest as incest survivors rather than incest victims. This minor language change provides an atmosphere of healing instead of one of emotional damage. A quote from Madanes et al. (1995) is useful when thinking about reporting suspected sexual abuse:

> If I believe in personal responsibility and I also believe that the only reality is in action—that not to act is to act—then I must recognize that in my therapy I need to protect human rights and to prevent violence. To avoid action, to remain neutral, is to be on the side of violence and abuse. (p. 9)

In the introduction to their training manual promoting adoptive families as a healing resource for children who have been sexually abused, Minshew and Hooper (1990) wrote:

> Sexual abuse is the ultimate violation of childhood. Not only are children violated physically and denied the right of ownership of their own bodies, but they quickly learn that adults, in most cases parents, cannot be trusted. It is generally acknowledged by psychiatrists, psychologists, and child development specialists that the trust relationship between children and parents is absolutely essential to the children's emotional development, for upon this first trust relationship depends their future ability to give and receive love, as well as their view of themselves as persons worthy of being loved. (p. 3)

Similar issues are addressed in a book edited by Blacher (1994), which focuses on alternative options for children not living with their natural families. A chapter within this text, by Weisz, concerns placement for children who have been abused.

Hollander (1992) focused on making young children aware of sexual abuse. The roles of the school and school counselor were discussed. Curriculum development was addressed, and materials were listed and described.

A book by Trute, Adkins, MacDonald, McCannel, and Herbert (1994), titled *Coordinating Child Sexual Abuse Services in Rural Communities,* provides helpful information on a community-wide basis. Although the book is based on a research project that was not aimed at schools, it is a useful text for understanding coordinated services, particularly in rural communities.

Incest is certainly not the only form of sexual abuse. Children are also victimized by other adults in their lives and by strangers. Schools that help parents know how to prevent child abduction and molestation are providing a much needed service. Fontana and Moolman (1991, p. 27) listed 10 rules for lowering the risk of child abduction and molestation:

1. Always know where your children are and be sure they know where you are. Require them to call you when they arrive at their destination.

2. Never leave your children unattended while shopping.

3. Go to public restrooms with your children or send a trusted person along.

4. Do not leave your children unattended in a car while you are shopping.

5. Be sure your children have adult supervision when they are playing outdoors in secluded places.

6. Provide schools with authorization about who can pick your children up.

7. Be sure your children can make an emergency phone call to the police or operator. Teach them their address and phone number, including the area code.

8. Find responsible baby-sitters who come with glowing recommendations for your children. Ask your children about the baby-sitter and listen to what they say.

9. Teach your children to run away if someone tries to pick them up or to give them a present when they are away from home.

10. Teach your children to say NO to adults who ask for assistance, offer gifts or rides, or offer to take their picture. Be sure they know that they should come to you immediately and tell you what happened should any of those situations occur.

A list such as this can be provided to parents in the form of a printed card, a flyer sent home with other school information, or a newsletter article. In addition, it can be printed on posters placed strategically in the community.

Finally, particularly for younger students, a school curriculum that deals with appropriate and inappropriate touching, privacy issues, asking for help, the expression of feelings, and self-protection may help to increase the incidence of reporting. The school social worker and/or counselor can help with developing such a curriculum.

PRINCIPLES OF EFFECTIVE SCHOOLS AND TEACHERS

Children from dysfunctional families are at risk for failure in school and society. Being at risk means it is tough to beat the odds against you; however, it is still possible to be resilient. It is important for school professionals to be a voice for children beyond the schools so that social policy and laws support research-based means of prevention and intervention. Professionals are inextricably woven into a world that requires no less than an unwavering commitment to making a difference for children and youth who are at risk.

School professionals have children's best interest at heart, but even more is needed. To support changes being made in the United States, professionals may wish to read *The Book of David* (Gelles, 1996), *Save the Family, Save the Child* (Fontana & Moolman, 1991), and *The Vulnerable Child* (Weissbourd, 1996). To make change happen requires no less than becoming an advocate and going beyond the classroom doors. As Edmund Burke said, "All it takes for evil to prevail is for good men to do nothing." As school professionals and citizens, we *can* make a difference.

It is the responsibility of every educator to find ways to lower the risk for failure of students from dysfunctional families and increase the possibility of their becoming resilient. Weissbourd's (1996) principles of effective schools and teachers, presented in Chapter 6, pertains as well to at-risk students from dysfunctional families as it does to students from nontraditional families.

CONCLUSIONS

Children from dysfunctional families who are at risk for academic, emotional, and behavioral problems should be identified early and should be provided with the support needed to prevent or reduce future problems. It is essential that school professionals accept the reality that they will be working with children from dysfunctional families and take steps to help strengthen these vulnerable children (Weissbourd, 1996).

CASE EXAMPLE

Bob is a 14-year-old boy whose father abandoned the family when his mother got pregnant with him. Bob's mother, who works as a clerk at the nearby convenience market on a part-time basis, drinks and is dating an alcoholic who physically abuses her. Bob has come home to find his mother passed out from alcohol. He has also seen her fight with her boyfriend and end up with a black eye regularly. Bob has a 15-year-old sister in foster care because one of his mother's boyfriends sexually abused her when she was 13. Bob feels responsible for protecting his mother so that her boyfriend does not hurt her. He worries about her driving and drinking.

Because Bob has been truant and talks back to authority figures at school, he has been in a class for students with behavioral disorders for over a year. He does have some physical education and exploratory classes, which involve rotating through subjects such as art, music, and foreign language during the 9-week grading periods, with the general education students. Recently, he has been having trouble with the female teachers at school.

Questions and Comments

1. *What family systems concepts described in Chapters 1 through 4 are operational in this family? How do these factors relate to what has been seen in the school setting? Given the information provided, what hypotheses might you draw?*

   Bob is a parentified child as evidenced from desire to take care of his mother. There is an inversion of the hierarchy, with Bob acting more as the parent than the mother. Boundaries are enmeshed, with Bob assuming a spousal role with his mother when he protects her from the boyfriend.

   Bob may be acting out against authority figures at school because he is angry that his mother does not take care of him. Since she is obviously dysfunctional, he chooses not to attack her but to transfer his anger to other women. Female teachers in particular are the brunt of his verbal attacks.

2. *How would you describe this family's dysfunction related to the topics of this chapter?*

   Bob has lived in a single-parent home from birth. It is likely that his family falls in the lower socioeconomic status category. There is likely alcoholism and certainly alcohol abuse in the mother. Bob is witnessing violence and abuse of the mother by the boyfriend. Bob is also neglected by the mother.

3. *To help Bob in school, what might the teacher in the class for students with behavioral disorders focus on?*

    She might first assist him in identifying his feelings. Then, he would benefit from learning to direct them to the right person or by letting off steam in the gym.

    If Bob were to say negative things to the teacher, she could reply, "I don't think I have said anything disrespectful to you. What is going on that makes you seem upset with me?"

    The teacher could also pair Bob with another teacher whom he likes as a mentor. This would provide Bob with a substitute caregiver to augment what is provided to him at home. Another teacher as mentor would allow the teacher in the class for students with behavioral disorders to serve without role conflicts of mentor/caregiver and provide firm, fair, consistent rules.

4. *What might the teachers in the general education classes do to help Bob when he is obviously struggling?*

    If the teachers realize that Bob is "brewing up" (e.g., picking a fight), they can send him to the guidance counselor for a visit or to the gym to use the punching bag. An alternative strategy would be to send him to the principal's office for up to 10 minutes of quiet time, not as a punishment. He would, however, be required to return to class after the 10 minutes if he had not already self-selected back into the class.

5. *How might the teacher in the class for students with behavioral disorders approach the mother?*

    She could ask Bob, "Can I talk to your mom about your being upset that her boyfriend beats her up . . . and that you worry about her drinking?" When meeting with the mother, the teacher could describe the behaviors she has witnessed at school and ask, "How can we work together to help Bob?" Bob may or may not be there at the time, depending upon his preference about being around when the teacher brings up the abuse and drinking. Bob may want to enter at the end of the meeting with the teacher, after the topics have been discussed between the two of them. Because trust is a major issue, it is important not to violate Bob's request for confidentiality.

EXTENSION ACTIVITIES

Reflection: In recent years, the media have focused heavily on the violation of children in our society. Consider situations you have known, heard of, seen in a movie, read about, or experienced in which alcoholism, neglect, abuse, incest, or violence directly affected a child. Simply let yourself recall incidents and your reactions to them, including what you thought and how you felt at the time.

Journal: How has your increased knowledge about the topic of violation of children affected your willingness to suspend judgment of perpetrators? What questions do you still have about the violation of our children?

Excursion: Attend one or more of the following open meetings in your area: Al-Anon, Alcoholics Anonymous (AA), Adult Children of Alcoholics, Adult Children of Dysfunctional Families, Gamblers Anonymous, Overeaters Anonymous, Women for Sobriety, or other Anonymous meetings. Your local newspaper likely lists meeting times and places at least on a weekly basis. Note that you may attend only open meetings unless you are an individual in one of the categories. Call your local AA phone number, and ask if someone can speak with you about attending a meeting. There will probably be someone available who can guide you to the meeting that is most appropriate for your interests.

Journal: Write about your impressions of the Anonymous meeting(s) you attended. What did you think and feel? What was your greatest challenge? What surprised you the most? How could you share your insights with others?

In-Class/Training Discussion: How can you share your insights with others in your class or session. What questions have surfaced from attending the Anonymous meeting(s)?

In-Class/Training Panel Discussion Leader Instructions: Ask for students/group members to volunteer to serve on a panel and speak about their personal experiences related to being in one of the following categories: adult child of alcoholic parent(s); observed violence in the home; abused. Invite each member of the panel to prepare a 5-minute talk about his or her background to be used as a springboard for the question-and-answer session. Those who are not on the panel will write questions they would like answered on cards while the panel members are speaking. A moderator will facilitate the brief background-sharing session and the question-and-answer session. He or she will collect all of the question cards and pose the questions to the panel members.

AND/OR

In-Class/Panel Discussion Leader Instruction: Ask for students/group members to volunteer to serve on a panel and speak about their personal experiences or the experiences of someone they have known closely who fits into one of the following categories of recovery: alcoholic parent, neglectful parent, abusive parent. Invite each member of the panel to prepare a 5-minute talk about their backgrounds to be used as a springboard for the question-and-answer session. Those not on panel will write questions they would like answered on cards while the panel members are speaking. A moderator will facilitate a brief background-sharing period prior to the question-and-answer session. The moderator will collect all of the question cards and pose the questions for panel members.

In-Class/Training Discussion: How has your understanding and way of responding to abuse shifted in your life over time, and to what do you attribute any shift(s) that have occurred? What surprised you the most about what you read in this chapter? What did you find difficult to read or believe? How do you think you could contribute to improving the life of children who experience dysfunction such as neglect, abuse, violence, or incest? What could you do in the school setting to help other school professionals understand and work with such families? What questions do you still have about neglectful, abusive, violent, or incestuous families?

In-Class/Training Speaker Panel Leader Instruction: Have the whole class/group work together to invite a variety of people from the external community who are in recovery from addictions to serve on a panel for the class/group. Have the class/group members write down questions they'd like the speakers to address and send them to the speakers a week prior to their arrival. That way, the speakers will be able to tailor their remarks to the interests and knowledge of the class/group. This exercise is designed to prepare the students/group members to replicate this type of activity for their schools when they are working as school professionals. [If the students/group members do not know how to locate people in recovery, have them call the local AA phone number and ask for assistance in finding such people. If the AA staff is unable to help, have them call a local outpatient provider facility for chemical dependency and addictions. The staff will likely be able to provide names and numbers of potential speakers.]

OR

In-Class/Training Panel of Students Leader Instructions: Find high school students who are willing, able, and stable enough to attend a class/group session and serve on a panel of teens in recovery from addiction. A local chapter of Alateen may be able to ask teens to volunteer to call you. You may want to focus on speakers who are from addictive family systems, speakers who are in recovery for addictions, or a mix of both. Alternatively, you could invite university undergraduate students who are in recovery from addictions to sit on the panel.

In-Class/Training Expert Speakers: In a small group or as a whole class/group activity, work together to arrange for one expert or a panel of experts to come to the class/session to address the dysfunctional areas (addiction, abuse, neglect, incest) covered in this chapter. You might want to arrange for a series of speakers, one of whom could talk for a half hour at each class/session, or you might prefer to have several speakers come at once to cover diverse topics related to addiction, neglect, abuse, and incest. If you have trouble finding speakers, you can call the American Association for Marriage and Family Therapy at (800) 374-2638 to request names of licensed professionals in your area. Be sure to prepare the speaker(s) by discussing the audience characteristics, including their range of experiences, whether remuneration is available, what you would like them to cover and how, whether other experts will be there, what the audience has read concerning the topic, how long their talk should be, and whether questions will be asked. By taking part in arranging this type of activity you will learn what is involved so that you will be able to replicate such activities in the future.

Invitational Principals' Panel Leader Instruction: In a small or large group, arrange for a panel of principals from elementary, middle, and high schools to speak to your class/session about the impact on schools of the at-risk students covered in this chapter. If possible, include principals who represent urban, suburban, and rural schools. Prior to the talks, provide the speakers with similar kinds of information as discussed for the panel on topics related to addiction, abuse, neglect, and incest.

Special-Needs Students From Dysfunctional Family Systems

C hapters 2 and 3 provided a background on the family life cycle and the structural concepts of hierarchy, boundaries, communication patterns, and subsystem functioning. These concepts form the basis for a deeper and more specific understanding of families who have children with special needs. Building upon structural family principles, this chapter provides a framework for looking at how some families become dysfunctional in response to the stresses of dealing with a child or adolescent with a disability. It concludes with a case example of a girl with diabetes who is a member of a dysfunctional family system. While most families having children with disabilities do not fall into the category of being dysfunctional, some do. It is important for school personnel to learn the general characteristics of families that are dysfunctional so that they can better understand and serve them.

INTRODUCTION

The focus in this chapter is on helping the school professional understand the structure of families faced with the particular challenges posed by four broad groups of disabilities: physical disabilities and chronic illness, behavioral and emotional disorders, learning disabilities, and mental retardation. Suggestions for school personnel are provided throughout the chapter. Part III of this book offers additional suggestions for responding to these challenges by presenting applications of the concepts outlined in Parts I and II.

It is helpful for educators to learn the general patterns that researchers have observed in families of a child with recurring behavioral, emotional, or physical symptoms (Fishman, 1993). These include predictable family changes, family reorganization, life cycle adjustments, and, in dysfunctional families, predictable family characteristics. By recognizing these patterns in the families they serve, educators can have more realistic expectations. In addition, this information enables teachers, counselors, principals, and other school personnel to relate to families in a more authentic manner, thus promoting trust and mutuality of problem solving. Parents who hear understanding in the voice of school personnel are far more likely to accept and support their efforts.

Family Changes

When a child is diagnosed with special needs, a number of predictable and important changes occur within the family. Initially, the parents are required to focus extra energy on the diagnosed child to ensure that the child receives help from the available resources. The parents may need to obtain evaluations of the child, medical follow-up, and special tutoring (Buscaglia, 1983; Darling, 1991; Seligman, 1991a; Winton, 1996).

Some writers suggest that another family change occurs when siblings are made aware of the problem. In the view of these writers, siblings are expected to make allowances for the special child (LeClere & Kowalewski, 1994; Powell & Gallagher, 1993; Seligman, 1991c). Research by Meyer and Vadasy (1994) and Coleman (1990, cited in Meyer & Vadasy, 1994) indicates conflicting conclusions in the area of sibling expectations. As the sibling of a brother with a disability, I was expected to make allowances both as a child and as an adult, and thus I agree with the observation of the former writers.

Another change occurs when professionals outside the usual family structure are included in important family decisions. These professionals receive information about the workings of the family that previously had been private (Upshur, 1991). Enmeshed families may find this acceptable; however, it poses a challenge for more rigidly bounded or disengaged families.

In an article dealing with families' levels of meaning associated with stressful life events, Patterson and Garwick (1994) focused on what families view as the cause of the problem and on how families deal with the problem. Families faced with a stressful life event form either an internal locus of control and see themselves as responsible for their life situations or an external locus of control by attributing situations they face to chance or powerful others. The authors indicated that those who believe in chance may not connect well with the health care system. If they believe in powerful others, they may search endlessly for cures or become passive in terms of dealing with the illness. Those who have a high internal locus of control, however, will likely be more active in managing the chronic illness or disability.

When a child is diagnosed with special needs, the family often begins to form a common identity that is related to the child. For example, people may refer to them as "the family with the Down syndrome child" or "the family with the delinquent kid" rather than "the Jones family" or "the lawyer's family." Thus, another development that occurs when a child is diagnosed is the feeling experienced by many families of being stigmatized as a result of the identified child's problem (Goffman, 1963). The more visible and profound the disability, the greater the potential for stigmatizing the family.

Patterson and Garwick (1994) affirmed the family illness identity described by Goffman but suggested that the opposite also occurs. In facing adversity together, the family may strengthen its identity, and shared meaning can evolve from the presence of the disability or illness within the family.

Reiss, Steinglass, and Howe (1993) described the *family paradigm* or *family identity,* stating that it "refers to implicit emotionally charged conceptions shared by members of the same family. . . . These shared conceptions guide and constrain the behavior patterns of the family, setting a stable base for the transactional patterns that provide for the needs of the members" (p. 175). These writers focused on the family's organization around illness.

Another important change that may occur because of the special problems associated with caring for a child with a disability is that parents may begin to feel more tied to their homes and thus more isolated and lonely (Kew, 1975; Tavormina, Boll, Dunn, Luscomb, & Taylor, 1981; Upshur, 1991; Vetere, 1994).

Finally, parents may feel that they have lost control over their lives to physicians, diagnosticians, educators, and counselors (Sloman & Konstantareas, 1990). Heller (1993) indicated, "When faced with stress, those who have low estimations of their ability to cope with upcoming situations and to control their outcomes tend to give up easily and experience high levels of anxiety or depression" (p. 196). Empowering parents is crucial to helping them to regain an internal locus of control and to helping them be better parents for their children.

All of these changes bring both stress and the opportunity for growth and for coming together as a family. Garland (1993) described the positive impact family systems perspectives can have on family adaptation. He emphasized the value of everyone involved by taking the whole family unit into consideration rather than merely focusing on the individual with a disability. It is crucial that professionals hold a realistic and positive view of the child. This viewpoint serves as a model to the family members and helps them realign their perspective by focusing on capacities rather than deficits (Malatchi, 1997).

Family Reorganization

The basic family changes just described begin a process of reorganization in the daily family life and structure that is far-reaching in its implications (Marion, 1992). Just as the movement of the first domino will impact an entire chain of dominoes, the diagnosis of one child with a disability within a family system will affect all of the other members of that system. Adapting to the diagnosis of a child requires flexibility on the part of all family members. Following the diagnosis, boundaries that had been clearly defined are renegotiated, and functional roles of family members change. For example, parents who both work outside of the home and have established patterns for taking care of housework, meals, and errands often must face the challenge of adjusting their schedules so that one parent can be free to take a child to doctors' appointments or special treatment facilities.

It is important that professionals neither minimize the challenges faced nor canonize the parents as saints. Instead, they should show respect as they provide guidance in framing the situation as a challenge (Patterson & Garwick, 1994) and help the family to find personal and family meaning. By doing so, professionals will, again, focus on assets rather than deficits (Malatchi, 1997).

Life Cycle Adjustments

Just as in families of children without special needs (see Chapter 2), effective reorganization of the family around a child with special needs requires changes at each developmental stage of the family life cycle (Heller, 1993). A family with a toddler with a disability will face the struggles of toilet training, setting limits, and nurturing. As the special-needs child becomes a teenager, the family will have to meet the demands of biological changes, independence issues, and identity formation.

As in all families, these varied life cycle demands require flexibility and adaptability. In families with a child having special needs, the life cycle of the family is often interrupted (Marshak & Seligman, 1993) and sometimes arrested at the point of diagnosis (Hughes, Berger, & Wright, 1978; Kew, 1975; Wilchesky & Reynolds, 1986). For these families, the diagnosis is such a crisis that the family is unable to adapt and maintain flexibility. Thus, the family structure "freezes" at the life cycle stage it was experiencing at the time of the crisis.

As discussed in Chapters 2 and 4, the specific process of how a family makes life cycle adjustments will depend somewhat upon the family constellation and sibling position of the child with a disability. A family with four children ranging in age from infancy to 15 years old, the youngest of whom is diagnosed with spina bifida, will have more potential caretakers to share the load than a family in which the diagnosed child is an only child. However, the parents in the former family, to ensure normal development for their older children, will have to juggle car-pooling for various functions, entertaining peers, and other activities with taking care of the infant with a disability. The parent with an only child will have none of those demands.

In addition, the extent of family adjustment will depend upon whether there is a parent available in the home on a full-time basis and the level of social network supports available to the family (Burke & Cigno, 1996; Gallagher, Beckman, & Cross, 1983; Knoll, 1992; Meadow-Orlans, 1994; Seligman, 1991a). Thus, when looking at family adjustments, it is important for the school professional to know something of the makeup of the family of the identified student. Specifically, important information would include numbers and ages of siblings, sibling position of the student, parents' work status, and involvement with extended family. Knowing these pieces of family information, the educator can build the relationships that are essential for collaboration between parents and school.

None of the family adjustments that have been described in this section is a problem in and of itself. In fact, these adaptations of parents, siblings, and professionals are essential when a child presents physical, emotional, or intellectual symptoms. Problems arise in families, however, when these changes become frozen in time. For example, when parents continue to focus the same amount of energy on the special child as they did at the initial diagnostic stage, the child's independence may be compromised (Marshak & Seligman, 1993). When parents continue to expect nondisabled siblings to treat the diagnosed child as different, the siblings will eventually begin to resent the expectations (Powell & Gallagher, 1993), and the child with special needs will end up feeling isolated and incompetent. When professionals continue to delve into the daily life of the family, all family members may begin to feel compromised and intruded upon. In the immediacy of the situation, the normal boundaries between the family and the external systems become more pliant, which may create further stress, especially for families that occupy the disengaged end of the continuum.

Family Characteristics

Teachers, counselors, and other school professionals working with a student with a disability who continues to have difficulties adjusting to classroom demands should look for the following family characteristics, which are symptomatic of chronic family dysfunction (see Chapter 3):

- Dysfunctional family boundaries
- Overprotection
- Lack of conflict resolution
- Parental asymmetry and marital relationship subordinate to parental roles

As with children without disabilities, the presence of these structural characteristics will inhibit the child's school adjustment.

Not all families of children with disabilities experience these dysfunctional characteristics, but when they do, these diagnostic signs are indicators that the family either has not faced and resolved the implications of the child's disability or has not been able to move past the initial adjustments required when the child was first diagnosed. The specifics of how these characteristics manifest themselves differ from family to family. Within areas of disability, however, there are some predictable indicators of family distress that fall into the categories listed above. The following sections are designed to provide the school professional with an understanding of the common struggles faced by families with a child having special needs. Such understanding provides the basis of relationship building that allows for mutual problem solving between families and schools.

PHYSICAL DISABILITIES AND CHRONIC ILLNESSES

In this section, patterns are described that have been observed in dysfunctional families having a child with a chronic illness or physical disability. For the purposes of this discussion, the category "Physical Disabilities and Chronic Illnesses" includes diabetes, asthma, chronic allergies, chronic pain, and mild cases of spina bifida, cerebral palsy, or multiple sclerosis. The impact of more serious illnesses such as cancer, leukemia, or AIDS has not been considered.

The mere presence of a chronic illness or physical disability in a child does not predict whether the family will be dysfunctional (Ferrari, Matthews, & Barabas, 1983; Seligman, 1991a; Upshur, 1991). As Byng-Hall (1995) indicated, it is a mistake to view disability as always leading to dour circumstances (p. 267).

Dysfunctional Family Boundaries

In dysfunctional families in which a child has a physical disability or chronic illness, the individual differences of family members, such as likes and dislikes, opinions, and needs related to age, are often ignored or poorly tolerated. This characteristic is evidence of enmeshed boundaries and an enmeshed system (Marshak & Seligman, 1993). All children may have the same allowance, bedtime, and household rules regardless of age. Typically, little accommodation is made for the different developmental needs of children of different ages. As Liebman, Minuchin, and Baker (1974, cited in Minuchin, 1974), indicated, personal privacy is at a minimum. One 10-year-old child with seizures expressed:

> I went to my girlfriend's house, and she got dressed in the bathroom with the door shut. I couldn't believe it. At my house, you're not allowed to close doors. My parents think if you close a door you're trying to hide something, or maybe I'll have a seizure. What if I just want to get dressed without being seen?

Although the entire family tends to exhibit clear indicators of enmeshed family boundaries (Elman, 1991), the child with the physical problem is particularly vulnerable to the intrusiveness of other family members. In many ways, this pattern is a predictable outcome of having a medical problem. How many of us have commented on the lack of privacy in hospitals and other medical settings? When a child is required to undergo physically intrusive procedures on a regular basis, and his or her physical health and well-being depend on these procedures (e.g., catheterization), the entire family tends to be aware of the child's physical condition. In addition, older siblings, grandparents, and even close friends may be given permission to intervene in the child's physical routine or management. As a result, the child may have difficulty developing normal personal boundaries around hygiene and health.

Teachers may recognize the manifestations of enmeshment in these children. They may, for example, describe in detail the specifics of their physical routine, bowel habits, or eating habits in inappropriate ways in class, identifying themselves as peculiar within their peer network. Teachers need to help these children respect and guard their right to privacy in all possible ways. Any talking about physical symptoms should be done alone with a teacher or counselor, not in the classroom.

Overprotection

The line between adequate protection and overprotection is a difficult one in families with a chronically ill child. In dysfunctional families, the parents tend to be overprotective and have difficulty with the disabled child's natural attempts to become independent (Marshak & Seligman, 1993). Several studies, however, have reinforced the finding that children with chronic illnesses who are not overprotected feel more in control, less depressed, and more competent (Thompson, 1993). Results of a study of 60 children and adolescents with diabetes indicated that the children in families in which independence and participation in age-appropriate social and recreational activities were promoted perceived themselves as more competent and had better diabetes adjustment than the children in overprotective families (Hauser, Jacobson, Wertlieb, Brink, & Wentworth, 1985). Thus, family members who are overprotective may need to be exposed to the research about the impact of overprotection on the child who is chronically ill.

When a child is initially diagnosed with a chronic illness, the parents and family are required to focus almost exclusively on that child's physical needs to the exclusion of themselves and other children (Beckman-Bell, 1981; Heller, 1993; Shapiro, 1983). They are trained to look for physical signs of distress in their son or daughter and to respond to these signs in particular ways (e.g., by monitoring blood sugar or providing medication). Later, when the boy or girl matures and wants to take over his or her personal physical management, the parent who has been in charge may feel rejected or displaced. What is this parent to do with the extra time now that he or she is no longer needed in this way? Parents may need help at this point to develop a more normal, meaningful relationship with their child (J. Hall & Taylor, 1971) as well as to regain a balanced life by taking advantage of opportunities for personal time, obtaining respite, and seeking support from family, friends, neighbors, schools, religious institutions, and community services (Marshak & Seligman, 1993).

Laborde and Seligman (1991), focusing on parents who have difficulty when their child with disability is ready to transition to independent living, stressed that empathy and understanding for the family members' apprehension are critical. It is also important to help the family members focus on the continuity that will be maintained through contacts and the activities they will engage in with their child, just like what will happen when their other children leave home.

Overinvolved parents of children with a chronic illness or physical disability will often call teachers to make special requests on their child's behalf. It is very common for such parents to ask that their child be excused from physical education classes or certain classroom activities. Frequently, their action is in response to their child's complaint about gym suits, heat, dirt, or any of the uncomfortable aspects of the classroom—normal complaints for children their age. Rather than excusing the child, the teacher should integrate the child into the physical education and classroom plan through adapted exercises. Teachers must do what they can to prevent parents from perpetuating absenteeism because of their overprotective stances (Sexson & Madan-Swain, 1993). The important role for educators in these situations is to recognize overprotection, withhold judgment of parents, empathetically help parents see what is happening by normalizing their child's complaints, and maintain a firm policy of using only medical opinions to excuse students from any classroom activities.

Lack of Conflict Resolution

Other common characteristics of families having a child with a chronic illness are the avoidance of conflict and prohibition toward displaying anger (Elman, 1991; Koch, 1985). Some children become embroiled in forming a coalition with one parent against the other (Elman, 1991). However, detouring the expression of angry feelings in this way only solidifies the family pathology. As noted by Elmer (1991), "It is in avoidance of conflict that some families become overinvolved with a disabled child" (p. 384).

The members of dysfunctional families with a child who has a disability typically have difficulty expressing any wants, needs, or feelings other than physical discomfort. Again, because individual differences are ignored, how can an individual have a want or need that is different from that of the whole? Quite often, family members other than the child with a disability will have numerous physical complaints, such as headaches, stomachaches, or backaches. It seems that the physical dimension is the only one in which family members can express differences. School personnel should observe such occurrences to see if they eventually become part of a pattern that might suggest the need for counseling or outside referral for a student and his or her family.

As noted earlier, anger tends to be avoided in families with a child who has chronic illness or physical disability (Elman, 1991). Expressions of anger by the child are typically reinterpreted as expressions of physical discomfort. A child with diabetes explained, "Whenever I get upset, everyone starts to check my blood sugar. I must be low or high, I can't just be mad."

When conflicts do surface, they are usually ignored, with little opportunity for resolution. As a result, it is common to find long-held resentments in these families that have never been adequately discussed or understood. Their difficulty in dealing with anger often leaves family members feeling isolated from one another and from members of their social networks.

Children from these families will not typically pose a behavior problem in the classroom. Rather, they will frequently complain of physical symptoms, which often can be traced to a difficult interaction with a peer, teacher, or family member that was not settled. When possible, educators should attempt to help the child see those connections. An example of a question to pose is, "Joey, have you noticed any connection between when you have a stomachache and what is happening at home?"

Parental Asymmetry and Marital Subsystem

Finally, there is often an imbalance of parental roles in relation to the child with a disability. One parent, typically the mother, has usually taken over primary management of the child, and the other parent is usually underinvolved (Laborde & Seligman, 1991; Wickham-Searl, 1991). The parent who is in charge of "nurse duty" usually feels overwhelmed and misunderstood, while the other parent feels excluded. These dynamics understandably make for poor communication between the parents and emotional distance in the couple. Often school personnel reinforce this asymmetry by contacting the mother to discuss issues regarding the child rather than including both parents. Educators need to make every effort to include both parents in meetings and phone contacts.

In families with a child having a chronic illness, the marital subsystem is usually subordinate to all other subsystems. An early study by Tew, Lawrence, Payne, and Rawnsley (1977) reported a divorce rate in families with a child having a physical disability that is twice that of matched control families. Some studies cited by Laborde & Seligman (1991) dispute that finding, whereas studies by LeClere and Kowalewski (1994) and Upshur (1991) lend support to it. Singer and Nixon (1996) indicated that having a child with a disability results in the marital dyad being strengthened as well as impaired.

Parents having children with chronic illness or physical disability often feel compelled to put the disabled child's needs first, other siblings' needs second, and their own needs last on the list of priorities. As discussed earlier, this dynamic may be adaptive in the initial stages of the child's diagnosis and adjustment but becomes dysfunctional when it continues after the child has become more capable and mature. These parents may be willing to offer any amount of time to attend special school activities with their child or provide homework supervision, yet they may not have had time alone with their spouse for a vacation or even an evening for years. Teachers who are aware of this dynamic may suggest that the parents go out to dinner or lunch together before or after a school conference. By asking simple, probing questions and reinforcing parental time together teachers may help these families become aware of a new possibility in their relationship. Teachers can also refer the families for respite care in the community.

Some families having children with chronic illnesses or physical disabilities resemble psychosomatic families in terms of family patterns (Elman, 1991). Problems with family boundaries, overprotection, conflict resolution, and/or the parental and marital subsystems will exacerbate episodes of illness in the children. For this and other reasons it is important that dysfunctional families having a child with physical disabilities or chronic illness receive the counseling they need from a family systems counselor.

Many dysfunctional families having a child with a chronic illness or physical disability will not demonstrate all of the structural characteristics described in this section. The family dysfunction may be expressed in only one area or will be more obvious in one area than another, such as overprotection. The description of these characteristics is intended to give the educator a framework from which to observe and understand the family of a child with chronic illness or physical disability as well as to help the educator formulate some ideas of how to deal with the everyday manifestations of these characteristics in the classroom.

BEHAVIOR DISORDERS AND SOCIAL MALADJUSTMENT

The wide variety of symptoms that fall within this category precludes identifying many specific family characteristics. There are some broad patterns, however, that tend to characterize dysfunctional families with a child presenting behavior problems.

Dysfunctional Family Boundaries

Boundaries in dysfunctional families having children with emotional or behavior symptoms tend to be either enmeshed or disengaged. M. P. Nichols and R. C. Schwartz (1995) indicated that family members in enmeshed families are overreactive and intrusive, and the boundaries are diffuse. They stated, "Enmeshed parents create difficulties by hindering the development of more mature forms of behavior in their children and by interfering with their ability to solve their own problems" (p. 218).

Amatea and Sherrard (1995) summarized the typical enmeshment process of delinquent children and those with behavior problems. They characterized the family's enmeshed boundaries as tight and interlocking, with family members hyperaware of one another's emotional reactions. The result is triangulation of a third family member. For example, two family members disagree, a third joins one side or the other, and the issue is never resolved. The authors described the parents as intrusive, overinvolved, and overprotective or overrestrictive. R. J. Green (1989) indicated that when one or both parents are overinvolved, the symptoms in the child include "obsessional worry, performance anxiety, procrastination, passive-negativism, or oppositional behavior in reference to academic tasks" (p. 194).

Enmeshment is typically present in families in which a child is chronically depressed, in a repetitive conflict with a parent, or involved in the marital conflict of the parents (Safer, 1966). Enmeshed boundaries are indicated when, metaphorically, the child gets cut and the mother bleeds. In these families, when children are asked how they feel about something, a parent may answer for them. Language contains frequent references to "we" instead of "I." The parents tend to be overprotective in the same way as parents of the chronically ill are, involving themselves in the child's homework, style of dress, and choice of friends. The parents view indicators of normal differentiation or independence in their children as rebellious.

Enmeshment was clearly evident in a family seen for family therapy in which the 8-year-old daughter had crying spells. She would frequently cry at night, complaining about how difficult school was for her and how alone she felt. Her mother's response was to sit up talking with her daughter until the child finally fell asleep. Then the mother, who was also depressed, would stay awake all night worrying about her daughter's unhappiness. The next day, when the child was too tired to go to school, the mother would become angry at her.

Enmeshment is also apparent in single-parent families where the identified child has taken over the role as emotional supporter and confidant for the custodial parent. Due to the responsible nature of the parentified child (W. C. Nichols, 1996; Whetsell-Mitchell, 1995), school personnel may not actually view him or her as needing intervention. In reality, the child needs as much assistance as the acting-out or aggressive student. Family counseling may be necessary to help restore the appropriate parental hierarchy.

Families with disengaged boundaries are at the opposite end of the continuum from those with enmeshed boundaries. They can be characterized by excessive emotional distance and failure to mobilize support when it is needed (M.P. Nichols & Schwartz, 1995). The parents may not notice that their child is depressed or having problems in school until the problem is extreme and warranting a major intervention. R. J. Green (1989) indicated that these children have trouble with both attention and conduct. The parents often become very controlling and are inconsistent in enforcing rule infractions as well as the consequences of breaking rules. Depending upon their mood, they might let something slide or punish the child severely for the same infraction.

Parents with disengaged boundaries may provide few limits and be underreactive to their children's behavior (Fox & Savelle, 1987). In this type of family a child who steals may be described as "having this little problem with borrowing things." With children who externalize anxiety by acting out, the parents typically tend to ignore signs of difficulty until a crisis occurs or the problem is pointed out to them by someone outside the family. School personnel who observe parents as being distant and uninvolved with their child generally recognize that a problem may exist. The challenge is to help the families of these students see, with new eyes, the reality of the situation before it requires referral for special education.

Overprotection

In any family, overprotection can lead to problems in the children. Minuchin and Nichols (1993) described the situation in which the parent steps in to resolve small quarrels between siblings. Such overprotectiveness creates dependency and stunts growth in problem solving as well as negotiating. This type of situation can lead to the child never learning to fight his or her own battles.

A paradoxical form of overprotection can occur when children act out and are identified by the school or court authorities. The parents in these situations often feel compelled to protect their children from these outside influences (J. C. Johnston & Zemitzsch, 1988). The children thus have the parents' covert endorsement and avoid facing the consequences for their behavior. This type of overprotection operates externally to the family, with outside agencies or the school. As described in Chapter 4, this process involves triangulation between the student, the parents, and an outside authority. These triangles limit the emotional functioning of the student with a behavior disorder. Generally, overprotection in families of children with behavior or emotional disorders does not operate internally or around personal boundaries as it does in the families of children with chronic illnesses.

An example of how this type of overprotection might play out is provided by the following scenario. A student steals another student's watch. The parents know the truth but staunchly protect their child by offering some excuse. They might, for example, suggest that the other student forgot to retrieve the watch he had asked their child to hold. Generally, the parents exhibit anger toward school personnel in these instances.

In families with enmeshed boundaries, the overprotection tends to work in a different way. Instead of angrily lying, the parents would react as if they themselves had been accused of stealing. They would deny the possibility of their child stealing, and the thought of investigating that possibility would not likely cross their minds. These parents would tend to react defensively to contact by school personnel by withdrawing and becoming unavailable for discussion or mutual problem solving. Prior awareness of dysfunctional family boundaries may help the school professional plan contacts that take into account the family climate of overprotection.

It is important for school personnel to state the facts and corroborate observations among personnel. The principal must be careful to not become triangulated or to side with the family against anyone they might blame. Detriangling, which is discussed in Part III, is critical to effective interactions with these families.

Lack of Conflict Resolution

In dysfunctional families in which there is a child or adolescent with emotional or behavioral symptoms, the expression of anger and conflict tends to take one of two inappropriate forms. One of these forms is exhibited in families in which there is a high level of internal chaos and the parents tend to feel overwhelmed with the tasks of providing for and structuring family life. In these families, the parents are highly reactive to any expression of anger or potential conflict in their children. Discipline may be punitive or abusive in nature (Kamps & Tankersley, 1996), and the parents may be physically or verbally abusive of one another as well (M. J. Hanson & Carta, 1996; Minuchin et al., 1967). Educators may notice that these parents call their children names when trying to set limits on their behavior or when confronted with the slightest difficulty on the child's part. This type of family dynamic is usually multigenerational in nature. Families that exhibit this type of behavior may benefit from referral for outside counseling (H. Anderson & Goolishian, 1986).

Marital discord and divorce contribute to the disruption of parent-child interactions in these families (Kamps & Tankersley, 1996). Although professionals do not see divorce as the critical factor, the amount and intensity of conflict, as well as any violence that may be experienced or witnessed, will contribute to dysfunctional relationships. Another parental factor contributing to behavior problems is maternal insularity. What emerges from this dynamic are negative social contacts with the community and extended family, linked with the mother's belief that friends will not support her. Wahler and Sansbury (1990) recommended therapy for these mothers, as their children will be at risk for considerable emotional problems unless the mothers respond to therapeutic treatment.

The second type of difficulty with conflict resolution that is often seen in families with a child or adolescent with emotional or behavioral symptoms is the avoidance of anger and conflict resolution at all costs (M. P. Nichols & Schwartz, 1995). Enmeshed families will deny the conflict by "bickering, which allows them to vent feelings without pressing each other for change or resolution of the conflict" (M. P. Nichols & Schwartz, 1995, p. 219). Disengaged families will distance themselves from one another and avoid personal contact. In both types of families, children are taught, either covertly or overtly, that to be angry is to be bad. In contrast, feelings such as sadness, depression, or hurt are seen as acceptable and deserving of parental attention and intervention. Thus, any conflict or anger between family members is denied or expressed indirectly. Unresolved long-term resentments, however, may result in acting-out or chronic depressive symptoms that professionals will then witness in school. Referral for counseling may be in order because of the long-standing nature of the problem.

Parental Asymmetry and Marital Subsystem

In many families in which a child has an emotional or behavioral problem, considerable discord exists between the parents about the definition and handling of the problem. Bowen (1985) indicated that the three ways dysfunction is expressed in families are through fighting, through the parents projecting the problem onto the child (child-focused projection system), and through the development of illness (including addiction) by a family member. Students with behavioral disorders and social maladjustment are seen as products of a child-focused projection system. Bowen also indicated that the healthiest form of dysfunction was for the parents to fight with one another.

Parents may demonstrate a diversion of conflict by each spouse pulling the child in a different direction, leaving the child confused (Minuchin & Nichols, 1993). For example, the mother may identify her son as "depressed" while the father may view the son as "lazy." Playing struggles out in this way represents a combination of Bowen's child-focused projection system and marital conflict and often is a symptom of more extensive marital difficulties. School personnel confronted with differing parental views must avoid taking sides in the dispute. It is important to elicit input from both parents. The parents may be willing to learn to work together for the benefit of their child, whereas they would not be motivated to settle their differences solely for their own happiness. Here, as in other situations described, the marital subsystem takes a back seat to the functions of the parental subsystem.

In this section dealing with behavior disorders, references have been made to a wide variety of children's problems and symptoms that may be observed in the school. Family dynamics have also been described to help familiarize you with some of the ways in which problems are manifested in dysfunctional families. These descriptions are not intended, however, as exhaustive examples of all the possible ways family dysfunction may be exhibited. When school professionals become aware of family dysfunction in families with children with behavior or emotional disorders, a referral for counseling made in a sensitive, nonjudgmental manner is important, as is having available a list of referral sources in the area.

LEARNING DISABILITIES

The category *learning disabilities* includes many different types of learning problems and consequent behaviors. Children with learning disabilities range from those with severe disabilities who cannot function in a normal classroom to those who are mild underachievers, receiving C's and D's when they are capable of making A's.

The structural dynamics in families of children with learning disabilities depend upon when and how the diagnosis of learning disability was made and severity of the disability. Unique to this category of special needs is the elusive quality of the disability. In contrast to, for example, diabetes or mental retardation, children with learning disabilities may have experienced difficulties that have gone undiagnosed for years (Abrams & Kaslow, 1977).

Often these children have experienced a series of failures that have led them to feel insecure, poorly motivated, and ignorant. Parents and teachers may have been involved in a variety of attempts to correct the child's school failures, including homework monitoring, behavioral checklists, punishment, and coaxing (Sloman & Konstantareas, 1990).

A study by Rasku-Puttonen, Lyytinen, Poikkeus, Laakso, and Ahonen (1994) examined maternal communication in mothers with children with learning disabilities. They found that these mothers gave less exact instructions as well as more ambiguous messages to their children than did mothers whose children did not have learning disabilities. The boys with learning disabilities did not, however, request clarification any more than the boys without learning disabilities did. Thus, it is important to help these mothers with their instructions to their children.

Dysfunctional Family Boundaries

The possibility for poor communication between families and the school system is greater in this disability area than in any other due to the subtlety of the diagnosis ("Our Son Has Had Trouble," 1986). Frequently, parents have seen more than one outside professional about their child's problems and may have requested various evaluations of the child that resulted in little or no progress. Without an understanding of the child's disability, parents may blame teachers for poor instruction and classroom management (Kottman, Robert, & Baker, 1995), and teachers may blame parents for inconsistency or lack of support in an effort to explain a child's school failure. A letter from a mother of a child with a learning disability illustrates this cycle of blame:

> His nursery school teacher said I babied him because he couldn't button or zip. . . .
> His kindergarten teacher said I should discipline him more because he was too lazy
> to learn his letters and numbers. His first-grade teacher called one parent conference
> after another. I tried to help Henry sit still and learn his letters. . . . [My husband]
> says I spoil him. . . . His folks say, "A few good spankings will set him straight."
> Mother says I just need patience. Dad says, "He's all boy." . . . The pediatrician says
> . . . he's a late bloomer. . . . I'm trying everything I know how to do. I'm exhausted
> from trying. (S. L. Smith, 1981, p. 150)

In these families, boundary problems often arise between the family and external resources. From their history of involvement with the school system and other professionals, the parents and the child with special needs may have developed a "we/them" mentality. Often, the family's external boundaries become rigid and inflexible, which may lead to a sense of isolation for all family members. School professionals observing this situation should remain patient, validate their justifiable concerns, and continue to strive for alliances with these types of families.

Overprotection

Some parents with a child having a learning disability are overprotective and show enmeshed boundaries (Amerikaner & Omizo, 1984; R. J. Green, 1989). These family dynamics frequently appear in situations in which the diagnosis of the child was delayed and there has been confusion or conflict between the parents and the school system. Many times, but not always, these students have overall levels of intelligence in the average or low-average range and may have been identified as *slow learners* or as having *mental retardation*. The parent who feels that his or her child does not have retardation, having seen evidence of the child's intellectual abilities in the home, may feel compelled to protect the child from teasing, labeling, and incorrect school placement.

R. J. Green (1995) wrote, "In these families, the parents tend to be too involved and too controlling of the child's school performance—taking over, cajoling, pressuring, demanding, dominating. The child may be perceived as 'lazy' or as 'weak and incompetent'" (p. 219). He also indicated that the over involvement of the parents in the child's schoolwork usually backfires.

Overorganized, enmeshed parents of children with learning disabilities have been described as negatively impacting their child's school performance (R. J. Green, 1992). Parental overinvolvement leads to worry, performance anxiety, and procrastination in the children around academic tasks. Either the overinvolved parents assume too much responsibility and the children with learning disabilities assume too little responsibility for achievement, or the children rebel.

Another example of overprotection can be seen with the most serious, severe, and all-encompassing disabilities such as dyslexia (Perosa & Perosa, 1981). A child who has a high score on an intelligence test but who cannot read will usually be diagnosed early in the schools. Due to the student's high intelligence, it may be difficult for parents to reconcile themselves to the fact that their child cannot read normally. They may overprotect their child by lashing out at the schools for poor instruction or programming (L. B. Silver, 1984). It is important for teachers to remain patient with these parents until the parents learn enough about their child's disabilities to understand the symptoms.

As with other disorders, parental protection and advocacy may be important and adaptive following the diagnosis of a learning disability. When the parent continues to be overprotective, however, long after diagnosis and placement issues have been resolved, dysfunctional family dynamics will ensue. Referral for counseling is likely the best course a school professional can take.

Conflict Resolution

The longer a child has school problems with an undiagnosed learning disability, the more likely the child, parents, and school professionals will be frustrated and angry with one another about the struggles around the child's problems. Because of the frequent challenges school personnel face with "resistant, angry, and uncooperative" parents, Kottman et al. (1995) investigated the perspectives of parents of boys with attention-deficit/hyperactivity disorder (ADHD). They found that most of the parents saw schools in a negative light. They concluded that ADHD is associated with high stress in parents, which negatively affects their interactions with school personnel as well as their child's performance. They encouraged counselors to design programs that would help the parents of children with ADHD communicate more successfully with school personnel and recommended that they give the following suggestions to parents:

1. At the beginning of every year, go in and meet your child's teacher and discuss [your child's] behavioral and academic difficulties. Be ready to discuss specific strategies that have worked in the past to help your child become more productive in the classroom.

2. Make arrangements with your child's teacher to provide concrete feedback on your child's behavior and academic progress on a daily basis. One method that works for this is a note that the teacher sends home every day describing the day's behavior, homework, and any other important information.

3. Do not always side with your child in every dispute with the teacher. Remember that your child is difficult to live with and is also difficult to teach.

4. Ask the teacher if he or she is willing to establish some kind of reward system to reinforce your child for on-task behavior.

5. Suggest to the teacher that your child works best if he or she is allowed to have some type of "sanctioned" movement at least once every hour. If the teacher will build sanctioned movement into the class, your child will have less of a need to move in ways that require discipline. (p. 149)

Parental Asymmetry and Marital Relationship

The stress of identifying and dealing with a child having learning disabilities tends to intensify any parental disagreements or lack of cohesion (Kottman et al., 1995). Frequently, one parent is well versed in the nuances of the child's diagnosis, while the other parent has only a vague idea of how the child's learning disability affects his or her educational performance. Because of this difference, the parent with the most knowledge tends to be the primary person who helps the child with remediation or organization. Bearing this dysfunctional system in mind, school professionals should work to ensure that both parents receive copies of diagnostic reports, attend planning meetings, and have an opportunity to ask questions about their child's disability.

Because of the link between learning disabilities and motivational problems, many parents will have experienced problems with discipline issues. One parent may feel that the child is trying his or her hardest and should be reinforced for trying, while the other parent may focus on grades and assume a lack of motivation. Behavioral systems may have been tried and failed, leaving both parents feeling as if they, themselves, are failures. These types of conflict may lead to increased distance between the couple and less focus on the positive aspects of the marital subsystem ("He Pits Jane and Me," 1988).

School professionals working with families of students with learning disabilities need to observe, probe, and use their experience with each family to get a clear picture of the underlying dynamics of acceptance and integration of the student. Educators should not assume that what families present on the surface is the complete picture of their struggle or dynamics in relation to the student.

MENTAL RETARDATION

When discussing structure and dysfunction in families of children with mental retardation, at least two broad subgroups must be considered: children with milder retardation and children with more severe retardation. With the current movement toward inclusion, general educators can anticipate more interaction with families who have children with milder as well as more serious forms of mental retardation. Therefore, information concerning the family dynamics of both groups is provided here.

Dysfunctional Family Boundaries

All parents with children who have been labeled as having *retardation* must go through a process of dealing with the realities of their child's limitations and altering their hopes, dreams, and expectations for a "normal" child (Kew, 1975; Laborde & Seligman, 1991;

Marion, 1992; Strom, Rees, Slaughter, & Wurster, 1981; Vetere, 1994). With children having milder retardation, parents may notice some differences in their child as compared to other children or some delay in developmental milestones, but they may continue to deny the reality of their perceptions until the child reaches school age and is identified by an outside professional. For children with more severe forms of retardation, it is likely that the diagnosis was made soon after the child's birth and that intervention was begun in infancy. The family situation with a child diagnosed with retardation is ripe for enmeshment and for the family to identify having a child with a disability as the central important characteristic of the family, which leads to the loss of personal identity.

Within families in which boundaries are weak and the structure enmeshed, there is often an understanding that the child with retardation will never leave home and be on his or her own. Siblings may be expected to assume parental responsibility (Vetere, 1994). Family members may be apprised of their future responsibility for the child, and family plans are made with the understanding that the person having retardation will be a permanent member of the nuclear family. Older siblings may be told early on that it will be their responsibility to support this child and to take him or her into their households when the parents can no longer provide the necessary support ("I'm Not Going to Be," 1987).

The dynamics of enmeshment are particularly evident when working with teenagers with retardation. Professionals will find that the parents frequently deny the implications of peer relationships, sexual development, and vocational issues for their child. For example, many parents do not assume the responsibility for providing guidance regarding interest in members of the opposite sex, sexual protection, or basic family life education that they would normally provide to their nondisabled children (J. Beavers, Hampson, Hulgus, & Beavers, 1986). From a study of the sexual knowledge and experience, as well as the feelings and needs, of individuals with mild intellectual disability, McCabe and Cummins (1996) reported that these individuals have not been given the necessary information and that they have a higher incidence of unwanted pregnancy and sexually transmitted diseases than nondisabled individuals. Their lack of knowledge in this area indicates that their families may be overprotective.

Overprotection

Despite the fact that family members are reminded daily that the child with retardation is not "normal" and that adjustments must be made to accommodate his or her disabilities, the extent to which the retardation will interfere with the child's life depends, in large part, on how far the family will be able to go in helping the child be treated as normally as possible (Heller, 1993; Mink, Meyers, & Nihira, 1984). Overprotective parents often believe it is cruel to push a child with retardation to reach for achievements that may be outside his or her capabilities. So the parents set in their own minds what they consider to be the limits of the child's functioning. Unfortunately, their assessment may underestimate the child's potential and work to keep the child within those limits. Further, parents may believe that their child will be ridiculed or used by society if they are not there to protect him or her. If the overprotective parent communicates fear of the world to the child, then the child will be disabled not only intellectually but also socially.

Vetere (1994) offered an alternative interpretation of overprotection in parents of children with disabilities. She indicated that parents may feel hostility and guilt about the disability, with corresponding feelings of rejection toward the child. Overprotection may be a defense against these feelings. Vetere indicated this dynamic usually leads to infantilization of the child with a disability.

Dudley (1983) conducted an interesting sociological study of 27 adults labeled as having retardation, in which he lived with each of the individuals for a period of time so that he could experience their lifestyle firsthand. He found that those who had been allowed to openly discuss the realities of their retardation, the realities of societal fear and stigma about retardation, and the demands of adulthood were more likely to be able to adjust than those who had been overprotected.

When dealing with overprotective parents, school personnel should observe without judgment and help the parents to free their child gradually from their own fears. Providing an arena for children to openly discuss such questions as "What does retardation mean? Will I always have retardation? How can people tell that I have retardation?" with their parents may help to improve family communication.

Lack of Conflict Resolution

In an extensive longitudinal study of 104 children with more serious retardation and their families, Nihira, Mink, and Meyers (1981) found that the most important factor in the school adjustment of these children was the harmony and quality of parenting. Based on this information, it is clear that conflict resolution is an important skill for parents of a student with retardation.

School professionals may find two types of dysfunction in the area of conflict resolution in families of students with retardation. One type of dysfunction involves parents who have few or no skills in advocating for their children with retardation. Some of these families have multiple problems (M. J. Hanson & Carta, 1996), including cultural deprivation, poverty, and intellectual slowness on the part of the parents. Professionals may find that these parents act very compliant and agreeable during discussions but then fail to follow through with school requests or training programs.

These parents tend to have few assertiveness skills and may feel that attempts to disagree with school personnel or even to ask questions will not help to change their situation. Often, these parents are accustomed to heavy questioning and to complying with agency rules in order to obtain food for their children, shelter, and medical help. Their nonassertiveness may have developed in response to these other experiences. School professionals should help these parents formulate and express questions and disagreements, communicate their unique perceptions of the child, and develop a mutual working relationship with the school system over time. School personnel may also provide parents with help in networking. For suggestions about networking, see Chapter 9 and Appendix D.

The other dysfunctional pattern that is common in these families is a heightened level of conflict with agencies, schools, and any professionals who are involved with the student with retardation. Typically, the conflict with schools centers around placement issues and labeling during the student's school career. Families with this dysfunctional pattern often direct a high level of general anger toward people outside and/or within the home. As a result, the families tend to be isolated and have little social network involvement to help with the child having retardation. From my experience the intense anger appears to be a mask for overwhelming sadness and guilt that the parents feel toward their child. Because emotional expressiveness in families with a child having retardation is often limited (Margalit & Raviv, 1983), the parents may have had no one with whom they could express their feelings of sadness and guilt. Over the course of years, they may have begun to project blame onto outside sources in an effort to avoid looking at their own feelings of blame and doubt.

Parental Asymmetry and Marital Subsystem

Families with a child with retardation tend to develop the classic situation in which the mother accepts primary responsibility for the child's management. As M. Berger (1984b) stated:

> Because the task of arranging for the youngster's treatment falls mostly on mothers, a predictable structure for families . . . is one in which there is a very close mother/child dyad. The closeness of this dyad is reinforced by the fact that when agencies that serve handicapped children seek "parent involvement," they tend to mean mother involvement. (p. 144)

This intense closeness is particularly evident in families with a child with retardation because the long-term training in many functional living and personal hygiene skills for people with retardation typically falls into the mother's domain. Thus, the close-mother/distant-father dynamic that was discussed as troublesome in families of students with other disabilities easily evolves in families having a child with retardation (Laborde & Seligman, 1991).

Corrales, Kostoryz, Ro-Trock, and Smith (1983) interviewed and observed 24 families with children having intellectual and developmental delays. They reported significant marital distress in 16 of the 24 couples. In addition, in almost all of the families with high marital distress one parent had formed a coalition with the child who had a disability. School professionals can help parents to become aware of this dynamic over time and to develop strategies for intervening on their own behalf.

Another process that often occurs in couples with a child having retardation is mutual blaming, guilt, and grieving (Laborde & Seligman, 1991; A. L. Turner, 1980; Vetere, 1994). Asking themselves the question, "Why do we have a child with retardation?" one or both parents will often look to genetic history or prenatal care and focus blame on the other parent. Of course, some of this questioning and wrestling with themselves and with God is a natural part of the process of accepting a child with disabilities. It is when this dynamic continues over a prolonged period that marital distance and dysfunction are inevitable.

Vetere (1994) related a study by Carr that focused on mothers of Down syndrome children and the mothers' views of the effects of those children on their family lives. The mothers reported that they carried significant burdens; that they had less time for their other children; and that their marriages were negatively impacted. Compared to the control group, the mothers of the Down syndrome children had significantly poorer health as well as higher rates of depression.

Couples need to be helped to understand that the process of grieving for the lost "normal" child and feeling angry about the reality of having a child with retardation are predictable stages for parents of children with disabilities. Rather than turning on each other, the couple needs to be helped to turn to each other for support and resolution of the grieving process.

Poyadue (1993) referred to the stage parents reach after they have moved through the typical steps of grieving and anger as the "all right" stage. She framed this stage as going beyond acceptance, for now the family realizes the disability is *all right*. She cautioned professionals against leading family members to see the child as negatively impacting their family.

Support groups are invaluable in helping parents with acceptance and grieving. Information about the availability of these groups can and should be provided by schools. Parent Helping Parent (PHP), a parent-directed family resource center, is another effective support for families in California (Poyadue, 1993). Further, there are 55 statewide Parent Training and Information Centers (PTIs) that are funded by the federal government. Any of these can be contacted by school professionals for information about services offered. (See Chapter 9 and Appendix D for further information on referring parents to external resources.)

H. Berk (1993) provided charts on skills achieved by children with mild and moderate mental retardation. The skills were further divided into those learned by the end of elementary school and those learned by the end of high school. Such a listing might be helpful for parents. It can help them know what they can expect so that they hold neither unrealistically high nor unrealistically low expectations for their children.

As a final note, general educators may wish to network with special education professionals who are more familiar with these family dynamics in order to develop a better understanding of families having children with retardation. Inclusion of these students provides an opportunity for consultation and cohesion between staff from various educational disciplines. Such networking often results in learning on all fronts.

SUMMARY

This chapter has provided a framework for assessing dysfunctional patterns in families having a child with special needs. Four broad categories of students with special needs were discussed: those with physical disabilities and chronic illnesses, those with behavior disorders, those with learning disabilities, and those with mental retardation.

The following case example pulls together the content of this chapter by tracing one family through the four structural concepts (dysfunctional family boundaries, overprotection, lack of conflict resolution, and parental asymmetry and subordination of the marital subsystem) that have been highlighted. This example is not intended to indicate how a school system should specifically intervene with a family presenting these symptoms.

Instead, its purpose is to provide the reader with experience in integrating information and observations for the purpose of hypothesizing about the dynamics of a particular family.

CASE EXAMPLE

This case example involves the family of 11-year-old Nora, a sixth-grade student. Nora, the youngest of two children, had been diagnosed with insulin-dependent diabetes at the age of 8. Her older brother, a senior in high school, was described as a model child. He played on the school football team, was an A student, and participated in student government. His plans for the future included attending college, and he had already received early acceptance notices from two colleges. In contrast, 11-year-old Nora was viewed as a very difficult child. Her grades were in the low C range with occasional D's and F's, despite testing that indicated an above-average IQ. Nora had few friends and was somewhat overweight.

During the current school year, Nora had been absent from school an average of once per week. In addition, she had frequently asked to leave the classroom to go to the school clinic due to what she described as "low blood sugars." At these times, the school nurse would give her orange juice or a protein snack, if necessary. The nurse would also call Nora's mother, a former nurse, to receive instructions. Recently, Nora had been going to the clinic on the average of three times per day. Needless to say, this time out of the classroom was contributing to her poor grades. When Nora's mother was contacted by one of Nora's teachers about her missed work, the mother became indignant because the teacher would not agree to require less work of Nora due to her frequent absences. The mother had then called the school principal about the "unfair treatment" her daughter was receiving. At that time the principal called a meeting of Nora's teachers.

Based on information they received over the year, the team of Nora's five teachers and the principal made the following observations about the family structure.

Dysfunctional Family Boundaries

The father, who owned his own business, worked long hours and was essentially unavailable for family time. He appeared to have a better relationship with his son than with Nora. He regularly attended his son's football games but was not involved in his son's other activities or in providing significant emotional support to him. The mother had always been the backbone of this family's life. Prior to Nora's diagnosis with diabetes, she had been very involved in both her children's achievements and had worked part-time as a tutor. She had been president of the booster club at her son's high school and had led her daughter's Girl Scout troop.

After the diagnosis, Nora had become this mother's mission in life. Nora no longer attended Girl Scouts because she felt that the other girls made fun of her because of her diabetes. On a daily basis the mother began to cook specific meals at her daughter's request in an attempt to keep her blood sugar in check. The mother quit her job because she felt she had to be available for intervening in her daughter's blood-sugar monitoring. Nora had begun to have tantrums at home when she did not get her way. The mother identified these outbursts as "high-blood-sugar attacks" and would try to calm Nora by giving her what she wanted. As the mother became more involved with Nora, the father became more distant. He felt that the mother's approach to his daughter was "spoiling" her and making her "weak." The mother felt that her husband did not understand the medical implications of diabetes and thus could not provide sound judgments about managing Nora's behavior.

Overprotection

Previous to the diagnosis, Nora had played on a soccer team and had attended Girl Scouts. Following her diagnosis, she quit both of these activities and began to spend more time at home. Her mother often allowed her to stay home from school because of the slightest physical complaint. Over the past 2 years, Nora had become less functional with peers and more dependent on her mother in all areas of her life. The mother's request to be called by the school nurse each time her blood sugar was monitored was another example of the overprotection. The school nurse was highly trained in diabetes management, and Nora's blood sugar level was often found to be normal despite her complaints. The mother's attention to these "spells" only served to reinforce Nora's dependence.

Lack of Conflict Resolution

Rather than Nora's parents openly arguing about or discussing their differing opinions, the mother had become more involved with protecting Nora, and the father had become more involved with his business and with ignoring his daughter's complaints. Although the son may have resented the changes in his family due to their handling of his sister's illness, he had not expressed his feelings to either parent. He had also adapted by becoming more involved in his own activities and life outside the home.

When Nora reported that she felt she was being "made fun of" by her peers in her Girl Scout troop, her mother allowed her to quit going to Scouts rather than to help her reach some resolution in her relationships. The mother was very reactive to any perceived mistreatment of her daughter by peers, teachers, bus drivers, or extended family members. Her way of managing her anger was to keep Nora out of school as often as possible, to drive Nora to school so she would not have to deal with the driver or students on the bus, to instruct Nora to avoid peer interactions, and to withdraw from extended family relationships. All of these choices indicated that conflict was avoided rather than resolved.

Parental Asymmetry

The mother had taken over sole management of Nora's life, while the father had withdrawn from interaction. The mother made all significant decisions regarding the physical and emotional functioning of the family. No one within the school system had ever spoken with or met the father. Although he was a respected businessman in the community, he had little power in influencing the day-to-day workings of his family.

Marital Relationship Subordinate to Parental Roles

Although the school personnel had little information about Nora's parents' relationship, they could hypothesize that it was not going well. The parents had not been out of the home together in the 2 years since Nora's diagnosis since Nora felt she was too old for baby-sitters and her mother would not allow her to stay home alone due to fear of a blood-sugar crisis. It was probable that the father's anger toward his wife because of her unavailability to anyone other than her daughter, and the wife's anger toward her husband because of his withdrawal from family life, contributed to significant tension and distance between the couple.

Questions and Comments

1. *What are the dysfunctional characteristics of this girl's family? What information did you use to diagnose these dysfunctional components?*

   This family displayed enmeshed boundaries between the mother and Nora and disengaged boundaries between the father and Nora. [Cite evidence.] The family also showed indications of problems with conflict resolution both within the family and in dealings with the outside world. [Cite evidence.]

   Nora's mother was extremely overprotective of her daughter following her diagnosis with diabetes. [Cite evidence.]

   Within the family, it appeared that the parents had avoided dealing with their basic differences about management of Nora. [Cite evidence.]

   It was clear that the balance of power between this couple was very one-sided. [Cite evidence.]

2. *What intervention strategies could be used by the school to help change this family's dysfunctional structure? Develop your own ideas before reading the example below.*

   The team of Nora's teachers and the principal could request a meeting of both of Nora's parents with all of the school personnel involved with Nora. At this meeting, they might ask the mother, because of her nursing experience, to provide in-service education to all of them regarding diabetes, its management, and its complications. The teachers could ask specific questions about symptoms of low and high blood sugar so that they could feel comfortable dealing with Nora in the classroom.

   In addition, the teachers and school nurse could present an intervention plan to the parents for dealing with Nora's frequent trips to the school clinic. Each time Nora went to the clinic, her blood sugar could be monitored and the level written in a log to be sent home at the end of the day. Nora would carry the log with her at all times so that, if she asked to leave a classroom, the teacher could check the log for the time of her most recent blood-sugar monitoring and the intervention. The parents would be asked to agree that monitoring Nora's blood sugar more often than once every 2 hours was not necessary unless Nora was exhibiting severe physical symptoms (which could be described by the mother in the meeting). If Nora asked to leave the classroom and she had been checked within the past 2 hours, her request could be refused. If she insisted that she was experiencing a "low," she could be given a container of orange juice that each teacher would keep in the classroom. In addition, each time that Nora did visit the clinic, both parents would be called with a report on her blood-sugar monitoring. The father could be asked to carry a beeper so that he could be reached at his office or while on outside calls. The parents could be asked to agree that each night before Nora went to bed they would look over her blood-sugar log with her and discuss any questions.

Finally, the teachers could send home a weekly progress report for Nora in each subject. If Nora had a weekly average of B or above in any class, she would receive reinforcement from the teacher of that particular class and from her parents. This intervention would replace some of the negative attention that Nora had been receiving with more positive time with her teachers and parents.

EXTENSION ACTIVITIES

Journal for those with prior professional experience: Reflect on past experiences you have had with dysfunctional families of students having special needs. Using hindsight, view these families through a family systems lens. Then write about the kinds of dysfunction you now see these families had. How do you think your new understanding will make a difference in your professional role in the future?

Journal for those with no prior professional experience: You may have read novels or biographies in the past about individuals with disabilities. Consider one that presented enough information about families for you to use the family system lens to determine the types of dysfunction present. You may not find dysfunction, but at least look into and write about the areas described in this chapter.

In-Class/Training Exploration: [The instructor or group members should bring in copies of case studies of students with chronic illnesses, behavior disorders, learning disorders, and mental retardation.] Using case studies of students with special needs, identify any family dysfunction, noting examples of dysfunctional family boundaries, overprotection, lack of conflict resolution, parental asymmetry, and marital subsystem dysfunction.

In-Class/Training Discussion for those with prior professional experience: Without going into long case study information, describe examples or vignettes of each of the dysfunctions discussed in this chapter (i.e., family boundary dysfunction, overprotection, lack of conflict resolution, and parental asymmetry and marital subsystem dysfunction).

OR

In-Class/Training Discussion for those without prior professional experience: Describe hypothetical examples of each of the dysfunctions discussed in this chapter (i.e., family boundary dysfunction, overprotection, lack of conflict resolution, and parental asymmetry and marital subsystem dysfunction). Your examples should include chronic illnesses, behavior disorders, learning disabilities, and mental retardation.

In-Class/Training Discussion: How can school principals, counselors, social workers, and psychologists benefit from an understanding of the four dysfunctions presented in this chapter?

Deliberation and Preparation: As a professor or in-service trainer, where could you locate additional information on the dysfunctions covered in this chapter to use in classes/training? Who are some speakers (or who might know of some) who could meet with your students? If your students do not have prior experience with families with these dysfunctions, who are some people they could interview for information on dysfunctional families of students with special needs? What are some novels (or who might know of some) you could use as examples to highlight dysfunction in classes/training? What are some videos or movies (or who might know of some) that could be shown to highlight different dysfunctions?

Reflection: As a principal, how could you disseminate the information presented in this chapter to your staff members? What further information do you feel you need about dysfunctional families of students with special needs and how can you find it?

Resiliency and the Village

Resilience in at-risk children and youth has become a topic of interest within the field of education during the last two decades. Studying resilience in children who would otherwise be expected to fail in school or life provides us with clues for helping children and youth who are living under similar circumstances. What is resilience? Simply put, resilience is about *beating the odds* (Haggerty, Sherrod, Garmezy, & Rutter, 1994; Masten, Best, & Garmezy, 1990; Wang & Haertel, 1995). Peng, Wang, and Walberg (1992) found that about 19% of students who are at risk are resilient. As caring educators, our challenge is to increase the number of children who fall into the resilient category. Protective factors, or buffers, were found to be associated with recovery in high risk populations (Garmezy, 1991; Werner & Smith, 1992, 1998).

This chapter on resiliency and the village serves as a bridge from the second to the third parts of this book. It includes both the primarily descriptive focus of Part II and the application focus of Part III. Resiliency is associated with family systems models that this text covers (D. R. Hawley & DeHaan, 1996; H. I. McCubbin, M. A. McCubbin, A. I. Thompson, & E. A. Thompson, 1995; J. M. Patterson, 1997; G. E. Richardson & Hawks, 1995; F. Walsh, 1996). Resilience is a valuable topic for this text because it focuses on the positive that can accompany challenging life circumstances (Cowan, Cowan, & Schulz, 1996; Kaplan, Turner, Norman, & Stillson, 1996). Clearly, the village relates to family systems concepts, in particular with regard to family resources.

In writing the second edition of this text, the greatest change I noticed in the disciplines that intersect in this book is an even greater dedication to focus on the positive. Educators, mental health professionals, sociologists, as well as their professors are focusing on possibilities and abilities; shared meaning, values, power, and experience; as well as the importance of developing an internal locus of control within students and their families.

At times, I wondered if this emphasis on the positive was a Pollyanna means of dealing with tightening budgets, shifting interests on the part of society, or a denial of overwhelming pain in the face of perceived hopelessness. My conclusion is that, indeed, *if you train your eye to look in the right direction you will see much beauty.* I consider myself to have been a resilient child who overcame many family life and personal challenges. Nietzsche wrote, "That which does not kill me makes me stronger." Perhaps all of us who succeed are resilient and have something to offer in our stories of resiliency (Henderson & Milstein, 1996). All of us have painful stories others would never guess . . . stories like those told by the girls of the Phoenix Group, adolescents in a residential treatment program who are working to *beat the odds* and are being taught by a teacher who has beaten the odds in spite of adversity. So, where we choose to train our eyes and the example that gives to others become important in our efforts to increase resilience. The eye to the positive is a voyage of discovering how our vulnerable children can rise from the ashes like the phoenix of mythology.

Professionals who have beaten the odds and risen from the ashes can make excellent models, especially when they speak from experience, offer compassion, and have chosen *a path with heart* (Shepard, 1995). This chapter is about them and for them. It is about our communities joining to be part of the whole, serving not as islands but as part of the main. In being allowed the opportunity to give, we are vital links in the chain, and we know it—we are valuable.

Research demonstrates that resilient individuals beat the odds because they recover from or adapt to stress and problems found in life (J. McMillan & Reed, 1994; W. A. Rhodes & Brown, 1991; Werner, 1986, 1989, 1993, 1994, 1995). Educators benefit from knowing what protective factors contribute to resiliency so programs can be reinforced, thereby increasing resiliency (Garmezy, 1991).

Today, school personnel speak about a school population in which the dropout rate reaches 30 to 50%, in which more and more students are impoverished, are classified for special education, come from various ethnic and cultural backgrounds, and have academic difficulties in our schools (Barr & Parrett, 1995). At the same time, our economy is becoming less tolerant of individuals without skills and the ability to learn and adapt. If the schools do not address the at-risk population effectively, the consequences for at-risk children and our society are clear. With the growing numbers of at-risk children and youth in America (Barr & Parrett, 1995), we must find ways of helping our schools and communities increase the numbers of resilient, as-risk students. Increasing resiliency among at-risk children is a community responsibility, rather than the school's responsibility alone (Garmezy, 1991; Waddock, 1995).

Many have written on resiliency and children. This chapter reports aspects of resilient children and successful school programs (Garmezy & Rutter, 1983; Haggerty et al., 1994; Henderson & Milstein, 1996; Hetherington & Blechman, 1996; Joseph, 1994; W. A. Rhodes & Brown, 1991; Wang & Gordon, 1994; Weissbourd, 1996). As part of ongoing research conducted by the Metropolitan Educational Research Consortium at Virginia Commonwealth University, Westfall and Pisapia (1994) provided a brief on at-risk students. Factors they found to be characteristic of at-risk students were covered in Chapter 1 of this text. In this chapter, protective factors that are related to resilient at-risk students are described in terms of personal factors, family factors, and school factors. That description is followed by characteristics of successful school programs. The remainder of the chapter is devoted to increasing resiliency by promoting the wise use of resources from many contexts, including family, social supports, school-community, and the community at large. School professionals are encouraged to help develop a caring community (Noddings, 1995).

FACTORS RELATED TO RESILIENT AT-RISK STUDENTS

This section describes three areas that are related to resilience: personal factors, family factors, and school factors. Understanding these protective factors will enable professionals to influence and develop programs and interventions within schools and communities. All are pertinent to at-risk and special-needs students, each is reviewed.

Personal Factors

Resilient children have been described by teachers as social, optimistic, energetic, cooperative, inquisitive, attentive, helpful, punctual, and on-task (Sagor, 1996). They laugh at their own mistakes (Young-Eisendrath, 1996). The resilient child has a personality, manifested in early childhood, that elicits a positive response from others. These children are affectionate, good-natured, cuddly, and easy to get along with (J. McMillan & Reed, 1994), and they actively seek out relationships (Wolin & Wolin, 1996). As they grow older, they play alone and with others comfortably, and as they seek challenging experiences, they appear to be self-reliant and have little fear. They use art, play, and humor as creative outlets that help them escape painful circumstances (Wolin & Wolin, 1996).

They also request and receive help from adults when required (Werner, 1984, 1992, 1994, 1995). Positive reciprocity emerges at an early age. Resilient youth reach out to others assuming they can receive help. Thus, their affirming attitude results in responsiveness from others. Resilient children view the world as positive in spite of challenging circumstances. Their positive attitude relates to respect for others, being prepared for school, volunteering, and being at ease with school (McMillan & Reed, 1994).

Additionally, resilient at-risk children have an internal locus of control and are highly motivated to succeed (Henderson & Milstein, 1996). They feel personally responsible for their success, which they view as their own (J. McMillan & Reed, 1994; Wolin & Wolin, 1996). They do not blame others or their environments (external locus of control) for their failures or their situations. They have clearly defined goals that are articulated in a mature manner, and they recognize the importance of goal-setting as a method by which they can improve their situations. Thus, mastery of new experiences is important for all at-risk students. Teachers who provide self-fulfilling activities for their students also reinforce an internal locus of control.

Resilience is seen in the potential individuals have for creative development (Young-Eisendrath, 1996). Resilient students often seek refuge from their troubled environments in extracurricular activities. These activities may keep them away from potentially detrimental activities such as drug abuse. Resilient youth welcome alternative positive experiences such as sports and academic clubs (McMillan & Reed, 1994). Working successfully in groups with peers and emerging as a leader within one's peer group can be rewarding for the resilient child or youth. The recognition associated with extracurricular activities can motivate students to participate. Teachers can do much to enhance belief in the student's ability to succeed.

Choosing to volunteer is another personal factor related to resilient children and youth (Henderson & Milstein, 1996). Werner (1992, 1994, 1995, 1997) spoke of the importance of required helpfulness at home. Other volunteer opportunities are tutoring, helping in the home, and visiting nursing homes. Having a purpose that aids others is associated with resiliency (Keith, 1997; Werner & Smith, 1992, 1998). Young Eisendrath (1996) wrote of the desire as well as ability to "feel and understand the needs of others" and "the ability to compromise and to delay meeting one's own desires in order to meet the needs of others" (pp. 71-72). Equally valuable in extracurricular activities and volunteering alike is the exposure to a positive adult who leads or facilitates the activities and serves as a role model for resilient behavior. This factor is described in a later section of this chapter.

The personal protective factors of resilient children and youth help them find success in the face of adversity. They have achieved a wisdom that allows them to engage life's meaning as well as their personal limitations (Young-Eisendrath, 1996). Resilient children in dysfunctional and abusive homes have the capacity to develop insights about their circumstances and don't blame themselves for their family's troubles. They seek safety for themselves by creating physical and emotional distance from unpredictable parents and find productive activities to fill their time (Wolin & Wolin, 1996). Some at-risk children from families having a parent who has a psychological disorder are able to maintain a sense of separateness from their parents, making peace with them and assuming a resilient life (Rak & Patterson, 1996; Werner, 1994, 1995; Werner & Smith, 1992).

Though peers may struggle in school as well as daily life, the resilient child emerges from a stressful environment able to cope successfully. Resilient children are the kind of people that other people want to be around. They survive and thrive despite the odds against them. A resilient child is our modern-day phoenix. This child rises with much to teach us about life, and, if we listen and observe, we will more ably serve all children and youth and their families.

Family Factors

Family demographic factors are not predictive of resiliency. Children in intact families have no higher incidence of resiliency than single-parent families do. What influences resiliency is a strong parent-child relationship and support (Hetherington & Blechman, 1996). Parental commitment gives the family a sense of coherence. Out of this family experience, resilient children learn to feel that life makes sense and that they can exercise control of their lives. This sense of meaning is basic to their motivation.

Receiving family support is another important protective family factor that can promote resiliency in children (Liontos, 1991). Parents of resilient children have higher educational expectations for their children, which in turn influences the children's achievement orientation; and resilient children have more of the necessary tools and materials for learning at home and are more frequently taken to community educational activities than are those who are nonresilient (Henderson & Milstein, 1996). Undereducation of parents does relate to nonresiliency. Werner and Smith (1992, 1998) reported that mother's educational level impacted resilience at age two. Peng et al. (1992) found that fewer than 11% of children were resilient in families in which the parents had not earned a high school diploma. Of students whose parents had at least a high school diploma, 23% were considered resilient. These findings alone point to the need for parent training in low-income and high dropout areas.

A hallmark of resilient children is that, at an early age, they seek out and access adults whom they can trust (Hetherington & Blechman, 1996; J. McMillan & Reed, 1994; Rak & Patterson, 1996; Werner & Smith, 1992, 1998). Trust is established in the early years. It forms the building blocks for later life adjustment at school, translating to reciprocal relationships with teachers and other role models. It is difficult to "exaggerate the importance of anchors in their lives—children and adults outside their families who are caring and attentive over time" (p. 63, Weissbourd, 1996).

Parents, though important, are not essential to building this trust. Other adults may provide the necessary ingredient. These other adults often become as close as family. Many resilient adults recount stories of a special neighbor or teacher who took an interest in them (Wolin & Wolin, 1993). This connection made the children feel confident in their ability to build other strong relationships.

A personal recollection from a resilient adult follows:

> I remember when it seemed as if everything in our family life was a struggle. My father was ill and had to retire in his 40s. My mother was overwhelmed with the responsibilities of her nursing job, my father's heart attacks and strokes, and raising us kids. When I was in sixth grade, my father went into the hospital, and the day he got out my mother went in.
>
> A friend of my mother's, Elena, stepped in and filled some empty spaces in my life. Elena continued to be an important person in my life throughout life. I can still hear some of the things she would say, and they serve as guides to me today. She was fun to be with and had lots of advice about dating.
>
> When my grandmother died, Elena was right there with me at eighth-grade graduation while my mother was at the funeral across the country. She was also right beside me a few months later when my dad died. Even today I think of her as one of the most important influences in my life. She was a teacher of mine in grade school and for life. She taught me a lot about people and how to lighten up. I don't think I would have made it without her presence in my life.

School Factors

Children who are resilient find support outside of the home (Werner, 1997; Werner & Smith, 1992, 1998). This often takes the form of support in school. Resilient children usually get along well with their peers and have at least one close confidant from their school. They have an informal network of people whom they can access in crisis as well as for help in academic and other areas (McMillan & Reed, 1994).

These students like school though they may not want to be labeled as gifted because that might conflict with their peer relationships. They become involved in learning and find that school goes beyond the academics. Resilient children usually are involved in extra-curricular activities and find them to be supportive, providing a sense of belonging and increased self-esteem (Werner, 1984).

Service learning has become a major thrust in education, and taking advantage of the opportunities it presents will help build resiliency (Henderson & Milstein, 1996; Keith, 1997). Resilient students often mention that teachers and other school staff have provided personal interest in and support for them (Geary, 1988; Coburn & Nelson, 1989) that influence them to succeed. Resilient students find the interpersonal relationships as well as the competence of these adults to be important (Geary, 1988). The resilient student wants teachers to demonstrate caring, respect them for who they are, be able to get along with ease, listen without being intrusive, take them seriously, be available and understanding, provide encouragement, and share humor. In terms of competence, the resilient student wants the teacher to foster group goals, listen beneath the surface before disciplining, be fair in grading and instruction, encourage success, and know them academically and personally (McMillan & Reed, 1994). Schools have the opportunity to increase protective factors.

CHARACTERISTICS OF SUCCESSFUL SCHOOL PROGRAMS

Richard Sagor (1996) identified five attributes that schools can integrate within the curriculum to encourage resiliency: competence, belonging, usefulness, potency, and optimism. Sagor asserted that educators must incorporate these attributes in educational experiences. This is neither difficult nor time consuming. Sagor (1996) pointed out that teaching and resiliency-building are the same. Educators continue to do what already works—what already helps instill resiliency within students.

Ten attributes of successful programs have been identified for at-risk students (McMillan & Reed, 1993; Westfall & Pisapia, 1994). These ten categories, expanded upon in the following pages, are related to characteristics and challenges faced by at-risk students.

Early Intervention

As has been learned from experiences such as Head Start and special education (Fewell, 1995), early educational experiences in quality preschool programs can serve to decrease school failure stemming from poverty (Berrueta-Clement, 1984, cited in Trachtman, 1991). Early monitoring of progress and providing assistance can help at-risk students avoid the all too frequent school failure and high drop out rates associated with challenging life circumstances. Early education has been related to better intellectual performance, reduction in the dropout rate, and reduction of placement in special education (Trachtman, 1991). Early educational intervention can also unlink negative family patterns and habits from low school success rates and increase early exposure to resiliency-building factors.

School Climate

A welcoming and pleasant school atmosphere will help students enjoy coming to school and increase the likelihood of their success. Noddings (1995) wrote that personal manifestations of care are "more important in children's lives than any particular curriculum or pattern of pedagogy" (p. 676). Cooperative learning (Johnson & Johnson, 1994), a sense of belonging (Edwards, 1995), and a positive environment (Mullis & Fincher, 1996) can be encouraged through alternative and enrichment activities, total school programs, more direct contact with teachers, counselors, and administrators, and the use of positive reenforcement. Lewis, Schaps, and Watson (1995) wrote of developing the child's ethical and social aspects through a caring community. They said formation of trust and mutually satisfying relationships are important features of schools.

School Personnel

The teacher plays a significant role in creating a positive school climate and in motivating students (Hetherington & Blechman, 1996). Teachers must be positive and believe that they and their students can be successful. To be successful, school professionals must be flexible, approaching each student as an individual with different needs, providing activities that lead to the development of an internal locus of control and a positive self-image, and offering students visible touchstones of their success. School professionals do well to keep themselves focused on the positive and the possible rather than on deficits. Thus, we must include students in creating a classroom community through classroom meetings, problem solving, and democratic procedures (Lewis, Schaps, & Watson, 1995).

Small Class and School Size

Class and school size affect how much individual attention a school professional can provide, how flexible the professional can be in meeting individual needs, and how quickly a teacher will be able to notice and address problems as they develop. Small classes make it easier to provide a positive school climate and to interact personally and in a timely manner with parents, resulting in fewer behavior problems and higher achievement (Achilles, 1996, 1997; Finn, 1998).

Beyond class size, Sergiovanni (1995), focused on size of high school, reiterating Goodlad's findings in *A Place Called School,* and the value of smaller schools. Wynne and Walberg (1995) seconded this value on smaller schools, especially intimacy in education that can be developed more easily in smaller schools. According to Weissbourd (1996), many larger high schools are "creating more personal environments—environments in which children spend the bulk of their day with the same group of teachers and students" (p. 63). He pointed to their clustering students with teachers as well as the creation of schools within schools and houses within schools.

Parent Involvement

When parents work with their children to prepare them for preschool, the children experience fewer difficulties when they do enter school. Counselors can impact growing families when they work with parents of students who have preschool siblings. Later, parents should be invited to be participants in their child's education both at home and in the school building (Slavin et al., 1996). James Comer (1996) focused on families and schools, eventually developing a model for the nation that is holistic in nature. Empowering parents as co-planners in their child's education is an effective way to increase their participation and to encourage them to reinforce academic activities at home. Special education, with its emphasis on parental involvement, is a model that general education can borrow for at-risk families (Pell & Cohen, 1995).

Counselors can advocate for meaningful family involvement in the schools by helping teachers and administrators recognize its importance and overall positive impact on adjustment, achievement, and self-esteem of students (Christiansen, 1997). Henry (1996) challenges us to communicate with parents in ways that encourage collaboration, value diverse perspectives, and utilize problem solving to benefit the child.

Self-Esteem Building and Support

Increasing self-esteem is critical with at risk-students (Joseph, 1994). The first step in increasing self-esteem may be finding an area in which a student can be successful and recognizing the student for the success. This can serve to hook the student on success. Positive reinforcement for valued behavior should be a continual focus. Success in academics is paramount for building self-esteem in students.

Volunteer projects and service learning can provide students with opportunities to feel good about themselves and their ability to contribute to their worlds (Keith, 1997; Lewis, Schaps, & Watson, 1995; Yoder, Retish, & Wade, 1996). Including students in decision making also helps to build a sense of ownership and control in the school community. Groups led by counselors can focus on increasing self-esteem/self-efficacy of students (Sonnenblick, 1997).

Guidance and Mental Health Counseling

Schools should provide opportunities for counseling support for students as well as their families, both at school and in the home (Edwards & Foster, 1995; Rak & Patterson, 1996). Confidentiality must be maintained and meetings held discreetly so students and families remain comfortable with the process. Counselors who remain creative, flexible, and non-judgmental can work successfully with this population. Brief, solution-focused approaches should recognize cultural diversity. Consultation services (Kaplan, Turner, Norman, & Stillson, 1997) are invaluable with at-risk families and students.

Social and Life Skills/Vocational Education

Good vocational programs as well as social and life skills training make education relevant to students and increase their feeling that education is worthwhile (McMillan & Reed, 1993). Students involved in vocational education tend to complete school. Also, vocational classes tend to provide many of the positive attributes described earlier, including smaller classes and positive classroom climate.

Prerequisites for school success are having and using social skills (Sugai & Lewis, 1996). Counselors can use the group context effectively to help students who come to school with insufficiently developed social skills to develop appropriate human interaction skills.

Although some (e.g., Barr & Parrett, 1995) question the success of vocational and career education programs with at-risk students, others (McMillan & Reed, 1993; Westfall & Pisapia, 1994) indicate that students involved in vocational education tend to complete school. They also related that vocational classes tend to provide many of the positive attributes described previously, including smaller classes and positive classroom climate. Teachers and counselors are in a unique position to point out these advantages to the family and students who are at risk for school failure. They can also be instrumental in countering the stigma that vocational education has in some communities. Comprehensive career guidance programs, coordinated by the counselor, should include community and family involvement and emphasize social and life-skills.

Extracurricular Activities

Many positive benefits are associated with extracurricular activities, including a sense of belonging and community, as well as a greater opportunity to pursue interests and learn new things, both of which can increase student self-esteem (Geary, 1988; McMillan & Reed, 1994; Werner 1984). After-school activities provide students with a safe, supervised atmosphere. Evidence cited in a review of at-risk students, by McMillan & Reed (1993), also suggests that extracurricular activities decrease the likelihood that a student will drop out of school.

We do have to do more than offer these activities, though, because at-risk youth often do not feel connected to the school community. School personnel need to invite and encourage youth to participate and recognize the importance of positive leisure activities in developing resiliency. Extracurricular involvement must be seen as an integral part of the education experience that fosters resiliency and wellness.

Easing Grade Level Transitions

Because students tend to drop out of school when they are making the transition between grades and school levels, such as between middle and high school, it is important for schools to provide activities and services that prepare students for and support them through the transitions. The counselor's role in this is paramount. Assistance with transitions and orientation of students, a traditional counselor role, fosters resiliency in students. Looping teachers with classes across grades is another way of dealing with transition problems (Lewis, Schaps, & Watson, 1995). Noddings (1995) encouraged this practice as a means of strengthening relationships. Small groups providing support for students who are retained a grade level are effective in countering the sense of loss and failure that students may experience when they are retained.

Together, these 10 characteristics of school programs can serve as a guide for educators to increase resiliency in students who are at risk for failure. Chapter 6 presented additional principles for teachers and for schools that also serve as a guide for educators. School programs alone, however, will not foster resiliency to the extent desired. The environment beyond the school must be actively engaged as well (Waddock, 1995) if we are to increase protective factors (Werner & Smith, 1992, 1998) and foster resilience.

RESOURCING AND CREATING COMMUNITY

A child's behavior is influenced by many factors, including environment, biological constitution, disposition, and developmental level. This section focuses on the role that environment plays in fostering resilient behaviors by increasing the protective factors in at-risk families.

Systems theory holds that behavior is affected by many interrelated systems. Thus, change in one subsystem—for example, the community—will reverberate throughout other interrelated systems such as the classroom and schools. Contending that resilience "provides a conceptual base for an intervention that calls for responsive classroom, school, and community environments" Wang and Haertel (1995, p. 159) made clear the importance of community joining with schools to build resilience in youth. School counselors are naturals to serve a coordinating function (Keys, Bemak, Carpenter, & King-Sears, 1998) for creating community.

One of the most successful methods for encouraging resiliency is to create a school community that is positive and fosters a sense of belonging (Wang, Haertel, & Walberg, 1994). The African proverb says, "It takes a village to raise a child." In postmodern America the heart of that village is the school. Through collaboration with external resources (businesses, volunteers, retirees, YM/WCAs, mosques, synagogues and churches, as well as social-service agencies), schools have the opportunity to become the hub of a community that links and provides services that support and enhance everyone's efforts to raise healthy and whole children (Fowler & Corley, 1996). Resourcing and creating community provides for the exploration of opportunities that schools offer to strengthen the proverbial village through linking families and students to professional service providers and, perhaps more important, through creating a supportive and nurturing community by which students and families are connected in a caring manner (Lewis, Schaps, & Watson, 1995; Noddings, 1995; Wynne & Walberg, 1995). Such opportunities increase the protective factors, or buffers, that augment resilience (Werner, 1992, 1993, 1994, 1997).

Rationale for Creating Community

There is no better time than now for transforming our communities to build resiliency in children and youth. Our society is on the edge of possibility. Our families are changing demographically, and technology has revolutionized our worlds of home and work. Yet the rise of poverty, crime, sexual promiscuity, drugs, and depression has made it difficult for families and schools to support and care for the nation's youth the way they once did. Zill and Nord (1994) and Waddock (1993) concluded that families today are less able to provide nurturing, supportive, safe, and secure environments where children can develop and learn. Communities must take stock and rearrange our resources to help children grow up to become responsible and actively productive members of this society (Dryfoos, 1994).

With the intention of building better learners, school personnel have an opportunity to lead the way as family and child advocates.

With a vision of social transformation, educators can become partners not only in the development of a child but also in the preservation and development of the entire community (Booth & Dunn, 1996; Dryfoos, 1994). For schools to achieve such partnership, Haas (1993) suggested that schools must move away from the factory model of production with raw materials and move into a new era where they adopt the metaphor of family resource schools—where schools, as extensions of a child's family, provide the scaffolding for the child's growth that was once provided solely by relatives and neighbors. This will require a shift of attitudes about the roles of the school and of school personnel that must expand and evolve to meet the needs of the at-risk population. Comer (1996) provides a model for holism that involves all aspects of the lives of children. The text is titled "Rallying the Whole Village: The Comer Process for Reforming Education." School counselors have been challenged to become advocates for school and community partnerships and to coordinate networks of resources for children and youth who are considered at-risk (Hart & Jacobi, 1992). Schools must go beyond the traditional "three Rs" and include the teaching and nurturing that parents have traditionally been expected to provide. Counselors and other school personnel must also reach out to parents through parent education, training, and support groups.

Schools can focus on and assist families as well as help them to link with community assistance for their developing children. Although schools cannot be all things to all people, they must become more things to more people than they have in the past. Schools are in a unique position to help increase resiliency in children and youth by becoming part of a cohesive community that meets the needs of families of at-risk and special-needs students. This is critical, not only for individual students and their families but also for the continued health and viability of our society. As an outgrowth of the work of The National Commission on Children, Nicholas Hobbs (1975) wrote *The Futures of Children,* in which he indicated that by not acting in the present generations to come will suffer from our neglect. Further, Hobbs saw investing in children as a national imperative. This point is as appropriate as it was in 1975, and the evidence of Hobbs' grave warning echoes through our cities and our people.

As mentioned in Chapter 2, the presence of a support network is one of the most important protective factors in family adjustment during life-cycle changes and stresses. Schools can encourage support and should act as liaisons, linking at-risk and special-needs students with public and private institutions, businesses, churches, retirees, and volunteers interested in and capable of providing services. The heart of the service is in the relationship that is formed, and relationships are best formed through interpersonal contact (Beck, 1994). The heart of service is in the relationship that is formed through interpersonal contact (Noddings, 1995). Schools can and should diagnose needs, collaborate and network, and share information as well as resources. They must also keep in mind that it is relationship that builds resiliency (Noddings, 1995). Mentoring, lunch buddies, Big Sisters/Brothers, tutoring by retirees, e-mail pen pals that link students with professors, and similar experiences will provide opportunity for the relationship building that fosters resilience (Rak & Patterson, 1996).

Schools must become part of the fabric that *gives back* to the community. Native-American cultures emphasize giving back (Attneave, 1982), and those who give to others are held in highest regard. Service learning provides an opportunity for the school to connect with the community (Keith, 1997; Kleinbard, 1997). A class of adolescent students might, in a program for troubled youth, provide tutoring to kindergarten children, who benefit from hearing stories from supportive people. These same adolescents may be visited by senior citizens from the nearby community for retirees who can share with the experience of gardening. Werner (1992, 1994, 1995, 1997) spoke of required helpfulness and its positive impact on children and youth. In this way all involved benefit and realize the vital part they play in community life. In community we are inexorably linked with one another in ways that are critical, yet we often forget the importance of sharing, community, and relationship—the human connection that gives meaning to our lives (Noddings, 1995). A gentler nation is one that is aware of its potential and in touch with its soul, connected across generations.

Coleman (1987) concluded that the success students experience in parochial schools could be attributed to the crossing of generations encountered by religious organizations. "They are among the few in which the social capital of an adult community is available to children and youth" (p. 37). Therefore, community involvement is important for the success of children in school and as adults. Schools have to take a proactive stance to include citizens of all ages in meaningful relationships with children and youth, and members of the community must view themselves as central to the school's mission (Waddock, 1995).

At times, families need access to professional resources from the community. The goal of resourcing or referral is not to encourage family dependency on outside resources. Nor should families be expected to solve all their problems alone or be responsible for meeting all the needs of its members. Services are provided with the goal of reminding each family of its own resources, so that, working together, the family members can draw out, through mutual clear and honest communication, the strengths, knowledge and wisdom that are already there. The underlying belief here is reflected by the poet Gibran (1923) in the section from *The Prophet* titled "Teaching."

> No man can reveal to you aught but that which already lies half asleep in the dawning of your knowledge. . . .
>
> If he is indeed wise he does not bid you enter the house of his wisdom, but rather leads you to the threshold of your own mind. . . .
>
> For the vision of one man lends not its wings to another man. . . . (pp. 56–57)

Frames of Reference

The professional's understanding of the concepts of family resources and deficits will affect his or her plans for, as well as interactions with, family members. The family may not be able to interpret the professional's attitude; however, when they deal with professionals who respect and view them as resourceful and consult with them as equal partners, trust is more likely to develop. To focus on the resources of an individual and family, the professional must assume that each family has a wealth of assets that can be tapped (Dunst, Trivette, & Deal, 1994b; Hawley, & DeHaan, 1996; H. I. McCubbin, M. A. McCubbin, 1988; J. M. Patterson, 1997; G. E. Richardson & Hawks, 1995). This does not mean that professionals ignore the family's deficits. Both resources and deficits can be acknowledged at the same time. The goal is to view the family's wholeness and strength.

Professionals must deal with and think about their frames of reference—how they view people in general as well as how they view specific individuals. Discounting those who are at risk and assuming their lives are tenuous will lead to further losses and, in a subtle manner, may support self-fulfilling prophecies of those at risk for failure in school or life (Rak & Patterson, 1996). If professionals' expectations for families who have a child with special needs are negative, they may miss the family resources as well as the possibilities the resources present for wholeness. Our society has had a jaundiced view of at-risk individuals and has focused for decades upon the deficits among those who have special needs—thereby failing to attend to the possibilities and resources.

The conceptualization of families as resourceful is an essential view with which to engage family members (Cameron & Vanderwoerd, 1997; Hawley & DeHaan, 1996; H. I. McCubbin, M. A. McCubbin, 1988; J. M. Patterson, 1997; G. E. Richardson & Hawks, 1995). When professionals view the family as resourceful and as a positive resource, they recognize that the need for additional resources is secondary and temporary. They also recognize that at certain times in the family's life cycle, the family may face an overload when attempting to meet demands. An appropriate analogy was presented by Imber-Black (1986): "The family has not suddenly become bankrupt in terms of its own resources, although its assets may be temporarily frozen or creating no interest" (p. 149).

A resource model of family functioning assumes that families continually create their own norms as they interact with history, culture, ethnicity, social class, politics, interpersonal relationships, individual quirks, and so forth. School professionals can frame their views of the family with this in mind and recognize the impact of context. Seeing context as significant, the professional is better able to make sense of family observations instead of seeing the family as abnormal. This view focuses on the assets of the family while recognizing but not emphasizing its deficits. More specific information on recognizing and utilizing family resources is presented in the "Resourcing" subsection.

Sharing Information with Families

This subsection is rooted in family systems tenets. It furnishes the basis for the remainder of the chapter. It provides information important to resourcing, focusing on areas in which school professionals can serve as family liaisons that link traditional and nontraditional families with supportive resources, thereby precluding their students from falling through the cracks (Greenawalt, 1994).

Helping individuals and family members to not be overly dependent upon outside resources is certainly good, but being independent does not mean having to meet all needs alone or within one's own family. The focus here is on sharing information that allows family members to learn more about family life and healthy communication and to know how to link with beneficial resources. Interdependence is the outgrowth of connection with others and builds the fabric of the community, which is relationship. This is a critical protective factor in producing resiliency.

Although sharing information with most families of at-risk and special-needs students will present no difficulty, some will resist input from school professionals (Campbell, 1993). Some parents will consider it to be bordering on an invasion of privacy or indicative of perceived failure or inadequacy.

For example, in one family the suggestion that a child join a Little League team may be considered a positive intervention that fits the child's developmental level and offers a social outlet. In another family, the same suggestion may be seen as squelching the boy's natural creativity by requiring him to take part in an organized sport rather than allowing exploration of unique physical and social needs. The professional who is aware of the differences between the families might recommend to the second family that they take time to play as a family and explore each individual's creativity through interaction. Suzuki, a form of teaching a musical instrument that involves teaching the parent as well, or the family learning a foreign language together would fit such a family.

There are many valuable concepts in the family systems approaches that can help professionals more effectively share information with family members of at-risk and special-needs students. Information presented in Chapter 13 on classroom extension of family intervention will also be helpful when assisting with resourcing.

Resourcing

Not all at-risk families or those who have children with special needs are dysfunctional; however, most would benefit from having resources available at times of increased stress. This subsection focuses on helping any family, functional or dysfunctional, with a child who is at risk or who has special needs. Assistance in resourcing can allow families to take better advantage of their family and social networks as well as any number of free or low-cost social services. Resourcing can also increase the likelihood that families will have more resources with which to assist their child. As mentioned in Chapter 2, a support system is one of the most important protective factors in family adjustment to life cycle changes and stresses. This subsection also addresses the importance of joining support groups, as well as referral to counseling, and focuses on locating as well as linking family members with these groups and services. Support includes: family resourcing, social systems resourcing, school-community resourcing, and external resourcing.

Family Resourcing

Family resourcing encourages school personnel to identify family strengths (Hawley & DeHaan, 1996; J. M. Patterson, 1997; G. E. Richardson & Hawks, 1995; F. Walsh, 1996) and builds on Weissbourd's (1996) principles of collaboration, covered in an earlier chapter, highlighting the interdependence of systems. This section on family resourcing initially defines family resources, then provides information about four family resource areas that can be tapped during interactions with the family members. School personnel can catalog resources and problems for later use. Cataloging means tracking family patterns on a family-by-family basis. This allows for a greater use of family resources. Strategies for school personnel to encourage the wise use of family resources follow.

Definition of family resources. Several types of family resources have been identified in the literature (Attneave & Verhulst, 1986; Dunst, Trivette, & Deal, 1994c; J. C. Hansen & Falicov, 1983; J. C. Hansen & E. I. Coppersmith, 1984; Karpel, 1986a; J. M. Patterson, 1997). Karpel (1986b) defined family resources as "those individual and systemic characteristics among family members that promote coping and survival, limit destructive patterns, and enrich daily life" (p. 176). He was not referring to finances or other material trappings, nor was he including social service resources within the community.

Karpel's (1986b) first element of family resource is the ability to access coping and survival techniques. As described in Chapter 2, families face a variety of predictable as well as unexpected stressors throughout the family life cycle. Families, particularly those with children having special needs, will vary widely in their resources for promoting coping and survival (Pell & Cohen, 1995). Some of these families cope well with the challenges, while others struggle. Those who struggle with daily coping may benefit from family resourcing. Assistance can be a means of promoting resiliency in all family members.

Another element of family resource identified by Karpel (1986a) is the ability of the family to limit possible destructive patterns. This both relates to external stressors and to internal patterns, such as attacking, demeaning, neglecting, or diminishing another. Limiting destructive patterns helps prevent the "pile-up" mentioned in Chapter 2 (H. I. McCubbin & Patterson, 1982; H. I. McCubbin, M. A. McCubbin, A. I Thompson, & E. A. Thompson, 1995). Some families seem to resist destructive patterns, which Karpel (1986a) paralleled with immunological resistance. Examples of such resistance are a wife's resisting her husband's invitation for a co-alcoholic marriage, parents exercising a clear hierarchy over an acting-out teenager, and a child's resistance to being triangled into the parents' conflicts.

A third element of family resource relates to the ability to enrich and enjoy daily life (Karpel, 1986a). This element goes beyond dealing with problems and focuses on life's more rewarding aspects—caring and sharing, satisfaction and pleasure (G. E. Richardson, & Hawks, 1995). The ability to bounce back—one characteristic of resiliency—is enhanced by the family's ability to enjoy simple aspects of daily life.

Karpel (1986a) expanded upon this three-element definition by describing personal resources as well as relational resources in families. Examples of personal resources include self-respect, protectiveness, hope, tolerance, and affection. Relational resources include respect, reciprocity, reliability, repair, flexibility, family pride, and loops of interaction.

Personal and relational resources within families are affected by three characteristics: capacity, rules, and active efforts. For example, consider that the relational resource of reciprocity, or give-and-take, in a family relates to how the family balances and holds fair play. Professionals can assess each family member's capacity for reciprocity and consider those capacities in conjunction with the family rules (e.g., Dad is the disciplinarian). Finally, active efforts by family members to initiate and collaborate on reciprocity can be considered. Counselors, school social workers, and psychologists are the professionals most likely to look closely at these factors. Observations can be added to the catalog of family process (mentioned in a later chapter), noting strengths and challenges faced by family members.

Areas of family resource. Imber-Black (1986) described four family resource areas that direct professionals' attention to the family's strengths as opposed to their deficits. The first area has to do with *religious, cultural, and racial identity.* As referenced in a previous chapter, McGoldrick et al. (1996) have addressed the issue of ethnicity and family therapy, and R. T. Carter (1995) has focused on the importance of racial identity.

Avoiding stereotypical thinking about people from other backgrounds is beneficial to healthy family-professional interactions. Professionals should be aware of their own values and any prejudices they may have. Looking for the strengths in others' ethnic backgrounds is helpful, and being aware of differences is critical to avoid misinterpreting behavior. For example, Mexican-American families are typically cooperative rather than competitive. A school professional who tries to use a competitive strategy to motivate a Mexican-American child may get lackluster results, which are often misunderstood. This child could easily be seen as unmotivated, whereas in truth the child might be easily motivated by a cooperative learning task. The cooperative task would serve as a resiliency-building strategy as well.

School professionals should observe family interactions with an eye toward recognizing and cataloging family identity. This is covered in more detail in a later chapter. Families also identify with religious groups, and these allegiances serve as a family resource. Some church groups will have considerable resources that might be tapped in helping families. Racial identity was focused upon by R. T. Carter (1995) and is another resource to tap. Such linkages are important as schools reach out to community resources and form partnerships for mentoring and other resiliency-building programs.

A second area of resource described by Imber-Black (1986) relates to the family's *inner language,* which identifies them as a family to both family members and to others. The professional should look for myths, metaphors, jokes, humor, and words or phrases with special meaning to the family members, note any examples, and use them at appropriate times. For example, a family may refer to themselves as having "dogged determination." When the family is going through a particularly rough time, the professional could provide support and encouragement in terms of the family members' own view of themselves by complimenting them on "hanging in there with dogged determination," a resiliency characteristic to be reinforced.

A third area of resource categorized by Imber-Black relates to *individual and family commitments, loyalties, or a sense of connections.* School professionals should be aware of and publicly recognize commitments and loyalties. Examples are a grandmother who takes over the custody and rearing of her unmarried teenage daughter's child, and a family that will go to all ends to be sure that the wheelchair-bound child does not miss out on family outings. Professionals should validate family convictions about including everyone in the family fun, thus reinforcing several aspects of resiliency.

The fourth area (Imber-Black, 1986) relates to the *capacity of the family to interact with the outside world* in such a way that preserves and enhances its integrity as a family. The outside world is defined as everything beyond the family. Families have rules for dealing with the external world, beyond family, in the same way that rules develop for family relationships. Professionals should build upon family resources for dealing positively with people outside the family. School professionals are members of that outside world, and it is valuable to know how the family has interacted in the past with school professionals. If prior experiences with the schools have been negative, the current school professionals should attempt to engage the family members, which may mean overcoming negative expectations on both sides.

For example, former school professionals may have seen parents as recalcitrant. If the professional views the family as having been protective rather than antagonistic, however, he or she will be better able to focus on the family's positive resources and functional survival skills for making it through an antagonistic situation.

Strategies. School professionals can assess, monitor, and reinforce all four areas of family resources. Again, when collaborating with any family it is good to look for resources versus deficits (Malatchi, 1997; J. M. Patterson, 1997). Everyone who has contact with the family of at-risk students or one with special needs can contribute to the cataloging process. A file on each student is valuable, to which information on family resources can be added. The file can be divided into the resource areas described here or according to any other system that meets the needs of the school system.

There is good reason to include family members in the process of recognizing their resources (J. M. Patterson, 1997; G. E. Richardson & Hawks, 1995). Team meetings might include an agenda item on family resources. When family members attend meetings, professionals can observe the family's use of inner language, as well as how they interact with the outside world.

It is important not only to note but also to reinforce family resources. When school professionals are in meetings with family members or in one-to-one interactions, they should take every opportunity to validate family resources related to resiliency. For example, a teacher might tell a mother, "I can see your son Timmy takes after the rest of your family when it comes to being gentle. I wish you had seen him with the new student from Iran."

It is also important to validate and encourage healthy family functioning that enhances resiliency. The healthy functioning of the spousal system is a particular function to be encouraged by school professionals. When spouses are going to take a vacation together and tell the school that they will be out of town, the school professionals should verbally reinforce their taking care of their marriage and encourage them to not worry about the child at school with words like, "We can handle whatever might come up here."

The sibling subsystem should also be validated as a source of support and a valuable family resource. Too often, people think that the siblings are in a rivalry. Professionals need to help frame existing or potential sibling relationships positively (Meyer & Vadasy, 1994; Powell & Gallagher, 1993; Seligman, 1991c). In an excellent chapter about the sibling subsystem, Kahn (1986) focuses on bonds of intensity, loyalty, and endurance. Knowing whether the family is either disengaged or enmeshed can also be helpful when making comments that might encourage balance and sibling support. When the family is disengaged, the school professional can facilitate alignment between siblings, fostering the resiliency-producing protective factor of relationship bond. For example, "I have noticed that you and your brother act quite differently, but it seems as though the two of you have had a very similar experience in your family."

Dysfunctional family interaction patterns or roles, such as scapegoating (Satir, 1988), can be changed. For example, the professional might say, "It looks as if Sandy is the 'fall guy' in this family. I wonder if she might be bringing a fresh perspective instead?" Another dysfunctional role that can be transformed is that of parentified child, frequently the oldest daughter in families that are extremely stressed. School professionals can suggest the family allow the daughter an opportunity for extracurricular activities, thereby fostering resiliency. Professionals should not unwittingly reinforce *parentifying* (W. C. Nichols, 1996). For instance, comments about what a "great little mother" a child is are inappropriate.

Another resource of potential strength lies in the extended family. Family members may overlook the real possibilities that the extended family has to offer. We can learn from African-American families in which extended family members often pitch in, not only to care for but also to participate in, rearing the children in their families (Hines & Boyd-Franklin, 1996). The school professional can ask whether a grandparent, aunt, uncle, or other relative might be able to help out with different functions. A simple suggestion that an unmarried aunt or uncle baby-sit once a week so that the spouses can have time together might never have occurred to the family. Extended family members can serve as important role models for coping with stress and for increasing resiliency in children and youth. The school professional who makes such suggestions is providing a valuable service.

Family retreats, family play-group counseling, and parent education groups can be implemented using flexible scheduling, with babysitting provided for infants and toddlers. When focusing on family as resource, the school professional can be creative and energizing. Many possibilities exist. It is up to the creative professional to make these possibilities real and to bring them to the school's attention.

Social Systems Resourcing

Cameron and Vanderwoerd (1997) defined social networks as "the actual, reoccurring linkages between a focal person and significant others in her or his environment" (p. 27). Social support comes from the "instrumental, educational, social, and psychological assistance actually received by the focal person" (p. 27).

Extensive research shows that social support helps some individuals and families to cope better with a stressful event and improve health (Hobfoll & Stephens, 1990), life expectancy (Kennedy, Kiecolt-Glaser, & Glaser, 1990), and increased success on exams and other academic tasks (Goldsmith & Albrecht, 1993). Paradoxically, other evidence suggests that some forms of support may be detrimental (Goldsmith, 1992; Kaplan & Toshima, 1990; Swann & Brown, 1990). Advocating for continued social support, Burleson, Albrecht, and Sarason (1994) stated:

> In short, supportive communication can contribute (positively and negatively) to how well people recover from illness, cope with loss or transition, manage chronic health conditions, deal with everyday upsets and disruptions, perform on a variety of tasks, and generally feel about themselves and their quality of life. (p. xiii)

Families should be encouraged to pursue supportive relationships that reduce their stress and increase their well-being. Schools can help to facilitate social support by connecting people with others who face similar challenges or to people in their community who could serve as positive role models (Comer & Haynes, 1991). School professionals, for example, could designate a room for families to meet with other families who share the same needs or with parents who have already overcome similar obstacles. The room should be inviting, and careful attention should be paid when selecting the leaders to facilitate the meetings. Counselors, psychologists, and social workers should all be particularly aware of the impact that social support networks have on individuals and families. Group co-leadership by a helping professional and a "veteran" successful parent can facilitate interaction and minimize the resistance of individuals who are defensive or mistrust professionals.

A number of professionals interested in at-risk families and those having children with special needs have written about social network interventions and the value of social support (M. Berger, 1984a; Coopersmith, 1983; Dunst, Trivette, & Cross, 1986; Dunst et al., 1994b; Friedrich & Friedrich, 1981; Intagliata & Doyle, 1984; Kazak, 1987; Kazak & Marvin, 1984; Rueveni, 1979). Just as the resources of the immediate and extended family are valuable, so too, are the resources of the family's social network.

Families who face a high level of stress will look to their social network for resources that might enable them to reduce and better cope with that stress. Unfortunately, the social network system may unwittingly add to the stress by providing contradictory and competing suggestions. Parents often turn to family members and friends for advice on how to handle problems. Although they have good intentions and they care, these family members and friends may not realize the parent is searching for advice among many people. One person will suggest a favorite intervention and another might offer a diametrically opposing idea. This can be very confusing. Thus social network interventions can be invaluable in getting all interested parties to understand and support realistic strategies.

This subsection on social systems networking includes background information on systems and the influence of external environments on family functioning. Next, social support systems are explained. Finally, findings and strategies are presented, particularly with regard to social systems networking with families having an at-risk child.

Background. Systems theorists propose that social networks, with their attendant support, directly and indirectly influence attitudes, expectations, behavior, and knowledge of both family members and other members of the network. Bronfenbrenner (1979) described ecological units or social networks topologically. He saw them as a nesting of concentric structures, one embedded within the other. The child and family are the center. Broader ecological systems move out in concentric circles, including relatives, friends, neighbors, and other acquaintances. Beyond that are larger social units (discussed in the next section on external networking) that include the neighborhood, churches, mosques, and synagogues, as well as social organizations, the workplace, play areas, and schools.

Waddock (1993) also described ecological units or social networks topologically. She saw them as spider webs of influence moving outward from the center, which is the child and the school. Moving outward, the broader ecological systems include family and social workers, then the larger community where services are provided, then state policies. At the outer edge of the web lies the nation and federal government. Counselors can serve as web weavers to develop linkages that promote resiliency-building for families and students between and among these systems.

Social systems theorists contend that these ecological units do not function in isolation but, rather, interact within and between levels. Thus, changes in one unit or subsystem will reverberate and impact upon other units or subsystems. When professionals understand this dynamic, reciprocal, systemic relationship, they will be more likely to plan appropriate interventions that promote resiliency by considering input from the school, the family, and the community, and its impact on at-risk students.

Definition of social support systems. Social support networks are links among individuals and groups. These links relate to size, satisfaction, density, connectedness, and frequency of contacts. As Dunst et al. (1986) indicated:

> Social support is a multidimensional construct that includes physical and instrumental assistance, attitude transmission, resource and information sharing, and emotional and psychological support. There is general consensus among social systems theorists that social support networks function to nurture and sustain linkages among persons that are supportive on both a day-to-day basis and in times of need and crises. (p. 403)

R. Turner (1981) described social support as an aspect of psychological well-being. Although he did not study at-risk families or those of children with special needs, he did study four diverse populations, one of which was adults with hearing losses. He also traced research about social support and concluded that social support is most important in stressful circumstances. In his study, Turner adopted Cobb's (1976) view that social support consists of information. Turner related social support as

> information belonging to one or more of three classes: (1) information leading the subject to believe that he or she is cared for and loved; (2) information leading the subject to believe that he or she is esteemed and valued; and (3) information leading the subject to believe that he or she belongs to a network of communication and mutual obligation in which others can be counted on should the need arise. (pp. 358–359)

Findings and strategies for social systems resourcing. Social networks, with their attendant support, directly and indirectly influence the attitudes, expectations, behavior, and knowledge of both family members and other members of the network alike. In this web of influence, professional educators have the distinct opportunity, through the "collective anchoring of the individual life" (Haas, 1993 , p. 215), to develop students by providing the tools that allow them to forge a tranquil, thriving and equitable society.

The Harvard Family Research Project (1995), stated, "The heart of family support programs is the web of relationships connecting staff with families, parents with children, and parents with other parents" (p. 11). This study found that schools had to overcome some formidable obstacles including the negative images held toward schools, reaching families that are poor and isolated, and overcoming transportation and child-care barriers that make parents reluctant to leave their neighborhoods. Thus, professionals must be willing to go into the communities to meet parents in their homes, or possibly, at a neutral establishment such as a library, mosque, church, synagogue, or fast-food restaurant to strengthen relationships and to provide the necessary assistance.

As the Harvard Family Research Project (1995) found, outreach programs are complex and difficult. Professionals must be adept at disarming resistant and often dysfunctional attitudes, and also be able to convince the family of their need for assistance. Many valuable concepts in family systems approaches can help professionals effectively share information with parents of at-risk and special-needs students, thereby promoting resiliency and reducing harmful stress. Information in the chapter on classroom extension of family intervention will also be helpful when serving as family-liaison.

A variety of findings presented in the literature on social network systems indicate the value of considering social systems as essential assets in reducing stress on family members. Dunst et al. (1986) examined effects of social support on parents of children with mental retardation and physical impairment, as well as developmentally at-risk children. These researchers were concerned with the impact of social support on "personal well-being, parental attitudes toward their child, family integrity, parental perceptions of child functioning, parent-child play opportunities and child behavior and development" (p. 403). Their findings supported the positive impact of social support systems on families having children with disabilities.

Kazak and Marvin (1984) studied stress and characteristics of social support networks of families with and without a child with a disability. They found that mothers are particularly subject to personal stress. Unlike previous research findings, they did not find a significant difference in the stress levels of marital dyads. They suggested that professionals view the differences between families (and their networks) as appropriate accommodations to raising a child with a disability. Specifically, they found both the overinvolvement of the mother and child and the peripheral role of the father in parenting to be appropriate and to be respected by professionals, "unless there is ample evidence that the marital relationship is impaired" (p. 75).

Kazak (1987) examined mothers and fathers of children with disabilities or chronic illnesses and compared them with matched parents of children without disabilities. She considered personal stress, marital satisfaction, and social network size and density of the social network. She found that only the mothers of the children with disabilities experienced higher levels of stress. Again, her findings indicate no differences in marital satisfaction. Finally, she found that mothers of children with disabilities had higher-density social networks than comparison mothers.

Intagliata and Doyle (1984) examined the effect of training in interpersonal problem-solving skills on enhancing social support for parents of children with developmental disabilities. From this pilot study, they concluded that enhancing problem-solving skills of these parents was relevant and could be a helpful intervention.

Friedrich and Friedrich (1981) compared parents of children with a disability with a control group of parents of children without disabilities. One of the many measures they investigated was social support. They concluded that "an appropriate avenue of intervention might increase the availability of social support for these parents to help them cope with this additional stress" (p. 553).

Minuchin and Fishman (1981) described the technique of enactment. In enactment, people act out the problem as contrasted with simply talking about the problem in the family. For example, if a student is disobedient to the parents during a social systems networking session, the teacher might ask the parents what they plan to do. This allows the teacher to see the problem as it evolves naturally. It may also present an opportunity for the teacher to intervene while serving as a model for the whole social systems network.

M. Berger (1984a) recommended the use of enactments in network interventions. He suggested creating a context in which those in attendance act differently toward one another. This is helpful when attempting to look at the family and social network as valuable resources. He described network interventions as "especially powerful contexts for the use of enactments that alter network members' definition of the handicapping condition or of what needs to be done about that condition (p. 134)."

Social support has a positive impact upon families with children with special needs as well as those who are at risk for failure. School professionals must consider this when relating to families (Rak & Patterson, 1996). Counselors, psychologists, and social workers in the schools should be particularly aware of the influence of social systems on building resilience.

School-Community Resourcing

The following subsections look at the types of possible services schools can provide both within the school setting and through linking with local community services, along with some studies that have examined the merit of support services in regard to children and families. Characteristics of effective school and community programs with some suggestions for establishing effective services follows.

Schools as a source of support. Outside the informal support families receive from friends, relatives, and one another, the schools or teachers are often the main source of support for families who need assistance (Burke & Cigno, 1996). Quite often the schools are the first to recognize a problem and to contact the parent when a problem arises (Comer & Haynes, 1991).

Poverty, drug abuse, learning problems, health problems, child neglect and abuse, teen pregnancy, single-parent families and two-parent families where both parents work, and even homelessness are just a few of the challenges that students face and bring with them when they enter school. Thus, schools have become a place where education alone is not enough. It is imperative that families, schools, and external agencies collaborate to provide education and other services so that our troubled children do not fall through the cracks (Greenawalt, 1994b).

Slavin et al. (1996) described a familiar scenario about a child from the Baltimore slums. The story is repeated regularly in schools across America. The child had completed kindergarten the year before, and his teachers already saw him as being in serious trouble. His anger and disruptiveness precluded his learning much in school. He was frequently absent and usually 2 hours late. His teenage mother loved her son but felt helpless as she reexperienced her own childhood school history through him. When he was angry, he was aggressive just like his mother. When the school contacted the mother the first week of school, she stomped into school cursing and threatening to take her son out of the school.

The social worker made an effort to make the mother feel valued and accepted, and the mother began to collaborate with the teachers, the facilitator, a family support team, and the attendance monitor. As a result, the boy's attendance, performance, and behavior improved. He was also provided academic help and the mother received training.

This scenario, in one variation or another, can play out in many forms across our nation. Unfortunately, all too often, a student's problems are left to the teacher or building principal and are eventually passed on from elementary to middle school or junior high and on to high school, where a once preventable problem grows to crisis magnitude.

When to offer support. The kinds of support services provided should depend on the family's desires and needs, the community, and the specific challenges encountered. In today's complex society, no family can meet all of its needs. Sooner or later all families will need and benefit from different kinds and levels of support. Although one might expect that two-parent, nonminority homes experience low stress and are able to cope, communicate, and parent effectively, this is unfounded (Allen, Brown, & Finlay, 1992). Whereas middle-income families are less likely to need financial help to pay for child care or health services, they can benefit from peer support or parenting classes as well as a number of other services matched to their needs.

Supportive school programs. At any given time, an observer can find an example of almost any variety of human services located in or facilitated by the school. According to Dryfoos (1994), these include school health teams; school-based dental health and general health clinics; mental health services; psychosocial counseling programs for substance abuse, teen pregnancy, and school failure; social skills training; family or parenting skills training; occupational selection assistance; mentoring programs; recreation and cultural enrichment classes; and after-school centers for academic tutoring or job training with links with businesses, universities, and nonprofit organizations (Dryfoos, 1994). Programs show up in all shapes and sizes and reflect the needs of the communities that they serve.

As described by Fowler and Corley (1996), prior to the opening of Saltonstall Elementary School to students, linkages with city officials, college faculty, and teachers were in place. One feature that was developed was the *Friday Club*. Every Friday, community partners teach elementary students how to do a variety of things. One volunteer teaches students how to build doll houses and then to paint, wallpaper, and decorate the interior. Another volunteer teaches students how to play soccer. All this is done from 8:00 to 10:00 while teachers spend the 2 hours planning lessons.

In Monticello, Arkansas, schools work with HIPPY (Home Instruction Program for Pre-school Youngsters) coordinators to help parents develop social and interpersonal skills that can reduce their feelings of isolation (Greenawalt, 1994b; Harvard Family Research Project, 1995). In one meeting with the school counselor, parents of children entering kindergarten shared their feelings of inadequacy. One mother told the group that she never hugged any of her five children or told them that she loved them. Through the help of a HIPPY coordinator who followed up on the case and with the mother's own desire to show more affection, the mother began to hug her children every day. It became clear that the family was changing fundamentally when the youngest child began to tell the mother, "I love you Mommy. You are so special to me."

Schools in Indianapolis, Indiana, indicated that they wanted more contact with parents and more parent participation in the schools. Working with Parents in Touch (PIT), schools there have set aside 20 minutes a day for parent-teacher conferences, created activity calendars to inform and make suggestions to parents, and set up homework contracts, homework hotlines, call-in services, parent workshops, and even medical and dental services. Many also have received other assistance through the various services the school system provides (Harvard Family Research Project, 1995).

Schools and school districts must decide what they want to achieve and provide before they can effectively begin to create programs and links to help their students and their families. There are many agencies, support groups, counseling services, and other possibilities at the local, state, and national levels.

According to The Harvard Family Research Project's report, *Raising Our Future* (1995), after 25 years of scientific research, Ramey and Ramey (1992) determined that effective programs embody the following seven characteristics:

- Begin earlier and continue longer.
- Interact more frequently with participants.
- Provide direct learning experience to children.
- Offer comprehensive services to children and families.
- Tailor services to match children's learning styles and risk conditions.
- Provide continuing supports as children make the transition into elementary school.
- Build up cultural beliefs, traditions, and practices. (Harvard Family Research Project, p. 5)

In Oakland, California the Unified School District was facing big problems with its students. Two of the schools in the district, the Health Academy and the Media Academy, sought solutions. Based on a concept first employed successfully in Philadelphia, the schools linked with community resources to offer students academic and career-oriented services in a school-within-a-school setting. Subsequent findings revealed that the students in these schools had improved attitudes toward school, were less disruptive, and were better able to work in cooperative groups. Several students and teachers indicated that Academy students were better mannered and often more "driven" to success than their nonacademy peers (Guthrie & Guthrie, 1993).

External Resourcing

External resource networking has to do with helping families form supportive links with resources outside their family, school, or social network. This type of networking might include tapping into volunteer groups, social service agencies, support groups, counseling services, and a number of other possibilities. This subsection initially suggests means of finding available resources in a local area as well as at state or national levels. It then suggests means of gaining access to support groups and of referring families to support groups or counseling.

Finding resources. There are a host of potentially valuable resources available in every community and state, as well at the national level, that most professionals know about only generally. Every school should have a resource file that all professionals can consult in their efforts to provide resource information to families. As professionals learn about additional resources, they can add to the file. School professionals might even find beneficial resources for themselves or their families in the file. Appendix D lists a variety of resources that could be included.

Each file should also contain evaluation information, that is, feedback from family members who have used the resources. Family members should be asked to respond to a brief questionnaire covering their impressions and reactions to different resources. There should also be a space for their general comments. If any school professionals have used a resource or know someone who did, they can also add their comments to the evaluation. Neither parents nor professionals should be required to sign the questionnaire. Further, they should not quote or identify by name anyone receiving confidential services. For obvious reasons some people would not like to be identified as having attended, for example, an alcoholics' support group or a group for parents who have abused their children.

It is important to check and purge files at least once a year. Telephone numbers and contact people change regularly, as do opportunities for group as well as individual support. It is frustrating for family members to hear of a resource that is no longer available. When this happens, they may decide not to follow any other leads.

To generate a file, a group of professionals can get together and divide the workload. A search of resources in the community begins with contacting the local school board for brochures or information on different agencies and services available to families. Then the community mental health center should be contacted for information on its services as well as other resources with which its staff are familiar. The community parks and recreation associations can also be contacted. Local churches and synagogues are another important source of services. The local phone book is a great resource for recent telephone numbers.

Beyond the local community, the professionals can contact state agencies such as the Department of Education for information on state-level services and opportunities for networking with families of at-risk and special-needs children. The division responsible for special education in the state should definitely be contacted, along with the Department of Mental Health. The division on volunteerism within the state government may also be of service.

National agencies should also be investigated. Many would be useful contacts for a variety of types of disabilities. Addresses and phone numbers are often listed in national directories. Examples of agencies that may prove helpful are the Association for Retarded Citizens (ARC), the Learning Disability Association of America (LDA), and Bereaved Parents. Appendix D contains information on a variety of resources.

Gaining access to support groups and referrals for counseling. Support groups and counseling for parents as well as siblings of at-risk and special-needs children are invaluable in helping to reduce stress. Whether the school system or a community resource provides the resource, the school professional must make the family member aware of the opportunity. Few parents know on their own about the variety of support groups or counseling services that are available in the community.

The school resource file will allow the professional to select relevant support groups for the family member who needs support. When making a referral, it is important to recognize the family member's need for privacy. Some family members will be embarrassed to be considered in need of a support group or counseling, whereas others will not know anything about these opportunities. Do not assume that anyone will understand anything about these possibilities. It is better to repeat information people already have than to leave them wondering about your referral.

Who makes the referral is important. Someone familiar with the family member, who has established a positive rapport with that person, is the best professional to make a referral for a support group or counseling. If the familiar professional is not comfortable making a referral, the next most familiar individual can assume that task.

The context or place for making the referral is also important. The family member should come to the school for a meeting, or the referral should be made during an already scheduled meeting. A phone call is not an appropriate way to convey a referral for a support group or counseling. During the meeting, time should be invested in building rapport before actually suggesting counseling or a support group. The situation that has led to the recommendation should be retraced so that the parent or sibling understands the reason for the referral. Then the school professional can present the opportunity and describe its value. The professional should indicate that the school personnel recommend that such services be considered by the family member(s). The purpose for the recommendation should be made very clear, and follow-up information should be provided. If there is a brochure or flyer available with phone numbers, contact persons, and a description of services, it should be provided. Cost of services and possibility of insurance coverage should also be discussed.

In some rare cases the school professional might prefer to allow the family member(s) to ask for information about contacting the resource. This is an effective way to handle people who try to make others responsible for them. Waiting for the family member to request further information allows the family member to be more in charge of the personal process and does not leave the responsibility solely on the professional. In such cases, the professional might simply provide contact names and tell the family member where to find phone numbers.

Some family members will appreciate hearing about how other families have benefited from the recommended resource. Some people will be willing to be contacted by phone to discuss their own experiences with a resource such as a support group or counselor. At other times the professional can relate what other family members have told without providing the names of those involved.

Family members should always be given time to ask questions regarding the referral. The professional should recommend that they consider the possibility and call later if they have further questions before making contact with the support group leader or counselor.

Again, Chapter 13 contains important information on metaphor and reframing that can be used when making recommendations for counseling or support groups. Reframing is helpful when families resist a recommendation. It is invaluable to provide constructive frames when recommending support services.

SUMMARY

This chapter has presented information concerning the school becoming a hub of a community that responds through loose and more formal links with one another to help meet the needs of children and their families. Protective factors related to at-risk students were initially described as they relate to personal, family, and school domains. Characteristics of successful school programs followed. Family systems views on the sharing of information with family members were initially described to set the stage for resourcing as it relates to the family network, the social systems network, school-community, and resourcing beyond family, friends, and schools. The school professional is essential in helping family members of at-risk or special-needs children receive the support they need, thereby increasing resilience.

CASE EXAMPLE

Harry is a teacher who went to the flagship university in his state after graduating from a rural high school. His story of resilience and beating the odds is presented here because the outcome can be traced over time. Harry was the oldest of two boys and the child of an alcoholic father who was verbally abusive, uninvolved, and frequently drunk on week-ends. While the father was hard on Harry, most of the father's worst abuse, which was at times physical, was directed toward the mother. Harry would often disappear as the battles between his parents raged. When the noise quieted, he would reappear to comfort his mother, whose only source of emotional support came from Harry. Harry's mother, in turn, spent all her energies on her children, reading to them when they were very young, taking them to the library weekly, and supporting them in their various interests. Harry does not recall a time period in his youth when his father did not have a problem with alcohol. Harry recalled that any expression of anger, sadness, or disappointment was interpreted by his father as a sign of ungratefulness.

As Harry grew up, he became very involved in school and had a series of teachers who encouraged and supported him in his interests and encouraged him to go to college. He became involved in extracurricular activities in high school. Though he excelled in high school, Harry began "partying" at the age of 13 but never got into any real trouble. He was popular, but he also suffered from occasional bouts with despair and anger.

During college, Harry had begun to experiment with drugs and was probably close to addiction by the time he was 20. By the age of 24, he entered therapy for his growing despair and depression. He did not quit using drugs until he was 26.

After graduating from college, Harry entered the field of business and succeeded. He eventually realized he wanted another life and career path, and at 27 he began to work with adolescents who were from troubled families. For a number of years, he served as a youth counselor before taking a position teaching adolescents in a residential facility. As one who is resilient, he can relate to his students and knows the pitfalls of low self-esteem and an external locus of control.

Questions

1. *What are the dysfunctional structural characteristics of Harry's family of origin? How did you arrive at your hypotheses?*

2. *What are the behaviors that demonstrate Harry's resilience?*

3. *What might have been done for Harry when he was in public school that might have helped him so that he did not face the cycle of despair he met while in high school.*

EXTENSION ACTIVITIES

Reading: Read children's and young adult literature depicting resilient children and youth. Your librarian will likely be able to make recommendations.

Reflection or Journal on Reading: What has your reading shown you about kids who *beat the odds?* How could you use this literature with students who are at risk or to help sensitize others to their lives?

In-class/Training Discussion Based on Children's and Young Adult Literature: If you read any stories with information on family life, can you glean anything about structural patterns or historical factors that demonstrate risk or resilience? In what ways do the stories point out environmental factors as causative factors for risk? To what do you attribute resiliency in each story read, and did any common themes emerge across the stories? How do these relate to what you learned in the preceding four chapters?

Movie/Video: Use the same structure described in the preceding activity.

Guest Speaker(s) Trainer Instructions: Invite an individual or individuals who have *beaten the odds* to class or training session(s). Provide them with information about the class/group and questions that participants would like answered. A panel with a moderator could also be assembled.

In-class/Training Discussion: Reminisce about novels you have read that portray individuals who are resilient. Discuss common factors that contributed to their resilience. The same can be done for movies. Discuss how these novels/movies could be used with students to increase resilience.

Part III
Applications of
Family Systems

Part III focuses on the application of family systems concepts in educational contexts. Chapter 10 is an introductory chapter on team functioning and family involvement. Although it does not relate specifically to family systems concepts, it is integral to the family systems perspective, since the needs of many at-risk students will be considered by educational teams, and by legal stipulation, the needs of all students with disabilities must be considered by a team.

Chapters 11 through 13 integrate family systems concepts with concrete and useful applications for school professionals. These chapters include information about informal and formal meetings with families, as well as the application of family systems concepts when working with groups and in the classroom.

Chapter 14 provides insights into how to strengthen possibilities for the adoption of systems models in schools. Also discussed are barriers to working with families, as well as strategies for avoiding or dealing with barriers. A change model from the family systems field is presented at the end of the chapter in recognition of the reality that bringing family systems into schools will require a major change process.

Team Functioning and Family Involvement

This chapter is designed to help you understand effective team functioning, with families being a focus of, as well as cooperating in, the team process. Although much of the information presented here is related to the education of students with special needs, the information is also pertinent to at-risk students and their families. Three different educational team approaches familiar to special education are described. Then, information is provided about the people who serve on such teams. Next is an introduction to educational touchpoints, particular situations in education in which the team can help parents and children deepen their relationships. A discussion of important aspects in planning and implementing an effective team process follows. The discussion then turns to team characteristics and avoiding problems on teams, with subsections on stages of team development, the triaxial model for teams, and challenges faced by teams. The chapter concludes with information on involving families in teamwork, specifically in the areas of reviewing test data, reviewing options for service delivery models, decision making, and goal setting. Although this chapter focuses mainly on professionals working on teams to serve students with special needs, the sections on screening and on teacher and student support teams are also related to at-risk students and their families. Chapters 11 and 12 focus more equally on at-risk and special-needs students. It is important to remember, in reading this chapter, that the main focus of this text is on family systems approaches. Family systems concepts are woven throughout all of Part III.

TEAM APPROACHES IN EDUCATION

What is a team? Briggs (1997) defined a team as "a group of individuals who are committed to a shared purpose, to each other, and to working together to achieve common goals" (p. 14). In considering the elements inherent in this definition, Briggs examined five aspects: individuals, shared purpose, commitment, goals, and uniqueness. Having diverse individuals serving on an education team leads to an enriched experience that will benefit the student served. Each member's experiences, personality, biases, and contributions become part of the rich mix that allows for greater gains by students and their families. A shared purpose brings interdependence and is based on trust. Commitment leads to ownership, and thus the necessary investment of energy of the part of the team members will follow. A team must have a goal or purpose in order to exist, and that goal or purpose brings meaning into the group. Though goals change, the underlying mission or purpose must be what drives the team. Finally, a unique identity evolves within a team as the members work together. They form their own subculture within the organization with operating norms and shared values evolving over time. Some teams choose a name or logo to represent how they feel about their group and its work together. The song title "We Are the World," for example, could be a motto a team might adopt.

Three different team approaches for working with students with special needs are commonly referred to in the literature: multidisciplinary, interdisciplinary, and transdisciplinary teams. Because most school programs for students with special needs use one of these three models, or a variation of one, it is helpful to have an overview of all three. The models are described briefly so that you can identify which type is used in your program and become familiar with its strengths and weaknesses. If you work with more than one program, two or perhaps all three of the descriptions may be applicable.

Multidisciplinary Team Approach

In the multidisciplinary model, professionals from various disciplines, such as education, psychology, occupational therapy, and art therapy, each work individually with the student or family. That is, the professionals work in isolation from one another as they evaluate students and provide services. The multidisciplinary model originally was developed to serve patients with medical problems that could be relegated to one particular discipline, and it is still used in this way today. In this approach, the different professionals working with the same patient often do not even regard themselves as part of a team (Orelove & Sobsey, 1996).

Coordinating services to an individual student can be very difficult using the multidisciplinary approach. A major disadvantage of the multidisciplinary model is the potential for failure to consider the whole child. Another disadvantage is that two or more professionals can make recommendations that conflict with one another. For example, a therapist may be encouraging parents who are overly involved in their child's education to back off, while at the same time, the school counselor might be working independently to involve parents in a home-school behavior management program. When the professionals from the different disciplines meet, sorting through their recommendations can be a complex task. In some schools, multidisciplinary team members provide their different recommendations and then leave the teacher to sort through their ideas and implement suggestions.

Interdisciplinary Team Approach

The interdisciplinary team approach is considered more sophisticated than the multidisciplinary model (Briggs, 1997; Morsink, Thomas, & Correa, 1991; Orelove & Sobsey, 1996). The interdisciplinary model provides a formal structure allowing interaction and communication among team members. In this approach, each professional performs his or her own assessment and implementation; however, programming decisions are made by the group. As Fordyce (1981) indicated, with interdisciplinary teams, the outcome is accomplished only by an interactive effort with all disciplines involved in the contributions. Orelove and Sobsey (1996) stated that "although program planning is more collaborative than in the multidisciplinary model, program implementation remains isolated" (p. 10).

This model is an improvement over the isolated functioning of the multidisciplinary team, but it is subject to a number of the same disadvantages. Decisions are affected by the orientations of each professional and may, therefore, result in disjointed outcomes for students. The difficulties inherent in group interaction also can cause problems.

In an article on physicians' involvement in interdisciplinary teams, F. Bennett (1982) looked at a variety of problems inherent in interdisciplinary teamwork. He stated: "Parents may become confused, rather than enlightened, by the interdisciplinary process if sufficient care is not taken to coordinate and synthesize the numerous professional evaluations" (p. 313). He also suggested several other problems, such as turf issues, differences in assessment approaches and management strategies, and the discouragement of strong, effective leadership if one discipline views leadership attempts as arrogant.

Transdisciplinary Team Approach

Discussing early intervention teams for children with special needs, Briggs (1997) described four key components of the transdisciplinary model:

- Many disciplines are involved in the delivery of services.
- Collaborating to reach a consensus for a decision is standard practice. All members help plan and monitor intervention even if they are not directly involved in the service delivery. Each member of the team is committed to learning from the others as well as teaching others.
- Essential to the team are family members. They choose their degree of involvement in assessment, planning, implementation as well as evaluation. Training of family members varies based on need and over time. The ultimate authority to make decisions resides with family members.
- Finally, there is a designated team member in charge of the child so that families are not intruded upon too frequently. The role of the coordinator of care is to incorporate team decisions and integrate other disciplines' goals into a treatment program. A family member may choose to serve in this role or one member of the team may be assigned this task. (adapted from p. 94)

Others also have focused upon these key components in essentially the same way (Morsink et al., 1991; Orelove & Sobsey, 1996; O'Toole & Switlick, 1997).

As might be expected, the transdisciplinary model presents some difficulties in coordinating services. For example, some professionals have trouble with the notion of training other team members to implement procedures that they consider to be their areas of expertise. This notion, called role release (Orelove & Sobsey, 1996), can result in interpersonal difficulties. For example, if a counselor is required to train a parent to implement a program, the counselor might feel demeaned when the parent is seen as capable of implementing a program that the counselor needed a master's degree to learn.

The integrated therapy model is a feature of the transdisciplinary model wherein therapy services become integrated within education. Therapy goals are integrated within educational goals on individualized education programs (IEPs). This feature is based on the assumption that therapists and teachers work together in program assessment, planning, and delivery. For more information on the integrated therapy model, Rainforth, York, and Macdonald (1992) is a good resource. The integrated therapy model focuses on students with severe disabilities but is meaningful for all professionals interested in becoming more familiar with integrated therapy models.

Benefits to parents ascribed to the transdisciplinary model abound (Orelove, 1995). Foremost of these benefits is that family members are treated with respect and decide for themselves their degree of involvement in the decision-making process. Further, the family can turn to a single professional on the team, who serves as a synthesizer of information, for answers to their questions. The parents do not have to contact each team member in order to understand something about their child's education. In addition, the new information and skills the family members gain as part of the team help them to improve their understanding of their child's behavior and learning.

Orelove (1995) noted that students benefit from more appropriate solutions and support, which draw from the diverse backgrounds of the team members; the team's holistic view of the learner, which results in a more cohesive approach to working with the student; more humanistic means of dealing with challenging behaviors; and an integrated therapy that preserves the continuity of learning, focuses on naturally occurring activities, and yields more effective results.

Familiarity with the three models just described is useful for all school professionals. Not only may they change jobs, moving into a school system that uses a different team model than the one that was used in their previous job, but they may also be faced with working with a student who has transferred into the school from a system that used a different model. Having an understanding of how decisions were made and implemented in the previous system is vital to effectively working with the student and his or her family.

EDUCATIONAL TEAM MEMBERS

A variety of people contribute to the educational team process. Working together for the benefit of a student with special needs, they share their theories, philosophies, beliefs, experiences, and skills. Differences of opinion are expected and are most beneficial when viewed as contributing to a whole picture as opposed to being seen as competing with other members' perspectives.

This section deals with the various people who serve on the educational team. It is important for each team member to gain an understanding of the other members' beliefs, knowledge, and skills. Doing so will help the team members respect and collaborate with one another, enabling them to better meet the needs of the students.

Family Members

Parents and other family members are not usually in the schools on a regular basis. For this reason, many textbook discussions of teams either fail to include family members as part of the team or relegate them to insignificant roles. In this book, however, the family comes first, since responsibility for the final decision regarding treatment resides with the parents. Beyond parents' legal rights to participate in assessment and planning, schools should invite their participation and view them as competent to provide information and suggestions (Losen & Losen, 1994; Switlick & Bradley, 1997; Turnbull & Turnbull, 1996). Parents will vary in the degree to which they would like, or be able, to participate. Recognizing and responding to the different preferences shows respect for them as parents.

Teacher

The teacher has the primary responsibility for the education of the student with special needs. The general education classroom teachers in elementary and secondary schools can provide a great deal of insight into the needs of students. From their observations of students within and outside the classroom they can develop concrete descriptions on which the team can build a realistic picture and base its recommendations. Suggestions provided by team members are filtered through the general education teacher's lens for practicality.

Special Educator

The responsibility of the special education teacher is to teach students with special needs who have been found eligible for special education or related services. The special educator also serves as a liaison between the family of the student and the school system. Serving as a member or coordinator of a team of professionals working with the student, the special educator plays a unique role in the education of students with special needs. The special educator is an advocate for the student and provides the expertise of advanced training in a specialized field or fields of education.

Paraprofessional

The paraprofessional, or teacher's aide, often plays an important role in the education of the student with special needs. The paraprofessional can provide valuable information about the student's functioning as well as suggestions about the practicality of interventions. Too often school professionals do not recognize the value of paraprofessionals' wisdom.

Psychologist

The psychologist in most of the schools across America functions as an evaluator of students' intellectual and emotional abilities. During the assessment process, he or she measures the cognitive and affective functioning level of the student.

In addition to that responsibility, school psychologists also may be called upon to assess the student's learning style or problem-solving approaches. Some researchers have suggested that such testing should be requested only if the teacher cannot make educational program decisions without it (Moran, 1978). In such cases, the teacher should provide the psychologist with a statement of the presenting problem in the form of a question whose answer will lead to effective instruction of the student being referred. Suzuki and Kugler (1995) focused on cultural bias and stressed the importance of knowing the background of the student being assessed.

Many school psychologists have assumed the role of helping to develop behavioral strategies to be employed in the school or home. Some psychologists also are trained to work with families regarding issues of grief and loss. Increasingly, psychologists are receiving training in family systems models so that they can assist in interventions that consider the whole family system as opposed to just the individual student.

Counselor

Counselors provide some of the same services as psychologists, depending upon their training and the needs of the school system. Some school districts have counselors in every elementary building and more than one counselor in each secondary school.

As part of the educational team, counselors can provide diagnostic information as well as input on family matters. Increasing numbers of counselors are being trained in family systems concepts and are able to provide an intervention focus that reflects the family unit. They may also provide input on current group process opportunities in the school. For example, the counselor may lead a group for students who need follow-through after in-patient substance abuse treatment or a group for students whose parents are divorcing.

Educational Diagnostician

Most school systems employ educational diagnosticians. Educational diagnosticians are experienced special educators who have received additional training. They assess students' academic abilities and achievements and provide essential information on which team members rely. The diagnostician administers both formal, standardized measures as well as informal tests of academic functioning. They often engage in trial teaching to determine the method by which the student learns best.

Social Worker

The school social worker will be the person on the team most familiar with family matters. He or she serves as a family advocate with extensive training in the realm of family functioning. The social worker is also most familiar with community resources that might benefit students with special needs and their families.

The social worker might even be the person the team appoints to coordinate services among the community, school, and home. Not all social workers, however, are familiar with the specialized concepts of family systems. While well trained in aspects of family concerns, social workers may not have been exposed to the concepts of family systems approaches presented in Part I of this book.

Administrator

The administrator is responsible for policy and decision making as well as implementation of matters of placement, transportation, related services, equipment, and scheduling. Administrators are also responsible for ensuring compliance with regulations. In many school systems, administrators head prereferral and eligibility teams.

Administrators who sit on teams include principals, program directors or specialists, and special education coordinators. Administrators can free up material, time, personnel, and financial resources, thereby facilitating the implementation of programs and related services for students with special needs. To facilitate effective family interventions, it is important that administrators have some training in family systems concepts.

Nurse

The school nurse is frequently the team member with the most realistic information on the physical health of students with special needs. Among other areas, nurses are trained to deal with first aid, seizures, and medication, as well as to provide information on hygiene and diet. There is a growing emphasis on schools being a hub of the community (Guthrie & Guthrie, 1993) and on the development *full-service schools* (Dryfoos, 1994) that provide wrap-around services (Fowler & Corley, 1996). This emphasis stems from children not receiving the medical services they need (Allen et al., 1992; Harvard Family Research Project, 1995) and professionals in human services looking for creative means of meeting their needs.

Other Specialists

A variety of other specialists may be included on teams for particular students with special needs. Physicians can help the team by providing input on health and medication (Orelove & Sobsey, 1996) as well as by screening for common medical problems. Although few physicians actually attend team meetings, they can provide valuable input by phone or written communication. Physicians vary widely in their ability to deal with, as well as their interest in, school-related problems (Levine, 1982). F. Bennett (1982) underscored the increasing involvement of physicians on interdisciplinary teams. Morsink et al. (1991) saw the role of the physician as primarily a consultant to the team. Most beneficial is ongoing communication between the physician and the staff at the school.

At times, occupational or physical therapists will be included on a team for a student with special needs. Occupational therapists work with fine-motor skill development, including such skills as buttoning, zipping, writing, and typing. They also frequently work with students with severe physical impairments on daily living skills, such as eating. Physical therapists work with gross-motor skill development, including skills such as walking, balancing, skipping, playing ball, relaxing, and general coordination. Physical therapists assist students with more severe physical disabilities.

Student

Even though federal and state laws clearly state that students may attend meetings, many school systems overlook the student as a potential contributor to the team (Brendtro & Bacon, 1995). With the current emphasis on personal involvement in growth processes (Field, 1996), students likely will become more frequent members of teams. In 1991 the United States Department of Education funded a project on self-determination by individuals with disabilities. This was followed in 1993 with funds for research on self-determination. Field's (1996) article focused on self-determination instructional strategies for youth with learning disabilities, and it has an expansive reference listing.

Generally, elementary school students will not attend team meetings, although elementary students have been consulted about their preferences for pull-out, in-class, or integrated service delivery models (Jenkins & Heinen, 1989). Secondary-level students may be able to provide input about their educational programs. They also can provide realistic and accurate information about family considerations. In a heartrending commentary, Greer (1989) described his mistake of not including a secondary student as a team member or asking for her input about the service delivery model used. His former student told him years later that he had ruined her life because he had not left her in a special education classroom. Turnbull and Turnbull (1996) suggested ways for students to be involved in discussing evaluation results during conferences.

TEAM FUNCTIONING DURING EDUCATIONAL TOUCHPOINTS

T. Berry Brazelton (1992), a well-known American pediatrician, discussed particular situations that offer parents and children opportunities to deepen their relationships. These *touchpoints* can delight or challenge the relationship, but the intent is to help the child and parent become closer.

The process of meeting the educational needs of at-risk and special-needs learners also involves several touchpoints, though most students will not go through all of them. These are times for strengthening parent and child relationships as well as parent and professional relationships. This section includes information on the educational touchpoints of screening, prereferral, referral and evaluation, eligibility, and individualized educational programs.

Screening

Screening is a process of selecting students who may be at risk for school difficulties and is the domain of the general education classroom teacher. When a student has a problem in school, the teacher should be concerned, whether the problem is academic, organizational, or behavioral. Solutions will vary according to the nature of the problem; however, crucial to the resolution of all problems is an understanding of the cause of the problem. Understanding the cause requires careful and systematic exploration of the student's performance, behavior, prior school experiences, developmental age, disability, and family life.

Because the classroom teacher has responsibility for the student's education, he or she is the most appropriate person to begin exploring most problems. Classroom teachers also have the most knowledge of, and experience with, the students in their classrooms. The teacher has the opportunity to observe the student in a variety of situations and thus can make more sound decisions than those that are based upon a short observation under nonclassroom conditions. The teacher also has the opportunity to observe the child across the whole day and week, which is particularly helpful for tracking and understanding underlying family problems. For example, the teacher might observe that Mondays are particularly stressful for a student and wonder about what occurs on the weekend at home.

A wise teacher will involve the family in determining the cause of a problem he or she has observed. The teacher can approach parents so that they are not alarmed but feel invited to help wrestle with the challenge they are facing together. The involvement of parents has been seen as particularly crucial to the achievement of at-risk children (Slavin et al., 1996). Leithwood (1997) corroborated the relationship between achievement and parental involvement.

Perhaps most important the teacher is responsible for creating positive change by using information gathered during the screening process. The teacher analyzes problems and attempts interventions based on the analysis. He or she carefully documents these interventions for future use if the need arises. When changes or interventions attempted by a teacher do not produce results, or if the teacher runs out of solutions, then it is time to ask for assistance from a team of other professionals and continue to involve the family.

Prereferral—Teacher and Student Assistance Teams

Most school systems have committees or teams that operate more or less formally to help teachers who need assistance with at-risk or special-needs students. This process has been referred to as teacher collaboration or consultation (D. F. Bradley & Switlick, 1997; Friend & Cook, 1996; Graden & Bauer, 1991; Idol, Nevin, & Paolucci-Whitcomb, 1994). All teams that provide teacher assistance skirt the process of determining eligibility for special education and can help achieve the goal of inclusion.

This step is not the beginning of the special education process. The purpose of the teacher and student assistance team is to help the teacher and student solve the specific problems that led to the request for assistance. This team tries to assist the teacher and student by analyzing information and suggesting possible modifications that may include involving families (Switlick, 1997). Chapter 11 of this text includes more extensive information about teams that assist teachers early on in the process of identifying challenges and discusses family involvement in those teams.

At one time, professionals viewed all problems as deficits within the student. Today, most professionals recognize the importance of context. In the classroom, the student is influenced by such variables as teaching style and organizational arrangement; however, it is difficult for teachers to judge the effects of these variables on the achievement and behavior of a particular student. Also, different students respond differently to the same teaching techniques and behavior management strategies. When academic troubles or inappropriate student behaviors occur, adaptations in instruction, differing management strategies, or fresh strategies in the home may reduce the problem. Members of the teacher and student assistance team are viewed as consultants whose aim is to help the classroom teacher and student devise strategies for overcoming learning or behavior problems.

It is important for educators to consult with parents when a teacher and student assistance team is convened. Professionals should share their concerns and proposed interventions with parents during team meetings, regularly scheduled parent-teacher conferences, or specially arranged conferences. Effective communication skills are critical in all of these processes. Professionals will not take family members by surprise if they have kept them continually informed or involved as team members. In addition, family members are a valuable source of information about their child. When a student's performance varies tremendously between different contexts such as home and school, the teacher should examine potential causes of that discrepancy. Also, family members sometimes suggest the very intervention that the teacher successfully adopted, thus precluding the need to refer a student for an evaluation.

Unfortunately, there are times when this type of intervention does not succeed. The next stage in the process of attempting to meet the student's needs then becomes referral and evaluation.

Referral and Evaluation

Referral and evaluation is the process by which students and their families may enter special education. The probability that a family will have a positive experience is increased if all professionals handle this process in a sensitive and efficient manner, respectful of family members' contributions as well as their fears and apprehensions. Professionals must keep in mind that families likely will feel vulnerable at this touchpoint.

The classroom teacher develops the referral for evaluation. He or she communicates the student's status, reports prior interventions used, specifies the referral question, and prepares the student for referral. The referral question (Suzuki & Kugler, 1995) specifies what the teacher would like to determine from the assessment that will follow. An example of a referral question is, "Would Tom benefit from remedial instruction in reading?"

Once the referral is made, the building administrator ensures that parents are informed of their rights and that they consent, in writing, to an evaluation. The administrator also must ensure that appropriate evaluations are conducted by qualified personnel and that an eligibility determination discussed later in this section is made within a predetermined number of working days. Evaluations must be free from cultural bias.

The topic of informing parents of their legal rights deserves further mention. School districts should always provide written information, called *procedural safeguards,* to parents regarding their legal rights. It is helpful for a professional to review that information to ensure that it is clear enough for the parents in a particular community to understand. All parents must receive such information before giving consent for evaluation. School professionals should also be sure to obtain and read a copy of the procedural safeguards. In addition, school professionals should find out who has the responsibility for providing this information to parents, since that responsibility may vary from one school system to another.

Parents also must be provided with a description of any action to be taken with their child, rationale for that action, and alternatives proposed by the school. At this point in the referral and evaluation process, the proposed action is evaluation of a child to determine whether a disability exists and what types of individual programming would be most appropriate.

Next, parents must be informed about assessment procedures, data, and other information that will be employed to decide whether to pursue evaluation. Names and purposes of tests that will most likely be used are helpful for parents.

Following the assessment, parents must be provided with the information that the committee used to make a decision to refer their child. Typically, the information relates to academic functioning, peer relationships, and health status.

Eligibility

After the formal assessment of the student is completed and the reports that interpret the assessment results are written, a new team, referred to in this text as the eligibility team, meets to evaluate the results (D. F. Bradley, King-Sears, & Tessier-Switlick, 1997). Who serves on this team, the procedures employed during eligibility team meetings, and record-keeping procedures are discussed in the following sections.

Membership

The members of the eligibility team include someone capable of interpreting the tests administered; the special education administrator or someone with expertise in the field of special education designated to take that person's place; a person who has observed the student or been directly involved in the assessment process; the teacher; and other professionals, as necessary. The membership should have a broad base to ensure that the decisions made represent the best thinking from a variety of perspectives.

Some school systems also include the parents on this team. I am in favor of parents having the opportunity to be involved in the eligibility meeting. Although the process may take longer when parents are included, they can add a great deal of important information. Including parents is not a legal requirement at this stage. However, it is a legal requirement for the next stage, developing the individualized education program.

Guterman (1995) investigated students in high school receiving learning disabilities services in separate classrooms and found that while the students did not view the special education classroom as efficacious, they valued it because of the unresponsive system in general education. If students are able to be involved in making decisions about their education, results such as these, when provided to them, may help them in their decision-making process.

Determination of Eligibility

In examining the results and interpretations of the various professionals who have evaluated the student, the eligibility team must make two important determinations. They must first determine whether the student qualifies as exceptional according to federal and state guidelines. Just as important, they must determine whether the student needs special education services to profit from the educational experience (King-Sears, 1997).

Both conditions must exist before the student is eligible for special education. It is possible that a particular student might meet only one of the standards and thus not qualify for special education. For example, it might be determined that a student is indeed performing poorly in school and that the services of a special education teacher in a resource setting might be beneficial, but the student does not meet the state and federal definitions of any of the disabilities. In this case, it would be illegal to use the term *special education* to label the student "disabled" just so that he or she can receive special educational services.

If the team decides that a student has a disability that requires special education or related services, the committee must identify the disability and recommend what, if any, services are required. These recommendations relate to the educational and other related services that the student needs if he or she is to receive an education appropriate to his or her learning needs and abilities.

Records

The eligibility team keeps a written record of its meeting that must be signed by each member. Any member who does not agree with the consensus of the group has the right to refuse to sign the minutes. That individual then submits a written report explaining his or her reasons for disagreement with the determination of the team. Once signed, the minutes of the meeting are placed in the student's confidential folder.

If the eligibility team determines that the student is eligible for special education services, then a summary of this report is prepared. This summary is used by the next committee, which is the individualized education program team.

Individualized Education Program

The individualized education program (IEP) is meant to be the cornerstone of educational programming for students with disabilities. It is the vehicle used to develop programs that provide free and appropriate educational experiences for each of these students.

The IEP must be developed before the student is placed in any special education program. The student's parent(s) also must agree to the program before it may be implemented. These conditions are designed to ensure that the program the child receives meets his or her unique learning needs, not that the individual student meets the requirements of a given program. In other words, a program is designed to fit the individual student; the student is not made to fit a program. The stipulation that the IEP be developed before a student is placed in a program is intended to avoid previous practices that placed a student in a program according to a label such as *learning disabilities* with the expectation that all students so labeled would profit from identical educational experiences. IEPs are part of what makes special education *special*.

The IEP team members include a person who is qualified either to supervise or to provide special education, the student's teacher, the parent or guardian, other individual(s) chosen by the school or parent, and the student when appropriate. Students are required to participate when transition services are addressed. If student participation does not occur in a meeting at which participation is not mandatory, the school must document "how the student's needs and preferences are addressed in the IEP" (King-Sears, 1997, p. 29). The meeting must be scheduled at a time that is convenient for both the school personnel and the parent(s).

An IEP is similar to a contract. It delineates the educational program and related services, if any, the school system is obligated to provide for each student with a disability. The school system and teacher are not, however, legally responsible if the goals of the educational program are not met. The law and its reauthorizations recognize that education is a complex endeavor. While educational personnel can be held responsible for providing the opportunities for success, they cannot be held responsible for ensuring that each student will be successful. Chapter 12 in this book includes more extensive information on IEPs and involving parents in that process.

As this section on team functioning during educational touchpoints shows, a professional could belong to a number of teams. Beyond that, imagine the parents trying to keep up with all of these teams and also to provide meaningful input for their child. Clearly, providing the best educational opportunities for the student requires careful planning and implementation of the team process. Without such consideration, these teams would not be able to function effectively.

PLANNING AND IMPLEMENTING TEAM PROCESS

There are four primary factors that are important to effective planning and implementation of team process. First, clarity of purpose is critical to productive team functioning. Second, smoothly functioning teams must employ effective task behaviors (e.g., giving information, summarizing) and maintenance behaviors (e.g., encouraging, harmonizing). Third, leadership is best when it is shared, and the chairperson is most effective when assuming a democratic style. Finally, the involvement of all team members is critical to effective team functioning.

Purpose

Groups that work effectively together perform as a collection of individuals with clarity of purpose and goals (C. E. Larson & LaFasto, 1989). Teams that meet to help learners with special needs usually meet to plan or review educational or behavioral programs. For the at-risk student the team meetings are usually oriented toward problem solving.

The following activities are typical for planning meetings: (a) meeting in a collaborative setting to problem solve; (b) meeting before a referral to review information and provide suggestions; (c) reviewing referrals for special education services; (d) deciding whether a student is eligible for special education; (e) determining placement options in the least restrictive environment; (f) considering related services; and (g) developing an IEP. Awareness of the activity to be conducted allows team members to know their purpose from the beginning. Having a clarity of purpose about assigned activities is one way to improve team functioning (Garner, 1994).

Review is required for monitoring the IEP as well as for modifying the student's educational program, related services, or placement. The review process must be completed at least once a year.

Task and Maintenance Behaviors

Any behavior of a team member that supports the purpose of the team can be classified according to its basic function. When promoting the purpose of the team, team members speak either with the intent to get the group task accomplished, known as *task behavior*, or to improve relationships among members, known as *maintenance behavior*. Benne and Sheats (1948) provided the classic and time-honored work in this area. Table 10.1 lists the types of behavior that correlate to task functions and provides an example of each that is related to teams in schools. Of course, not all team processes are about task functions. Maintenance functions are critical for the team to function smoothly within a supportive climate that maximizes the use of each team member. Group maintenance functions are described in Table 10.2.

Together, task and maintenance behaviors allow team members to get their jobs done smoothly and efficiently. All of these behaviors are the responsibility of each team member. It is helpful to observe these behaviors in others as well as to note their absence. You may choose to set a goal of increasing your repertoire of these behaviors or of calling what typically occurs in your team meetings to the attention of the other team members.

Leadership

Leadership is the responsibility of all members of the team and should be shared by all. The chair of the team cannot be responsible for all of the task and maintenance behaviors, nor would that be desirable. Shared responsibility makes for more effective team functioning (Garner, 1994).

Beyond each team member's responsibility for assuming a role in leadership, the role of the chair of the team is important (Briggs, 1997). In particular, it is essential for the leader to empower all team members to assume leadership. In 1980, Pfeiffer examined studies on the effects of leadership styles on the special education team. He found that when the chair is too directive in resolving problems, his or her ideas are often seen as unacceptable and may lead to hostility on the part of other team members. The team members in the study considered it important to be given a voice in decision making and in sharing ideas and suggestions.

TABLE 10.1 • Team Task Functions

---

1. *Initiating.* For effective team functioning, someone must take the initiative. Proposing tasks, actions, goals, suggesting a procedure, and defining group problems are examples of initiating. Someone might say, "Let's build an agenda" or "Let's write the suggestions on the board so we don't forget them."

2. *Seeking or giving information, or openness.* For a task to be accomplished, there must be a clear and efficient flow of information, facts, and opinions. An example of information giving is, "I have some research data that might help in making our decision." This sharing of information ensures that any decisions are based on as much information as possible. Like information giving, information seeking helps the entire group, not just the one asking the questions or providing the information. An example of information seeking is, "How did Charlie perform during resource activities?"

3. *Clarifying and elaborating.* This behavior involves interpreting ideas or suggestions as well as clarifying issues before the team. Such statements communicate a collaborative stance. Examples are, "Let me elaborate and build upon that idea" and "I think what Mr. Jones means is that he doesn't know whether his son has the self-confidence to make himself comfortable enough to return to the general education classroom full-time. I agree and . . ."

4. *Summarizing.* This behavior involves pulling together related ideas and suggestions or offering a decision or conclusion for team consideration. Summarizing allows the entire group to reflect on where they have been, where they are, and where they must go. Summarizing statements are interjected at various times during a team meeting, not just in concluding the meeting. An example might be, "It seems as though so far we have made these points . . ."

5. *Consensus testing.* Although not all decisions can or should be made by consensus, much teamwork is a result of consensus decisions. Consensus testing involves making statements that check with team members to determine the amount of agreement that has been achieved. For example, "Have we made a decision about his speech therapy?" Such a statement reminds team members that they must sooner or later commit to a decision, thus adding positive work tension to the team process.

Pfeiffer also found that team members do not want problems handed to one discipline or individual to solve. He maintained that at least two team members from different disciplines should be involved in all aspects of the problem-solving process.

Sharing responsibility for team process does not simply happen, and team members need training to help them become contributing members (Losen & Losen, 1994). Effective sharing of responsibility must be nurtured and reinforced by the chair as well as by other team members. Losen and Losen (1985) recommended that the chair offer guiding suggestions, provide information timed to be of value, stimulate self-direction, appreciate others' values and views, and respect differences in opinions. The authors also recommended the chair *not* provide direct orders, interrupt proceedings with personal suggestions, ignore

---

TABLE 10.2 • Team Maintenance Functions

---

1. *Gatekeeping.* Without gatekeeping, information is lost, multiple conversations develop, and quieter team members can be cut off and withdraw. Gatekeeping statements attempt to keep the channels of communication open, facilitate participation by team members, and focus on sharing. Examples are, "Mary never had the opportunity to explain her suggestion" and "If we would all speak one at a time, we could hear everyone's ideas."
2. *Encouraging.* This behavior allows relevant information to be shared, heard, and considered. It involves being respectful, warm, and friendly toward others. An example is, "Mrs. Guissepe, is there something you would like to add before we move on?"
3. *Harmonizing and compromising.* The aims of harmonizing are to reconcile disagreement, reduce tensions, and allow team members to explore differences. An example is, "It would be beneficial if each of you would specify your objections to the other rather than name call." An example of compromising would be, "It looks as if Dan and I both have viable suggestions. Also, the team looks evenly divided about these two suggestions. In order to move forward in the meeting, I would like to focus on Dan's suggestion and retract mine." It is important to not overuse these types of statements. In addition, it is easy to use them inappropriately and thereby reduce the effectiveness of the team. You do not want to harmonize or compromise if it results in masking important issues or discounting creative solutions.
4. *Standard setting and testing.* This behavior focuses on the effectiveness of the task and maintenance behaviors of the team members at a particular point in time. It is a matter of watching to see how the group is operating and then sharing your perceptions with the other team members. An example would be, "Are we off task?" or "I can't keep up. Could someone summarize this discussion for me?"

---

team members' suggestions, withhold praise or encouragement, make general critical or nonobjective comments, or demand respect or allegiance.

Orelove and Sobsey (1996) and Sobsey (1994) suggested steps that administrators can take to facilitate a transdisciplinary approach for individuals with severe disabilities. The following ideas are adaptations of leadership activities, especially on the part of the principal, that encourage team process:

1. Encourage individual team members to see themselves as responsible to the team.

2. Encourage the team to see itself as responsible to the student and family and to see the learner from a family systems perspective.

3. Encourage family members to become involved at the level they choose.

4. Encourage the team to develop a mission statement.

5. Arrange school schedules to allow for regular team meetings, with coverage of classrooms when necessary.

6. Demonstrate effective communication skills during team meetings.

7. Encourage teachers and related services personnel to work together with family members to assess students and to develop goals and objectives.

8. During meetings, encourage the use of clear, simple language that parents and other professionals can understand.

9. Do not prevent conflict; help to resolve it when it occurs.

10. Promote respect for team members' diversity and differences.

11. Reaffirm who has been assigned each task/objective and who has primary responsibility.

Involvement

Involvement of all members of the team, including parents, must be encouraged. Some studies have pointed out differences between staff and parents as members of a team. Their training is different, their goals are different at times, and the parents' status on the team is different (Cooper & Rascon, 1994; Giangreco, 1994). Other studies have shown that parents and general education classroom teachers tend not to be involved in team process (Pfeiffer, 1980; Ysseldyke, Algozzine, & Allen, 1982). Yet Yoshida, Fenton, Maxwell, and Kaufman (1978) found that the level of satisfaction of team members increase with higher levels of participation on the team. Thus, involving all team members, especially parents, is critical to effective team functioning (Carney & Gamel-McCormick, 1996; Idol et al., 1994).

Focusing on time barriers to team participation, J. West (1990, cited by Turnbull and Turnbull, 1996) recommended the use of a permanent floating substitute so that teachers can attend IEP-related tasks. This author also suggested having volunteers or paraprofessionals teach so that teachers can be released for meetings and earmarking one time block a week and one day a marking period for collaboration. Pfeiffer (1980) recommended that a general education teacher serve as a constant team member to represent general education. Being a standing team member would enhance the status as well as involvement of that teacher. A standing team member would be more likely to help the occasional member feel more comfortable and be more involved in team process.

The findings of Yoshida et al. (1978) concerning the lack of involvement by general education classroom teachers in team meetings were built upon by Trailor (1982). She investigated the effects of role clarification on the participation level of classroom teachers on teams. General education classroom teachers in an experimental group helped develop 17 role statements for classroom teachers as participating team members. Those teachers who helped define their roles as team members (i.e., clarified their roles) contributed significantly more than the other teachers during team meetings. The finding that greater role clarification positively affects participation during team meetings has strong implications for training team members. Losen and Losen (1994) agreed with this finding, stating that without preparation team members' contributions "may, at best, prove meaningless, and, at worst, disruptive" (p. 121).

Fisher (1980) identified three types of factors that influence team effectiveness: intrapersonal factors, interpersonal factors, and group identity factors. Each of these types of factors, described in the following sections, has implications for the involvement of team members. The research-based literature of C. E. Larson and F. M. LaFasto (1989) and the writing of Garner (1994, 1995a) also focused on characteristics of teams that function effectively.

Intrapersonal Factors and Teamwork

Each team member should be open-minded about potential outcomes and sensitive to the feelings and beliefs of other team members. Each person must be committed to the team and its process and be willing to commit time and energy for that purpose (Garner, 1995a).

Each team member must actively share responsibility for the team's decisions (Garner, 1995a). Team members should also share their honest feelings and ideas, even when they feel they may be off-track. Along the same lines, they should express their views even when they feel they may be criticized for them. They must also find ways to criticize constructively, especially during team meetings.

Effective team members are *competent*. C. E. Larson and F. M. LaFasto (1989) looked at different aspects of competence. They found that, in teams, technical competence is important, as is personal skill in collaboration. Problem-solving teams need individuals with integrity—people who can be trusted as well as trust others. Creative teams thrive with independent thinkers who are confident, tenacious, and have initiative.

Interpersonal Factors and Teamwork

Collaboration is critical to effective team functioning. For group decision making to be effective, all team members must participate and encourage the participation of other members. Clear roles, responsibilities, and lines of communication are essential aspects of collaborative efforts, as is underlying trust. Without trust, it is difficult for team members to be honest, thus allowing negativity to fester. Trust promotes the open expression of personal interests as well as strengths and weaknesses. This communication leads to a more realistic division of labor based on both expertise and interest. Rather than hiding inadequacies, team members can obtain the help they need from, and rely on, those with strengths in their areas of inadequacy. Likewise, that can absorb team responsibility for their areas of strength.

Team effectiveness increases when members are skilled in communication. Team members should consider it their responsibility to learn effective communication skills. Supportive and accepting communication that is not defensive is most effective.

Members should evaluate problems and issues, not other members. A climate of mutual trust evolves from such communication. To be effective, team members must clarify communications that are unclear. They need to check others' reactions and describe ideas in detail so that others can respond with their observations and opinions. If members disagree with an idea, they should describe their reservations rather than react in a judgmental manner.

Groups and Teamwork

Focusing on the group *goal* is critical to effective team functioning. It is important that all members are clear about their objective. Having a clear purpose allows the team to focus their energy and effectively and efficiently conduct their important, rewarding, and necessary work.

Focusing on *results* is also important to the group. Of the different types of teams they studied, C. E. Larson and F. M. LaFasto (1989) found problem-solving, creative, and tactical teams to be most successful. Trust was found to be important for problem-solving teams, autonomy was found to be crucial for creative teams, and tactical teams were found to succeed when they reinforced clarity (C. E. Larson & LaFasto, 1989).

Patience with group process is necessary, especially during the early stages when the team is being established. It is important for members to be given ample opportunity to think through ideas, allowing for greater creativity and the development of more effective decisions. The team should avoid unrealistic "formula answers" to difficult problems.

Team members who are sensitive to group process will know when to communicate a particular idea. Team members who do not contribute should be encouraged to resign. A member who is not committed to the team will negatively affect the group process.

A *unified commitment* is critical to highly effective teams. In such teams an *esprit de corps* is palpable, and team members are loyal as well as dedicated to the team. Unlike the individualism prevalent in U.S. society, effective team members identify with being part of something larger than the self.

Other Factors Related to Teamwork

Garnering *external support* and *recognition* is essential to highly effective teams (C. E. Larson & LaFasto, 1989). Without the necessary human and nonhuman resources, a team will wither and die.

Teams must also develop *standards of excellence,* which convey the important values held by the team. They focus on the quantity and quality of the team's work as well as the human interaction demonstrated by the team members. Standards may stem from an individual drive, team pressure, or consequences of actions taken by the team; they may also derive from outside pressures, such as funding and legislation. The leader of the team has an impact on the standards of excellence, with different leadership styles impacting teams in different ways. Some leaders are demanding, others lead with a clear and shared vision. Some facilitate and are barely noticed, while others encourage and cheerlead. Some support and provide the basics, while others inspire.

A final factor influencing team effectiveness is *principled leadership,* which C. E. Larson and F. M. LaFasto (1989) defined as leadership that communicates a vision, creates change, and unleashes talent. It confronts and resolves problems of inadequate performance by team members and narrows priorities to allow for team success. For teams to succeed, the leader must support collaboration and focus on participatory decision making, share power, delegate responsibilities, model effective communication and human interaction, and train members to best utilize their capacities. Leadership is everyone's responsibility, and principled leadership is important for each team member to possess.

As a group, the team can use the factors related to gathering external support, recognition, standards of excellence, and principled leadership to evaluate their work. They provide a guide, and when used as indicators of healthy functioning, can point to areas that can be celebrated as well as those that need strengthening. Celebration of successful functioning is as important as recognition for the work accomplished.

TEAM CHARACTERISTICS AND AVOIDING PROBLEMS ON TEAMS

Understanding the characteristics of teamwork will help team members avoid problems (Briggs, 1997). Insight into specific characteristics of teams, including teamwork as an evolutionary process, was provided by Lowe and Herranen (1981). Another view of the team process was contributed by Bailey (1984), whose triaxial model can be used to help prevent problems in team functioning. Following a discussion of the stages of team development and Bailey's triaxial model, this section concludes with a discussion of potential challenges that team members face. An understanding of these three topics will better prepare the professional to avoid or deal with problems on teams.

Stages of Team Development

Different models of the stages of team development have been conceptualized. Two are related in this section. The first has been applied universally in the analysis of team process. The second was used originally for teamwork in hospital settings. Both are directly transferable to the discipline of education.

Five Stages of Team Development

Professionals in the field of education have described stages of team development that are meaningful to schools (Briggs, 1997; Garner, 1995a). Based on the work of Tuckman (1965), the stages are forming, storming, norming, performing, and transforming. Briggs (1997), writing about early intervention teams, provided a lengthy description of each stage and gave case examples. She also provided suggestions for ways to improve the group process within each stage. Her work is worthwhile reading regardless of the level of student your team serves.

Stage 1—Forming. When a team first forms, there is confusion, uncertainty, anxiety, and ambiguity, as well as excitement and enthusiasm. Team members are figuring out what their mission and purpose are and whether they have the resources necessary to be a member of the team. Because members are hesitant to speak openly, interactions may be superficial. In this phase of team development, a strong leader capable of navigating the uncharted waters is necessary. Identifying resources and establishing norms are parts of this phase.

Stage 2—Storming. As the team moves from observation to participation, relationships among team members become more contentious and fractious. The leader often becomes the whipping boy or girl, and hostility and disagreement are not uncommon. Underlying this friction is the movement toward reconciliation of two common fears, isolation and absorption. The resolution of the disagreements leads to affiliation. Although uncomfortable, this chaos is a necessary step in the right direction.

Stage 3—Norming. Over time, harmony develops, and team members become more aware of their similarities as opposed to their differences. The oil has greased the machine, and work moves along well. People on the team know what is expected of them and the other members. Definite ways of coming together and being apart are well established.

Stage 4—Performing. This is a time of balance and stability. Cohesion and collaboration are obvious among team members. Team members are more comfortable working as a team, and they have a sense of pride in their teamwork. A definite *esprit de corps* has evolved.

Stage 5—Transforming. As its work comes to a conclusion, the team seeks new challenges or disbands. Not dependent upon one person or a leader, the team is *one* organism. Personal mastery is evident, and people feel fulfilled.

Six Phases of Team Development

Lowe and Herranen (1981) identified six phases in the development of a team. They described patterns of interactions, common emotions, and team productivity for each of the six phases. Although this model analyzed teamwork in hospital settings, it relates well to the field of education.

Phase 1: Becoming acquainted. People bring different perspectives to the team. Some enter the team because their involvement is mandated, others enter by choice and in recognition of the team's value. While team members are becoming acquainted, the leadership style might be autocratic, democratic, or absent. Generally, there is a hierarchical structure with the professional at the top of the pecking order anointed as leader. Interaction patterns are polite and impersonal; and are social in nature. There is no group consensus regarding goals; each professional on the team sees his or her goals as most important. Emotions are held in check, and there are few conflicts. Phase 1 is characterized by high individual productivity and low team productivity.

Phase 2: Trial and error. Once professionals recognize the need to collaborate on common goals, this phase begins. Pairing with an ally is the typical interaction pattern that emerges. Such pairing, however, increases individual productivity rather than group productivity. Role conflict, role ambiguity, and role overload stem from team members' testing the waters. The nature of the team is similar to that in Phase 1; members are concerned about turf issues.

Phase 3: Collective indecision. In this phase members are attempting to avoid conflict and achieve equilibrium. Boundaries begin to develop. Team members are aware of the appeal of groups as well as their disadvantages. Little is accomplished because there is no emphasis on accountability. There is a lack of leadership; conformity is expected. Role conflict is not dealt with, and there is low morale and covert anger. As might be expected, both team and individual productivity suffer. No one feels heard by other team members.

Phase 4: Crisis. As a result of a crisis stemming from collective indecision, roles and responsibilities are defined and boundaries are drawn. An informal and formal leader develop, and aspects of group process become a focus of attention. Negative emotions are expressed because they can now be handled. Team members begin to value one another for their particular expertise and potential assistance in achieving the team's goal. Team productivity continues to be low.

Phase 5: Resolution. Teamwork finally has begun when the team members commit to working as a unit. Open communication leads to a sharing of leadership, decision making, and responsibility. Accountability is important for the individual and the team. Team productivity is high. This phase is fragile; the team needs to move to the next phase, maintenance.

Phase 6: Team maintenance. Sharing by team members allows the focus to be on the team's goals. In the school setting, all team members see the student from a holistic view and value other members' expertise. Effectiveness depends upon internal group processes and how conflicts are handled. Expectations are clarified continuously, norms evolve, team members respect self and others, accountability is important, and a common language develops. According to Lowe and Herranen (1981), this is the critical phase in team development.

As Orelove and Sobsey (1996) indicated, all of these phases are not experienced by every team, "nor will teams go through each stage in a fixed sequence. It does seem clear, however, that virtually every team experiences growing pains as a normal part of the process of evolving into a smoothly operating unit" (p. 21).

The Triaxial Model

Bailey (1984) proposed a triaxial model (described in Table 10.3) for understanding processes within teams that focus on individuals who are at risk or who have special needs. The model shows the complex and difficult task of organizing effective teams and provides insight into avoiding, recognizing, and ameliorating problems experienced by team members.

Bailey's model is based on the work of Tseng and McDermott (1979). Three premises, called "axes," form the basis for the model:

1. Team growth is a developmental process. Some problems in team functioning can be attributed to the stage of development at which the team is functioning.

2. Teams are composed of individuals. Thus some problems may result from interpersonal problems or subsystems within the team.

3. The team is a functioning unit. Some problems can, therefore, be expected to stem from whole-team dysfunction.

TABLE 10.3 • The Triaxial Model

Axis I. Team growth is a developmental process. Problems related to the developmental stage of a team can occur during a given team meeting. There are six typical steps in IEP meetings: review assessments, discuss present status, develop a long-range plan, make placement decision, determine instructional objectives, and design an implementation plan. Team members should analyze their interactions within meetings to determine whether a pattern of dysfunction emerges. One particular step might show up as problematic. In other cases, the actual sequencing of steps might need to be changed.

Axis II. Teams are composed of individuals. The ideal team will have a leader present who performed previously as a member of the team. Each member possesses equal power and influence. On the ideal team, conflicts and disagreements are based not on personality conflicts but on substantive issues. There are seven potential problems relating to individuals.

A dominant leader may arise who is resented by others, cuts down on discussion, or fosters dependency. The purpose of the team is collaboration, so even if domination is not resented it is inappropriate.

Dominant team member(s) may arise. Who they are stems from personalities, hierarchies, or perceived power. Dominant behavior is counterproductive when the person exhibiting that power will not listen to others' opinions. Not all domination is obvious. It may be very subtle, such as professional domination by a psychiatrist.

Inferior team member(s) may arise. An inferior team member could be any person. Often, teachers and parents are inferior members. Their opinions may be viewed by others or themselves as less worthy than other members' opinions. People who are viewed as inferior eventually stop making contributions. That withdrawal reinforces the others' view of them as inferior. It is important for team functioning to equally value all contributions.

Specific conflict between two members may occur, resulting in team dysfunction. Conflict is a natural and expected part of team functioning; however, when it pervades all meetings and interferes with planning, it is dysfunctional. An example of such a conflict is when two members always take diametrically opposed positions, regardless of usual opinions.

One member may continually conflict with all others. Such behavior is highly disruptive of team functioning. It is even more dysfunctional when the person is highly vocal. Eventually such a person is rejected, regardless of the quality of the input.

Factions within the team may occur when subsystems compete with one another. Winning should not take precedence over the task of the team, which is meeting the student's needs.

One member may feel isolated from the group. This member does not appear to belong to the team socially. A feeling of being in the "out crowd" is not conducive to healthy team functioning.

(continued)

Source: Drawn from "A Triaxial Model of the Interdisciplinary Team and Group Process" by D. Bailey, 1984, *Exceptional Children, 51*(1), pp. 17–25.

TABLE 10.3 • *continued*

Axis III. The whole team is a functioning unit. In Axis III the structure or organization of the whole team is the subject of scrutiny. Ideal teams are well organized, possess clarity of roles, and are structured yet flexible. There are four types of whole team dysfunction.

The Underperforming Team occurs when team members are unskilled or not invested in the team process. The task is not completed due to whole-team dysfunction. Team tasks are perfunctory. Often the underperforming team has an ineffective leader, and members are unable or unwilling to take responsibility for seeing that the team accomplishes its goals.

The Overstructured Team occurs when members' roles are rigidly defined. Meetings are usually inflexible, with substance taking a back seat to structure and the agenda. Rigidity in roles and routines restricts interactions and prevents the discussion of social and emotional content.

The Team With Ambiguous Roles occurs when members are unclear about who does what. Planning is not integrated due to territoriality or confusion and withdrawal. Basically, no one takes responsibility for team process, and the result is inadequate planning for the student.

The Disorganized Team lacks leadership, direction, and structure. Meetings may appear chaotic. This problem stems from either poor leadership or confusion about roles and purpose. Members sometimes become overly involved in discussing their social lives. At other times, different members are flowing in and out of the meetings due to late arrivals, early departures, and telephone calls.

This three-dimensional model allows the determination of the level of dysfunction—team development, team subsystems, or whole-team functioning. This breakdown allows for a considered diagnosis of team dysfunction and improves the likelihood of teams being functional in the school context.

An understanding of the processes teams experience can help team members pinpoint the focus of analysis and intervention for problems that occur.

Challenges

A variety of challenges to team functioning are covered in this section. The discussion is, by no means, conclusive; many other challenges may surface. The purpose in focusing on challenges is to help you recognize and avoid, as well as resolve, these very human situations. These challenges are divided into four categories: philosophical and theoretical differences, isolation of family members, interpersonal challenges, and resistance to change. In any group, it is important to frame challenges as potentially resolvable, rather than as impossible situations.

Differences in Philosophical and Theoretical Orientations

Team members must often confront differences in their training as well as theoretical and philosophical orientations (Courtnage & Smith-Davis, 1987). Therapists typically are trained in a medical model that emphasizes determining the underlying cause of the behavior and then focuses therapy on that "cause." Family systems therapists are, however, trained in theoretical models that view challenging situations less linearly (W. M. Walsh & Williams, 1997). The emphasis on individual versus systemic thinking may be cause for misunderstanding among team members. Further, it is likely to result in fundamental differences in approaches to students as well as family members.

This difficulty is intensified by the isolated preparation of professionals such as teachers, counselors, therapists, nurses, and occupational therapists. Professionals frequently use their own jargon when meeting in teams. Others, especially parents, may not understand the terminology and may become frustrated when trying to provide input or simply to follow the team discussion. Briggs (1997) pointed to the importance of recognizing and identifying the differences in team members' philosophies and theoretical orientations and saw these differences as contributions that strengthened team functioning.

Philosophical and theoretical challenges to team functioning can be intensified or reduced by the team model employed. A multidisciplinary approach has a greater likelihood of facing philosophical and theoretical problems. The nature of the approach lends itself to such misunderstandings. It is highly difficult to understand, coordinate, and value the orientations of other team members when their approaches are not integrated, which follows from the multidisciplinary team approach. Due to its interactive nature, the interdisciplinary team model has a greater likelihood of team collaboration with fewer theoretical and philosophical challenges.

Isolation of Parents or Other Family Member

Another challenge to effective team functioning is the isolation of family members. Parents may be apprised of their rights; however, whether they typically understand those rights have been questioned (Armstrong, 1995; Roit & Pfohl, 1984). Parents also may be confused by the educational processes used in the schools. If parents are involved only at the stage of developing the IEP, their isolation is exacerbated even further. It is important to afford family members opportunities to be involved throughout the process—from the initial request for assistance to planning the educational program. Long-term involvement will reduce the sense of isolation on the part of any family members who choose to be involved to a greater degree in the educational life of the student with special needs.

Interpersonal Challenges

Professionals trained in a medical model may feel threatened by the egalitarian nature of teams that include parents and paraprofessionals. Trusting others to provide helpful information is imperative in the effective functioning of such teams. Rising to that challenge is difficult for some professionals. In time, however, most of those who were threatened originally will find that the risk-taking is worth the effort.

Another aspect of interpersonal struggles is a lack of clarity regarding team members' responsibilities. Each person's role must, therefore, be clarified continuously. Role conflict will ensue if team members are unsure of their current functions.

Resistance to Change

People resist change for a variety of reasons. While resistance should be viewed as a normal and expected aspect of any change process, leaving it unchecked can be destructive. Therefore, it is important to recognize reasons for resisting change.

Team members may resist change because they (a) feel inadequate, (b) fear the unknown, (c) lack trust, or (d) are unable to see the larger picture. Generally speaking, when team members become more familiar with team functioning, they overcome their feelings of inadequacy.

The fear of the unknown, which may surface when professionals are faced with working collaboratively on an egalitarian team, can be reduced through effective communication. Training that responds to questions and concerns effectively lowers the level of fear about new team functioning.

There is a lack of trust when the people involved do not have faith in those initiating change. As changes are being planned, representatives should be involved in planning and decision making. This allows those involved in change to consult trusted colleagues about their concerns.

Inability to see the larger picture occurs when team members are not part of the change process from the beginning. It is difficult for them to understand the goals and need for change. Once they understand the benefits to the total team functioning, it is likely that they will be more supportive.

Again, this focus on challenges is intended to be positive. The purpose is to help you recognize and avoid or resolve problems. Chapter 14 covers resistance to change in more detail.

INVOLVING FAMILIES IN TEAMS

Involving families in reviewing test data and options for service delivery models, as well as in decision making and goal setting, is important to the team process. As discussed by Losen and Losen (1994), it is critical to involve parents in a preteam meeting to explain the evaluation procedures used and their child's test results. This allows for a smoother and more effective team meeting.

Reviewing Test Data

During the eligibility team meeting, it is valuable to refer to the parents' reactions to the test data that were shared at the preteam meeting. Such a statement might be,

> Mrs. Smith probably remembers that, during the preteam meeting, I suggested her daughter Kristie could be experiencing greater anxiety than we originally anticipated. When we reviewed the results of the tests, I was able to demonstrate the level

on which Kristie is functioning as compared with other students in kindergarten. As a result, I think Mrs. Smith understands why Kristie needs special help. Placement in special education is meaningful in particular as Kristie regains her self-esteem and confidence in her ability to function successfully at school tasks. Mrs. Smith, do you have anything further to discuss about your reactions?

It is important that the eligibility team meeting not be the first time that parents receive test results that have important implications for their child, particularly when the test results involve categorization or labeling (Losen & Losen, 1994). Falik (1995) has written about family reactions to having a child with a learning disability. Imagine having your own child being labeled with retardation or learning disability at a meeting. You would likely be unable to participate further in providing input or suggestions, or to be involved in decision making, if this was your first awareness of the label being assigned to your child. Sensitivity and empathy are necessary. One positive strategy for developing empathy is to use imagery, imagining yourself walking a mile in the other person's moccasins.

Information provided during IEP team meetings should be summaries of test results. Going point-by-point through test data takes too much time. Having already viewed test data and having an opportunity to react, parents will not mind summaries, as long as their particular reactions to those results are included with the summaries.

Charts, outlines, or descriptions of tests may be helpful when providing summaries. Family members will find data provided in this way easier to follow than test protocol results alone. It may be helpful to include brief written descriptions of each of the subtests used. Such descriptions can be used with many different families. It is critical to write those descriptions in lay terms and at the level of the reader. This practice also indicates to the family members that you are interested in helping them understand what kinds of tests have been administered and what information was found about their child.

Family members should feel comfortable asking questions about summaries, charts, or descriptions. It is the professionals' responsibility to make the family members feel comfortable by summarizing the test results at their level of understanding. Otherwise, the family members may not even be able to formulate their questions. Professionals can help the family members clarify what they do not understand or what they find questionable.

Family members also should be informed about the psychometric properties of the tests. Reliability and validity may need to be discussed if some test data are not as valuable as other test data. This is often the case when independent evaluations, requested by the parents, include results from tests with questionable reliability or validity.

Consideration of the Service Delivery Model

For schools in which inclusion is the preferred base (Gamel-McCormick, 1995; Guterman, 1995; P. J. McWilliam & Bailey, 1993), discussing the value of inclusive schools with parents is important. Parents will benefit from hearing about the training that has been and will continue to be provided to the teachers who work in inclusive schools. Parents are more likely to become advocates for inclusive schools if they know what support will be made available for their child to succeed in an inclusive setting.

Parents are involved in the consideration of service delivery options for their child. It is important that they are familiar with the variety of alternative service delivery models. They should know that within one model there are choices (D. F. Bradley & Switlick, 1997), such as the variations of collaborative services including co-teaching with its complementary instruction, supportive learning activities, and team teaching, as well as indirect services including problem solving, group problem solving, and peer coaching.

If possible, the parents should learn about the options for service delivery at an early stage so they are more likely to understand the reasons for the combination of placements recommended or why one type of placement is recommended over all the others. This practice could result in fewer due process hearings initiated by parents. It is also a good check and balance for team members so that they do not recommend too quickly a particular delivery model for a student. When parents are involved in listening to those deliberations, professionals are more likely to be deliberative.

As the team considers placement for a student, the parents will benefit from a review of the advantages and disadvantages of different delivery models. With this knowledge, parents can contribute to decision making, as well as understand that there are ways that disadvantages can be overcome or minimized.

When the number of general education classroom activities in which a given student might engage is being considered, team members can indicate how time spent in the general education program may benefit the student more than the special classroom involvement. Switlick (1997b) provided various scenarios of flowing in and out of general education and special classrooms in a flexible manner. She indicated that success depends on:

- Teacher attitude toward the disability (especially emotional disabilities)
- Team teaching and collaboration between the general educator and the special educator
- Student-centered (not content-centered) instruction in the general education setting
- Integration of specialized curricular objectives in the general education setting (p. 255)

In addition, Orelove and Malatchi (1996) recommended that the IEP team develop a matrix of the goals for the student and the time/activity blocks of the school day. Together, these ideas may help parents examine the inclusive delivery of services in a more favorable manner.

Decision Making

Once test results and service delivery model options have been reviewed, a decision must be made about the student's placement and program. If parents are involved in the steps prior to this point, it is more likely that they will support any professional recommendations that are made.

In actuality, recommendations or suggestions for a particular placement may be considered by the parent or professional prior to the meeting when the decision will be made. It is important to have all the information that is needed available at the meeting so that the decision regarding placement will not be delayed.

When team members do not agree on the program, it is important to discuss the reasons for their disagreement and try to resolve them. Reaching consensus is preferable to a vote that results in a decision made on the basis of one vote tipping the balance for a particular placement. When team members do not agree about the program placement, the decision can be deferred. It may be necessary that certain points of contention be researched prior to a decision being reached.

Often, the process of reviewing the alternatives makes the best decision obvious and the decision simply needs to be confirmed. When there is no consensus on a decision, however, it is important to listen to family preferences. Gamel-McCormick (1995), writing about family preferences, particularly recommended listening to the parents of elementary-aged students when they want inclusive education.

Goal Setting

After a recommendation for placement is made, related services and the student's IEP must be considered. Parents also are involved in these determinations. All objectives should be written in simple, clear language that the family members and student can understand.

In addition, the parents and student should be informed about the length of time it generally takes to achieve a particular goal or objective. The parents will also benefit from knowing that the IEP is not a binding contract but a working agreement with stated goals for their child as well as related services on which they can count.

Whenever family members are involved in team meetings, professionals must make them feel comfortable and wanted as well as view them as capable of contributing meaningful input. Parents should never be pressured into accepting a delivery model or program if they feel there is another, more appropriate option. Schools should let parents know that their participation is desired and that they have an important contribution to make in the planning process.

General Guidelines for Family Involvement

Carney and Gamel-McCormick (1996) summarized the school professional's responsibility with regard to family involvement on interdisciplinary teams as follows:

1. Appreciating and valuing parents' involvement in the team at the level they desire to be involved

2. Remembering that the family is in the midst of a typical process of change and adjustment and at the same time are experiencing an event that is very different from other families

3. Recognizing that the child's fit within the family might be a priority concern

4. Respecting the family's cultural patterns and beliefs and the impact they will have on whether and how the family participates on a program planning team

5. Communicating accurately and honestly with parents (p. 464)

SUMMARY

The focus of this chapter has been on team functioning for those working to meet the needs of special-needs and at-risk students. Collaboration and respect are critical to successful team functioning, and family involvement is a key to meeting the needs of the student. Trust and honesty are important characteristics of all individuals contributing to the education of students.

Family Conferences and Teacher-Student Support Teams

The family conference is a crucial component of family–school professional interaction and an important mechanism for identifying unmet needs of both at-risk and special-needs students who are in the general education classroom. The earlier the family involvement, the better. In fact, the literature has shown that if school professionals include the family in the early stages of the identification process, the chances increase that referral for special education will not be needed (Fuchs, Fuchs, & Bahr, 1990; Fuchs, Fuchs, Bahr, Fernstrom, & Steker, 1990). Embedding family systems concepts and practices in teacher-student support teams will likely reduce referrals even more.

This chapter begins with a discussion of three considerations basic to productive interactions between school and home and then addresses general applications of family systems concepts that professionals can use to improve family-school communication. These applications involve many of the concepts described in Appendix A. Next, information on planning, implementing, and evaluating family conferences is provided, followed by a discussion of teacher-student support teams and how to obtain the family support that is needed to ensure student success. As in Chapter 10, this chapter builds on the concepts presented in Parts I and II and focuses on family involvement from a family systems perspective.

BASIC CONSIDERATIONS FOR SCHOOL-HOME INTERACTIONS

Classroom teachers, as well as principals, are in a special position for relating to families of at-risk and special-needs students. Many family members do not interact with school counselors, social workers, psychologists, or other helping professionals. Their contact with these specialists is frequently irregular and in response to problems. The teacher, however, has frequent opportunities for routine contact with family members.

This contact provides a basis for establishing and maintaining a trusting relationship. Whereas the family member may view the school psychologist as intimidating and judgmental, the teacher is often seen as an understanding and nonthreatening source of valuable information. Parents view teachers in the most positive light of all of the school professionals. The different contexts in which teachers and family members relate to the student enrich the information and idea exchange between family members and the school and provide the teacher with opportunities to build upon the parents' trust.

This section discusses three considerations that are fundamental to all human interactions between school and home and are central to the family systems perspective. They are sensitivity, climate, and locus of influence.

Sensitivity

Simpson (1990, 1996) indicated that successful interaction with others stems from an interest in, as well as a sensitivity toward, people. Those who serve students and families need to have an authentic interest in others as well as a desire to invest time and energy in joint problem solving.

The success of a family-professional interaction always hinges on the attitudes, values, sensitivity, and understanding of the professional. Fortunately, it is possible for professionals to learn the many important and beneficial human interaction skills for building relationships (D. Johnson, 1997). Acquiring these skills is not sufficient, however; the professionals must also be committed to meeting the needs of the families. Although both professionals and family members should assume the responsibility for sound working relations, it is incumbent upon the professional to have the attitude and motivation necessary for helpful interactions to occur. Such development is a basic part of professionalism on the part of the school representative. Nel Noddings (1984), writing about caring on the part of professionals in education, offers food for thought on this topic.

Climate/Mood

The most important characteristic of a successful family-professional interaction is trust. Trust emerges if people feel safe enough to take interpersonal risks. The risk taking can then result in successful, productive relationships.

Several interactive elements are essential for the development of trust in the family-professional relationship. They include the willingness of both the family and the professional to invest time and energy in a shared commitment to the student, to advocate assertively for the student, to maintain sensitivity to one another's needs, to confront as well as reinforce one another, and to maintain a positive, honest outlook.

In their interactions, family members and school professionals need to be honest and direct, even though that may involve a significant degree of interpersonal risk. It is critical to effective human interaction that professionals have these qualities and take the lead in modeling appropriate risk-taking behavior. In his text *Conferencing Parents of Exceptional*

Children, Simpson (1990) provided a questionnaire listing 20 risk-taking situations that professionals often face in relation to parents. It is reprinted in Table 11.1. A useful exercise for educators is to complete the questionnaire and then answer the following five questions:

1. What items were you surprised to see on the questionnaire?

2. Are there any items you feel are inappropriate to interaction with families?

3. Did you learn anything new about yourself? If so, what? If not, why?

4. Which items are more difficult for you personally?

5. Are there items you would add to the questionnaire?

Also beneficial is to discuss your answers to these questions with others who have read this book and completed the questionnaire. You may find some interesting differences in your answers. Understanding the reasons for those differences can provide insight into the management of risk-taking situations.

It is natural for professionals to feel uncomfortable with some of the items in Simpson's (1990) list. To develop a climate of trust, however, professionals must manage their discomfort effectively. Realizing that, as a professional, you must take risks and recognizing your feelings about risk taking will help you empathize with parents as they take even greater risks.

Locus of Influence

Effective human interaction is a mutual, shared activity. Regardless of the specific purpose of the interaction, all interchanges provide opportunities to trade information and views, share feelings, and make joint decisions. The preservation of trust and the establishment of a sound working relationship require the maintenance of a shared locus of influence, that is, that the professional, the student, and the family members mutually share influence in decision making (Gamel-McCormick, 1995).

If family members think that professionals are interfering with their ability to influence decisions affecting their child they may become anxious, frustrated, and angry. Professionals must make sure that parents know they not only will have the opportunity but will be expected to influence decisions. Empowerment of the students (Brendtro & Bacon, 1995) and family (Dunst, Trivette, & Deal, 1994a) is critical to effective family-professional interactions. Shared influence and joint decisions are generally more difficult to achieve than unilateral decisions. Sharing the influence, however, maximizes the investment of all of the involved parties in the outcome.

The basic considerations of sensitivity, climate/mood, and locus of influence are relevant to all forms of interactions with families, whether related to family conferences, obtaining assistance for a student, or other school-initiated interactions. They are critical to effective human interaction, and, while they are not linked directly to family systems concepts, they maximize the use of family systems concepts by school professionals.

TABLE 11.1 • Risk Taking Questionnaire

How comfortable are you in . . .	Very Comfortable	Somewhat Comfortable	Neutral	Somewhat Uncomfortable	Very Uncomfortable
1. Telling parents you don't know	___	___	___	___	___
2. Telling parents that you made a mistake	___	___	___	___	___
3. Suggesting to parents that another professional made an error	___	___	___	___	___
4. Suggesting to parents that they should consider therapy for themselves	___	___	___	___	___
5. Telling parents that there are behaviors displayed by their children that you dislike	___	___	___	___	___
6. Displaying your emotions in parent-educator conference	___	___	___	___	___
7. Confronting parents with their failure to follow through on agreed-upon plans	___	___	___	___	___
8. Talking about your own problems in a parent-educator conference	___	___	___	___	___
9. Praising parents for things they do well	___	___	___	___	___
10. Having parents take notes during conferences	___	___	___	___	___
11. Allowing parents to observe in your class while you are teaching	___	___	___	___	___
12. Allowing parents to tutor their child at home	___	___	___	___	___
13. Allowing parents to use behavior modification procedures with their child at home	___	___	___	___	___
14. Telling parents their "rights" under PL 94-142	___	___	___	___	___
15. Having parents assume an active role during individualized education program conferences	___	___	___	___	___
16. Having parents ask you to defend your teaching strategies	___	___	___	___	___
17. Having parents bring a friend to individualized education program conferences	___	___	___	___	___
18. Having parents call you at home about a problem their child is having at school	___	___	___	___	___
19. Having parents recommend specific curriculum	___	___	___	___	___
20. Having parents review school records	___	___	___	___	___

Source: From *Conferencing Parents of Exceptional Children* (2nd ed.) by R. Simpson, 1990, Austin, TX: PRO-ED. Reprinted by permission of PRO-ED.

GENERAL APPLICATIONS OF FAMILY SYSTEMS CONCEPTS

As stated in the introduction to this chapter, many of the ideas in this section relate to the family systems concepts described in Appendix A. Reviewing the information in Appendix A on the Satir Communication Process Model and Bowen theory will provide a framework for the following discussion of systems concepts.

The section begins with a discussion of Satir's process for transforming family rules into guidelines, an aspect vital to change and growth. The discussion then turns to Satir's *five freedoms,* the heart of her view of healthy communication. School professionals will benefit by being able to help family members use these processes in their relationships. Finally, the Bowen theory is revisited, with attention directed to detriangling, a process that requires considerable time and attention and is one of the most difficult processes to achieve (Kerr & Bowen, 1988).

Transformation of Family Rules Into Guidelines

Satir (1983a) believed it was possible to find something useful in any rule. Recognizing that some family rules are outdated, inflexible, or restrictive, she focused her energies on helping individuals transform the dysfunctional rules with which they grew up. Such transformation allows the rules, in a new form, to guide the individual while also providing protection (Schwab, 1990). An example of a rigid rule is, "I should never be angry." This is not always possible, nor is it healthy. Expressing anger may be a significant way to lead to positive change in a situation as well as to discharge pent-up energy that might otherwise explode in unproductive ways or cause health problems like ulcers. Satir would have helped a person who adhered to this rigid family rule, transform it into a guideline by going through a series of transformative steps, as described in the following section.

Steps for Transforming Family Rules

Satir would have begun by evaluating the first-order transformation, "I can always be angry," with the person. Most people would say, "No, not always." Then a second-order transformation, "I can sometimes be angry," would be discussed. Most people who have grown up with the "I can never be angry" rule would say, when faced with a professional aware of what constitutes healthy family rules, "Well, maybe." The third-order transformation would be, "I can be angry when [and then three occasions would be listed]. "Examples would be "when (a) it will make me feel better, (b) there would be a possibility for change, and (c) I might eventually feel closer to the person with whom I am upset." This type of transformation allows the individual to use the family rule in a way that can continue to provide guidance for life. This process of transformation is elaborated upon in later subsections of this section on implementation and further exploration.

Questions for Evaluating Family Rules

Satir and Baldwin (1983) provided a list of questions for evaluating family rules (see Table 11.2). The professional and family member can use these questions to determine whether

TABLE 11.2 • Satir's Questions for Evaluating Family Rules

The following series of questions can be used by school professionals to help determine what family rules need transformation. The first two questions can help the professional determine potential rules for transformation into guidelines. The following three questions can help the professional probe areas of human interaction that might reveal a rule in need of transformation. Most ineffective family rules stem from aspects of information sharing, differentness, and expression of feelings, thoughts, or opinions within the context of the family.

1. Are the rules humanly possible?
2. Are the rules up to date and relevant to a changing situation?
3. What are the rules governing differentness?
4. What rules surround the sharing of information?
5. What rules govern what family members can say about what they are feeling, seeing, and hearing?

Source: From *Satir, Step by Step* (pp. 202–205) by V. Satir and M. Baldwin, 1983, Palo Alto, CA: Science and Behavior Books.

family rules are in need of transformation. The professional can also use these questions when attempting to identify what the family rules are.

A review of these questions can help family members gain insight into the rules that govern their lives, examine other possibilities, and transform the rules that interrupt their lives. Improved communication and higher self-esteem generally follow such revisions of dysfunctional family rules. These are two of the most important aspects of healthy human functioning.

Implementation

Although it is not always possible to help family members transform obsolete, rigid, or ineffective rules, there are occasions when school professionals can be of assistance. For example, a professional can introduce to a family the concept of the need to transform a rule by relating the following story:

> A newlywed couple argued profusely for their first two Thanksgivings about how to cook the turkey. The husband insisted that the legs had to be cut off and placed beside the turkey in the pan. The wife was equally adamant that the legs not be removed. One day, when they were visiting the husband's parents, the wife asked her mother-in-law why she had always cooked the turkey with the legs removed. The mother-in-law replied, "We didn't have a large enough pan in which to cook the turkey, so we had to cut off its legs."

Counselors can then apply Satir's rule transformation technique to help transform an actual family rule. For example, consider the case of a father and his 16-year-old son who came to counseling because they argued frequently and, on occasion, came close to exchanging blows. In the process of counseling, the counselor learned that the parents had imposed the rigid family rule that "children never question rules established by a parent." While this rule may have been appropriate for the father's 4-year-old son, it did not fit the adolescent's situation. In fact, it could, by its very nature, instigate authority problems with any adolescent. In counseling, the father and son were led through a process of transforming that rule. The father was taught that his 16-year-old son had become old enough to think about which of the family's rules did and did not fit for him. The father began to realize that respect for elders is not automatic but is earned by flexible and supportive rules that fit the age of the children and the situation involved.

As noted in Chapter 2, parents need to adapt family rules to the developmental level of each child. The emphasis in the following example of rule transformation is on what the counselor (C) would say to the parent (P).

C: Mr. Emmerson, I'm glad we have this opportunity to continue discussing the situation with your son Tim. I have thought about the early curfew Tim has on the weekends. Tell me how that came about.

P: Tim has the same rule as our other son, Ralph. Since it would be too late for Ralph to come home after 9:00, my wife and I decided that Tim would also have to come in at 9:00. We cannot see how we could allow Tim to come in later, when Ralph has to be home by 9:00.

C: How old is Ralph?

P: 12.

C: So Tim is 4 years older than Ralph, and he still has to live by the same rules. Is that the way it was in your house when you grew up?

P: No, my older brother got away with murder. He was always coming in late and waking me up. My parents let him come in whenever he wanted, and he got in a lot of trouble. Then, later, they cracked down on me and made me come in earlier than he did at my age.

C: I can see how that could affect the kind of rules you have designed for your two children. Mr. Emmerson, could you imagine Tim always having a 2:00 a.m. curfew?

P: No. That's not in the realm of possibility.

C: Then, could you just imagine that on some occasion Tim might be allowed to have a later curfew?

P: I suppose so, like for the junior prom.

C: What might be some other times Tim could have a later curfew?

P: I guess when there's a movie he is seeing that won't be over in time for him to get home. . . . Also, perhaps when another parent has offered to go bowling with them, he could come in later.

C: Do you think there are big enough differences in a 12-year-old and a 16-year-old that they might need different rules?

P: I don't want Ralph to think we're favoring Tim!

C: It might be a good idea to talk with Ralph and explain why his rule for curfew is different from Tim's. Most kids even look forward to the time when they are old enough for their curfew times to change. I think that when we are most comfortable with our rule differences, our children test us less regarding those inequities. What we are talking about is a recognition, as well as an acceptance, of the fact that age makes a difference for all kinds of things.

P: I suppose so. I could even give Ralph the example of Tim being old enough to drive.

C: Right. I think that your agreeing to change his curfew will make a real difference for Tim. I appreciate your openness to these thoughts. By the way, I have a good article I think you might like to read about age differences in families.

Not all family-professional interactions are appropriate for working on transforming family rules. Sometimes, there will not be enough time; in other instances, the issue at hand will have nothing to do with rules. Sometimes, family members may not be open to the suggestion of transforming family rules; on other occasions, the mix of people may not be appropriate.

When coaching parents regarding family rules, it is important to keep in mind that although a family rule may not fit for you and your family, it may not be ineffective, inflexible, or restrictive. The test of whether a family rule would benefit from being transformed is whether it results in forwarding or restricting the growth of the individual and other family members. The questions in Table 11.2 can be used to assist the professional and family member in making that decision.

Further Exploration

Before helping family members transform their rules, it is beneficial for professionals to practice on themselves. The exercise in Table 11.3 is designed to provide you with that opportunity. In addition, I have found it beneficial to practice and share with other professionals my own transformed family rules and their resulting impact on my life. This has helped me assist families in transforming their worn-out, inflexible, or ineffective rules. It is very difficult to help families do something that you have not accomplished yourself.

Professionals, parents, the student, and siblings would all benefit from reading Satir's work, in particular, *The New Peoplemaking* (1988) and *Your Many Faces* (1978). These books are highly readable and can be understood by anyone with a fifth-grade reading level.

TABLE 11.3 • Transforming a Family Rule

State a family rule that was not healthy. Usually these are dogmatic statements like, "You can never _____" or "You should/ought to _____."

Your family rule: _____

_____

Transform your family rule in the following three steps:

I can always _____

I can sometimes _____

I can _____when:

a. _____

b. _____

c. _____

Complete another family rule transformation if it suits you!

Origin of Family Rules

Most family rules have been passed down for generations and thus are strongly affected by family history. Cultural and ethnic influences also affect family rules. McGoldrick et al.'s edited book on family therapy and ethnicity (McGoldrick et al., 1996) is an excellent source for information that can help you better understand and hypothesize about the families of students in your school and their culturally governed rules. An example of a culturally grounded rule, cited in Chapter 5 of this text, is that children of some ethnic backgrounds should not look adults in the eyes when being reprimanded; other ethnic backgrounds have the opposite rule.

Satir's Five Freedoms

Satir saw the following five freedoms as the cornerstone to effective human communication (Schwab, 1990):

1. To see and hear what is here, instead of what should be, was, or will be.

2. To say what one feels and thinks instead of what one should.

3. To feel what one feels, instead of what one ought.

4. To ask for what one wants, instead of always waiting for permission.

5. To take risks in one's own behalf, instead of choosing to be only "secure" and not rocking the boat. (Satir & Baldwin, 1983, pp. 168–169)

Flexible family rules that are based in reality provide these five freedoms. The mother-father-child triad is the source of the most powerful rules for behavior. Parents who set their children free by providing realistic and flexible rules are usually the children of parents who were able to do the same for them. Inflexible rules result in a suppression of these freedoms and unhealthy relationships within and outside the family.

When people are more concerned with conforming to a rule than with the people and situation at hand, they are violating a number of their basic freedoms promoting healthy functioning. An example would be if the children of a man with Alzheimer's disease continued operating under the family rule, "You do not interfere in another family member's business." People with Alzheimer's disease need others who love and care for them to become involved in their life. By continuing to adhere to an obsolete family rule that is no longer functional for the person and situation at hand, these children would not be helping their father and would be violating their own basic freedoms. As Satir said, people need to "give themselves permission" to see what is there, to say what they think, or to take a risk. Old family rules can be tenacious, as well as destructive. Adults usually are unaware that their behavior may arise from a lack of understanding about the impact of dysfunctional rules and not giving themselves permission to change their traditional patterns. Even when they are aware of this, the grip with which these rules are held can be like a vise.

Professionals clearly face formidable odds when encouraging the five freedoms. Nevertheless, it is their responsibility to help families promote these five freedoms. Furthermore, since schools are another source of rule-making in our society, it is equally important for professionals to reflect upon the rules created by schools to see whether the students are free at school in the sense of the five freedoms. If the students are not "free," professionals need to take steps to change that situation.

Implementation

School professionals who wish to encourage the five freedoms can, first and foremost, model healthy communication. Ways to encourage healthy communication include:

- Talking about the five freedoms and what they mean. Initially, all school professionals would benefit from training in the five freedoms.
- Talking about the five freedoms in classes, when appropriate.
- Making posters of the five freedoms for display in the school.
- Establishing groups for students that focus on the five freedoms.
- Encouraging families to be free by helping them understand and relate to the five freedoms.
- Devoting parent-teacher organization meetings to the five freedoms.
- Arranging for mental health professionals on the staff of the school or for an outsider to deliver large-group information sessions on the five freedoms.
- Implementing follow-up sessions in which school professionals lead the small-group interactions.

The most important aspect of working to help others fulfill the five freedoms is recognizing that knowing what they mean and actually living them are two different things.

Some autocratic leaders will not understand how to implement the five freedoms because they cannot allow others to be free to think their own thoughts and feel their own feelings. They see others' freedom as a threat.

As mentioned in Appendix A, reality is subjective. Individuals react based on their own backgrounds; they view their experiences through their own special filters. Thus, it behooves professionals not to encourage others, subtly or obviously, to adopt their views of any situation. That is the beginning point of living Satir's five freedoms.

For example, if a student becomes manipulative, the professional should tell the student how he or she sees the student manipulating the situation. In such a scenario, the professional is exercising the freedom to see and hear what is occurring and the freedom to say what he or she feels and thinks. Using the five freedoms as a guide, the professional is remaining true to himself or herself while serving as a model for the student.

Of course, an individual's interpretation of a situation can be off the mark or in direct opposition to someone else's. Consider the case of the person who loves an argument and the one who hates any conflict. The professional would have a difficult time convincing either of them of the legitimacy of the other's view of reality. In such instances, it is important that the professional assist the individuals in testing their realities without violating their freedom to view those realities from their own perspectives.

Detriangling

Another family systems concept professionals can use to improve family-school communication is detriangling (see Bowen theory in Appendix A). Like other human interactions, detriangling is a complex process. One must be able to identify subtle and obvious means of being triangled as well as triangling others. Words are not the only means of communicating a triangling message. Facial expression, tone of voice, and other nonverbal cues such as eye contact help communicate a conscious or unconscious intent to triangle.

Kerr (1988) stated that detriangling is "probably the most important technique in family systems therapy" (p. 56). When it is used only as technique, however, it will most likely be ineffective. Appendix A points out that Bowen theory focuses on theory, not technique. When an individual understands the systemic situation, he or she can relate the cause of the struggle to the emotional process linking people and events, rather than seeing the cause of the struggle as being the person or event itself. However, most people do not have the capacity to grasp and live comfortably with this understanding. Generally, people are so emotionally embroiled in a situation that they do not observe systems or process. Kerr and Bowen contended that being emotionally neutral fosters detriangling. As Kerr (1988) stated:

> Emotional neutrality does not mean a refusal to approve or disapprove of particular aspects of human behavior, and it does not mean making rules for oneself about not passing judgment on people's actions. A person who adheres to rules usually appears to be more neutral than he actually is. Nor does neutrality mean straddling fences or being wishy-washy. One can have a very clear position with respect to what occurs in a family and in society and still be emotionally neutral. Dogmatic positions, a lack of position, and efforts to change others all betray the absence of

emotional neutrality. In essence, neutrality is reflected in the ability to define self without being emotionally invested in one's own viewpoint or in changing the viewpoints of others. (p. 57)

Thus, detachment is of value when detriangling. Being able to remain emotionally neutral when two other people are attempting to triangle you is critical. If you can see both sides of an argument, you will know that you are on the right track. And, if you can keep your thought processes clear and do not *put onto* anyone else what you think *should* be, you are even in better shape. Kerr (1988) made it clear that judging other people's process is being intolerant and indicates that you are being triangled.

Kerr (1988) admitted that seeing both sides of a relationship problem can be quite demanding, since one person may look like the *cause* of the other person's problem. One appears to be a victim and the other, the victimizer. Worse, one looks sick and the other as though he or she is making the best of a bad situation. Nevertheless, seeing both sides of a problem or argument is an essential part of the detriangling process.

Implementation

To detriangle, the school professional must first accurately see the triangling process. Second, he or she must censor personal emotions and detach from judgments or resentments. Recognizing how feelings affect behavior will allow the professional to gain control over automatic responses stemming from those feelings. Then, the professional can interact with family members by making statements indicating that he or she is not embroiled within the triangle and can be neutral. A statement about the observed triangulation will most likely not have the desired impact of eliminating or even reducing the process of triangulation because the other persons will have their own view of the situation that probably will not include seeing triangulation. Also, teaching anything in a straightforward manner violates the Bowen theory premise that direct attempts to influence others are counter to the process of differentiating a self and, in fact, nullify that process.

It should be obvious, therefore, that differentiating a self is important to detriangling. Kerr probably best stated it this way, "Maintaining one's differentiation and detriangling is not an attempt to manipulate or control others but a way of dealing with others' attempts to manipulate and control oneself" (p. 58). Further, when professionals are able to detriangle, it is far more likely that they will be able to improve the relationship of the other two people in the triangle. According to Bowen theory, when a detached third person sustains a higher level of differentiation than the other two, the other two will raise their functional levels of differentiation. For further information on detriangling, see Kerr's 1988 article, particularly the interesting case example presented on pages 58 and 59.

Further Exploration

School professionals who are involved with families would learn much from investigating the triangling that occurred in their own families. That is best accomplished with the assistance of a family systems therapist. Not all professionals trained in family work are trained in family systems approaches or emphasize triangulation. A quick way to locate a person who can help you investigate triangulation in your family of origin is to ask local members of the American Association of Marriage and Family Therapists (see Appendix D) if they are familiar with Bowen concepts.

Professionals should learn more about all aspects of their own family process. Bowen's training model, intended for family therapists who would continually be in situations that lent themselves directly to triangulation, included lifelong work dealing with one's family of origin. Lifelong investigation of personal family process may not be needed by school professionals, yet a minimum of a year of family investigation would be beneficial. This training would help the school professional see the natural triangle that forms in schools between student, parent, and professional. Seeing a therapist weekly is not necessary to pursue family process. An excellent place to begin is to read Bowen's chapter, "Toward the Differentiation of Self in One's Family-of-Origin" (Bowen, 1985), which relates Bowen's journey with his own family-edition.

Further, it might be possible to employ a family systems therapist to meet with a small group of professionals in the school who are interested in investigating family process. In such a group, professionals would learn not only about their own family process, but also about that of others in the group. This would make it easier for them to understand different family processes and to use this understanding in the schools for the benefit of students and families.

FAMILY CONFERENCES

As indicated earlier, the family conference is an important part of family-professional interaction. The purposes of the conferences include, but are not limited to, getting to know one another; enlisting and providing support; reporting student progress; and problem solving. Focusing on conferences with families who have children who are at risk or have special needs, this section provides information on planning, implementing, and evaluating conferences. Throughout the discussion, the focus is on family systems concepts. This section is not intended to provide a nuts-and-bolts approach to parent-teacher conferences but, in keeping with the focus of this text, to suggest ways to embed family systems concepts in the practical life of those in schools. For further discussion of family conferences for families of at-risk as well as special-needs students, see Kroth and Edge (1997) and Simpson (1996).

It is important to realize that students may well be included in planning for, implementing, and evaluating conferences. Austin's (1994) book, *Changing the View,* discusses student-led parent conferences. If our aim in education is to lead students to the threshold of their own knowledge, then it is important to help them hold the reigns. Written with this goal in mind, Austin's book is highly recommend to all school professionals as a means of helping students assume responsibility for their lives. From my point of view, that is a major purpose of all schools.

Planning

As with so many other activities, good preparation for family conferences can lead to comfort, relaxation, and a sense of being on top of things. Prepared professionals are more confident professionals. The same is true for students involved in conferences. To this end, students can benefit from Austin's (1994) book as well. Several aspects of planning related to family systems concepts can help school professionals set the scene and improve the likelihood of a successful family-professional conference. These are discussed in the following sections.

Prepare the Setting in Advance

There are many features to consider related to the physical setting that can enhance or detract from effective family conferences. For example, there must be adequate and comfortable seating. No adult wants to sit in a chair designed for a 6-year-old for 30 to 60 minutes! Beyond the physical discomfort, uncomfortable chairs might signal to family members that the school is not able to meet their needs. Family members may or may not realize consciously that they have doubts about the professional's ability to provide for them, and those who are aware of their doubts may or may not know the root of the doubts, but any such doubts will affect the family-school interactions. The professional(s) seated in an adult chair while the adult family members are seated in short chairs also signals a hierarchical structure that should be avoided.

Another consideration in planning the setting is to allow for privacy. No one wants his or her personal life aired in public. Providing such a setting would signal enmeshed boundaries on the part of the professional. It is the professional's responsibility to ensure privacy. A closed door, as opposed to open space, signals privacy and sensitivity to the families' needs. In addition, a room appropriate for the number of people at the conference is conducive to a sense of confidentiality. It is uncomfortable for three people to meet in a room than can hold 100 people. Think about what you would want for yourself or a loved one in terms of privacy. Providing an appropriate space is a signal of healthy, semipermeable boundaries on the part of the professional who has arranged the setting.

Freedom from interruptions is another major consideration in planning the setting. It is intrusive to have phone call interruptions or people walking in and out of the conference space. Allowing such interruptions is another signal of enmeshed boundaries. Perhaps more important, these interruptions are automatic signals to the family that they are not all that is on the professional's mind, or that the professional is more important than they are, signaling a hierarchy dysfunction. Family members also may draw the conclusion that the professional does not have time for them and their child.

Issues of control and turf may arise when family members meet in the teacher's classroom. When family members are invited into a classroom, they are in the teacher's territory. That automatically puts the family members and teacher on unequal ground, setting the stage for a possible hierarchy dysfunction. A room designed for conferences is best used for family conferences that have sensitive content. Control and turf issues often do not arise; however, their possibility needs to be considered in any potentially fragile situation.

Another important consideration in the environment is the seating arrangement. The best arrangement is to sit in a circle at a round table or in comfortable chairs without a barrier between family members and professionals. The professional should not sit behind the teacher's or principal's desk during the conferences; doing so puts an automatic barrier between the professional and the family. It further signals the "threat and reward" style of interaction described in Appendix A. Parents sitting on the other side of the principal's desk naturally might remember times when they were young and sitting in the same position. The circle or round table is a more egalitarian approach. The structural concept of power, described in Chapter 3, comes to bear in seating arrangements in obvious ways.

If an outsider can tell where the professional(s) will sit when they walk into the conference room, the seating arrangement is probably not egalitarian. It is amazing how subtle the signs of authority can be and how easily such signs can make family members feel inferior. Alternatively, signs of authority can set up a situation where a family member reacts in a hostile and angry manner due to unresolved authority problems. That person may not even realize why he or she is reacting in that way. Even with thorough grounding in Satir's seed model, which contrasts with the threat and reward model (see Appendix A), the professional may not be able to ensure that family members will not react to the setting by feeling inferior or being overly authoritative. Attention to detail, however, can help prevent or minimize problems and allow the family members to see the professional as a collaborator rather than an adversary.

Know Your Purpose

It is essential that professionals know their purpose in calling for a conference. The purpose should be the focal point throughout the planning and implementation. It is easy to become sidetracked when interacting with family members, whether or not an issue is involved. A stated purpose, known to all parties including professional, student, and family members, will help keep everyone on track.

Knowing the purpose for the conference, the professional is able to focus all of his or her energy on achieving that goal, be it problem solving or simply getting to know one another. Beyond that clearly framed goal or purpose, other purposes should pervade all conferences. These include, but are not limited to, building rapport and trust and gleaning additional family information. A caring interaction process will allow rapport to grow. However, as discussed in the next section, a plan is important for learning additional information about family considerations.

Make a Plan

Formulating a plan is essential to the success of any family-professional interaction. Some professionals believe that an evolving process will carry them through a conference; they do not bother to plan how they will achieve their purpose. Seldom do they fully achieve their aims.

Clearly, the first plan made should concern the stated purpose, such as reporting student progress. The professional can easily plan for that purpose by thinking about how to open the conference, the order for sharing content, and how to close the conference. Each of these aspects is important. The plan should allow the professional to achieve not only the stated purpose but also the other two overarching purposes of building rapport and getting to know more about the family unit.

It is also wise to involve the student in the planning for the conference. Additionally, professionals who want to include family members in planning for conferences can call them prior to making the plan to state the purpose and to ask if a parent or another family member would like to contribute to the plan. This action signals an egalitarian/seed model approach to conferences from an early point in the process.

In selecting or designing an opening to a meeting, the professional should use whatever information he or she already knows about the family. Greetings should match the family's style of interaction. If the family members are formal and proper or disengaged, a greeting in the interaction style with which they are most accustomed should help them feel at ease. People who are distant by nature are unlikely to respond to an effusive greeting. This does not mean that the professional should not act naturally. Everyone has the capacity to vary responses as well as actions, depending upon the situation at hand.

Satir was a master at matching clients. She was, in fact, an "object" of research study regarding her style (Bandler & Grinder, 1979). In that research, the observers found that a critical aspect of Satir's style was that she matched the level of the client. For example, when a client would refer to something using a visual metaphor such as "It really looked good to me," Satir would respond with a visual response, such as "I get the picture." This is a very simplistic example of a complex yet powerful process known as neurolinguistic programming (NLP).

The professional does not need to remain at the same energy level and style as the family throughout the conference. In fact, in NLP training, professionals are taught to initially match the level and speech patterns of the individual, to alter gradually their own, and to let the other follow suit. For example, if a parent asks a question in a clipped and anxious tone, the professional would deliver his or her first sentence in the same clipped style and then gradually flow into his or her natural style. Doing so will help lead the parent to another energy level with less anxiety attached to the content. As you can imagine, the parent will be able to derive more benefit from a more relaxed and receptive manner. Basically, in such an interaction, the professional subtly validates the parent's view of the situation while even more subtly implying that another frame of the situation can easily be cast.

Deciding the order or sequence for the sharing of student progress should be as strategic as planning the opening to the meeting. Most people would like to have any negatives deeply buried in the middle of many positives. Thus, it is important, in reporting student progress, to begin and end on a positive note. Because it is easy for families of students with special needs to expect and focus on weaknesses, the professional should, when possible, describe weaknesses in terms of challenges, thus helping reshape the family members' view of the situation. For example, the professional can refer to Joe's "hard-fought battle with mainstreaming for English class" instead of Joe's "failure to adjust in the mainstream." Malatchi (1997) focused on a capacity versus a deficit view of functioning.

Reframing, covered elsewhere in this book, is an important aspect of working with families. The professional should plan to present positive frames of reference and to have several *reframes* available to present if the need occurs.

Prepare the Family in Advance

Family members should be informed about the purpose of the conference in advance and, as mentioned earlier, be given the opportunity to provide input to the agenda for the meeting. Uncertainty about purpose may result in anxiety on the part of the family. For example, if school professionals call parents to a meeting to get to know one another better but don't inform them of the purpose in advance, the parents may assume their child has done something wrong or is having big problems. Prior to the conference, the parents may be on pins and needles about the meeting.

The professional should also let the family members know whether anyone besides the family and the teacher will be present at the conference and why those other people will attend. For example, if a family member doesn't know that a psychologist will be at a conference, he or she may assume, upon arriving and seeing the psychologist, that things are worse than anticipated. Parents can intuitively interpret such surprises as a boundary violation without even realizing what felt uncomfortable. Such surprises are damaging to trust and to the working relationship between the teacher and the family member. Informing parents about people who will attend and inviting them to ask questions will help reduce potential anxiety.

Other aspects of preparing family members include giving them clear directions concerning where and when the meeting will be held and telling them what materials they will need to bring or what preparations they can make for the conference. Families who are prepared in advance will be better able to see the collaborative and egalitarian aspects of the upcoming conference.

Implementing Family Conferences

Traditional recommendations for how to conduct family conferences are the subject of other texts and articles (Austin, 1994; Kroth & Edge, 1997; Lawler, 1991; Simpson, 1996), which should be consulted for a refresher on the basics of conducting conferences with parents of students with special needs and those who are at risk. The focus here is upon how to implement family systems concepts during family conferences.

Employ Family Systems Applications

Earlier in this chapter, several applications stemming from family systems concepts were described. It is important to employ those principles, as appropriate, during family conferences. For example, there may be a perfect opportunity to assist the family in transforming an ineffective family rule into a guideline that works for them. The professional definitely will want to model Satir's five freedoms by respecting, encouraging, and validating the family members' opinions and feelings. Remaining objective and noting triangling also will be beneficial, as will detriangling when possible. Cataloging family process (see later section of this chapter) can provide useful information for enhancing future family school interactions.

Maintain a Self

When meeting with family members, professionals need to continually stand for what they are as individuals. This is important in all family-professional interactions but is especially important during conferences. People have a tendency to attribute things to other people with no basis. When meeting someone for the first time or interacting with someone you do not know very well, you may have automatic reactions to them that do not fit the reality of that person. Think of a time when you first met someone and automatically disliked her or him. Later, you may have realized that the person had reminded you of someone who had treated you poorly in the past, and you may have changed your view correspondingly. If the professional stands his or her ground and continues being natural, usually the family will come to recognize the professional for who he or she is.

Satir used to say to people who appeared to have confused her with someone else, "I think you've put a hat on me." Recognizing this phenomenon, accepting it as human, and being yourself is probably the best approach professionals can assume. It may take a long time for family members to realize that the professional is not the kind of person they thought he or she was, but usually they will come to that realization. In schools it is not unusual for family members to confuse current professionals with other professionals with whom they have dealt in the past. If the professional is fortunate, those interactions were positive. If they were not, building trust may be an arduous process.

Popular pop singer Billy Joel has a song about the process of being who you are regardless of what others see in you that truly does not fit reality. The title of his song is "An Innocent Man." Although he wrote the song about his relationship with a new woman in his life, it shows a clear understanding of the task anyone has with new relationships. He firmly establishes his understanding of the woman's prior hurt as well as his patience in helping her overcome that hurt in order to be able to risk again.

Professionals may need that level of understanding and commitment to reach some family members. A long time may elapse before trust is established, and the professional may feel as though he or she is taking an undeserved beating at times. In such instances, the professional might reach the family member by saying, "I think you've put a hat on me." Be warned, though, that such words might spur greater agitation. Some people do not like to be caught with their hands in the proverbial cookie jar.

Another way to communicate the same message is to say something along the following lines: "I wonder if Todd's former principal did things that way. Here at Crestwood High, the students and teachers mutually write conduct rules at the beginning of the year. My role has been to help enforce rules developed by the students." Clearly, this principal ascribes to the seed model view of the world (see Appendix A).

Catalog Family Process

Thorough familiarity with family theory and process is helpful when cataloging family patterns. Each conference presents the professional with an opportunity to develop further his or her understanding of family process for a particular student and his or her family.

Just as professionals keep an academic file on each student, keeping a family file on family process is most helpful. Sections in such a file would include information on the family life cycle, family interaction patterns, historical factors, environmental factors, family configuration, and the nature of any special needs. The last part of this book presents a major case study focusing on the family. All of the information presented in that case study relates to areas that can be included in the family file. When the professional first meets with family members, he or she begins compiling the file on family process. As more is learned about the family during conferences, additional information can be cataloged.

The objective in cataloging family process is to identify patterns that occur with some regularity. Of particular interest are any dysfunctional patterns that emerge—for example, a family rule that has hampered growth and development over the generations or the negative results of a triangle between grandmother and parents that has been transmitted down through generations.

The purpose of cataloging current life circumstances and dysfunctional patterns is not to emphasize or dwell on the negative. It is to provide professionals with information they can use to help family members change patterns that stunt the growth of the family unit as well as the student. Of course, educational professionals cannot replace the services of family systems therapists. Educational professionals catalog family process to better understand a family and, therefore, to plan more effective future interventions. They should not make suggestions that are beyond the family's capability to implement. Nor should they elicit negative reactions by proposing what family members perceive as impossible demands and unrealistic expectations. An understanding of family process and circumstance will help the professional avoid those situations.

Some observations can be cataloged as facts; others should be cataloged as hypotheses. The family's place in the family life cycle is factual. The type of family configuration, cultural factors, and socioeconomic status are also facts. Although these factors are not always cataloged by school professionals, they constitute important considerations in any recommendations made to the family.

What are not simply factual are observations about interaction patterns and historical factors, such as triangulation or level of differentiation as well as dysfunctional patterns related to the student. It is important to maintain any such observations as hypotheses until several professionals confirm the opinions.

Once patterns or facts about the family have been cataloged and discussed with other professionals, it is important to use that information during future conferences. For example, if the professional has corroborated a hypothesis that the oldest daughter is a parentified child, that observation can be discussed with the family during a conference. The professional might find out that this was also true in the mother's family and that it has become a transgenerational pattern with more intensity driving it.

Use Mutual Processes, When Appropriate

If there is one underlying theme in Satir's seed model (Schwab, 1990), it is working with people as equals. Using mutual processes means that the family members and professionals jointly engage in any planning, problem solving, and student progress reporting. The professional should be as interested in hearing about the student's progress on the home front as in sharing the student's progress in school. In other words, reporting student progress is a two-way street. When family members realize that professionals are as interested in hearing about their accomplishments and challenges as in telling about progress in school, they will begin to make the shift from bystander to collaborator.

Of course, some family members will not be interested in mutual processes, and the needs of families should be determined on a family-by-family basis (Gamel-McCormick, 1995). Knowledge of the family life, such as environmental factors and family life cycle stage may help explain parents' desires and needs. Although some family members may not want to share in the problem-solving process, others may be overwhelmed or under-organized (R. J. Green, 1995) rather than uninvolved.

This section has provided several guidelines relating to a family systems perspective that can be used for implementing conferences. More could certainly be ferreted out from the literature on family systems, but the four guidelines presented here are a worthwhile beginning for school professionals.

Evaluating

The professional should evaluate his or her use of family systems concepts in the process of planning and conducting conferences as well as after completing the cycle of family conferences. The suggestions provided in this section can help point you in the direction of using more of what works for you as well as help you determine ways to make your practices that have rough edges more workable.

Evaluate Your Planning

The purpose of evaluating your planning efforts is to determine what to change or replicate in the future. Did your planning produce the results that you wanted? To answer this question, professionals need to look back on the setting, primary and secondary purposes, planning process and product, as well as on how the family was prepared for the conference. Answering the questions in Table 11.4 can help professionals evaluate their planning efforts.

Question 7 concerns how the family members viewed the conference. Professionals should design a checklist for family members to complete after each conference. The checklist would provide feedback and remove part of the burden of evaluation from the professional's shoulders.

Evaluate Your Implementation

Just as planning must be evaluated, so too must implementation be assessed. The professional should ask himself or herself about each of the implementation guidelines covered in this chapter. For example, did he or she employ family systems principles? If not, what blocked that process? Once the professional understands what caused the block, he or she can determine a strategy so that the next occasion will not yield the same results. Perhaps there simply was no opportunity to transform a family rule; however, the professional could always model the five freedoms. If the professional did not recognize triangling, he or she might decide to tape-record a future conference for further analysis in this regard.

Another good question for the professional to review is whether or not he or she was able to *maintain a self*. If not, what factors contributed to the downfall? Can the professional point to any behavior pattern, across families, that might suggest when he or she gets pulled into the families' web and does not maintain a sense of self? Does one type of family resonate with any struggle in the professional's own life and, therefore, contribute to less effective strategies?

TABLE 11.4 • Evaluating the Planning

Focus on the following questions. In answering them, consider how you might better plan for family conferences in the future. Any answers with which you are not satisfied should be pursued.

1. Did the setting facilitate open, honest, and confidential communication?
2. Was the seating arrangement comfortable?
3. Did your focal point remain the central theme of the conference?
4. Was your opening effective?
5. Did you close on a mutually supportive note?
6. Did the sequence of the conference facilitate open, helpful communication?
7. Was the family prepared so that they were comfortable participating in the conference? How do you know?
8. Did the family indicate anything else you could consider in the future?

Other questions to ask include: Was I able to learn new information at the conference about family process or facts related to the family life cycle, environmental concerns, or family configuration? If so, can any of the information help me confirm or deny hypotheses I've established? How will I use that information in the future? If I met a dead end in cataloging family process, what contributed to the lack of information? How might I obtain more information in the future? Am I possibly colluding with the family in any way by helping the family deny a reality that is difficult to confront?

Was I able to use mutual processes that fit the situation? If so, how might I use those strategies again in the future? If not, what could I change in the future to enhance mutual processes? What factors about this family might make it difficult for me to facilitate mutual processes during family conferences?

This series of questions can help professionals modify their ways of conducting future conferences with families. Evaluation should be a learning process that affords insights as well as direction. Furthermore, it should make conducting conferences easier in the future with new and different families.

This section on conferences with families of at-risk and special-needs students has focused on family systems concepts rather than presenting the full spectrum of information on planning, implementing, and evaluating family conferences. More information is available in other texts written with a focus on other aspects of family conferencing with students having special needs (see, e.g., Kroth & Edge, 1997; Simpson, 1996).

TEACHER-STUDENT SUPPORT TEAMS

Over the years, many researchers have focused on various aspects of educating students with special needs in general education classrooms (see, e.g., C. Alexander & Strain, 1978;

Bailey & Winton, 1987; Banerji & Dailey, 1995; Brucker, 1994; Carr, 1993; Farlow, 1996; Fuchs & Fuchs, 1994; S. K. Green & Shinn, 1995; Hardin & McNelis, 1996; Jenkins & Heinen, 1989; Patton, 1994; Power-deFur & Orelove, 1997; Putnam, Spiegel, & Bruininks, 1995; Stainback, Stainback, East, & Sapon-Shevin, 1994; B. R. Taylor, 1994; Wang & Birch, 1984; Will, 1986; Ysseldyke et al., 1994). The research and experience have shown that general education classroom interventions are appropriate for both at-risk and special-needs students. While not all students can be educated full-time in general education classrooms, at-risk students and most students with special needs can succeed in these classes (Giangreco, 1996b; Power-deFur & Orelove, 1997; Pugach & Seidl, 1995; Pugach & Wesson, 1995; Thousand, Villa, & Nevin, 1994; Villa, Thousand, Stainback, & Stainback, 1992). With integrated models, professionals can help meet the needs of many students with disabilities while they remain in regular classrooms (Affleck, Madge, Adams, & Lowenbraun, 1988; Elliott, 1997; Miller, 1996; O'Toole & Switlick, 1997; Power-deFur & Orelove, 1997). Before referring children for special education assessment, general education classroom teachers should consider multiple educational interventions (Lambert, 1988) as well as intervention assistance (Ysseldyke, Christenson, & Kovaleski, 1994), which is the focus of this section.

The discussion begins with basic information about preferral intervention, or teacher-student support teams. The discussion includes a description of the teams, their membership, and the process generally followed. Then, the role of the general education classroom teacher and other professionals in involving families in this assistance is addressed.

The approach to teacher-student support that is described here illustrates a way of implementing Satir's organic and seed model (Satir & Baldwin, 1983; Schwab, 1990), described in Appendix A, on a team basis in schools. Alignment with Satir's systemically oriented, organic and seed model is seen in the egalitarian nature of this team model that values uniqueness while searching for alternatives.

Introduction

The term *prereferral intervention* was used initially by Graden, Casey, and Christenson in 1985 (Graden, 1989). Today, many people prefer to use the term *teacher-student support teams,* since the purpose of the support is to prevent later referral for special education. At-risk students are often considered for such interventions, which are characterized by collaborative consultation (Giangreco, 1996a; Hudson & Glomb, 1997; Idol, 1997; Idol et al., 1994; Pugach & Seidl, 1995; Pugach & Wesson, 1995; Thousand et al., 1994; Villa et al., 1992) and the use of problem-solving teams, such as teacher assistance teams or intervention assistance teams (Algozzine & Ysseldyke, 1992). Intervention made before problems become compounded can reduce the need for referral to special education (Fuchs, Fuchs, & Bahr, 1990; Fuchs, Fuchs, Bahr, Fernstrom, & Stecker, 1990). A useful resource on school consultation is a 1987 article by West and Idol, the first part of which focused on theoretical bases and reviewed 10 different models of consultation.

Many articles have been written on prereferral intervention (J. Carter & Sugai, 1989; Fuchs, Fuchs, & Bahr, 1990; Fuchs, Fuchs, Bahr, Fernstrom, & Stecker, 1990; Phillips & McCullough, 1990; Tindal, Shinn, & Rodden-Nord, 1990). In addition, a study has been completed on general education classroom teachers' prereferral interventions for students with behavior problems (Sevcik & Ysseldyke, 1986). Fuchs, Fuchs, Bahr, Fernstrom, and Stecker (1990) defined prereferral intervention as modifications made to instruction or classroom management aimed at accommodating a student without disabilities before a referral is made. They saw this definition as incorporating a preventive intent—preventing inappropriate referrals from being made and lessening future problems faced by students by helping the teacher learn to deal more effectively with a diversity of students.

The typical prereferral intervention, like other forms of intervening when early signs of challenging situations are noticed, involves the collaboration of professionals rather than the involvement of families and students in problem solving (Turnbull & Turnbull, 1996). I believe better practice is to involve families early on and to help them become part of the process of helping solve their child's problems. Idol et al. (1994) also noted that parents need to be involved, stating,

> If a child is having sufficient difficulties in the general classroom to warrant either (a) referral to any collaborative problem-solving group such as child study teams or (b) consideration of using the Collaborative Consultation Model as a means of providing an appropriate education, then parents should be informed and included in decision making. (p. 80)

Besides being involved in partnership with teams, a simple way families can help is by assisting with homework (Kay, Fitzgerald, Paradee, & Mellencamp, 1994; Patton, 1994). Ysseldyke et al. (1994) discussed five components of home support for learning: expectations and attributions, discipline orientation, home effective environment, parent participation, and structure for learning. Taken into consideration by professionals, these components can be used to increase student success.

Membership

Members of the various teams that provide assistance to teachers differ from one school system to another; however, the teams generally include the principal or the assistant principal, the referring person, the consulting teacher, and other specialists, such as a counselor, school psychologist, or special educator, as appropriate. Some teams involve fewer people, perhaps including three professionals working together to develop viable solutions. Usually, the composition of the team is based upon the chairperson's selection of relevant members, given the nature of the individual situation.

Phases of Support

First Phase

The process of gaining assistance begins with the classroom teacher and student requesting help for a particular challenge. The teacher and student describe the academic, social, or motor behaviors that are of concern. The teacher also shares the information that has been gathered and explains past efforts to solve the problems. Different schools have different procedures for these requests. Some are informal; others require a more formal, written request for assistance.

Whether formal or informal, the next step is consultation with the referring teacher and student, if appropriate. One or more members of the team meet with the referring teacher and student for problem solving. Typically, an assessment is made of the discrepancy between the student's current level of performance and the level of performance expected or desired by the teacher and student. Relevant classroom variables are analyzed for their influence on this discrepancy between actual and desired performance. Together, the referring teacher and members of the team, which should include the student and a family member, design an intervention. Interventions are implemented and evaluated. If they are successful, the process ends. If they are unsuccessful, the process moves to the next phase.

Second Phase

The next phase of the support process typically involves classroom observations by other professionals and sometimes a family member. The purpose of these observations is to collect information on important variables in the classroom setting. Observation also allows the observer to compare the student in question with other members of the class. Classroom observations are not the only type of observation considered. A social worker, visiting teacher, teacher, other professional, or family member might observe the student in the home or in a community setting. Such observations help corroborate the student's functioning as well as point to possible causes.

The observers make note of the curriculum, the tasks and demands of the academic program, and the student's response to these variables. Also noted, in relation to the student in question and the class or situation in general, are the actions and language of the teacher, family members, siblings, or other relevant individuals. In addition, they look at the way work and space are organized in the classroom, including seating arrangements, grouping patterns, and interaction patterns. Then they make attempts to describe the causes and consequences of the student's behaviors.

Third Phase

Following the observations, the members of the teacher-student support team meet to design collaborative interventions based upon the observations. Interventions might include changes in instruction in the classroom, changes in the way work and space are organized, the implementation of behavioral procedures in the home or school, or the use of other resources available in the school, such as tutoring, sessions with the guidance counselor, or help from a remedial specialist. A family-school intervention also might be planned. If a parent does not attend this meeting, then a subsequent meeting is scheduled with the student or family to discuss the proposed instructional or behavioral changes.

Family Involvement

This section discusses training for professionals in the process of obtaining assistance, the formal request for assistance, and guidelines for intervention. The section concludes with a case example highlighting parental involvement.

Training

All teachers should receive in-service training on the process of obtaining needed assistance. The training should communicate the belief that families and the student are important parts of the process. Actual cases from the school can be described to highlight the value of families being involved from an early juncture.

Training might also involve an introduction to relevant family systems concepts. The school social worker or counselor can provide in-service training for incoming teachers. Alternatively, teachers and other new staff can be required to read this book or another that covers similar information.

Request for Assistance

In schools with a formal process in place for requesting assistance, the teacher writes a written request for intervention. Students old enough to be involved in making the request can contribute to its formulation. It is recommended that teachers be required to consult with parents before filing a request for assistance. When that is a requirement the request for assistance should include a description of family member involvement to date. Covered in the description should be the responses of the family members and their suggestions. If their suggestions have been given any attention in the classroom, or if combined school-home interventions have been attempted, the results should be reported. Reporting results is necessary so that others do not waste time thinking about ideas that have already proven ineffective.

Family process information is also helpful. Any information the teacher has about the family should be presented in the written request, including information on demographics, family life cycle, special family configurations, historical and environmental factors, and family interaction patterns related to subsystems, boundaries, hierarchy, and power.

Guidelines

The teacher should not alarm family members unduly before or after making a request for assistance. At the same time, this is the perfect opportunity to apply pressure on the family, if that might nip a problem in the bud. In some cases, families are reluctant to apply necessary consequences at home. As a result, students arrive at school thinking they can get away with unacceptable behaviors. The teacher might have exhorted the parents to apply appropriate consequences for inappropriate behaviors on the part of their child, with no results. When the parents realize that their child is one step from being referred for special educational services, they may begin to do what is necessary to achieve change in their otherwise unruly child.

In other cases the parents may not have followed through with the kind of help their child needed. The teacher may have asked the parents to provide a quiet space as well as paper and pencil for the student to complete homework assignments. When the parents realize that their lack of attention to these suggestions is about to result in a more formal request for assistance, that in itself may elicit the results desired. This type of problem may stem from what Aponte (1994) referred to as "underorganization," another factor such as "pile up" (H. I. McCubbin & Patterson, 1982), mentioned in Chapter 2, or a dysfunctional family, as referred to in Chapters 7 and 8. Naturally, other causes also can explain such situations.

The first guideline—to not alarm family members unduly but to apply pressure when appropriate—might look like arm-twisting, and in a way it is. It is, however, a very real effort on the part of the teacher to receive assistance from the family members in under-standing and solving a problem. The guideline is actually designed to avoid eliciting an overreaction and to apply the right amount of pressure at the right time to family members who have not responded in the past. It is a systems concept referred to as *gaining leverage* (Senge, 1990).

Another guideline is to *encourage mutual problem solving* among professionals and family members, including the student when appropriate. Once the request for assistance has been made, it is assumed that the family and teacher were not able to solve the situation together.

When other professionals are involved, it is wise to involve the family as well as the student in the problem-solving process. Imagine clarifying the nature of a problem without the family present only to find out much later, when the child is receiving special education services, that the situation would have been quite easily resolvable. A home-school intervention program that required the use of an inexpensive resource might have taken care of the problem! Just such an intervention might have been made possible by, for example, the school principal, who could have recommended and funded a tutor for one night a week.

A third guideline is to *prepare family members* to contribute to the intervention process. Family members should already be familiar with the process through information presented at school meetings and in newsletters. Once the parents are approached about the specific situation with their child and have assisted the teacher in clarifying the problem, planning ideas, and implementing the plan, the parents need further information on team process. A written description of the purpose, nature, and process of requesting assistance and intervening should be provided to family members. A school professional should also be available to answer questions and provide any other assistance necessary.

Case Example

A first-grade student, Raheem, was rambunctious and disturbing other students in the classroom, making it difficult for them to concentrate and complete their seat work. The teacher tried several strategies. Finally, feeling discouraged at the lack of progress, she called Raheem's parents. The teacher explained the situation and dis-cussed the interventions she had attempted. The parents indicated that their older son, too, had been rambunctious in school. They shared Raheem's IQ score of 140 with the teacher. They believed that, like his brother, Raheem might be bored and frustrated with having little to do once he completed his seat work. The teacher had not seen Raheem's test scores because the family had recently moved from the Mid-dle East, and the children's school reports did not follow them. She enlisted the par-ents' support in a home-school intervention. The intervention involved the teacher sending a note home each day reporting on Raheem's disturbing others who were working. When he had a day with no disturbances, the parents would provide praise and spend time reading to Raheem about his favorite subject, outer space. The teacher would also provide Raheem with two options after he completed each assignment. Both options were enrichment activities that would allow him to fulfill his intellectual curiosity about outer space. This intervention was effective. Raheem settled down and became a model student.

This intervention was tried only because the teacher knew that prior to a request for assistance she was required to consult the parents to help solve the problem. Had that not been the requirement, she would have simply made a request without having consulted the family.

This section has been devoted to the process of teachers and students obtaining assistance from other professionals and family members to increase the likelihood that a student will succeed in the general education classroom. The process focuses predominantly on children who are at risk and their families, although it has also been documented to minimize special education services being required for students who may have special needs (Fuchs, Fuchs, & Bahr, 1990; Fuchs, Fuchs, Bahr, Fernstrom, & Stecker, 1990).

SUMMARY

The first section of this chapter considered sensitivity, climate/mood, and locus of influence important for home-school communication. This was followed by general applications of family systems concepts as they relate to schools. The next section of this chapter focused on family conferences for both at-risk and special needs students and was followed by a section on the collaborative process of teachers and students receiving assistance from other professionals and family members. Ways in which the family systems perspective can be embedded within the on-going processes found in schools were highlighted. The teacher-student support team model that was presented illustrated one way of putting Satir's family systems concepts into practice in the schools. Most schools have some version of teacher-student assistance; but few of these efforts involve a family systems perspective. Many of the family systems concepts and practices discussed in this chapter are valuable not only for conferences and support teams but also for other school-family interactions.

Family Involvement and Planning for FFIs and IEPs

T his chapter builds upon the information about teamwork presented in Chapters 10 and 11 as well as Parts I and II of this book. It focuses on two processes that involve families: family-focused interventions (FFIS) and individualized education programs (IEPS). The premise of any school-based intervention is that something in the student's school life is not functioning as well as could be hoped. Academic, social, and emotional interventions are often implemented, but most are made on an individual basis, without family involvement. It is unusual to find schools conducting family interventions, though this is gradually changing with the current emphasis on early intervention (Garland, 1994). In this chapter, family systems concepts are interwoven throughout the descriptions of the FFI and IEP, with school-related examples provided.

RATIONALE FOR FAMILY INVOLVEMENT

Sussell, Carr, and Hartman (1996), writing about family-school partnerships, indicated that students benefit from such linkages because they have more available resources and greater consistency between home and school expectations and approaches. The parents, having received needed support, are more able to transfer that support to their children and thus their efforts are more successful.

As stated earlier in this text, Leithwood (1997) found that parental involvement in children's education accounted for 50% of the variance in children's school achievement. Tittler, Friedman, Blotcky, and Stedrak (1982) noted that children's progress in school appeared to be significantly related to their family's willingness to become involved with the schools and to cooperate within the educational setting. The findings in support of parental involvement do not negate, however, the warning expressed in Chapter 10 that families should not be forced into involvement beyond the capacity they perceive themselves to possess.

From their research on ways of making homework successful, Kay et al. (1994) found that students with learning disabilities responded in a more favorable manner when assignments were made "in the context of a strong support system of teachers, parents, and peers" (p. 551). Emerging from their data were five themes:

> (a) Parents felt ill-prepared to help their children with homework; (b) parents needed more information about the classroom teachers' expectations of their child and of their own roles in helping with homework; (c) parents wanted their children to be given homework assignments that were appropriate for them as individual learners; (d) parents valued and even enjoyed hands-on homework and projects in which the whole family could participate; (e) parents wanted an extensive, two-way communication system that would allow them to become partners on their child's instructional team. (p. 554)

It is clear that involvement of family members in children's education is important. Furthermore, such involvement is linked directly with achievement. Beyond the research supporting the rationale for involving families in children's education, parental involvement in the education of children with special needs is required by law.

The family systems concepts found throughout this chapter were presented in detail in Parts I and II of this text as well as in Appendix A, so the literature is not repeated in this chapter. Any new family systems information, however, is referenced.

FAMILY-FOCUSED INTERVENTIONS

The field of early intervention has been at the forefront in promoting extensive family involvement in education (Garland, 1994). In fact, as a result of PL 99-457, all children enrolled in early intervention programs must have an individual family service plan (IFSP) (King-Sears, 1997). Recognizing that child and family truly cannot be separated, the early intervention field did not make individualized education programs the focus of intervention. Instead, they made IFSPs paramount and required parental membership on the assessment team. (Garland, 1995). We can learn an important lesson from this branch of education.

Although laws change and reauthorization may bring modifications in requirements, King-Sears' (1997) description of the conceptual and procedural mandates of the IFSP, and Turnbull and Turnbull's (1996) clear description of the differences between the IEP and the IFSP, are instructive. It is important to be aware of changes in the law and to note that school systems are responsible for providing training on modifications that result from any shifts in governmental requirements.

The underlying belief of proponents of family-focused interventions is that educators must individualize services for families with children who have special needs (Garland, 1995; Malatchi, 1997; P. J. McWilliam, 1996; Turnbull & Turnbull, 1996). As Miller (1996) indicated, this should be true for the families of all students, not just those with special needs. However, the involvement of families is particularly important for at-risk students, since intervention services must be tailored to important characteristics that differentiate families (Gamel-McCormick, 1995). These characteristics relate to differences in family structure, family interactional patterns, and family life cycle as well as other family characteristics discussed in Part I. Carney and Gamel-McCormick (1996) stated that multidisciplinary teams "must consider not only the concerns and preferences, but also the service and support needs, of parents and other family members" (p. 451). The Harvard Family Research Project (1995), writing about the importance of family involvement with children, provided a resource guide of family support and education programs across the country.

The family-focused intervention model, like the IFSP, consists of a sequence of specific activities related to planning, implementing, and evaluating family services (Dunst et al., 1994c). Unlike the IFSP, which relates specifically to early intervention in special education, the term FFI was selected to broaden the range for family intervention to include at-risk students, all ages of students with special needs, and their families. Because of its broader focus I have chosen to discuss the FFI, rather than the IFSP, here. Much in the discussion has been borrowed, however, from IFSPs and the literature relating to this vital process. Covered in this section are the underlying features of family-focused interventions, processes of intervening, and types of assistance provided.

Underlying Features

The three underlying features that must be considered when planning family-focused interventions are family uniqueness, goodness of fit, and networking. Family systems concepts fit into these features in interesting ways.

Family Uniqueness

As stated earlier, families differ on a number of important dimensions (P. J. McWilliam, 1996), including family life cycle stage and family interaction patterns, which relate to boundaries, hierarchy, and power. Also relevant to family uniqueness are cultural and socioeconomic background; historical factors within the family, such as triangulation and sibling position; family configuration, such as blended families; as well as the type and severity of special needs of the child and their impact upon the family. Each at-risk student, as well as each student with special needs, has a unique mixture of skills, feelings, behaviors, values (Winton, 1996), and potentials. Thus, it is necessary to individualize all family service plans and educational programs to meet the child's personal needs (P. J. McWilliam, 1996). Likewise, to relate to families in supportive ways, the plans and programs must respond to the intricate design that each family presents. Like snowflakes, families come in infinite varieties.

To elaborate further upon this theme, two different families are described in Tables 12.1 and 12.2. Read the first table, about Bobby and his family, and then complete the outline given under the case information. Your notes should concern family life cycle, needs, cultural and socioeconomic factors, any historical information noted, family configuration, and family structure, including subsystems, boundaries, and hierarchy. It might be helpful

TABLE 12.1 • Case Study: Bobby

Bobby is an 8-year-old boy who has been in a self-contained classroom for children with emotional disturbance since kindergarten. A very shy, withdrawn child, he did not speak to anyone but the teacher during his first year of school. He is now being mainstreamed for most of the school day.

Bobby is the oldest child in his family. He has a sister 4 years younger than he. His sister is not really aware that her brother has had a problem.

Bobby's parents are overprotective and continually hover around him. They pick him up from school daily, even though he could take the school bus home. They appear to be happily married and to support each other, though they spend an inordinate amount of time with Bobby. It is hard to tell if he is Mommy's or Daddy's little boy.

Bobby's mother is originally from Puerto Rico and makes most decisions regarding child rearing. The parents together, however, make the rules in the house. This family is deeply spiritual. They talk as though they have a sense that all is well with the world. The parents often speak of a "grand design." They have many friends and relatives with whom they interact and from whom they regularly seek assistance. They have, however, seen few professionals over the years regarding Bobby. They have said that Bobby will "grow out of" his shyness. The father even mentioned that he, too, is painfully shy. The father described an uncle of Bobby's who was much like Bobby when he was young. The parents seem resolved in many ways about their only son having serious emotional problems. However, they are currently involved with locating resources that can tell them more about Bobby's problem.

NOTES

Demographics: 8 years old; part-time general education classroom

Family life cycle:

Structure:
          Subsystems
          Boundaries
          Hierarchy

Historical factors:

Cultural and socioeconomic factors:

Bobby's special needs:

Family configuration:

TABLE 12.2 • Case Study: Chris

Chris is a 12-year-old student who has been in a classroom for children with emotional problems for 3½ years. He is a "motor-driven" hyperactive youth who talks to anyone who will listen. His mouth and feet are in constant motion. Currently, Chris is being mainstreamed for a portion of the school day.

He has an older half-brother, Leroy, who is 16 years old. They have a very close relationship. Leroy protects Chris in the neighborhood and, in fact, probably fights too many of Chris's battles for him. On occasion, Leroy feels embarrassed by Chris, especially when Leroy's adolescent friends are visiting and Chris gets rambunctious.

Chris's mother is a single parent. She and Chris's father, who is a carpenter, are divorced. Chris has been very upset about that loss and has befriended many of the adult males around in the school building. He is good friends with a custodian and speaks with the assistant principal regularly, both of whom are males. Further, he has made a special friend of the floating substitute, who is also male. Chris's mother seems to realize that she is in a lifelong struggle with him. She has few social supports in friends or family; however, being a social worker, she knows many professionals in the predominately black neighborhood where she works. The mother's main feelings appear to be frustration and isolation. She seems to feel alone in shouldering the responsibilities of the family and has little time to herself.

NOTES

Demographics: 12 years old; part-time general education classes

Family life cycle:

Structure:
      Subsystems
      Boundaries
      Hierarchy

Cultural and socioeconomic factors:

Chris's special needs:

Family configuration:

to discuss your notes on Bobby with others who have read the text. Comparing your notes with others can be helpful in clarifying your knowledge.

Next, read the information regarding Chris in Table 12.2. After you have read the case study, take notes as before, using the outline provided. Again, you may want to discuss your notes with others. The purpose of including the descriptions of these two different families in this text was to make the meaning of *family uniqueness* more obvious.

Goodness of Fit

The second underlying feature of which professionals should be aware when planning a family-focused intervention is *goodness of fit*. Describing a specific methodology for family-focused interventions in relation to early intervention, Bailey et al. (1988) referred to goodness of fit as a comfortable, beneficial meshing of the unique family needs with professionals that must exist if educators are to help both the student with special needs and his or her family. The same type of fit is essential for at-risk students and their families.

Think back to the case studies of Bobby and Chris. What suggestions do you have for helping these families? You may want to discuss your ideas with someone else who has read the same information. Remember that there must be a fit between your suggestions and the specific needs of each family. It also might be useful to recall a time in your childhood when your family of origin experienced pile-up, stress, or a bumpy transition from one family life cycle stage to another. At least one of these situations, if not all, will occur in the life of every family. Think about what was attempted to bring greater balance to the family unit. Considering whether what was attempted *fit* with your family will help make this concept more visceral and will likely help you relate it to other families in the future.

Networking

It is important that school professionals maintain role perspective when making family-focused interventions. They cannot be everything to everybody. They need to view themselves, first and foremost, as being responsible for their primary role—teaching.

Teachers are in a distinctive position in relation to parents of at-risk and special-needs students, however. They share with the students' families the mutual responsibility for educating the child. As such, they have the opportunity to establish a close working relationship with the families. The teachers frequently become confidants to parents and function as trusted professionals on whom the family can rely. The counselor, school social worker, consulting teacher, or psychologist might also play the role of confidant.

The teacher, however, functions best not as an isolated intervener but as a "hub" through which a network of resources can positively affect families. See Chapter 9 for more information on networking. The teacher cannot realistically maintain, on his or her own, both the parent-teacher relationship and the primary role of teaching while trying to satisfy the diverse needs of these families. The teacher should see it as his or her responsibility to serve as a *facilitator* in helping parents to access a variety of resources that are available in the educational system and larger community. Appendix D provides suggestions for resources across the country. These resources can be shared on an individual basis or put out in printed form for all families to access.

Before moving on to the section on processes of intervening, you may want to check your understanding of the material covered in this section by completing the exercise in Table 12.3. The exercise will give you the opportunity to identify violations of the underlying features of effective family-focused interventions in three proposed courses of action.

Processes of Intervening

Family-focused interventions, like all other types of interventions, involve the four processes of assessment, planning, implementation, and evaluation. As with the other types of interventions, organization is a key factor in effective family intervention. Interventions should be based on the best available data, carefully planned, implemented responsibly, and evaluated critically. Dunst and Deal (1994) listed eight elements to consider and include in developing and implementing family plans that empower and strengthen families: family concerns, family needs, outcome statement, resources and supports, courses of action, family strengths, partnership, and evaluation. These elements are incorporated into the following discussion of the family-focused intervention process.

Assessment

Sound assessment is the foundation on which effective intervention rests. Can you imagine a physician prescribing a drug before he or she diagnosed what was wrong? Or, worse yet, imagine being operated on before the need for an operation had been established!

There are two complementary parts to assessment for family-focused interventions. The first component is determining the status of the family on such dimensions as family life cycle, interaction patterns, historical factors such as sibling position and triangulation, cultural or socioeconomic factors, family configuration, the needs of the student, and the desires of student and family.

The second component of assessment in family-focused interventions is eliciting the family's needs and determining the family's resources. A relationship involving trust and mutual commitment will allow family members to feel comfortable enough to provide information to professionals about those needs. The professional can then use that information to draw conclusions about the family's life cycle, interactions patterns, and other aspects of family systems.

Once conclusions have been drawn, the professional reflects the information back to the family. For example, the professional might say, "Mr. and Mrs. Estevas, to me it sounds as though Miguel's older sister, Maria, is really feeling the pinch of your spending so much time helping Miguel with his homework. It also seems as though the two of you are overloaded with your 2-year-old twins." Of course, much more could be reflected over time. Once a professional reflects and confirms the information, he or she has created a data base that is held jointly with the parents.

The data and conclusion should be explicit. Consider the scenario of a family with an adolescent child and a younger child with a physical disability. The family has asked the adolescent to help the younger child find friends. The parents also expect the adolescent to come home after school, wait for the sibling to arrive, take care of the child, take the child around the neighborhood, and be sure that the child is content. Having all this information,

---

TABLE 12.3 • Case Study Analysis

Refer to the case of Chris in Table 12.2. Then evaluate each of the following three suggestions for any violations of the three features that underlie effective family-focused interventions.

Suggestion 1:   Chris is referred to the medical center for further evaluation of his hyperactivity.

Suggestion 2:   Since Chris's mother is a social worker, she is asked to chair a "parent group" for parents of students in Chris's middle school. The meetings will be held in the morning. The teacher assumes the responsibility of interviewing and finding a "big brother" for Chris.

Suggestion 3:   Leroy, Chris's brother, is to be seen by Chris's teacher weekly for counseling sessions.

Your Analysis of Violations of the Three Underlying Features

Uniqueness: _____

_____

_____

_____

Goodness of Fit:_____

_____

_____

_____

Networking: _____

_____

_____

_____

the professional might reach the conclusion, "This looks like a family that is enmeshed with a parentified older sibling."

In reflecting the conclusion back to the family, no professional would want to say, "Maybe you are expecting too much from your adolescent" without enough information to confirm that fact. Neither would one say to the parent, "Your family seems to be enmeshed." Instead, the professional would make comments to help the parents realize that adolescents have needs of their own. Providing information about the family life cycle and differing demands at each stage of development would help the parents realistically view the needs of their adolescent.

As conclusions are developed and agreed upon, problems and needs are prioritized in terms of the immediacy and seriousness felt by the family. Professionals often find it helpful to make a list of the needs as they surface in the conversation. A simple listing is all that is needed. For example, in the Estevas family just mentioned, the list might include time for spouses to be together, help with Miguel's homework, time for Maria to do her own homework, time for the mother to be by herself, and the siblings' need for information on genetics and possible impact on their own future families.

Later, the professional shares the list with the family members and potential solutions are discussed and prioritized. Family members will decide that there are some things that are more serious than others and some things that need immediate attention. This prioritization process reflects both seriousness and immediacy.

Professionals will benefit from reading Dunst et al.'s (1994c) book on methods, strategies, and practices for supporting and strengthening families. Most of the chapters are devoted to information useful in assessing the eight components the authors define for IFSPs. This text highlights family systems concepts that can be embedded within those processes.

Also available are structured assessment tools, particularly in the area of family needs. Turnbull and Turnbull (1986) provided a Family Information Preference Inventory that can be reproduced for noncommercial purposes. Such an instrument is helpful in the assessment step of the family-focused intervention process. Mothers should not be the only ones to complete questionnaires. Concerns shared by more than one family member will likely be given higher priority; individual concerns might be resolved through joint discussion of family members. Morsink et al. (1991) provided a list of assessment instruments and cautioned that they be used responsibly.

When assessing the functioning of the family, it is important to assess relevant child variables as well as adult variables. It is also important to establish how family members view their own needs for support, information, or training (Losen & Losen, 1994). Observations of parent-child interactions are another rich source of assessment data. From the information gleaned and observations made, teachers, social workers, other professionals, and family members develop tentative hypotheses about family needs.

Once the functioning and characteristics of the family are known, including all the dimensions of family systems as well as what the family sees itself as needing, it is time to move into the planning process. It is impossible to move into this second step unless professionals have invested considerable time with family members to gain an understanding of their particular characteristics as well as their personal needs and desires.

Planning

In person-centered planning, information is gathered during the assessment process "from the child, family, and others supporting the child, considering strengths, interests, needs, and dreams for the future" (Malatchi, 1977, p. 92). Team planning allows school professionals to validate the needs of the family, reprioritize those needs when indicated, and elicit family members' suggestions about what solutions might fit them. Generally, professionals have a list of areas to pursue while talking with the family.

From the data base that is developed and summarized into a prioritized listing of needs and problems, goals can be generated. A goal is essentially a description of what will occur when the problem or need no longer exists. Goals should be outcome-oriented, time-limited, and stated in measurable terms. It is more functional to state goals in relative as opposed to absolute terms. For example, reducing temper tantrums to one an evening as opposed to eliminating them entirely is a realistic, functional goal. Another example would be having an adolescent complete homework three out of the four nights that he has it each week, as opposed to completing it four out of four nights of the week.

Notari-Syverson and Shuster (1995) presented guidelines for developing educational goals and objectives for family-focused interventions and individualized education programs. From their review of the literature, they found that high-quality goals and objectives had the following characteristics: "functionality, generality, ease of integration within the instructional context, measurability, and hierarchical relationship between long-range goal and short-term objective" (p. 29). Their list of 10 questions to ask to determine the viability of educational goals and objectives is useful reading.

Goals are critical to the planning process. They serve as a map to reach the destination. Once educational goals have been established, professionals can work with the family to generate plans for achieving those goals.

Plans are best established according to the three W's: What action is to be taken toward achieving a particular goal? Who will be responsible for that action? When will the action be completed? In family-focused interventions, such planning must be a process involving parents, the student, and professionals.

Examples of plans that might be developed during a conversation with the Estevas family include having the grandmother tutor Miguel, allowing time alone for the spouses at least every other evening, and having an aunt baby-sit while the mother has three mornings out a week. Any plans that are developed should be based upon family input and the family's prioritization of their needs.

Forest and Pearpoint (1992) described a process for strategic planning and problem solving in education that involves making action plans and tracing the path that will lead to the plans being implemented successfully (Pearpoint, O'Brien, & Forest, 1995). Although their focus was on inclusion, the process they suggested can be adapted to other areas of planning for both at-risk and special-needs students. The beauty of their work is in the involvement of a host of people who are committed to being involved in the student's life and to helping the student not only generate ideas and plans but also implement solutions. Videotapes of their work are available through Inclusion Press in Toronto, Canada. Because the time involved in such planning is extensive, it is impossible to provide the experience for all students for whom FFIs are being written. For those in need of more involved family and support processes, however, it is an excellent possibility.

The necessity of joint planning involving professionals and parents cannot be emphasized strongly enough. Investment is highest when all parties have had the opportunity to examine alternatives, express concerns, and influence decisions (Winton, 1996).

Implementation

It has been said that no decision has really been made until action has been taken. Likewise, the best of plans are only good intentions until they are implemented. If any party to a plan is reluctant to proceed to implementation, a reexamination of the data and the planning process may be warranted. A critical question to ask in such a case is, "What has prevented individuals from freely expressing their concerns during the planning part of the process?" It may be that there was a violation of Satir's five freedoms or that the individual was generalizing to the planning process a prior experience in which one or more of the five freedoms were restricted.

Lack of freedom to express concerns, perceived or real, is not the only explanation for lack of implementation. Unforeseen barriers to implementation may also be the cause of the reluctance. For example, perhaps the grandparents, who were going to help the child with his homework, had to be hospitalized and could no longer offer assistance. When such barriers develop, the professional should model flexibility by initiating conversation about the new circumstances. Flexible rules are a sign of healthy functioning, and some parents may need encouragement to bend the rules under unusual circumstances. Families with rigid boundaries are less likely to adapt easily to changing circumstances.

Types of interventions typical of family-focused interventions are covered in detail later in this chapter. In general, Bailey et al. (1988) listed three types of direct professional support: informational support, instrumental support that helps families achieve tasks or functions, and socioemotional support such as listening. The authors also discussed indirect support such as facilitating services and case management. They cautioned professionals against attempting to provide services in which they were not skilled. For example, in good faith and with the best intent, a teacher might attempt to provide counseling for parents bereaved by the loss of a child. Unskilled and untrained in counseling, the teacher might do more harm than good. Although a caring and supportive teacher can, and actually should, talk with the parents about the death of a child whom he or she taught; the teacher should not assume the role of counselor in those interactions.

Evaluation

Once a plan is implemented, it is time for the final component in the process, evaluation. Good plans contain built-in evaluation in terms of measurable and time-limited goals. Goal attainment is always helpful in evaluation. Evaluation also might include readministration of the inventory used earlier to assess family need.

During evaluation of family-focused interventions, it is critical to assess more than simply the degree to which the desired outcome was achieved. Each family member's level of satisfaction with the process should be determined. It is also helpful to ascertain what was ineffective as well as what worked. This evaluation, combined with results from the readministration of any family inventory or assessment procedure, can then become the basis for an updated assessment to use in the development of a new intervention cycle.

The four steps of assessment, planning, implementation, and evaluation result in a dynamic interrelated process for change, not a start-and-stop model. It is a cyclical process in which each new round builds on the successes of the last, leading to increased impact and effectiveness.

When the parents, student, and professionals evaluate where they are in the process, they realize they have worthwhile assessment information relating to the first step in the process. This allows family-focused interventions to recycle at deeper and deeper levels.

Table 12.4 presents questions to answer about the four processes of intervening. I recommend discussing those questions with others.

TABLE 12.4 • Discussion Starters on the Four Processes of Intervening

1. What are some reasons trust is so important in the assessment process?
2. The assessment step is considered critical to the family-focused intervention process. To what do you attribute that?
3. Goals seem to be time managers' answer to the world. Why so?
4. Provide a well-stated goal for a family-focused intervention and defend its aspects and value.
5. Mutuality in planning appears to be a "sacred cow." Why?
6. How do you see evaluation fitting into the process of family-focused intervention?

Types of Assistance

Having covered underlying features and the four-step process of family-focused intervention, the discussion now turns to consideration of specific types of assistance provided by professionals.

Emotional Support

Families will not necessarily identify the emotional support that school professionals provide as a need. Professionals can assume, however, that all families will benefit from emotional support. This is especially true of those families with children who are at risk or who have special needs. At the same time, it is also important to ask parents as well as students what forms of emotional support they want.

Many families with children who have special needs suffer from feelings of grief, isolation, anxiety, or frustration. It is crucial that professionals provide an atmosphere of trust and safety (Miller, 1996) when relating to these families. Conveying a sense of understanding and caring is a most basic and powerful way to assist a family (Morsink et al., 1991). Burleson (1994) indicated that comforting is important to the health and well-being of all people.

Reflection of feelings may be the best way for school professionals who are not trained for in-depth responses to provide emotional support. Client-centered therapy, developed by Carl Rogers, evolved around the concept of active listening and the idea that it is supportive simply to listen to someone who is in emotional pain. It can be very distracting when a professional hurries to suggest solutions rather than being at the feeling level of the person. Professionals all too often respond with solutions rather than react to the family member at his or her level of emotional response.

Again, showing the family that they are understood is, by itself, a powerful way of providing assistance. Active listening, with its emotional support, often leads to more specific strategies, such as those described in the following sections.

Resource Identification

Few family members know of all the useful resources available to them. Chapter 9 described means of linking families with community resources. Resource identification is particularly important for at-risk students and their families (Booth & Dunn, 1996; Dryfoos, 1994; Harvard Family Research Project, 1995; Slavin et al., 1996).

Appendix D provides a list of national resources available for adults and children, some of which have web sites. It is very important that schools find a way to help families learn about these and other resources. Appendices B and C provide reading lists for adults and children/youth on topics of interest to families. Making such a book list available is helpful, but providing copies of the books in a Family Resource Center in the school is even more worthwhile. Although disengaged families are less likely to make use of such resources, it may be possible to find one member within the family who can link with the resource(s) and connect them with others in the family. It is important to be aware of *goodness of fit* in linking people with resources. For example, playing up the internet as a resource for a family having a member who is involved with computers is a good strategy.

For families of special-needs students, resource identification might include making written information available about the child's special needs, rights and responsibilities, and the procedures to be followed, as well as due process procedures. Links with specialized personnel within the school and community should be provided frequently.

One of the most valuable resources for parents of children with special needs is information about parent groups (Turnbull & Turnbull, 1996), of which there are three basic types. First, parent support groups focus on coming together to share emotional support and assist one another in learning to cope with the facts of having a child with special needs. Second, parent education groups are oriented toward providing information about particular conditions such as learning disabilities. They also may train parents in management techniques or other topics such as time management. Third, parent advocacy groups center around teaching and encouraging parents to become strong advocates for their children. The Association for Children With Learning Disabilities is one such group.

Resource identification may involve helping parents locate and gain access to another parent or helping them find ways of gaining needed experiences, such as by sitting in on IEP meetings or visiting alternative programs (Turnbull & Turnbull, 1996). As stated earlier, further information concerning parent groups and other resources are included in Chapter 9 and Appendix D of this text.

Technical Assistance

Professionals may intervene directly with families by suggesting at-home management strategies, training techniques, or helpful hints about working with specific behavior problems. This information, of course, would be provided because family members had indicated the need for it. However, it may be an outgrowth of observations made, hypotheses tested, and conclusions drawn by professionals. In some cases, professionals would recognize family characteristics, such as enmeshment, and use the family's language to convey areas that need attention.

While the best collaborations between parents and teachers tend to preserve their respective roles—that is, teachers teach and parents parent—much of what works in one setting can be applied to the other. The exchange of what works between parents and professionals frequently enhances the effectiveness of both. Such sharing can easily be accommodated during parent-professional conferences, discussed in Chapter 11.

Referral

Another type of intervention is referral to family therapy or medical, counseling, psychological, or financial services. Referrals are made when the specialized needs of families go beyond what the professionals in the schools can reasonably be expected to provide.

In particular, teachers should not become so involved with families that they rob themselves of personal discretionary time. Families having children with special needs are frequently desperate for someone to listen to them, and it is natural for teachers to want to help them in any way possible. Teachers should be particularly cautious about stepping out of their roles. At the same time, they can play a valuable role in using the trust and mutual commitment they have established with parents to help link families with other needed services.

Family therapy is a prominent option for referral when the professional can identify structural or interactional patterns in the family that warrant such an intervention. Part I of this book covered these types of patterns. Sibling groups are another option for referral, either when problems arise among siblings or simply for mutual support (Meyer & Vadasy, 1994). Sibling issues were discussed in Chapters 2 and 8 of this text, and part of Chapter 9 focused on the process of referring family members for other services.

Normalization

Professionals have pointed out the difficulty both parents and school professionals face in maintaining perspective by avoiding an overemphasis on the deficits of the student with special needs (Malatchi, 1997). Professionals can help parents who are overemphasizing deficits by helping them view their child's behavior as normal.

Many parents perceive their child's behavior through a *disability filter*. They often do not realize that most actions of even the most atypical child are age-appropriate and normal. For instance, *normal* students have bad days at school every now and then. They also have minor problems at home. The same behaviors in a child with special needs tend to be thought of as symptomatic. Teachers have a marvelous opportunity to help the family develop a normalizing perspective, as do the other professionals in the school.

Reframing

Reframing is a type of intervention that is sometimes used in normalization. Reframing involves offering alternative interpretations of behavior or events that essentially change the meaning of the behavior for the family (Bardill, 1997; Nardone & Watzlawick, 1993). Its objective is to alter the pattern of the interaction.

For example, many children with attention-deficit disorder have difficulty following complex directions and therefore do not do anything to comply with directions. A father may label his child's lack of compliance as defiance. If the school professional can help the father to relabel the behavior as "confused," it might change the emotional loading and the sequence of interactions. Similarly, a parent who complains of a child's pestering may respond differently if the child's need for affection and reassurance is emphasized.

Appendix A describes Virginia Satir's Communication Process model. Satir was a master of the art of reframing. By itself, reframing can be an effective intervention provided by school professionals. Satir (1983a) referred to helping families to see situations with "new eyes." She might have characteristically said, "Yes, that is how you saw your son yesterday. Now you've learned so much about yourself, your parents, and their parents. How do you see your son now?" The concept of reframing is discussed in detail in Chapter 13.

Contextualization

Contextualization shares some similarities with normalization and reframing. It is a process of helping parents and family members to interpret behavior *in and through* the context in which it occurs. This process is the heart of systems thinking!

For example, physical complaints may develop when a child is confronted with demands on his performance that he feels inadequate to meet. Consider a kindergarten child, Emma, who was the only child in her class unable to recognize the letters of the alphabet. She began to complain about headaches and wanted to go to the infirmary every time the teacher taught letter recognition in class. Or consider John, an adolescent who became withdrawn or rejecting toward his siblings after a difficult social encounter with peers at school. As another example, being afraid of a classmate can induce a child to become aggressive or threatening toward that classmate in order to decrease their social differences. An example of this was seen with an adolescent, Shawn, who was afraid of a peer's size and threatening manner. Shawn would tell the peer that he had a black belt in karate and invite him to fight, when, in fact, Shawn had never even attended a karate class.

School professionals can assist parents and other family members to respond effectively to a child's behavior by helping them become tuned in to significant contextual factors. Once the parents and family members notice and understand the context from which the behavior springs, it is much easier for them to accept and respond to the student. The intervention actually attunes the family members to the context. How the family members respond once they notice and understand the context depends upon the situation. In the example of Emma, the family members could be coached to support her by commenting on the way they would feel if they were in a class for which they were unprepared. In the second example, John's siblings might be coached not to bother him until he had time to come to terms with the situation at school. Such advise would be especially important for enmeshed families, who might tend to get in the middle of the special-needs student's own problems. If Shawn's family (in the third example) was disengaged, after attuning the family to the context, the school professional might coach the family to reach out to Shawn by commenting on how threatened they might themselves feel in similar situations. This intervention could lead to stronger positive alignments between the needs of the adolescent and the family members as well as healthier cohesion in the family interaction pattern.

The family-focused intervention is a relatively informal process. IEPs, to be discussed next, are a formal process. Family-focused interventions can be used with both at-risk and special-needs students, whereas IEPs are required only for students with disabilities.

INDIVIDUALIZED EDUCATION PROGRAMS

The individualized education program is intended to be the cornerstone of educational programming for students with disabilities. The IEP is the vehicle used to develop programs that provide free and appropriate educational experiences for students who are determined to be eligible for special education (Strickland & Turnbull, 1990).

The local school system may choose to also write IEPs for at-risk students. School systems providing IEPs for students who are *not* determined to be eligible for special education do not have to follow federal or state regulations regarding content or process. Since they are free from regulations when developing IEPS for at-risk students, they may select the elements of IEPs that most fit for their systems.

This section presents background information on IEPs for special education students and then addresses potential challenges or barriers to the effective inclusion of parents in the IEP process. Finally, ways to involve families in the IEP process are described and related specifically to family systems concepts.

Background

An individualized education program written for a student must be developed by a committee and include the parent in the process. Furthermore, this process must be completed before the student can be placed in a special education program. The parents must agree to the program before it may be implemented. As stated in Chapter 10, these conditions are intended to ensure that the program the student receives is designed to meet his or her unique learning needs, rather than having the individual student meet the requirements of a given program.

The IEP outlines the educational program for a student with a disability for the period of 1 year (King-Sears, 1997). It sets learning goals for the student and specifies the related services, such as family counseling or occupational therapy, that will be required to help the student meet those goals.

This introductory section concerning IEPs includes information on components of IEPs, improving IEPs, research results relating to family involvement in the IEP process, and advantages and disadvantages of IEPs. It is followed by a section on barriers to IEP development identified by parents as well as teachers. This book does not tell how to write

IEPs; its focus is on family involvement. For further information on developing and implementing IEPs, refer to Strickland and Turnbull (1990). Bear in mind, however, that changes in requirements have occurred since that text was published, in particular the transition component.

Components

The first component of an IEP is a description of the child's current level of educational performance or functioning. This statement should include strengths as well as weaknesses. Just as it is important to take into account family resources when assessing families, it is valuable to state strengths of the student in the IEP (Malatchi, 1997). This information is gleaned from the assessment process.

Annual goals and short-term objectives for reaching those goals follow the statement of the student's level of functioning. Goals and objectives must be tied to the student's strengths and weaknesses. Family involvement in the process of determining goals is critical. King-Sears (1997) recommended that peers of students with disabilities also contribute information and ideas for the IEP.

A statement of the specific special education and related services required is provided, along with a statement of the extent to which the student will participate in general education programs. The IEP must specify the date when services will be initiated and how long these services are expected to last. Parents should be involved in the decision making about the delivery model (see Chapter 10) as well as the related services desired. Winton (1996) indicated that parents should be the ultimate decision makers.

A statement of the transition services to be implemented is needed for students age 16 and older, including linkages before the student leaves school. For some students, such a statement is appropriate at age 14 or younger.

Criteria for the achievement of specific objectives must be indicated. Dates when objectives will be introduced and when they are expected to be mastered also are specified.

Another important component is evaluation of the individualized education program. The IEP must state when, how, and by whom the program will be evaluated. By law, it is required that all IEPs be evaluated at least annually. During the annual review, the student's program is examined in its entirety. The progress made in accomplishing short-term objectives and long-term goals is determined. In addition, the continued appropriateness of the student's present educational placement must be reviewed.

PL 101-476 (the Individuals With Disabilities Education Act, or IDEA), which was the 1990 reauthorization of PL 94-142, added another required component to individualized education programs. Now, a statement must be included concerning transition services that aid the movement from school to postschool life. The statement should detail a coordinated set of activities in postsecondary education, vocational training, integrated employment (including supported employment), continuing education, adult services, independent living, or community participation. School and agency responsibilities must be included for students age 16 and over.

Finally, a complete evaluation of each student receiving special education must be performed every 3 years. At that time, the student must undergo a new comprehensive assessment that includes all of the components present in the original assessment process.

Parents or professionals may request a comprehensive assessment sooner if they feel the present educational program is not meeting the needs of the student.

Improving IEPs

King-Sears (1997) indicated that IEPs become more useful and meaningful when:

- students are part of developing and implementing the goals and objectives;
- peers of students with severe disabilities who contribute ideas about these students can be included in classes as well as social occasions;
- families take an active role in forming and implementing the IEP;
- the IEP content is determined with the assistance of general educators.

Research Results Related to Family Involvement

Grigal, Test, Beattie, and Wood (1997) studied the transition component of IEPs for high-school students. They examined the format, compliance with mandates, and consideration of best practices as well as differences in these aspects across disability categories. They found the letter of the law was met but that the transition components did not reflect best practices.

An examination of culturally sensitive practices related to IEPs was conducted by Dennis and Giangreco (1996). They interviewed 14 special education professionals who were members of minority groups in the United States. From the conversations, six keys to being culturally sensitive emerged: appreciation for the unique nature of each family; awareness of how influential the professional is; recognition of personal cultural biases; actively expanding knowledge of different cultures; developing awareness of cultural norms; and learning with the families. In the article, the authors presented numerous suggestions to help professionals be more culturally sensitive, including seeking assistance from "cultural interpreters" prior to the IEP meeting; determining the literacy and language status of family members; involving families in planning for the meetings; previewing the meeting with families; being flexible and responding to the interaction style of the family; adapting the time frame so that family needs are met; and examining the questions they pose. Many of the authors' suggestions are included in an informative two-page chart in the article. I highly recommend that permission to reprint the chart be requested and that the chart be distributed to all professionals involved in IEPs. The suggestions, when followed, will lead to improved family-professional relationships. The authors can be reached via e-mail: rdennis@moose.uvm.edu or mgiangre@moose.uvm.edu.

A 3-year study of families participating in IEPs was conducted by Harry, Allen, and McLaughlin (1995). In the first year, 16 of the 18 parents participated in the IEP conference for their child. This number declined to 11 in the third year. Queried about why they did not attend, the parents sited work conflict, late notice with little time to schedule, and feeling ignored. A third of the parents in the study believed they had influenced the decision-making process. However, the parents did not view the conferences, which typically lasted for 20 to 30 minutes, as eliciting their participation and commented that jargon was used throughout the meetings.

S. W. Smith (1990) reviewed both data-based research and position papers on IEPs published between 1975 and 1989. He described the literature as falling into normative, analytic, and technology-reaction categories. The normative literature described norms and procedures for IEPs as well as professional concerns about the IEP process. The analytic literature included data-based research and found teacher involvement and perceptions, parental involvement, and the team approach to be important. The technology-reaction literature focused on computer-assisted systems that could manage the IEP process and provide documentation.

Of particular interest here is the information Smith related about parental involvement described in the analytic literature. He cited four studies as representative of professionals' perceptions of the parents' roles, the actual roles of the parents, the parents' perception of their roles during the IEP conference, and the parents' satisfaction with their roles in the IEP conference. His summary of the studies indicated "little interaction by parents when they attended the IEP meeting, with parents being perceived by school professionals as recipients of information. Despite this passive role, parents have generally been satisfied with the IEP conference and its outcomes" (p. 9). The entire article by Smith (1990) is excellent reading.

As early as 1979, Gilliam noted the importance of increasing participation in the decision-making process. He also specifically mentioned the need for encouraging parents and professionals "to share their knowledge about the child and the placement functions" (pp. 467–468).

Even earlier, Yoshida Fenton, Kaufman, and Maxwell (1978) noted "that planning team members' attitudes toward parental participation will be a major factor in determining the actual role parents take during planning team meetings" (p. 531). They found that parents were expected to provide information to the team but not to be involved actively in making decisions about their own child's educational program.

In another study, Goldstein, Strickland, Turnbull, and Curry (1980) observed 14 IEP conferences and found that only one was devoted to parents and educators writing goals and objectives together. The father of the student for whom the IEP was being written was a psychologist and familiar with IEPs. The student's mother attended the meeting and participated in writing the goals and objectives.

Advantages and Disadvantages

There are many advantages to writing IEPs. They form a working guide that helps parents keep focused on current goals and objectives for their child, thus providing parents with the opportunity to reinforce skills at home that are being covered in school. The IEP process also requires parents to interact with teachers in a constructive manner. Additionally, the focus in IEP meetings is on possibilities rather than problems. Another advantage is that a written document (the IEP) is taken home, and parents do not have to rely on their memories. At the high-school level, the IEP meeting allows for discussion about the type of diploma or certificate toward which the student is working. Such discussion prevents parental disappointment and alienation later about the type of diploma or certificate their child received.

There are also disadvantages to IEPs. Considerable time is required to develop these plans as well as to coordinate meeting times for all involved. Parents may have their own struggles with the IEP process, such as masking their lack of understanding or acceptance of the IEP, transportation problems, or difficulty accepting their child's disability and level of functioning. The parents may have unrealistic expectations of their child or of the professionals who implement the IEP. No process or document is perfect; however, like pregnancy and delivery of a child, the outcome of the IEP is definitely worth the trouble.

In considering the research on IEPs and IFSPs, Turnbull and Turnbull (1996) concluded that schools are merely complying with mandates and not supporting families in becoming part of the collaborative process. They indicated that the IEP process "falls short of being a reliable alliance that fosters collaboration leading to empowerment" (p. 231), although they also indicated that it is possible to empower families.

Barriers

From both the teachers' and the parents' points of view, there are some barriers to involving parents in the IEP process. Those will be described before moving to the phases of the IEP conference and how to involve parents in each phase.

Barriers for Parents

As described in Turnbull and Turnbull (1986, 1990), parents have identified several barriers to their involvement in IEPs. Among those barriers are logistical problems, communication problems, lack of understanding of the school system, and feelings of inferiority.

Logistical problems. Examples of logistical problems are difficulty with transportation, child-care problems, problems with involving fathers, and time constraints. The unique resources and interaction patterns of families will lead to these barriers. Some families are disengaged and may not want to be involved. Others may be overwhelmed, having few available resources. Still others are what Aponte (1994) called "underorganized." This problem is most frequently observed in schools in areas where families are of low socioeconomic status.

Professionals should find ways to ameliorate these barriers so that parents can participate in the development of IEPs. Solutions may include networking to assist with transportation and baby-sitting as well as arranging meeting times that are convenient for parents. Information on networking was provided in Chapter 9. An understanding of family systems concepts and family characteristics is helpful in responding to barriers stemming from unique family characteristics.

Communication. A common problem parents have identified in the area of communication relates to language and cultural barriers. Certainly professionals can find ways to work with minorities. For example, home visits, translators, written texts, and outreach can be used to counteract these barriers. Whoever chairs the IEP conference should be able to relate effectively to the family's cultural and socioeconomic background (Turnbull & Turnbull, 1996) as well as to overcome any language barriers.

Lack of understanding of the school system. Parents may also need help from professionals in understanding the school system and their parental rights and responsibilities. They may also need help in understanding the ways in which they can call upon their rights. In reference to explaining parental rights to parents, Losen and Losen (1994) stated that school staff should be straightforward with parents about

> the fact that they have a right to invite advocates to future meetings, to obtain an independent evaluation at school expense, to employ the counsel of an attorney, to challenge recommendations, and so on. It should be made clear to the parents that they do not have to agree to the staff's classification of their child's needs or to any proposed special education placement. They need to understand that they have the right to request additional or different services, or a different placement, and that their request will be seriously considered. (p. 124)

Turnbull and Turnbull (1990) cited a study by Thompson involving training parents to be involved in IEP meetings through lecture, discussion, audiovisual materials, and simulated activities. Mothers who received the training were twice as likely to contribute to the IEP conference as those who did not receive the training.

Feelings of inferiority. Professionals must let parents know that they are valued. They must convey the role and value of partnership between home and school. It is easy for parents to feel overwhelmed by large committee meetings. They need to know that professionals value and appreciate their input. Again, employing an IEP chair with a link to the family can be very helpful. For example, a Puerto Rican family would probably find it easier to have an IEP chair who speaks Spanish or is of Spanish descent.

Barriers for Teachers

Teachers have identified other barriers to involving parents in the IEP process. Among them are parental apathy, professional time constraints, parents' lack of time, and the schools' devaluation of parent input.

Parental apathy. Parental apathy should be taken in stride by the teacher and not personalized. Professionals are not responsible for motivating everyone! It is helpful for the teacher to consider what is known about the particular family characteristics and to recognize that there are good reasons for parental apathy. The parents, for example, may not have the personal resources at the time to be involved in one more activity. They may consider IEP involvement as the "straw that would break the camel's back." Professionals need to recognize situations that will not change and conserve their personal energy.

Professional constraints. Time is a major factor in developing IEPs. Teachers have indicated that they spend approximately 6 hours on developing each new IEP (Price & Goodman, 1980). Turnbull and Turnbull (1996) reaffirmed time constraints as a problem. It is important that professionals provide sufficient time for preparing for conferences, even if they have to lean on others to do some tasks. Dictating reports, using volunteers for scheduling, and receiving in-service training on time management are all helpful.

Time barriers can work against effective and clear communication with parents. It is common for professionals facing time constraints to inform parents about their "rights" and not to encourage them to participate in decision making. The results are predictable—the parents become adversaries rather than advocates. Time well spent early in the IEP process will save time over the long term, especially as related to parental involvement.

Family Involvement

Family involvement in the IEP process is typically seen as parental involvement. It is important that professionals view parental involvement in IEPs as important. The federal government did so when it required parental involvement in the development of IEPs.

There are eight components of the IFSP/IEP conference:

- preconference preparation,
- the initial conference proceedings, an important part of which is connecting with the family members,
- the sharing of visions and expectations for the student by family members and friends as well as by professionals,
- review of the formal evaluation and current levels of performance,
- the sharing of resources as well as priorities and concerns,
- the development of goals and objectives,
- the determination of placement and related services, and
- closing the conference by summarizing and concluding (Turnbull & Turnbull, 1996).

Each of these components is now described. Highlighted in the discussion are family involvement and the ways in which dysfunctional families might operate in that phase of the IEP process.

Not all school systems link determination of placement and related services to the IEP process; they hold meetings for those purposes separate from the IEP meeting. Whether a part of the IEP meeting or separate from it, parental involvement obviously is beneficial during that stage.

Preconference Preparation

During the assessment process, much information concerning the family's unique characteristics and process was accumulated. Those on the team who know the most about the family systems approaches should meet with the professionals who will be involved in the IEP conference to explain or review family functioning so that their ideas will be taken into consideration. Further, the knowledge they provide about the family's process will help the professionals provide input that fits the given family. For example, professionals would not want to encourage increased parent-child involvement for field trips if it was already determined that the parents were overly involved with their child. All professionals will want family characteristics to be utmost in their minds as they begin mutual program planning.

The chair chosen for the IEP conference should be the person who is the best fit for the particular family. Some professionals will work better with enmeshed families; others will be more effective with disengaged families. A member of a minority group might offer to chair the conference of a minority family. A single parent might be the best chair for a single parent of a student with special needs.

The chairperson's responsibilities are to coordinate the preconference proceedings, chair the actual IEP meeting(s), and provide follow-up support. It is easy to see why some type of matching of family to chairperson is important.

Connecting and Initial Conference Proceedings

The beginning of any conference sets the tone for what is to come. Most people have heard about or attended large conferences with a keynote speaker whose skills and sensitivities prompted the audience to look forward to the remainder of the conference. It is equally important to get off to a good start in a small conference dealing with one student. Professionals concern themselves with many students. During an IEP conference, professionals and the family members are concerned about one child only.

Critical to effective human interaction is allowing all other concerns or unresolved problems to recede from your mind. The skill of putting all other things from your mind and focusing wholly on the present concern is essential. Counselors and therapists must regularly employ this clear focusing of their energies; other professionals at the meeting may not be as adept at such specific focusing. Prior to walking into the meeting, professionals would benefit from taking a minute to clear other concerns from their minds. Thirty seconds of deep breathing followed by a quick review of the child's records and unique family characteristics will help the professional to focus. In addition, the professional may want to use an affirmation such as, "This student and family [name and family] are my only concern at this time. I give them my full attention." These suggestions are components of low-stress living and abound in the literature on stress.

It is important that the chairperson speak with the family members, including the student, while everyone is arriving. People who are unfamiliar with one another should be introduced, and everyone should have a chance to interact informally before the meeting becomes more formal. On occasion, with contentious parents, informal introductions may not be in order; in such cases a formal introduction will have to do.

A number of authors have noted the importance of greeting family members and any others they have invited to the initial meeting. The student might be invited to make introductions before a professional reviews the agenda and provides time schedules. It may also be necessary to provide information on legal rights before going any further. These are all basic to effective initial conference proceedings (Idol et al., 1994; Losen & Losen, 1994; Turnbull & Turnbull, 1996).

All professionals need to keep distinctive family characteristics foremost in their mind during this and other stages of the conference. If family members respond coolly to a professional's greeting, the professional should review their family patterns. They may be disengaged within the family and generalizing this type of functioning outside of the family. Certainly, most people operate in similar ways within and outside of the family. Also, as mentioned in the chapter on cultural factors, cultural background should be considered.

Someone from a northern European background might have a more reserved style than a southern European, who might be more extraverted.

Sharing Visions and Expectations

This component of the IEP conference allows the student, family members, friends, and professionals to share what they see as rich possibilities for the student. All involved should be encouraged to use imagery to go beyond the edge of possibilities now experienced by the child and his or her family and friends. Family members who are disengaged may have trouble becoming involved in this process. Until they follow the uplifting energy being created, the rest of the team will need to lead the way.

Turnbull and Turnbull (1996) recommended that if the family and/or friends have previously been engaged in a MAPs process—a process of developing an action plan—they review that plan with the professionals. Such sharing creates a momentum that buoys the educational process.

The focus of visions ranges from home to work to the community to friendships to the support needed to achieve the vision. In the latter regard, Forest and Pearpoint (1992), reported that they generate enthusiasm and energy by training personnel around the country to use MAPs and CIRCLES (a group of supportive friends organized to help achieve the inclusion goals established during the MAPs process) to plan and problem solve so that students can be educated in general education classes.

Review of Formal Evaluation and Current Levels of Performance

If the professionals on the team have done their homework adequately, the chairperson already will have received the information on test results and covered that information with the family members. Chapter 10 recommended the use of a premeeting conference for presenting test results prior to determination of eligibility (Losen & Losen, 1994). Having already absorbed this information, families can join the group of professionals in planning the educational program at the IEP conference. It is helpful, however, to review the test results at the conference so that everyone remembers the student's current level of functioning and strengths and weaknesses. During IEP conferences that are held after the initial conference, the teacher(s) should present information on progress to date for goals and objectives set at earlier IEP conferences.

Sharing Resources, Priorities, and Concerns

If the African saying *It Takes a Village to Raise a Child* is true, then it is important that everyone involved in the IEP process contributes resources to the goal of educating the student. Parents can speak about the ways in which they can be involved in their child's education. Their contributions plus the sharing of unique resources by other team members allows for a complete picture of what the student can count on from the team.

It is important to bolster family and friends who may feel impoverished in their offerings by asking them questions that will call forth their beneficial gifts. Dysfunctional family members may have such low self-esteem that they do not even know they have gifts that are important to the student's educational experience. A team member can encourage these individuals by making comments such as, "When I was a child, the most meaningful collaboration I had with my father was when he helped me study my spelling words. The gift you offer may seem small to you yet very important to your child." Beyond that, sharing resources is a statement of commitment from all involved. Thus the student will experience the sense of connection as well as feel the web of support surrounding him or her.

The priorities of the team members, which are linked to the expectations expressed earlier in the conference, are also discussed at this stage. Examining priorities early in the process can lead to a more productive meeting and help the team members know one another better.

Finally, here and throughout the meeting, it is important to share any concerns or worries about the goals, objectives, or plan. Without expressing concerns, it will not be possible to ensure that the student and family needs are met. This process also helps members of the team to feel supported as well as heard.

Development of Goals and Objectives

An earlier section of this chapter covered the components of IEPs. Important among them were goals and objectives. Family members, including the student when possible, can contribute to developing the goals and objectives. They should also feel comfortable responding to their impression of the goals and objectives presented by the professionals.

When parents are aware of the goals and objectives for their child, it is much easier for them to follow up on them at home. Certainly parents want their child's learning to generalize to other situations. Their involvement can focus the rest of the family on common purposes and tasks. Siblings may also be able to participate in reinforcing learning goals.

As in other steps of the IEP conference, the professionals must keep family considerations in mind during the discussion of goals and objectives. Some families from lower socioeconomic strata might find it difficult to relate to the goals and objectives presented. It is important to invest time in conferences with such parents so that they can become familiar with the educational program and come to value it.

Other parents might be unwilling to let school professionals know that they do not understand the goals and objectives presented. They appear to be attending the meeting simply out of a sense of obligation. When this situation occurs, professionals should hypothesize how the parents might be reacting and respond to their situation. It is important to put the parents at ease by sharing realistic expectations in language they can understand. Allowing them to ask questions is also helpful. Professionals should empower parents rather than letting them stay in the dark. Clarification of goals and objectives is most helpful, and as in all stages of the IEP process, language at family members' levels is imperative.

Person and family-centered approaches include dreaming about possibilities (Malatchi, 1997). Creative means of developing possibilities with families have evolved over the years, and the IEP meetings can be infused with energy and enthusiasm. Malatchi wrote of *dream catchers* and the importance of involving families and professionals in focusing on capacities and possibilities.

Beyond those commonsense ways of joining, it is beneficial to consider family functioning from a family systems perspective. If a student is presenting his or her ideas with excessive strength and the parents are acquiescent, it might confirm a professional's hypothesis that there is an inversion of hierarchy in the family. It may not be possible to address this situation completely in the IEP meeting; however, school professionals should at least note the situation and later convey it to the appropriate professionals. The social worker, counselor, and psychologist might find the information helpful in future meetings with parents. Such objective and descriptive information could also be valuable if the family is seeing a therapist. Educators must not, however, volunteer such information outside the school system without a signed release from the parents.

In the example of the overly assertive adolescent, one way of intervening could be to acknowledge the situation and place the parent(s) at the top of the hierarchy with a statement such as, "Ken, I notice that you are being really assertive here. I would also like to hear from your father and mother. Mr. and Mrs. Takayima, what are your thoughts and feelings about this goal?" Whether this will be a viable option will, of course, depend upon the situation. As with any intervention, professional discretion is advised. With that said, support for healthy family interactions should be given whenever possible. The modeling of effective human interaction by professionals is a beneficial strategy.

There are endless situations in which parents and students will demonstrate their family functioning. The discussion of goals and objectives is a choice time for confirming as well as establishing hypotheses regarding unique family characteristics. What is observed also might help professionals plan strategy for future family involvement as well as help refer families for family systems therapy or other counseling.

Determination of Placement and Related Services

As stated earlier, some school systems do not determine placement and related services at the same time that they develop the IEP. Whatever the practice, parents should receive information that allows them to comprehend the different placement options as well as their respective advantages and disadvantages. Information about related services must also be provided.

The general practice in most schools is to merely recommend a particular delivery model and assume the parents will not object. Instead, parents should be encouraged to offer their views. Parents might even benefit from visiting classrooms to further investigate the options. Professionals should not make any recommendation until the parents have expressed their thoughts and opinions. If a parent suggests an option that is obviously not in the child's best interest, the professionals should provide information on their views. An example is, "Mrs. Bellissimo, I have heard parents who have said the same thing in the past. In your shoes, I might say the same thing. What I am not sure is evident is the fact that a few months in a self-contained classroom might be less restrictive than 2 years in the resource model." Effective communicators will validate the parents' thoughts, even when holding another view. They will then voice their professional thoughts and opinions.

With effective human interaction skills, the professionals and family members can reach a decision together on placement and related services.

During this discussion, too, all of the distinctive family characteristics will come into play. Professionals sometimes, in the interest of time, allow reticent parents to withhold their views. When everyone is involved in the decision-making process, however, parents will be more likely to support the path taken. Unless they are able to share their views, family members will not feel a part of the process and may subvert the results without even realizing it. Thus, it behooves professionals to solicit family involvement.

Summarizing and Concluding the Conference

In this final phase of the conference, the chairperson summarizes the conference, lists follow-up tasks, and assigns responsibility for those tasks. Before concluding the conference, the chairperson also makes explicit a timeline for review and establishes means of regular communication between the family and school. Disengaged families, in particular, would likely benefit from more frequent family-school interactions. Enmeshed families, conversely, might benefit from less involvement in the student's progress. The main thing for professionals to consider is that any plans for continued follow-up activities should fit the unique family characteristics. A family with three preschool children may not have the time for much involvement with detailed follow-up activities. Recognizing the reality of the family situation helps guide the kinds of plans made.

Concluding remarks are best focused on the value of shared decision-making and the expression of appreciation for family and professional collaboration. The end of the conference is the perfect opportunity for professionals to again show their appreciation for and value of family involvement.

One caveat about IEP conferences; professionals and family members alike should commit themselves to attending full meetings and not just dropping by to provide their input. To provide meaningful input and involvement, parents and professionals must make a commitment that they honor in all ways.

SUMMARY

This chapter described family-focused intervention for both at-risk and special-needs students and detailed the IEP process as it relates to involving family members. Interwoven within the discussions of both the FFI and IEP processes were insights and methods arising from family systems approaches. Now that family systems has been shown as a base for team and collaborative processes involving families, classroom and group extensions of family systems concepts are logical next steps on which to focus.

Classroom and Group Extension of Family Systems Concepts

The focus of this chapter is the extension of family systems concepts into the classroom as well as into educational, support, and counseling groups held in schools for family members. Family systems concepts and methods can be used to pursue goals in both the cognitive/academic and affective/social domains. The chapter begins with information on the extension of family systems perspectives into the academic worlds of curriculum and then instruction. Those discussions are followed by information on techniques, including metaphor and reframing, as they relate to family systems concepts. The chapter concludes with a section on socialization, which discusses in detail a family systems method called *temperature reading*.

ACADEMIC CURRICULUM

This section initially focuses on Satir's (1988) five communication *stances,* which are characterizations of human behavior. Four of the five are dysfunctional; the last is a functional, congruent stance. Information on these stances could be considered a curriculum content area in its own right, and family members might also benefit from the information. Further, understanding the stances can help school professionals in networking, making referrals to groups, as well as in counseling families. In other words, school professionals should be familiar with the stances and how the knowledge can help them when interacting with at-risk and special-needs students and their families. Following this discussion a new focus is engaged—concerns of parents about new and controversial curricula that are being considered or have been implemented in the schools.

Communication Stances as a Curriculum Area

An understanding of communication stances (Satir, 1988) can help school professionals to refine their personal communication styles so that they present a single-level, congruent message. Professionals can also use knowledge about the stances to identify dysfunctional communication in the schools and then to intervene to help others recognize incongruent communication and begin to use congruent communication. Satir (1983b, 1988) provided many examples of ways in which trained professionals can help others recognize and change their communication stances so that they are congruent most of the time.

This section provides a brief background on Satir's communication stances, describes each of the five stances, and provides examples of the use of communication stances as a curricular area for students. The discussion then turns to the implementation of such a curriculum with suggestions given for exploring personal communication stances and ways to respond to the stances of students and family members.

Background Information

In two of her books, *Peoplemaking* (1972) and *The New Peoplemaking* (1988), Satir described the four dysfunctional communication stances she had found in families throughout the world: placating, blaming, superreasonable, and irrelevant. Satir and Baldwin (1983) described these stances as "different ways to hide the reality of one's feelings from oneself and from others" (p. 199). Satir also represented the functional stance of being congruent as a healthy way of expressing oneself. Satir's (1983b) text *Conjoint Family Therapy* provides excellent suggestions for activities that a trained social worker, counselor, or psychologist can use to further the understanding of family members about their communication patterns.

All four dysfunctional stances begin during infancy within the primary triad of mother-father-child, yet they all have potential for renovation through what Satir referred to as a process of transformation and atrophy (Satir & Baldwin, 1983). All of these stances are systemic in nature; none is able to persist without the support of another. Thus, a family might present a teaming up of two "supportive," or reciprocal, stances, for example, the placater and the blamer.

The Stances

This section describes each of Satir's (1988) five stances from the perspective of how these stances look to others. It also looks at the internal states of people assuming these stances and the underlying reasons for taking on the dysfunctional stances. Further, it describes how the dysfunctional stances appear when they have been renovated or transformed, with strengths growing out of former weaknesses. Finally, the aspects of communication—self, other, and context, including purpose, time, and place of communication—that are violated or discounted with each type of dysfunctional communication are delineated (Satir, 1988).

Placating. One who assumes a placating stance is trying to conceal personal vulnerability by striving to please others. The placater will go along with something out of the need for emotional survival rather than because of personal commitment and interest. A placater rejects or discounts self when doing what others expect; his or her actions derive from not wanting to be rejected by others. The placater seems like a *nice* person who avoids conflict and turning others down. Although protective of others, this person is really quite dependent and fragile.

Through a transformative process and letting go of past dysfunction, the placater makes choices that affirm self as opposed to seeing self as worthless unless approved of by others. The placater who has gained a sense of personal worth has the capacity for being tender and compassionate. Transformed, the placater genuinely cares for others.

Blaming. The individual who takes a blaming stance is attempting to mask personal vulnerability by trying to control others as well as by indiscriminately disagreeing with them. This stance allows the blamer to feel a greater sense of personal importance in spite of the experience of loneliness and personal sense of failure. This person will complain, bullying others and finding fault with them. One who assumes a blaming stance discounts the other person or people.

Blaming can be transformed into being assertive and taking a stand for oneself. When standing up for oneself, the blamer learns to assert self realistically, as opposed to having a knee-jerk reaction to others.

Superreasonable (the computer). A person assuming the stance of superreasonable seeks to disguise vulnerability with a detached control that focuses on intellectual experience. This focus allows the person to skirt emotions and thereby anesthetize feelings. This person is cool, aloof, reasonable, and intellectual; his or her clear persuasiveness should not be confused with congruent communication. This type of communication discounts both self and other.

A person who is superreasonable can learn to use his or her intelligence creatively, as opposed to using intelligence to protect self. The professional will sense the connection with emotions in the transformed superreasonable and be aware of this person's wisdom.

Irrelevant (the distractor). The individual who takes on the irrelevant stance is pretending that the stressor is nonexistent. He or she diverts the focus from the present, feeling-laden situation to something else. To others, that diversion may appear quite off-the-wall. Non sequiturs and scatterbrained comments frequently are observed. This type of communication discounts self, others, and context.

Transformed, the formerly irrelevant person has the ability to be spontaneous and have fun. This person becomes a creative individual capable of congruent interactions, having no need to discount self, others, or context.

Congruent. According to Satir (1988), a congruent person provides leveling responses in which the outward expression, actions, and tone of voice fit the spoken word. Not feeling a need to hide or conceal personal feelings, this person has high self-esteem and loves and values self. Furthermore, others and context do not need to be discounted. This person is balanced; he or she is centered in the truth of his or her own feelings and beliefs. Not afraid to challenge the status quo, a congruent individual takes risks to grow and change. He or she also assumes responsibility for personal thoughts, feelings, and actions.

The Stances as a Curricular Area

At-risk and special-needs students can and should go through a curriculum that teaches them about the five communication stances. It might be part of an existing health curriculum or separate from that with its own particular designation. The school might choose to teach students about many of the family systems concepts or simply about the communication stances.

A well-versed teacher could certainly teach this content, as could the school counselor, social worker, or psychologist. The school might choose to teach the designated content to all students, just at-risk students, those with special needs, or another target group. Different circumstances will warrant different decisions.

Though Satir's books are written at the fifth-grade level, an age by which students have certainly experienced both the congruent as well as dysfunctional stances, this curricular content is generally more appropriate in middle and high school when students have the maturity and cognitive capacity to comprehend the concepts (Piaget & Inhelder, 1958). This does not mean that aspects of these concepts cannot be taught to elementary-aged students. It simply would not be a formal curricular area to be covered.

Preparing to Implement Curricula on Stances

Prior to implementing a curriculum on stances, it is advisable to become familiar with one's own stances and with ways to respond to the dysfunctional stances of others. These topics are covered in this section.

Exploring personal stances. The professional who explores his or her own stances and their impact on communication will be more likely to give congruent messages and will be better able to recognize and respond congruently to the stances of others. Because stances that are dysfunctional indicate low self-esteem, transformation to a more functional stance involves improving personal feelings of self-worth.

Satir made it clear that everyone engages in dysfunctional communication stances. She believed that all of us are capable of assuming all four stances but that we rely on some more than others. As Satir (1972) stated, "What is so sad is that these four ways have become the most frequently used among people and are viewed by many as the most possible ways of achieving communication" (p. 78). Satir (1988) estimated that within a typical group of people 50% will be placaters, 30% will be blamers, 15% will be superreasonable computers, 0.5% will be irrelevant distractors, and only 4.5% will be congruent.

Satir was not saying that people use dysfunctional communication almost 96% of the time during which they are interacting with others. She believed that people fall back on those incongruent stances, learned as children, when they are in stressful situations. Thus, some students and family members relate in a congruent fashion most of the time and slip into incongruent stances when under duress.

It is helpful for professionals to invest time into considering the communication stances with which they are most familiar, both from the perspective of assuming the stances as well as from the perspective of being on the other side of a stance. To better understand yourself and the family in which you were raised, it helps to recall some significant interactions from your early, middle, and later childhood. Examining these interactions in terms of the five communication stances has the potential of producing growth. Considering the stances you favored will be helpful, and recognizing the favored stances of each member of your family will lead to even further understanding. It is particularly helpful to note family members in reciprocal stances, such as placating father and blaming mother.

After examining the stances from your youth, consider your current life at home and work or school. Examining your communication stances in a variety of recent interactions will reveal the degree to which you have continued to follow the patterns established in your childhood. Determining the people with whom you assume different stances may help show how relating to different people in your current life resonates with your past circumstances. Are there any parallels between your childhood patterns and current life? When is it easy to be congruent? What types of situations call forth the different stances?

After reminiscing about your childhood and comparing patterns established in your younger years with the present, think about a recent situation in which you felt threatened and relied upon one of the four dysfunctional communication stances. As clearly as possible recall the sequence of events and determine the dysfunctional stances assumed by each principal character. Then recreate the scene in your mind but imagine yourself assuming a congruent stance as opposed to a dysfunctional stance. This exercise will make it easier for you to be more congruent in the future. While creating the new scene in your imagination, think about how the other person would react given a new and congruent response, and then imagine responding with another congruent message. Following the imagery through to a new conclusion and using congruent responses throughout the interactions will provide a mental rehearsal for new situations.

Although this exploration and opportunity for rehearsal occurs solely in the mind, it is a powerful means of changing patterns in current life circumstances. The last technique described, which required you to conceive a new possibility, is called *covert rehearsal*. Many mental health professionals believe that to the degree one can visualize or imagine a new behavior, one can execute that behavior. Thus, employing this technique can lead to positive change in the use of functional, leveling, congruent messages.

Another challenge is to look for a new situation in which to employ a congruent stance when you might normally employ one of the dysfunctional stances. Later analysis of your communication, as well as that of the other person, will allow a determination of the communication stances used. If you were not congruent, you could use covert rehearsal to imagine a different scenario.

Another helpful technique is to observe the use of congruent communication by other people or by characters on television or in movies, videos, or plays. Such observations can further your own expression of congruent messages.

Dysfunctional stances stem from low self-worth, and mimicking others is not the answer to higher self-esteem. Yet people who have not dealt with many others who are congruent will find it useful to have models that help them expand and grow. If only 4.5% of the population is congruent in their communication all of the time, then it is valuable to search for functional communicators and use their interactions as models from which to expand.

Responding to stances. As might be imagined, an individual who understands his or her personal stances will be better able to be congruent when interacting with others. Communicating congruently is especially important when relating to family members of at-risk students and those with special needs but is also important when interacting with other school professionals. Remembering Satir's (1988) estimate that only 4.5% of the population communicates congruently all of the time should help professionals be patient with themselves, their students, and their families. It is not realistic to expect that peers will communicate congruently. Professionals should assume major personal responsibility for communicating congruently and realize that others will at least have congruent communication as a model.

Responding to dysfunctional communication is a challenge. The school professional must first identify the stance assumed by the other person. Next, the professional needs to think about the root causes of the stance, for example, low self-worth. Then the professional needs to recall any information about the family background of the person speaking. These steps will help the professional remain centered and balanced and keep the professional from moving in the direction of a dysfunctional stance.

The professional who is balanced can then communicate with single-level, congruent messages. It is important not to placate, blame, distract, or become superreasonable in the face of any of those types of communication. The professional's sole responsibility is to communicate in a congruent manner.

For example, consider the responses a principal might make when faced with a parent who, taking a blaming stance, has remarked, "Why don't the teachers ever listen to us? I can't believe Jon is that much of a problem in school. Everything is fine at home." The principal might be inclined to counter-blame or placate. Or he or she might become superreasonable, providing facts or quoting experts. The best option, however, is to be congruent with a statement such as, "Mrs. Wickham, I realize it is frustrating to keep getting reports about aggression by Jonathan. The fact remains that Jon has slugged his teacher twice in the last week, leaving bruise marks. So far the teacher has elected not to call in the police. If this occurs again, she has said that she will call the police. She has already filed a report regarding the last assault. As before, we recommend family counseling. . . ."

As another example, consider this remark by a parent: "I know I have done a terrible job of raising Henry. I'm just a miserable mess of a parent." The school professional, recognizing the placating stance assumed by this mother, might choose to point out the placating stance. Another professional might tend to back off from people when they placate, afraid to kick a person who is already down. A better course than either of these is to remain congruent with a comment such as, "Mrs. Lathrop, all of us struggle in raising our children. I also have had many learning experiences. I agree that there are practices you can change to better respond to your son's needs. To that end, we are recommending a parent effectiveness training group that begins. . . ." With this response the professional has shared information regarding the problem and also has responded to the discounting of self by the mother by normalizing her child-rearing struggles.

When communicating with a person who is superreasonable, who discounts both self and others, any response should focus on both self and others as important. Consider the following example, in which a parent is interacting with the school counselor about home issues between two of his children that spill over into school. The father is explaining, "I read several child psychology books in my undergraduate years. I read that when you ignore the behavior of the child you do not feed the situation by giving the child attention for inappropriate behavior. Dr. Benjamin Spock said not to be hard on your children. Additionally, Dr. . . . ." To an onslaught like this the school counselor, well aware of the super-reasonable nature of the communication, might say, "Mr. Mafigliano, when I am in the halls and see your two sons changing classes and getting into it with one another, I have a hunch about what I see. I get the feeling that they are not really looking for attention from adults. My intuitive hunch is that Joe is a bit embarrassed by Rich's antics and tries to disown him and then Rich feels abandoned and hurt by Joe's embarrassment. I wonder if you might consider a sibling support group for Joe that is offered at the mental health center in the county. There is no fee and . . . ." In this situation, the counselor indicated by example that simply responding to what one sees may be more important than any textbook offering. Furthermore, the counselor validated self by relying on personal intuition.

The most difficult dysfunctional communication to respond to is the irrelevant stance. This type of communication discounts self, other, and context. It is critical that school professionals recognize the nature of the communication and not judge the person as not caring about the situation. Although such a judgment can come easily, a person's comments sound unrelated to the topic at hand. As an example, consider the following situation in which a teacher is speaking to a parent about her daughter's inappropriate dress at school: "Mrs. Jones," the teacher says, "I'm sure Shironda doesn't leave home looking like she does in school. She turns over the waistband in her skirts so they are much shorter. She has served in-school suspension for breaking the dress code five times this month, and I am concerned about her grades and what she has learned this grading period." To which Mrs. Jones replies, "Did I tell you my husband has a case of the flu? Seems like everybody in our neighborhood is having that old flu these days." The teacher might be tempted to respond in a number of ways. However, the best option is a congruent response such as, "I realize that it is hard to connect with low grades, in-school suspension, and a daughter who is defying school rules. These are critical matters, and I assume you feel the struggle of dealing with this. I also have been concerned that our procedures of serving in-school suspension have not worked. I'd like to meet with you and Shironda about this situation. Before we do that, I'd like to map out a strategy about how we can approach her regarding her blatant violation of the school dress code. . . ." With such a response, the teacher has initially refocused on the very real situation or context and then has focused on the parental concern, tying it to his or her personal concern for Shironda. Further, the teacher has offered to form a joint plan for dealing with the situation, thus focusing again on self and other.

This section has presented several examples of dysfunctional communication by a parent with a functional, congruent response by a school professional. With practice, professionals will become more fluent while interacting with family members and at-risk and special-needs students who engage in incongruent communication.

Parental Concern

When school professionals are considering any new academic curriculum, but especially when the curriculum involves new and controversial ideas, parental concerns may surface.

With a grounding in family systems concepts, including all of the concepts presented in Parts I and II, professionals can predict such concerns and better interact to alleviate them. An understanding of family systems concepts will both help school professionals plan strategies for considering new curricula and provide a grounding for meeting parents who are unhappy with a curricular change process.

One topic that has received a lot of recent attention in many states has been family life curriculum. The legislatures of many states have joined in the controversy by requiring that schools provide a family life curriculum (sometimes including sex education). It is to be expected that parents, who had the major responsibility in the past for providing this part of their children's education, are concerned about school professionals crossing that traditional boundary.

Professionals need to recognize that, for some families, the boundary issue is a major concern. For some of those families, the concern can be alleviated easily with basic information. Other families may be enmeshed and overinvolved, becoming quite agitated about what their children may be learning. School professionals probably will see more of these families directly raising their concerns and issues. Children from disengaged families often will act out the concerns of the parents, yet professionals will not be told the nature of the parents' concern. By recognizing the boundary issues and having a firm grounding in the principles of family systems, it is easier to face parental concerns with less personal reaction and a greater sense of confidence.

Those professionals who have cataloged the family systems processes for the families of their at-risk and special-needs students will find it easier to predict the concerns of those families when curricular change is planned. They also will know how to approach the families to prevent problems from developing. Further, they will be able to use their knowledge of family processes during all of their interactions with these families, as well as with the families of their other students. As has been noted many times throughout this text, few families of students with special needs are dysfunctional. The same is true of the at-risk and general population. If a professional is aware, however, that a particular family has boundary problems or a hierarchy dysfunction, he or she can use this information as a basic framework in any interaction with the family.

ACADEMIC INSTRUCTION

Families may have concerns about academic instruction that can be divided into two areas: curricular topics other than the family systems curriculum and the family systems curriculum.

Non–Family Systems Curricula

With a non-family systems curriculum, at least three areas of potential struggle exist with regard to instructional practice and families. First, parents may have concerns about the instructional approaches used in the schools. Second, teachers may have concerns about a parent's knowledge of an instructional practice and the need for the practice to remain consistent at school and home. And third, both parents and teachers may have concerns about homework. The following sections elaborate on each of these concerns.

Instructional Practice Concerns

Parental concerns regarding unusual instructional approaches are not uncommon. Because teachers use more unique instructional approaches with students with special needs than with most other students, parental concerns are more likely to surface. To prevent such concerns, professionals should inform parents upfront about the nature of any unusual instruction and its estimated duration.

It may help to provide a demonstration or videotape of the instructional practice. Some practices, such as the Neurological Impress Method (NIM), may appear particularly time consuming and confusing to parents. The NIM method of teaching reading is highly intensive, with a trained professional working one-on-one with a student. Professionals often prefer that students not read on their own or to their parents while receiving instruction in this method. Once the parents see the intensity of the method, they frequently understand why the teacher is requiring a different approach at home, for the time being, than what they had been using.

It is not always possible, however, to prevent parents from being concerned about instructional practices. When concerns arise, professionals should try to lower the anxiety. For example, if a mother is concerned that her daughter is learning "Touch Math," not realizing that the title refers to the child touching points on paper as opposed to humans interacting through touch, the teacher could easily provide a demonstration or information. If, however, the mother's concern is that "Touch Math" might make her child dependent upon an external crutch, the situation is entirely different. All of the family systems concepts and techniques will be helpful when working with parents who have this type of concern. The professional should reexamine the catalog of family process to be clear about the typical family process. Then the professional will be better prepared to join the family in resolving their concerns.

Coordinating Home-School Instruction

In the second area of concern, the teacher struggles to coordinate instructional practices between home and school. Again, providing information regarding the instructional practice is the best means of preventing concern. For example, a student with a reading problem might learn to spell best by practicing with a tactile instructional technique. It is good prevention to talk with the parents about this method, explaining how it was chosen (e.g., as a result of trial teaching) and providing information on the instructional practice. It is also helpful to train parents, when appropriate, to help their child practice his or her spelling words according to the tactile method. The professional, however, should be familiar with the family characteristics, life cycle, and process. Some families will not have the time for the added responsibility; others will only make things worse for a child who already needs some distance from an overly involved parent. Examining the catalog of family process, characteristics, and other relevant information will be helpful in making decisions about how to approach parents.

Informing the parents about special approaches also can prevent school-home conflict. To extend the example above, if the parents do not know about the instructional practice and are trying to get their child to practice spelling with a *look and say* method that served them well, the child might become confused. Further, the child's spelling test scores might become lower because of that confusion. Wanting to please both the parents and the teacher, the child might not mention any such differences in practice techniques. If, however, the parents see the child using a tactile practice method at home and ask the teacher about it, the teacher has the chance to provide the necessary information and to work to improve the parents' trust level. Again, knowledge of the family's process, life cycle, and characteristics will be valuable when meeting with parents under such circumstances.

Homework and Families

The third possible problem area relates to homework. A number of professionals have written about this potentially thorny problem (Kay et al., 1994; Patton, 1994). The focus here is on the types of homework struggles occurring in the home. Some parents may be overly involved in the child's homework. Other parents may not provide the needed supplies or study space due to a disengaged pattern. Yet other parents may be unable to help their child due to unavailability, lack of knowledge, or lack of concern.

Consideration of family characteristics, life cycle, interaction patterns, and environmental factors, and discussion of these factors with others who know the family or during team meetings, will be of great assistance in determining how to handle homework challenges. When dealing with an overly involved parent, the professional's objective should be to decrease the involvement. How that can best be done will be dictated on a case-by-case basis. The same is true in dealing with parents who do not provide the necessary supplies or study space or who are unable to help their child. Disorganization of some single parents and the underorganization of poor parents were addressed in Chapters 5 and 6. Both of those circumstances require an empathic and patient response from school personnel. Schools can support the successful completion of homework in creative ways; however, discovering the root of the problem is necessary before forces can be marshaled.

Family Systems Curricula

The earlier section on curricula provided basic information on communication stances as curricular content. A well-versed teacher can provide the curricular content to the students. School counselors, social workers, and psychologists are excellent resources for providing that information to the parents and siblings.

The actual instruction or teaching techniques to be used are not that different from those with any other type of instruction. The instructor would prepare an overall unit plan with daily lessons detailing objectives, methodology, materials, and evaluation. Satir's characterizations of the people assuming each of the four stances are a valuable media prop. Satir's book *The New Peoplemaking* (1988) is excellent for use as a required text.

The most important aspect of instruction is the enactment of the communication stances. After describing the four stances, Satir had people pose in the stances. She then had them work in groups and practice employing each stance by going round-robin, alternating the stances employed. A group of four or five people would reenact the basic family structure. Individuals who participated recognized familiar and unfamiliar stances from their own experiences.

A similar experience is valuable today for students and their family members. Participants benefit from demonstrations of the four stances and feedback on their interpretation of those stances. For example, with the superreasonable/computer stance, a participant may need feedback on how to stand straighter and stiffer. It is important that the physical body is aware of and registers the deleterious impact of assuming such a role. This realization helps the participants relate to others and to recognize the impact of incongruent communication upon themselves and others. Satir (1983b, 1988) provided many suggestions for activities that allow individuals to explore the communication stances. Those suggestions should be employed when providing basic instruction regarding the communication stances.

TECHNIQUES USED IN FAMILY SYSTEMS APPROACHES

Marshall McLuhan (1967) is credited with saying "the medium is the message." His words are highly applicable to the manner in which a school professional delivers a message. This section focuses on two techniques used in family systems approaches in which the medium is indeed the message. These are the techniques of using metaphor and reframing. It is particularly valuable to use positive metaphors and to reframe any negative views about disabilities when helping others gain access to resources or engage in counseling.

Metaphor

A metaphor is a figure of speech that uses a term or phrase in connection with something to which it cannot be applied literally in order to suggest a characteristic of one to the other. When one invokes any image or association from one arena to highlight the similarities, differences, or ambiguities in another arena, one is using metaphor. This medium allows people to develop a new awareness by connecting or linking two characteristics, events, ideas, or meanings. In using metaphor, one describes experience and creates new patterns of consciousness, thereby extending the boundaries of subjective experience. Thus, this technique or medium is quite helpful in teaching, counseling, and therapy. Metaphors allow people to access information in a nonthreatening way; they can reinforce learning as well.

In *Therapeutic Metaphors for Children and the Child Within,* Mills and Crowley (1986) described the use of metaphor in general and specifically its use with children. In their introduction to the first chapter they stated that metaphor, a style of symbolic language used throughout the ages, can be found in parables in the bible, the Kabbalah, Zen Buddhist koans, allegorical literature, poetry, and fairy tales. In all of these, metaphor indirectly yet more significantly conveys the central message.

Metaphor can be used effectively with child and parent alike. This technique, or medium, is not one that can be easily taught because it is as much artistic as it is technical. To prepare for the use of metaphor, professionals may want to read the text by Mills and Crowley. An example of a metaphor that might be used when a student is taking on too much is, "It seems as if Joey might be too big for his britches." Another metaphor could be, "Is it possible that Kentu is tied to his mother's apron strings?"

Reframing

Reframing was described briefly in Chapter 12. This technique is used widely in family systems approaches (Breulin et al., 1992; Dallos, 1991; Holmes, 1993; Jameson & Alexander, 1994; Minuchin & Fishman, 1981; M. P. Nichols & Schwartz, 1995; Piercy & Wetchler, 1996; Satir & Baldwin, 1983; Watzlawick, Weakland, & Fisch, 1974) as well as in other approaches to counseling and psychotherapy.

Underlying all reframing is the desire to help others bring a larger and different perspective to a life situation. It is not an attempt to whitewash or minimize suffering on the part of others. It is a legitimate effort to improve a person's situation by altering his or her view to encompass a new way of *seeing*.

Background Information

The following story from the Taoist tradition serves as a good introduction to this section on reframing.

> There once was a farmer who had a wonderful horse that the farmer's family depended upon for their livelihood. His horse ran away one day and all his neighbors said how awful was his fate. To this the farmer replied, "Maybe." A couple of days later the horse returned with a herd of wild horses. The neighbors told him how lucky he was. The farmer said, "Maybe." Soon the farmer's oldest son tried to break in one of the wild horses and was thrown and broke his leg. Again the neighbors said how awful and the farmer said, "Maybe." The next day the people in charge of drafting soldiers rejected his oldest son because of his injury. The neighbors thought he again was very fortunate and he thought, "Maybe." (J. Daniel, personal communication)

Reframing is about transforming the frame a person holds of events so that a different meaning can be attached. With the change in meaning come changes in responses and behaviors. As Watzlawick et al. (1974) stated:

> To reframe, then, means to change the conceptual and/or emotional setting or viewpoint in relation to which a situation is experienced and to place it in another frame which fits the "facts" of the same concrete situation equally well or even better, and thereby changes its entire meaning. (p. 95)

Like metaphor, reframing can be used with children and youth as well as adults. In the field of family systems, the professional usually is redefining the treatment unit to be the whole family as opposed to the symptom bearer or problematic child, which is the framework so often seen in schools. Reframing is intended to affect the interrelated cognitive, emotional, and behavioral spheres. Reframing generally results in a change in how people think, feel, and act.

Types of Reframing

There are many uses of reframing. In all of them it is the process of bringing a different context into play that brings a deeper meaning to the experience. Karpel (1986b) stated:

> Reframing may be used to accomplish different ends. Like psychoanalytic interpre-
> tation, which it resembles, it may be intended to foster insight. In other cases it may
> be used to make alternative patterns of interaction easier to enact or to make it much
> more difficult to persist in problematic patterns. From a resource perspective, it is
> probably most often used to identify resources that are inherent in the presenting
> problem itself, as in the use of statements that throw light on patterns of loyalty,
> concern, and protectiveness in what would otherwise look like destructive or
> self-destructive behavior. (p. 200)

Reframing can be used to maintain or increase a person's self-worth. Satir and Bald-win (1983) reported the value of helping people to focus on observing what occurred in an incident instead of blaming another person for the situation. Satir referred to this as using an "observing ego" to help a client reduce blame and increase trust.

Reframing can also be used to diffuse negative feelings. An example would be when one family member is angry and his temper is flaring and others are upset because he has broken the family rule that one should not express angry feelings. The school professional might reframe the temper to be seen as a "way of bringing out his thoughts." Another example would be to reframe blame into searching for information.

In addition, reframing may be used to clarify what has been said by a family member. An example provided in *Satir, Step by Step* (Satir & Baldwin, 1983) is that of a father who struggled with making compliments and would beat around the bush with them. A reframe could be to state that the father had complimented or admired someone.

In many ways, this technique may be used to reframe liabilities and perceived weak-nesses as strengths. In so doing, the professional may be able to transform meaning attached to the frame. For example, a single mother taking her adolescent for therapy could be framed as "caring enough about her daughter to find the resources she needed."

Reframing With Children and Youth

When using reframing with children, it is important to consider their cognitive level. For example, children who are 7 years old or younger overgeneralize how they see their strengths and weaknesses (Piaget & Inhelder, 1969). It may not be effective, then, for an adult to speak about only one aspect of what the child does as a problem. The child may not have the cognitive capacity to understand that difference, and, therefore, a reframing will not be possible. For example, a teacher trying to reframe the fighting of two 5-year-olds as a sign of liking one another may find that the attempt falls on deaf ears.

While young children may not be able to follow a reframe cognitively, they may be able to follow a shift related to emotions. For example, a child sensitive to nonverbal changes in the emotional climate, such as making a joke and laughing about the child's irritability, will be able to benefit from this nonverbal reframing. This type of reframing is at an experiential level as opposed to a cognitive one.

Once children reach approximately age 7, they will be able to understand reframing that relates to concrete as opposed to abstract thinking. At approximately age 12, the child is able to respond to higher-order thinking when a reframe is presented. A reframing statement such as "You do not argue with those you do not care about" could be understood by children at this cognitive level.

Also important in reframing with children and youth is for professionals to have the view that reframing does apply to them. When the professional can see a child's distracting behavior both positively and negatively, then he or she will be more able to reframe the situation for the student. For example, there are times when bullying may be desirable. Satir was famous for asking people to look at any weakness and discover times that such a weakness could be a strength. She used that type of reframing consistently in her *Part's Parties* (Bitter, 1993; Satir & Baldwin, 1983). *Part's Parties* use experiential technique to help an individual become more aware of the many parts of the self. The party introduces each to the others because many parts of the self are not used, overused, used poorly, or ignored. They take from 2–4 hours.

Timing

The timing of reframing cannot be guided externally but must be felt or intuited to be appropriate by the professional, given the readiness of the family member or student. Used at a poorly chosen time, or at too abstract a level, reframing can cause a sense of misconnection as well as anger at the professional for having misperceived the situation.

One timing guideline is to wait until any highly intense feelings of grief or anger have been diffused. For example, if a family has learned recently that their child has Down syndrome, the timing is not right for sharing an example of a parent who is in acceptance. In time, the professional may sense that the family is moving out of shock, denial, or anger. The timing would then be appropriate for the use of reframing.

Use Language of the Family

In reframing, professionals should use language that speaks to the family. For example, a New Testament Bible story might be used to reframe something for a Christian family. For an artistic family, a reframe regarding drawing or other visual imagery might be effective. Likewise, a musical family would appreciate a reframe that is auditory in nature.

Case Example

A 7-year-old boy whose father had recently committed suicide had begun to act out by talking back to his mother and resisting directions. The mother tended to interpret the behavior as *oppositional/defiant* and to react by intensifying her disciplining efforts. When the mother mentioned this problem to the boy's teacher, he commented that the behavior appeared to be designed to keep the mother intensely involved with the boy and could be interpreted as the equivalent of *anxious, clingy* behavior. In the context of recent loss, the mother found the idea that her son would be *anxious and clingy* to be much more acceptable than her previous interpretation of defiance and anger. Her response, then, was to become more nurturing, which resulted in a reduction of the boy's anxiety and acting-out behavior. The teacher's ability to reframe the child's behavior resulted in a positive shift in the family system. This shift allowed the mother and son to help each other through their mutual grief and avoided prolonging a painful symptom.

SOCIALIZATION

Shifting from *academics* and the cognitive domain, this section focuses on *socialization* and the affective domain, discussing in detail a family systems strategy called *temperature reading* (Schwab, 1990). Adapted from Satir (1983a), this strategy provides a method of *clearing the air* in group interactions (Azpeitia & Zahnd, 1991) that can be used easily in classrooms as well as during regularly scheduled meetings of ongoing groups. Temperature reading can also be used with families, once parents learn the procedure. If the parents do not attend meetings where this technique is used, they would need training in the method to carry it forward in the home.

Background

Temperature reading is one of Satir's lesser known communication processes, though it is used widely by those who attended her training. Its two basic purposes are for group members to share feelings and to help detoxify negativity on the part of group members. It could be used in a class session or homeroom as well as during educational, support, or counseling groups.

Features

Satir (1983a) included five types of expressions in a temperature reading: appreciations, complaints and recommendations, puzzles, new information, and hopes and wishes (Azpeitia & Zahnd, 1991). Not all five features need to be included, during a temperature reading, but it should be possible to include them.

Appreciations

Appreciations should be shared directly with the person being appreciated. In the classroom a teacher might say, "Tim, you are doing an excellent job of assisting Helen in making the transition to a whole new set of instructional materials. I appreciate your help in this matter." In another example, a teacher might tell a parent, "Mr. Juval, I am so glad you told me about the support group you have attended. Now I can tell other parents about your findings. Thanks."

In a parental training session in which a family has given a demonstration where the parent did not directly appreciate another family member, the professional could say, "Mr.

Jones, let me play you in a scenario. . . . Joey, come on over here and look me in the eye. I am going to role-play being your dad. 'You know, Joey, I am so glad you raked the yard this weekend without being asked. It meant a lot to me and gave us time to watch that video together. Thanks, son.'" Following this modeling, the professional could ask the father if he would be willing to try again and ask for feedback. If the father and son succeed in engaging in an authentic sending and receiving of appreciation, the professional might ask each one how the interaction felt. If they respond that they feel a little stiff about it, the professional can compare the situation to putting on a *new shoe* that needs some wearing before it becomes comfortable. If they feel closer or even misty-eyed, it may help to reinforce that by simply saying, "Take that feeling in, and remember how it feels."

There is no need to fabricate an appreciation. If there is one, the temperature reading is the perfect time to share this communication. The communication helps focus on the positive and provides examples for others of directly sharing an appreciation. Eye contact and tone of voice are important aspects of sharing an appreciation. Appreciations honor humanness and lead to authentic human connection. As models for children, parents and teachers can help increase the sharing of appreciations in our children and youth.

Complaints and Recommendations

Complaints are a major reason for conducting temperature readings. Voicing complaints can provide the opportunity to detoxify negativity as well as a structure that allows an individual to voice a complaint. According to Azpeitia and Zahnd (1991), "A complaint with a recommendation is the reporting of a discrepancy between what is and an idea or awareness of how things could be better" (p. 86). Such a sharing brings validation. When unexpressed, complaints can lead to negative interactions and restrict the necessary openness that brings vitality, commitment, and flexibility to relationships. Sharing a complaint allows a person to discharge negative feelings, allowing more room for closeness.

Satir (1983a) recommended that any complaint be accompanied with a recommendation for change. Others should not promote dependency by allowing a person who has expressed a complaint to not provide a recommendation. The recommendation for solving the problem does not have to be carried out. The strategy is simply intended to help the person look toward solutions as opposed to merely voicing a complaint. Of course, even the registering of a complaint and being heard are very important.

A classroom example of a complaint expressed during a temperature reading would be a student saying, "I am having a hard time catching up with all the new algebra since I was in the hospital for a week. I hate slowing the class down and wonder if someone might have the time to help me during study hall in the afternoons." Another example of a complaint during a support group meeting would be a father saying to the counselor, "I have a problem with the time of these meetings. I cannot get from work to home and feed my son before coming here at 6:00. I find the group beneficial and would like to have the time moved to no earlier than 7:00."

Puzzles

The third feature of a temperature reading is presenting a puzzle, confusion, question, rumor, or piece of gossip. It is used where the person presenting the puzzle has heard something but does not understand fully what he or she heard. Expressing the puzzle allows rumors to be affirmed or denied. The rumor might be about something others could look forward to, something the individual feared, or something the individual was worried about. In any event, the puzzle has not been addressed adequately. Surfacing the puzzle lessens uncertainty and confusion.

An example of a puzzle expressed during a temperature reading in the classroom is, "I was wondering if it is true that anyone who earns two thousand points will be able to attend a showing of the newest Star Trek movie next Friday afternoon?" Another example of presenting a puzzle would be a parent querying a social worker, "I overheard a parent at the basketball game telling someone else that there was a support group called Compassionate Friends. I am wondering if you know how I can get in touch with them in this county? My wife and I are still grieving over the loss of our daughter."

New Information

New information simply allows individuals to let others know about an upcoming event, activity, or other opportunity. It involves forecasting a new possibility so that others might avail themselves of the occasion. It also helps to prevent rumors from spreading as well as helps to prevent anyone from being left out or being the last to find out about something with which others are familiar.

A classroom example of providing new information would be a teacher saying, "We have a great speaker who will be at our assembly during third period on Tuesday. Her name is Carol Scearce. She is the president of Enlightening Enterprises outside Boston along the coast in Beverly. She is the best speaker I have ever heard. She will be teaching you to make mind maps. That is a special and creative form of taking notes developed by Tony Buzan, from England. She has agreed to provide a special 2-hour presentation to the students in our program on Tuesday afternoon. I hope no one misses school on Tuesday."

Another example of providing new information would be a school psychologist telling a parent group, "I have an announcement I know all of you will be interested in hearing. We now have an easier referral process to the county mental health center. Some of you will remember that the center's waiting list for family counseling was several months long. The center has hired two new family systems therapists, and the waiting period is nonexistent. Be sure to thank Dr. Wojinski when you see her. She was responsible for finding the funds for these new additions."

Hopes and Wishes

Hopes and wishes are simply a statement about something that is desired. If a desire remains unarticulated, it has little chance of being fulfilled. Satir (1983a) was concerned that every member of a family or group be able to give voice to their hopes and wishes. She had found that many people will reserve their wishes when they do not have a structure for voicing them.

A classroom example of the expression of a hope or wish is a student saying, "Mrs. Anthony, I was wondering if we could have a popcorn party this Friday afternoon. My brother will be home from the service, and he wanted to visit my school. He will be here this Friday afternoon, and I hoped everyone could meet him and visit with him." Another example of expressing a hope or wish is a parent commenting before the start of a parent effectiveness training session, "I wish somebody would develop a list of child-care opportunities for our younger children so that it would be easier to attend these parent training workshops."

Guidelines

Satir recommended that temperature readings be conducted in families, in groups, and as part of any work group. The following guidelines for temperature readings focus on frequency, leadership, structure, and the training of professionals and parents.

Frequency

Satir (1983a) provided the following guideline about the frequency of conducting this process. She recommended that temperature readings be conducted daily whenever a new group is formed. She noted that once the group stabilizes, the frequency of temperature readings can be lowered gradually, although she indicated that they would be most beneficial if held at least weekly. The more struggles there are within a group or family, the more frequently temperature readings should be conducted. Groups that meet less than weekly should conduct temperature readings before the beginning of each meeting.

In a newly formed classroom, temperature readings are best conducted daily for the first week and then gradually reduced to meet the needs of the class. However, they should never be held less than weekly. Homeroom is a good time to conduct temperature readings in secondary schools. If a teacher has a totally different group of students each period, it is not likely that he or she will be able to invest the time in temperature reading at the expense of academic time. In elementary school, temperature readings can be conducted first thing in the morning, when all students have arrived in the classroom but before the start of the academic day.

Family members who are part of a temperature reading process in the school will find it easier to implement a similar process at home. Thus, the temperature reading conducted during school activities serves as a model for the parents. The tougher the situation to which they see professionals respond, the better their opportunity to learn from experience.

Leadership

In large groups that met regularly, Satir (1983a) would have the person making a contribution stand next to her. She would often hold the contributor's hand while he or she was speaking, lending support by her presence. Not many professionals have the presence of Satir in holding a contributor's hand during a temperature reading; the leader should do so only if he or she is comfortable with that style and has the personal savvy to carry it off.

Temperature readings are generally most effective when one school professional is in charge of conducting them. In the classroom, that one person is the teacher. This is not a situation to turn over to shared leadership on a rotating basis. It is best that a professional comfortable in providing congruent messages, and in helping others to do the same, lead the temperature reading in nonclassroom groups.

Structure

While introducing a temperature reading, the professional conducting it initially states the purposes and then describes the five features. Next, the leader shares personal experiences with temperature readings. Following that, a brief role-play of a temperature reading is conducted. Concluding with a question-and-answer session helps eliminate concerns about the process and content.

Temperature readings are valuable for all ongoing groups that operate in schools. Teams that meet regularly would also benefit from conducting temperature readings at each meeting, as would all ongoing parent groups, be they PTO/PTA, support groups, parenting training sessions, or less structured yet regularly held meetings. The temperature reading does not take much time, though those that include complaints and puzzles will likely be longer. Temperature readings should be conducted at the beginning of meetings, allowing the air to be cleared prior to engaging in new business and thereby increasing the effectiveness of the actual meeting.

Satir (1983a) would help the individual share the offering, assisting with any statements made so that the person provided congruent messages. She also would reframe any complaints so that the person would be open to other possibilities when viewing the situation.

To help parents understand the possibilities of this process, the leader should connect the value of temperature readings with family life situations. The leader can recommend that the parents conduct this process at home and share personal and others' experiences with temperature reading in family situations. The leader can also recommend that families wait to conduct temperature readings at home until they are more familiar with how they work in the school group that is using the process.

Training/Preparation

Probably the most effective training for school professionals in conducting temperature readings is to conduct them regularly in their own work groups. This emphasizes "learning by doing," recognizing that there is seldom a better teacher than experience. In conducting real (not practice) temperature readings, professionals will face many touchy or confusing situations. Having real-life experience with this activity in their work groups will allow them to plan better how they will respond to sensitive or difficult situations. Such situations occur quite naturally in a spontaneous and open sharing of feelings and thoughts in a group context. Difficult situations should be expected and should not take a professional by surprise.

Preparing parents to be involved in temperature readings is also important. Parents may never have experienced such an open exchange of thoughts and feelings. Furthermore, they might not believe that their thoughts and feelings are being valued by professionals during the temperature reading. It may take a few sessions to establish trust in the process. Therefore, professionals should not be surprised if the first several temperature readings focus largely upon appreciations, hopes and wishes, and new information, which are less threatening than expressing complaints or puzzles. When a student or parent shares his or her first complaint or puzzle, it is important to validate his or her concerns before moving on with the elaboration.

SUMMARY

This chapter has focused on the extension of family systems concepts into the classroom and into education, support, or counseling groups. New possibilities for applying these concepts abound in the literature; school professionals should be creative in their design and implementation of the family systems concepts they use. Communication stances, reframing, metaphor, and temperature readings can be used with both classroom and group instruction.

Strengthening the Possibilities for a Systems Paradigm

The focus of this chapter is on improving the likelihood that the systems recommendations presented in this book will be implemented in schools. Potential barriers to implementing change may be related to parents, professionals, or the school context. The intention behind this chapter is to help school professionals prevent barriers from forming, whenever possible, and to minimize barriers that do arise. A systems change model is presented as a means of facilitating movement toward integrating family systems concepts into schools.

The chapter opens with a discussion of communication skills, focusing predominately on means of communicating more effectively. Next, psychological issues that can result in barriers to the implementation of family systems ideas in the school context are considered, with a focus on demanding parents, psychiatric difficulties, and angry parents. The discussion then turns to problem solving and a five-step process leading to conflict resolution. A section on interaction between families and schools follows, highlighting five aspects of working with families. Potential limitations to using family systems concepts in schools that stem from lack of training, school norms, and school procedures are then discussed, followed by a discussion of the reality constraints of time, money, and availability of trained personnel. The final section of this chapter focuses on attitudes, resistance, and change. This section identifies the stages of response to change, addresses concerns about change, and ends with a major focus on Satir's model for change.

COMMUNICATION SKILLS

Parents' communication skills vary widely. Some parents are quite articulate, while others struggle to make even the simplest point. Some parents will not even try to communicate because they are afraid that they will sound foolish or inadequate. Beyond parents' communications skills lie the communication skills of everyone else involved in school-family interactions, including professionals, others in the student's life, and the student. This section begins with a discussion of parental communication, focusing on reasons for communication problems and the need for parent training. The focus then shifts to the many different levels on which people communicate, which Satir (1983a) referred to as the *ingredients of an interaction*. An understanding of these ingredients is important for preventing miscommunication.

Parental Communication

It is important to help parents learn the communication skills needed to articulate their views and not feel overwhelmed by their team experiences. It is infinitely possible for parents to help one another by sharing their experiences; however, Morsink et al. (1991) questioned using parents as teachers. Whether parents or professionals provide the training, it is important to augment parenting skills if children are to succeed in school. In *Raising Our Future* (1995), the Harvard Family Research Project presented a national resource guide for families. Many of the resources listed include training for parents.

Inadequate Processing of Information

Communication problems can arise because parents are unfamiliar with the procedures employed on teams or because they have not mastered effective communication skills. These problems are relatively easily remedied. There are also parents who may be inarticulate due to a personal disability. Some parents with retardation may have trouble processing information given to them by the schools. Losen and Losen (1985) suggested that someone might accompany them to IEP conferences to interpret what is happening. If a case worker is assigned to the family, that person is a logical possibility because he or she has already formed a trusting relationship with the parents. Some parents who do not understand the IEP process or what is being said may become disruptive and be unwilling to admit their lack of understanding. When these parents refuse to sign off on a placement recommendation, the school system can request a due process hearing. Seldom would one want to use that alternative, but it is a possibility. Miller (1996) recommended that parents bring a trusted person with them to school functions to increase the likelihood of their continued involvement with the school.

Parent Training

A number of professionals have written about parental/family involvement with special-needs children and youth (S. K. Green & Shinn, 1995; Jenson, Sheridan, Olympia, & Andrews, 1994; Kay et al., 1994; Sussell et al., 1996; Turnbull & Turnbull, 1996). This literature has focused on parental involvement, parents as teachers, parents as partners, homework, teamwork, and attitudes toward the delivery of services. However, finding research on the training provided to parents is difficult. Most articles and books are devoted to involving parents in activities that don't involve training or on descriptions of the different kinds of parent effectiveness training aimed at the general population, such as Systematic Training for Effective Parenting (STEP).

McLoughlin (1981) described a parent/teacher education model for the joint training of teachers and parents of children with disabilities. The model involved competency-based, skills-oriented training and focused on "training together to work together," with the outcome being enhanced cooperation and interaction. The project demonstrated that joint training can be effective in gaining the involvement and support of these parents.

As noted earlier in this text, Leithwood (1997) found that parental involvement in children's education accounted for 50% of the variance in the school achievement of children. Based on this finding it is incumbent upon educators to provide training to parents. Many others agree. Yet, still, for some school professionals, the idea of training parents to be involved in their child's education remains a low priority. Turnbull and Turnbull (1996) reported that there are 71 Parent Training and Information Centers funded by the federal Department of Education. Each state has at least one PTI, as do Palau and Puerto Rico. Turnbull and Turnbull listed the centers in an appendix in their text.

Ingredients of an Interaction

Parents, students, and professionals will better meet students' needs if they communicate more effectively. It can be confusing to wade through the levels of human interactions to determine the meaning intended as well as the meaning ascribed to interactions. By learning about Satir's ingredients of an interaction professionals will be better able to sort out as well as respond to the various *ingredients,* thereby improving their communication.

So, what are the ingredients of an interaction? They are everything that goes into making communication (Baldwin, 1993; Schwab, 1990). Satir (1983a) compared communication to a recipe with many different ingredients. A person's interactions with others can be seen as enjoyable and as complex as making that new recipe for the evening meal. It is easy to misread communication if you are not aware of all of the ingredients. Just as leaving out the baking powder in a recipe can result in flattened cookies, failure to understand, recognize, or respond to an ingredient of an interaction can result in flattened communication.

Ingredients

Satir described seven ingredients in communication (Azpeitia & Zahnd, 1991; Satir, 1983a; Schwab, 1990). Figure 14.1 shows these ingredients for a two-person interaction involving spoken communication. Point 1 is the initiating point, and point 8 is the responding point of the communication.

Person A, named Adam, initiates a message to Person B, Betty. The other six ingredients of the interaction (points 2–7) are part of Betty's internal process before she responds at point 8.

Point 2 represents Betty's internal process of figuring out what she sees and hears. She uses her eyes, ears, skin, and so forth, to determine what she sees and hears. If she cannot see because she is on the phone or she is blind, she will not have all those avenues of determination open to her. Assuming that she can see, Betty will take in Adam's facial expression, body position, muscle tone, skin color, scent, smell, breathing, voice tone and pace,

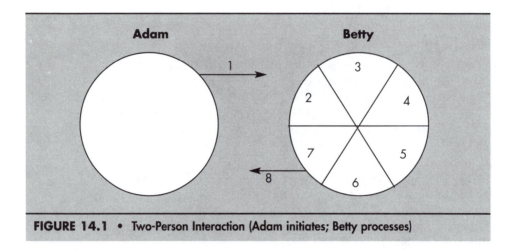

FIGURE 14.1 • Two-Person Interaction (Adam initiates; Betty processes)

as well as movement. These factors are called paralinguistics; they provide well over half of the meaning of the message. Adam's words are only part of the message. How Adam delivers the words will convey much meaning. Betty will select what she hears and sees from all the possibilities.

Next, point 3 is Betty's connecting with past experiences and learning, which will determine the meaning she will make of what she sees and hears. Betty might well ask herself, while forming the meaning of the message, how aware of the past and present she is as they relate to self, other, and context. Those three dimensions were described in the last chapter under the five communication stances. She also could ask herself whether she was aware of any past experiences that could contaminate the meaning she makes of the message from Adam.

Point 4 in the diagram represents the feelings triggered within Betty about the meaning she made of the message conveyed by Adam. Betty might ask herself the question, "What feelings do I have about the meaning I have made of the communication?" Note that Satir (1983a), like many people in the field of mental health, believed that feeling stems from the meaning or belief a person holds about an event, situation, or communication (M. P. Nichols & Schwartz, 1995).

In turn, the feelings activate point 5, which is related to feelings about the feelings. Satir (1983a) asked the question, "What are my feelings about the feelings about the meaning?" At first this may seem roundabout. Consider, however, that Betty may feel angry about the meaning and feel guilty about feeling angry. The feelings associated with the feelings about the meaning need to be sorted out. It is one situation if Betty feels that her feeling of anger is fine and another if she feels guilty about feeling angry. Both communication stances (Chapter 13) and family rules (Chapter 11) come into play. The feelings about the feelings activate survival rules. Thus, coping stances will come into play if the person discounts self, other, context, or two or three of these. The person is easily caught in an old web of feelings.

Point 6 stems from point 5 and relates to defenses Betty uses. These include such defense mechanisms as denying, projecting, and distorting. If she is using defenses, Betty could look to see whether she would cope by blaming, placating, being superreasonable, or being irrelevant. If, however, Betty owns and accepts her feelings, she does not have to defend herself and can decide how she chooses to respond.

Point 7 represents rules for commenting. The five freedoms, described in Chapter 11, come into play here. Must Betty see what she "should," say what is expected, feel what she "ought," and wait for permission, choosing to be secure and not rock the boat? Or can Betty exercise the five freedoms? In owning and accepting her feelings, she creates internal safety and does not have to defend herself. She is free to take risks and has choices for what and how she would like to respond to Adam.

At point 8 Betty responds with a message. Ideally, Betty will have made a meaning that matches the meaning intended by Adam. By accepting and owning her feelings, acknowledging and valuing Adam's feelings, as well as considering the context, Betty can take responsibility for her response and express herself in a congruent mode.

The communication, however, is not over yet. Now Adam must go through the same process that Betty just did. Figure 14.2 represents points 9 through 15, as Adam goes through the same steps in the process that Betty went through in points 2 through 8.

As indicated by this discussion, communication is more complex than is immediately obvious. There are many places where problems or snags might be found. Understanding one's own process is necessary before understanding that of others.

Effect of Communication Stances

The complex communication process becomes even more complex when one or both people are not communicating congruently. Several variations are possible. Both partners could communicate congruently, or both could communicate incongruently. Person A

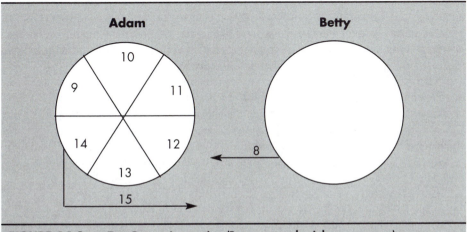

FIGURE 14.2 • Two-Person Interaction (Betty responds; Adam processes)

might be congruent and person B, incongruent. Person B might be congruent and person A, incongruent. Imagine the possibilities within a family!

Each person in an interaction must consider the internal process of the other. There are many possible ways of misinterpreting others, and miscommunication is more than occasional. That is understandable in light of the variations in stances that may exist. Being aware of the four possibilities is essential when communicating with others. To be unaware of the possibility that one's partner might be incongruent or congruent, and that you might also be either one, would lead to even greater problems when communicating. Recognizing how easy it is to miscommunicate underscores the need to clarify any communication that seems unclear or that you are unable to read accurately.

When trying to clarify what another person means by a message, you can look to the ingredients of the interaction for potential assistance. You will need to think about how the person made meaning from your original message, how he or she felt about that meaning and about the feeling about the meaning. Then you will need to try to decipher the defenses employed or the stances assumed as well as determine any freedoms violated by the person's rules for commenting. Before trying to understand another person's process, it helps to have examined your own.

Examining Personal Process

Understanding your own process is the first step in being able to use your knowledge about the ingredients of an interaction. Beginning your investigation with a current interaction is laudable; however, it might be easier to start by recollecting a recent, simple, meaningful interaction. It is valuable to recall, as well as memory allows, each of the components in that interaction. You should think back to the first comment made during the interaction by the other person and then determine the meaning you attached to it as well as the feelings you experienced about that meaning. You should then determine your feelings about these feelings, even if you were not aware of them at the time. Look to what defenses you used as well as what rules operated to determine whether you violated any of the five freedoms (see Chapter 11). That type of analysis can help you better understand your response. There is no way to know the internal process of another without engaging in what is called *mind rape*. You might, however, try to infer each of the components that form the internal process of the other person. This is merely inference and good practice.

After analyzing a past interaction, you can benefit from analyzing several other past interactions to see if any patterns emerge. Are there certain types of meaning made from a particular type of message? Are there feelings attached to meanings that provide a better picture of yourself? Can you determine defenses or rules operating under different feelings about feelings? By answering these questions, you can analyze your personal communication style. This type of analysis will serve professionals well when they attempt to transform family rules that would perform better as guidelines, as described in Chapter 11.

The next task is to analyze the ingredients while an interaction is occurring. For one day, while interactions are occurring, analyze those interactions that present a low level of threat. Once you have successfully finished that task, the next step is to analyze the ingredients of a current interaction that is potentially emotionally laden. It is important to not make too large a leap from an interaction that is low threat to one that is high threat, or your internal process may be too hard to follow. The amazing thing about communication is that everyone unconsciously and continually goes through this internal process throughout each day, giving little thought to the internal process.

Application Process

Although it is not possible to *apply* the ingredients of an interaction, an *awareness* of these ingredients is helpful for overcoming barriers to working with families as well as for gaining access to support groups, networking, and referring to counseling.

Miscommunication often occurs when a professional conveys to parents the need for additional assistance. Parents frequently mistake that comment as a judgment about their adequacy as a family or as individuals. Clearly, they are uncomfortable when others judge them to be inadequate. Knowing that parents might interpret any recommendation as a judgment of inadequacy can help professionals prepare their communications so that they are more likely to be understood as intended.

Any referral recommendation should begin with statements about realities within the family and should be followed by comments about the positive effects of the intervention on other families or individuals. It is important to use a positive frame when presenting any recommendations. For example, the professional could say, "All of us could use external assistance at times of stress and transition. This is not a sign of inadequacy or even dysfunction, but a normal reaction to stress." Then the specific issues can be linked to the need for additional assistance. When the professional is aligned with the family, they are less likely to see the professional as having judged them as inadequate.

PSYCHOLOGICAL ISSUES

School professionals, unlike professionals in mental health centers and child guidance clinics, often do not have the luxury of working with parents who recognize that they may be contributing to their child's problems. What is often found in schools is that parents are unaware that they have somehow played into their child's school difficulties. Losen and Losen (1994) discussed passive parents who defer to school professionals and seem unaware of their own collusion through being uninvolved.

Losen and Losen (1985) also stated that no matter how experienced the team members are in family dynamics, "parents may not be willing to accept even the hint of a suggestion during a team meeting that they are in any way responsible for their child's problems" (p. 113). Such parents should not be confronted in team meetings. Instead, it is important to ensure parental cooperation *before* including parents in team meetings during which decisions about their child will be made.

Although infrequent, problems involving parents who are defensive or belligerent do occur. These problems frequently stem from alcoholism, divorce, and psychiatric difficulties. The next sections briefly discuss aspects of these types of problems and suggests means for dealing with them. Chapters 6–8 of this text covered these kinds of problems in a more comprehensive manner.

Demanding Parents

Most legalistic and demanding parents have experienced prior incidents that led them to mistrust authority. They may easily misread the school's efforts to provide procedural due process as trying to "pull a fast one on them." It may be helpful to allow a trusted friend of the family or a professional to act as a go-between with the school. At all times, it is important to keep the focus on the best interest of the student. Eventually, parents will hear the call to what is in their child's best interest. An outside evaluation, conducted by an impartial evaluator, may help some parents feel better. If parents consider such an option, any evaluators recommended by the school should be independent and not vanguards of the system. The following case example illustrates why independent evaluations can be useful.

> The parents of a student with a chronic physical illness had a history of demanding special treatment for their son. Frequently, if their demands were not met, they would call the superintendent of schools and threaten a lawsuit. School personnel became so numb to parental complaints that they failed to take note when the boy continued to make poor grades through the fifth grade. It was only after independent evaluations were suggested and completed that the boy's severe learning disability in reading was discovered. In this case, parental symptomatic behavior had obscured the focus on the best interest of the student.

There are some rules of thumb (Losen & Losen, 1994) that will help school professionals when dealing with demanding and legalistic parents. As suggested earlier, parents should not be confronted during team meetings. If a conflict erupts unexpectedly during a team meeting, it is best to table any decisions until the conflict has been resolved. Any hostility or mistrust should be validated, and, obviously, strong feelings should not be denied or ignored. The school professionals should discuss with the parents the origin of their concerns as well as their underlying fears.

The team also should let the parents know when they are on target in making a fully intelligible and defensible point of view. A good comment is, "If I were in your place I probably would be feeling the same way," or "Although I do not see it that way, I do understand your belief and thus the feelings you have about this situation."

When parents become flexible, school professionals must be sure not to remain rigid in response. It is better to have a good beginning toward what is best for the student than a due process hearing that may make things worse.

Psychiatric Difficulties

Parents with emotional problems may be unsupportive and unresponsive, needy and seeking continual input and reassurance, or emotionally unstable and disruptive as well as irresponsible. Working with such parents may leave any school professional feeling in a *one down* position.

Regardless of the type of disruption, it is important that the professional reassure the parents of his or her commitment to their child. It may also be necessary to clarify and explain rationale and procedures. Further, the team needs to work with irrational parents prior to conducting any meetings. Parents can meet individually with the professional with whom they share the best rapport. Some parents would benefit from referral for family systems therapy; the social worker could make this recommendation while meeting with them. It is more likely that the parent will provide more meaningful and honest input with one open and supportive professional than at a team meeting.

An alcoholic parent should not be invited to a private conference. Alcoholics' behavior may be unpredictable, and they may be difficult people. If they insist on attending and are obviously under the influence of alcohol or other drugs, the meeting should be terminated immediately. Professionals must be careful, however, that such parents do not feel put down by this action and should help them in any way possible to reclaim their self-esteem. Following the meeting, it might be helpful to share information with the nonalcoholic parent about local Alcoholics Anonymous or Al-Anon chapters (see Appendix D).

Professionals (Losen & Losen, 1985, 1994; Morsink et al., 1991; Turnbull & Turnbull, 1996) have suggested many effective strategies for working with unstable parents. Some recommendations are that the professional attempt to clarify the parents' understanding of their child's problem, that the professional provides more reassurance than is usually needed, that a strong relationship be established between one team member and the parents during individual conferences as a precursor to team meetings, and that school comments be directed to the most stable or rational parent. When working with unstable parents, refraining from exchanging angry words is a must. However, professionals should not refrain from calling upon external resources such as police, friends, or a minister. Chapters 7 and 8 elaborate upon families with a dysfunctional parent and provide recommendations for school professionals about working with them.

Angry Parents

Dealing with angry or aggressive parents has been addressed by various professionals (Armstrong, 1995; Losen & Losen, 1994; Morsink et al., 1991; Turnbull & Turnbull, 1996). Margolis and Brannigan (1986) published a useful article titled "Relating to Angry Parents." Dealing with angry and aggressive parents is part of a professional's job in the schools, yet maintaining composure under direct attack and confrontation is not an easily developed skill. Even more difficult is empathizing with parental fears and frustrations. These are important skills for all school professionals.

Even sane, rational parents may become angry and let their anger show. School professionals need to recognize that parents may have valid complaints, or that a mistake may have been made. Working with the parents to help them vent their feelings and share their understanding of the problem is critical. However, it is definitely not advisable to give in to aggressive parents when the option is not in the child's best interest.

The following are some rules of thumb for dealing with angry parents. Professionals should always make eye contact and be courteous. They should not try to interject their own opinions. Instead, they should listen to the parents. If the professional does not understand the underlying concern because of the level of anger being expressed, a clarification should be requested. The professional should listen actively, reflecting the parents' beliefs and feelings. Summarization of the parents' points also may be helpful. If the parents disown any mention of their anger, the professional should steer clear of further comments and relate to the parents' beliefs. The important point in dealing with angry parents is to not try to solve the situation but instead to build trust by demonstrating caring and concern.

The professional should also try to distinguish true issues from pseudo concerns, asking questions that assist in this process. The questions should be open-ended, such as, "How is it that this came about?" Questions that begin with "why" should be avoided because they may lead to defensiveness in the parents. Once everything is out in the open, the professional should summarize the points of agreement as well as disagreement. The professional should then determine if the parents have anything to add that would further clarify everyone's understanding.

All of these steps provide for exploration and understanding of the problem from the parent's point of view. As noted earlier, the emphasis is on connecting and building trust. The next step is problem solving. D. Johnson (1997) presented a number of exercises designed to help professionals, students, and parents in developing and refining their human interaction skills. Chapters in Johnson's textbook relate to psychological issues and focus on listening, resolving interpersonal conflicts, and managing feelings related to anger and stress. Though oriented toward the preparation of professionals, the exercises can be used in training parents as well as students in healthy human interaction skills. The problem-solving process will now be discussed briefly.

PROBLEM SOLVING

Problem solving is a multistep process that leads to conflict resolution. The five steps presented in this section are critical to group problem solving. The steps are time-honored; most problem-solving models are only slightly different variations of the one described here. Teams are involved in continual problem solving concerning team process issues as well as content concerns (Losen & Losen, 1994).

Step 1: Define the Problem

No one can effectively solve a problem that is not well defined. Although most team members expect that defining the problem will be an easy step in the process of problem solving, in reality, it is a challenging step.

It is important that all team members focus on the underlying cause of the problem and not on the symptoms. People often become wrapped up in symptoms and fail to see the forest for the trees. If, for example, a student is having trouble concentrating and staying in his seat in school, many professionals will focus on the surface manifestations of the problem—that is, the student's in-school behavioral excesses. By more thoroughly examining the problem, however, the team might find that no parent is available to supervise the student in the mornings before school. Lacking supervision, the student might be getting hyped up by eating junk food and watching overstimulating videos before going to school. Thus, the problem would be accurately defined as one that originates at home rather than in the classroom.

Step 2: Collect Facts and Opinions

Once the problem is understood, the team members gather the facts and opinions needed for further understanding the situation. It may not be possible to obtain all the facts, but it is important to move forward and not allow the situation to become a crisis. It is critical to find out what the situation is, what happened, who is involved, and what policies and procedures are involved. All of those factors will help team members design realistic solutions.

Step 3: Generate Solutions

This step involves brainstorming for possible solutions. No idea should be criticized at this point. When team members criticize or evaluate ideas at this stage, they effectively shut off the production of creative solutions. This step should be freewheeling and fast-moving, with everyone on the team providing potential solutions.

Step 4: Select the Solution

There are two aspects to the fourth step. First, the team must clearly specify the goals, or end results, they expect from the solution. Then, they must evaluate each of the solutions generated in the previous step in light of the agreed-upon goals. The few solutions that come out on top should be put to the tests of potential feasibility and maximization of resources. Based on those tests, the best solution is selected.

Step 5: Implement the Solution

Timetables for the solution should be established by team members. Further, the team should specify the evaluation techniques to be used and make plans for follow-through.

INTERACTION BETWEEN FAMILIES AND SCHOOLS

This section focuses on four aspects of working with families. First, the need, desire, and availability of family members to be involved in the education of the at-risk or special-needs learner are considered. Second, a family systems perspective on team issues is addressed. Third, reasons for nonparticipation, and fourth, ways to overcome unwanted nonparticipation, and means of involving families who want to participate are covered.

Need, Desire, and Availability of Family Members

It is important that team members consider the desires and availability of family members for involvement on the team (Armstrong, 1995; Carney & Gamel-McCormick, 1996; Foster et al., 1981; Losen & Losen, 1994; Power-deFur & Orelove, 1997; Turnbull & Turnbull, 1996; Winton & Turnbull, 1981). Some parents might want to be more involved than their schedules and responsibilities allow. Other parents might not be interested in involvement, regardless of other responsibilities, and their choice should be respected by educational professionals. Bjorck-Akesson and Granlund (1995) reconfirmed the 1981 findings of C. Lusthaus, E. Lusthaus, and H. Gibbs that parents wanted to be involved in schools by giving and receiving information. Parents also were found to be interested in being involved with decisions about the "kinds of information kept on their children; medical services for their children; and transfer of their children to other schools" (p. 257).

Professionals currently maintain that school personnel should encourage family involvement while also recognizing that there are a variety of reasons for limited participation or nonparticipation. Those reasons are elaborated upon later in this chapter. Z. P. Solomon (1991) reported on California's policy relating to parental involvement in schools. California recommended six ways to design programs to involve parents:

1. Help parents develop parenting skills and foster conditions at home that support learning;

2. provide parents with the knowledge of techniques designed to assist children in learning at home;

3. provide access to and coordinate community support services for children and families;

4. promote clear two-way communication between the school and the family as to the school programs and children's progress;

5. involve parents, after appropriate training, in instructional and support roles at school; and

6. support parents as decision-makers and develop their leadership in governance, advisory, and advocacy roles. (p. 361)

These guidelines are as pertinent to at-risk and special-needs families as they are to all other families. More specific ways to involve parents in schools were described by Bjorck-Akesson and Granlund (1995), Chapman (1991), D'Angelo and Adler (1991), Z. P. Solomon (1991), and Sussell et al. (1996).

After researching family involvement, Winton and Turnbull (1981) suggested that schools match parental involvement to the individual needs of families. They further indicated that parental uninvolvement will sometimes be a tremendous contribution to the school program. Although professionals may assume that they are acting in the best interests of the student by encouraging parental involvement in their program, in some cases this is not true.

Turnbull and Turnbull (1996) indicated that parents should be provided with options for involvement. One option would be uninvolvement with the school program as a matter of choice. Another option would be involvement through being informed about, but not participating in developing, goals and objectives. A third option would be full and equal decision-making opportunities for parents who choose to participate at that level.

Family Systems Perspective

The focus of an edited text by W. M. Walsh and G. R. Williams (1997) is on the use of family systems theory and therapy to resolve school problems. A book about change, it focuses on a paradigm shift that leads people toward systems thinking. The editors wrote, "When we conceptualize students' problems as a part of an interactional dynamic within a system and work to change those interactions and ultimately the system, students improve" (p. xiii).

Peeks (1997) suggested that the revolution in counseling related to the theory and practice of family therapy should provide the basis for a revolution in public education. She proposed that "one of the important elements of educational reform be focused on the relationship among parents, students and school professionals. Students should be helped by their parents and school working as a cooperative problem solving team" (pp. 5–6). Students who are problem-free were described as able to achieve to their potential, thus improving the collective achievement in the school. It also was suggested that students would benefit by observing their parents' involvement in their education. According to Peeks, as problems of students are solved by parental input, higher quality education would follow.

Malatchi (1997) framed the educational paradigmatic shift in relationship to the education of children with special needs. She saw the shift as a movement from a system-centered approach to one that is family/person-centered. The edited text (Power-deFur & Orelove, 1997) in which her chapter appears elaborates on how to put such an approach into action in the schools. Briggs (1997), focusing on family systems as a base for early intervention, stated, "Professionals can learn to move their focus away from treating the child with special needs as the identified patient. With a broader focus, the family system is no longer a problem but part of the solution" (p. 107).

As early as 1983, Pfeiffer and Tittler described how eligibility teams could benefit by adopting a family systems orientation. Their approach recognized that families and schools are intimately interrelated and linked through the student. By shifting to a family focus, the referred student is no longer viewed in isolation but within the context of his or her family. By observing the family, team members can better understand and predict the student's behavior in school as well as social functioning in the family. Also, if other family members can be helped to redirect some stress from the student, the student's dysfunction should lessen, with an increase in the possibility for remediation in school.

Reasons for Nonparticipation

Carney and Gamel-McCormick (1996), as well as Morsink et al. (1991), indicated that while it is important for professionals to respect the right of parents to choose not to participate in their child's educational program, it is also important to determine whether the nonparticipation is based upon an informed choice. Lack of parental participation might be related to specific child and family characteristics rather than choice. D. L. McMillan and A. P. Turnbull (1983) had previously reached the same conclusion, as had Suelzle and Keenan (1981), whose findings indicated that families with lower incomes, older children, and children with more severe disabilities were less likely to be involved in their child's education.

Weber and Stoneman (1986) investigated the differences in family characteristics, maternal knowledge about the IEP process, and the mother's knowledge about the IEP itself for parents who did and did not attend IEP meetings. They found that poor families with limited parental education who were nonwhite and who were headed by single parents were overrepresented in the group of parents who did not attend the meetings. Mothers who viewed teachers and other professionals as responsible for their child's education were often nonparticipants. The authors considered it important to reach out to families, to provide programs responsive to their particular needs that are sensitive to the demands faced by the parents, to empower the parents, and to provide them with a sense of control. They indicated that parents are able to make informed choices about participation in their child's education when they fully understand both the rights and the opportunities that are available from the schools. They concluded that many parents lack basic information that is needed to make informed choices.

Parental anxiety contributes to lack of participation (Losen & Losen, 1994). Parents may be anxious for a variety of reasons. First, they may be concerned about what is happening to the child and feel that they don't have the answers (Miller, 1996). Especially early in the process, parents tend to depend upon team members to identify their child's difficulties and to provide remedial services (Armstrong, 1995). Thus, they may feel somewhat at the mercy of the expertise of the professionals, especially if they are not knowledgeable about their child's problem. Second, parents may be worried that they will appear stupid, confused, or indecisive. Thus, they may restrict their input and be passive during the team meetings they do attend.

Third, parents may feel that they have failed their child. Such a sense of guilt is common among parents of children with special needs (Losen & Losen, 1994). Parents may be concerned that their parenting skills are being judged or evaluated negatively by professionals and that they have made mistakes that resulted in their child's disability. These thoughts would naturally lead to passivity on the part of parents. They might think that the professionals involved would have better solutions.

Fourth, parents may mistrust the school staff. They may believe that the professionals had misdiagnosed their child or that the professionals might not be competent to deal with the special needs of their child (Losen & Losen, 1994). Some of these parents resign themselves to professional input; others, feeling a sense of helplessness, resist any efforts to reassure them. Concern and doubt about the competence of professionals also could reflect the parents' own personal doubts about how to deal with the needs of their child. Miller (1996) indicated that it is important that school professionals realize that trust is not automatic and that it grows over time and with positive experience. By requesting information from the family and making them part of the team, professionals can help parents realize that their concerns and issues will be addressed and that they are held in respect.

Fifth, parents may be concerned that involvement in special education will cause their child to be seen negatively by other teachers as well as peers. Parents with this fear have generally found it difficult to accept their child's level of need and, thus, remain doubtful about the differences between their child and other classmates (Losen & Losen, 1994). They may allow the schools to plan programs for their child yet not be supportive of those programs in the home.

Sixth, parental guilt feelings may involve a fear of criticism (Miller, 1996). Feeling that they have failed their children with special needs and others in the process, parents may fear that friends and relatives will learn about their perceived poor parenting skills unless they comply with the recommendations of the school. This is particularly true of parents of children who are belligerent and act out.

An additional reason for parental passivity and lack of involvement with their child's educational program stems from prior negative experiences with schools. For example, a prior teacher, principal, or other professional may have led the parents to conclude that to obtain the best for their child they should remain silent. Parents also may fear that their child will be mistreated, or that a more restrictive environment will be recommended if they contribute their own personal opinions to the process. Even though these negative expectations may be unrealistic, it is important to get them out on the table. For example, a parent may have heard through the grapevine that a particular principal is a strict disciplinarian, or that a social worker might be more negative while interacting alone with parents than during a team meeting. Such concerns need to be aired and dealt with if parental involvement is to be achieved.

Overcoming Nonparticipation

Losen & Losen (1994) suggested that information be presented to parents prior to team meetings. Their advice is equally applicable to all of the other team participants. When all participants have received information prior to the meeting, more of the meeting time can be devoted to discussion, which increases the likelihood of participation. Further, Losen and Losen suggested that a preteam meeting between the parents and one professional can alleviate sources of nonparticipation and anxiety. They recommended that a professional with good communication skills meet with the parents to discuss procedures used and their child's test results. All questions the parents might have would be answered, and the professional would maintain an egalitarian attitude.

This preteam meeting allows the professional to explain the test results in lay terms and provides parents with the opportunity to raise issues and questions about the process or results without wasting other team members' time. In addition, parents can be made aware of the purposes for the upcoming full team meeting. They may want to suggest that alternative procedures be employed prior to that meeting, such as observing their child in different settings.

By helping to ensure that the parents understand the procedures used, the preteam meeting should help decrease their passivity, defensiveness, or resistance during the team meeting. The preteam meeting also provides an opportunity to deal with parental doubts, guilt, and sense of inadequacy. It is far easier to deal with these issues in an intimate conference than a full team meeting.

Plus, the meeting prevents the pitfall of parents' first learning about significant results of the assessment during the full team meeting. No humane professional would expect parents to be able to respond to learning that their child has, for example, mental retardation, and also help plan their child's education during the same meeting. Falik (1995) wrote about how families react to having a child with a learning disability.

To involve parents meaningfully in the team process, it also may be necessary to provide services such as baby-sitters and transportation. Pfeiffer (1980) indicated that such strategies were highly successful in increasing parental involvement.

LIMITATIONS

This section covers limitations on using family systems concepts and approaches in schools. Many of the limitations stem from lack of training, current norms in the schools, and traditional school procedures.

Training

Traditional university training in general education and special education does not require a course in communication between home and school. Often school principals are the only school professionals required to take a course in school and community relations, and, typically, parents are just one of many topics covered. Realizing that universities generally require no separate course on working with families, one can see that the family systems approach is infrequently considered in teacher-training institutions.

Further, few counselor-education programs do not require a course on working with families, and none require a course in family systems. School social workers have always been trained to work with families. In fact, that is their major responsibility in most schools. Not all schools of social work, however, train students in family systems approaches. Few school psychologists have training in family systems, though that does appear to be changing. Experts are beginning to recognize that schools have students for only 9% of their lives and are increasing their curricular focus to include a holistic view (W. M. Walsh & Williams, 1997).

Although special educators are obviously required to interact with parents on an ongoing basis, they usually are not required to take a separate course in working with families. Special education is a vast subject area, and family systems concepts may not even be included in elective courses. It is more likely that general educators will have taken a course dealing with families, yet few of those courses focus on family systems.

Thus, there is a very large deficit to overcome before people are able to call upon university professors or schools of social work or psychology to teach content such as that found in this book. Preservice training is very limited, and the in-service needs of all of the professionals already working in schools compound the problem. At a time when requirements for teacher recertification are being relaxed, it is even less likely that teachers will take courses that will prepare them in family systems concepts.

University systems are slow to change program requirements. Although higher education has been in the process of restructuring, it is unlikely that, without pressure, institutions of higher education will spontaneously provide coursework on family systems. Thus, it behooves those who recognize the value of family systems to assume responsibility for generating interest in such a course. Typically, they will be greeted with a response such as, "We already have an elective course on working with parents" or "We can incorporate that into another existing course." Neither response is appropriate. As can be seen from this text, family systems is a complex field that requires in-depth study, understanding, and training. W. M. Walsh and G. R. Williams (1997) have chapters on training school counselors in family systems.

Other potential ways to promote preservice family systems training include legislative mandate and school system recommendation. Many states require, by legislative mandate, a separate course in special education. Other states require that special education be covered within the education program, thus allowing colleges and universities to cover the field of special education for general educators within a portion of another existing course. Similar mandates could be recommended for family systems training. Further, informed superintendents might advise schools of education to provide preservice coursework in family systems. Most institutions of higher education respond to input from superintendents.

In-service training is another matter. Although they have changed dramatically in recent years, staff development activities seldom focus upon family systems training for school professionals. The Commonwealth of Virginia did develop a training module on family systems (Lambie, 1987). The school professionals deeply appreciated the content from both a personal and a professional perspective. A trainer-of-trainers model and the use of a team to provide training are highly recommended. It is helpful if one member of the team is knowledgeable about the content and can field questions. The school social worker would be an excellent professional for that perspective.

So far, this section has dealt with limitations in the training of professionals. Another training limitation is the lack of programs that respond to the training needs of parents of at-risk and special-needs students. Few schools provide more than written literature concerning the child study or eligibility process. Parents need more than that. At the very least, parents should be coached in effective communication skills. After all, more effective communicators are also more effective team members.

Norms

A well-established norm for school professionals is to not become too involved with family matters. With the exception of Project Head Start, schools generally have considered family matters to be the responsibility of agencies external to the schools. Referral to mental health centers is not a common approach taken by school professionals. Due to concern about the cost of related services to the school system, school professionals are even less likely to suggest these types of services for students with special needs.

Another norm in schools and elsewhere is to consider the symptom bearer to be the unit of intervention. For students with special needs, this norm should shift to viewing the whole family as the unit of intervention. This norm would likely shift if training in family systems concepts were to begin to make an impression on school professionals.

Shifts in norms are slow to occur and most likely follow training. It seems that a grass-roots or top-down authoritative pronouncement would be the only ways in which a shift in norms initially could be generated in the school system. Since a grass-roots approach is unlikely, someone in the school system would presumably have to assume responsibility for generating interest in family systems. School professionals would need to be given permission not only to know about the family systems concepts but also to use what they have learned without feeling they have crossed a professional boundary. The notion of role release described in Chapter 10 is an important factor in realizing this change.

School Procedures

Many school procedures make it difficult for school professionals to implement or teach their knowledge about family systems. Social workers who are familiar with family systems concepts may have such large case loads that they do not have the time to help other school professionals learn about family systems approaches. With budgetary problems and shrinking dollars, it is unlikely that school procedures will change in the near future.

The past emphasis on the placement of school counselors in each elementary school building was a hopeful sign that the use of family systems approaches could increase and develop. It augured well for the investment of energies and money in family systems concepts. Recent changes in state policy in Virginia, however, have shifted the responsibility for this decision to the local schools.

Adding to the problem, school counselors may be unfamiliar with family systems concepts or may not have the time to implement their knowledge and skills learned about family systems. Many elementary school counselors work with children rather than families. They often work quickly with a group of children for a short period and then move on to another group so that more may be served.

Secondary school counselors are almost always in charge of scheduling and have little, if any, time for counseling students, let alone families. Secondary schools are oriented toward noninterference with families. Students are viewed as old enough to be responsible for themselves and to accept natural consequences of behavior. Trying to elicit family support is often seen by professionals and families as enabling students to remain immature and dependent.

Finally, most educational teams do not function in a way that would allow collaboration with family systems. The teams often do not meet regularly and communicate mainly through written report; they may have only enough time for the barest of information sharing during team meetings. Once a student is determined to be eligible for special education, the collaboration of team members often decelerates. The teachers are often on their own until the IEP is revisited a year later.

REALITY CONSTRAINTS

A number of reality constraints also limit the use of family systems concepts and approaches in the school. The three reality constraints of time, money, and availability of trained personnel are seen most frequently.

Time

The constraint of insufficient time is a concern of all school professionals. However, once school staff have been trained and are competent in implementing family systems concepts, their knowledge will save them time. Over the long term, less time will be expended mired in an individual perspective when a family systems perspective will more easily resolve the problem.

Money

Finding money for staff development and for the release of personnel to attend training sessions is a real concern. With shrinking dollars, staff development funds may be among the first to be decreased. However, over the long term, the full implementation of family systems concepts may save dollars. Consider the example of students with emotional and behavioral disorders. If the whole family were seen as the unit of treatment, many of the problems would be resolved and the students would remain in classes for the seriously emotionally disturbed for less time. It is also likely that fewer due process hearings, which are very expensive, would be needed.

Training

The lack of trained personnel is another reality constraint. As mentioned earlier, changes in the institutions of higher education are slow to develop. With the emphasis on restructuring in the past several years, little energy is left for new endeavors and changing programs of study. Arends (1990) pointed to the slowness of universities to respond to criticism. He suggested that "teacher preparation of the future could be under the auspices of inspired and well-funded district-based human resource development units or state-based special academies for teachers" (p. 117–143).

The expenditure of initial funds for staff development in school systems would be invaluable. Again, a trainer-of-trainers model that allows more people to be reached with fewer funds is useful. Furthermore, schools of social work and psychology at universities and colleges are excellent resources for those who might design modules as well as train trainers.

ATTITUDES, RESISTANCE, AND CHANGE

Attitudes are an intriguing phenomenon. They are defined as strong beliefs or feelings toward people and situations. We acquire attitudes, both favorable and unfavorable, throughout our lives. Attitudes involve a *for* or *against* quality that makes them obviously an attitude as opposed to an opinion. A poster often seen in schools bears the slogan, "Attitudes are contagious—are yours worth catching?" This a great way to think about attitudes. It becomes obvious that individuals with positive attitudes toward change will bring about positive results.

M. Scott Peck (1978), the author of *The Road Less Traveled* and other wonderful books, stated, "It is only through a vast amount of experience and a lengthy and successful maturation that we gain the capacity to see the world and our place in it realistically, and thus are enabled to realistically assess our responsibility for ourselves and the world" (p. 37).

Negative attitudes and resistance to change can greatly limit the incorporation of family systems concepts into the school system. Both must be understood to make way for effective change. Further, a model for change is helpful in understanding, expecting, and validating concerns of employees about the change process.

Negative Attitudes

The most prevalent attitude that limits the use of family systems concepts in schools is: "It is someone else's responsibility to work with those families. I do not have enough time. What do they expect from us anyway? It is not in our job description. Our local education association or federation will support us on that."

Another negative attitude toward change stems from fear of failure and associated repercussions. Teachers and principals, in particular, might be concerned about employing strategies usually reserved for counselors, social workers, and psychologists. A natural concern relates to how the use of change strategies might result in a setback, as opposed to the growth and development, of the family. Without extensive training and well-understood boundaries regarding who employs these strategies, these fears would be well grounded. Obviously, this is a fear that needs to be addressed by anyone implementing change.

Negative contagion, a third attitude problem, may occur in some schools where teachers have bonded together to block anything new and different. They denounce new endeavors as "old wine in new bottles." As a group, they form a prodigious force that is hard to convert.

Resistance

It is important to recognize that resistance to change is normal human behavior. Orelove and Sobsey (1996) recommended that school professionals expect resistance to change, confront it, and focus on the common goals of the team that benefit children. People resist change for a variety of reasons. In an edited text on teamwork in education, Roy (1995) listed reasons for people's resistance to change:

- New goals are not accepted.
- People fear the unknown.
- People fear failure in the new situation.
- People like the current situation and arrangement.
- Reasons for change are not communicated well enough.
- People do not like or trust the individual or group initiating the change.
- New goals are unimportant to people.
- The changing environment is seen as an opportunity to oppose management.
- People fear loss of status, rights, and privileges.
- People resist change because it's change. (p. 86)

Focusing on the human side of change, Rosabeth Moss Kanter (1995) listed the following reasons people most commonly resist change in organizations: loss of control, excess uncertainty, Surprise? Surprise?, the "difference" effect, loss of face, concerns about future competence, ripple effects, more work, past resentments, and sometimes the threat is real. She suggested tactics for working with resistance and identified 14 ways to build commitment to change:

- Allow room for participation in the planning of the change.
- Leave choices within the overall decision to change.

- Provide a clear picture of the change, a "vision" with details about the new state.
- Share information about change plans to the fullest extent possible.
- Divide a big change into more manageable and familiar steps; let people take a small step first.
- Minimize surprises; give people advance warning about new requirements.
- Allow for digestion of change requests—a chance to become accustomed to the ideas of change before making a commitment.
- Repeatedly demonstrate your own commitment to the change.
- Make standards and requirements clear—tell exactly what is expected of people in the change.
- Offer positive reinforcement for competence; let people know they can do it.
- Look for and reward pioneers, innovators, and early successes to serve as models.
- Help people find or feel compensated for the extra time and energy change requires.
- Avoid creating obvious "losers" from the change. (But if there are some, be honest with them—early on.)
- Allow expressions of nostalgia and grief for the past—then create excitement about the future. (p. 679)

These are lessons that everyone can take to heart when participating in a school renewal or other change processes.

According to Reece and Brandt (1987), some individuals resist change because they feel inadequate. Some feel their security is threatened; others may not trust those in charge of the change process. Some individuals who resist change have such a narrow focus that they simply do not see the larger picture.

Feelings of Inadequacy

When people learn new skills, they generally accept additional responsibility. That, in turn, may stretch their abilities and make them feel a lack of self-confidence. For example, most school professionals felt uncomfortable with computers until they became computer literate. The same will be true with family systems concepts. It is very important to support professionals who are learning these new skills. All professionals should feel that they can and will make mistakes as they learn; permission to learn from mistakes is important. Sharing stories with others and exchanging ideas for problem solving also can be very helpful. Those who are newly implementing family systems concepts and strategies will learn quickly that they are not the only ones who lack confidence and feel inadequate. Groups are great vehicles for mirroring and learning more about oneself.

Issues of Security

As Maslow (1970) made clear, personal security, both physical and psychological, is a very basic need. When the expectations for school professionals change and they are faced with making major changes in their work, some may worry that if they are unable to keep abreast of the changes they may be phased out or seen as less worthy. It is therefore important to make certain that school professionals know that the individuals in charge of the change process have the responsibility of preparing them adequately for the implementation of family systems strategies. Any lack of understanding or failure of implementation should be met with a careful check on the preparation of the employee and the necessary coaching provided to reach an appropriate mastery level.

Issues of Trust

Lack of trust is another reason people resist change. Where the implementation of family systems concepts is concerned, mistrust is aimed at those responsible for directing and implementing change. There may be large differences among schools within one system, depending upon how much the principal is trusted. When school professionals are let in on upcoming changes only after all of the decisions and planning are complete, they are less likely to trust and therefore may resist even the most appealing change. It behooves the change makers to solicit input from representatives of all levels and types of school professionals. Furthermore, these representatives should be professionals who are trusted by their peers. Anyone perceived as a *Yes Wo/man* will not engender automatic trust.

Narrow Focus

Many school professionals will be unable to see the larger picture and will not understand that the learning of family systems concepts will pay off in the long run in terms of both time and money. Furthermore, they may not see the most important benefit, which is that the needs of at-risk and special-needs students will be met in a more satisfactory manner. To eliminate or minimize this form of resistance, it is imperative to explain the overall picture and reasons for the change, including family systems concepts and strategies.

Change: Response Stages, Concerns About Change, and Stages of Growth

The process of effecting lasting and meaningful change is complex and challenging. The literature on change is replete with advice about initiating change within educational institutions (D. F. Bradley & King-Sears, 1997; Briggs, 1997; Caine & Caine, 1997; Corbett, Firestone, & Rossman, 1987; Evans, 1993; Giangreco, Dennis, Cloninger, Edelman, & Schattman, 1993; Guskey, 1986; Haimes, 1995; G. E. Hall & Hord, 1987; Sarason, 1982, 1996a, 1996b; Showers, Joyce, & Bennett, 1987). This section discusses stages of response to change, concerns about change, and stages of growth.

Stages of Response to Change

M. Moore and P. Gergen (1989, cited in Haimes, 1995) identified four stages experienced by staff members in response to change: shock, defensive retreat, acknowledgment, and adaptation. Initially, people feel threatened by change, and their ability to relate to the change is impaired by their feelings. It is important to provide the necessary time for them to adjust to the changes and to discover what their roles in the change process will be. They need to be able to express their concerns, fears, and frustrations before planning is even broached.

Next, defensive retreat occurs, where people try to return to the "old way" of doing things. I conduct a training exercise where I have everyone stand up, bring their arms out to their sides in mid-air, then bring their hands together clasping them with fingers interlocked. Then I tell them to note which thumb is on top. I instruct them to pull their arms apart again and reclasp them with the nondominant thumb on top. We go through a series of these simulations (e.g., putting an arm in a jacket, jumping out to an imaginary rock), each time alternating the customary way and the new way. We then discuss which way feels better and which they plan to use the next time they put on a jacket, jump to a rock, or clasp their hands. Nobody wants to move out of their comfort zones, and it is critical to honor that human trait. During the time of defensive retreat, leaders can let staff members know what will not change, as well as what areas will likely be uncomfortable. Clear expectation about roles is important during this stage of reaction to change.

Acknowledgment involves school professionals' recognition that something good may result from the change for them and the students. The sense of loss is being replaced by excitement and anticipation as well as interest in their personal involvement. Planning commences, and people look to the future. Risk taking should be reinforced, as should be a focus on what people are learning.

Adaptation relates to the assumption of roles, routines, and methods that are new. During this implementation phase, those people who are not on board will become evident. They may be simply stuck in an earlier phase longer than the rest and not really resistant to change. Some of these individuals eventually will move through the earlier phase into the adaptation stage. Some, however, may not find it possible to make the adaptation.

Concerns-Based Adoption Model

This section presents information on the Concerns-Based Adoption Model (CBAM). It is highlighted because of its attention to the *concerns* of school professionals and, therefore, its ability to affect *attitudes* toward change. The model focuses on personal aspects of change. Change is seen as a process and not an event (G. E. Hall & Hord, 1987). Further, it emphasizes the need to understand the point of view of participants who are involved in the change process. Idol et al. (1994) used CBAM in implementing Collaborative Consultation, as did Erb (1995) in relation to teamwork in middle school education. This model continues to be seen as a viable aid in the family systems field.

The CBAM model has three dimensions: stages of concern, levels of use, and innovation configurations. This discussion addresses only the stages of concern. Discussion of the other dimensions can be found in Hall and Hord (1987).

G. E. Hall, R. C. Wallace, and W. Dossett (1973), and later G. E. Hall and S. M. Hord (1987), delineated seven levels of concern about change that relate to how school professionals feel about an innovation. They called the lowest stage of concern *Awareness* and assigned it a value of zero. In this stage, school professionals have little concern about or interest in the innovation. This is the level of concern people have toward something about which they know little or nothing.

The next stage of concern, *Informational,* reflects a general awareness of the innovation. The professional will have an interest in learning more about the innovation or change. At this stage, professionals are not concerned about how the change will affect them. They generally are concerned about aspects of the innovation such as its characteristics, requirements for use, and effects of the change. The developers of the model assigned a value of 1 to the informational stage of concern.

Personal concern, assigned a value of 2, occurs when the professional is uncertain about the professional demands of the innovation as well as his or her personal adequacy in meeting those demands. The professional might analyze his or her role in relation to rewards in the organization and in relation to decision-making processes and find these to be of personal concern at this time. Potential conflicts with current commitments also could be of concern. Financial and status implications are other potential personal concerns.

At the next level of concern, *Management,* professionals focus their attention upon the processes and tasks involved in using the innovation as well as the best use of information and resources. Of prime concern are issues that relate to organizing, managing, and scheduling the innovation, as well as efficiency and time considerations. This level of concern was assigned a value of 3.

A value of 4 was assigned to the stage referred to as *Consequence.* In this stage, professionals focus their concerns on the impact of the innovation on their particular students. Relevance to the lives of their students is of concern, as are outcomes and changes needed to increase the outcomes of the students.

The *Collaboration* stage, with a value of 5, has to do with concerns about coordinating with others. Professionals will want to know about ways to cooperate with peers in using the innovation.

In the final stage, *Refocusing,* with a value of 6, professionals are concerned with how the innovation might benefit others. Some professionals might be concerned about alternative innovations. It is certain that professionals will have definite ideas and opinions about proposed or existing forms of the innovation.

With knowledge of this model, professionals can anticipate what will occur during a change process. A basic premise of the model is that anyone can be a change facilitator. Anyone can expedite the change process and facilitate, rather than manipulate, change. The facilitator would know about individual concerns and respond to them so that others would be more effective in applying innovations. Understanding the CBAM model can help the professional in any change effort he or she might initiate.

Stages of Growth and the Process of Change

Virginia Satir spoke and wrote about the *stages of growth* we go through in life as individuals, couples, families, and organizations (Dodson, 1991). She identified the stages as status quo, introduction of the foreign element and resistance, chaos, new integration and practice, and finally the new status quo. Satir's change model is highlighted here because of its family systems perspective.

Rosabeth Moss Kanter, mentioned earlier in this chapter, referred to those assuming responsibility for change in an organizational system as change-masters. I use this terminology in this section, even though it was not one of Satir's terms.

Dodson (1991) wrote, "Concepts behind Virginia's model for change were systems theory, life as a process, the inner healer in everyone and the need for education to aid change" (p. 122). Satir saw her model for growth and change as applicable to all domains. Her view of change stemmed from her seeing the world through what she called the systemic organic and seed model (see Appendix A). The organic model is influenced by holistic concepts that hold that human beings have an inner drive to grow and develop. In awakening the healer(s) within, individuals and groups can engage in conscious choices to individuate and contribute to an expanding world. Essential to the growth process that Satir spoke of is self-esteem, and essential to the development of high self-esteem is an environment rich in nurturance and the freedom to explore and to know, as well as comment on, what is experienced. Satir applied her model for change "to education, prevention, individual, couple, family therapy and world healing" (Dodson, p. 122).

In the educational context, becoming conscious of change is critical for individuals, families, and schools. Otherwise, change is random and haphazard, and neither professionals, students, or their families will *own* the change process or outcome. A description of each of Satir's five stages follows. Within the descriptions, I have provided examples from my experience of being a university faculty liaison with urban schools moving toward site-based management.

Status quo. We are all familiar with the status quo. Things operate as usual, and we know what to expect, which may be that problems will pop up daily. The status quo may be very painful, yet is known and feels safe. Although we may realize that change is needed, we are fearful because we do not know what will happen if we move out of our comfort zones, even if they are unhealthy and unreasonable.

When an individual, family, or group such as a school consciously chooses to reach out toward something different, the motivation to do so generally stems from one of three stimuli. An individual, family, or group, such as a school or a team within a school, will want to change because the way things are operating is intolerable. Another version is that an individual, family, or group sees a possibility for something more enriching. Here, the vision of one person or group can provide the necessary motivation for change to begin. In the last version, the individual, family, or group is experiencing so much pain that it feels as if change must occur.

When I was a liaison with urban schools, the motivation for change came from the second stimulus, a vision. In this case, a grant provided funds to link schools with university liaisons and training so that site-based management could evolve more easily. The schools decided whether or not they bought into the vision.

Obviously, the three motivations mentioned go against the homeostasis described in Appendix A. It is not unusual for the problem that initiates a change process to relate to coping mechanisms that once served a useful purpose but no longer meet the needs of the individual or group. Whatever the motivation, in this first conscious stage of change people must become aware of what no longer functions to serve them. Because people fear change, they will resist (see preceding section on resistance) coming into awareness about their current function/dysfunction.

When people are in this phase of resisting yet obviously needing to grow, the change-master serves the growth process best by instilling visions for new possibilities. Imagery exercises are useful for this purpose. Imagery speaks to the deeper self, and that part of the self that has hope can speak to the part of the self that is fearful. In a group, the change-master can ask one person to take the hopeless and fearful side with regard to a proposed change and another person to respond from the hopeful or visionary side. Fear must be validated and not squashed before moving forward. Once the fear is validated, it becomes possible to dream of new possibilities. Some Native American tribes have *dream catchers* (Malatchi, 1997) that serve this purpose. It is important to unleash the process of dreaming for change to move forward.

Questions for the change-master to pose to facilitate the process of dreaming were offered by Dodson (1991):

1. "If I visited you and the change that you want had happened, what would I see?"

2. "If you had a magic wand and could make one thing different in your life (in your family [team/school]), what would you most want to make different? If that were different, how would that help you?" (p. 124)

Dodson indicated that it is important to be very aware of the body language of the person who is responding to these questions. It is possible to see fear and gauge your next response accordingly. Again, fear must be validated, or it will control the process of change. Empathy as well as patience are also important for change-masters. When this level of sensitivity is displayed, individuals within groups will begin to trust the leader and the relationship will deepen, a necessary ingredient for later stages in the process. The leader serves as a partner in exploring the new possibilities by encouraging the people involved to see, hear, feel, know, and share their experiences as well as their desires.

With the group having moved this far, the next step is to explore more deeply the nature of the status quo. What has been implied can be made explicit. What has been unconsciously done can be brought into awareness. Then a conscious choice can be made for growth and change. The change-master will find the techniques of reframing and metaphor, discussed in Chapter 13, useful in this stage.

Satir had a few particular examples that she used in this phase (Dodson, 1991). In demonstrating the status quo, Satir would speak about a mobile over a baby's crib and how all the figures in their place kept it in balance. Removing one would affect all the others, and the status quo would be disrupted. She likened this to what happens when change affects members within a family or teams within a school.

A second image Satir used was that of a teeter-totter with a heavy person on one side and a light person on the other. The heavier person, sitting close to the center for balance, is not having much fun. The lighter person, having to lean far back, is on the edge. Neither person is in a comfortable position, although they are keeping things balanced. She used this imagery to help others recognize the price that is paid for balance.

Satir's third image was that of an individual (and I would add group, team, or school) standing in concrete. The individual may be upright, but he or she cannot move. This very real imagery conjures up feelings of entrapment, of being frozen or stifled.

Generally, a change-master will offer an image and will then invite those involved to bring their own images to the table, making the exercise more meaningful. The images offered by the group members speak to the deeper self and, therefore, have more power to catalyze energy for change.

During this stage, as well as all the others, it is important that the leader accept the experiences shared and not judge, criticize, or put anyone down either verbally or nonverbally. Satir believed that all human beings have the capacity for change and that anything anyone has done can be rehabilitated. The more successful change-masters are those who are able to accept and forgive as well as nurture and support.

Introduction of the foreign element and resistance. The next stage in Satir's model of growth and change involves the introduction of a foreign element and resistance to that element. Foreign elements include new as well as inner desires to make changes. Resistance to change, described in a preceding section of this chapter, is an expected and normal part of the process of change. Satir (1988) referred to this stage as reshaping the status quo.

Change involves a form of loss or death of a part of the self or loss of the typical patterns for functioning in a group. In the same way that the body rejects a transplanted organ, we will resist and reject changes in our typical patterns. We are not comfortable wearing, and do not want to wear, a "tight, new pair of shoes." When we resist change, we are trying to maintain balance or homeostasis.

Change-masters need to be attuned to the natural tendency people have to direct their discomfort with change toward the agent of change. People may express anger toward or criticize the leader of change. The change-master may feel inadequate or think he or she is not doing things the right way. Alternatively, he or she may view the individual, family, or group/team as impossible. These are all signals that the group is in the stage of resistance. In this stage, it is important for the change-master to be in a place of nonattachment to the results of the change process.

When I served as a faculty liaison in urban schools, I experienced the discomfort of the professionals the planning and management team were attempting to "bring on board." The team members, a vital and energized group of trained professionals, were excited about the prospects of site-based management. At 3:00 on a Friday afternoon, they asked me to make a presentation at an in-service the following Monday morning to explain more about the process to their colleagues. Needless to say, it was a setup. Fortunately for me, I had been trained in Seymour Sarason's psychoeducational model during my doctoral program at the University of Kansas. I knew what to expect, even if I could not mitigate the losses I anticipated.

I was the brunt of some very strong anger. There were teachers sitting in the back of the room doing other things and not participating in the experiential exercises. This was obviously the norm in the school, as everyone acted as if "the Elephant in the Cafeteria wasn't there"! I stayed steady, did my best to be authentic, and discussed the situation with the principal during a break. She had never dealt with the nonparticipating teachers successfully and referred to them as her nemesis. It appeared that I was experiencing guilt by association.

The change-master during this stage must draw on his or her personal sense of satisfaction and appreciation. He or she must be self-supporting rather than dependent upon others for recognition. Aligning with the momentum of positive energetic change is critical, whether it is with an individual or group/team. Almost paradoxically, the leader must also be aware of and honor the fear others have about change. Change is a *both/and* proposition—both hopeful and anxiety provoking.

A graphic way of depicting the pull on individuals at this stage is to have one person stand up, have a second person, representing the force for hope, pull that person from the front, and have a third person, representing the force of fear and speaking in *shoulds* and *oughts,* pull the person from behind. The change-master would focus all three on how it feels to be in their respective positions and may have two of the people dialogue with *each other.* Satir also was known to have a fourth person play the observing ego or evolved self. This part would speak with the other parts and provide advice when a stalemate occurred as well as at other opportune times.

It is also beneficial for the change-master to help the individual or group/team focus on the courageous aspect of the self that has chosen to be involved in the change process. The person or group/team could be asked to get in touch with the courageous aspect of the self and journal or dialogue out loud with that part of the self, moving back and forth from the fear part to the courageous part.

Also, the change-master might find an opportunity to address the fear and hopelessness that runs deep in some people and groups. If a person were to say, "I don't know what makes you think anything will be any different," the change-master could respond with a more direct statement like, "It sounds as if you think I may fail you as others have and then you will be in a worse place because you would have made another commitment and be disappointed again." Satir said such interaction allows the leader to *make contact* with the person. It allows the change-master to go beyond the resistance and be in a deeper place with the person's fears and losses, rather than with the anger often stirred in resistance. It also allows for contact with the higher self of the person, that which the person is capable of becoming.

Chaos. Whereas the status quo is predictable and comfortable, Satir's third stage, chaos, is anything but that. It is not unusual for individuals, families, teams, and schools to ask for help with change when they are in crisis. Often, what they are really seeking is help in returning to the homeostasis that preceded the crisis. Yet, the crisis may be the very thing that will allow for a shift in a healthier direction that will move the individual or group past where things were before the crisis and into an improved pattern of being. Thus crisis, which the Chinese depict as two characters, brings both danger and opportunity.

Crises signal a need for people to listen more deeply, whether to the deeper self or to others. A responsibility of the change-master at this stage is to help people listen more deeply, thus helping them move toward new possibilities. As in the previous stage, imagery is helpful because it speaks to the deeper self. It is also important for the change-master to know and communicate to others that chaos is a positive and necessary step in the right direction. I recall Satir saying something like, "I am concerned when everything is going along well because when there is no chaos, there is no change."

Feeling vulnerable is part and parcel of this stage. Thus, another task of the change-master is to help people feel safe. If the change-master can protect people from being harmed by others, through reframing and other means, he or she will be more successful in charting these turbulent waters. If people open up to their vulnerabilities, they will more likely discover their inner truths.

When people feel vulnerable, they may get upset and sound off. When someone over-reacts in this way, the leader needs to do some detective work to determine what set the person off. It may be that a situation recreated an earlier wound, and the infusion of energy was really related to past history. The person may not even realize he or she was over-reacting. It may help to direct the person who is upset to look within, to be still in order to see what is underneath the expression of feelings in the outburst. Going deeper will certainly bring another foreign element into play, but that is part of the movement forward. Most people will need time to reflect on such circumstances before they will be able to use them to move forward in their growth process.

Because individuals and teams may perceive this stage as a backward movement, it is incumbent upon the change-master to frame the chaos as necessary. It is helpful to have mentioned ahead of time, during Stages 1 and 2, that chaos is predictable and painful and necessary for growth. When people experience what was expected, it is usually easier to frame the experience in a more positive manner.

The change-master must remain rock solid during this stage. Serving as a model, the leader helps people move into and through fear-based views of the world. Being congruent (see Chapter 13) is a necessity. While remaining neutral and nonjudgmental, the leader can point out the dysfunctional stances described in previous chapters.

Satir (1983a) maintained that "the problem is not the problem." It is the way of coping with the concern that is the problem. This is true in all domains. To help people change unhealthy coping mechanisms, the change-master can encourage them to honor the five freedoms, remain congruent, and help them be in touch with their inner experiences as well as their feelings about these experiences. The feeling about the feeling is important. It is one thing to feel angry and another to feel guilty about feeling angry. Once these feelings are discovered, coping mechanisms used in the past can be changed.

Chaos theory is a current interpretation disorder with a systems perspective. Professionals from many different fields of science theorize in order to make sense of the world. For a long time, scientists theorized about the world as predictable. In chaos theory, scientists look at nature as complex and dynamic, and they see it as whole. Chaos theory holds that underneath disorder and unpredictability is pattern. One must wade through the disorder to find the pattern. Similarly, where change is concerned, disorder is part and parcel of the movement forward, and those involved must learn to flow with the disarray or at least to tolerate it as a necessary step in the right direction.

During the chaos stage, I always try to remember that the worst that can happen is that things will return to the way they were before. This helps me to not become overwhelmed by the chaos or its impact upon others. In one of the urban schools for which I served as faculty liaison, I was careful to predict the stage of chaos ahead of time. The members of the planning and management team, aware of the necessity for chaos, would joke about this "sign of progress" and stay centered, while the rest of the school professionals lumbered about, trying to avoid ownership of the site-based concept.

In the same school, I advocated that I or someone else facilitate a workshop during which people who were not on board would be given the opportunity to place their fears and frustrations on the table. I got nowhere with this idea and had to let it go. The school professionals were not ready for that much authenticity and had not reached a point of trusting me, or anyone else on the team, enough to let all of their negative feelings about site-based management surface. There was even resistance to that level of intimacy within the planning and management team. Members of the team feared that opening themselves up would result in the creation of bigger barriers rather than the breaking down of barriers. From that response, I unfortunately went into a place of less hope and pulled back from my involvement. I do not believe it is possible for individuals to effect authentic, system-wide change if they are holding back out of a realistic fear of reprisal.

New integration and practice. This stage is a time of growing comfort with the new. The old, automatic responses and ways of interacting and doing things have gone, and new possibilities have replaced them. Hope is rebirthed, and it feels a little like springtime internally. Once the individual, family, team, or group has moved out of chaos, it is time to integrate and practice the new patterns. Practice is necessary to validate, confirm, and reconnect to oneself and others. It is a time of being conscious of one's actions and not doing things on automatic pilot.

In this phase the change-master needs to remove him- or herself from a directive role and turn power over to the individuals, group, or team. In my role as faculty liaison, I had the experience in one school of observing the principal rotate out of the responsibility for facilitating the planning and management team meeting. The principal consciously chose to continue being just another voice on the team. The team eventually moved on without her presence as facilitator. While she would have been ill-advised to be absent frequently during the first three stages, I always considered it a gift that she was not always present during later stages because it showed her respect for the team process in decision making, and it helped the team members absorb the new possibility—that of leadership being everyone's responsibility.

As part of the shift in power, the change-master needs to restrict him- or herself to asking questions rather than answering them. In the school just mentioned, I frequently had to bite my tongue when I was asked "how things *should* work" by the team members. Whereas in the earlier stages I needed to play a more direct role, the point of moving to site-based management was to empower people and to share leadership so that the ownership would flow over and result in better things happening for the students. My stance, as well as the principal's, allowed the team to practice their new ways of being together and their newly established patterns of shared leadership and it gave them the opportunity to learn from their mistakes as well as their successes.

The change-master's role at this stage is to cheer and validate the new growth by pointing it out and focusing on it in concrete ways. At the opening meeting of the planning and management team in the second year of my involvement with one school, I chose to use my part of the meeting to share a list of all the things that I thought the team had learned and the processes that were working well for them as a leadership team. Equally important is to support people in authentic ways when they are straying off target or reverting to old patterns. Without support, the person or group may, out of fear, revert to the old ways. The role of the change-master is exquisite when done well. It is a matter of being totally present, aware, and supportive.

In one school, when we were in this phase of practice, I did take a directive role in recommending that the team look at the process they were now using in comparison to what they had earlier identified as their preferred pattern. Team membership had become so large that participation had dropped off. Furthermore, the team members had become overworked from what seemed to me to be too frequent meetings and had lost some of their enthusiasm. When presented with my observations, they agreed that I was on target. We moved to reduce membership and meet less frequently. The results were positive for all involved.

The new status quo. The adage "Good better best, never let it rest, until the good is better and the better best" fits in this final stage of Satir's growth model. The practice has paid off, and people are no longer in danger of regressing to their old patterns. Usually people feel more creative, energetic, vital, and connected. And, as they have achieved another status quo, they eventually will move into another period of growth and change. I have worked with schools that moved quite a distance in a short time and then needed time to settle and function normally for a while. It takes considerable energy to move through planned change, and it is not necessary to be actively involved in change processes at all times. In fact, there are times when that is ill-advised.

What is important is to look underneath the new status quo situation and see what is driving it. If fear lurks, it is a signal that people are not being authentic or not listening deeply to themselves and others. It signals that there is an imbalance, and in such cases it is important to move into a new process of change. Renewal is the catchword of the day, and its importance can't be overemphasized in the context of the ever-changing universe to which we all must respond. It is infinitely possible to be growing while maintaining a form of status quo. Staying in touch with one's experiences—what one sees, hears, thinks, feels, wants—and commenting on them is critical to healthy living.

I have found Virginia Satir's model for growth to be one that makes intuitive sense. I have also found it to be an excellent resource when professionals want me to consult with them on organizational transformation. I teach the model to prospective leaders at the university and always find that it opens doors rather than closes them. If leadership is everyone's responsibility, which I believe it is, then the model provides vital information for everyone.

I leave you with one of my favorite readings. Attributed to Lao Tzu in the sixth century B.C., it speaks to the heart of my vision of leadership. For anyone wishing to implement systems models, perspectives, and approaches in their work lives, this philosophy of leadership will serve you well. It is a philosophy I adopted long ago. Like a compass, it helps me find my center on a daily basis.

Of the best leaders, the people only know that they exist.
The next best they love and praise,

And the next they fear and revile.
When they do not command the people's faith
Others will lose faith in them and resort to recriminations
But of the best, when their work is done
The people will all remark, "we have done it ourselves."

SUMMARY

I believe in possibilities. Experience has taught me that challenges can be met and that barriers can be broken. Books and articles abound on change. Change is a way of life, and problems associated with change are expected as well as predictable. The effort to use family systems concepts and approaches with at-risk and special-needs students will have a better chance for survival if professionals are more aware of the aspects of change and understand the implications of these aspects in school settings.

Dr. Debbie Daniels-Mohring, co-author of the first edition of this text, and I are available to help you find family systems professionals within your state who can provide consultation or training in this field. Family systems approaches can make a significant contribution to your at-risk and special-needs students. Furthermore, all of your students will benefit from such growth and development by the professional staff. I wish you the best in your endeavors to implement change and benefit from the knowledge of family systems concepts in your life and schools.

EXTENSION ACTIVITY

Know, Want to Know, Learned (KWL): You may want to revisit the KWL list you composed at the end of Chapter 1 and then discuss or reflect on what you have learned. Musing about what more you now *want to know* may help focus your continuing education.

Part IV
Family Systems
Case Study

15 • Case Study

Case Study

This case study is intended to consolidate your understanding of the principles discussed in this book. It illustrates how family of origin issues (Chapter 4) can affect a nuclear family many generations in the future. The concepts of family structure (Chapter 3) and the family life cycle (Chapter 2) are clear in this family's issues, surrounding lack of parental cohesion and the relocation of the family. The effects of socioeconomic and cultural concerns (Chapter 5) upon the type of intervention planned for this family are also portrayed. The contribution of the mother's depression and the family's rigidity (Chapters 6 and 7) to this boy's symptoms are examined as well. Finally, the case illustrates the role of the school professional in networking and family referral (Chapter 9) as well as collaboration with the family and outside professionals.

SCHOOL INTERVENTIONS

This case involves a 13-year-old boy, Mike, who was referred for therapy by his school counselor. The presenting problem was Mike's refusal to go to school; it had lasted six months. Before referring Mike for outpatient psychotherapy, school professionals had attempted the following interventions:

1. Phone contacts to the mother, Mrs. Wright, from Mike's teachers and the school principal asking about his health and offering assistance.

2. Letters to the family from the school principal and county superintendent of schools requesting that the parents contact school officials about their son's repeated absences.

3. Referral to a child study team who had enlisted Mike, after 3 months of absence, in homebound instruction. The referral for psychotherapy was made after 6 months'

absence as was a request for the therapist's opinion about whether homebound instruction should be continued.

4. Referral to a probation officer for school truancy.

The latter intervention resulted in a home visit by the probation officer and threats of a jail term for the mother if Mike did not begin attending school. However, there had been no follow-through on these threats.

HISTORICAL INFORMATION

The outpatient therapist initially met with Mrs. Wright to gather information about Mike's problem. Although the appointment had been scheduled for both parents, Mrs. Wright stated that her husband refused to attend therapy. The therapist then made contact with Mike's school counselor and his probation officer. From these three conversations, the therapist had gathered the following information about Mike and his family:

Mike was the youngest of three sons of Mr. and Mrs. Wright. His parents had been high-school sweethearts and had married immediately following their graduation from high school. They had been married for 22 years and lived in the same home in a small town in rural Georgia for all of that time. Both sets of Mike's grandparents also lived in this town and maintained close ties with Mike's nuclear family. The family genogram is depicted in Figure 15.1

Mr. Wright was the older of two boys; Mrs. Wright was the youngest of three girls. She was extremely close to her family, the Thomases. She reported having at least one telephone conversation with each sister and her mother every day since her marriage. The

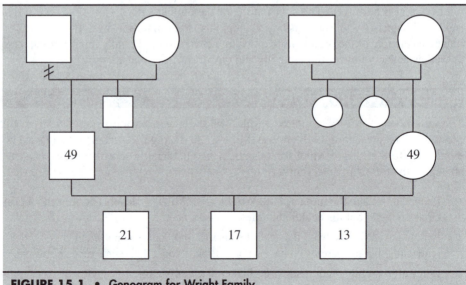

FIGURE 15.1 • Genogram for Wright Family

Thomas family attended the same church as the Wrights and shared in socializing and entertainment. In addition, when her boys were growing up, Mrs. Wright shared baby-sitting with her sisters and mother. As she was the only sister who was not employed outside of the home, Mrs. Wright kept her sister's children during the week and allowed her children to spend time with her parents and sisters on the weekends. Mrs. Wright described her father as a "stable, devoted" man who supported the family and "spoiled" her. He owned a store in the community and was well respected.

Mr. Wright's family was involved with Mike's family through more "male" activities. The uncle and Mr. Wright took the boys fishing or hunting and attended sporting events together. Mr. Wright was close to his mother, who had worked two jobs all of her life to support him and his brothers. Mr. Wright had served the function of "man of the house" since his father, who was an alcoholic, disappeared when Mr. Wright was 6 years old and left the family penniless. Mr. Wright had worked after school and became a manager in a local grocery store. If he had not met his wife and decided to get married, he had planned to go to college on a business scholarship provided by the store. As it was, he was a married man and a father within a year of graduation. He had stayed with the grocery store for 22 years and remained a manager.

According to Mrs. Wright, she had never learned to drive because she had always depended upon her husband or family for transportation. She had never worked outside of the home, although her sisters had paid her for baby-sitting their children while they were working. In addition, her father gave her money whenever she asked. Mrs. Wright used her creative energies to sew, cook, garden, and make crafts. She stated that she had always kept busy with these activities because her husband had worked 60 to 70 hours a week for most of their married life.

HISTORY OF PRESENTING PROBLEM

By 1996 Mike's father had saved enough money to buy his own store. This had been a dream of his for a long time. When he finally had enough money in savings, he began a search for a good investment opportunity. Although he looked, there were no such opportunities available in the small town in which he and his family lived. After a year of searching, he found a gas station for sale in the suburbs of Atlanta, about 80 miles from his hometown. Against his wife's wishes, he bought the business 6 months later. In May 1997, he and his oldest son left for Atlanta to work in the gas station. May through August of that year, Mr. Wright and the eldest son lived in an apartment in Atlanta, while Mrs. Wright and the 17- and 13-year-old sons remained in their home.

The business took almost all of Mr. Wright's time, and he was unable to travel home during these 4 months. Mrs. Wright and one of her sisters came to Atlanta for a weekend and Mrs. Wright decided that she "hated the city." However, when she confided to her mother and sisters that she missed her husband, they urged her to move to Atlanta and support his decision. In September, the eldest son moved back into the family home and began attending a local junior college, Mrs. Wright and Mike moved to Atlanta, and the 17-year-old son moved in with his maternal grandparents so that he could complete his senior year of high school in the same school.

Mike was enrolled in the eighth grade in a large suburban high school. His mother took him to school on the first day to make sure that he arrived safely. He attended that one day of school and refused to return to the high school for the next 6 months. At first, Mike had complained of being ill. His aunt came to Atlanta to get him and took him back to their home-town to see the family doctor. He was pronounced healthy and was urged to return to school.

After a month's absence, Mike's father began urging him to return to school. Accord-ing to Mrs.Wright, Mr. Wright threatened Mike with grounding, removal of his allowance, and finally physical punishment. Mrs. Wright, who described her husband as "hot tem-pered," forbade her husband to spank Mike. In addition, although Mike was grounded by his father, it was Mrs. Wright who was left to enforce the grounding while her husband worked in the store. Because Mrs. Wright felt sorry for Mike, she was never able to stick to her guns about grounding him.

When Mr. Wright discovered that Mike and his mother had been returning to their hometown on weekends and Mike had been allowed to spend time with his friends, he became angry and confronted his wife. She accused him of being gone all the time and being unwilling to give her emotional support. She stated that she was not able to deny Mike time with his friends because she thought he was refusing to go to school because he was depressed about moving. She hoped that if he spent time enjoying himself, he would become less depressed and more accepting of the move. In her eyes, he would then return to school voluntarily.

Mr. Wright, who felt that Mike's refusal to attend school was rebellious in nature, then withdrew even more from the family. According to his wife, he had become angry and sullen when he was home and often drank too many beers. He began working longer and longer hours; the mother and Mike spent more and more time together watching soap operas and playing cards. Neither one of them had made friends in their new neighbor-hood, and neither one of them were able to drive. Mrs. Wright and Mike continued to return to their hometown every weekend, without Mr. Wright.

DIAGNOSIS

Mrs. Wright, who was very dependent and lonely, was overinvolved with Mike. She depended upon him for her daily entertainment and company. Mike's symptom served the function of keeping her busy and helping her avoid confronting her own loneliness and the distance in her marriage. Mrs. Wright was aligned with the sibling subsystem in a coali-tion against the father. Mr. Wright, the functioning parent, was undermined by this alliance. He became ineffective and withdrew from interaction with both his wife and Mike. In addition, Mrs. Wright's family of origin was involved in undermining Mr. Wright by continuing to provide transportation and money to her and Mike.

INTERVENTION

The therapist asked Mrs. Wright's permission to contact her husband at work and request his presence at a meeting concerning his son. Contrary to his wife's characterization of him, Mr. Wright was more than willing to attend the meeting. He talked to the therapist at length about his frustration regarding his son and said that he would be willing to do anything that would solve the problem. The therapist then scheduled a meeting, at the high school, to include the child study team, the homebound teacher, the parents, the probation officer, and Mike.

During the first part of the meeting, Mike was asked to wait outside. The therapist made this request purposefully to indicate to Mike that he was not part of the executive subsystem and that the adults would make the decision as to how to proceed with his problem. In addition, excluding him from this part of the meeting broke up the alliance between Mike and his mother.

The meeting began with a ventilation of feelings of frustration on the part of the parents, teachers, and probation officer. The therapist then asked questions about Mike's intelligence and physical and emotional development. As the meeting progressed, it became clear to everyone that Mike was capable of attending high school. However, the homebound instructor said that Mike was not motivated and that, even with the one-to-one attention, he was not keeping up with his school assignments. The therapist began to reframe Mike's problem as a developmental lag. The therapist used evidence that had been presented by those present to convince the parents that Mike needed to be given nurturing, support, and structure to begin to grow up and face the challenges of being a high-school student. The explanation was centered on Mike's need, like that experienced by younger children, for structure and help in becoming motivated to complete homework, chores, and other skills of growing up.

With this reframe in mind, the therapist advised that Mike had not been receiving enough structure and reinforcement. The parents were asked if they would be willing to work together to provide for these needs. In step one of the intervention, the mother was assigned as Mike's homebound instructor. She agreed to structure a mock classroom for teaching Mike about attending school and growing up. For 6 hours per day, she was to instruct Mike in his various high-school subjects. The probation officer agreed that if the mother were tutoring her son, the threats and charges against her regarding the truancy would stop. Mike's teachers agreed to provide weekly lesson plans for her to follow, and the homebound tutor agreed to come to her home once a week to help her plan assignments and clarify any information about which she was unclear. In addition, the teachers offered to be available by telephone if Mrs. Wright had any questions about assignments. The purpose of this intervention was to intensify Mike's and his mother's dependency upon one another so that they would, eventually, become unhappy with this arrangement.

Step two was to elicit the father's help. He agreed to be in charge of waking Mike up each morning and helping him get showered, dressed, and fed in preparation for his day at "school." Because the father needed to be at his store by 7:00 each morning, Mike's school day was scheduled to begin by 7:30 and end at 2:30, with an hour break for lunch. This intervention was designed to decrease the distance between Mike and his father and to give Mrs. Wright the message that she was supported by her husband.

Step three was to define Mike's visit to his hometown each weekend as "confusing" to a child with his "delayed developmental level." If he was to be helped to adapt to his new home and to the structure of school, he needed to have the stability that living in one place provided. In this regard, the mother agreed that they would visit their hometown only every other weekend and then only for a day. Mike, because of his "delays," needed to sleep in the same house consistently. Mr. Wright agreed to take Sundays off and spend time with his wife and Mike. He also agreed to begin exploring options for a local church with his family.

This three-part intervention served many purposes. By identifying Mike as "delayed," the team created a situation in which the only way Mike could convince the adults otherwise was to return to school. As long as he was "delayed," he was "incapable" of spending every weekend in his hometown. Thus, he was, essentially, put on the same grounding schedule that his father had threatened but ostensibly for very different reasons. It was hypothesized that if Mrs. Wright and Mike were no longer able to get their social needs met on weekends in their hometown, they might begin to search for connections with other people in Atlanta. Finally, Mr. Wright agreed to become more involved with and supportive of his wife so that her loneliness would decrease and her need for Mike as her support system would diminish.

As the final step in the intervention, Mike was asked to join the meeting. His position as the baby of his family was emphasized, and he was told the reframe that his school refusal indicated his "delay in growing up." His parents then advised him of the plan that had been designed by the adults and pledged their mutual support of his efforts to "catch up" in development. Clearly, Mike was less than happy about these proceedings.

OUTCOME

After 2 weeks of home schooling, Mike returned to high school. His mother offered to attend his first day with him, but he declined, saying that would be "babyish." His teachers introduced him as a new student who had recently moved to Atlanta so that he did not have to face the stigma of being absent for so long. In addition, Mike received supportive services from his school counselor to help him cope with joining this new social arena. With coaxing, he tried out for baseball in the spring and made the team.

Mike and his parents continued in periodic family therapy. With help, Mr. and Mrs. Wright were able to set up a reinforcement schedule for Mike through which he could earn visits to his hometown or trips to movies, sports events, and other events in Atlanta. Any absence from school, unless accompanied by high fever or vomiting, resulted in no privileges for the weekend. At first, Mike almost exclusively chose visits back "home" as his reinforcement. As time went by and he began to develop friends on his baseball team and at school, his request for visits became less frequent.

Through therapy, Mrs. Wright was helped to look at her own loneliness and isolation. She obtained a bus schedule and, with support, began shopping and sightseeing in Atlanta by herself. She asked one of her sisters to begin teaching her how to drive and got a promise from her husband that, as soon as she got her license, they would buy her a car. She began helping her husband in the store on a part-time basis. Eventually, she was able to use her skills at crafts to help him make buying and display decisions for the store. Mr. Wright continued to take Sundays off and spend them with his wife, even when Mike no longer needed the support.

This case study represents successful collaboration between the school professionals, an outpatient psychotherapist, a probation officer, and parents. Without this collaboration, the interventions would not have been possible.

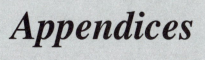

Appendices

Conceptual Frameworks of Family Systems Models

This appendix describes the conceptual frameworks of the four major family systems models: the Satir Communication Process Model, Bowen's multigenerational theory, structural family therapy, and strategic family therapy. The frameworks presented can assist in better understanding families. The explanation of each of these four models includes a brief historical account of the development of the theory as well as specific theoretical concepts and principles from each perspective. Following those descriptions is a brief section on family assessment that is new to this edition. Although not targeted by theoretical perspectives, this information may be helpful to some professionals (e.g., psychologists, social workers, counselors) working in the schools. The information in this appendix can enrich your understanding of family systems concepts and will form an important base for understanding Part I of this text, which undergirds Parts II and III.

SATIR'S PROCESS MODEL

This section overviews the Satir Communication Process Model. A brief historical account of its development is followed by a description of Satir's philosophical view of humanity, systems orientation, and homeostasis. This is followed by a description of six concepts central to Satir's work. Satir's model contrasts with the theoretical concepts of Murray Bowen's theory, which are presented next. Satir did not spend time propounding theory. Her approach was more conceptually and methodologically based than theoretically grounded.

Historical Information

Virginia Satir, like Murray Bowen, was one of the earliest pioneers in the field of family systems. She popularized the family therapy movement with her engaging presence as well as her exciting and practical methods. Her method was described by Guerin and Chabot (1992) as "highly personalized, experiential, and immensely popular" (p. 250).

Satir was a teacher from 1936 to 1941. She became interested in families while teaching children and making home visits. She later received a master's degree in social work from the University of Chicago. From 1955 to 1958 she was an instructor in the Family Dynamics Residency Program at the Illinois State Psychiatric Institute in Chicago. In 1959 Satir moved to California and joined the staff at the Mental Research Institute in Palo Alto where she developed a formal training program in family systems therapy. She left Palo Alto to join the staff at the Esalen Institute in Big Sur, California. She was director of residential training at the Esalen Institute from 1963 to 1965.

According to Guerin and Chabot (1992),

> Satir speaks of the family as a "balanced" system and, in her assessment, seeks to determine the price individual family members pay to maintain this balance. She views symptoms as blockages to growth which help to maintain the family status quo. She is more important as a skilled clinician and teacher than as an original theorist. However, her impact on the practices of family therapists was far from minor. Indeed, she may be the most influential of all the people mentioned in this chapter. (p. 250)

In 1964 Satir published the first of many books, *Conjoint Family Therapy*, which is currently in its third edition (1983b). In 1972 she published *Peoplemaking*, which was intended for the general public and written at a fifth-grade level so children could also benefit from the book. Satir continued to write a variety of professional and popular books, updating her concepts and methodology. *Peoplemaking* was published again in 1988 as *The New Peoplemaking*, an expanded version of the popular book.

Satir founded the AVANTA Network, an organization devoted to promoting her process model throughout the world, and the network continues her work today. She held month-long training seminars for professionals in the summers of 1981 through 1987 in Crested Butte, Colorado. The AVANTA Network continues to offer that training; it is one of many different training opportunities in the Communication Process Model. Satir presented a variety of other training seminars and speaking engagements around the world until she became ill in the summer of 1988. Virginia Satir died in October 1988. The January/February 1989 issue of the *Networker,* a professional journal devoted to family systems approaches, contained a tribute to Satir entitled "The Legacy of Virginia Satir." It is excellent reading for those who would like more of a flavor of her life and being.

Satir received many awards for her work. One of the most notable was being named in Germany in 1982 as one of the 10 living people who had made a positive difference in the world. Satir is remembered for her charisma, emphasis on positive intentions, solution-oriented focus on the present and future, accent on equality, and action orientation.

Background Information

Satir was assured of, and convinced about, the potential for goodness and wholeness of people and the world. She believed in human potential and the individual's ability to transform his or her own life.

A description of Satir's "ways of viewing the world" is helpful as a basis for understanding her work. According to Satir, there are two ways of viewing the world. One, which is hierarchical in nature, is known as the threat and reward model and is familiar to Americans. She referred to the other by several different terms, including the "organic and seed" model. These two ways of viewing the world were described by Satir and Baldwin (1983) in the book *Satir, Step by Step* and presented as a chart by Schwab (1990).

The threat and reward model regards people as inherently bad and weak by nature. Thus, a hierarchy is necessary to determine and maintain standards of behavior. People at the top of the hierarchy believe that they are acting for the good of all. They use rewards and punishments to enforce the standards. From this practice dominance and submission evolve. People are viewed in terms of their degree of conformity to the standards. Those at the top of the hierarchy do not take kindly to difference. In turn, they do not see themselves as individuals. Instead, they obtain their identity from their prescribed roles. For those beneath them on the hierarchy, the consequences of these ways of defining people and their relationships include stagnation, fear, despair, hopelessness, and rebellion. Those at the top may appear happier with their jobs.

In the threat and reward model, events are seen as linear. Any lack of conformity is interpreted as the hierarchy failing to maintain conformity. This cause-and-effect view of the world results in blame and fault finding. Change is not welcome because it is a threat to the status quo.

In families that operate by this model, parents are dictatorial and accept little input from their children. Family members frequently blame others; there is little acceptance of responsibility for personal behavior. Threats are common, and rules are enforced with punishments. The parents would set the standards for behavior and hold to those standards even when they no longer fit the situation. For example, a boy might be told that men do not cry. Even when a situation would legitimately warrant crying, his parents would reject that appropriate behavior.

Most school professionals have seen children who come from families that operate within this model. The children may find it confusing at schools in which rules and standards are not carved in stone and punishments are few and far between. It then becomes the task of the school professionals to work with them to help them understand expectations and disciplinary procedures that are not consistent between the home and school.

There are also some schools that function from a threat and reward model and professionals within schools who operate from such a position. Satir and Baldwin (1983) provided an example: "The student must follow directions and look at his teacher to prove that he is paying attention, regardless of whether he actually concentrates better by attending in a different way" (p. 162). The schools can expect resentment and hostility under these circumstances.

The seed model contrasts with the threat and reward model. In the seed model, people are seen as having an innate potential for goodness and wholeness. That which is unique within individuals is cause for celebration and support. People are defined in terms of their uniqueness and encouraged to know and value themselves. Relationships are based on mutual appreciation of the uniqueness of self and others and are egalitarian in nature. Change is a by-product of this way of being in the world. A growth orientation is the outcome.

The seed model is a systemic paradigm, with relationships existing between all components. Events are viewed as a result of many variables rather than being linear, as with the threat and reward model. Events within people's lives are understood as a result of complex, interrelated variables, rather than in terms of cause and effect or blame.

School professionals will find children whose families ascribe to the seed view of the world to be vastly different from those who grow up in families ascribing to the threat and reward model. Interestingly, a school system may operate from a threat and reward model and have students who have grown up with a seed model family life. Confusion will arise for students who face dramatically different sets of expectations in the two different contexts.

In reality, the contrast between these two models may not be so obvious. There are more shades of gray than there are actual extreme opposites. It is possible, however, to determine whether a person, family, or school ascribes to a threat and reward model or a seed model.

By determining the model from which the pupil comes and understanding the two models, the professional becomes better able to work with families and pupils in the school. Rather than blaming a child for not complying with the system in place, the professional can step back and recognize that the family's view has shaped the pupil's behavior. In ways that are constructive, professionals can work together to help the student be successfully educated within a system that may be quite different than the home in which the pupil has been raised.

In addition to becoming knowledgeable about these two views of humanity, it is helpful to understand Satir's perspective on systems. Satir and Baldwin (1983) stated that in a family, "every part is related to the other parts in a way such that a change in one brings about a change in all the others. Indeed, in the family, everyone and everything impacts and is impacted by every other person, event, and thing" (p. 191).

They further described two types of systems, *open* and *closed*. Closed systems operate on the rigid application of rules regardless of their appropriateness. They described the closed system as "dominated by power, obedience, deprivation, conformity, and guilt. It cannot allow any changes, for changes will upset the balance" (Satir & Baldwin, 1983, p. 192). The family members are ruled by fear, punishment, guilt, and dominance. Self-worth is quite low in these families. Symptoms develop when someone from such a system reaches the end of his or her coping abilities.

An open system is just that—open to change with changing contexts. These systems accept all expression and feelings, including hope, love, anger, frustration, sadness, joy, and compassion. As would be expected, members from such systems have higher levels of self-worth.

Satir also ascribed to the systems perspective of *homeostasis* (Guerin & Chabot, 1992). Homeostasis involves the innate tendency to establish a dynamic balance amidst changing conditions and relationships. Within families one will find that family members exhibit complementary and predictable patterns of communication. Family members operate to maintain the survival of the family and achieve balance within the family system. Satir believed that families attempt to preserve homeostasis by finding different means of adapting and adjusting to change. In particular, they establish rules for behavior as well as communication styles. From the efforts to preserve homeostasis stem behaviors that, rather than restoring homeostasis in times of transition, may actually result in symptoms. A frequent example of a symptom given by Satir was delinquency on the part of a youth. She saw delinquency as indicating imbalance in the family system.

Finally, Satir continually emphasized the *process* versus the *content* of human interactions. Her focus for intervention was the way in which family members dealt with a problem rather than the content of the problem. She was famous for saying, "The problem is not the problem; the problem is the process." She also contended that once a new process for resolving one situation was learned, then other situations could be resolved with the newly learned process.

Conceptual Understandings

Satir's two models of the world provide a background from which her family systems concepts can be appreciated. As stated earlier, Satir was pragmatically oriented rather than theoretically governed. Even so, Bernhard (1991) wrote a chapter titled "Theory and Practice of the Satir System." This section provides a framework that will allow the professional to better understand family systems and thus better profit from information contained in the remainder of this textbook.

Six of Satir's concepts are briefly described: triangles and the development of self-identity and personhood, the aspects of the self, learning and change, self-worth, rules, and communication patterns used as coping mechanisms.

Triangles and the Development of Self-Identify and Personhood

Most children have parents who provide them with the basics for human survival. Those parents also provide their initial schooling about the world. The child perceives the world through his or her senses, and anything that is not understood is fabricated. Thus, memories from the early childhood years are a combination of truth and fabrication. The child unwittingly misinterprets information while trying to make sense of what occurs in the family. The more dysfunctional the family, the more misinterpretation occurs. Frequently this misinterpretation follows the child in later life and affects his or her coping abilities. Thus, the family has the initial impact upon coping with difficulties later in life. Satir saw the:

> experience of the primary triad (father, mother, and child) as the essential source of identity of the "self." On the basis of his learning experience in the primary triad, the child determines how he fits into the world and how much trust he can put in his relationships with other people. (Satir & Baldwin, 1983, p. 170)

The patterns of responding to stress used later in life develop when the child is very young, according to Satir (Baldwin, 1991).

The child also learns about contradictions in communication or inconsistencies between what is seen and what is said or between what he or she feels and hears. An example of such an incongruent message would be a little boy noticing that his mother looked angry and wondering what was wrong. The nonverbal aspects of the communication would affect the child, who attends to voice tone, touch, and looks. The mother, whose parents had taught her that family members must never be angry, would respond by denying feeling angry and indicate that everything was fine. The child would then have to decipher that discrepancy. Further, the child probably would consider himself to be a possible cause of the anger. Such mixed messages damage the child.

In the mother-father-child triad, it is usual for one individual to feel excluded at times. If the child interprets communications between the parents as being a rejection of him or her, the child will develop a low sense of self-worth. The child learns about being included and excluded from the primary triad. These experiences help shape the personality of the child.

Also developing from the primary triad is the child's sense of personal power. There are many possible points children can learn about personal power. They might learn that they have the power to generate negative feelings between their parents. Another possibility is learning that they have no power. A third is that they can have a positive impact on their parents.

As was typical of her outlook, Satir saw the possibilities of the triad as being supportive, powerful, and resourceful. She emphasized that functional families with high levels of self-worth are cooperative and suggested cooperation as a possible goal for everyone interested in transformation. Summarizing Satir's view of the primary triad, Baldwin (1991) wrote:

> The reason Virginia Satir puts so much emphasis on the primary triad of father, mother and child is that the triad is the place where the individual begins the formation of his personhood and his self-concept. On the basis of his experience in the primary triad, the child determines his place in the world and how much he can trust his relationships with other people. (p. 29)

The Aspects of the Self

Satir used the Eastern concept of the mandala (Figure A.1) to illustrate her holistic view of the eight aspects of the self. The mandala is a symbol with concentric circles that represent parts of the whole. When taken together, these parts create more than the sum of the parts (Schwab, 1990).

As shown in Figure A.1, in Satir's conceptualization of the self has eight aspects: physical, emotional, intellectual, sensual, nutritional, interactional, contextual, and spiritual. The eight aspects interact with one another and influence the individual's health. At the center of the mandala is the core of the human being that Satir referred to as the "I Am" or the "Self." Together the eight aspects of the self and the "I am" core create a system.

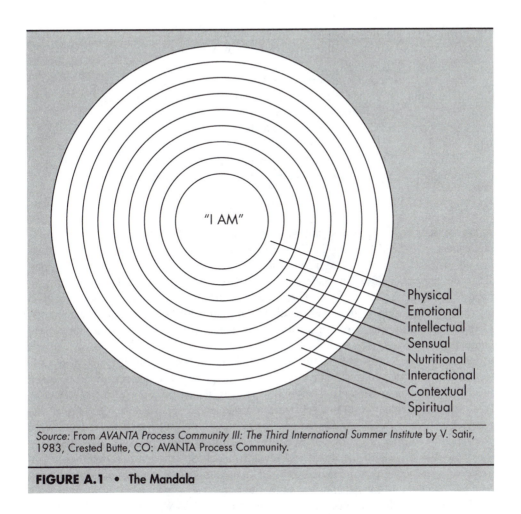

"I AM"

Physical
Emotional
Intellectual
Sensual
Nutritional
Interactional
Contextual
Spiritual

Source: From *AVANTA Process Community III: The Third International Summer Institute* by V. Satir, 1983, Crested Butte, CO: AVANTA Process Community.

FIGURE A.1 • **The Mandala**

Learning and Change

Becoming more fully human was Satir's theme. She had banners with this theme hanging in her training rooms and devoted her life to enabling people to become more fully human by learning and changing.

Some people change because they are in pain; others because they want to mature and grow (Dodson, 1991). The process of change Satir promoted was similar for both types of people. To change, individuals need to learn to feel their *life force* as well as be willing to take risks. Ability and willingness to learn at both the cognitive and emotional levels are essential.

According to Satir, we have all *learned* how to be human and we can all *learn* to be more fully human. As ingrained as some experiences from a stressful childhood might be, we have the capacity to replace our old *learnings* with new and more beneficial *learnings*.

Satir focused on learning as opposed to unlearning. She believed that old, no longer needed or wanted learnings will atrophy or fade away when they are replaced with new and more beneficial learnings.

Satir also focused on the importance of being supported when taking risks to change, although she did not negate the need for helpers to use tough love when needed. The importance of the help of others is a natural evolution from the seed model.

Satir recommended that helpers enable individuals to find their own answers as opposed to having ready-made answers and static rules for communication. Further, she believed that we all have within us answers that can be rediscovered. The helper thus assumes the role of a guide, helping the individual to find personal answers.

Self-Worth

Central to Satir's work and teaching was the concept of self-worth (I. Goldenberg & H. Goldenberg, 1991; M. West, 1991). The value an individual assigns to himself or herself, the self-love and respect that are distinct from anyone else's view of the individual, constitute the person's self-worth. Satir viewed the first 5 years of a child's life as critical when considering the level of self-worth. Later in life, significant others and a positive environment can improve the level of self-worth. Satir also believed that how a family communicates is indicative of the members' feelings of self-worth (I. Goldenberg & H. Goldenberg, 1991).

Individuals with low self-worth are anxious and unsure of themselves. They are hypersensitive to how others see them. They may interpret exclusion from a dyad as rejection and become more anxious. The eight aspects of the self are not well integrated or developed in individuals with low self-worth. These people oppose change and prefer the safety of conformity.

Parents with low levels of self-worth beget children with low levels of self-worth. These families ascribe to the threat and reward model. Submission and dominance are prevalent, and incongruent messages are common. Although Bowen used different constructs to explain this, his beliefs were similar to Satir's.

Satir believed that raising the self-worth of individuals was an essential focus for intervention. She also contended that most problems seen in therapy were associated with low self-worth. She explored this topic in depth in *The New Peoplemaking* (1988).

Rules

Each family has a set of rules unique in the expectations and standards that are set. Rules include those that are overt, such as who does what chores, and those that are covert, such as "no complaining allowed" (Satir, Bitter, & Krestensen, 1988). The rules of the system dictate how family members are defined and behave. The rules affect the expectations individuals have of others (Schwab, 1990). People assume that others have the same rules as their family. They expect to observe in the rest of the world the same situations that occurred in their families.

Indeed, rules are not only valuable they are truly necessary for survival. They establish beneficial norms for behavior. It is when rules are inflexible and rigid that they no longer benefit the individuals in the family. Those who rigidly apply the rules have damaging "shoulds," "oughts," and "musts" in their repertoire.

Satir focused her energies on helping people to transform rules they grew up with in the family. An example of a rigid rule is, "I should never complain." To never complain is not always possible or healthy. Complaining may be a significant way to lead to positive change in a situation.

The helper's role is to assist family members in knowing more about and transforming the rules that impact their lives (Schwab, 1990). With a change in the rules comes improved communication and self-worth. Part III of this text presents information on how to help families work to change ineffective or rigidly held rules.

Communication Patterns

Discussing Satir's beliefs, I. Goldenberg and H. Goldenberg (1991) related that "dysfunctional communication (indirect, unclear, incomplete, unclarified, inaccurate, distorted, inappropriate) characterizes a dysfunctional family system" (p.135). In *Peoplemaking* and *The New Peoplemaking,* Satir (1972, 1988) described four dysfunctional communication styles she found in use around the world. Established out of low self-worth, these patterns are those of the placator, the blamer, the superreasonable person, and the irrelevant person. These communication patterns are described here as they function in the family; Chapter 13 includes information on dealing with these patterns, or stances, in the schools.

These communication styles, or coping mechanisms, begin in the primary triad as a means of dealing with family stresses. To better understand the four dysfunctional stances, it is important to know about the dimensions of an interaction. Schwab (1990), as well as Satir, Stachowiak, and Taschman (1975), delineated three dimensions of all interactions: self, other, and context. The self is the communicator, the other is the person to whom the interaction is being sent, and the context is the situation in which the communication occurs. Healthy communication contains a balance of all three dimensions.

The placator, with feelings of low self-worth, will try to please others at the expense of self. Incongruent communication results when the self is denied. Placating conceals feelings of inferiority.

The blamer, also feeling low self-worth, tries to control others or is disagreeable. This person is seen by others as hostile and tyrannical. Blamers disregard the other in favor of self and context. Underneath, blamers feel vulnerable and like failures.

Superreasonables also feel diminished self-worth. They deny feelings and intellectualize. Those with whom they work might describe them as rigid, intellectual, or manipulative. The context becomes the whole focus of the superreasonable. When self and other are restrained, incongruency occurs. Superreasonable people feel very vulnerable.

The irrelevant individual, too, experiences low self-worth. Self, other, and context are all discounted in communications. This person appears erratic and inappropriate and feels anxious and lonely.

Nevertheless, congruent communication does exist. It emanates from people with high self-worth. They do not distort communication and clarify as well as improve interactions. There is a balance of self, other, and context in their communications.

All people have patterns on which they rely most heavily. In times of great stress, normally congruent people usually fall back on one of the four dysfunctional patterns. The dysfunctional patterns are complementary and systemic in nature. For example, the blamer and placator need one another to function. Satir emphasized the capacity of all people to relearn what was originally a learned communication style. She believed that individuals can learn to be congruent in their interactions and cease to rely on the four dysfunctional stances.

Although they have been quite briefly described here, Satir's concepts are highly pertinent to this text. This information is a foundation on which to build further concepts as well as methodology. Other chapters focus on how to use this foundation when working with families of at-risk and special needs children and youth.

THE BOWEN THEORY

This section provides an overview of a transgenerational process, the Bowen theory. A brief historical account of the development of this theory is presented, followed by an explanation of two variables important to understanding the Bowen theory: togetherness–separateness and intellectual–emotional functioning. This discussion is followed by a description of Bowen's eight key concepts of human functioning. An understanding of these theoretical concepts is beneficial to education professionals who are working with students who are at risk or have special needs.

Historical Information

Murray Bowen was a pioneer in the field of family systems therapy. He developed the Bowen theory between 1957 and 1966 from observations he made while examining families with a schizophrenic family member. A physician and psychiatrist, Bowen worked at the Menninger Clinic in Topeka, Kansas, and then moved to the National Institute for Mental Health (NIMH) in Washington, DC. Under Bowen's direction, whole families with schizophrenic members were hospitalized while he was working at NIMH. He was later affiliated with the Medical College of Virginia in Richmond, and finally with the Georgetown Family Center, a part of Georgetown University in Washington, DC. Bowen died in October 1990. The March/April (1991) issue of the *Family Therapy Networker,* a journal devoted to family systems approaches, contains a special feature on Bowen's life and work.

Early in the development of his theory on family systems, Bowen decided that a new language, with a systems viewpoint, would be critical for the accurate description of families. He was influenced by systemic concepts of biology, which furnished him with a framework for defining the basic concepts of his theory. Kerr and Bowen (1988) clearly stated that general systems theory is "not a satisfactory integrative theory. It is a kind of 'umbrella' theory that has been imposed on a variety of natural systems" (p. x). They further wrote that people and families are "driven and guided by processes that are 'written in nature.' In this sense, the human family is a natural system. It is a particular kind of natural system called an *emotional system*" (p. 26).

In the Bowen theory the connection between theory and practice is paramount. Theory and therapy are seen as too intertwined to separate. There is essentially no therapy without theory; theory dictates what will be accomplished in therapy. Between 1959 and 1975 Bowen developed eight concepts that constitute the core of his theory. These were described in a collection of Bowen's works, *Family Therapy in Clinical Practice,* first published in 1978.

Many influential students of Bowen continue using Bowen theory. Some of them collaborated with him until he died, and others branched off on their own over time and/or trained others. Those interested in reading the current literature that uses Bowen theory as a base are directed to the works of Betty Carter, Thomas Fogarty, James Framo, Edwin Friedman, Philip Guerin, Michael Kerr, Monica McGoldrick, Daniel Papero, Peggy Papp, Olga Silverstein, and Marianne Walters.

Background Information

According to Bowen, biological processes account for a person's affinity for individuality and togetherness. Individuals function differently based upon learning. The more emotionally reactive the person, the more the biological process has the upper hand. The more neutrality and choice the individual demonstrates, the more cognitive and feeling resources are being used.

Individuality (or separateness) and closeness (or togetherness) are two counterbalancing processes within human relationships. Rooted in instinctive drives for autonomy and connection, these forces are by nature fluid and variable. When a person experiences too much separateness, then he or she feels the desire for togetherness, and vice versa. Bowen saw the movement to seek equilibrium between these forces as characteristic of all human relationships (M. P. Nichols & Schwartz, 1995).

The opposing functions of intellect and emotion similarly seek a balance. The use of logic and reason to describe the world and behave rationally are characteristic of the intellectual system. The automatic functions of the autonomic nervous system, the instinctive states that derive from basic life processes, and the subjective, feeling states are characteristic of the emotional system. The balancing of these two systems results in a continual interplay between the functions. In Bowen theory the balance between the two is achieved when their characters are maintained as separate, interacting entities (Guerin & Chabot, 1992). An imbalance results in the loss of distinction, or fusion, of the intellectual and emotional systems. The intellectual function is abandoned, with resulting reliance on the emotional function.

Choice is limited when a person is overreliant on the emotional system. A person capable of achieving a balance between the emotional and intellectual systems is able to make choices about separateness and closeness (M. P. Nichols & Schwartz, 1995). Imbalances result in a reactive individual with little initiative for separateness. Boundaries between self and others are affected, and emotions dominate relationships. These people live in conflict, withdrawal, and dependence. Differentiated people are those who are less responsive to their emotional reactivity. That neutrality allows for choice in how to handle separateness and closeness. It stems from combining both feeling and cognitive resources.

Balancing the force for togetherness with the force for separateness as well as balancing intellectual functioning with emotional functioning are important principles to understand. Balancing or maintaining equilibrium between these two principles determines the degree of integration of a self and thus the health of the individual (M. P. Nichols & Schwartz, 1995). Different degrees of balance between togetherness-separateness and emotional-intellectual functioning are required of different relationships (Kerr, 1988). For example, in marriage one expects to see more togetherness than in friendships.

Varying movement along the continuum of togetherness and separateness and that of intellectual and emotional functioning results from the naturally occurring changing circumstances within relationships. Two main variables, the degree of anxiety and the degree of integration of self, govern the equilibrium between the intellectual and emotional systems as well as the forces toward togetherness and separateness. When anxiety is high, or chronic, the tension results in a fusion of the intellectual and emotional systems, with a concomitant increase in the togetherness force. Physical, emotional, or social symptoms are seen as a result of this fusion.

The integration of self is the ability to differentiate one's self from others. Bowen posited that the degree to which one can use intellect to monitor and control emotions while surrounded by the emotional intensity of family relationships determines one's level of integration or differentiation. Also indicative of integration of self is the ability to remain in relationships with others while maintaining a sense of self apart from others during a time of emotional intensity.

Physical, emotional, or social symptoms occur when an individual does not adapt to tension. Chronic anxiety stresses the person, and symptoms develop (Jacobson & Gurman, 1995). Substance abuse, emotional disturbances within children or their parents, and physical symptoms such as asthma and diabetes can have manifestations in school that appear to be related to stress in the home.

Theoretical Concepts

Bowen's observation of the togetherness-separateness forces as well as the intellectual-emotional systems and their relationship to the integration of self, the impact of anxiety, and the emergence of symptoms led him to develop eight key concepts of human functioning (M. P. Nichols & Schwartz, 1995). The concepts are differentiation of self, triangles, nuclear family emotional system, family projection process, emotional cutoff, sibling position, multigenerational transmission process, and societal regression. The concepts that more directly affect children will be elaborated upon in greater depth than the others in the following sections. To read the original work see Bowen (1966, 1976, 1985) and Kerr and Bowen (1988).

Differentiation of Self

Pivotal to understanding Bowen's theory is the concept of differentiation of self (Roberto, 1992). This concept describes people in terms of their ability to keep their intellectual and emotional systems from becoming fused. People whose systems are fused are dominated by the emotional system and the force for togetherness. People who are able to balance their intellectual and emotional systems are able to make choices about how they will deal with life experiences. Although differentiation describes a capacity to make a choice, Kerr and Bowen (1988) made it clear that this capacity does not determine the correct or best choice.

According to Bowen, differentiation of self and chronic anxiety are the two main variables that explain level of functioning. The level of differentiation within one's family of origin affects one's own level of differentiation (Guerin & Chabot, 1992).

Anxiety also affects one's level of differentiation of self. As Kerr (1988) stated, "Acute anxiety is fed by fear of what is; chronic anxiety is fed by fear of what might be" (p. 47). Higher levels of chronic anxiety place a greater strain on people's adaptive capabilities. Individuals who are better at differentiating between their own intellectual and emotional systems have more functional means for and choices about adapting to anxiety. They will have fewer symptoms in their lives.

In terms of understanding levels of differentiation of self, Bowen (1978) described the *solid self* and the *pseudoself*. He viewed the solid self as the part of a person that is resistant to fusion of the intellectual and emotional systems. It is able to maintain a healthy balance between the forces for togetherness and separateness. The solid self embodies the individual's beliefs, principles, attitudes, and opinions that are nonnegotiable under any circumstance.

The pseudoself is quite different (Roberto, 1992). A fusion of the processes of the emotional and intellectual system results from anxiety and stress. Bowen (1978) referred to the pseudoself as the "pretend" self. It has soft beliefs and principles; thus, it takes its beliefs and principles from someone else. The expected return for this action is belonging to the other and a sense of togetherness.

The levels of solid self and pseudoself are different among individuals and within an individual over time, depending upon life circumstances. When experiencing few stresses, an individual with a low level of solid self may appear to have a strong solid self. However, when a stressful situation results in anxiety, the actual level of the pseudoself will emerge. Having a child with a disability is an example of a stress on parents that can bring out their pseudoselves.

When the intellectual and emotional systems are fused, couples will be at the lower levels of differentiation because the emotional system will have the upper hand in the relationship. One member of the marital dyad may adapt for a long time and may even lose parts of the solid self he or she once possessed. Chronic physical illness and psychoses are examples of this situation in its most extreme form.

In the Bowen model, differentiation is separate from being an individual. Sometimes people reactively function on a pseudoself level. They claim their individuality and manifest emotional reactivity to the desires of another. Instead of being closer to the other person, they become further apart.

Triangles

Bowen saw the triangle or three-person unit as the smallest stable relationship system. In families and groups, the triangle is the basic building block of relationships; creating this type of system is part of a human's instinctive nature (Kerr & Bowen, 1988).

Bowen (1978) maintained that when anxiety is low a triangle will consist of a comfortable twosome and a less comfortable outsider. The twosome will strive to maintain togetherness. A third person is drawn in by the twosome when the anxiety level increases, which results in a lowering of anxiety within the twosome and creates a triangle. When high levels of anxiety affect the members of the triangle, the outsider position may be more attractive because the outsider can escape the intensity of anxiety.

Kerr (1988) described a typical example of how a triangle operates.

> A husband, on the outside (in fact or fantasy) of the relationship between his wife and his oldest daughter, becomes sullen. The wife predictably reacts to his sullenness by focusing more on him and attempting to cheer him up. The daughter, in reaction to being on the outside in relation to her two parents, becomes overly solicitous toward her father. The mother, reacting to being on the outside in relation to her husband and her daughter, criticizes the daughter's physical appearance. The daughter responds defensively, and she and her mother have a long discussion to resolve their differences. (p. 53)

The emotional system, with its force toward togetherness, drives triangles. Individuals who have higher levels of differentiation of self are more able to observe and handle the relationships within the triangle. Individuals with lower levels of differentiation of self, who fall back on the emotional system and need for togetherness, are reactive to any tensions within the triangle.

Kerr (1988) noted that anxiety created by family systems often spreads to outside systems. Under stress, anxiety may be spread to the schools, the workplace, or some other agency. Kerr also explained that

> parents never want such an outcome [impaired functioning] for any of their children. For the most part, they dedicate themselves to preventing it. However, their anxiety that things go well may obscure their ability to see that they are acting in ways that foster the very outcome they most want to prevent. (p. 55)

Kerr (1988) perceived triangles in families as lasting forever. He viewed the "emotional circuitry" of a triangle as outliving the people who are its members. When one family member in the triangle dies, another person generally replaces that individual. Through the generations the family members may be involved in acting out a conflict that was never resolved between grandparents or great-grandparents. As Kerr (1988) stated, "So a particular triangle was not necessarily created by its present participants; nor do triangles form anew or completely dissolve with the ebb and flow of anxiety" (p. 53).

School professionals would do well to consider Kerr's (1988) statement that "intolerance of aspects of the human process is a manifestation of being triangled into it" (p. 57). It is critical for professionals to understand human process and their own vulnerabilities and to detriangle from families. Frustrations and intolerance experienced by professionals are signs of a need for them to become better informed about human processes, in particular systemic processes, as well as to develop new ways of working with families or family members.

Nuclear Family Emotional System

This system includes processes and patterns of emotional functioning within a single generation of a family that replicate those of past generations and will be repeated in future generations. Bowen contended that individuals with similar levels of differentiation marry one another. Spouses with higher levels of differentiation balance their emotional and intellectual systems with little fusion. They generally have few problems in their marriage. Spouses with lower levels of differentiation, with fusion of the emotional and intellectual systems, have more pseudo-self than solid self. For them, each process or pattern of symptoms is magnified by anxiety.

The patterns or processes of symptoms fall into three categories of dysfunction within the nuclear family: marital conflict, illness in a spouse, and impairment of one or more children. The symptoms are physical illness, emotional illness, or social illness. All of these are viewed through the family systems lens as being linked to the same basic patterns of emotional functioning within the nuclear family. In other words, the patterns that contribute to the development of an emotional illness are the same as those that contribute to a physical or social illness. Kerr and Bowen (1988) made it clear, however, that "this does not mean that patterns of emotional functioning in a family cause physical, emotional, or social illness; the creation of a specific illness depends on the combination of many factors" (p. 164). More on the impairment of children is found in Chapter 4.

Family Projection Process

This process was first described by Bowen in 1966. In later writings, Kerr and Bowen (1988) subsumed this concept under the concepts of *nuclear family emotional system* and *differentiation of self.*

The family projection process begins with anxiety in the mother regarding some aspect of her child's functioning, which the child responds to with anxiety. The mother might become anxious about something her child said or did, something she feared her child might say or do, or something she imagined her child to have said or done. The child's anxious response is interpreted by the mother as a problem with the child. The mother might become overprotective in response to the child. Her view of the child stems more from her own anxiety than from the child. However, the mother begins to act as though her view of the child is truth. Eventually the child acts like the mother's image, and the mother begins to calm down. With the mother's greater calm comes the child's greater calm. Finally the child internalizes the mother's perception and behaves like the mother's picture of the child.

Bowen contended that the family projection process is part of every family, varying in content and degree. The content within the same family even varies from child to child. Parents may become anxious about a particular trait or behavior in one child and about a different trait or behavior in another child. Kerr and Bowen (1988) stated that "the mother is not malicious; she is just anxious. She is as much a prisoner of the situation as the child" (p. 201). This realization can help school professionals to be nonjudgmental and more patient while working with parents.

Emotional Cutoff

This theoretical concept, which Bowen added to his theory in the 1970s, describes a way of gaining distance from fusion in the family of origin. Cutoffs range from minor to major significance. The person who institutes the cutoff is trying to reduce anxiety. The cutoff may in fact reduce anxiety; however, that is not always the case. Not dealing with a difficult situation is relatively easy for most people. It can also result in losing potentially positive relationships and support as well as opportunities for learning about oneself within the context of the family.

Emotional cutoff describes the manner in which people deal with emotional reactivity between the generations. The greater the emotional reactivity, or fusion, the higher the probability that the two generations will cut off. Cutoffs occur in the forms of both physical distance and emotional withdrawal.

As Kerr (1981) indicated, emotional cutoff reflects a problem of fusion, solves a problem with distance, and creates another problem. Cutoffs are only temporary solutions; the unresolved emotional attachment to the parent continues despite the child's determination to distance from it. In the future the unresolved emotional attachments are carried over into the child's own marriage or parenting, and the fusion continues. When people use cutoff as a means of dealing with the past, they are using emotional distance in the present. The lower the level of differentiation, the more one can be expected to see cutoff used as an attempt to gain distance.

Adolescence is a time of particular emotional vulnerability. Choosing friends of which their parents disapprove, getting into trouble with the law, and abusing substances are ways adolescents try to cut off from parents. This declaration of independence from family is not the same as differentiation of self. It in no way resolves the emotional fusion with the parent.

Sibling Position

Bowen based his understanding of sibling position on the original work of Walter Toman (1969), in which Toman delineated 10 important categories of sibling position that affect future relationships. The latest edition of Toman's text was published in 1993. Bowen (1978) stated that there was no single piece of information more important to understanding family systems functioning than the sibling position of family members in present and past generations.

The Bowen theory stresses the importance of understanding functional sibling position when diagnosing emotional reactivity. A child might function as an oldest child in terms of responsibility or as a youngest child in terms of impulsivity, risk-taking, and dependency. Bowen saw shifts in the functional nature of sibling positions as resulting from the family projection process within the family of origin. When siblings function as would be expected by their sibling position, there is likely a low incidence of projection and higher level of differentiation within the family.

Also important is the degree to which an individual actually fits the profile that would be expected. If an oldest child acted more like a youngest child, the hypothesis would be that the oldest child was the focus of the family projection process. An exaggeration of the characteristics, such as a youngest child being extremely impulsive, leads to the observation that there was a high level of fusion in the family of origin and present marriage.

Multigenerational Transmission Process

This concept describes the family projection process through multiple generations. Children who are the object of the family projection process will have a lower degree of differentiation than their parents. Then, as adults, they will project emotional reactivity and lower levels of differentiation on their own children, and that will be passed down to the next generation (M. P. Nichols & Schwartz, 1995). Bowen believed that as lower and lower levels of differentiation emerged, a schizophrenic child would develop. He indicated that it would take 8 to 10 generations to produce a schizophrenic individual.

The concept of multigenerational transmission centers on a gradual regression to lower levels of differentiation and emotional reactivity, with the fusion of the intellectual and emotional systems being passed through successive generations. Bowen contended that individuals marry individuals with an equivalent degree of differentiation. Thus, their children would be expected to develop the same or a lower level of differentiation than the parents.

In accordance with Bowen theory, professionals within the schools need to realize that what is observed in the classroom is the result of many generations of this transmission process. This perspective makes it easier to be patient with and understand families and their schoolchildren.

Societal Regression

The last of Bowen's eight theoretical concepts, societal regression, is based upon the degree of anxiety in society. Bowen hypothesized that the same process of gradual regression to lower functioning that occurs in families is also occurring in society. When there is increasing chronic societal anxiety, society reacts with decisions based on emotion rather than intellect. This process parallels the fusion of the emotional and intellectual systems that leads to lower levels of differentiation and inability to define a self.

In 1978 Bowen published a text with a chapter titled "Societal Regression as Viewed Through Family Systems Therapy." In this chapter he outlined the reasons for his belief that society is regressing. In particular he pointed to the environmental crisis people have created, the increase in crime and the use of drugs, as well as the new norms for sexuality. He predicted a series of crises before a major final crisis prior to the middle of the 21st century. Those who survive will, he predicted, be the ones "who can live in better harmony with nature" (p. 281).

The concept of societal regression may not be relevant to understanding families with children having special needs; however, it does demonstrate the value of understanding systems theory. It is easier to understand any system, such as cultures, institutions, businesses, or schools, when one understands theory from the perspective of the smallest relationship system, the family. The concepts of family systems enable professionals to better understand other systems in which they live and work as well as the people found in those systems, including themselves.

STRUCTURAL FAMILY THERAPY

This section provides an overview of the conceptual framework undergirding structural family therapy. A brief historical account of the development of this model is presented, followed by a description of three general concepts basic to understanding how families can be described in structural terms. These concepts are subsystems, boundaries, and hierarchy.

Historical Information

In the 1960s, Salvadore Minuchin, a pediatrician turned psychiatrist, and his co-workers at the Wiltwyck School for Boys near New York City began developing a model of family therapy designed to deal with delinquent youngsters from low socioeconomic backgrounds. Their book, *Families of the Slums: An Exploration of Their Structure and Treatment* (Minuchin et al., 1967), was the result of 3 years of research funded by a grant from the National Institute for Mental Health. The approach they developed, which they called structural family therapy focused on helping chaotic, multiproblem families change those patterns of behavior that had led to the placement of one of their members at the School for Boys. Structural family therapy involves a focus on the present rather than the past, on changing behaviors rather than gaining intellectual insight, and on short-term rather than extensive treatment.

In 1965, Minuchin and Braulio Montalvo, a colleague from the Wiltwyck School, moved to the Philadelphia Child Guidance Clinic, where they began to develop a family-oriented treatment team. This inner-city, traditional child guidance clinic was to become transformed into the Mecca of structural family therapy. Many clinicians who eventually became well known as family therapists, including Jay Haley (Haley & Hoffman, 1967), M. Duncan Stanton and Tom Todd (Stanton et al., 1982), Lynn Hoffman (1981), Harry Aponte (1976b), and Marianne Walters (1972), originally worked with families from a structural perspective at the Philadelphia Child Guidance Clinic.

Minuchin's next book, *Families and Family Therapy* (1974), delineated a model of effective family functioning that included the qualities of openness, flexibility, and organization. These three basic traits and the language that Minuchin developed to describe them are discussed in greater detail later in this section. Minuchin also introduced in this book the technique of structurally mapping families to help the therapist develop specific goals for treatment. Further, he discussed the need for the therapist to join in the family's process and language in order to effect change. In Minuchin's approach, it is only after listening to the family and joining with them to bring about change that the therapist can begin to restructure patterns in communication and behavior.

Minuchin's writing not only introduced his theory to the psychological community but also included transcripts from actual sessions in which a structural family therapy approach had been used. Minuchin's therapy style was unique in that he was directive with his patients and very active during the sessions, frequently walking around the room and asking family members to change seats. Considered bold and controversial, he was one of the first trainers in the field to videotape family therapy sessions and show the videotapes to provide examples of principles of structural family therapy. This format later became a strategy of choice in training for all approaches to family systems therapy.

Although Minuchin's original therapy approach was based on the nuclear family as the unit of treatment, in the epilogue to *Families and Family Therapy* (1974) he opened the door for including extended family and other social networks in the concept of "family." He wrote, "To include the entire family as a factor . . . enlarges the perspective from the traditional concentration on the individual. . . . Yet even this focus distorts the view . . . for it ignores the linkages between family and society" (p. 255). In the 1980s, structural family therapy began to include an emphasis upon extended systems that interact with the nuclear family and generational patterns that influence the family.

Although structural family therapy was originally developed from applications to families of lower socioeconomic status, the approach was generalized in the 1970s and 1980s to include all families. This extension came about as a result of 10 years of research Minuchin and his colleagues conducted at the Philadelphia Child Guidance Clinic funded by a grant for work with children having psychosomatic illness. The research involved children who were suffering from diabetes, asthma, and anorexia nervosa. Both the children with diabetes and those with asthma had numerous hospitalizations resulting from episodes of ketoacidosis or breathing difficulties that did not respond to conventional medical treatment.

As part of this research, the identified patients were videotaped with their parents and at least two siblings engaging in a series of interactive family tasks. The videotapes were then coded on dimensions of family structure by *blind* observers. This videotaped interview included phases during which the identified patient witnessed parental conflict from behind a one-way mirror and sat in the room during a conflict between his or her parents.

Comparison of the results of these interactions with interviews conducted with "normal" children and their parents revealed that the identified patients were much more involved in their parents' conflict than normal children. The patients tended to serve as mediators of parental conflict and to become involved in alliances with one parent against the other. In addition, there was evidence that the children with diabetes had an exaggerated response to parental conflict that resulted in an increase of free fatty acids in the bloodstream.

This research also involved a therapy component in which the principles and techniques of structural family therapy were applied in working with the families. Minuchin, Rosman, and Baker (1978) stated, "Our findings clearly indicate that, when significant family interactional patterns are changed, significant changes in the symptoms of psychosomatic illness also occur" (p. 21).

Minuchin continued his work at the Philadelphia Child Guidance Clinic until 1982, when he went into private practice. During his time at the clinic, he and his colleagues expanded the principles of structural family therapy to working with families coming together as a result of a remarriage, families with a schizophrenic child, families of adolescent drug abusers, as well as numerous other types of families who came for treatment. Minuchin continues to present workshops both nationally and internationally on the principles and practice of structural family therapy.

Background Information

The theory underlying structural family therapy is descriptive in nature. Based on specific values that deal with how the family should function, the therapy is practical and directive. This section describes some of the underlying premises and values that resulted in development of the approach known as structural family therapy.

Minuchin (1974) clearly identified a necessary balance between the general systems principles of homeostasis and adaptability when he wrote:

> The continued existence of the family as a system depends on a sufficient range of (transactional) patterns . . . and the flexibility to mobilize them when necessary. The family must . . . be able to transform itself in ways that meet new circumstances without losing the continuity that provides a frame of reference for its members. (p. 52)

The concepts of structural family therapy stem from the premise that family members interact with one another in predictable patterns that can be observed and that are repeated over time. Therapy is aimed at changing these patterns by changing the organization or structure of the family. Structure should not, however, be seen as fixed. The structure may be for a brief period and should be seen as dynamic (I. Goldenberg & H. Goldenberg, 1991). Minuchin and his colleagues believed that as the behavior of family members changed, the basic patterns and structure of the family would change. As the structure was transformed, the experience of the individuals in the family would be different (Fishman, 1993).

Minuchin (1974) wrote that the primary job of the family was to "enhance the psychosocial growth of each member" (p. 51). To accomplish this task, the family must operate with some predictability and stability. For instance, children should be able to forecast that each time they misbehave they will receive a similar response from their parents. A classic example of the effects of lack of predictability comes from families in which there is an alcoholic parent. Children in these families learn early in life that they cannot depend on the alcoholic parent's reaction to their behavior. Only when they become older are they able to understand that the source of the instability is the parent's drinking behavior.

In addition to creating and maintaining stability, the family must also be able to respond to changing circumstances with some degree of flexibility. Stress upon the family such as moving, financial problems, the illness or death of an extended family member, or the identification of a child with physical or learning problems can overload the general functioning of the family system. If the family is not capable of responding to these demands by changing roles and communication patterns, family conflict and dysfunctional behavior will result.

The role of the therapist is to help families adapt to changing circumstances with changes in the structure of the family. Once the family experiences the changes and the adaptation that goes with the new structure, the homeostatic mechanism of the family should operate to continue the new structural pattern (Fishman, 1993). In families where restructuring changes do not continue or where conflicts are not resolved, what began as a problem of a family in transition may continue as dysfunctional patterns. Eventually, according to Minuchin's theory, these dysfunctional family patterns will result in the identification of a family member (usually a child) with behavioral, emotional, or physical symptoms.

Theoretical Concepts

Minuchin's view of the family as a relational context with predictable structural patterns led to the development of three theoretical constructs regarding family functioning: subsystems, boundaries, and hierarchy.

Subsystems

A two-parent nuclear family is composed of four major subsystems, each with its own interaction patterns and functions. These subsystems include the spousal or marital subsystem, composed of the husband and wife; the parental subsystem, which includes the parents as executives or decision makers for the family; the sibling subsystem; and the extrafamilial subsystem, including extended family, friends, and social supports.

The individuals included in each subsystem differ from family to family. For example, in single-parent families there is no spousal subsystem, and the parental subsystem often includes a grandparent or an older sibling who has parental permission to make decisions regarding younger siblings. The extrafamilial subsystem may include aunts, uncles, and cousins who live nearby or may be composed mostly of family friends or colleagues.

Each member of a family may belong to several subsystems. For example, a teenage child may be allowed periodic entrance into the parental subsystem in the form of baby-sitting. This same child will also be a member of the sibling subsystem. In addition, if the teenager is involved in extracurricular school activities, he or she will be an integral member of the extrafamilial subsystem.

Membership in each subsystem will demand different interaction skills and ways of functioning in relationships. When interacting with parents, a teenager must know about respect and authority. When acting in a parental role, such as when baby-sitting, he or she must know about leadership and responsibility. Interacting with siblings or peers, this same child must learn about sharing, cooperation, and empathy.

Each subsystem has particular functions for the family system. The spousal subsystem promotes interdependence of the marital couple, conflict resolution between the pair, and sexual and emotional satisfaction. Although information about this area is not readily available to school professionals, some general observations can give them a sense of the patterns of interaction between a couple.

The functions of the parental subsystem include the emotional and physical support of children, the establishment of family rules, the dispensing of appropriate discipline, and the socialization of children. School professionals will find dysfunction in the parental subsystem in the form of abusive, unpredictable, or absent authority. Further discussion of the effects of imbalance in the parental subsystem is contained in Chapter 3.

The sibling subsystem provides recreation, companionship, and role modeling for its members. Interaction with siblings provides a social laboratory for learning negotiation, cooperation, and competition with peers of different ages. The child's identity is formed, in large part, from positive and negative experiences within his or her sibling group (Bank & Kahn, 1975).

Finally, the extrafamilial subsystem provides a social network with which the family can socialize and compare ways of interacting and family rules. The network offers emotional and instrumental support such as through the sharing of family celebrations and values and training in general life skills. Often families with a child with special needs become isolated from social supports, resulting in increased tension within the nuclear family.

Boundaries

According to Minuchin, the boundaries of a subsystem are defined by rules that govern who functions within that subsystem and how each person carries out his or her function. An example of a rule that defines a boundary would be, "The children in the family do not make decisions about how bills are paid." This rule places a boundary between the sibling subsystem and the parental subsystem.

For subsystems to function appropriately, boundaries must be clear enough to allow subsystem members to carry out their functions without interference from those outside the subsystem. For example, young couples quite often have marital difficulties if there is frequent involvement with and input from in-laws into their early marriage negotiations. If the couple purposefully goes to their in-laws for advice on specific issues, such as money management, there need not be a blurring of boundaries.

In healthy family interactions, boundaries are clear and permeable. When boundaries are blurred, subsystems have problems functioning. In families with blurred boundaries, parents tend to be overprotective and have difficulty with their children's attempts to become appropriately independent. There is little individual privacy. Aponte (Aponte & Van Deusen, 1981) stated that in these types of families, members function as if they were part of one another. Minuchin (1974) coined the term *enmeshed* to describe families with blurred, unclear, or undifferentiated boundaries.

At the other end of the continuum are families in which boundaries are inappropriately rigid and impermeable. Family members have little to do with one another; there is very little emotional support or closeness in these families. Only a severe crisis or a high level of stress can activate parental involvement. These types of families are called *disengaged* by Minuchin and his colleagues.

Hierarchy

Minuchin used the term "hierarchy" to describe the distribution of power in families. The member at the top of the hierarchy is the one who has the most relational power within the family. Families operate best when there is a clear hierarchy with parents occupying the upper levels, adolescents or older children next, and younger children at the lower levels.

There are many different ways in which hierarchy problems occur in families. One type of problem occurs in families with weak or ineffective parents. In these families, children tend to not listen to their parents' directions, and there is often much sibling conflict. In many low income or highly stressed families with multiple problems, the weak parental subsystem may be exacerbated by a general disorganization at all levels. Bills are left unpaid, phone calls go unanswered, and there is a general sense of a lack of leadership.

A second type of hierarchy problem occurs when a child functions regularly in the parental subsystem. This child assumes an inappropriate level of responsibility within the family and often misses out on age-appropriate experiences and activities. A child in this position is referred to as a *parentified* child (Minuchin & Fishman, 1981). Parentification occurs in families in which there is a highly inappropriate involvement between a parent and child.

Another hierarchy difficulty is found in families where members repeatedly align together across subsystem boundaries against another family member. An inflexible alignment is known as a *coalition*. This type of problem is frequently seen in families where parents avoid dealing with their marital conflict by focusing on problems in a child. For example, an adolescent who complains about his mom's nagging is often acting out his father's resistance to what his father perceives as his wife's nagging. Rather than the father confronting his wife, the adolescent, in a coalition with his father, acts out the conflict from across generational boundaries.

In summary, Minuchin used these three constructs to describe family dynamics and to identify the forces that lead to the development of problems in the family system. Subsystems with identified functions serve as the structural elements in the family. Boundaries are the mechanisms by which the family balances between stability and flexibility. Hierarchy is the organizing principle by which subsystems are arranged. By their articulation and extension of these constructs, Minuchin and his collaborators have provided a useful model for applying general systems theory to the problem of family dysfunction.

An Ecostructural Assessment Process

Aponte (1994) described an ecostructural assessment process that professionals can effectively use during the family-school interview. The process is explained here so that professionals involved in an ecostructural family-school interview will have a better understanding of what structural therapists who come to schools to assist with troublesome pupils are using in their typical assessment process.

The components of the ecostructural assessment process include: the target issue on which the assessment process is focused; diagnostic hypotheses, which are related to structural and functional hypotheses; and, finally, therapeutic hypotheses that are related to the target issue(s), the client (pupil, family, and/or community), and the professional. Aponte made it clear that these components should be seen as dynamic, with the professional revising and gathering new data and testing hypotheses on an ongoing basis. It is important to consider each of the subsystems, described earlier in this chapter, that influence the target issue when an ecostructural assessment is used as a base for the family-school interview.

Target Issue(s)

The pupil and, as appropriate, the family and/or community members negotiate the target issue(s) that will be the focus of the intervention process. The target issue(s) should be directly related to the current concerns that need intervention. When possible, the statement of the target issue(s) should be worded in a way that indicates the possibility for change. Therefore, it is important to include achievable goals. It is also important to consider the whole school-family-community system so that the target statement accurately reflects the degree of control the pupil has in relation to the situation. A child living with a dying parent or an alcoholic parent, for example, cannot change that situation. A statement of target issues that takes realities into consideration follows:

> The target of the intervention is Pat's truancy. Pat's absences are nearing the number of days at which a student must repeat the grade, and it is only January. Although nothing can be done to change the fact that Pat's grandfather is dying, it is important for Pat to come to terms with this loss and focus on the job of obtaining the education that will allow her to graduate from high school this year, enroll in college, and pursue her interest in becoming a physician. Mr. and Mrs. Little need to work on refocusing their energies so that they can be available to help Pat focus on her loss in a healthy way instead of being truant.

Diagnostic Hypotheses

The diagnostic hypotheses state tentative explanations concerning the source and nature of the target issue(s) described by school staff and the pupil as well as the family and/or community members (the latter being involved when the problems spill over from the school to the community). Diagnostic hypotheses include both structural and functional hypotheses. Together these hypotheses serve as guides for professionals who are working with a pupil with a particularly challenging issue.

Structural Hypotheses. This part of the diagnostic-hypothesizing process specifies what is going on now in the pupil's ecosystem in relation to the target issue(s). The professional needs to determine the systems (school, family, and/or community) in which the issues are rooted. Additionally, the structure of the relationships within those systems, as related to the target issue(s), must be identified. Thus, boundaries, alignments, and hierarchies need to be considered.

Boundaries. Boundaries must be considered when determining which systems are involved in the issue. Is it merely school-related, or does it also include home and/or community? As conveyed earlier in this appendix, boundaries are defined by unstated rules for inclusion as well as for how people participate with one another. It is important to sort out how the interlacing systems within which the pupil lives and interacts impact one another in terms of the target issue(s). Are the boundaries enmeshed or disengaged, and, if so, where and in what ways? An understanding of the boundaries within which the pupil functions will allow the professional to speculate and to improve his or her probability of intervening in meaningful and necessary subsystems. In the example of Pat, the truant senior, there is enmeshment in the symbiotic and overprotective relationship between the mother and daughter, and the father is distant and disengaged from his wife as well as his children, spending many evenings at work and golfing on weekends. He functions as an absent father.

Alignments. Only those alliances/coalitions and opposition relating to the people within the subsystems connected to the focal issue are considered. Alignments and opposition are usually thought of as who is "in" and who is "out" of a relationship. For example, the paternal grandfather and Pat are positively aligned with one another. The father is left out of the family relationship and spends most of his time at work; the mother and daughter keep secrets from the father and do not invite him on outings.

Hierarchy. Influence-wielding related to the issue must also be considered. Important questions are who has the power, how is the power wielded, and what transactional patterns occur related to the focal issue. Order and balance are influenced by hierarchy. Order is established by the natural pecking order of parents being on top in terms of power and, in their absence, by the oldest sibling taking that position. Balance is established or maintained by the degree of shared power in decision making. If the youngest child independently makes all of the important decisions and dictates family direction, there is a problem related to balance. If the marital dyad shares equally in decision making, there is balance. An example of a hierarchy problem is Pat calling the shots in her school attendance. The spouses do not have balance in terms of decision making because Pat and her mother collude to steer the direction of the family.

Together, the statement of boundary, alignment, and power structures constitutes the structural hypothesis. An example of a well-stated structural hypothesis is: The school unwittingly has colluded with the symbiotic relationship of the mother and Pat, thus supporting the ongoing dysfunction. This situation has developed because the school has not followed through on Pat's truancy and was overly lenient because her grandfather is dying.

Functional hypotheses. In relationship to the target issue(s), functional hypotheses speak to the meaning and significance of what is occurring. These hypotheses explain "why" the issue is transpiring. Specifically, they relate to "history, social conditions, culture, family relationships, individual psychology, motivation, etc." (Aponte, 1994, p. 36). They include value, motivational, and historical hypotheses.

Value hypotheses. Value hypotheses are related to the meaning and purpose of the underlying issue. For Aponte (1994), values pertain to "ethnicity, culture, race, gender, religion, spirituality, and any other influence on principles, standards, morality, and priorities giving personal significance to life and its problems" (p. 36). Pat, the truant senior, has an absence of spiritual or religious roots to guide her in dealing with the death of the grandfather.

Motivational hypotheses. The motivational hypotheses explain behaviors based on social conditions, family relationships, and individual psychology. They involve such catalysts as the mission of social institutions and family needs as well as individual drives and defenses.

The professional working with Pat would see that she has been unable to deal with the loss of her grandfather and as a result has checked out from school on a regular basis. Having grown up close to her grandfather and distant from her father, she has been angry at her father for not being more like his father. There has been continued strain between Pat's father and grandfather, and the problems of the past remain unresolved. Pat's truancy appears to take the pressure off her father and grandfather, relieving both of them from dealing straightforwardly with one another.

Historical hypotheses. Historical hypotheses focus on the past. They describe sources and antecedents of the target issue(s) that are of a social, family, and personal nature. Events, family stories and legacies, as well as individual emotional struggles are considered.

The maxim that one who does not know the past is condemned to repeat it is true of family history. The intensity or force of the transgenerational transmission of dysfunctional interaction patterns is an important focus of family systems perspectives. Realizing that the past is prologue, professionals are wise to ascertain historical information so that they will more quickly reach conclusions and be able to plan more effective interventions. Without knowing the history, it is easy to simply treat the symptom rather than work on the underlying cause of the problem. If professionals ignore history, their interventions may not work and frustration will likely result.

Therapeutic Hypotheses

Therapeutic hypotheses relate to the planned intervention strategies. For the purposes of this text, this discussion is limited to hypotheses about the issue(s) and hypotheses about the pupil, family, and community. Goals of the intervention, available resources, and the potential of the pupil and subsystems for change are taken into account.

Hypotheses about issue(s). School professionals look at the key issues that need to be considered to help the pupil. The professionals work with the pupil, family, and/or community in this process and focus the issue(s) so that the goals of the intervention are a natural outgrowth of their work.

Hypotheses about pupil, family, and community. Available resources must also be considered when establishing an intervention strategy. These resources include the motivation, commitment, and freedom to change on the part of the pupil, the family, and sometimes the community.

Together, these three types of hypotheses—functional, diagnostic, and therapeutic—form an assessment process that is continually updated and revised as new data are gathered. This kind of assessment process informs the therapeutic process directly and dramatically increases the likelihood that an intervention will be successful. In haste, schools frequently try to solve problems by applying Band-Aids and treating surface symptoms. If, however, professionals can discipline themselves to use this assessment process with cases that are particularly difficult or of long standing, they will improve their likelihood of meeting with greater success.

STRATEGIC FAMILY THERAPY

This section describes the general theoretical principles underlying the practice of strategic therapy. A brief historical account of the development of this model is presented, followed by a discussion of the basic theory of change from a strategic perspective.

Historical Information

The term *strategic* is most often used to describe family therapy approaches that focus on identifying the function served by psychiatric symptoms within the family system. Further, the strategic therapist assumes responsibility for directly intervening in the system to effect change. Finally, the focus of strategic therapy is on here-and-now behaviors, with little or no attention paid to historical events. This focus contrasts with that of Bowen's and Satir's approaches, which treat the individual within a context of family history.

The two settings historically associated with the strategic approach are the Mental Research Institute (MRI) in Palo Alto, California, and the Family Therapy Institute in Washington, DC. Although each setting is known for its use of particular strategic therapy techniques, this discussion focuses on the commonalities in theory rather than the differences between their approaches. For a more detailed discussion of strategic therapy techniques, consult the relevant sources included in the reference list at the end of this book.

Many of the clinicians who have been important in the strategic therapy movement were originally trained and influenced by two men, Gregory Bateson (1972) and Milton Erickson. Bateson, an anthropologist, directed a 10-year grant project in the 1950s to investigate communication among both animals and people. Jay Haley, John Weakland, and Don Jackson, all of whom made major contributions to strategic therapy, worked on Bateson's grant project.

Milton Erickson, a physician, developed a unique brand of psychotherapy techniques based on hypnosis and paradoxical instruction. As Haley (1985) stated:

> Erickson had one major concern in his professional life—finding ways to influence people. . . . He seems to have been the first major therapist to expect clinicians to innovate ways to solve . . . problems and to say that the responsibility for . . . change lies with the therapist. (p. vii)

Haley, Jackson, and Weakland all studied extensively with Erickson; the influence of his beliefs can be seen in their later work as advocates of the strategic approach.

In 1959, Jackson left Bateson's research project and formed the Mental Research Institute. Several important contributions to strategic therapy have evolved from the MRI group, including brief therapy techniques designed to effect change in families in 10 sessions. In addition, this group maintained that therapeutic change could occur whether or not the entire family was involved in treatment. At MRI, motivated members of the family are advised how to change their own behavior so that the dysfunctional family patterns would then change.

Jay Haley moved from Bateson's project in 1967 to the Philadelphia Child Guidance Clinic, where he worked for 9 years with Minuchin and his colleagues. Haley then moved to Washington, DC, and began the Family Therapy Institute. Haley has contributed to the field of family therapy by training therapists in specific interviewing techniques designed to discover behavioral and communicational patterns within the family. He has also developed a model for treating severely disturbed young adults that focuses on the family's failure to allow the person to leave home and become independent.

Although Jackson, Bateson, and Erickson have all died, the ideas that they germinated continue to grow in the field of family therapy. The Mental Research Institute and the Family Therapy Institute continue to provide training and therapy. Both Haley and Weakland, who are prolific writers, provide supervision to therapy trainees and conduct national workshops on strategic therapy approaches.

Theoretical Concepts

Strategic therapy is grounded primarily on the general systems principles of homeostasis and levels of interaction. Probably the best-known concepts arising from the strategic therapy movement are those of family homeostasis and the double bind as a communication pattern in the etiology or cause of schizophrenia. The concept of the double bind was the first theory in the area of paradoxical communication. The double bind communication pattern occurs when an individual appears to offer a choice to another; however, no matter which option is chosen by the respondent, he or she ends up in a bind.

For example, a mother buys a red sweater and a blue sweater for her son's birthday and presents them both to him with the question, "Which one will you wear to the party?" The boy answers that either sweater will be fine. The mother then insists that the boy choose one of the sweaters. If the boy asks for the red sweater, she responds, "You don't like the blue one?" If he chooses the blue one, she asks why he does not like the red one. In other words, he is given the illusion of choice, but he will lose in this communication no matter which "choice" he makes. The study of this type of communication pattern within families led strategic therapists to develop general theoretical concepts regarding family homeostasis and the importance of family development and problem definition.

Family Homeostasis and Symptom Development

In 1957, Jackson first discussed the idea of psychiatric symptoms in an individual as systemic responses to family communication. In other words, people within a family govern one another's behavior by their responses to one another. Jackson believed that families have a natural movement toward stability or homeostasis, just as other living systems do.

According to strategic therapy (Watzlawick et al., 1974), psychiatric symptoms result from attempts by family members to change an existing difficulty. When difficulties arise in daily living, parents or spouses usually attempt to apply a solution to make things better. For example, if someone is depressed, family members try to cheer up the individual. If initial attempts at cheering up do not work, the family members increase their efforts. Once a symptom is present and a family attempts to treat the symptom, however, they often only succeed in making it worse. The solution then becomes entrenched as the family's behavior for dealing with the problem. The symptom is maintained by a particular sequence of behaviors within the family.

Consider the following scenario: Johnny looks depressed, so his family tries to cheer him up. If their efforts are not successful, they try harder. Johnny sees his family working hard to make him feel better, but he still feels depressed. Only now he also feels guilty about being depressed and taking so much family energy. In addition, his family is angry that they are trying so hard and Johnny is not responding, so they begin to withdraw from Johnny. Johnny then becomes more depressed. This sequence of behaviors is circular. If the therapist can discover this circular sequence and help change the family's reactions at any point along that circle, strategic therapy proponents maintain that the symptomatic behavior will then change.

Life Cycle

Strategic therapists look at the family's stage of development as an important factor in understanding the etiology of symptoms. Families are seen as prone to developing problems at transitional points, such as the birth of a child or a family relocation. At these times, due to the stress of transition, families are less able to adjust their interactions to accommodate necessary changes. In other words, the forces for homeostasis outweigh the forces for flexibility. Haley (1980) related this phenomenon to movement on a stairway. The family must make adjustments to move from one step to the next. Families with a symptomatic member have become "stuck" on one step and cannot move on to the next step in the life cycle. It is the therapist's job to help the family introduce new behaviors that will help them move on up the stairway.

All families become unbalanced at times and react to stress with nonproductive interpersonal cycles. Many people understand this process as a "button-pushing" phenomenon. Once a particular topic is broached or once a particular action takes place, each family member can predict how the other family members will react. It is as if the family is watching a very familiar one-act play but they cannot seem to change their lines to come up with a more productive outcome. In healthy families, there comes a point when someone does "change his or her lines," and the nonproductive cycle is broken. In pathological families, these cycles continue to repeat over and over for months or years at a time. In these families, the cycles repeat until a crisis ensues. Even then the system does not change, because family members develop symptoms to provide a stabilizing force toward resolving family stress.

Just as the saying goes that people will pull together in times of crisis, the family tends to pull together around the symptomatic member, who is usually a child, and thus avoids making any real changes in the family patterns that caused the initial crisis. This pulling together around the symptom-bearing member might make it look to observers as though the family had changed its dysfunctional patterns and was functioning better. The essence of the system, however, has not changed, and the dysfunctional process will resurface as the problematic family member begins to function more healthily.

Haley (1980) viewed many severely disturbed young people as being stuck at the leaving-home stage of the family life cycle. In these families, the parents need to have their own lives and identities that are oriented around something other than child-rearing. If child-rearing is a mother's only purpose in life, then the underlying fear of the child leaving home is that the mother will no longer have a job. A strategic therapist would identify the young person as suffering from problems in maturity and independence. He or she would then work to have the parents in this situation become more controlling and demanding of their symptomatic child to help the child mature. As the parents effectively assert their control, the child's concern becomes how to get out from under this structure. The child then begins to work toward gaining independence and leaving home rather than on maintaining the parent's symptom. Once the child has given up the symptom, the family is then unstuck and can begin to introduce more adaptive behaviors. The mother can then give up her focus on the young person and devote her energy to managing her own needs as her role naturally changes.

Problem Definition

According to the theory of strategic therapy, there is no objective reality. How one looks at things determines what one sees. What one sees determines how one behaves. How one behaves determines how others respond.

Families usually seek help from a therapist long after symptoms have developed in a family member. The family has already applied its solution to the problem, and no change has occurred. The family members are demoralized by their maladaptive solution but cannot see how to approach the problem differently. They see the symptom as beyond their control and resistant to change.

In strategic therapy, it is the therapist's job to help the family define the problem in a way that a solution is possible. How one defines the problem determines what one will do about it. Therefore, much of the skill in strategic therapy lies in asking questions that help the family begin to entertain alternative views of the symptom. The therapeutic process of expanding the family's definition of the problem is known as *reframing*. When family members begin to view the problem differently, the therapist then gives directives concerning how individuals can begin to behave differently. In this model, action or strategy replaces traditional interpretation and insight therapy.

Different ways in which reality can be defined can be seen in the following classroom example: A first-grader has begun to destroy property in the classroom and to hit other students. At first, the teacher views this behavior as angry and aggressive. She responds by setting limits on the child and using time-outs. The teacher later finds out from the school counselor that the child's parents have recently decided to get a divorce. At this point, she views the same behavior as depressed in nature. The next time the child acts out, she takes him aside and asks him about his feelings about the divorce. In each case, the teacher's perspective on reality governed her behavior.

The strategic family therapy approach was developing on the West Coast at about the same time that the structural family therapy approach was developing on the East Coast. Both approaches differ from those of Bowen and Satir in that their focus is on the behavior and communication of the family in the present. Structural therapists tend to develop goals aimed at helping the family members change roles and behaviors in the here and now. Much of strategic therapy is oriented to techniques used by the therapist to induce change in communication patterns in the family system. In fact, the strategic therapy approach is known for being long on technique and short on theory. The three theoretical concepts discussed here—family homeostasis, life cycle, and problem definition—are used to help the therapist determine where to direct his or her efforts toward change.

FAMILY EVALUATION/ASSESSMENT

My experience in using family systems assessment instruments is that none has completely met my needs. I have, however, found the use of genograms helpful in describing family systems. The genogram, described earlier in this book, organizes family data and tracks relationship processes as well as allows for the tracking of key triangles during treatment. *Genograms in Family Assessment,* by McGoldrick and Gerson (1985), provides a useful guide to working with genograms.

Beyond genograms, I have found ecostructural assessment (Aponte, 1994) useful. Aponte (1994) provided a clear description of this model, which expands structural family therapy to include the individual, the family, and the community, which can include schools. The focus of Aponte's book is on the poor, and, thus, his model speaks in particular to at-risk pupils and their families. Though Aponte's book is written for therapists, it is useful for all school professionals.

Although most professionals working within schools will not be involved in the assessment of family functioning, it is helpful for psychologists, social workers, and counselors to have some knowledge of this area within family studies. Kerr and Bowen (1988) wrote a text that focuses on family evaluation as it relates to Bowen theory. Bowen's concepts, described earlier in this appendix, are used as a means for measurement. The text by L'Abate and Bagarozzi (1993) is an excellent sourcebook of marriage and family evaluation. Trained professionals will find this text useful for selecting appropriate instruments. Others will find it useful for learning more about what each instrument covers and how the different strands are evaluated.

Jacob and Tennenbaum (1988) described a variety of assessment instruments related to families, as did Fredman and Sherman (1987). Grotevant and Carlson (1989) reviewed and discussed family assessment measures, including in their discussion observational coding schemes, global rating scales, and self-report measures.

Assessing family functioning through a family systems lens is a complex and multi-faceted process. Many of the different facets have been investigated. Kantor and Lehr (1975), for example, developed a means for determining which basic family type—open, closed, or random—families cluster around. Each type represents different structures of internal relationships as well as different levels of access to and exchange with the external world. They found each of the three types to have its own rules, boundary arrangements, and tactics for achieving and maintaining homeostasis and viewed each of the three types as potentially flawed.

Kantor and Lehr described open families as democratic and balanced in terms of boundaries. In these families honest interchange with outsiders is encouraged. Order exists without rigidity, flexibility is a priority, and negotiation is encouraged. In the open family, adaptation through consensus, respect for individual rights, and loyalty to self and family are the norms.

Closed families require that individuals within the family subordinate their needs to the whole. Rules and the hierarchy drive the norms. An observer would typically find doors being locked, reading and television programs being screened, children being required to report all engagements. In these families strangers are not trusted, and daily schedules are rigidly adhered to. These families are looking for stability through stasis, which is in contrast to open families, which encourage adaptability.

Random families were described as fragmented. There is a lack of interconnectedness with what different family members are doing. Family rules are few, and boundaries are blurred and easily transgressed. People come and go in irregular patterns, and meals are seldom shared. The purpose of this type of family is exploration through intuition.

Olson and colleagues (1983) attempted to design a reliable and valid typology to classify and measure changes in families. Known as the Circumplex Model, their typology looks at two dimensions: family cohesion and family adaptability. The self-report instrument, Family Adapted and Cohesion Evaluation Scales (FACES), has been through many revisions.

The McMaster Model (Epstein, Baldwin, & Bishop, 1982; Epstein, Baldwin, & Bishop, 1983), which includes a questionnaire referred to as the Family Assessment Device, probes for six aspects of functioning within the family: family problem solving, family communication, family roles, affective responsiveness, affective involvement, and a behavior control. A collective family health/pathology score is provided.

In an attempt to assess the impact of the family environment on both individual and family functioning, Moos (1974, described in I. Goldenberg and H. Goldenberg, 1991) developed a Family Environment Scale. His scale includes 10 subscales within three dimensions (Relationship, Personal Growth, and System Maintenance).

In reality, few family systems professionals use standardized assessment instruments (M. P. Nichols & Schwartz, 1995). A study by M. P. Nichols and R. C. Schwartz (1995) found that only 13% of the therapists they surveyed used standardized instruments for family therapy, and only 29% used them for marital therapy. Furthermore, the instruments used usually were individual rather than family assessment instruments and, thus, did not provide meaningful information from the family systems perspective.

Books for Professionals and Family Members

ABUSE AND VIOLENCE

Bahr, A. C. (1986). *It's O.K. to say no: A book for parents and children to read together.* New York: Grosset & Dunlap.

Bass, E., & Thornton, L., Eds. (1991). *I never told anyone.* New York: Harper Perennial. Writings by female survivors of child sexual abuse.

Besharov, D. J. (1990). *Recognizing child abuse: A guide for the concerned.* New York: The Free Press. Written for those interested in making a difference for children who are abused.

Crewdson, J. (1988). *By silence betrayed: Sexual abuse of children in America.* Boston: Little, Brown.

Farmer, S. (1989). *Adult children of abusive parents.* New York: RGA Publishing Group, Inc. A healing program for those who have been physically, sexually, or emotionally abused.

Fontana, V. J., & Moolman, V. (1991). *Save the family, save the child: What we can do to help children at risk.* New York, NY: Dutton/Penquin. Graphic and focused on changing our society at all levels. For professionals.

Furniss, T. (1991). *The multi-professional handbook of child sexual abuse: Integrated management, therapy and legal intervention.* London: Routledge.

Gelles, R. J. (1996). *The book of David: How preserving families can cost children's lives.* New York: BasicBooks.

Gil, E. (1996). *Systematic treatment of families who abuse.* San Francisco: Jossey-Bass Publishers.

Gil, E. (1995). *Outgrowing the pain: A book for and about adults abused as children.* New York: Dell Publishing Company. This book helps illuminate destructive patterns and gives new insight to abuse survivors.

Gil, E. (1991). *The healing power of play: Working with abused children.* New York: The Guilford Press. How play therapy can work.

Gore, T. (1987). *Raising PG kids in an X-rated society*. Nashville: Abingdon Press.

Hagans, K. B., & Case, J. (1988). *When your child has been molested: A parent's guide to healing and recovery*. Lexington, MA: D.C. Heath and Company. Includes practical and topical issues for parents to "put the pieces back together." Focuses on a variety of areas related to self, professionals, feelings, coping, interacting with others, court, and incest. Glossary is provided.

Janko, S. (1994). *Vulnerable children, vulnerable families: The social construction of child abuse*. New York: Teachers College Press.

Johnson, B. C. (1992). *For their sake: Recognizing, responding to and reporting child abuse*. Martinsville, IN: American Camping Association.

Justice, B. (1990). *The abusing family*. New York: Plenum Press.

Mufson, S., & Kranz, R. (1991). *Straight talk about child abuse*. New York: Facts On File.

Murdock. R. L. (1992). *Suffer the children: A pediatrician's reflections on abuse*. Santa Fe, NM: Health Press.

National Center on Child Abuse and Neglect. (1992). *Consortium of clearinghouses on child abuse and neglect*. Washington, DC: NCCAN.

Patton, M. (Ed.). (1991). *Family sexual abuse: Frontline research and evaluation*. Newbury Park, CA: Sage Publications.

Peled, E., Jaffe, P. G., & Edleson, J. (Eds.). (1995). *Ending the cycle of violence: Community responses to children of battered women*. Thousand Oaks, CA: Sage.

Pelzer, D. (1995). *A child called "it": An abused child's journey from victim to victor*. Deerfield Beach, FL: Health Communications, Inc. A victim's first-hand account of overcoming childhood abuse..

Rench, J. E. (1992). *Family violence: How to recognize it and survive it*. Minneapolis, MN: Lerner Publishing Company. This book discusses various forms of violence, including child abuse and incest, and explains the ways a family can get help.

Royce, D. (1994). *How do I know it's abuse: Identifying and countering emotional mistreatment from friends and family members*. Springfield, IL: Thomas.

Rushford, P. H. (1996). *The Jack and Jill syndrome: Healing for broken children*. Ada, MI: Fleming H. Revell Company. The book describes the wounds experienced by a child who has known physical, sexual or emotional abuse and neglect.

Terr, L. (1990). *Too scared to cry*. New York: Basic Books. How trauma affects childen and us all.

Trute, B. (1994). *Coordinating child sexual abuse services in rural communities*. Toronto: University of Toronto Press.

ADDICTION

Balcerzak, A. M. (1981). *Hope for young people with alcoholic parents*. Center City, MN: Hazelden. Dealing with major crises and big family changes.

Bates, C., & Wigtil, J. (1994). *Skill building activities for alcohol and drug education*. Boston: Jones and Bartlett Publisher. Developed to help teach people to confront individual and societal drug behaviors, and can be adapted for secondary schools.

Bagnall, G.(1991). *Educating young drinkers.* New York: Routledge. Classroom experiment in alcohol education with a primary prevention orientation.

Baron, J.D. (1984). *Kids & drugs: A parent's handbook of drug abuse, prevention, and treatment.* New York: Perigee Books.

Brooks, C. S., & Rice, K. F. (1997). *Families in recovery: Coming full circle.* Baltimore: Paul H. Brookes. Book focuses on recognizing and accepting addiction and abuse as political, social, health, educational, and spiritual crises.

Center for Substance Abuse Prevention. (1996). *Just the facts.* Washington, DC: CSAP.

Center for Substance Abuse Prevention. (1996). *Keeping youth drug-free: A guide for parents, grandparents, elders, mentors, and other caregivers.* Washington, DC: CSAP.

Department of Education. (1993). *Growing up drug free: A parent's guide to prevention.* Washington, DC: DOE.

DeStefano, S. (1991). *Drugs and the family.* Frederick, MD: Twenty-First Century Books.

Dulfano, C. (1992). *Families, Alcoholism, & Recovery.* San Francisco: Jossey-Bass. Helpful to professionals as well as family members.

Friend, M., & Cook, L. (1996). *Interactions: Collaboration skills for school professionals* (3rd ed.). New York: Longman.

Glantz, M., & Pickens, R. (Eds.). (1992). *Vulnerability to Drug Abuse.* Washington, DC: American Psychological Association.

Goode, E. (1992). *Drugs in American Society* (4th ed.). New York: McGraw-Hill.

Hanson, D. J. (1996). *Alcohol education: What we must do.* Westport, CN: Praeger. Promotes "development and evaluation of diverse responsible alcohol use curricula based on a sociocultural understanding of how best to reduce alcohol abuse."

Heuer, M. (1994). *Teen addiction.* New York: Ballantine Books. A book of hope for the parents, teachers, and counselors of chemically dependent adolescents.

Johnson, D. W., & Johnson, R. (1991). *Teaching students to be peacemakers.* Edina, MN: Interactions Books.

Koffinke C. (1991). *I'll never do that to my kids: The parenting traps of adult children.* Minneapolis, MN: Deaconess Press. Focuses on typical traps faced by adults who grew up in dysfunctional families.

Marshall, S. (1992). *Teenage addicts can recover: Treating the addict, not the age.* Littleton, CO: Gylantic Publishing.

Nastasi, B. K., & DeZolt, D. M. (1994). *School interventions for children of alcoholics.* New York: Guilford Press. "Tells the story of children and families whose lives are affected by alcohol, and provides a guide to school personnel who are interested in developing programs for COAs."

National Institute on Drug Abuse. (1996). *Don't harm yourself! Arm yourself with knowledge about drugs!* Washington, DC: NIDA.

National Institute on Drug Abuse. (1997). *Preventing drug abuse among children and adolescents.* Washington, DC: NIDA.

Neff, P. (1996). *Tough love: How parents can deal with drug abuse.* (Rev. ed.). Nashville, TN: Abingdon Press.

Noddings, N. (1992). *The challenge to care in schools: An alternative approach to education.* New York: Teacher's College Press.

Ruben, D. H. (1993). *Family addiction: An analytical guide.* New York: Garland Publishers.

Schaefer, C. E., & DiGeronimo, T. F. (1994). *How to talk to your kids about really important things: For children four to twelve.* San Francisco: Jossey-Bass. Believing that what children don't know can hurt them, this book is divided by topical areas related to major crises and big family changes as well as concerns of youth. Topics include such things as alcoholic parent and drug abuse, among many others.

Schlesinger, S. (1988). *Taking charge: How families can climb out of the chaos of addiction — and flourish.* New York: Simon & Schuster.

Sher, K. J. (1991). *Children of alcoholics: A critical appraisal of theory and research.* Chicago: University of Chicago Press.

Taylor, D. B., & Taylor, P. M. (1990). *Coping with a dysfunctional family.* New York: Rosen. Focuses on alcohol and drug abuse, physical and verbal abuse, sexual abuse and emotional neglect.

ADOPTION

Aigner, H. (1992). *Adoption in America coming of age.* (Rev. ed.). Grenbriar, CA: Paradigm Press.

Askin, J., & Oskam, B. (1992). *Search: A handbook for adoptees and birthparents.* (2nd ed.). New York: Harper and Row.

Bartholet, E. (1993). *Family bonds: Adoption and the politics of parenting.* Boston: Houghton Mifflin. Written by a female attorney and law professor who twice adopted from Peru as a single parent.

Bothun, L. (1987). *When friends ask about Adoption: Questions and answers guide for non-adoptive parents and other caring adults.* Chevy Chase, MD: Swan.

Brodzinsky, D. M., Schechter, M. D., & Henig, R. M. (1992). *Being adopted: The lifelong search for self.* Tauted as different than other books on adoption, this book shares a model of normal adjustment to being adopted, across the life span. Includes the ups and downs of psychological adaptation of well-adjusted adoptees.

Caplan, L. (1990). *Open adoption.* New York: Farrar, Straus & Giroux.

Gilman, L. (1992). *The adoption resource book* (Rev. ed.). New York: Harper Perennial.

Godwin-Beauvas, L., & Godwin, R. (1997). *The complete adoption book.* Holbrook, MA: Adams Media Corporation. Everything you need to know to adopt the child you want in less than 1 year.

Gritter, J. L. (1989). *Adoption without fear.* San Antonio, TX: Corona Publishing.

Hoffman-Reim, C. (1990). *The adopted child: Family life with double parenthood.* New Brunswick: Transaction Publishers. Study of adoption in Germany.

Kremetz, J. (1988). *How it feels to be adopted.* New York: Alfred A. Knopf.

Lancaster, K. (1996). *Keys to parenting an adopted child.* New York: Barron. Help for parents who must cope with the details of raising adopted children in the often-demanding contemporary environment.

Lifton, B. J. (1979). *Lost and found: The adoption experience.* New York: Harper Collins. Others share their experience with adoption.

Liptak, K. (1993). *Adoption controversies.* New York: Franklin Watts. Examines the various forms of adoption, as well as foster care and surrogate mothering.

Melina, L. R. (1989). *Making sense of adoption: A parent's guide.* Grand Rapids, MI: Perennial Library. Dealing with major crises and big family changes for parents and adults.

Minshew, D. (1990). *The adoptive family as a healing resource for the sexually abused child: A training manual.* Washington DC: Child Welfare League of America.

Plumez, J. H. (1987). *Successful adoption.* New York: Harmony Books. Dealing with major crises and big family changes for parents and adults.

Pohl, C., & Harris, K. (1992). *Transracial adoption: Children and parents speak.* New York: Franklin Watts.

Register, C. (1991). *"Are those kids yours?": American families with children adopted from other countries.* New York: The Free Press.

Reitz, M. (1992). *Adoption and the family system: Strategies for treatment.* New York: Guilford Press.

Schaefer, C. (1991). *The other mother: A true story.* New York: Soho Press. A woman's love for the child she gave up for adoption.

Schaefer, C. E., & DiGeronimo, T. F. (1994). *How to talk to your kids about really important things: For children four to twelve.* San Francisco: Jossey-Bass. Believing that what children don't know can hurt them, this book is divided by topical areas related to major crises and big family changes as well as concerns of youth.

Schaffer, J., & Lindstrom, C. (1989). *How to raise an adopted child.* New York: Penguin Group. A guide to help your child flourish from infancy through adolescence.

Silber, K., & Speedlin, P. (1991). *Dear birthmother: Thank you for our baby.* (2nd ed.). Dallas: Corona Publishing Co. Explores myths of adoption and the evolution of open adoption.

Silber, K., & Martinez, P. (1990). *Children of open adoption.* San Antonio, TX: Corona Publishing.

Simon, R. (1992). *Adoption, race and identity: From infancy through adolescence.* New York: Praeger.

Simon, R., & Alstein, H. (Eds.). (1991). *Intercountry adoption: A multinational perspective.* New York: Praeger.

Simon, R., & Alstein, H. (1987). *Transracial adoptees and their families.* New York: Praeger.

Watkins, M., & Fisher, S. (1993). *Talking with young children about adoption.* New Haven: Yale University Press. Useful to parents who adopt.

Webster, H. (1991). *Family secrets: How telling and not telling affect our children, our relationships, and our lives.* Reading, MA: Addison Wesley.

CHILDREN WITH SPECIAL NEEDS

Albrecht, D. G. (1995). *Raising a child who has a physical disability.* New York: John Wiley & Song, Inc. Compassionate, helpful and based on real-life experiences.

Alexander-Roberts, C. (1994). *The ADHD parenting handbook: Practical advice for parents from parents.* Dallas: Taylor Publishing Company.

Anderson, W., Chitwood, S., & Hayden, D. (1990). *Negotiating the special education maze: A guide for parents and teachers.* Rockville, MD: Woodbine

House. Helpful information for parents about special education.

Baker, B. L., & Brightman, A. J. (1989). *Steps to independence: A skills training guide for parents and teachers of children with special needs*. (2nd ed.). Baltimore: Paul H. Brookes Publishing Company. Step by step approach for teaching skills to children with disabilities.

Barkley, R. A. (1995). *Taking charge of ADHD: The complete, authoritative guide for parents*. New York: The Guilford Press. Become an empowered parent, learn how to help your child and help yourself.

Batshaw, M. L., & Perret, Y. M. (1992). *Children with disabilities: A medical primer*. (3rd ed.). Baltimore: Paul H. Brookes Publishing Co. Information on the nature, assessment, and causes of mental retardation, as well as information on genetics and genetic disorders.

Batshaw, M. L. (1991). *Your child has a disability: A complete sourcebook of daily and medical care*. Boston: Little, Brown & Company.

Berube, M. (1996). *Life as we know it: A father, a family, and an exceptional child*. New York: Pantheon. A father's account of raising a child with Down's Syndrome.

Blank, J. (1976). *Nineteen steps up the mountain: The story of the DeBolt family*. Philadelphia: J. B. Lippincott.

Bloom, J. (1990). *Help me to help my child: A sourcebook for parents of learning disabled children*. Boston: Little, Brown & Co.

Bloom, B., & Seljeskog, E. (1988). *A parent's guide to spina bifida*. Minneapolis: University of Minnesota Press. Designed to help parents and children, professionals and educators understand and cope with spina bifida.

Boyles, N. S. & Contadino, D. (1997). *Parenting a child with attention deficit/hyperactivity disorder*. Los Angeles: Lowell House.

Brewer, E. J., & Angel, K. C. (1992). *Parenting a child with arthritis: A practical, empathetic guide to help you and your child live with arthritis*. Los Angeles: Lowell House.

Brill, M. T. (1994). *Keys to parenting the child with autism*. Hauppauge, NY: Barron's.

Buck, P. S. (1992). *The child who never grew*. (2nd ed.). Vineland, NJ: Woodbine House. A mother's struggle to understand and help her mentally-retarded daughter.

Buscaglia, L. (1983). *The disabled and their parents: A counseling challenge*. New York: Holt, Rinehart & Winston.

Buscaglia, L. (1983). *Living, loving, and learning*. New York: Ballantine Books/Random House.

Buscaglia, L. (1972). *Because I am human*. Thorofare, NJ: Charles B. Slack.

Callahan, C. R. (1990). *Since Owen: A parent-to-parent guide for care of the disabled child*. Baltimore, MD: The Johns Hopkins University Press.

Christopher, W. & Christopher, B. (1989). *Mixed blessing*. Nashville: Abingdon Press. A parent's story of an autistic son.

Cicchetti, D. & Beeghly, M. (Eds.). (1993). *Children with Down syndrome: A developmental perspective*. New York: Cambridge University Press. Review of what is known about young children with Down's Syndrome.

Cohen, L. H. (1994). *Train go sorry: Inside a deaf world*. New York: Houghton Mifflin Company. Comprehensive work about the missed connections between the deaf and the hearing.

Colin, A. (1997). *Willie: Raising and loving a child with attention deficit disorder.* New York: Viking. A mother journals her son's first five years.

Commerce Clearing House Editorial Staff. (1990). *Americans with disabilities act of 1990: Law and explanation.* Chicago: CCH Inc. A readable version of the law.

Davis, H. (1993). *Counselling parents of children with chronic illness or disability.* Leicester, Great Britain: The British Psychological Society. Provides medical professionals with the skills needed to effectively communicate with parents.

Davis, R. D. (1994). *The gift of dyslexia: Why some of the smartest people can't read...and how they can learn.* New York: The Berkley Publishing Group. Teachers, parents, therapists or dyslexics can use these procedures to overcome the difficulties of dyslexia.

Des Jardins, C. (1980). *How to get services by being assertive.* Chicago: Coordinating Council for Handicapped Children. Advice on how to advocate for needed services for children with disabilities.

Devencenzi, J., & Pendergast, S. (1988). *Belonging: Self and social discovery for children of all ages.* San Luis Obispo, CA: Belonging.

Diagnostic and statistical manual of mental disorders. (1987). (3rd ed.). Washington DC: American Psychiatric Association. Information regarding mental retardation, causes, prevalence and diagnosis.

Dickman, I., & Gordon, S. (1985). *One miracle at a time: How to get help for your disabled child.* New York: Simon & Schuster. Parents share their experiences with obtaining services for their disabled children.

Dendy, C. (1995). *Teenagers with ADD: A parents' guide.* Bethesda, MD: Woodbine House. Looks at special issues and challenges faced by these teens, their families, teachers and treatment professionals.

Dickman, I. (1985). *One miracle at a time: How to get help for your disabled child.* New York: Simon & Schuster.

Doman, G. (1994). *What to do about your brain-injured child.* Honesdale, PA: Avery Publishing Group.

Dorris, M. (1989). *The broken cord: A family's ongoing struggle with fetal alcohol syndrome.* New York: Harper & Row. An adoptive father's feelings concerning the alcohol abuse that was the source of his son's disability.

Dougan, T., Isbell, L., & Vyas, P. (1983). *We have been there: A guidebook for families of people with mental retardation.* Nashville: Abingdon. Parent and sibling essays regarding various topics associated with raising a child with a disability.

Elliott, J. (1990). *If your child has diabetes: An answer book for parents.* New York: Putnam Publishing Group.

Featherstone, H. (1982). *A difference in the family: Life with a disabled child.* New York: Penguin. A parent writes about life with a son who has severe disabilities.

Feshbach, N., Feshbach, S., Fauvre, M., & Ballard-Campbell, M. (1983). *Learning to care.* Glenview, IL: Scott, Foresman.

Finston, P. (1990). *Parenting plus: Raising children with special health needs.* New York: Dutton. Insight and practical advice.

Fowler, M. (1993). *Maybe you know my kid.* New York: Carol Publishing Group. A parents' guide to identifying, understanding, and helping your child with attention-deficit hyperactivity disorder.

Fox, R. M. & Azrin, N. H. (1973). *Toilet training persons with developmental disabilities: A rapid program for day and nighttime independent toileting.* Champaign, IL: Research Press.

Freeman, J. M., Vining, E., & Pillas, D. J. (1997). *Seizures and epilepsy in childhood: A guide for parents.* (2nd ed.). Baltimore: The Johns Hopkins University Press. Comprehensive medical information for parents.

Gallagher, H. G. (1985). *FDR's splendid deception.* New York: Dodd, Mead Publishers.

Garber, S. W., Garber, M. D. & Spizman, R. F. (1990). *If your child is hyperactive, inattentive, impulsive, distractable...: Helping the ADHD child.* New York: Villard Books. A practical program for changing your child's behavior with and without medication.

Geralis, E. (Ed.). (1991). *Children with cerebral palsy: A parent's guide.* Bethesda, MD: Woodbine House. The facts about cerebral-palsy and how it will affect a child and the family.

Getskow, V., & Konczal, D. (1996). *Kids with special needs: Information and activities to promote awareness and understanding.* Reston, VA: Council for Exceptional Children. Sourcebook including simulations, games, and activities for developing empathy.

Gliedman, J., & Roth, W. (1980). *The unexpected minority: Handicapped children in America.* New York: Harcourt Brace Jovanovich.

Goldstein, S., & Goldstein, M. (1992). *Hyperactivity: Why won't my child pay attention?* New York: John Wiley & Sons, Inc. A complete guide to ADD for parents, teachers, and community agencies.

Grandin, T. (1995). *Thinking in pictures: And other reports from my life with autism.* New York: Vintage Books. One woman's first-hand account of living with autism.

Greenfield, J. (1986). *A client called Noah: A family journey continued.* New York: Henry Holt & Company. A parent's journal entries regarding his brain-damaged son.

Haerle, T., Ed. (1992). *Children with Tourette syndrome: A parent's guide.* Rockville, MD: Woodbine House. A handbook for parents of children and teenagers with Tourette Syndrome.

Hallowell, E. (1996). *When you worry about the child you love: Emotional and learning problems in children.* New York: Simon and Schuster. Helps parents identify problems and advises when to seek help.

Hallowell, E. M. & Ratey, J. J. (1994). *Driven to distraction: Recognizing and coping with attention deficit disorder from childhood through adulthood.* New York: Simon and Schuster. Professionals share the stories of the experiences of their patients.

Hamaguchi, P. (1995). *Childhood speech, language & listening problems: What every parent needs to know.* New York: John Wiley & Sons, Inc. Valuable information for parents.

Harris, S. L. (1994). *Siblings of children with autism: A guide for families.* Bethesda, MD: Woodbine House. Guide to understanding sibling relationships and how they are affected by autism.

Hart, C. A. (1993). *A parent's guide to autism: Answers to the most common questions.* New York: Simon & Schuster.

Hartmann, T. (1993). *Attention deficit disorder: A different perception.* Grass

Valley, CA: Mythical Intelligence, Inc. Answers common questions regarding ADD.

Holbrook, M. C. (Ed.). (1996). *Children with visual impairments: A parent's guide*. Bethesda, MD: Woodbine House. Written by parents and professionals.

Hoskins, R. (1995). *Meeting the challenge of inclusive schools*. Reston, VA: Council for Exceptional Children. For administrators, teachers, and special education staff. A practical guide containing strategies and processes.

Hunsucker, G. (1993). *Attention deficit disorder*. (Rev. ed.). Fort Worth, TX: Forrest Publishing. The author explores a common but often overlooked disorder of children.

Ingersoll, B. D., & Goldstein, S. (1993). *Attention deficit disorder and learning disabilities: Realities, myths and controversial treatments*. New York: Dell Publishing. Information for parents.

Irlen, H. (1991). *Reading by the colors: Overcoming dyslexia and other reading disabilities through the Irlen method*. Garden City Park, NY: Avery Publishing Group. Techniques are discussed to improve reading difficulties.

Jablow, M. M. (1982). *Cara: Growing with a retarded child*. Philadelphia: Temple University Press. A mother's account of life with her Down Syndrome daughter.

Jablow, M. M. (1992). *A parent's guide to eating disorders and obesity*. New York: Dell Publishing.

Jordon, J. B., Gallagher, J. J., Hutinger, P. L., & Karners, M. B. (Eds.). (1988). *Early childhood special education: Birth to three*. Reston, VA: CEC-ERIC Clearinghouse. Describes model early intervention programs and approaches.

Kamien, J. (1979). *What if I couldn't...? A book about special needs*. New York: Charles Scribner's Sons.

Kaufman, S. Z. (1988). *Retarded isn't stupid, mom!* Baltimore, MD: Paul H. Brookes Publishing Co. One family's story of coping with the joys and challenges of a mentally retarded child.

Kegal, B. (1986). *Sports for the leg amputee*. Redmond, WA: Medic Publishing Co.

Kennedy, P., Terdal, L. & Fusetti, L. (1993). *The hyperactive child book*. New York: St. Martin's Press. Treating, educating, and living with your ADHD child.

Konczal, D., & Petetski, L. (1983). *We all come in different packages: Activities to increase handicap awareness*. Santa Barbara, CA: The Learning Works.

Krishef, C. H. (1983). *An introduction to mental retardation*. Springfield, IL: C. C. Thomas. Mental retardation, classification and educational labels.

Kumin, L. (1994). *Communication skills in children with Down syndrome*. Bethesda, MD: Woodbine House. Provides parents with information about speech and language development.

Landy, L. (1988). *Child support through small group counseling*. Mount Dora, FL: KIDSRIGHTS.

Lavin, R. P. (1989). *Parenting the overactive child: Alternatives to drug therapy*. New York: Madison Books.

Lechtenberg, R. (1984). *Epilepsy and the family*. Cambridge, MA: Harvard University Press. For those who have epilepsy and those who are close to them.

Levin, T. (1992). *A guide for the special needs child*. North Miami Beach, FL: Starlight Publishing Company, Inc. Good resource for anyone dealing with children who have birth defects.

Loring, G. (1991). *Parenting a diabetic child: A practical, empathetic guide to help you and your child live with diabetes.* Los Angeles: Lowell House.

Lukens, K. (1989). *Song of David.* Nanuet, NY: Venture Press. A family discovers that their child has autism and mental retardation.

Marsh, J. (Ed.). (1994). *From the heart: On being the mother of a child with special needs.* Bethesda, MD: Woodbine House.

Maurice, C. (1993). *Let me hear your voice: A family's triumph over autism.* New York: Randomhouse. A mother's account of how one family triumphed over autism.

McArthur, S. (1982). *Raising your hearing-impaired child: A guide for parents.* Washington DC: Alexander Graham Bell. Practical advice on teaching and caring for a child with a hearing impairment.

McConnell, N. (1982). *Different and alike.* Colorado Springs: Current, Inc.

McElroy, E. (Ed.). (1988). *Children and adolescents with mental illness: A parent's guide.* Bethesda, MD: Woodbine Press.

McWilliam P. J., & Bailey, D. B. (1993). *Working together with children and families: Case studies in early intervention.* Baltimore, MD: Paul H. Brookes. Wide variety of topics for case studies with discussion questions following each chapter.

Meyer, D. J. (1995). *Uncommon fathers: Reflections on raising a child with a disability.* Bethesda, MD: Woodbine House. Collection of essays by fathers who were asked to reflect on the experience of having a child with a disability.

Meyers, J. (1980). *One of a kind.* Maryland Heights, MO: Sunrise Publishing.

Miezio, P. (1983). *Parenting children with disabilities: A professional source for physicians and a guide for parents.* Levittown, PA: Phoenix Society.

Moller, K. T., Starr, C. D., & Johnson, S. A. (1990). *A parent's guide to cleft lip and palate.* Minneapolis: University of Minnesota Press. The nature, causes, diagnosis, and treatment of the disorder is discussed, as well as ways the child can cope.

Moore, C. (1990). *A reader's guide for parents of children with mental, physical or emotional disabilities.* Rockville, MD: Woodbine House. Annotated bibliography of books on topics regarding disabilities.

Naseef, R. A. (1997). *Special children, challenged parents.* Secaucus, NJ: Carol Publishing Group. The struggles and rewards of raising a child with a disability.

Neill, C. A., Clark, E. B., & Clark, C. (1992). *The heart of a child: What families need to know about heart disorders in children.* Baltimore: Johns Hopkins University Press. A summary of what parents need to know to be effective partners in caring for children who have heart disorders.

Nordic Committee on Disability. (1985). *The more we do together.* New York: World Rehabilitation Fund.

Nowicki, S., & Duke, M. P. (1992). *Helping the child who doesn't fit in.* Atlanta: Peachtree Publishers. Two child psychologists advise how to help children labeled as misfits by their peers.

Ordover, E. L., & Boundy, K. B. (1991). *Educational rights of children with disabilities: A primer for advocates.* Cambridge, MA: Center for Law and Education. Information on educational advocacy.

Paltin, D. M. (1993). *The parents' hyper-activity handbook: Helping the fidgety child.* New York: Plenum Press.

Parker, H. C. (1994). *The ADD hyperactivity workbook for parents, teachers and kids.* (2nd ed.). Plantation, FL: Specialty Press, Inc.

Pennington, B. F. (1991). *Diagnosing learning disorders: A neuropsychological framework.* New York: The Guilford Press. The latest research on the neuropsychology of learning disorders and down-to-earth advice for clinical practice.

Perske, R. (1988). *Circles of friends.* Nashville: Abingdon. How friendships among people with disabilities enrich lives.

Perske, R. (1981). *Hope for the families: New directions for parents of persons with retardation and other disabilities.* Nashville: Abingdon. Written by parents of a child with a developmental disability.

Pincus, D. (1990). *Feeling good about yourself.* Carthage, IL: Good Apple.

Plaut, T. F. (1995). *Children with asthma: A manual for parents.* Amherst, MD: Pedipress, Inc. Much needed information for parents, along with first-person stories.

Powers, M. D. (Ed.). (1989). *Children with autism: A parents' guide.* Rockville, MD: Woodbine House. Explains autism and gives suggestions for parents.

Pueschel, S. M. (1990). *A parent's guide to down syndrome: Towards a brighter future.* Baltimore: Paul H. Brookes. Informative, easy to understand guide for parents and professionals.

Pueschel, S., Scola, P. S., Weidenman, L. E. & Bernier, J. C. (1995). *The special child: A source book for parents of children with developmental disabilities.*

(2nd ed.). Baltimore: Paul H. Brookes. Information to help parents face questions about children with disabilities.

Reaves, J., & Austin, J. B. (1990). *How to find help for your troubled kid: A parent's guide to programs and services for adolescents.* New York: Henry Holt. For parents of adolescents. Helps them when they have exhausted their personal resources and are looking for help.

Reisner, H. (Ed.). (1988). *Children with epilepsy: A parent's guide.* Bethesda, MD: Woodbine House.

Ripley, H. (1988). *Children with epilepsy: A parent's guide.* Rockville, MD: Woodbine House. Discusses epilepsy and how parents and children can cope.

Rosenberg, B. (1989). *From catastrophe to help for the retarded.* New York: Rivercross Publishing. Firsthand account of a parent who has crusaded for the rights of children with mental retardation.

Routburg, M. (1987). *On becoming a special parent, a mini-support group in a book.* Chicago: Parent/Professional Publications.

Russell, L. M., Grant, A. E., Joseph, S. M. & Fee, R. W. (1994). *Planning for the future: Providing a meaningful life for a child with a disability after your death.* Evanston, IL: American Publishing Company. Practical ideas and information for parents.

Russell, P. (1985). *The wheelchair child: How handicapped children can enjoy life to its fullest.* Englewood Cliffs, NJ: Prentice Hall, Inc.

Schopmeyer, B. B. & Fonda, L. (1992). *The fragile X child.* San Diego: Singular Publishing Group. Genetic information regarding X, and descriptions of children's behavioral and developmental characteristics.

Schwartz, L. (1978). *I am special*. Santa Barbara, CA: The Learning Works.

Schwartz, S. (Ed.). (1987). *Choices in deafness: A parent's guide*. Washington, DC: Woodbine House. Professionals and parents talk about the choices parents have in raising deaf children.

Schwier, K. (1990). *Speakeasy: People with mental handicaps talk about their lives in institutions and in the community*. Austin: Pro-Ed. Adults with mental retardation tell of their experiences in institutions.

Scott, E. P., Jan, J. E., & Freeman, R. D. (1985). *Can't your child see? A guide for parents of visually impaired children*. (2nd ed.). Austin: Pro-Ed. Helps parents raise a child with visual impairments from infancy to adulthood.

Setouguchi, Y., & Rosenfelder, R. (1982). *The limb deficient child*. Springfield, IL: Charles C. Thomas.

Shapiro, B. L., & Heussner Jr., R. C. (1991). *A parent's guide to cystic fibrosis*. Minneapolis: University of Minnesota Press. Helps parents, children, professionals and educators understand cystic fibrosis.

Siegel, B. (1986). *Love, medicine and miracles*. New York; Harper & Row. Written by a premier physician who work with exceptional cancer patients.

Siegel, B. (1989). *Peace, loving and healing*. New York: Harper & Row. Written by a premier physician who works with exceptional cancer patients.

Siminerio, L., & Betschart, J. (1995). *Raising a child with diabetes: A guide for parents*. Alexandria, VA: American Diabetes Association. Two diabetes educators help parents care for children with diabetes.

Simon, C. (1997). *Mad house: Growing up in the shadow of mentally ill siblings*.

New York: Doubleday Publishing. One adult's account of growing up sane in the midst of madness.

Simons, R. (1987). *After the tears: Parenting talk about raising a child with a disability*. Orlando, FL: Harcourt Brace Jovanovich.

Smith, C., & Strick, L. (1997). *Learning disabilities: A to Z*. New York: Free Press. A parent's complete guide to learning disabilities from preschool to adulthood.

Smith, R. (1993). *Children with mental retardation: A parents' guide*. Rockville, MD: Woodbine House. An edited book focusing on a variety of topics from "What is Mental Retardation?" to "Advocacy." Chapters are written both by professionals and parents. Includes glossary, list of frequently used instruments for evaluation, extensive reading list, and resource guide.

Smith, S. L. (1992). *No easy answers: The learning disabled child at home and at school*. New York: Bantam Books. A guide to childhood learning disabilities written especially for parents and teachers.

Spiegle, J. A., & van den Pol, R. A. (1993). *Making changes: Family voices on living with disabilities*. Cambridge, MA: Brookline Books. Provocative self-reports examine the daily impact on the family with children with disabilities.

Stehli, A. (1991). *The sound of a miracle: A child's triumph over autism*. New York: Doubleday. A mother's struggles associated with caring for an autistic daughter.

Stehli, A. (Ed.). (1995). *Dancing in the rain: Stories of exceptional progress by parents of children with special needs*. Westport, CT: The Georgiana Organization, Inc. A guide to learning disabilities, developmental delay and autism through first-hand accounts from parents.

Stein, B. (1984). *About handicaps: An open family book for parents and children*. New York: Walker & Co.

Stevens, M. (1991). *Breathing easy: A parent's guide to dealing with your child's asthma*. New York: Prentice Hall Press.

Strey-Gundersen, K. (1986). *Babies with down syndrome: A new parents' guide*. Rockville, MD: Woodbine House. Information on the issues involved in raising a child with Down Syndrome.

Sullivan, T. (1995). *Special parent, special child: Parents of children with disabilities share their trials, triumphs, and hard-won wisdom*. New York: G. P. Putnam's Sons.

Taylor, J. F. (1990). *Helping your hyperactive child*. Rocklin, CA: Prima Publishing. From effective treatments and developing discipline and self-esteem to helping your family adjust.

Trainer, M. (1991). *Differences in common: Straight talk on mental retardation, down syndrome, and life*. Bethesda, MD: Woodbine House. An essay collection which speaks to every parent of a child who is "different."

Treiber, P. M. (1993). *Keys to dealing with stuttering*. Hauppage, NY: Barron's. Help for parents with children who stutter.

Turnbull, A. P., Patterson, J. M., Behr, S. K., Murphy, D. L., Marquis, J. G., & Blue-Banning, M. J. (1993). *Cognitive coping, families and disability*. Baltimore, MD: Paul H. Brookes. An edited book for professionals on cognitive coping of parents having a child with a developmental disability.

Turnbull, A., & Turnbull, H. R. (1985). *Parents speak out: Then and now*. New York: Macmillan. Parents tell what it is like to raise a child with disabilities.

Turnbull, A., & Turnbull III, H. R. (1986). *Families, professionals, and exceptionality*. Columbus, OH: Merrill. Discusses effective teaming of parents and special education professionals.

Turnbull III, H. R., Turnbull, A. P., Bronicki, G. J., Summers, J. A., & Roeder-Gordon, C. (1989). *Disability and the family: A guide to decisions for adulthood*. Baltimore: Paul H. Brookes. Information on government programs, legal definitions, and rights of children with disabilities.

Tuttle, C. (1996). *Challenging voices*. Los Angeles: Lowell House. Writings by, for, and about people with learning disabilities.

Unruh, J. F. (1994). *Down syndrome*. Eugene, OR: Fern Ridge Press. Help for parenting a child with Down Syndrome.

Waller, S. (1981). *Circle of hope*. New York: Evans Publishing Company.

Weiss, E. B. (1989). *Mothers talk about learning disabilities: Personal feelings, practical advice*. New York: Prentice Hall Press. Mothers talk about dealing with a child's learning disability.

Wieland, B., & Brown, S. N. (1989). *One step at a time*. Grand Rapids, MI: Zondervan Publishers.

Wodrich, D. L. (1994). *Attention deficit hyperactivity disorder: What every parent wants to know*. Baltimore: Paul H. Brookes Publishing Company. Information is given regarding ADHD.

DEPRESSION AND SUICIDE

Berger, D., & Berger, L. (1991). *We heard angels of madness: A family guide to coping with manic depression.* New York: Quill.

Crook, M. (1992). *Listen to me! Your guide to understanding teenagers and suicide.* (2nd ed.). Bellingham, WA: Self-Counsel Press.

Cytryn, L., & McKnew, D. (1996). *Growing up sad: Childhood depression and its treatment.* New York: W. W. Norton. An overview of childhood depression by two clinician-scholars.

Dubuque, S. E. (1996). *A parent's survival guide to childhood depression.* King of Prussia, PA: The Center for Applied Psychology, Inc.

Oster, G. D., & Montgomery, S. S. (1995). *Helping your depressed teenager: A guide for parents and caregivers.* New York: John Wiley & Sons, Inc.

Schaefer, C. E., & DiGeronimo, T. F. (1994). *How to talk to your kids about really important things: For children four to twelve.* San Francisco: Jossey-Bass.

Slaby, A., & Garfinkel, L. F. (1994). *No one saw my pain: Why teenagers kill themselves.* New York: W. W. Norton.

Williams, K. (1995). *A parent's guide for suicidal and depressed teens.* Center City, MN: Hazelden. Help for recognizing if a child is in crisis and what to do about it.

DIVORCE, REMARRIAGE AND CHANGING FAMILIES

Benedek, E. P., & Brown, C. F. (1995). *How to help your child overcome your divorce.* Washington, DC: American Psychiatric Press. Written by child psychiatrists and aimed to help parents raise emotionally balanced children in spite of divorce.

Blau, M. (1994). *Families apart: Ten keys to successful co-parenting.* New York: Putnam.

Burns, C. (1986). *Stepmotherhood: How to survive without feeling frustrated, left out or wicked.* New York: HarperColllins.

Chambers, C. A. (1991). *Child support: How to get what your child needs and deserves.* New York: Summit Books.

Cohen, M. (1989). *Long distance parenting: A guide for divorced parents.* New York: New American Library.

Cohen, M. (1991). *The joint custody handbook.* Philadelphia: Running Press.

Emery, R. (1988). *Marriage, divorce, and children's readjustment.* Newbury Park, CA: Sage Publications.

Engel, M., & Gould, D. (1992). *The divorce decisions workbook.* New York: McGraw-Hill.

Everett, S.V., & Everett, C. A. (1994). *Healthy divorce.* San Francisco: Jossey-Bass.

Fisher, B. (1992). *Rebuilding when your relationship ends.* San Luis Obispo, CA: Impact.

Francke, L. B. (1983). *Growing up divorced.* New York: Fawcett Crest. How to help your child cope with every stage—from infancy through the teens.

Gardner, R. (1991). *The parents book about divorce.* New York: Bantam Books. Help for parents to get their children through the stress of divorce.

Gold, L. (1992). *Between love and hate: A guide to civilized divorce.* New York: Plenum.

Goldstein, S., & Solnit, A. (1984). *Divorce and your child: Practical suggestions for parents.* New Haven, CT: Yale University Press.

Gregg, C. (1995). *Single fatherhood: The complete guide.* New York: Sulzburger & Graham Publishing, Ltd. From what you need to know about single father-hood to emotional aspects.

Hickey, E., & Dalton, E. (1994). *Healing Hearts: Helping children and adults recover from divorce.* Carson City, NV: Gold Leaf Press.

Howard, J., & Shepherd, G. (1987). *Conciliation, children and divorce: A family systems approach.* London: Trafalgar.

Jakes, T. D. (1996). *Help! I'm raising my child alone: A guide for single parents and those who sometimes feel they are.* Orlando: Creation House.

Johnson, L., & Rosenfield, G. (1990). *Divorced kids: What you need to know to help kids survive a divorce.* Nashville: Thomas Nelson.

Kalter, N. (1990). *Growing up with divorce: Helping your child avoid immediate and later emotional problems.* New York: Free Press.

Kline, K., & Pew, S. (1992). *For the sake of the children.* Rocklin, CA: Prima Publishing.

McLanahan, S., & Sandefur, G. (1994). *Growing up with a single parent: What hurts, what helps.* Cambridge, MA: Harvard University Press. Research based information provided on single parenting and its affects on children.

Prilik, P. (1990). *Stepmothering: Another kind of love: A caring, commonsense guide to stepfamily.* New York: Berkley Books.

Rosenburg, M. B. (1990). *Talking about stepfamilies.* New York: Bradbury Press.

Stinson, K. M. (1991). *Adolescents, family, and friends: Social support after parents' divorce or remarriage.* New York: Praeger. Focuses on the importance of interrelatedness of youth, especially those from divided or blended families.

Teyber, E. (1994). *Helping children cope with divorce.* New York: Lexington Books. Assists parents in helping their child(ren) to succeed and adjust to divorce.

Thomas, S. (1995). *Parents are forever.* Longmont, CO: Springboard Publications. A step-by-step guide to becoming successful co-parents after divorce.

de Toledo, S., & Brown, D. (1995). *Grandparents as parents: A survival guide for raising a second family.* New York: The Guilford Press.

Trafford, A. (1984). *Crazy time: Surviving divorce.* New York: Bantam Books.

Virtue, D. (1988). *My kids don't live with me anymore.* Minneapolis: CompCare Publishers.

Visher, E., & Visher, J. (1991). *How to win as a step-family* (2nd ed.). New York: Brunner/Mazel. Latest edition of excellent text by professionals who have lived the path of stepfamilies, raising eight children. Invaluable for professionals and families.

DIVERSITY

Aboud, F. (1988). *Children and prejudice.* Cambridge, MA: Blackwell Publishers. Concerns of youth when dealing with prejudice.

Bates, J. D. (1993). *Gift children.* New York, NY: Ticknor & Fields. Story told by a Caucasian father about the adoption of two African-American daughters.

Brown, D. (1975). *Bury my heart at wounded knee.* New York: Bantam. A story about Native American history.

Brown, W., & Ling, A. (Eds.). (1991). *Imagining America: Stories from the promised land.* New York: Persea Books.

Brown, W., & Ling, A. (Eds.). (1991). *Visions of America: Personal narratives from the promised land.* New York: Persea Books.

Chideya, F. (1995). *Don't believe the hype: Fighting cultural misinformation about African-Americans.* New York: Plume Books. Facts and statistics regarding misinformation about African-Americans.

Clark, K. B. (1988). *Prejudice and your child.* Hanover, NH: University Press of New England.

Comer, J., & Poussaint, A. (1992). *Raising black children: Questions and answers for parents and teachers.* New York: Penguin. Focuses on parents and addresses concerns of educators of black children.

Cose, E. (1993). *The rage of the privileged class.* New York: Harper Collins. Examines the racism middle class African-Americans confront.

Dew, R. F. (1994). *The family heart: a memoir of when our son came out.* New York: Ballantine Books. A mother's story about learning to accept her son's homosexuality.

Dog, M. C. (1990). *Lakota woman.* New York: Harper Collins. Autobiography of Mary Brace Bird, a Sioux woman who faces tremendous challenges.

Edelman, M. W. (1992). *The measure of our success: A letter to my children and yours.* Boston: Beacon. In a letter to her three sons, Marian Wright Edelman details important lessons of her life.

Faludi, S. (1991). *The undeclared war against American women.* New York: Crown Publishers. An analysis of the attacks on the women's movement.

Fernandez, J. (1994). *Conquered peoples in America* (5th ed.). Dubuque, IA: Kendall-Hunt. Overview of conquered peoples in the United States.

Frackenburg, R. (1993). *White women, race matters: The social construction of whiteness.* Minneapolis: University of Minnesota. Examines racial identity.

Franklin, J. H. (1994). *From slavery to freedom.* New York: Alfred Knopf. History of African-Americans in America.

Gates, H. L. (1995). *Colored people.* New York: Vintage. Autobiography of Henry Louis Gates.

Golden, M. (1995). *Saving our sons: Raising black children in a turbulent world.* New York: Doubleday. A mother of a teenager shares her feelings about raising African-American males.

Kadi, J. (1994). *Food for our grandmothers.* Boston: South End Press. Collection of pieces relating to Arab American and Arab Canadian feminists.

Kanter, R. M. (1993). *Men and women of the corporation.* New York: Basic Books. Examines institutional racism.

Kivel, P. (1996). *Uprooting racism: How white people can work for racial justice.* Philadelphia: New Society Press. A book to help white people understand racism in America.

Kohn, Alfie. *No contest: The case against competition.* Boston: Houghton Mifflin Company. An examination of the destructive nature of competition.

Ladner, J. (1995). *Tomorrow's tomorrow: The black woman.* New York: Doubleday. An examination of theories about African-American women and their families.

Lim, S. G. (Ed.). (1989). *The forbidden stitch: An Asian American women's anthology.* Short stories and poetry about and for Asian American women.

Marable, M. (1995). *Beyond black and white: Transforming African-American politics.* New York: Verso.

Meier, M., & Rivera, F. (1993). *Mexican Americans, American Mexicans: From*

Conquistadors to Chicanos. New York: Hill and Wang. History of the Mexican experience in America.

Miedzian, M. (1991). *Boys will be boys: Breaking the link between masculinity and violence.* Examines relationship between being male and being violent.

Moody, A. (1992). *Coming of age in Mississippi.* New York: Dell. A story of an African-American woman growing up in the south.

Morrison, T. (1993). *The bluest eye.* New York: Penguin. Examines racism and sexism.

Orenstein, P. (1994). *School girls: Young women, self-esteem and the confidence gap.* New York: Anchor Books. Examines issues surrounding self-esteem and confidences in eighth grade girls.

Paley, V. G. (1995). *Kwanzaa and me: A teacher's story.* Cambridge, MA: Harvard University Press. A discussion about multicultural classrooms.

Papajohn, J., and Spiegel, J. (1995). *Transactions in families: Resolving cultural and generational conflicts.* Northvale, NJ: Jason Aronson, Inc. Detailed family case histories show therapists how to understand and change family conflict.

Pipher, M. (1994). *Reviving Ophelia: Saving the selves of adolescent girls.* New York: Ballantine. Examines the effects of sexism on adolescent girls.

Rafkin, L. (Ed.). (1990). *Different daughters.* Pittsburgh: Cleis Press. Interviews with mother whose daughters are lesbian.

Reddy, M. T. (1994). *Crossing the color line: Race, parenting and culture.* New Brunswick, New Jersey: Rutgers University Press.

Shorris, E. (1992). *A biography of people.* New York: Avon. A history of Latinos/as in the United States.

Takaki, R. (1993). *A different mirror: A history of multicultural America.* New York: Little, Brown.

Tatum, B. (1997). *Why are all the black kids sitting together in the cafeteria: And other conversations about racial identity.* New York: Basic Books.

Tizard, B., & Phoenix, A. (1993). *Black, white or mixed race?: Race and racism in the lives of young people of mixed parentage.* New York: The Guilford Press.

Walker, A. (1967). *In love and trouble: Stories of black women.* New York: Harcourt Brace.

West, C. (1993). *Race matters.* Boston: Beacon Press.

GENERAL

Aldinger, L. E., Warger, C. L., & Eavy, P. W. (1991). *Strategies for teacher collaboration.* Reston, VA: Council for Exceptional Children. For school-based teams. Includes 18 inservice activities.

Annunziatia, J., & Jacobsen-Kram, P. (1994). *Solving your problems together: Family therapy for the whole family.* Washington, DC: American Psychological Association. Excellent resource aimed at helping professionals refer families to family therapy. Contains illustrations and is written so that most adults can understand the concepts presented.

Apter, T. (1990). *Altered Lives: Mothers and daughters during adolescence.* New York: Fawcett Columbine.

Bauwens, J., & Hourcade, J. J. (1995). *Cooperative teaching: rebuilding the schoolhouse for all students.* Reston, VA: Council for Exceptional Children.

Bennett, T., Lingerfelt, B. F., & Nelson, D. E. (1990). *Developing individualized family support plans: A training manual.* Cambridge, MA: Brookline Books. Information for professionals on writing IFSPs.

Bowen, M. (1994). *Family therapy in clinical practice.* Northvale, NJ: Jason Aronson, Inc.

Brazelton, B. T. (1969). *Infants and mothers.* New York: Dell Publishing.

Brazelton, B. T. (1974). *Toddlers and parents.* New York: Dell Publishing.

Clark, L. (1985). *SOS! Help for parents.* Bowling Green, KY: Parents Press. How to manage everyday problems of children's behavior.

Clark, L. (1989). *The time-out solution.* Chicago: Contemporary Books Inc.

Coleman, J. G. (1993). *The early intervention dictionary: A multidisciplinary guide to terminology.* Rockville, MD: Woodbine House. Defines terminology in the early intervention field.

Douglas, M. (1966). *How to make a habit of succeeding.* Grand Rapids, MI: Zondervan Publishing.

Dreikurs, R., & Satz, V. (1964). *Children: The challenge.* New York: Hawthorne Books.

Eyre, L., & Eyre, R. (1993). *Teaching your children values.* New York: Fireside Books, Simon and Schuster.

Fabers, A., & Mazlish, E. (1982). *How to talk so kids will listen and listen so kids will talk.* New York: Avon Books.

Friend, M., & Cook, L. (1996). *Interactions: Collaboration skills for school professionals.* Reston, VA: Council for Exceptional Children. Information on team meetings, parent conferencing, co-teaching, problem-solving with colleagues.

Holley, T. E. (1997). *My mother's keeper.* New York: William Morrow & Company, Inc. A daughter's memoir of growing up in the shadow of schizophrenia.

Glenn, H. S., & Nelson, J. (1988). *Raising self-reliant children in a self-indulgent world.* Rocklin, CA: Prima Publishing and Communications.

Ilg, F., Ames, L., & Baker, S. (1981). *Child behavior.* New York: Barnes & Noble.

Imber-Black, E. (1988). *Families and larger systems: A family therapist's guide through the labyrinth.* New York: The Guilford Press. Designed specifically for the practicing therapist. Offers descriptions of families and interactional patterns.

Jampolski, G. (1993). *Teach only love.* New York: Bantam Books.

Johns, B. H., & Keenan, J. P. (1997). *Techniques for managing a safe school.* Reston, VA: Council for Exceptional Children. Checklist provides for evaluating safety of school, legal consideration proper procedures, judicial and law enforcement, gang prevention, searches, and sexual harassment topics. Billed for school community, especially leadership teams.

Leman, K. (1993). *Bringing up kids without tearing them down.* New York: Delacorte Press.

Magid, K., & McKelvey, C. A. (1987). *High risk: Children without a conscience.* New York: Bantam Books. Case histories and suggestions for raising healthy children and protecting them.

Melda, K. (Ed.). (1992). *The family support syndicate: An information sharing network* (Vol. 1). Salem, OR: Human Services Research Institute.

Melda, K. (Ed.). (1993). *The family support syndicate: An information sharing network.* (Vol. 2). Salem, OR: Human Services Research Institute.

Miller, M. S. (1982). *Child-stress! Understanding and answering stress signals of infants, children, and teenagers.* New York: Doubleday.

Nachman, P. (1997). *You and your only child: The joys, myths and challenges of raising an only child.* New York: Harper Collins.

Napier, A. (1988). *The fragile bond: In search of an equal, intimate and enduring marriage.* New York: Harper Perennial. Renowned therapist uses his own marriage and other cases to illustrate obstacles we face within ourselves as we try to create an enduring modern marriage.

Newman, S. (1990). *Parenting an only child: The joys and challenges of raising your one and only.* New York: Doubleday. Debunking the myths and practical advice.

Novello, J. (1981). *Bringing up kids American style.* New York: A and W Publishers.

Novello, J. (1988). *How to survive your kids.* New York: McGraw-Hill.

O'Reilly, C. D. (1995). *Family connections: A family support project, families making communities — book 1: An introduction.* Lexington, KY: Interdisciplinary Human Development Institute.

O'Reilly, C. D. (1995). *Family connections: A family support project, families making communities — book 2: Getting started.* Lexington, KY: Interdisciplinary Human Development Institute.

O'Reilly, C. D. (1995). *Family connections: A family support project, families making communities — book 3: Sharing our stories, sharing our lives.* Lexington, KY: Interdisciplinary Human Development Institute.

O'Reilly, C. D. (1995). *Family connections: A family support project, families making communities — book 4: Families empowering themselves.* Lexington,

KY; Interdisciplinary Human Development Institute.

Paquette, P., and Tuttle, C. (1995). *Parenting a child with a behavior problem.* Los Angeles: Lowell House. Practical and effective guidance for parents to help the child become a better family member and person.

Peck, M. S. (1978). *The road less traveled.* New York: Simon & Schuster/Touchstone.

Rubin, L. (1996). *The transcendent child: Tales of triumph over the past.* New York: NY: BasicBooks/Harper Collins. Real stories of adults who overcame childhood traumas. Focuses on triumph over adversity.

Runyon, B. (1992). *The overloving parent: Making love work for you and your child.* Dallas: Taylor Publishing Co. Helps identify parenting style, provides techniques and solutions to common problems.

Samenow, S. (1989). *Before it's too late.* New York: Times Books. Explains why some kids get into trouble and what parents can do about it.

Scarf, M. (1995). *Intimate worlds: How families thrive and why they fail.* New York: Random House. Examines the complex rules and patterns of family interactions.

Schwartz, S., & Miller, J. E. (1988). *The language of toys: Teaching communication skills to special-needs children.* Rockville, MD: Woodbine House. How to use toys to help your child's communication skills.

Seagal, M., & Adcock, D. (1985). *Your child at play.* New York: New Market Press. Information for parents covering the years from one to five and including suggestions for parents.

Singer, D. G. (1993). *Playing for their lives: Helping troubled children through play therapy*. New York: The Free Press. For parents, educators, and therapists — uses and examples of play therapy.

Sulloway, F. J. (1996). *Born to rebel: Birth order, family dynamics, and creative lives*. New York: Pantheon Books. Insights about family relationships for therapists.

Taffel, R. (1994). *Why parents disagree and what you can do about it*. New York: The Hearst Corporation. How to raise great kids while you strengthen your marriage.

Valette, B. (1988). *A parent's guide to eating disorders: Prevention and treatment of anorexia nervosa and bulimia*. New York: Avon Books. Essential aid every parent needs when trying to cope with an eating disorder.

Wahlroos, S. (1995). *Family communication* (4th ed.). Chicago: Contemporary Books. The essential rules for improving communication and making your relationships more loving, supportive and enriching.

Weisinger, H. (1985). *Anger work-out book*. New York: William Morrow & Co.

Weissbourd, R. (1995). *The vulnerable child*. Reading, MA: Addison-Wesley Publishing Co., Inc. What really hurts America's children and what we can do about it.

Winebrenner, S. (1996). *Teaching kids with learning difficulties in the regular classroom*. Reston, VA: Council for Exceptional Children.

ILLNESS AND DEATH

Adams, D. W., & Deveau, E. J. (1995). *Beyond the innocence of childhood: Helping children and adolescents cope with life-threatening illness and dying*. Amityville, NY. Baywood Publishing Company. Mainly for professionals, this book deals with how to help kids with chronic illnesses.

Bain, L. J. (1995). *A parent's guide to childhood cancer*. New York: Dell Publishing. Guide to take an active, positive role in a child's well-being.

Buckingham, R.W. (1983). *A special kind of love: Caring for the dying child*. New York: Continuum.

Chesler, M. A., & Chesler, B. K. (1996). *Cancer and self-help: Bridging the troubled waters of childhood illness*. Madison, WI: University of Wisconsin Press. Studies and information regarding self-help groups for parents of children with cancer are discussed.

Colgrove, M., Bloomfield, H., & McWilliams, P. (1977). *How to survive the loss of love*. New York: Bantam. Major crises and big family changes when dealing with death of a loved one.

Dailey, B.A. (1990). *Your child's recovery: A parent's guide for the child with a life-threatening illness*. New York: Macmillan.

Davis, D. L. (1995). *Empty cradle, broken heart: Surviving the death of your baby*. (Rev. ed.). Golden, CO: Fulcrum Publishing. Offers reassurance to parents who struggle with anger, guilt and despair after tragedy.

Davis, H. (1993). *Counselling parents of children with chronic illness or disability*. Baltimore: Paul H. Brookes.

Edelman, H. (1994). *Motherless Daughters: The legacy of loss*. New York: Dell Publishing. Interviews with mother-loss survivors.

Fumia, M. (1997). *Honor thy children*. Berkeley, CA: Conari Press. One family's experience from grief to healing, when a young man dies of AIDS.

Fitzgerald, H. (1992). *The grieving child: A parent's guide.* New York: Simon & Schuster. Practical, compassionate advice for helping a child cope with the death of a parent or loved one.

Grollman, E. A. (1990). *Talking about death: A dialogue between parent and child.* (3rd ed.). Boston: Beacon Press. Sensitive and helpful advice for families coping with loss.

Kubler-Ross, E. (1993). *On children and death.* New York: Macmillan Publishing Company. Offers families of dead and dying children the help and hope they need to survive.

Kushner, H. S. (1981). *When bad things happen to good people.* New York: Schocken. Major crises and big family changes when dealing with the death of a loved one.

La Tour, K. (1987). *For those who live: Helping children cope with the death of a brother or sister.* Omaha, NE: Centering Corp.

Levert, S. (1995). *When your child has a chronic illness: What you must know, what you can do, what you should expect.* New York: Dell Publishing Company. Straightforward compassionate advice for parents.

Lingard, J. (1991). *Between two worlds.* New York: Lodestar Books.

Lonetto, R. (1980). *Children's conception of death.* New York: Springer.

McCue, K., & Bonn, R. (1994). *How to help children through a parent's serious illness.* New York: St. Martin. This book explores what to tell a child about the illness and how a child's behavior may be affected.

Nieberg, H., & Fischer, A. (1982). *Pet loss: A thoughtful guide for adults and children.* New York: Harper & Row.

Obiakor, F. E., Mehring, T. A., & Schwenn, J. O. (1997). *Disruption, disaster, and death: Helping students deal with crises.* Reston, VA: Council for Exceptional Children.

Raab, R. (1989). *Coping with death.* New York: Rosen Publishing Group.

Sanders, C. (1992). *How to survive the loss of a child: Filling the emptiness and rebuilding your life.* Rocklin, CA: Prima Publishing. A psychologist and bereaved parent offers practical help.

Schaefer, C. E., & DiGeronimo, T. F. (1994). *How to talk to your kids about really important things: For children four to twelve.* San Francisco: Jossey-Bass. Believing that what children don't know can hurt them, this book is divided by topical areas related to major crises and big family changes as well as concerns of youth. Topics include such things as dying child, death of a pet, death of a loved one, among many others.

Scott, R. A. (1988). *Cradle song.* New York: Donald I. Fine, Inc.

Stein, S. B. (1974). *About dying.* New York: Walker.

U. S. Department of Health & Human Services. (1991). *Young people with cancer: A handbook for parents.* Bethesda, MD. Coping methods for parents are explored.

Walsh, F., & McGoldrick, M. (1991). *Living beyond loss: Death in the family.* New York, NY: W. W. Norton & Company. A family systems perspective on death. For professionals, an edited book providing range of topics including cultural differences in mourning, adolescent suicide, and helping families with loss.

Westburg, G. (1962). *Good grief.* Philadelphia: Fortress Press.

SIBLINGS

Burton, S. (1991). *KIDPOWER: A leader's guide for conducting KIDPOWER groups*. Moscow, ID: Idaho Center on Developmental Disabilities.

Faber, A. (1988). *Siblings without rivalry*. Chicago: Nightingale-Conant. Book-based lecture and workshop to help parents help their children live together and be able to express negative feelings without disrupting the family unit.

Harris, S. L. (1994). *Siblings of children with autism: A guide for families*. Bethesda, MD: Woodbine House. Understanding how autism affects sibling relationships.

Lobato, D. J. (1990). *Brothers, sisters, and special needs: Information and activities for helping young brothers and sisters of children with chronic illnesses and developmental disabilities*. Baltimore: Paul H. Brookes Publishing Co.

Merrell, S. (1995). *The accidental bond: How sibling connections influence adult relationships*. New York: Randomhouse. Examines competition, cooperation and comparison.

Meyer, D. J., & Vadasy, P. F. (1994). *Sibshops: Workshops for siblings of children with special needs*. Baltimore: Paul H. Brookes Publishing Company. Program brings 8 - 13 yr. olds to express their feelings about having siblings with disabilities.

Meyer, D. J., Vadasy, P. F., & Fewell, R. R. (1985). *Living with a brother or sister with special needs: A book for sibs*. Seattle: University of Washington Press.

Morgan, F. (Ed.). (1992). *The Pittsburgh sibling manual*. Pittsburgh: Easter Seal Society of Allegheny County.

Nollette, C. (1985). *Autism...a family affair: A curriculum for use with siblings of special needs children*. Minneapolis: Minneapolis Children's Medical Center.

Powell, T. H., & Ogle, P. A. (1985). *Brothers and sisters: A special part of exceptional families*. Baltimore: Paul H. Brookes. Siblings and experts write about being a brother or sister of a child with disabilities.

Ratto, L. L. (1992). *Coping with a physically challenged brother or sister*. New York: The Rosen Publishing Group. Written for those who share their lives with a physically challenged person. Covers a variety of topics related to feelings (shock, denial, anger, hate, jealousy, depression) as well as how to get life back in order. Glossary and resource list provided.

Reit, S. V. (1985). *Sibling Rivalry: Sound, reassuring advice for getting along as a family*. New York: Ballantine Books.

Samalin, N. (1996). *Loving each one best*. New York: Bantam Books. A caring and practical approach to raising siblings.

Twerski, A. (1992). *I didn't ask to be in this family*. New York: Henry Holt and Co. Sibling relationships and how they shape adult behavior.

Wiehe, V. R. (1991). *Perilous rivalry: When siblings become abusive*. Lexington, MA: Lexington Books.

Books for Children and Youth

ABUSE AND VIOLENCE

Aho, J. S., & Petras, J. W. (1985). *Learning about sexual abuse*. Hillside, NJ.: Enslow Publishers. Concerns of youth about sexual abuse for children aged nine to twelve.

Anderson, D., & Finne, M. (1986). *Jason's story*. Minneapolis: Dillon Press. A neglected baby is put into foster care and later returns when he becomes a victim of his mother's abuse.

Anderson, D., & Finne, M. (1986). *Michael's story*. Minneapolis: Dillon Press. An overweight boy suffers from verbal abuse from his parents and peers.

Berenstain, S., & Berenstain, J. (1984). *The Berenstain Bears and too much T.V.* New York: Random Books for Young Readers. Concerns of youth about television and media violence for children aged four to seven.

Byars, B. (1986). *The pinballs*. Mount Kisco, New York: Guidance Associates. Abused children live together in a foster home and find a game that symbolizes their situation.

Cormier, R. (1991). *We all fall down*. New York: Delacorte. This book explores the impact of random violence on individuals and their families.

Freeman, L. (1982). *It's my body*. Seattle: Parenting Press. Concerns of youth about sexual abuse for children aged four to eight.

Girard, L. W. (1984). *My body is private*. Niles, IL: A. Whitman. Concerns of youth about sexual abuse for children aged nine to twelve.

Hayden, T. L. (1991). *Ghost girl: The true story of a child in peril and the teacher who saved her*. New York: Little Brown. A teacher struggles to uncover the depth of abuse that has rendered a young girl speechless.

Hunt, I. (1976). *The lottery rose*. New York: Scribner. A young boy becomes fearful of adults after being abused by his mother and her boyfriend.

Johnsen, K. (1986). *The trouble with secrets.* Seattle: Parenting Press. Concerns of youth about sexual abuse for children aged four to eight.

Kellogg, M. (1972). *Like the lion's tooth.* New York: Random House. A young boy is sexually and physically abused by his father and meets other children who have been abused in a new school.

Lamb, W. (1993). *She's come undone.* New York: Pocket Star. A young girl finds strength after surviving her father's desertion, her mother's mental illness, and rape by a trusted person.

Mazer, H. (1978) *The war on villa street.* New York: Delacorte Press. An eight year-old abused boy runs away only to find life on the street never gets better.

Mowry, J. (1992). *Way past cool.* New York: Farrar, Straus and Giroux. Two gangs live in a hate-filled world.

Rench, J. E. (1992). *Family violence: How to recognize and survive it.* Minneapolis: Lerner Publications. Concerns of youth about sexual abuse for children aged nine to twelve.

Roberts, W. (1988). *Don't hurt Laurie.* Edgartown, MA: S&S Publisher. An eleven year old girl finally discloses her mother's abuse.

Sweet, P. (1981). *Something happened to me.* Racine, WI: Mother Courage Press. Concerns of youth about sexual abuse for children aged four to eight.

Tamar, E. (1993). *Fair game.* Niles, IL: Harcourt Brace. A community deals with gang-rape accusations.

Terkel, S. N. (1984). *Feeling safe, feeling strong: How to avoid sexual abuse and what to do if it happens to you.* Minneapolis: Lerner Publications. Concerns of youth about sexual abuse for children aged nine to twelve.

Wachter, O. (1983). *No more secrets for me.* Boston: Little, Brown & Co. A book for adults to share with children which helps families deal openly with the issue of sexual abuse.

White, R. (1992). *Weeping willow.* New York: Farrar, Straus and Giroux. A young girl is raped by her stepfather.

Williams, C. L. (1997). *The true colors of Caitlynne Jackson.* New York: Bantam Doubleday Dell Publishing. Two girls survive their mother's physical abuse.

ADDICTION

Adler, C. (1985). *With Westie and the Tin Man.* New York: Macmillan. Major crises and big family changes for children aged eight to twelve.

Berenstain, S., & Berenstain, J. (1993). *The Berenstain Bears and the drug free zone.* New York: Random Books for Young Readers. Concerns of youth about drug abuse for children aged five to seven.

Berger, G. (1992). *Meg's Story: Get real! Straight talk about drugs.* Brookfield, CT: Millbrook Press. Concerns of youth about drug abuse for children aged eight to twelve.

Berry, J. W. (1990). *Good answers to tough questions about substance abuse.* Chicago: Children's Press. Concerns of youth about drug abuse for children aged eight to twelve.

Brooks, C. (1989). *The Secret Everyone Knows.* Center City, MN: Hazeldon. Major crises and big family changes for children aged eight to twelve.

Carbone, E. L. (1992). *My dad's definitely not a drunk.* Burlington, VT: Waterfront Books. A twelve year-old girl wishes her dad did not drink.

Carter, A. R. (1991). *Up country*. New York: Scholastic. A teenager deals with the effects of his mother's alcoholism.

DeClements, B. (1987). *No Place for Me*. New York: Viking Kestrel. Major crises and big family changes for children aged eight to twelve.

DiGiovanni, K. (1986). *My house is different*. Burlington, VT: Waterfront Books. Alcoholism in the family, ages four through seven.

Ferry, C. (1992). *Binge*. Rochester, MI: Daisy Hill Press. This book illustrates the negative consequences which result from teenage binge drinking.

Friedman, D. P. (1990). *Focus on drugs and the brain*. (2nd ed.). New York: F. Watts. Concerns of youth about drug abuse for children aged eight to twelve.

Grant, C.D. (1992). *Shadow man*. New York: Atheneum. A community must deal with the death of a teenager as a result of drinking and driving.

Johnson, K. (1992). *Turning yourself around: Self-help strategies for troubled teens*. Alameda, CA: Hunter House. Stories of teens addicted to drugs help explain a program to help beat their addictions.

Kenny, K. (1980). *Sometimes My Mom Drinks Too Much*. Milwaukee: Raintree Childrens Books. Major crises and big family changes for children aged four to seven.

National Institute on Drug Abuse. (1995). *Marijuana: Facts for teens*. Washington, DC: NIDA.

Ryan, E. A. (1992). *Straight talk about drugs and alcohol*. New York: Laurel-Leaf/Dell. Information about the effects of societal, peer and family pressures on teenage use of drugs and alcohol.

Sanford, D. (1988). *I know the world's worst secret: A child's book about living with an alcoholic parent*. Burlington, VT: Waterfront Books. Alcoholism in the family for ages four through seven.

Sexas, J. S. (1987). *What they are, what they do*. New York: Greenwillow Books.

Silverstein, A., Silverstein, V., & Silverstein, R. (1992). *Steroids: Big muscles, big problems*. New York: Enslow. Understandable answers to questions about steroids are provided.

Stoehr, S. (1993). *Crosses*. New York: Laurel-Leaf/Dell. This book deals with a teenage girl's self-mutilation, drinking, smoking and drugs.

Super, G. (1990). *What are drugs?* Frederick, MD.: Twenty-First Century Books. Concerns of youth about drug abuse for children aged five to seven.

Super, G. (1990). *You can say "No" to drugs!* Frederick, MD: Twenty-First Century Books. Concerns of youth about drug abuse for children aged five to seven.

Vigna, J. (1990). *My big sister takes drugs*. Niles, IL.: Whitman. Concerns of youth about drug abuse for children aged five to seven.

Vigna, J. (1988). *I wish daddy didn't drink so much*. Niles, IL: A. Whitman. Major crises and big family changes for children aged four to seven.

Woods, G. (1986). *Drug use and drug abuse (2nd ed.)*. New York: F. Watts. Concerns of youth about drug abuse for children aged five to seven.

ADOPTION

Auch, M. J. (1988). *Pick of the litter*. New York: Holiday House. Major crises and big family changes for children aged eight to twelve.

Ballero, M. (1985). *My village in India*. Needham, MA: Silver Burdett & Ginn.

Banish, R. (1992). *A forever family.* New York: Harper Trophy. Major crises and big family changes for young children.

Bloom, S. (1990). *A family for Jamie: An adoption story.* New York: C. N. Potter. Major crises and big family changes for young children.

Burns, W. J., & Kim, D. (1987). *A letter from a Korean village.* Seoul, Korea Save the Children Federation and UNICEF/Korea.

Casagrande, L. B., & Johnson, S. (1986). *Focus on Mexico: Modern life in an ancient land.* Minneapolis: Lerner Publications.

Freudberg, J., & Geiss, T. (1992). *Susan and Gordon adopt a baby.* New York: Random House Books for Young Readers. Major crises and big family changes for young children.

Girard, L. W. (1989). *We adopted you Benjamin Koo.* Niles, IL: A. Whitman. Major crises and big family changes for young children.

Greenberg, J. E. (1997). *Adopted.* New York: F. Watts. Major crises and big family change for young children.

Jenness, A., & Kroeber, L. (1975). *A life of their own: An Indian family in Latin America.* New York: Harper and Row Junior Books.

Keller, H. (1991). *Horace.* New York: Greenwillow Books. Major crises and big family changes for young children.

Krementz, J. (1992). *How it feels to be adopted.* New York: Knopf. Major crises and big family changes for children aged eight to twelve.

Myers, W. D. (1992). *Mop, moondance, and the Nagasaki Knights.* New York: Delacorte Press. Major crises and big family changes for children aged eight to twelve.

Powledge, F. (1982). *So you're adopted.* New York: Scribners. Major crises and big family changes for children aged eight to twelve.

Rosenberg, M. B. (1989). *Growing up adopted.* New York: Bradbury Press. Major crises and big family changes for children aged eight to twelve.

CHILDREN WITH SPECIAL NEEDS

Adams, B. (1979). *Like it is: Facts and feelings about handicaps from kids who know.* New York: Walker & Co.

Anderson, P. (1985). *Children's Hospital.* New York: Harper & Row.

Arnold, K. (1982). *Anna joins in.* Nashville, TN: Abingdon Press. Cystic fibrosis.

Baldwin, A. N. (1978). *A little time.* New York: Viking Press. Developmental disabilities.

Berger, G. (1979). *Physical disabilities.* New York: Franklin Watts.

Bergman, T. (1989). *We laugh, we love, we cry: Children living with mental retardation.* Milwaukee: Gareth Stevens. The experiences of two sisters who have mental retardation are shared.

Bodenheimer, C. (1979). *Everybody is a person: A book for brothers and sisters of autistic kids.* Syracuse, NY: Jowonio/The Learning Place.

Bradbury, B. (1970). *Nancy and her Johnny O.* New York: Ives Washburn, Inc. Developmental disabilities.

Brown, T., and Ortiz, F. (1984). *Someone special just like you.* New York: Holt, Rinehart & Winston.

Byars, B. (1970). *The summer of the swans.* New York: Viking Press. Developmental Disabilities.

Carrick, C. (1989). *Stay away from Simon.* New York: Clarion Books. Mental Retardation.

Cleaver, V. (1973). *Me too.* Philadelphia: J. B. Lippincott. Developmental Disabilities.

Clifton, L. (1980). *My friend Jacob.* New York: E.P. Dutton. Developmental Disabilities.

Cosgrove, J. (1982). *Cap'n Smudge: So if you see someone different than you and me.* Los Angeles: Price/Stern/Sloan.

Deford, F. (1986). *Alex: The life of a child.* Washington, DC: Cystic Fibrosis Foundation.

Donovan, P. (1982). *Carol Johnston: The one-armed gymnast.* Chicago: Children's Press.

Dwyer, K. M. (1991). *What do you mean I have a learning disability?* New York: Walker and Co. One child's true story about dealing with his learning disability.

Edwards, J., & Dawson, D. (1983). *My friend David.* Portland, OR: Ednick Communications. Developmental Disabilities.

Evans, S. (1986). *Don't look at me.* Portland, OR: Multnomah Press. Learning disabilities.

Eyerly, J. (1981). *The seeing summer.* Philadelphia: J. B. Lippincott. Visual impairement.

Fassler, J. (1975). *Howie helps himself.* Morton Grove, IL: Albert Whitman & Co. Cerebral Palsy.

Feingold, S. N., & Miller, N. (1982). *Your future: A guide for the handicapped teenager.* New York: Richards Rosen Press.

Ferris, C. (1980). *A hug just isn't enough.* Washington, DC: Gallaudet College Press.

Fleming, V. (1993). *Be good to Eddie Lee.* Lee, NY: Philomel Books. Developmental disabilities.

Forecki, M. C. (1989). *Speak to me.* (2nd ed.). Washington, DC: Gallaudet College Press.

Fisher, G., & Cummings, R. (1990). *The survival guide for kids with LD.* Minneapolis, MN: Free Spirit Publishing, Inc. Answers to common questions children have about their learning disabilities.

Frank, K., & Smith, S. J. (1994). *Getting a grip on ADD: A kid's guide to understanding and coping with attention disorders.* Minneapolis, MN: Educational Media Corporation. A resource for elementary and middle school students coping with ADD.

Friis-Baastad, B. (1967). *Don't take Teddy.* New York: Charles Scribner's Sons. Developmental disabilities.

Garrigue, S. (1978). *Between friends.* Scarsdale, NY: Bradbury Press. A young girl's friendship with a girl who has Down Syndrome is tested.

Gehert, J. (1992). *I'm somebody too.* Fairport, NY: Verbal Images Press. Emotional/behavioral/attention deficit disorder.

Gillhan, B. (1981). *My brother Barry.* London: Andre Duetsch Ltd. Developmental disabilities.

Gold, P. (1975). *Please don't say hello.* New York: Human Sciences Press. Autism.

Gray, D. (1997). *Yes, you can Heather!* Grand Rapids, MI: Zondervan Publishing House. Adolescents can gain inspiration from the story of the 1995 Miss America's struggle to overcome severe hearing loss.

Greenfield, E., & Revis, A. (1981). *Alesia.* New York: Philomel. Physical disabilities.

Hall, D. E. (1993). *Living with learning disabilities: A guide for students*. Minneapolis, MN: Lerner. Factual information about learning disabilities, along with coping methods are explained.

Hall, L. (1982). *Half the battle*. New York: Charles Scribner's Sons. Visual impairment.

Hansen, M. (1985). *Straight from the heart*. Saskatoon, Saskatchewan, Canada: Saskatchewan Association for the Mentally Retarded.

Hesse, K. (1991). *Wish on a unicorn*. New York: Henry Holt & Co. Developmental disabilities.

Hirsch, K. (1977). *My sister*. Minneapolis, MN: Carolrhoda Books. Developmental disabilities.

Hlibok, B. (1981). *Silent dancer*. New York: Messner. Hearing impairment.

Hyman, J. (1980). *Deafness*. New York: Franklin Watts.

Kamlen, J. (1979). *What if you couldn't...? A book about special needs*. New York: Charles Scribner's Sons.

Keller, H. (1982). *Cromwell's glasses*. New York: Greenwillow Books. Hearing impairment.

Kent, D. (1979). *Belonging*. New York: Ace Books. Visual impairment.

Konschuh, S. J. (1991). *My sister*. Calgary, Alberta, Canada: Paperworks Press Ltd. Developmental disabilities.

Laird, E. (1989). *Loving Ben*. New York: Delacorte Press. Developmental disabilities.

Larsen, H. (1974). *Don't forget about Tom*. New York: Thomas Y. Crowell. A day in the life of a nine-year-old with mental retardation.

Lasker, J. (1974). *He's my brother*. Morton Grove, IL: Albert Whitman & Co. Developmental disabilities.

Litchfield, A. (1982). *Captain Hook, that's me*. New York: Walker & Co.

Litchfield, A. (1984). *Making room for Uncle Joe*. Morton Grove, IL: Albert Whitman & Co.

Little, J. (1962). *Mine for keeps*. Boston: Little, Brown. Cerebral Palsy.

Little, J. (1968). *Take wing*. Boston: Little, Brown. Learning disabilities.

Little, J. (1972). *From Anna*. New York: Harper & Row. Visual impairment.

Little, J. (1988). *Listen for the singing*. New York: E. P. Dutton. Visual impairment.

Lynch, M. (1979). *Mary Fran and me*. New York: St. Martin's Press. Developmental disabilities.

Marcus, R. (1981). *Being blind*. Mamaroneck, NY: Hastings House.

McConnell, N. P. (1982). *Different and alike*. Colorado Springs, CO: Current Inc.

McPhee, R. (1981). *Tom and bear*. New York: Thomas Y. Crowell. Visual impairment.

Metzger, L. (1992). *Barry's sister*. New York: Atheneum. Cerebral Palsy.

Miner, J. C. (1982). *She's my sister: Having a retarded sister*. Mankato, MN: Crestwood House.

Moss, D. (1989). *Shelley, the hyperactive turtle*. Rockville, MD: Woodbine House. A turtle learns how to cope with his sometimes out of control behavior.

Muldoon, K. M. (1989). *Princess Pooh*. Morton Grove, IL: Albert Whitman & Co. Physical disabilities.

Nolan, C. (1987). *Under the eye of the clock*. New York: St. Martin's Press. Cerebral Palsy.

O'Shaughnessy, E. (1992). *Somebody called me retarded today . . . and my heart felt sad*. Glendale, CA: Crestwood House, Inc. Developmental disabilities.

Parker, R. (1974). *He's your brother*. Nashville, TN: Thomas Nelson. Autism.

Parker, R. N. (1992). *Making the grade: An adolescent's struggle with ADD*. Plantation, FL: Specialty Press, Inc. Fiction for kids. Heartwarming story of 7th grader's struggle to succeed in school.

Perske, R. (1984). *Show me no mercy*. Nashville, TN: Abingdon Press. Developmental disabilities.

Perske, R. (1986). *Don't stop the music*. Nashville, TN: Abingdon Press. Cerebral Palsy.

Pevsner, S. (1977). *Keep stompin' till the music stops*. New York: Seabury. Learning disabilities.

Quinn, P. O. (1995). *Adolescents and ADD: Gaining the advantage*. New York: Magination Press. For teens - coping skills.

Rabe, B. (1981). *The balancing girl*. New York: E. P. Dutton. Cerebral Palsy.

Rabe, B. (1988). *Where's chimpy?* Niels, IL: Albert Whitman and Co. Down Syndrome.

Robinet, H. G. (1980). *Ride the red cycle*. Boston: Houghton Mifflin. Cerebral Palsy.

Rodowsky, C. (1976). *What about me?* New York: Franklin Watts. Developmental disabilities.

Rubin, S. G. (1993). Emily good as gold. New York: Harcourt Brace and Co. Developmental disabilities.

Rosenberg, M. B. (1983). *My friend Leslie*. New York: Lothrop, Lee & Shepard. Physical disabilities.

Schwier, K. M. (1992). *Keith Edward's different day*. San Luis Obispo, CA: Impact Pubs Cal.

Shapiro, L. (1994). *Jumpin' Jake settles down: A workbook to help impulsive children learn to think before they act*.

King of Prussia, PA: The Center for Applied Psychology, Inc.

Shyer, M. (1978). *Welcome home, Jellybean*. New York: Scribner. Developmental disabilities.

Siegel, I. M. (1991). *Everybody's different, nobody's perfect*. Tucson, AZ: Muscular Dystrophy Association.

Slepian, J. (1980). *The Alfred summer*. New York: MacMillan. Cerebral Palsy.

Slepian, J. (1990). *Risk n' roses*. New York: Philomel Books. Developmental disabilities.

Smith, D. B. (1975). *Kelly's creek*. New York: Harper & Row. Learning disabilities.

Southall, I. (1968). *Let the balloon go*. New York: St. Martin's Press. Cerebral Palsy.

Spence, E. (1977). *The devil hole*. New York: Lothrop, Lee & Shepard. Autism.

Stein, S. B. (1974). *About handicaps*. New York: Walker & Co.

Testa, M. (1994). *Thumbs up Rico!* Morton Grove, IL: Albert Whitman and Co. Down Syndrome.

Walker, L. A. (1985). *Amy: The story of a deaf child*. New York: E. P. Dutton.

Weiss, M. E. (1980). *Blindness*. New York: Franklin Watts.

Welch, S. K. (1990). *Don't call me Marda*. Wayne, PA: Our Child Press.

White, P. (1978). *Janet at school*. New York: Crowell. Spina bifida.

Wolf, B. (1976). *Connie's new eyes*. New York: Harper & Row. Visual impairment.

Wolf, B. (1974). *Don't feel sorry for Paul*. New York: J. B. Lippincott.

Wright, B. R. (1981). *My sister is different*. Milwaukee, WI: Raintree Children's Books. Developmental disabilities.

Yashima, T. (1976). *Crow boy*. New York: Puffin Books. Autism.

Yolen, J. (1977). *The seeing stick*. New York: Thomas Y. Crowell.

DIVERSITY

Bennett, J. (1994). *Dakota dream*. New York: Scholastic. Non-native American follows dream to become a native Dakota warrior.

Bernardo, A. (1996). *Fitting in*. Houston, TX: Arle Publico Press. A collection of stories of the problems encountered by young Cuban girls who immigrated to the United States.

Berridge, C. (1987). *Going swimming*. New York: Random House. Concerns of youth about prejudice for children aged four to seven.

Boas, J. (1995). *We are witnesses: Five diaries of teenagers who died in the Holocaust*. New York: Scholastic. Life depicted during the Holocaust from diaries of five women who did not survive.

Carlson, N. S. (1965). *The empty schoolhouse*. New York: Harper & Row. Concerns of youth about prejudice for children aged eight to twelve.

Chocolate, D. (1991). *On the day you were born*. New York: Scholastic. Chronicles the birth of a child in a large African-American family.

Clements, A. (1988). *Big Al*. Saxonville, MA: Picture Book Studio. A fish strives to fit in with the other fish.

Guy, R. (1992). *Edith Jackson*. New York: Laurel-Leaf/Dell. A young Black girl is faced with many challenges.

Holliday, L. (1997). *Children of "The Troubles": Our lives in the crossfire of Northern Ireland*. New York: Pocket Books. Autobiographical accounts of children and young adults in Northern Ireland.

Johnson, A. (1989). *Tell me a story, Mama*. New York: Orchard books. Concerns of youth about prejudice for children aged four to seven.

Kates, B. (1992). *We're different, we're the same*. New York: Random House. Diversity for young children.

Kim, H. (1996). *The long season of rain*. New York: Fawcett Juniper. A young Korean girl is faced with many challenges including traditional gender roles in the summer of 1969.

Lester, H. (1988). *Tacky the penguin*. Boston: Houghton Mifflin Co. A penguin strives to fit in with the other penguins.

Lester, J. (1995). *Othello: A novel*. New York: Scholastic. A tragic novel concerning the issues of marriage between a black man and a white woman.

Levine, E. (1989). *I hate English!* New York: Scholastic. Concerns of youth about prejudice for children aged eight to twelve.

Louie, D. W. (1992). *Pangs of love*. New York: Plume. Eleven short stories which deal with the experiences of a group of Chinese Americans. Topics include abortion, dating, and gay and lesbian lifestyles.

Martinez, V. (1996). *Parrot in the oven: Mi vida*. New York: Harper-Collins. Portrayal of a young Latino man growing up.

Mendez, P. (1989). *The snowman*. New York: Scholastic. Concerns of youth about prejudice for children aged eight to twelve.

Mizell, L. (1992). *Think about racism*. New York: Walker. Historical accounts and biographical profiles of those involved in the fight for civil rights are detailed.

Mori, K. (1993). *Shizuko's daughter*. New York: Fawcett Juniper. Un-romanticized account of Japanese culture, behavior, religion, and custom.

Myers, W. D. (1996). *Slam!* New York: Scholastic. Issues detailing the serious decisions of a young basketball player.

Myers, W.D. (1994). *The glory field.* New York: Scholastic. A fictional account of an African American family from slavery to the present.

Pfister, M. (1992). *The rainbow fish.* New York: North-South Books. Diversity for young children.

Pohl, C., & Harris, K. (1992). *Transracial adoption: Children and parents speak.* New York: Watts. This book takes a candid look at racially mixed families.

Rinaldi, A. (1996). *Hang a thousand trees with ribbons: The story of Phyllis Wheatley.* Orlando: Harcourt Brace. Fictional account of a female slave poet and the contradictions of her success in society.

Roy, J. (1992). *Soul Daddy.* Niles, IL: Gulliver Books/Harcourt Brace Jovanovich. A young girl whose mother is white and father is black, deals with her racial heritage.

Simon, N. (1976). *All kinds of families.* Niles, IL: A. Whitman. Concerns of youth about prejudice for children aged four to seven.

Simon, N. (1976). *Why am I different?* Mt. Rainer, MD: Gryphon House. Diversity for ages four through eight.

Soto, G. (1995). *New and selected poems.* San Francisco: Chronicle Books. Poems detailing the Latino view of the California barrio.

Taylor, M. D. (1989). *Mississippi Bridge.* New York: Dial Books For Young Readers. Concerns of youth about prejudice for children aged eight to twelve.

Taylor, M. D. (1987). *The Gold Cadillac.* New York: Dial Books For Young Readers. Concerns of youth about prejudice for children aged eight to twelve.

Taylor, M.D. (1987). *The Friendship.* New York: Dial Books For Young Readers. Concerns of youth about prejudice for children aged eight to twelve.

Tazewell, C. (1966). *The littlest angel.* Chicago: Children's Press. A story about finding something you are good at.

Wesley, V. W. (1993). *Where do I go from here?* New York: Scholastic. Two young African Americans experience the mainly white society.

DIVORCE, REMARRIAGE, AND CHANGING FAMILIES

Adler, C. S. (1992). *Tuna Fish Thanksgiving.* New York: Clarion Books. Major crises and big family changes for children aged eight to twelve.

Banks, A. (1990). *Me and my stepfamily: A kids' journal.* New York: Penguin Books.

Berman, C. (1992). *What am I doing in a stepfamily?* New York: Carol Publishing.

Berry, J. W. (1990). *Good answers to tough questions about stepfamilies.* Chicago: Children's Press. Remarriage and stepfamilies for children aged four to seven.

Black, J. R. (1994). *Alien under my bed.* New York: Bullseye Books. A young girl is miserable when her dad remarries and she finds an alien under her bed.

Boyd, L. (1990). *Sam is my half-brother.* New York: Viking. Remarriage and stepfamilies for children aged four to seven.

Brown, L. D., & Brown, M. (1986). *Dinosaurs divorce: A guide for changing families.* Boston: Joy Street Books. Major crises and big family changes for children aged four to seven.

Brown, L. K., & Brown, M. (1986). *The Dinosaurs Divorce: A Guide for Changing Families.* Boston, MA: Atlantic Monthly Press.

Cain, B., & Benedek, E. (1976). *What would you do? A Child's Book About Divorce.* Washington, DC: American Psychiatric Press Inc.

Christiansen, C. B. (1989). *My mother's house, my father's house.* New York: Atheneum. Major crises and big family changes for children aged four to seven.

Cleary, B. (1991). *Strider.* New York: Morrow. Major crises and big family changes for children aged eight to twelve.

Cleary, B. (1983). *Dear Mr. Henshaw.* New York: Morrow. Major crises and big family changes for children ages eight to twelve.

Danziger, P. (1985). *It's an Ardvark-eat-Turtle world.* New York: Delacorte Press. Remarriage and stepfamilies for children aged eight to twelve.

Danziger, P. (1982). *The divorce express.* New York, Delacorte Press. Major crises and big family changes for children aged eight to twelve.

Fassler, M. L., & Ives, S. B. (1988). *Changing Families: A Guide for Kids and Grownups.* Burlington, VT: Waterfront Books.

Gardner, R. (1992). *The boys & girls book about divorce.* New York: Bantam Books. Honest answers to children's frequently asked questions are provided, as well as an introduction for parents.

Glassman, B. (1988). *Everything you need to know about stepfamilies.* New York: Rosen Publishing Group. Remarriage and stepfamilies for children aged eight to twelve.

Hathorn, E. (1991). *Thunderwith.* Boston: Little, Brown. Remarriage and stepparenting for children aged eight to twelve.

Hazen, B. S. (1978). *Two homes to live in: A child's eye view of divorce.* New York: Human Sciences Press. Major crises and big family changes for children aged four to seven.

Helmering, D. W. (1981). *I have two families.* Nashville: Abingdon. Major crises and big family changes for children aged four to seven.

Ives, S. B., Fassler, D., & Lash, M. (1996). *The divorce workbook: An interactive guide for kids and families.* Burlington, VT: Waterfront Books.

Krasny-Brown, L., & Brown, M. (1988). *Dinosaurs divorce: A guide for changing families.* Boston: Little, Brown.

Leach, N. (1956). *My wicked step mother.* New York: Bookman Association. A boy tells about his stepmother who he believes is a witch.

Matthews, B., Adams, A., & Dockrey, K. (1994). *I only see Dad on weekends: Kids tell their stories about divorce and blended families.* Colorado Springs, CO: Chariot Family Publishing.

McClintock, N. (1991). *The stepfather game.* New York: Scholastic. Three step-sisters deal with their changing family.

Peck, R. (1992). *Don't look and it won't hurt.* New York: Laurel-Leaf/Dell. The story illustrates a young girl's growth and development through experiences with a changing family and other issues.

Ransom, C. F. (1995). *More than a name.* New York: Simon & Schuster. A young girl struggles with a new father, a new family, and fitting in.

Richards, A., & Willis, I. (1976). *How to get it together when your parents are coming apart.* New York: Bantam.

Rosenberg M. (1990). *Talking about stepfamilies.* New York: Bradbury Press. Remarriage and stepparenting for children aged eight to twelve.

Stolz, M. (1993). *What time of the night is it?* New York: Harper Keypoint. A family copes with the pain of divorce.

Turow, R. (1978). *Daddy doesn't live here anymore.* New York: Anchor.

Wartski, M. (1994). *Dark silence.* New York: Fawcett Juniper. A teenage girl deals with the loss of her mother, and her father's remarriage.

Willey, M. (1993). *The Melinda zone.* New York: Bantam. Youngsters deal with divorce.

Worth, R. (1992). *Single-parent families.* New York: Franklin Watts.

GENERAL

Berenstain, S., & Berenstain, J. (1982). *The Berenstain Bears get in a fight.* New York: Random House.

Berenstain, S., & Berenstain, J. (1984). *The Berenstain Bears and Mama's new job.* New York: Random House.

Berenstain S., & Berenstain, J. (1992). *The Berenstain bears and the trouble with grownups.* New York: Random House. The young bears put on a play to illustrate the trouble with grownups.

Cadnum, M. (1992). *Breaking the fall.* New York: Viking. A teenage boy forms a robbery habit.

Calvert, P. (1992). *When morning comes.* New York: Avon Flare. A young dropout in foster care has difficulty adapting to rules.

Wood, J. R. (1992). *The man who loved clowns.* New York: G. P. Putman's

Sons. A girl learns much about herself from her uncle, who has Down's Syndrome.

IDENTITY AND PRESSURE

Cohen, S., & Cohen, D. (1992). *Teenage stress.* New York: Laurel-Leaf. Methods for coping with stress are explored.

Haas, J. (1992). *Skipping school.* New York: Greenwillow. A boy deals with pressure by skipping school.

Klass, S. S. (1993). *Rhino.* New York: Scholastic Hardcover. A young girl worries about her nose.

Kolodyny, N. J. (1992). *When food's a foe: How to confront and conquer eating disorders.* New York: Little, Brown. Eating disorders are discussed, and activities to help those who suffer from these disorders are offered.

Kreiner, A. (1997). *In control: Learning to say no to sexual pressures.* New York: Rosen Publishing Group. The book discusses different types of sexual pressures, ways to negotiate sexual pressure, and how to determine one's own values and ethics with regard to sex.

LeShan, E. (1992). *What makes you so special?* New York: Dial. Real stories of young people help readers to understand and appreciate the unique qualities in themselves and others.

Ryan, E. A. (1992). *Straight talk about parents.* New York: Laurel-Leaf. Contemporary advice on problems today's teens face is discussed.

Schneider, M. F., & Meade, D. (Eds.). (1992). *Popularity has its ups and downs.* New York: Messner. Topics such as popularity, feeling good about yourself, friendship, and shyness are discussed.

Scoppettone, S. (1991). *Happy endings are all alike*. Los Angeles: Alyson Publications. A small town must handle different ideas on sexuality and sexual orientation.

ILLNESS AND DEATH

Amadeo, D. M. (1989). *There's a little bit of me in Jamey*. Morton Grove, IL: Albert Whitman & Co. Cancer.

Arrick, F. (1992). *What you don't know can kill you*. New York: Bantam. A teenager tests positive for HIV.

Bearison, D. J. (1991). *They never want to tell you: Children talk about cancer*. Cambridge, MA: Harvard University Press.

Bode, J. (1993). *Death is hard to live with: Teenagers and how they cope with loss*. New York: Delacorte. Interviews with bereaved teens show how to make peace with the feelings associated with death.

Brown, M. W. (1965). *The dead bird*. Reading, MA: Addison-Wesley, Young Scott Books. Concerns of youth for children aged four to seven.

Cannon, A. E. (1993). *Amazing Gracie*. New York: Laurel-Leaf/Dell. A teenager struggles to adapt to her mother's remarriage, a move to Salt Lake City, and the return of her mother's depression and attempted suicide.

Carlstrom, N. W. (1990). *Blow me a kiss, Miss Lilly*. New York: Harper & Row. Major crises and big family changes for children aged four to seven.

Carson, J. (1992). *You hold me and I'll hold you*. New York: Orchard Books. Major crises and big family changes for children aged four to seven.

Caseley, J. (1992). *My father, the nutcase*. New York: Knopf. A 15 year old deals with his father's mental illness.

Casely, J. (1986). *When grandpa came to stay*. New York: Greenwillow Books. Major crises and big family changes for children aged four to seven.

Clifton, L. (1983). *Everett Anderson's Goodbye*. New York: Holt, Rinehart & Winston. Major crises and big family changes for children aged four to seven.

Cohen, B. (1974). *Thank you, Jackie Robinson*. New York: Lothrop. Concerns of youth for children aged eight to twelve.

Cohn, J. (1987). *I had a friend named Peter*. New York: William Morrow. Major crises and big family changes for children aged four to seven.

Cossi, O. (1990). *The magic box*. New York: Penguin. A high school girl learns how to handle the news of her mother's cancer of the larynx.

Dabcovich, L. (1985). *Mrs Huggins and her hen Hannah*. New York: Dutton. Major crises and big family changes for children aged four to seven when dealing with pet loss.

Deaver, J. R. (1993). *You bet your life*. Scranton: PA: Harper Collins. A young girl (17) comes to grips with the suicide of her mother.

Fine, J. (1986). *Afraid to ask: A book for families to share about cancer*. New York: Beech Tree Books.

Gaes, J. (1987). *My book for kids with cancer: A child's autobiography of hope*. Aberdeen, SD: Melius & Peterson Publishing Corporation.

Grollman, E. A. (1993). *Straight talk about death for teenagers: How to cope with losing someone you love*. Boston: Beacon. Teens can learn what to expect when someone they love dies and what can help.

Hahn, M.D. (1993). *The wind blows backwards*. New York: Clarion. An interesting account of 18 year-olds who must learn to cope with the issues or life and death.

Hamilton, V. (1990). *Cousins.* New York: Philomel. Major crises and big family changes for children aged eight to twelve.

Heegard, M. (1992). *When someone has a very serious illness: Children learn to cope with loss and change.* Minneapolis, MN: Woodland Press. Art activities are used to help children cope with illness and loss.

Hermes, P. (1982). *You shouldn't have to say goodbye.* San Diego, CA: Harcourt Brace Jovanovich. Major crises and big family changes for children aged eight to twelve.

Hermes, P. (1980). *What if they knew?* New York: Harcourt Brace Jovanovich. Epilepsy.

Herzig, A., & Mali, J. L. (1982). *A season of secrets.* Boston: Little, Brown. Epilepsy.

Hickman, M. W. (1984). *Last week my brother Anthony died.* Nashville, TN: Abingdon Press.

Hines A.G. (1991). *Remember the butterflies.* New York: Dutton Children's Books. Major crises and big family changes for children aged four to seven.

Howe, J. (1981). *The hospital book.* New York: Crown Publishers.

Keller, H. (1987). *Goodbye, Max.* New York: Greenwillow Books. Major crises and big family changes for children aged four to seven when dealing with pet loss.

Kipnis, L., & Adler, S. (1979). *You can't catch diabetes from a friend.* Gainesville, FL: Triad Scientific Publishers.

Krementz, J. (1996). *How it feels when a parent dies.* New York: Alfred A. Knopf. Boys and girls speak about their experiences and feelings.

Kroll, V. L. (1992). *Helen the fish.* Niles, IL: A. Whitman. Major crises and big family changes for children aged four to seven when dealing with pet loss.

LaTour, K. (1983). *For those who live.* Omaha, NE: Centering Corp.

Marino, J. (1989). *Eighty-eight steps to September.* Boston: Little, Brown. Major crises and big family changes for children ages eight to twelve.

Martin, A.M. (1986). *With you and without you.* New York: Holiday House. Major crises and big family changes for children aged eight to twelve.

McDaniel, L. (1992). *Mother, help me live: One last wish series.* New York: Bantam. A teenager deals with her leukemia.

Moss, D. (1989). *Lee, the rabbit with epilepsy.* Rockville, MD: Woodbine House.

Orgel, D. (1986). *Whiskers, once and always.* New York: Viking Kestrel. Major crises and big family changes for children aged eight to twelve when dealing with pet loss.

Richter, E. (1982). *The teenage hospital experience.* New York: Cowan, McCann Geoghegan.

Rogers, F. (1988). *When a pet dies.* New York: Putnam. Major crises and big family changes for children aged eight to twelve when dealing with pet loss.

Rylant, C. (1992). *Missing May.* New York: Orchard. Young adults deal with death and grief issues.

Steel, D. (1989). *Max's daddy goes to the hospital.* New York: Delacorte Press. A small boy deals with his father's illness.

Stein, S. B. (1974). *About dying.* New York: Walker. Concerns of youth for children aged four to seven.

Stolz, M. (1991). *King Emmett the Second.* New York: Greenwillow Books. Major crises and big family changes for children aged eight to twelve when dealing with pet loss.

Tomey, I. (1993). *Savage carrot.* New York: Scribner. A young girl's experience regarding the accidental death of her father.

Vigna, J. (1991). *Saying goodbye to daddy.* Morton Grove, IL: Albert Whitman & Company. Fiction for children.

Viorst, J. (1971). *The tenth good thing about Barney.* New York: Athenuem. Major crises and big family changes for children aged eight to twelve when dealing with pet loss.

White, E. B. (1952). *Charlotte's web.* New York: Harper Collins Child books. Concerns of youth about death for children aged four to seven.

White, R. (1991). *Ryan White, my own story.* New York: Dial Books. Major crises and big family changes for children aged eight to twelve.

Wiener, L. S., Best, A., & Pizzo, P. A. (1994). *Be a friend: Children who live with HIV speak.* Morton Grove, IL: Albert Whitman & Co. For children.

Zim, H., & Bleeker, S. (1970). *Life and death.* New York: Morrow. Concerns for youth about death for children aged eight to twelve.

MENTAL HEALTH

Avery, C. (1992). *Everybody has feelings.* Mt. Rainer, MD: Gryphon House.

Crary, E. (1994). *I'm mad, I'm frustrated, I'm scared, I'm proud, I'm excited, I'm furious.* Burlington, VT: Waterfront Books. A series of books designed to deal with feelings.

Dubuque, S. and Dubuque, N. (1996). *Kid power tactics for dealing with depression.* King of Prussia, PA: The Center for Applied Psychology, Inc.

Godwin, P. (1993). *I feel orange today.* Mt. Rainer, MD: Gryphon House. Through the use of colors, children ages three through seven learn about feelings.

Mayer, M. (1989). *I was so mad.* New York: Dalton.

Moser, A. (1988). *Don't pop your cork on Mondays.* Kansas City: Landmark Editions Inc.

Simon, N. (1974). *I was so mad.* Chicago: Whitman.

Viorst, J. (1972). *Alexander and the terrible, horrible, no good, very bad day.* New York: Atheneum.

PREGNANCY

Bode, J. (1992). *Kids still having kids: People talk about teen pregnancy.* New York: Franklin Watts. Stories and factual information help the reader make wise decisions about teen pregnancy.

Gravelle, K. & Fischer, S. (1993). *Teenage fathers.* Old Tappan, NJ: Messner/Simon & Schuster. Thirteen interviews with teen fathers illustrate the problems of becoming a young parent.

Kaye, G. (1992). *Someone else's baby.* Westport, CT: Hyperion. A story of teenage pregnancy.

Williams-Garcia, R. (1995). *Like Sisters on the home front.* New York: Lodestar.

SIBLINGS

Adams, B. (1979). *Like it is: facts and feelings about handicaps from kids you know.* New York: Walker & Co. Nonfiction about general disabilities for middle school level readers.

Albert, L. (1976). *But I'm ready to go.* Scarsdale, NY: Bradbury. Fiction for middle to high school readers about learning disabilities.

Allen, A (1981). *Sports for the handicapped.* New York: Walker & Co. Nonfiction about physical disabilities for the primary reader.

Anders, R. (1976). *A look at mental retardation.* Minneapolis: Lerner Publications. Nonfiction for the primary reader about mental retardation.

Baldwin, A. N. (1978). *A little time.* New York: Viking Press. Fiction for middle to high school readers concerning mental retardation.

Barnes, E., & Berrigan, C. (1978). *What's the difference? Teaching positive attitudes toward people with disabilities.* New York: Human Policy press. Nonfiction concerning general disabilities that encourages discussion concerning issues such as stereotypes for those in high school level.

Berger, G. (1979). *Physical disabilities.* New York: Franklin Watts. Nonfiction for middle school readers.

Bodenheimer, C. (1979). *Everybody is a person: A book for brothers and sisters of autistic kids.* Syracuse, NY: The Learning Place. Nonfiction about autism for middle school readers.

Brightman, A. (1976). *Like me.* Boston: Little, Brown. Nonfiction for middle school readers about mental retardation.

Brown, T. (1984). *Someone special, just like you.* New York: Holt, Rinehart, & Winston. Nonfiction photobook for primary aged readers detailing general disabilities.

Byars, B. (1970). *The summer of the swans.* New York: Viking Press. Fiction about mental retardation for middle school readers.

Cairo, S. (1985). *Our brother has Down's Syndrome.* Toronto: Annick Press Ltd. Nonfiction for primary school readers concerning mental retardation.

Cleaver, V. (1973). *Me too.* Philadelphia: J. B. Lippincott Co. Fiction about mental retardation for middle school readers.

Clifton, L. (1980). *My friend Jacob.* New York: E. P. Dutton. Fiction for the primary school reader.

Edrington, M. J., Moss, S.A., & Young, J. (1978). *Friends.* Monmouth, OR: Instructional Development Corp. Nonfiction about general disabilities for primary to middle school readers.

Fanshawe, E. (1975). *Rachel.* Scarsdale, NY: Bradbury. Nonfiction about physical disabilities for middle school readers.

Fassler, J. (1975). *Howie helps himself.* Chicago: Albert Whitman & Co. Nonfiction about cerebral palsy for middle school readers.

Fassler, J. (1969). *Our little girl.* New York: Human Science. Nonfiction about learning disabilities for middle school readers.

Friis-Baastad, B. (1967). *Don't take Teddy.* New York: Charles Scribner's Sons. Fiction for the junior high reader about mental retardation.

Garrigue, S. (1978). *Between friends.* Scarsdale, NY: Bradbury. Fiction concerning mental retardation for the middle to high school reader.

Gillham, B. (1981). *My brother Barry.* Bergenfield, NJ: Andre Deutsch. Fiction for primary to middle school readers about learning disabilities.

Girion, B. (1981). *A handful of stars.* New York: Charles Scribner's Sons. Fiction for junior high school readers about epilepsy.

Glazzard, M. H. (1978). *Meet Camille and Danielle, they're special persons.* Lawrence, KS: H & H Enterprises. Biography written for the primary reader about the hearing impaired.

Glazzard, M. H. (1978). *Meet Scott, he's a special person.* Lawrence, KS: H & H Enterprises. Nonfiction for the primary reader about learning disabilities.

Gold, P. (1975). *Please don't say hello.* New York: Human Services. Fiction about autism for primary to middle school readers.

Green, P. (1978). *Walkie talkie.* Reading, MA: Addison-Wesley. Fictional account about emotional disturbances for readers on a middle school level.

Hanlon, E. (1981). *The Swing.* New York: Dell. Fiction for the high school reader about the hearing impaired.

Hanlon, E. (1978). *It's too late for sorry.* Scarsdale, NY: Bradbury. Fiction for middle to high school readers about mental retardation.

Haskins, J. & Stifle, J. M. (1979). *The quiet revolution: The struggle for the rights of disabled Americans.* New York: Thomas Y. Crowell. Nonfiction discussion of civil rights and general disabilities for the high school reader.

Hamilton-Paterson, J. (1970). *The house in the waves.* Chatham, NY: S. G. Phillips. Fiction for junior high school readers detailing emotional disturbances.

Hermes, P. (1980). *What if they knew?* San Diego: Harcourt, Brace, Jovanovich. Fictional account about epilepsy for middle school readers.

Hirsch, K. (1977). *My sister.* Minneapolis: Carol Rhoda Books. Fiction for the primary level reader about mental retardation.

Hlibok, B. (1981). *Silent dancer.* New York: Messner. Nonfiction for primary to middle school readers concerning the hearing impaired.

Hyman, J. (1980). *Deafness.* New York: Franklin Watts. Nonfiction about the hearing impaired for middle school readers.

Jampolsky, G. G., & Taylor, P. (1978). *There is a rainbow behind every dark cloud.* Tiburon, CA: Center for Attitudinal Healing. Nonfiction about cancer for primary to middle school readers.

Jampolsky, G. G., & Taylor, P. (1982). *Another look at the rainbow. Straight from the siblings.* Tiburon, CA: Center for Attitudinal Healing. Nonfiction about cancer for primary to middle school readers.

Kamien, J. (1979). *What if you couldn't....? A book about special needs.* New York: Charles Scribner's Sons. Nonfictional resource book that discusses various general disabilities in a detailed manner for middle to high school readers.

Kelley, S. (1976). *Trouble with explosives.* Scarsdale, NY: Bradbury. Fiction for the primary to middle school reader about language problems.

Kroll, V. (1992). *My sister, then and now: A book about mental illness.* Minneapolis, MN: Carol Rhoda Books.

Larson, H. (1978). *Don't forget Tom.* New York: Thomas Y. Cromwell. Fiction for primary level readers concerning mental retardation.

Lasker, J. (1974). *He's my brother.* Niles, IL: Alber Whitman and Company. Fiction for the preschool to primary school reader concerning learning disabilities.

Lenski, L. (1952). *We live in the south.* Philadelphia: J. B. Lippincott. Fiction concerning cardiac problems for primary school readers.

Levine, E. (1974). *Lisa and her soundless world.* New York: Human Sciences Press. Nonfiction about the hearing impaired for the primary reader.

Litchfield, A. (1976). *A button in her ear.* Chicago: Albert Whitman and Company.

Fiction for primary to middle school readers about the hearing impaired.

Lynch, M. (1979). *Mary Fran and me.* New York: St. Martin's Press. Nonfiction about mental retardation for high school readers.

McConnell, N. P., & Duell, N. (1982). *Different and alike.* Colorado Springs, CO: Current, Inc. Nonfictional book with suggestion for helping others with general disabilities for middle school readers.

Meyer, D. J., Vadasy, P. F., & Fewell, R. R. (1985). *Living with a brother or sister with special needs: A book for sibs.* Seattle: University of Washington Press.

Nollette, C. D., Lynch, T., Mitby, S., & Seyfried, D. (1985). *Having a brother like David.* Minneapolis: Minneapolis Children's Medical Center.

Ominsky, E. (1977). *Jon O: A special boy.* Englewood Cliffs, NJ: Prentice-Hall. Biography for primary readers about mental retardation.

Parker, R. (1974). *He is your brother.* Nashville: Thomas Nelson, Inc. Fiction for middle school readers concerning autism.

Perske, R. (1986). *Don't stop the music.* Nashville: Abingdon Press. Fiction for middle to high school readers about cerebral palsy.

Perske, R. (1987). *Show me no mercy.* Nashville: Abingdon Press. Fictions for middle to high school readers about mental retardation.

Peterson, W. (1982). *I have a sister, my sister is deaf.* New York: Harper & Row. Nonfiction concerning the hearing impaired for the primary school reader.

Pevsner, S. (1977). *Keep stompin' till the music stops.* New York: Seabury Press. Fiction about learning disabilities for middle school readers.

Prall, J. (1985). *My sister's special.* Chicago: Children's Press.

Reynolds, P. (1968). *A different kind of sister.* New York: Lothrop, Lee & Shepard.

Riokind, M. (1982). *Apple is my sign.* Boston: Houghton Mifflin. Fiction for the high school reader about the hearing impaired.

Robinson, V. (1965). *David in silence.* Philadelphia: J. B. Lippincott Co. Fiction concerning the hearing impaired for the junior high school reader.

Rosenberg, M. B. (1988). *Finding a way: Living with exceptional brothers and sisters.* New York: Lothrop, Lee & Shepard.

Shyer, M. F. (1978). *Welcome home, Jellybean.* New York: Charles Scribner's Sons. Fiction for middle school readers about mental retardation.

Silverstein, A., & Silverstein, V. B. (1978). *Itch, sniffle, and sneeze. All about asthma, hay fever and other allergies.* New York: Four Winds Press. Nonfiction about asthma and allergies for the primary aged reader.

Silverstein, A., & Silverstein, V. B. (1975). *Epilepsy.* Philadelphia: J. B. Lippincott Junior Books. Nonfiction for primary to middle school readers about epilepsy.

Slepian, J. (1980). *The Alfred summer.* New York: Macmillan Publishing Co. Fiction about mental retardation for middle school readers.

Smith, D. B. (1975). *Kelly's creek.* New York: Harper & Row. Fiction for the middle school reader about learning disabilities.

Smith, L. B. (1977). *A special kind of sister.* New York: Holt, Rinehart, & Winston. Fiction about mental retardation for primary school readers.

Sobol, H.L. (1977). *My brother Steven is retarded.* New York: Macmillan Publishing Co. Biography for primary readers about mental retardation.

Spence, E. (1977). *The devil hole.* New York: Lothrop, Lee, and Shepard Books. Fiction about autism and siblings for middle school readers.

Sullivan, M. B., & Bourke, L. (1980). *A show of hands.* Reading, MA: Addison-Wesley. Nonfiction for primary to middle school readers concerning the hearing impaired.

Sullivan, M. B., Brightman, A. J., & Blatt, J. (1979). *Feeling free.* Reading, MA: Addison-Wesley. Nonfiction concerning general disabilities for middle school readers.

Thompson, M. (1992). *My brother, Matthew.* Rockville, MD: Woodbine House.

Wartski, M. C. (1979). *My brother is special.* Philadelphia: Westminster Press.

Wolf, B. (1977). *Anna's silent world.* Philadelphia: J. B. Lippincott Co. Biography about the hearing impaired for the primary to middle school reader.

Wright, B. R. (1981). *My sister is different.* Milwaukee: Raintree Publishers, Inc. Fiction about mental retardation for primary readers.

Resources for Professionals and Families

Local Resources
(Local Telephone Directory)

Adult Children of Alcoholics
Al-Anon
Al-Ateen
Gamblers Anonymous
Narcotics Anonymous
Overeaters Anonymous
Sex Addicts Anonymous
Sex and Love Addicts Anonymous
Women for Sobriety

National Resources

Addiction Research Foundation
   Department
c/o Marketing Services
33 Russell St.
Toronto, Ontario, Canada M55 2S1
http://www.arf.org

Adult Children of Alcoholics World
   Service Organization (ACA WSO)
P. O. Box 3216
Torrance, CA 90510
(310) 534-1815
E-mail: aca@lafn.org
Web Site: www.lafn.org.community/aca

Al-Anon/Al-Ateen Family Group
   Headquarters
1600 Corporate Landing Parkway
Virginia Beach, VA 23454-5617
(800) 356-9996
www.Al-Anon-Alateen.org

Alcoholics Anonymous
475 Riverside Drive
New York, NY 10115
(212) 870-3400
http://www.alcoholics-anonymous.org
Alcoholics Anonymous: A worldwide
    fellowship of sober alcoholics, whose
    recovery is based on Twelve Steps; no
    dues or fees, self-supporting through
    voluntary, small contributions or
    members, accepts no outside funds;
    not affiliated with any other
    organization; our primary purpose: to
    carry the A.A. message to the
    alcoholic who still suffers.

American Coalition for Abuse Awareness
P. O. Box 27959
Washington, DC 20038-7959
http://www.sover.net/~schwcof/newshead.
    html

American Council for Drug Education
(800) 488-DRUG
http://www.acde.org

Center of Alcohol Studies,
    Rutgers University
Smithers Hall - Allison Road
Busch Campus
Piscataway, NJ 08855-0969
(908) 445-4442
http://www.info.rutgers.edu
    (or telnet info.rutgers.edu)

Center for Education and Drug Research
    (CEDAR)
Rita Santucci
Department of Psychiatry
Western Psychiatric Institute and Clinic
3811 O'Hara Street
Pittsburgh, PA 15213
http://www.pitt.edu/~mmv/cedar.html

Chemically Dependent Anonymous
    (CDA)
P. O. Box 423
Severna Park, MD 21146-0423
(888) CDA-HOPE
http://www.printing.presstar.com/cda

Cocaine Hotline
(800)COCAINE

Covenant House Nineline
    (kids in trouble)
(800) 999-9999

Domestic Violence Shelter Aid Hotline
(800) 333-SAFE

Drug Abuse Council
1828 L Street, NW
Washington, DC 20036

Drug Enforcement Administration
700 Army Navy Drive
Arlington, VA 22202
Web site: www.usdoj.gov/dea

Fetal Alcohol Education Program
School of Medicine
Boston University
7 Kent Street
Brookline, MA 02146

Indiana Prevention Resource Center
http://www.drugs.indiana.edu

Nar-Anon Family Group Headquarters,
    Inc.
P. O. Box 2562
Palos Verdes, CA 90274-0119
(213) 547-5800

Narcotics Anonymous
P. O. Box 9999
Van Nuys, CA 91409
(818) 773-9999
(818) 700-0700 - Fax
E-mail: info@wsoinc.com
Web Site: http://www.narconon.org

National Association for Children of
    Alcoholics
35182 Coast Highway, Suite B
South Laguna, CA 92677
(714) 499-3889

National Center for Alcohol Education
1901 N. Moore Street
Arlington, VA 22209

National Clearinghouse for Alcohol and
    Drug Information (NCADI)
P. O. Box 2345
Rockville, MD 20852
(301) 468-2600
http://www.health.org/index.htm

National Coordinating Council of
    Drug Education
1526 18th Street, NW
Washington, DC 20036

National Council on Alcoholism and Drug
    Dependency, Inc. (NCADD)
12 W. 21st Street
New York, NY 10010
(800) NCA-CALL
http://www.ncadd.org
national@ncadd.org

National Families in Action (NFIA)
2296 Henderson Mill Road, Suite 300
Atlanta, GA 30345-2739
(770) 934-6364
http://www.emory.edu/NFIA

National Institute on Alcohol Abuse and
    Alcoholism (NIAAA)
5600 Fishers Lane
Rockville, MD 20857
http://www.niaaa.nih.gov

National Organization on FAS
    (Fetal Alcohol Syndrome)
1815 H Street, NW
Suite 750
Washington, DC 20006

National Women's Resource Center
    (NWRC)
515 King Street, Suite 410
Alexandria, VA 22314
(800) 354-8824
http://www.nwrc.org

Overeaters Anonymous
P. O. Box 44020
Rio Rancho, NM 87174-4020
(505) 891-2664
http://www.overeatersanonymous.org
overeatr@technet.nm.org

Parents Anonymous
(800) 421-0353

Rational Recovery
5540 David Road
Davie, FL 33314-6066
(800) 328-4402
(305) 791-0298
http://rational.org/recovery

Runaway Hotline
(800) 621-4000

Rutgers Center of Alcohol Studies
P. O. Box 969
Piscataway, NJ 08903

The Safe and Drug-Free Schools Program
600 Independence Avenue S.W.
Portals Building, Suite 604
Washington, DC 20202-6123
(202) 260-3954
www.ed.gov/offices/OESE/SDFS

Talking about Alcohol: A Program for
    Parents of Preteens
P. O. Box 1799
Ridgely, MD 21681
(800) 732-4726

Teen Challenge
Turning Point
P. O. Box 22127
Chattanooga, TN 37422-2127
(423) 899-4770
http://www.teenchallenge.com

ADOPTION

Adoptee-Birthparent Support Network
PO Box 23674
L'Enfant Plaza Station
Washington, DC 20026-0674
(202) 686-4611
Search and support group for both
    adoptees and birthparents

Adoptees in Search
PO Box 41016
Bethesda, MD 20824
(301) 656-8555
Fax (301) 652-2106
E-mail AIS20824@AOL.com

Adoptees Liberty Movement Association
PO Box 727
New York, NY 0101-0727
(212) 581-1568

Adoption Advocates International
401 East Frong Street
Port Angeles, WA 98362
(360) 452-4777
Fax (360) 452-1107
aai@olympus.net
www.lbeecom/aai/default.asp
Foreign adoption

Adoptive Families of America
3333 Highway 100 N.
Minneapolis, MN 55422
(800) 372-3300
http://www.AdoptiveFam.org

American Adoption Congress
PO Box 20137
Cherokee Station
New York, NY 10028-0051
Search Hotline (505) 296-2198
Search, support, and education

National Council for Single Adoptive
    Parents
PO Box 15084
Chevy Chase, MD 20825
(202) 966-6367

Concerned United Birthparents
2000 Walker Street
Des Moines, IA 50317
(515) 263-9558

Holt International Children's Services
PO Box 2880
Eugene, OR 97402-9970
(541) 687-2202
Fax (541) 683-6175
e-mail info@holtin/.org
www.holtint/.org
foreign adoption agency

International Soundex Reunion Registry
PO Box 2312
Carson City, NV 89702-2198
(702) 882-7755
Matching registry without search.
    Free and open to 18 and older

National Adoption Center
1500 Walnut Street, Suite 701
Philadelphia, PA 19102
(215) 735-9988
Fax (215) 735-9410
e-mail nac@adopt.org
www.adopt.org

National Adoption Information
    Clearinghouse
P. O. Box 1182
Washington, DC 20013-1182
(703) 352-3488
Fax (703) 385-3200 or (888) 251-0075
e-mail naic@calib.com
http://www.calib.com/naic

National Association of Former
    Foster Children Inc. (NAFFC)
PO Box 060410
New Dorp Station
Staten Island, NY 10306
(212) 332-0078

National Council for Adoption
1930 17th St. NW
Washington, DC 20009
(202) 328-1200
Fax (202) 332-0935
e-mail ncfa@juneo.com
www.ncfa-usa.org

National Adoption Hotline
(202) 328-8072

National Organization for Birthfathers
    and Adoption Reform
PO Box 50
Punta Gorda, FL 33951

National Resource Center for
    Special Needs Adoption
16250 Northland Drive, Suite 120
Southfield, MI 48075
(248) 443-7080
Fax (248) 443-2845

CHILD ABUSE AND NEGLECT

National Resources

American Humane Association
American Association for
    Protecting Children
63 Inverness Drive, East
Englewood, CO 80112
(303) 792-9900 (800) 227-4645
e-mail child@amerhumane.org
http://www.amerhumans.org

American Professional Society for
    Abused Children (APSAC)
University of Oklahoma
Health Sciences, Department of Pediatrics
P. O. Box 26901
Oklahoma City, OK 71390
(405) 271-8858
http://www.apsac.org

Childhelp USA
15757 North 78th Street
Scottsdale, AZ 85260
(800) 4-A-CHILD
(800) 422-4453
WWW.CHILDHELPUSA.ORG

Children's Institute International
711 S. New Hampshire Avenue
Los Angeles, CA 90005
(213) 385-5100 (800) 747-5102
Fax (213) 251-3673
www.childreninstitute.org

Child Welfare Research Institute
919 Levering Avenue, Suite 208
Los Angeles, CA 90024

C. Henry Kempe Center for the
    Prevention and
Treatment of Child Abuse and Neglect
1825 Marion Street
Denver, CO 80218
(303) 321-3963
http://electricstores.com/kempe/default.
    html
kempe@kempecenter.org

Clearinghouse on Child Abuse and Neglect
P.O. Box 1182
Washington, DC 20013-1182
(800) FYI-3366; (703) 385-7565 Fax:
    (703) 385-3206
e-mail: nccanch@calib.com
www.calib.com/nccanch

National Center for the Prevention and
    Treatment of Child Abuse and Neglect
University of Colorado Medical Center
1825 Marion Street
Denver, CO 80218
(303) 864-5252
Fax (303) 864-5179

National Center on Child Abuse and
    Neglect
P. O. Box 1182
Washington, DC 20213

National Center for Missing and
    Exploited Children
2101 Wilson Blvd, Suite 550
Arlington, VA 22201
(703) 235-3900
e-mail: ncmec@cis.compuserv.com
www.missingkids.org

National Coalition on Abuse and
    Disabilities (NCAD)
Spectrum Institute, P.O. Box T
Culver City, CA 90230-0090
(310) 391-2420 Fax: (310) 390-6994

National Coalition Against
    Domestic Violence
P. O. Box 18749
Denver, CO 80218
(303) 839-1852
http://www.reeusda.gov/pavnet/cf/
    cfnatcoa.htm

National Committee for Prevention of
    Child Abuse (NCPCA)
332 S. Michigan Avenue, Suite 1600
Chicago, IL 60604
(312) 663-3520   TDD: (312) 663-3540
http://www.childabuse.org

National Domestic Violence Abuse
    Hotline
(800) 799-SAFE

National Runaway Switchboard
(800) 621-4000

National Network of Runaway and
    Youth Services, Inc.
1319 F Street NW, Suite 401
Washington, DC 20004
(202) 783-7949 Fax (202) 783-7955
e-mail: nn4youth@worldnet.att.net
www.nn4youth.org

Parents Anonymous
2810 Artesia Boulevard
Redondo Beach, CA 90278
http://www.korrnet.org/cfs/p_anon.htm

SEXUAL ABUSE

Local Resources
(local telephone directory)

Incest Survivors Anonymous
Survivors of Incest Anonymous

National Resources

Adults Molested as Children United
    (AMACU)
c/o Parents United
P. O. Box 952
San Jose, CA 95108
(408) 280-5055

Center for Adults Sexually Abused as
    Children
(212) 979-8613

Giaretto Institute on
    International Child Abuse
Treatment & Training Program
232 East Gish Road
San Jose, CA 95123
(408) 453-7616
www.giarretto.org
Giarretto@earthlink.net

Incest Resources
Women's Center
46 Pleasant Street
Cambridge, MA 02139
(617) 492-1818

Incest Survivors Anonymous
P. O. Box 17245
Long Beach, CA 90807-7245

Looking Up
P. O. Box K
Augusta, ME 04330
(207) 626-3402

SARAH, Inc.
741 Boston Post Road, Suite 103
Guilford, CT 06437
(203) 458-4040
www.sarah-inc.org/vol.html

Sex Information & Education Council of
    the United States (SIECUS)
130 West 42nd Street, Suite 350
New York, NY 10036
(212) 819-9770 Fax: (212) 819-9776
http://www.siecus.org
e-mail: siecus@siecus.org

Survivors of Incest Anonymous
P. O. Box 21817
Baltimore, MD 21222-6817
(410) 282-3400
(410) 433-2365
http://www1.shore.net/~tcfraser/sia.htm

Victims of Incest Can Emerge Survivors
    in Action, Inc. (VOICES)
P. O. Box 148309
Chicago, IL 60614
(800) 7-VOICE-8 (773) 327-1500
http://www.voices-action.org

CHILDREN WITH SPECIAL NEEDS

National Resources— Physical Disabilities

Accent on Information
P. O. Box 700
Bloomington, IL 61702
(309) 378-2961
information on services for disabled

American Amputee Foundation
P. O. Box 55218, Hillcrest Station
Little Rock, AR 72225

American Physical Therapy Association
1111 N. Fairfax Street
Alexandria, VA 22314
(703) 684-2782

Amputee Foundation of Greater Atlanta
120 Shady Brooke Walk
Fairburn, GA 30213

ARISE (Alternatives for Reaching
    Independence through Services and
    Engineering)
501 East Fayette Street
Syracuse, NY 13202

Arthritis Foundation
1330 W. Peachtree St.
Atlanta, GA 30309
(800) 283-7800
http://www.arthritis.org

The Association for Persons with
    Severe Handicaps (TASH)
7010 Roosevelt Way NE
Seattle, WA 98115
(206) 523-8446

Children's Hospital of St. Paul
345 North Smith Avenue
St. Paul, MN 55102
(312) 298-8504
(Cytomegalovirus - CMV)

Fifty-Two Association for the
    Handicapped, Inc.
    (a sports association)
441 Lexington Avenue
New York, NY 10017

Human Growth Foundation
    (growth-related disorders)
7777 Leesburg Pike Suite 202 South
Falls Church, VA 22043

International Center for the Disabled
Rehabilitation and Research Center
340 E. 24th Street
New York, NY 10010
(212) 585-6000
(212) 585-6060-TDD
(212) 585-6161- Fax

Kids R Kids, Inc.
P. O. Box 574
Quakertown, PA 18951
http://www.kidsrkids.org

Little People of America (dwarfism)
National Headquarters
P. O. Box 9897
Washington, DC 20016
(888) LPA-2001

Muscular Dystrophy Association
3561 East Sunrise Drive
Tucson, AZ 85718

National Amputee Golf Association
P. O. Box 1228
Amherst, NH 03031

National Easter Seal Society for
    Crippled Children and Adults
2023 W. Ogden Avenue
Chicago, IL 606012

National Handicapped Sports and
    Recreation Association (NHSRA)
P. O. Box 33141, Farragut Station
Washington, DC 20033

National Information Center for
    Handicapped Children and Youths
    (NICHCY)
P. O. Box 1492
Washington, DC 20013

National Organization on Disability
2100 Pennsylvania Avenue NW
Washington, DC 20037

National Rehabilitation Association
1910 Association Drive
Alexandria, VA 22091

National Scoliosis Foundation (NSF)
93 Concord Avenue
Belmont, MA 02178

New York Orthotic and Prosthetics
    Association (NYOPA)
50 Main Street
White Plains, NY 10606

PACT (Parents of Amputee Children)
Kessler Institute for Rehabilitation
Pleasant Valley Way
West Orange, NJ 07052

Paralympics
555 Ralph McGill Boulevard
Atlanta, GA 30312

Parent Advocacy Coalition for
    Educational Rights (PACER)
4826 Chicago Avenue S.
Minneapolis, MN 55417-1098
(612) 827-2966
Fax: (612) 827-3065
http://www.pacer.org

Roosevelt Warm Springs Institute for
    Rehabilitation
P. O. Box 1000
Warm Springs, GA 31830-0268

Spina Bifida Association of America
1700 Rockville Pike
Rockville, MD 20852
(800) 621-3141

United Cerebral Palsy Association
3399 Winton Road South
Rochester, NY 14623
(716) 334-6000
(212) 268-6655; (800) USA-1UCP

National Resources— Sensory Handicaps

Alexander Graham Bell Association for
    the Deaf
3417 Volta Place, NW
Washington, DC 20007-2778
(202)337-5220 (Voice/TDD)
(202)337-8314 Fax
E-mail: agbelld@aol.com
Web Site: www.agbell.org

American Council for the Blind
1155 15th St. NW
Suite 720
Washington, DC 20005
(202) 467-5081

American Foundation for the Blind
11 Penn Plaza Suite 300
New York, NY 10001
(212) 502-7600
http://www.igc.apc.org/afb

American Speech-Language-Hearing
    Association
10801 Rockville Pike
Rockville, MD 20852
(301) 897-5700

Association for Education and
    Rehabilitation of the Blind &
    Visually Impaired
4600 Duke Street, Suite 430
P. O. Box 22397
Alexandria, VA 22304-9239
(703) 823-9690
aernet@laser.net

Association for Education of the
    Visually Handicapped
206 N. Washington Street
Alexandria, VA 22314

Blind Children's Center
4120 Marathon Street
Los Angeles, CA 90059
(800) 222-3566
http://www/blindctr.org/bcc/text.htm

Braille Institute
(800) 808-2555
http://www/socialservices.com/vi/braille.
    html

Children of Deaf Adults (CODA)
8112 Russell Road
Alexandria, VA 22309
(703) 799-2239
http://www.gallaudet.edu/~rgpricke/coda

National Association for the Deaf
814 Thayer Avenue
Silver Springs, MD 20910-4500
(301) 587-1788
(301) 587-1789 TTY
(301) 587-1791 Fax
E-mail: NADHO@juno.com
Web Site: http://www.nad.org

National Association for Parents of
    Visually Impaired
2180 Linway Drive
Beloit, WI 53511
(800) 562-6265

National Association for the
    Visually Handicapped
22 West 21st Street, 6th Floor
New York, NY 10010
(212) 889-3141
E-mail: staff@navh.org
Website: http//www.navh.org

National Information Center on Deafness
Gallaudet University
Merrill Learning Center, Room LE-50
800 Florida Avenue, NE
Washington, DC 20002
(202) 651-5051; (202) 651-5052

Services for Children with
    Deaf-Blindness
Office of Special Education Programs
(202) 205-8165

The Shepherd Centre for Deaf Children
    and Their Parents
P. O. Box 871
Strawberry Hills
NSW 2012
Australia
http://www.sherpherd-centre.com

National Resources— Chronic Illness

AIDS Information
1132 West Peachtree Street, NW
Atlanta, GA 30309
(800) 342-2437; (800) 551-2728

American Cancer Society
1599 Clifton Road NE
Atlanta, GA 30379
(800) ACS-2345

American Diabetes Association
1660 Duke Street
Alexandria, VA 22314
(703) 549-1500
(703) 549-6995 Fax
http://www.diabetes.org

American Diabetes Association
149 Madison, 7th floor
New York, NY 10016
(212) 725-4925
(888) DIABETES

American Heart Association
1615 Stemmons Freeway
Dallas, TX 75207
(214) 748-7212
(214) 748-1307 - Fax
Web Site: www.amhrt.org/affili/tx/

Cancer Action, Inc.
255 Alexander Street
Rochester, NY 14607
(716) 423-9700
www.gkcreations.com/canceraction/index.
   htm
cancerac@frontiernet.net

Children's Cancer Society
1 Davis Boulevard Suite 604
Tampa, FL 33606
(813) 276-5726
http://mypage.ihost.com/ccc

Cystic Fibrosis Foundation
6931 Arlington Road
Bethesda, MD 20814
(800)344-4823

Epilepsy Foundation of America
4351 Garden City Drive
Landover, MD 20785-2267
(800) EFA-1000 - information services
(301) 459-3700 - main number
(800) EFA-4050 - professional library
E-mail: postmaster@efa.org
Website: www.efa.org

Families of Children with Cancer (FCC)
http://www.interlog.com/~fcc

Kidscope (for children with a parent who
   has cancer)
3400 Peachtree Road Suite 703
Atlanta, GA 30326
http://www.kidscope.org/kids.html

Leukemia Society of America National
   Headquarters
733 Third Avenue
New York, NY 10017

Make Today Count
1017 S. Union Street
Alexandria, VA 22314
(703) 548-9674
http://userpages.itis.com/lemoll/index.
   html

March of Dimes Foundation
1275 Mamoroneck Avenue
White Plains, NY 10605
(914) 428-7100

Muscular Dystrophy Association of
    America
3300 E. Sunrise Drive
Tucson, AZ 85718-3208
(520) 529-2000
(800) 572-1717
http://www.mdausa.org

National Easter Seal Society
70 East Lake Street
Chicago, IL 60601
(312) 726-6200; (312) 726-4258

National Foundation for Children with
    Aids
(305) 940-5437
http://www.childrenwithaids.org

National Hemophilia Foundation
110 Greene Street
New York, NY 10012

National Kidney Foundation
30 East 33rd Street
New York, NY 10016

National Multiple Sclerosis Society
205 E. 42nd Street, 3rd Floor
New York, NY 10017
http://www.nmss.org

The Neuroblastoma Children's
    Cancer Society
P. O. Box 957672
Hoffman Estates, IL 60195
(800) 532-5162
http://www.granitewebworks.com/nccs.
    htm

PediaAIDS Electronic News Network
    (PENN)
http://hypernet.com/itbic.html

Rubella Project
Developmental Disabilities Center
St. Luke's Roosevelt Hospital Center
428 West 59th Street
New York, NY 10019

National Resources— Learning Disabilities

Children and Adults with Attention
    Deficit Disorder (CHADD) -
499 NW 70th Avenue Suite 101
Plantation, FL 33317
(800) 233-4050

Children with Attention Deficit Disorders
    (CH.A.D.D.)
1859 N. Pine Island Road, Suite 185
Plantation, FL 33322
(305) 587-3700   (954) 587-3700
http://www.chadd.org

Information Resources for Adults with
    Disabilities (IRALD)
http://www.personal.u-net.
    com/~irald/IRALD_intro.htm

Learning Disabilities Association of
    America
4156 Library Road
Pittsburgh, PA 15234-1349
(412) 341-1515
(412) 344-0224 Fax
E-Mail: ldanatl@usaor.net
Web Site: http://www.ldanatl.org

National Network of Learning
    Disabled Adults
P. O. Box 3130
Richardson, TX 75080

National Resources— Emotional and Behavioral Disorders

Children's Behavioral Services
6171 W. Charleston
Las Vegas, NV 89158

National Institute of Mental Health
5600 Fishers Lane, Rm. 7C-02,
    MSC 8030
Rockville, MD 20892
(301) 443-4513
(301) 443-4279 Fax
E-mail: nimhpubs@nih.gov or
    nimhinfo@nih.gov
Web Site: http://www.nimh.nih.gov

Research and Training Center on Family
    Support & Children's Mental Health
Regional Research Institute
Portland State University
Attn: Kay Exo
P. O. Box 751
Portland, OR 97207-0751
(503) 725-4040   (503) 725-4180 Fax
E-mail: exok@rri.pdx.edu
Web Site: www.rtc.pdx.edu

Wediko Children's Services
264 Beacon Street
Boston, MA 02116
http://www.wediko.org

National Resources— Mental and Cognitive Disabilities

American Association on
    Mental Deficiency
5101 Wisconsin Avenue NW, Suite 405
Washington, DC 20016

Am. Assoc. of University Affiliated
    Programs for Persons with
    Developmental Disabilities
8605 Cameron Street, Suite 406
Silver Spring, MD 20910
(301) 522-8252

Autism Society of America
7910 Woodmont Avenue, Suite 650
Bethesda, MD 20814-3015
(301) 657-0881 (301) 657-0869 Fax
(800) 3AUTISM ext. 150
http://www.autism-society.org/

Association for the Help of
    Retarded Children
189 Wheatley Road
Brookville, NY 11545
(516) 626-1000
http://www.ahrc.org

Cornelia de Lange syndrome Foundation
60 Dyer Avenue
Collinsville, CT 06022
(800) 753-2357; (203) 693-0159

Down Syndrome Adoption Exchange
56 Midchester Avenue
White Plains, NY 10606
(914) 428-1236

Fragile X Southeast Network
Duke University Medical Center
Box 3364
Durham, NC 27710
(800) 654-FRAX

International Rett Syndrome Association
8511 Rose Marie Drive
Fort Washington, MD 20744
(301) 248-7031

Lowe's Syndrome Association
222 Lincoln Street
West Lafayette, IN 47906
(317) 743-3634

National Association for
    Retarded Citizens (ARC)
500 E. Border Street, Suite 300
Arlington, TX 76010
(817) 261-6003
http://TheArc.org/welcome.html

National Down Syndrome Congress
1800 Dempstre Street
Park Ridge, IL 60068-1146

National Down Syndrome Congress
1605 Chantilly Road
Atlanta, GA 30324
(800) 232-NDSC

National Down Syndrome Society
666 Broadway
New York, NY 10012
(800) 221-4602

National Fragile X Foundation
1441 York Street, Suite 215
Denver, CO 80206
(800) 688-8765; (303) 333-6155

National Society for Children and
    Adults with Autism
1234 Massachusetts Avenue NW,
    Suite 1017
Washington, DC 20005-4599

People, Inc. (Services for the
    developmentally disabled)
1219 N. Forest Road
P. O. Box 9033
Williamsville, NY 14231-9033
(888) 7PEOPLE

Prader-Willi Syndrome Association
6490 Excelsior Boulevard
Suite E-102
St. Louis Park, MN 55426
(612) 926-1947

The 5p Society
11609 Oakmont
Overland Park, KS 66210
(913) 469-8900
Cri du chat Syndrome

National Resources— Miscellaneous Special Needs

American Academy of Pediatrics
141 Northwest Point Blvd.
Elk Grove Village, IL 60007-1098
(847) 228-5005
http://www.aap.org
kidsdocs@aap.org

American Association for Gifted Children
1121 W. Main Street, Suite 100
Durham, NC 27701
(919) 683-1400
(919) 683-1742 - Fax
E-Mail: judyh@TIP.duke.edu
Web Site: http://www.jayi.com/aagc

American Medical Association
515 N. State St.
Chicago, IL 60610
http://www.ama-assn.org
WebAdmin@ama-assn.org

American Public Welfare Association
National Association of Public Child
    Welfare Administrators
810 First St. NE, Suite 500
Washington, DC 20002-4267
(202) 682-0100
http://www.apwa.org/

Association for the Care of
    Children's Health
3615 Wisconsin Avenue NW
Washington, DC 20016
(202) 244-1801

Association of Maternal Child Health
    Programs
275 E. Main Street
Frankfort, KY 40621
(502) 564-4830
http://www.parentsoup.com/

Child and Family, Inc.
901 E. Summit Hill Drive
Knoxville, TN 37915
http://www.korrnet.org/cfs/index.
    htm#menu

Children's Defense Fund
25 E. St. NW
Washington, DC 20001
(202) 628-8787
http://www.tmn.com/cdf/index.html
cdfinfo@childrensdefense.org

Children's Health Information Network
1561 Clark Drive
Yardley, PA 19067
www.tchin.org
mb@tchin.org

Clearinghouse on Disability Information
Office of Special Education and
    Rehabilitative Services
U.S. Department of Education
400 Maryland Avenue SW
Room 3132, Switzer Building
Washington, DC 20202-2524
(202) 205-8241

Closer Look
Parents' Campaign for Handicapped
    Children and Youth
P. O. Box 1492
Washington, DC 20013

Compassionate Friends, Inc.
National Office
P. O. Box 3696
Oak Brook, IL 60522-3696
(630) 990-0010
E-Mail: TCF_National@prodigy.com
Web Site: http://www.jjt.com/~tcf_
    national
Support to families who have experienced
    the death of a child

Council for Exceptional Children
1920 Association Drive
Reston, VA 22091
(703) 620-3660   (703) 264-9446 (TTY)
    (703) 620-4334 - Fax
E-Mail: cec@cec.sped.org
Web Site: http://www.cec.gped.org

Health Services and Mental Health
    Administration
Maternal and Child Health Services
Parklawn Building, Suite 739
5600 Fishers Lane
Rockville, MD 20852

IBM National Support Center for Persons
    with Disabilities
P. O. Box 2150
Atlanta, GA 30301
(800) IBM-2133; (800) 284-9482

National Academy for Child Development
P. O. Box 380
Huntsville, UT 84317
(801) 621-8606
http://www.nacd.org

National Association for the Education of
   Young Children
1834 Connecticut Avenue NW
Washington, DC 20009
(800) 424-2460; (202) 232-8777

National Association of Private Schools
   for Exceptional Children
1522 K Street NW
Suite 1032
Washington, DC 20005
(202) 408-3338

National Center for Youth with
   Disabilities (NCYD)
University of Minnesota, Box 721
420 Delaware Street S.E.
Minneapolis, MN 55455
(612) 626-2825 TDD: (612) 624-3939
   Fax: (612) 626-2134

National Clearinghouse for Professionals
   in Special Education
1920 Association Drive
Reston, VA 20191-1589
(703) 264-9476
Web Site: ncpse@cec.sped.org

National Information Center for Children
   and Youth with Disabilities (NICHCY)
P. O. Box 1492
Washington, DC 20013-1492
(703) 893-6061; (800) 999-5599
E-mail: nichcy@aed.org
Web Site: www.nichcy.org

Parent Care (Disabilities from
   Premature Birth)
101½ Union Street
Alexandria, VA 22314
(703) 836-4678

Rubenstein-Taybi Parent Group
414 East Kansas
Smith Center, KS 66967

Senate Document Room
Hart Building Washington, DC 20515
(202) 224-7860
House Document Room, Room B-18
House Annex #2
Washington, DC 20515
(202) 225-3456
federal bill or law copies

Sibling Information Network
Connecticut's University Affiliated
   Program on Developmental
   Disabilities
991 Main Street
East Hartford, CT 06108
(203) 282-7050

Special Olympics
1350 New York Avenue, NW
Suite 500
Washington, DC 20005
(202) 628-3630

THEOS (Loss of spouse)
322 Boulevard of the Allies, Suite 105
Pittsburg, PA 15222-1919
(412) 471-7779
(412) 471-7782—Fax

Tough Love
P. O. Box 1069
Doylestown, PA 18901
(800) 333-1069 (215) 348-7090

Williams Syndrome Association
P. O. Box 3297
Ballwin, MO 63022-3297
(314) 227-4411

CRIME VICTIMS

National Resources

American Bar Association Center
Howard A. Davidson, J.D., Director
Center on Children and the Law
740 15th St. NW
Washington, DC 20005
(202) 662-1720
http://dev.abanet.org/child/
ctrchildlaw@abanet.org

American Probation and
    Parole Association
P. O. Box 11910
Lexington, KY 40578-1910
(606) 244-8197
http://www.csa.org/appa/appa.htm
email: appa@csg.org

National Center for Missing and
    Exploited Children
2101 Wilson Boulevard
Arlington. VA 22201-3052
(703) 235-3900 TDD: (800) 826-7653
    Fax: (703) 235-4067
    Hotline: (800) 843-5678
http://www.missingkids.com

National Coalition Against Domestic
    Violence
PO Box 34103
Washington, DC 20043
(202) 638-6388

National Court Appointed Special
    Advocate (CASA) Association
100 W. Harrison, Suite 500
Seattle, WA 98119
http://www.nationalcasa.org

National Crime Victims Research &
    Treatment Center
Medical University of South Carolina
171 Ashley Avenue
Charleston, SC 29425-0743
http://www.musc.edu/cvc/

National Organization for
    Victim Assistance
1757 Park Road, NW
Washington, DC 20010
(202) 232-6682
nova@digex.net
http://www.access.digex.net/~nova

National Victim Center
307 W. Seventh Street, Suite 1001
Fort Worth, TX 76102
(817) 877-3355

Society for Pediatric Pathology
Providence Memorial Hospital
439 Eudora
El Paso, TX 79902
(915) 545-7323
http://path.upmc.edu/spp/about.htm

Victim Services
(212) 577-7777 (Hotline)
(212) 577-7700

DIVORCE

Academy of Family Mediators
1500 South Highway 100
Golden Valley, MN 55416
(612) 525-8670

American Association for Marriage and
    Family Therapy
1100 17th Street, NW, 10th Floor
Washington, DC 20036
(800) 374-2638

American Divorce Association of Men
   (ADAM)
1519 South Arlington Heights Road
Arlington Heights, IL 60005
(708) 364-1555

Association for Children for
   Enforcement of Support, Inc.
2260 Upton Avenue
Toledo, OH 43606
(800) 537-7072
(419) 472-6609
Fax (419) 472-6295
www.ISMI.NET/ACEC/INDEX.HTML

Divorce Anonymous
2600 Colorado Avenue, Suite 270
Santa Monica, CA 90404
(213) 315-6538

Joint Custody Association
10606 Wilkins Avenue
Los Angeles, CA 90024
(310) 475-5352

Mothers Without Custody
PO Box 27418
Houston, TX 77227
(800) 457-6962

North American Conference of
   Separated and Divorced Catholics
80 St. Mary's Drive
Cranston, RI 02920
(401) 943-7903

Parents Without Partners
(800) 637-7974
www.parentswithoutpartners.org
Check phonebook listing or newspaper

Stepfamily Association of America
650 J Street, Suite 205
Lincoln, NE 68508
(800) 735-0329 (402) 477-STEP
www.stepfam.org

Stepfamily Foundation, Inc.
333 West End Avenue
New York, NY 10023
(212) 877-3244
(212) 700-STEP
www.stepfamily.org

MULTI-CULTURAL

Anti-Defamation League of B'nai-B'rith
823 United Nations Plaza
New York, NY 10017
(212) 490-2525
www.ADL.org

Council on Interracial Books for Children
1841 Broadway
New York, NY 10023
(212) 757-5339

Mexican-American Legal Defense Fund
28 Geary Street
San Francisco, CA 94108

Multicultural Resource Center
8443 Crenshaw Boulevard
Englewood, CA 90305

Native American Rights Fund
1506 Broadway
Boulder, CO 80302
(303) 447-8760
(303) 443-7776 Fax

National Association for the
  Advancement of Colored People
4805 Mt. Hope Drive
Baltimore, MD 21215
(410) 358-8900

National Institute Against Prejudice and
  Violence
31 South Greene Street
Baltimore, MD 21201
(410) 706-5170

References

Abbott, D. A., & Meridith, W. H. (1986). Strengths of parents with retarded children. *Family Relations, 35,* 371–375.

Aber, J. L., Allen, J. P., Carlson, V., & Cicchetti, D. (1989). The effects of maltreatment on development during early childhood: Recent studies and their theoretical, clinical, and policy implications. In D. Cicchetti & V. Carlson (Eds.), *Child maltreatment: Theory and research on the causes and consequences of child abuse and neglect* (pp. 579–619). New York: Cambridge University Press.

Abi-Nader, J. (1991). Creating a vision of the future: Strategies for motivating minority students. *Phi Delta Kappan, 72,* 546–549.

Abramovitch, R., Corter, D., & Lando, B. (1979). Sibling interaction in the home. *Child Development, 50,* 997–1003.

Abramovitch, R., & Strayer, F. F. (1977). Preschool social organization: Agonistic, spacing and attentional behaviors. In P. Pliner, T. Kramer, & T. Alloway (Eds.), *Recent advances in the study of communication and affect* (Vol. 6). New York: Academic Press.

Abrams, J. C., & Kaslow, F. (1977). Family systems and the learning disabled child: Intervention and treatment. *Journal of Learning Disabilities, 10,* 86–90.

Achilles, C. M. (1996). Students achieve more in smaller classes. *Educational Leadership, 53,* 76–77.

Achilles, C. M. (1997). Small classes, big possibilities. *The School Administrator, October,* 6–15.

Ackerman, R. J. (1983). *Children of alcoholics: A guidebook for educators, therapists, and parents* (2nd ed.). Holmes Beach, FL: Learning Publications.

Ackerman, R. J. (Ed.). (1986). *Growing in the shadow: Children of alcoholics.* Deerfield Beach, FL: Health Communications.

Ackerman, R. J. (1989). *Perfect daughters: Adult daughters of alcoholics.* Deerfield Beach, FL: Health Communications.

Ackerman, R. J., & Graham, D. (1990). *Too old to cry: Abused teens in today's America.* Blue Ridge Summit, PA: Tab Books.

Adkins, P. G., & Young, R. G. (1976). Cultural perceptions in the treatment of handicapped school children of Mexican-American parentage. *Journal of Research and Development in Education, 9*(4), 83–90.

Adler, A. (1959). *Understanding human nature.* New York: Fawcett.

Affleck, J., Madge, S., Adams, A., & Lowenbraun, S. (1988). Integrated classroom versus resource model: Academic viability and effectiveness. *Exceptional Children, 54,* 339–348.

Aldous, J. (1978). *Family careers: Developmental change in families.* New York: Wiley.

Alexander, C., & Strain, P. S. (1978). A review of educators' attitudes toward handicapped children and the concept of mainstreaming. *Psychology in the Schools, 15,* 390–396.

Alexander, K. L., & Entwisle, D. R. (1996). Schools and children at risk. In A. Booth & J. F. Dunn (Eds.), *Family-school links: How do they affect educational outcomes?* (pp. 67–88). Mahwah, NJ: Erlbaum.

Algozzine, B., & Ysseldyke, J. (1992). *Strategies and tactics for effective instruction.* Longmont, CO: Sopris West.

Allen, M., Brown, P., & Finlay, B. (1992). *Helping children by strengthening families: A look at family support programs.* Washington, DC: Children's Defense Fund.

Amatea, E. S., & Sherrard, P. A. D. (1995). Inquiring into children's social worlds: A choice of lenses. In B. Ryan, G. Adams, T. Gullota, R. Weissberg, & R. Hampton (Eds.), *The family-school connection: Theory, research, and practice* (pp. 29–74). Thousand Oaks, CA: Sage.

Amerikaner, M. J., & Omizo, M. M. (1984). Family interaction and learning disabilities. *Journal of Learning Disabilities, 17,* 540–543.

Ammerman, R. T. (1990). Predisposing child factors. In R. T. Ammerman & M. Hersen (Eds.), *Children at risk: An evaluation of factors contributing to child abuse and neglect* (pp. 199–221). New York: Plenum Press.

Ammerman, R. T., & Hersen, M. (Eds.). (1990a). *Children at risk: An evaluation of factors contributing to child abuse and neglect.* New York: Plenum Press.

Ammerman, R. T., & Hersen, M. (Eds.). (1990c). *Treatment of family violence: A sourcebook.* New York: Wiley.

Ammerman, R. T., & Hersen, M. (1990b). Issues in the assessment and treatment of family violence. In R. T. Ammerman & M. Hersen (Eds.), *Treatment of family violence: A sourcebook* (pp. 3–14). New York: Wiley.

Ammerman, R. T., & Hersen, M. (Eds.). (1991). *Case studies in family violence.* New York: Plenum Press.

Ammerman, R. T., Lubetsky, M. J., & Drudy, K. F. (1991). Maltreatment of handicapped children. In R. T. Ammerman & M. Hersen (Eds.), *Case studies in family violence* (pp. 209–230). New York: Plenum Press.

Ammerman, R. T., Van Hasselt, V. B., Hersen, M., McGonigle, J. J., & Lubetsky, M. J. (1989). Abuse and neglect in psychiatrically hospitalized multihandicapped children. *Child Abuse & Neglect, 13,* 335–343.

Anderson, H., & Goolishian, H. (1986). Systems consultation with agencies dealing with domestic violence. In L. C. Wynne, S. H. McDaniel, & T. T. Weber (Eds.), *Systems consultation: A new perspective for family therapy* (pp. 284–299). New York: Guilford Press.

Anderson, J. A. (1988). Cognitive styles and multicultural populations. *Journal of Teacher Education, 29,* 2–9.

Aponte, H. J. (1976a). The family-school interview: An eco-structural approach. *Family Process, 15,* 303–311.

Aponte, H. J. (1976b). Underorganization in the poor family. In P. Guerin (Ed.), *Family therapy: Theory and practice* (pp. 432–448). New York: Gardner Press.

Aponte, H. J. (1994). *Bread and spirit: Therapy with the new poor.* New York: Norton.

Aponte, H. J., & Hoffman, L. (1973). The open door: A structural approach to a family with an anorectic child. *Family Process, 12,* 1–44.

Aponte, H. J., & Van Deusen, J. M. (1981). Structural family therapy. In A. S. Gurman & D. P. Kniskern (Eds.), *Handbook of family therapy* (pp. 310–361). New York: Brunner/Mazel.

Arditti, J. A., & Keith, T. Z. (1992). Visitation frequency, child support payment, and the father-child relationship postdivorce. *Journal of Marriage and the Family, 55,* 699–712.

Arends, R. I. (1990). Connecting the university to the school. In B. Joyce (Ed.), *Changing school culture through staff development* (pp. 117–143). Alexandria, VA: Association for Supervision and Curriculum Development.

Armstrong, D. (1995). *Power and partnership in education: Parents, children and special educational needs.* New York: Routledge.

Arroyo, W., & Eth, S. (1995). Assessment following violence-witnessing trauma. In E. Peled, P. G. Jaffe, & J. Edleson (Eds.), *Ending the cycle of violence: Community responses to children of battered women* (pp. 27–42). Thousand Oaks, CA: Sage.

Attneave, C. (1982). American Indians and Alaska Native families: Emigrants in their own homeland. In M. McGoldrick, J. K. Pearce, & J. Giordano (Eds.), *Ethnicity and family therapy* (pp. 55–82). New York: Guilford Press.

Attneave, C. L., & Verhulst, J. (1986). Teaching mental health professionals to see family strengths: Core network interventions in a hospital setting. In M. Karpel (Ed.), *Family resources: The hidden partner in family therapy* (pp. 259–271). New York: Guilford Press.

Austin, T. (1994). *Changing the view: Student-led parent conferences.* Portsmouth, NH: Heinemann.

Azpeitia, L. M., & Zahnd, W. F. (1991). Increasing couple intimacy using Virginia Satir's temperature reading. In B. J. Brothers (Ed.), *Virginia Satir: Foundational ideas* (pp. 83–101). New York: Haworth Press.

Baber, K. M., & Allen, K. R. (1992). *Women and families: Feminist reconstructions.* New York: Guilford Press.

Bagnall, G. (1991). *Educating young drinkers.* New York: Routledge.

Bailey, D. (1984). A triaxial model of the interdisciplinary team and group process. *Exceptional Children, 51,* 17–25.

Bailey, D. B., Jr., Simeonsson, R. J., Isbell, P., Huntington, G. S., Winton, P., Comfort, M., & Helm, J. (1988). Inservice training in family assessment and goal-setting for early interventionists: Outcomes and issues. *Journal of the Division for Early Childhood, 12,* 126–136.

Bailey, D. B., & Winton, P. J. (1987). Stability and change in parents' expectations about mainstreaming. *Topics in Early Childhood Special Education, 7,* 73–88.

Baldwin, M. (1991). The triadic concept in the work of Virginia Satir. In B. J. Brothers (Ed.) *Virginia Satir: Foundational ideas* (pp. 27–42). New York: The Haworth Press.

Baldwin, M. (1993). Ingredients of an interaction. In T. S. Nelson & T. S. Trepper (Eds.), *101 Interventions in family therapy* (pp. 17–21). New York: Haworth Press.

Bandler, R., & Grinder, J. (1979). *Frogs into princes: Neurolinguistic programming.* Moab, UT: Real People Press.

Banerji, M., & Dailey, R. A. (1995). A study of the effects of an inclusion model on students with specific learning disabilities. *Journal of Learning Disabilities, 28,* 511–522.

Bank, S. P., & Kahn, M. D. (1975). Sisterhood-brotherhood is powerful: Sibling subsystems and family therapy. *Family Process, 14,* 311–337.

Bank, S. P., & Kahn, M. D. (1982). *The sibling bond.* New York: Basic Books.

Bardill, D. R. (1997). *The relational systems model for family therapy: Living in the four realities.* New York: Haworth Press.

Barney, J. (1990). Stepfamilies: Second chance or second-rate? *Phi Delta Kappan, 72,* 144–148.

Barnhill, L. R., & Longo, D. (1978). Fixation and regression in the family life cycle. *Family Process, 17,* 469–478.

Barr, R. D., & Parrett, W. H. (1995). *Hope at last for at-risk youth.* Boston: Allyn & Bacon.

Barry, F., & Collins, P. (1997). The scope and history of child abuse and neglect. In J. Garbarino & J. Eckenrode (Eds.), *Understanding abusive families* (pp. 26–55). San Francisco: Jossey-Bass.

Barth, R., Berrick, J. D., & Gilbert, N. (Eds.). (1994). *Child welfare research review* (Vol. 1). New York: Columbia University Press.

Bartholet, E. (1993). *Family bonds: Adoption and the politics of parenting.* Boston: Houghton Mifflin.

Bates, C., & Wigtil, J. (1994). *Skill building activities for alcohol and drug education.* Boston: Jones & Bartlett.

Bateson, G. (1972). *Steps to an ecology of the mind.* New York: Ballantine Books.

Beal, E. W., & Hochman, G. (1991). *Adult children of divorce.* New York: Delacorte Press.

Beattie, M. (1987). *Codependent no more.* New York: Harper/Hazelden.

Beavers, J., Hampson, R. B., Hulgus, Y. F., & Beavers, W. R. (1986). Coping in families with a retarded child. *Family Process, 25,* 365–378.

Beck, V. (1994). "Opportunity plus": A school and community based tutorial program for elementary students. *Elementary School Guidance and Counseling, 29,* 156–159.

Beckman, P. J. (1983). Influence of selected child characteristics on stress in families of handicapped infants. *American Journal of Mental Deficiency, 88,* 150–156.

Beckman-Bell, P. (1981). Child-related stress in families of handicapped children. *Topics in Early Childhood Special Education, 1,* 45–53.

Benedek, E. P., & Brown, C. F. (1995). *How to help your child overcome your divorce.* Washington, DC: American Psychiatric Press.

Benne, K. D., & Sheats, P. (1948). Functional roles of group members. *Journal of Social Issues, 2,* 42–47.

Bennett, C. I. (1990). *Comprehensive multicultural education: Theory and practice.* Boston: Allyn & Bacon.

Bennett, F. (1982). The pediatrician and the interdisciplinary process. *Exceptional Children, 48,* 306–314.

Bennett, L. A., Wolin, S. J., Reiss, D., & Teitelbaum, M. A. (1987). Couples at risk for transmission of alcoholism: Protective influences. *Family Process, 26,* 111–129.

Berardo, F. M. (1980). Decade preview: Some trends and directions for family research and theory in the 1980s. *Journal of Marriage and the Family, 42,* 723–728.

Berger, A. (1985). Characteristics of abusing families. In L. L'Abate (Ed.), *The handbook of family psychology and therapy* (Vol. 2, pp. 900–936). Homewood, IL: Dorsey Press.

Berger, M. (1984a). Social network interventions for families that have a handicapped child. In J. C. Hansen & E. I. Coppersmith (Eds.), *Families with handicapped members* (pp. 127–136). Rockville, MD: Aspen.

Berger, M. (1984b). Special education programs. In M. Berger & G. J. Jurkovic (Eds.), *Practicing family therapy in diverse settings* (pp. 142–179). San Francisco: Jossey-Bass.

Berk, H. (1993). Early intervention and special education. In R. Smith (Ed.). *Children with mental retardation: A parent's guide* (p. 195). Bethesda, MD: Woodbine.

Berman, W. H., & Turk, D. C. (1981). Adaptation to divorce: Problems and coping strategies. *Journal of Marriage and the Family, 27,* 179–189.

Bernard, J. M. (1989). School interventions. In M. R. Textor (Ed.), *The divorce and divorce therapy handbook* (pp. 243–265). Northvale, NJ: Jason Aronson.

Bernhard, Y. M. (1991). Theory and practice of the Satir system. In B. J. Brothers (Ed.), *Virginia Satir: Foundational ideas* (pp. 21–25). New York: Haworth Press.

Besharov, D. J. (1990). *Recognizing child abuse: A guide for the concerned.* New York: Free Press.

Bitter, J. (1993). Satir's parts party with couples. In T. S. Nelson & T. S. Trepper (Eds.), *101 interventions in family therapy* (pp. 132–136). New York: Haworth Press.

Björck-Åkesson, E., & Granlund, M. (1995). Family involvement in assessment and intervention: Perceptions of Professionals and parents in Sweden. *Exceptional Children, 61,* 520–535.

Blacher, J. (1984). Sequential stages of parental adjustment to the birth of a child with handicaps: Fact or artifact? *Mental Retardation, 22*(2), 55–68.

Blumberg, B. D., Lewis, M. J., & Susman, E. J. (1984). Adolescence: A time of transition. In M. Eisenberg, L. Sutkin, & M. Jansen (Eds.), *Chronic illness and disability through the life span: Effects on self and family* (pp. 133–149). New York: Springer Publishing.

Bogolub, E. B. (1995). *Helping families through divorce: An eclectic approach.* New York: Springer.

Booth, A., & Dunn, J. F. (Eds.). (1996). *Family-school links: How do they affect educational outcomes?* Mahwah, NJ: Erlbaum.

Boszormenyi-Nagy, I., & Spark, G. M. (1973). *Invisible loyalties.* New York: Harper & Row.

Bowen, M. (1966). The use of family theory in clinical practice. *Comprehensive Psychiatry, 7,* 345–374.

Bowen, M. (1976). Theory in the practice of psychotherapy. In P. J. Guerin, Jr. (Ed.), *Family therapy: Theory and practice* (pp. 42–90). New York: Gardner Press.

Bowen, M. (1978). *Family therapy in clinical practice.* Northvale, NJ: Jason Aronson.

Bowen, M. (1985). *Family therapy in clinical practice* (3rd ed.). Northvale, NJ: Jason Aronson.

Boyd-Franklin, N. (1989). *Black families in therapy: Multisystems approach.* New York: Guilford Press.

Bradley, D. F., & King-Sears, M. E. (1997). The change process: Change for people and schools. In D. F. Bradley, M. E. King-Sears, & D. M. Tessier-Switlick (Eds.), *Teaching students in inclusive settings: From theory to practice* (pp. 56–82). Boston: Allyn & Bacon.

Bradley, D. F., King-Sears, M. E. & Tessier-Switlick, D. M. (Eds.). (1997). *Teaching students in inclusive settings: From theory to practice.* Boston: Allyn & Bacon.

Bradley, D. F. , & Switlick, D. M. (1997). From isolation to cooperation in teaching. In D. F. Bradley, M. E. King-Sears, & D. M. Tessier-Switlick (Eds.), *Teaching students in inclusive settings: From theory to practice* (pp. 109–128). Boston: Allyn & Bacon.

Bray, J. H., & Berger, S. H. (1993). Nonresidential parent-child relationship following divorce and remarriage: A longitudinal perspective. In C. E. Depner & J. H. Bray (Eds.), *Nonresidential parenting* (pp. 156–181). Newbury Park, CA: Sage.

Brazelton, T. B. (1992). *Touchpoints: Your child's emotional and behavioral development.* Reading, MA: Addison-Wesley.

Brendtro, L., & Bacon, J. (1994). Youth empowerment and teamwork. In H. G. Garner & F. P. Orelove (Eds.), *Teamwork in human services: Models and applications across the life span* (pp. 55–71). Boston: Butterworth-Heinemann.

Brendtro, L., Brokenleg, M., & Van Bockern, S. (1990). *Reclaiming youth at risk: Our hope for the future.* Bloomington, IN: National Educational Service.

Breslau, N. (1982). Siblings of disabled children: Birth order and age-spacing effects. *Journal of Abnormal Child Psychology, 10*(1), 85–96.

Breulin, D. C., Schwartz, R. C., & Kune-Karrer, B. (1992). *Metaframeworks: Transcending the models of family therapy.* San Francisco: Jossey-Bass.

Briggs, M. H. (1997). *Building early intervention teams.* Gaithersburg, MD: Aspen.

Broderick, C. B., & Schrader, S. S. (1991). The history of professional marriage and family therapy. In A. S. Gurman & D. P. Kniskern (Eds.), *Handbook of family therapy* (pp. 5–35). New York: Brunner/Mazel.

Brody, E. M. (1974). Aging and family personality: A developmental view. *Family Process, 13*(1), 23–37.

Brody, G. H., & Stoneman, Z. (1983, September). *Contextual issues in the study of sibling socialization.* Paper presented at the National Institute on Child Health and Development Conference on Research on Families With Retarded Persons, Baltimore, MD.

Brodzinsky, D. M. (1990). A stress and coping model of adoption adjustment. In D. M. Brodzinsky & M. D. Schechter (Eds.), *The psychology of adoption* (pp. 3–24). New York: Oxford University Press.

Brodzinsky, D. M., Schechter, M. D., & Henig, R. M. (1992). *Being adopted: The lifelong search for self.* New York: Doubleday.

Bronfenbrenner, U. (1979). *The ecology of human development.* Cambridge, MA: Harvard University Press.

Brooks, C. S., & Rice, K. F. (1997). *Families in recovery: Coming full circle.* Baltimore, MD: Paul H. Brookes.

Brown, F. H. (1989). The impact of death and serious illness on the family life cycle. In B. Carter & M. McGoldrick (Eds.), *The changing family life cycle: A framework for family therapy* (pp. 457–482). Boston: Allyn & Bacon.

Brucker, P. O. (1994). The advantages of inclusion for students with learning disabilities. *Journal of Learning Disabilities, 27,* 581–582.

Burgess, E. W. (1969) *Personality and the social group* (reprint of the 1929 ed.). Freeport, NY: Books for Libraries Press.

Burgess, E. W. (1926) The family as a unity of interacting personalities. *The Family, 7,* 3–9.

Burke, P., & Cigno, K. (1996). *Support for families: Helping children with learning disabilities.* Brookfield, VT: Ashgate.

Burleson, B. R. (1994). Comforting messages: Significance, approaches, and effects. In B. R. Burleson, T. L. Albrecht, & I. G. Sarason (Eds.), *Communication of social support: Messages, interactions, relationships, and community* (pp. 3–28). Thousand Oaks, CA: Sage.

Burleson, B. R., Albrecht, T. L., & Sarason, I. G. (Eds.). (1994). *Communication of social support: Messages, interactions, relationships, and community.* Thousand Oaks, CA: Sage.

Buscaglia, L. (1983). *The disabled and their parents: A counseling challenge* (rev. ed.). Thorofare, NJ: Slack.

Byers, P. (1992). The spiritual in the classroom. *Holistic Education Review, 5,* 6–11.

Byng-Hall, J. (1995). *Rewriting family scripts: Improvisation and systems change.* New York: Guilford Press.

Caine, R. N., & Caine, G. (1997). *Education on the edge of possibility.* Alexandria, VA: Association for Supervision and Curriculum Development.

Calof, D. L. (1988). *Adult children of incest and child abuse.* Workshop publication. Seattle: Family Psychotherapy Practice of Seattle.

Cameron, G., & Vanderwoerd, J. (1997). *Protecting children and supporting families: Promising programs and organizational realities.* Hawthorne, NY: Aldine.

Campbell, C. (1993). Strategies for reducing parent resistance to consultation in the schools. *Elementary School Guidance and Counseling, 28,* 83–91.

Carney, I., & Gamel-McCormick, M. (1996). Working with families. In F. P. Orelove & D. Sobsey, *Educating children with multiple disabilities: A transdisciplinary approach* (3rd ed., pp. 451–476). Baltimore, MD: Paul H. Brookes.

Carr, M. N. (1993). A mother's thought on inclusion. *Journal of Learning Disabilities, 26,* 590–592.

Carter, B., & McGoldrick, M. (Eds.). (1989a). *The changing family life cycle: A framework for family therapy* (2nd ed.). Boston: Allyn & Bacon.

Carter, B., & McGoldrick, M. (1989b). Overview: The changing family life cycle—A framework for family therapy. In B. Carter & M. McGoldrick (Eds.), *The changing family life cycle: A framework for family therapy* (2nd ed., pp. 3–28). Boston: Allyn & Bacon.

Carter, B., Papp, P., Silverstein, O., & Walters, M. (1986). The procrustean bed. *Family Process, 25,* 301–304.

Carter, E. A., & McGoldrick, M. (1980). *The family life cycle: A framework for family therapy.* New York: Gardner Press.

Carter, J., & Sugai, G. (1989). Survey on prereferral practices: Responses from state departments of education. *Exceptional Children, 55,* 298–302.

Carter, R. T. (1995). *The influence of race and racial identity in psychotherapy: Toward a racially inclusive model.* New York: Wiley.

Caspi, A., Elder, G. H., Jr., & Herbeno, E. S. (1990). Childhood personality and the prediction of life-course patterns. In L. N. Robbins & McRutter (Eds.), *Straight and devious pathways from childhood to adulthood* (pp. 13–33). Cambridge, UK: Cambridge University Press.

Chapman, W. (1991). The Illinois experience: State grants to improve schools through parent involvement. *Phi Delta Kappan, 72,* 355–358.

Chen, S. A., & True, R. H. (1994). Asian/Pacific Island Americans. In L. D. Eron, J. H. Gentry, & P. Schlegel (Eds.), *Reason to hope: A psychosocial perspective on violence and youth* (pp. 145–162). Washington, DC: American Psychological Association.

Cherlin, A. (1992). *Marriage, divorce, remarriage.* Cambridge, MA: Harvard University Press.

Christenbury, L., Beale, A. V., & Patch, S. S. (1996). Interactive bibliocounseling: Recent fiction and nonfiction for adolescents and their counselors. *The School Counselor, 44*(2), 133–145.

Christiansen, J. (1997). Helping teachers meet the needs of students at risk for failure. *Elementary School Guidance & Counseling, 31*(3), 204–210.

Cicirelli, V. G. (1972). The effect of sibling relationships on concept learning of young children taught by child teachers. *Child Development, 43,* 282–287.

Cleveland, D. W., & Miller, N. (1977). Attitudes and life commitments of older siblings of mentally retarded adults: An exploratory study. *Mental Retardation, 15*(3), 38–41.

Coates, D. L. (1990). Social network analysis as mental health intervention with African-American adolescents. In F. C. Serafica, A. I. Schwebel, R. K. Russell, P. D. Isaac, & L. B. Myers (Eds.), *Mental health of ethnic minorities* (pp. 230–253). New York: Praeger.

Cobb, S. (1976). Social support as a moderator of life stress. *Psychosomatic Medicine, 38,* 301–314.

Coburn, J., & Nelson, S. (1989). *Teachers do make a difference: What Indian graduates say about their school experience.* ERIC Document Reproduction Service No. ED 306 071.

Cohen, J. A., & Mannarino, A. P. (1991). Incest. In R. T. Ammerman & M. Hersen (Eds.), *Case studies in family violence* (pp. 171–186). New York: Plenum Press.

Cohen, R. (1969). Conceptual styles, culture conflict, and nonverbal tests of intelligence. *American Anthropologist, 71,* 828–856.

Colapinto, J. (1991). Structural family therapy. In A. S. Gurman & D. P. Kniskern (Eds.), *Handbook of family therapy* (Vol. 2, pp. 417–443). New York: Brunner/Mazel.

Colapinto, J. (1982). Structural family therapy. In A. Horne & B. Ohlsen (Eds.), *Family counseling and therapy* (pp. 112–140). Itasca, IL: Peacock.

Coleman, A. (1995). *Child abuse reporting: An urban profile.* New York: Garland.

Coleman, J. S. (1987). Families and schools. *Educational Researcher, 16*(6), 32–38.

Combrinck-Graham, L. (1983). The family life cycle and families with young children. In J. Hansen & H. Liddle (Eds.), *Clinical implications of the family life cycle* (pp. 35–53). Rockville, MD: Aspen.

Comer, J. P. (1996). *Rallying the whole village: The Comer process for reforming education.* New York: Teachers College Press.

Comer, J. P., & Haynes, N. M. (1991). Parent involvement in schools: An ecological approach. *Elementary School Journal, 91,* 271–277.

Cooper, K. L., & Rascon, L. (1994). *Building positive relationships on the border with parents of special students: Effective practices for the IEP* (Report No. RC 019 597). Paper presented 14th Annual American Council on Rural Special Education Conference (1994, March) Austin, TX: (ERIC Document Reproduction Service No. ED 369 627).

Coppersmith, E. I. (1983). The family and public service systems: An assessment method. In J. Hansen & E. Keene (Eds.), *Diagnosis and assessment in family therapy* (pp. 83–100). Rockville, MD: Aspen.

Corbett, H. D., Firestone, W. A., & Rossman, G. B. (1987). Resistance to planned change and the sacred in school cultures. *Educational Administration Quarterly, 33*(4), 36–59.

Corey, G. (1996). *Theory and practice of counseling and psychotherapy* (5th ed.). New York: Brooks/Cole.

Corrales, R. G., Kostoryz, J., Ro-Trock, L., & Smith, B. (1983). Family therapy with developmentally delayed children: An ecosystemic approach. In D. Bagarozzi, A. Jurich, & R. Jackson (Eds.), *Marital and family therapy: New perspectives in theory, research, and practice* (pp. 137–164). New York: Human Sciences Press.

Council for Exceptional Children. (1979). *We can help.* Reston, VA: Author. (ERIC Document Reproduction Service No. ED 177 754).

Courtnage, L., & Smith-Davis, J. (1987). Interdisciplinary team training: A national survey of special education teacher training programs. *Exceptional Children, 53,* 451–458.

Courtois, C. A. (1988). *Healing the incest wound: Adult survivors in therapy.* New York: Norton.

Cowan, P. A., Cowan, C. P., & Schulz, M. S. (1996). Thinking about risk and resilience in families. In E. M. Hetherington & E. A. Blechman, (Eds.), *Stress, coping, and resiliency in children and families* (pp. 1–38). Mahwah, NJ: Lawrence Erlbaum Associates.

Coyne, A., & Brown, M. E. (1985). Developmentally disabled children can be adopted. *Child Welfare, 64,* 607–615.

Cuban, L. (1989). The "at-risk" label and the problem of urban school reform. *Phi Delta Kappan, 70,* 780–784.

Cullen, J. C., MacLeod, J. A., Williams, P. D., & Williams, A. R. (1991). Coping, satisfaction, and the life cycle in families with mentally retarded persons. *Issues in Comprehensive Pediatric Nursing, 14,* 193–207.

Cummins, J. (1989). A theoretical framework for bilingual special education. *Exceptional Children, 56,* 111–119.

Cusinato, M. (1994). Parenting over the family life cycle. In L. L'Abate (Ed.), *Handbook of developmental family psychology and psychopathology* (pp. 83–115). New York: Wiley.

Dallos, R. (1991). *Family belief systems, therapy and change.* Philadelphia, PA: Open University Press.

D'Angelo, D. A., & Adler, C. R. (1991). Chapter 1: A catalyst for improving parent involvement. *Phi Delta Kappan, 72,* 350–354.

Daniels-Mohring, D. (1986). *Sibling relationships with an older sibling as identified patient.* Unpublished manuscript, Georgia State University, Atlanta.

Darling, R. B. (1991). Initial and continuing adaptation to the birth of a disabled child. In M. Seligman (Ed.), *The family with a handicapped child* (2nd ed., pp. 55–89). Boston: Allyn & Bacon.

Daro, D. (1990). Prevention of child physical abuse. In R. T. Ammerman & M. Hersen (Eds.), *Treatment of family violence: A sourcebook* (pp. 331–353). New York: Wiley.

Delaney, A. J. (Ed.). (1979). *Black task force report: Project on ethnicity.* New York: Family Service Association of America.

delCarmen, R. (1990). Assessment of Asian-Americans for family therapy. In F. C. Serafica, A. I. Schwebel, R. K. Russell, P. D. Isaac, & L. B. Myers (Eds.), *Mental health of ethnic minorities* (pp. 24–68). New York: Praeger.

De Luca, R. V., Hazen, A., & Cutler, J. (1993). Evaluation of a group counseling program for preadolescent female victims of incest. *Elementary School Guidance and Counseling, 28*(2), 104–114.

Dennis, R. E., & Giangreco, M. F. (1996). Creating conversation: Reflections on cultural sensitivity in family interviewing. *Exceptional Children, 63,* 103–116.

Depner, C. E., & Bray, J. H. (Eds.). (1993). *Nonresidential parenting.* Newbury Park, CA: Sage.

DeVillar, R. A., & Faltis, C. J. (1994). Reconciling cultural diversity and quality schooling: Paradigmatic elements of a socioacademic framework. In R. A. DeVillar, C. J. Faltis, & J. P. Cummins (Eds.), *Cultural diversity in schools: From rhetoric to practice* (pp. 1–22). Albany: State University of New York Press.

Dodson, L. S. (1991). Virginia Satir's process of change. In B. J. Brothers (Ed.), *Virginia Satir: Foundational ideas* (pp. 119–142). New York: Haworth Press.

Donnelly, D., & Finkelhor, D. (1992). Does equality in custody arrangements improve the quality of the parent-child relationship? *Journal of Marriage and the Family, 54,* 837–845.

Dowd, N. E. (1997). *In defense of single-parent families.* New York: New York University Press.

Downey, D., & Powell, B. (1993). Do children in single-parent households fare better living with same-sex parents? *Journal of Marriage and the Family, 55,* 55–71.

Dryfoos, J. G. (1994). *Full-service schools: A revolution in health and social services for children, youth, and families.* San Francisco: Jossey-Bass.

Dudley, J. (1983). *Living with stigma: The plight of the people who we label mentally retarded.* Springfield, IL: Charles C. Thomas.

Dulfano, C. (1992). *Families, alcoholism, & recovery.* San Francisco: Jossey-Bass.

Dunlap, W. R., & Hollinsworth, J. S. (1977). How does a handicapped child affect the family? Implications for practitioners. *The Family Coordinator, 26,* 286–293.

Dunn, J., & Kendrick, C. (1982). *Siblings.* Cambridge. MA: Harvard University Press.

Dunst, C. J., & Deal, A. G. (1994). A family-centered approach to developing individualized family support plans. In C. J. Dunst, C. M. Trivette, & A. G. Deal (Eds.), Supporting and strengthening families: Vol. 1. Methods, strategies and practices (pp. 73–88). Cambridge, MA: Brookline Books.

Dunst, C. J., Trivette, C. M., & Deal, A. G. (1988). *Enabling and empowering families: Principles and guidelines.* Cambridge, MA: Brookline Books.

Dunst, C. J., Trivette, C. M., & Deal, A. G. (1994a). Enabling and empowering families. In C. J. Dunst, C. M. Trivette, & A. G. Deal (Eds.), *Supporting and strengthening families: Vol. 1. Methods, strategies and practices* (pp. 2–11). Cambridge, MA: Brookline Books.

Dunst, C. J., Trivette, C. M., & Deal, A. G. (1994b). Resource-based family-centered intervention practices. In C. J. Dunst, C. M. Trivette, & A. G. Deal (Eds.), *Supporting and strengthening families: Vol. 1. Methods, strategies and practices* (pp. 140–151). Cambridge, MA: Brookline Books.

Dunst, C. J., Trivette, C. M., & Deal, A. G. (Eds.). (1994c). *Supporting and strengthening families: Vol. 1. Methods, strategies and practices.* Cambridge, MA: Brookline Books.

Dunst, C. J., Trivette, C. M., & Cross, A. H. (1986). Mediating influences of social support: Personal, family, and child outcomes. *American Journal of Mental Deficiency, 90,* 403–417.

Duvall, E. M. (1977). *Marriage and family development* (5th ed.). Philadelphia, PA: Lippincott.

Dyson, L., & Fewell, R. R. (1985). Stress and adaptation in parents of young handicapped and nonhandicapped children: A comparative study. *Journal of the Division for Early Childhood, 10,* 25–34.

Dyson, L., & Fewell, R. (1989). The self-concept of siblings of handicapped children: A comparison. *Journal of Early Intervention, 13,* 230–238.

Eckenrode, J., Powers, J., & Garbarino, J. (1997). Youth in trouble are youth who have been hurt. In J. Garbarino & J. Eckenrode (Eds.), *Understanding abusive families* (pp. 166–193). San Francisco: Jossey-Bass.

Edwards, D. L. (1995). The school counselor's role in helping teachers and students belong. *Elementary School Guidance and Counseling, 29,* 191–197.

Edwards, D. L., & Foster, M. A. (1995). Uniting the family and school systems: A process of empowering the school counselor. *The School Counselor, 42,* 277–282.

Egeland, B. (1993). A history of abuse is a major risk factor for abusing the next generation. In R. J. Gelles & D. R. Loseke (Eds.), *Current controversies on family violence* (pp. 197–208). Newbury Park, CA: Sage.

Eheart, B. K., & Ciccone, J. (1982). Special needs of low-income mothers of developmentally delayed children. *American Journal of Mental Deficiency, 87,* 26–33.

Elliott, J. (1997). Strategies for including students in elementary school programs. In L. A. Power-deFur & F. P. Orelove (Eds.), *Inclusive education: Practical implementation of the least restrictive environment* (pp. 153–166). Gaithersburg, MD: Aspen.

Elman, N. (1991). Family therapy. In M. Seligman (Ed.), *The family with a handicapped child* (2nd ed., pp. 369–406). Boston: Allyn & Bacon.

Entwisle, D. R. (1994). Subcultural diversity in American families. In L. L'Abate (Ed.), *Handbook of developmental family psychology and psychopathology* (pp. 132–156). New York: Wiley.

Epstein, N. B., Baldwin, L. M., & Bishop, D. S. (1983). The McMaster Family Assessment device. *Journal of Mental and Family Therapy, 9,* 171–180.

Epstein, N. B., Bishop, D. S., & Baldwin, L. N. (1982). McMaster model of family functioning: A view of the normal family. In F. Walsh (Ed.), *Normal family processes* (pp. 115–141). New York: Guilford.

Erb, T. O. (1995). Teamwork in middle school education. In H. G. Garner (Ed.), *Teamwork models and experience in education* (pp. 175–198). Boston: Allyn & Bacon.

Erikson, E. (1963). *Childhood and society.* New York: Norton.

Evans, R. (1993). The human face of reform. *Educational Leadership, 51*(1), 19–23.

Everett, C. A., & Everett, S. (1994). *Healthy divorce.* San Francisco: Jossey-Bass.

Falik, L. H. (1995). Family patterns of reaction to a child with a learning disability: A mediational perspective. *Journal of Learning Disabilities, 28,* 335–341.

Farlow, L. (1996). A quartet of success stories: How to make inclusion work. *Educational Leadership, 53*(5), 51–55.

Farmer, S., & Galaris, D. (1993). Support groups for children of divorce. *American Journal of Family Therapy, 21,* 40–50.

Featherstone, H. (1980). *A difference in the family.* New York: Basics Books.

Feiring, C., & Lewis, M. (1985). Changing characteristics of the U.S. family. In M. Lewis (Ed.), *Beyond the dyad* (pp. 59–90). New York: Plenum Press.

Feldman, L. B. (1992). *Integrating individual and family therapy.* New York: Brunner/Mazel.

Ferrari, M. (1984). Chronic illness: Psychosocial effects on siblings of chronically ill boys. *Journal of Child Psychology and Psychiatry, 25,* 459–476.

Ferrari, M., Matthews, W. S., & Barabas, G. (1983). The family and the child with epilepsy. *Family Process, 22,* 53–59.

Ferreiro, B. (1990). Presumption of joint custody: A family policy dilemma. *Family Relations, 39,* 420–426.

Fewell, R. R. (1995). Early education for disabled and at-risk children. In M.C. Wang, M. C. Reynolds, & H. J. Walberg (Eds.), *Handbook of special and remedial education: Research and practice* (2nd. ed., pp. 37–60). New York, NY: Elsevier Science Inc.

Field, S. (1996). Self-determination instructional strategies for youth with learning disabilities. *Journal of Learning Disabilities, 29,* 40–52.

Figley, C. R., & McCubbin, H. I. (Eds.). (1983). *Stress and the family: Vol. 2. Coping with catastrophe.* New York: Brunner/Mazel.

Fine, M. J., & Carlson, C. (Eds.). (1992). *The handbook of family-school intervention: A systems perspective.* Boston: Allyn & Bacon.

Finkelhor, D. (1987). The sexual abuse of children: Current research reviewed. *Psychiatric Annals, 17,* 233–241.

Finkelhor, D., Hotaling, G. T., & Yllö, K. (1988). *Stopping family violence: Research priorities for the coming decade.* Newbury Park, CA: Sage.

Finn, J. D. (1998). *Class size and students at risk: What is known? What is next.* Washington, DC: US Department of Education. [on-line www.ed.gov/offices/oeri/at-risk].

Fischgrund, J. E., Cohen, O. P., & Clarkson, R. L. (1987). Hearing-impaired children in black and Hispanic families. *Volta Review, 89*(5), 59–67.

Fisher, B. A. (1980). *Small group decision making* (2nd ed.). New York: McGraw-Hill.

Fishman, H. C. (1993). *Intensive Structural Therapy: Treating families in their social context.* New York: HarperCollins.

Fogarty, T. (1976). On emptiness and closeness, Part II. *The Family, 3*(2), 3–17.

Fontana, V. J., & Moolman, V. (1991). *Save the family, save the child: What we can do to help children at risk.* New York: Penguin Group.

Ford, B. A., & Jones, C. (1990). Ethnic feelings book: Created by students with developmental handicaps. *Teaching Exceptional Children, 33*(4), 36–39.

Ford, D. Y., & Harris, J. J. (1995). Underachievement among gifted African American students: Implications for school counselors. *The School Counselor, 42,* 196–203.

Fordyce, W. (1981). On interdisciplinary peers. *Archives of Physical Medicine and Rehabilitation, 62*(2), 51–53.

Forest, M., & Pearpoint, J. (1992). Common sense tools: MAPS and CIRCLES: for inclusive education. In J. Pearpoint, M. Forest, & J. Snow (Eds.), *The Inclusion papers: Strategies to make inclusion work* (pp. 40–51). Toronto, Ontario, Canada: Inclusion Press.

Foster, M. (1986). Families with young disabled children in family therapy. In J. C. Hansen & L. Combrinck-Graham (Eds.), *Treating young children in family therapy* (pp. 62–72). Rockville, MD: Aspen.

Foster, M., Berger, M., & McLean, M. (1981). Rethinking a good idea: A reassessment of parent involvement. *Topics in Early Childhood Special Education, 1,* 56–65.

Fowler, R. C., & Corley, K. K. (1996). Linking families, building community. *Educational Leadership, 53*(7), 24–26.

Fox, J., & Savelle, S. (1987). Social interaction research and families of behaviorally disordered children: A critical review and forward look. *Behavioral Disorders, 12,* 276–291.

Framo, J. L. (1981). The integration of marital therapy with sessions with family of origin. In A. S. Gurman & D. P. Kniskern (Eds.), *Handbook of family therapy* (pp. 133–158). New York: Brunner/Mazel.

Framo, J. L. (1992). *Family-of-origin therapy: An intergenerational approach.* New York: Brunner/ Mazel.

Framo, M. D. (1981). Common issues in recoupled families and therapy interventions. In A. S. Gurman (Ed.), *Questions and answers in the practice of family therapy* (pp. 333–337). New York: Brunner/Mazel.

Franklin, M. (1992). Culturally sensitive instructional practices for African-American learners with disabilities. *Exceptional Children, 59,* 115–122.

Fredman, N., & Sherman, R. (1987). *Handbook of measurements for marriage and family therapy.* New York: Brunner/Mazel.

Freedman, M. (1993). *The kindness of strangers: Adult mentors, urban youth, and the new volunteerism.* San Francisco: Jossey-Bass.

Friedman, A. S., & Granick, S. (Eds.). (1990). *Family therapy for adolescent drug abuse.* Lexington, MA: D. C. Heath.

Friedman, E. H. (1986). Emotional process in the marketplace: The family therapist as consultant to work systems. In L. C. Wynne, S. H. McDaniel, & T. T. Weber (Eds.), *Systems consultation: A new perspective for family therapy* (pp. 398–422). New York: Guilford Press.

Friedman, L. J. (1981). Common problems in stepfamilies. In A. S. Gurman (Ed.), *Questions and answers in the practice of family therapy* (pp. 329–332). New York: Brunner/Mazel.

Friedrich, W. N. (1979). Predictors of the coping behavior of mothers of handicapped children. *Journal of Consulting and Clinical Psychology, 47,* 1140–1141.

Friedrich, W. N., & Friedrich, W. L. (1981). Psychosocial assets of parents of handicapped and nonhandicapped children. *American Journal of Mental Deficiency, 85,* 551–553.

Friedrich, W. N., Wilturner, L. G., & Cohen, D. S. (1985). Coping resources and parenting mentally retarded children. *American Journal of Mental Deficiency, 90,* 130–139.

Friend, M., & Cook, L. (1996). *Interactions: Collaboration skills for school professionals* (3rd ed.). New York: Longman.

Frymier, J. (1992a). *Assessing and predicting risk among students in school.* Bloomington, IN: Phi Delta Kappa.

Frymier, J. (1992b). *Growing up is risky business, and schools are not to blame.* Bloomington, IN: Phi Delta Kappa.

Frymier, J., & Gansneder, B. (1989). The Phi Delta Kappan study of students at risk. *Phi Delta Kappan, 71,* 142–146.

Fuchs, D., & Fuchs, L. S. (1994). Inclusive schools movement and the radicalization of special education reform. *Exceptional Children, 60,* 294–309.

Fuchs, D., Fuchs, L., & Bahr, M. (1990). Mainstream assistance teams: A scientific basis for the art of consultation. *Exceptional Children, 57,* 128–139.

Fuchs, D., Fuchs, L., Bahr, M., Fernstrom, P., & Stecker, P. (1990). Prereferral intervention: A prescriptive approach. *Exceptional Children, 56,* 493–513.

Fulmer, R. (1989). Lower-income and professional families: A comparison of structure and life cycle process. In B. Carter & M. McGoldrick (Eds.), *The changing family life cycle: A framework for family therapy* (2nd ed., pp. 545–578). Boston: Allyn & Bacon.

Gabel, H., & Kotsch, L. S. (1981). Extended families and young handicapped children. *Topics in Early Childhood Special Education, 1,* 29–35.

Gallagher, J. J., Beckman, P., & Cross, A. H. (1983). Families of handicapped children: Sources of stress and its amelioration. *Exceptional Children, 50,* 10–19.

Gallagher, J. J., Cross, A., & Scharfman, W. (1981). Paternal adaptation to a young handicapped child: The father's role. *Journal of the Division for Early Childhood, 3,* 3–14.

Gamel-McCormick, M. (1995). Inclusive teams serving included students: Regular and special education teams working in integrated settings. In H. G. Garner (Ed.), *Teamwork models and experience in education* (pp. 157–174). Boston: Allyn & Bacon.

Garbarino, J., & Eckenrode, J. (1997a). The meaning of maltreatment. In J. Garbarino & J. Eckenrode (Eds.), *Understanding abusive families.* San Francisco: Jossey-Bass.

Garcia-Preto, N. (1996). Puerto Rican families. In M. McGoldrick, J. Pearce, & J. Giordano (Eds.),

Ethnicity and family therapy (2nd ed., pp. 183–199). New York: Guilford Press.

Garland, C. W. (1993). Beyond chronic sorrow: A new understanding of family adaptation. In A. P. Turnbull, J. M. Patterson, S. K. Behr, D. L. Murphy, J. G. Marquis, & M. J. Blue-Banning (Eds.), *Cognitive coping, families, and disability* (pp. 67–80). Baltimore, MD: Paul H. Brookes.

Garland, C. W. (1994). World of practice: Early intervention programs. In H. G. Garner & F. P. Orelove (Eds.), *Teamwork in human services: Models and applications across the life span* (pp. 89–116). Boston: Butterworth-Heinemann.

Garland, C. W. (1995). Moving toward teamwork in early intervention: Adapting models to meet program needs. In H. G. Garner (Ed.), *Teamwork models and experience in education* (pp. 139–155). Boston: Allyn & Bacon.

Garmezy, N. (1991). Resiliency and vulnerability to adverse developmental outcomes associated with poverty. *American Behavioral Scientist, 34,* 416–430.

Garmezy, N., & Rutter, M. (Eds.). (1983). *Stress, coping, and development in children.* New York: McGraw-Hill.

Garner, H. G. (1994). Critical issues in teamwork. In H. G. Garner & F. P. Orelove (Eds.), *Teamwork in human services: Models and applications across the life span* (pp. 1–18). Boston: Butterworth-Heinemann Publishers.

Garner, H. G. (1995a). Teamwork in education and child care. In H. G. Garner (Ed.), *Teamwork models and experience in education* (pp. 1–16). Boston: Allyn & Bacon.

Garrett, M. W. (1995). Between two worlds: Cultural discontinuity in the dropout of Native American youth. *The School Counselor, 42,* 186–195.

Geary, P. A. (1988). *"Defying the odds?": Academic success among at-risk minority teenagers in an urban high school.* ERIC Document Reproduction Service No. ED 296 055.

Gelles, R. (1996). *The book of David: How preserving families can cost children's lives.* New York: Basic Books.

Gelles, R. J., & Loseke, D. R. (Eds.). (1993). *Current controversies on family violence.* Newbury Park, CA: Sage.

Gergen, K. J. (1991). *The saturated self: Dilemmas of identity in contemporary life.* New York: Basic Books/Harper Collins.

Giangreco, M. F. (1994). Dressing your IEPs for the general education climate: Analysis of IEP goals and objectives for students with multiple disabilities. *Remedial and Special Education, 15,* 288–296.

Giangreco, M. F., Dennis, R., Cloninger, C., Edelman, S., & Schattman, R. (1993). "I've counted Jon": Transformational experiences of teachers educating students with disabilities. *Exceptional Children, 59,* 359–372.

Gibran, K. (1923). *The prophet.* New York: Knopf.

Gil, E. (1996). *Systematic treatment of families who abuse.* San Francisco: Jossey-Bass.

Gilliam, J. (1979). Contributions and status rankings of educational planning committee participants. *Exceptional Children, 45,* 466–468.

Giordano, J., & McGoldrick, M. (1996). Italian families. In M. McGoldrick, J. Giordano, & J. Pearce (Eds.), *Ethnicity and family therapy* (2nd ed., pp. 567–582). New York: Guilford Press.

Glidden, L. M. (1989). *Parents for children, children for parents: The adoption alternative.* Washington, DC: American Association on Mental Retardation.

Glidden, L. M. (1994). Not under my heart, but in it. In J. Blacher (Ed.), *When there's no place like home: Options for children living apart from their natural families* (pp. 181–209). Baltimore, MD: Paul H. Brookes.

Glover, G. L. (1994). The hero child in the alcoholic home: Recommendations for counselors. *The School Counselor, 41,* 185–190.

Goffman, E. (1963). *Stigma: Notes on the management of spoiled identity.* Englewood Cliffs, NJ: Prentice-Hall.

Goldenberg, I., & Goldenberg, H. (1991). *Family therapy: An overview* (3rd ed.). Monterey, CA: Brooks/Cole.

Goldsmith, D. (1992). Managing conflicting goals in supportive interaction: An integrative theoretical framework. *Communication Research, 19,* 264–286.

Goldsmith, D., & Albrecht, T. L. (1993). The impact of supportive communication networks on test anxiety and performance. *Communication Education, 42,* 142–158.

Goldstein, S., Strickland, B., Turnbull, A. P., & Curry, L. (1980). An observational analysis of the IEP conference. *Exceptional Children, 46,* 278–286.

Gorman, J. C., & Balter, L. (1997). Culturally sensitive parent education: A critical review of quantitative research. *Review of Educational Research, 67,* 339–369.

Gould, J. (1970). The phases of adult life: A study in developmental psychology. *American Journal of Psychiatry, 129*(5), 35–79.

Graden, J. (1989). Redefining "prereferral" intervention as intervention assistance: Collaboration between general and special education. *Exceptional Children, 56,* 227–231.

Graden, J. L., & Bauer, A. M. (1991). Using a collaborative approach to support students and teachers in inclusive classrooms. In S. Stainback & W. Stainback (Eds.), *Curriculum considerations in inclusive classrooms: Facilitating learning for all students* (pp. 85–100). Baltimore, MD: Paul H. Brookes.

Green, A. H. (1991). Child neglect. In R. T. Ammerman & M. Hersen (Eds.), *Case studies in family violence* (pp. 135–152). New York: Plenum Press.

Green, R. J. (1989). "Learning to learn" and the family system: New perspectives on underachievement and learning disorders. *Journal of Marital and Family Therapy, 15,* 187–203.

Green, R. J. (1992). "Learning to learn" and the family system: New perspectives on underachievement and learning disorders. In M. J. Fine & C. Carlson (Eds.), *The handbook of family-school intervention: A systems perspective* (pp. 157–174). Boston: Allyn & Bacon.

Green, R. J. (1995). High achievement, underachievement, and learning disabilities: A family systems model. In B. A. Ryan, G. R. Adams, T. P. Gullotta, R. P. Weissberg, & R. L. Hampton (Eds.), *The family-school connection: Theory, research and practice* (pp. 207–249). Thousand Oaks, CA: Sage.

Green, S. K., & Shinn, M. R. (1995). Parent attitudes about special education and reintegration: What is the role of student outcomes? *Exceptional Children, 61,* 269–281.

Greenawalt, C. E., II. (Ed.). (1994a). *Educational innovation: An agenda to frame the future.* Lanham, MD: University Press of America.

Greenawalt, C. E., II. (1994b). Educational outreach programs. In C. E. Greenawalt (Ed.), *Educational innovation: An agenda to frame the future* (pp. 413–433). Lanham, MD: University Press of America.

Greer, J. (1989). Another perspective and some immoderate proposals on "teacher empowerment." *Exceptional Children, 55,* 294–297.

Grigal, M., Test, D. W., Beattie, J., & Wood, W. M. (1997). An evaluation of transition components of individualized education programs. *Exceptional Children, 63,* 357–372.

Grossman, F. (1972). *Brothers and sisters of retarded children: An exploratory study.* Syracuse, NY: Syracuse University Press.

Grotevant, H. D., & Carlson, C. I. (1989). *Family assessment: A guide to methods and measures.* New York: Guilford Press.

Guerin, P. J. (Ed.). (1976). *Family therapy: Theory and practice.* New York: Gardner Press.

Guerin, P. J., & Chabot, D. R. (1992). Development of family systems theory. In D. K. Freedheim (Ed.), *History of psychotherapy: A century of change* (pp. 225–260). Washington, DC: American Psychological Association.

Guidubaldi, J., & Cleminshaw, H. (1985). Divorce, family health, and child adjustment. *Family Relations, 34,* 35–41.

Guskey, T. (1986). Staff development and the process of teacher change. *Educational Researcher, 15*(5), 5–12.

Gustafson, C. (1997). For a champion of racial harmony. *Educational Leadership, 54*(5), 67–69.

Guterman, B. R. (1995). The validity of categorical learning disabilities services: The consumer's view. *Exceptional Children, 62,* 111–124.

Guthrie, L. F., & Guthrie, G. P. (1993). Linking classrooms and communities: The health and media academies in Oakland. In G. A. Smith (Ed.), *Public schools that work: Creating community* (pp. 155–177). New York: Routledge.

Haas, T. (1993). School in communities: New ways to work together. In G. A. Smith (Ed.), *Public schools that work: Creating community* (pp. 215–245). New York: Routledge.

Hadley, T., Jacob, T., Miliones, J., Caplan, J., & Spitz, D. (1974). The relationship between family developmental crisis and the appearance of symptoms in a family member. *Family Process, 13,* 207–214.

Haggerty, R. J., Sherrod, L. R., Garmezy, N., & Rutter, M. (1994). *Stress, risk, and resilience in children and adolescents: Processes, mechanisms, and interventions.* Cambridge, UK: Cambridge University.

Haimes, R. (1995). Planning for change. In H. G. Garner (Ed.), *Teamwork models and experience in education* (pp. 73–83). Boston: Allyn & Bacon.

Hajal, F., & Rosenberg, E. B. (1991). The family life cycle in adoptive families. *American Orthopsychiatric Association, 61,* 78–85.

Hale, J. (1981). Black children: Their roots, culture, and learning styles. *Young Children, 36,* 37–50.

Hale-Benson, J. E. (1982). *Black children: Their roots, culture, and learning styles* (rev. ed.). Baltimore, MD: Johns Hopkins University Press.

Haley, J. (1980). *Leaving home: The therapy of disturbed young people.* New York: McGraw-Hill.

Haley, J. (Ed.). (1985). *Changing individuals: Conversations with Milton H. Erickson, M.D.* (Vol. 1). New York: Triangle Press.

Haley, J. (1987). *Problem-solving therapy* (2nd ed.). San Francisco: Jossey-Bass.

Haley, J., & Hoffman, L. (1967). *Techniques of family therapy.* New York: Basic Books.

Hall, C. S., & Lindzey, G. (1978). *Theories of personality* (3rd ed.). New York: John Wiley.

Hall, G. E., & Hord, S. M. (1987). *Change in schools: Facilitating the process.* Albany: State University of New York Press.

Hall, G. E., Wallace, R. C., Jr., & Dossett, W. (1973). *A developmental conceptualization of the adoption process within educational institutions.* Austin: The University of Texas at Austin, Research and Development Center for Teacher Education. (ERIC Document Reproduction Service No. ED 095 126).

Hall, J. A., & Maza, P. L. (1990). No fixed address: The effects of homelessness on families and children. *Child and Youth Services, 14*(1), 35–47.

Hall, J., & Taylor, K. (1971). The emergence of Eric: Co-therapy in the treatment of a family with a disabled child. *Family Process, 10,* 85–96.

Hammond, W. R., & Yung, B. R. (1994). African Americans. In L. D. Eron, J. H. Gentry & P. Schlegel (Eds.), *Reason to hope: A psychosocial perspective on violence and youth* (pp. 105–118). Washington, DC: American Psychological Association.

Hampton, R. L. (Ed.). (1991). *Black family violence: Current research and theory.* Lexington, MA: D.C. Heath.

Hampton, R. L., & Gelles, R. J. (1991). A profile of violence toward black children. In R. L. Hampton (Ed.), *Black family violence: Current research and theory* (pp. 21–34). Lexington, MA: D.C. Heath.

Hampton, R. L., Gelles, R. J., & Harrop, J. (1991). Is violence in black families increasing? A comparison of 1975 and 1985 national survey rates. In R. L. Hampton (Ed.), *Black family violence: Current research and theory* (pp. 3–18). Lexington, MA: D.C. Heath.

Hanline, M. F. (1991). Transitions and critical events in the family life cycle: Implications for providing support to families of children with disabilities. *Psychology in the Schools, 28,* 53–59.

Hansen, D. J., Conaway, L. P., & Christopher, J. S. (1990). In R. T. Ammerman & M. Hersen (Eds.), *Treatment of family violence: A sourcebook* (pp. 17–49). New York: Wiley.

Hansen, J. C., & Coppersmith, E. I. (Eds.). (1984). *Families with handicapped members.* Rockville, MD: Aspen.

Hansen, J. C., & Falicov, C. J. (Eds.). (1983). *Cultural perspectives in family therapy.* Rockville, MD: Aspen.

Hanson, D. J. (1996). *Alcohol education: What we must do.* Westport, CT: Praeger.

Hanson, M. J., & Carta, J. J. (1996). Addressing the challenges of families with multiple risks. *Exceptional Children, 62,* 201–212.

Hardin, D. E., & McNelis, S. J. (1996). The resource center: Hub of inclusive activities. *Educational Leadership, 53*(5), 41–43.

Harry, B. (1992). Making sense of disability: Low-income, Puerto Rican parents' theories of the problem. *Exceptional Children, 59,* 27–40.

Harry, B., Allen, N., & McLaughlin, M. (1995). Communication versus compliance: African-American parents' involvement in special education. *Exceptional Children, 61,* 364–377.

Hart, P. J., & Jacobi, M. (1992). *From gatekeepers to advocate: Transforming the role of the school counselor.* New York: College Entrance Examination Board.

Harvard Family Research Project. (1995). *Raising our future: Families, schools, and communities joining together.* Cambridge, MA: Author.

Hauser, S. T., Jacobson, A. M., Wertlieb, D., Brink, S., & Wentworth, S. (1985). The contribution of family environment to perceived competence and illness adjustment in diabetic and acutely ill adolescents. *Family Relations, 34,* 99–108.

Havinghurst, R. J. (1952). *Developmental tasks and education.* New York: Longmans, Green.

Hawkins, A. J., Christiansen, S. L., Sargent, K. P., & Hill, E. J. (1993). Rethinking fathers' involvement in child care: A developmental perspective. *Journal of Family Issues, 14,* 531–549.

Hawley, D. R., & DeHaan, L. (1996), Toward a definition of family resilience: Integrating life-span and family perspectives. *Family Process, 35,* 283–298.

Hayes, S. A. (1996). Cross-cultural learning in elementary guidance activities. *Elementary School Guidance and Counseling 30,* 264–274.

Hazzard, A. P. (1990). Prevention of child sexual abuse. In R. T. Ammerman & M. Hersen (Eds.), *Treatment of family violence: A sourcebook* (pp. 354–384). New York: Wiley.

"He pits Jane and me against each other!" Conflicting family styles. (1988). *Exceptional Parent, 18*(3), 62–68.

Heavey, C. L., Shenk, J. L., & Christensen, A. (1994). Marital conflict and divorce: A developmental family psychology perspective. In L. L'Abate (Ed.), *Handbook of developmental family psychology and psychopathology* (pp. 221–242). New York: Wiley.

Heller, T. (1993). Self-efficacy coping, active involvement, and caregiver well-being throughout the life course among families of persons with mental retardation. In A. P. Turnbull, J. M. Patterson, S. K. Behr, D. L. Murphy, J. G. Marquis, & M. J. Blue-Banning (Eds.), *Cognitive coping, families, and disability* (pp. 195–206). Baltimore, MD: Paul H. Brookes.

Henderson, N., & Milstein, M. M. (1996). *Resilience in schools: Making it happen for students and educators.* Thousand Oaks, CA: Corwin Press.

Hendrick, J. (1984). *The whole child: Early education for the eighties.* St. Louis, MO: C.V. Mosby.

Henry, M. (1996). *Parent-school collaboration: Feminist organizational structure and school leadership.* Albany, NY: State University of New York.

Herring, R. D., & Meggert, S. S. (1994). The use of humor as a counselor strategy with Native American Indian children. *Elementary School Guidance & Counseling, 29,* 67–76.

Hess, B. B., & Waring, J. M. (1978). Parent and child in later life: Rethinking the relationship. In R. Lerner & G. Spanier (Eds.), *Child influences on marital and family interaction: A life-span perspective* (pp. 241–275). New York: Academic Press.

Hesse-Biber, S., & Williamson, J. (1984). Resource theory and power in families: Life cycle considerations. *Family Process, 23,* 261–278.

Hetherington, E. M., & Blechman, E. A. (Eds.). (1996). *Stress, coping, and resiliency in children and families.* Mahwah, NJ: Erlbaum.

Hill, H. M., Soriano, S., Chen, A., & LaFromboise, T. D. (1994). In L. D. Eron, J. H. Gentry, & P. Schlegel (Eds.), *Reason to hope: A psychosocial perspective on violence and youth* (pp. 59–97). Washington, DC: American Psychological Association.

Hines, P. M. (1989). The family life cycle of poor black families. In B. Carter & M. McGoldrick (Eds.), *The changing family life cycle: A framework for family therapy* (2nd ed., pp. 513–544). Boston: Allyn & Bacon.

Hines, P. M. (1990). African-American mothers. *Journal of Feminist Family Therapy, 2*(2), 23–32.

Hines, P. M., & Boyd-Franklin, N. (1996). African American families. In M. McGoldrick, J. Giordano, & J. Pearce (Eds.), *Ethnicity and family therapy* (2nd ed., pp. 66–84). New York: Guilford Press.

Ho, M. K. (1992). *Minority children and adolescents in therapy.* Newbury Park, CA: Sage.

Hobbs, N. (1975). *Futures of children.* San Francisco: Jossey-Bass.

Hobfoll, S. E., & Stephens, M. A. P. (1990). Social support during extreme stress: Consequences and intervention. In B. R. Sarason, I. G. Sarason, & G. R. Pierce (Eds.), *Social support: An interactional view* (pp. 454–481). New York: Wiley.

Hodgkinson, H. L. (1990). *The demographics of American Indians: One percent of the people; fifty percent of the diversity.* Washington, DC: Institute for Educational Leadership.

Hoffman, L. (1981). *Foundations of family therapy.* New York: Basic Books.

Hoffman-Riem, C. (1990). *The adopted child: Family life with double parenthood.* New Brunswick, NJ: Transaction Publishers.

Hollander, S. (1992). Making young children aware of sexual abuse. *Elementary School Guidance and Counseling, 26*(4), 305–317.

Holman, T. B., & Burr, W. R. (1980). Beyond the beyond: The growth of family theories in the 1970s. *Journal of Marriage and the Family, 42,* 729–740.

Holmes, L. (1993). The special child: A multi-use reframe. In T. S. Nelson & T. S. Trepper (Eds.), *101 interventions in family therapy* (pp. 369–371). New York: Haworth Press.

Hoopes, J. L. (1990). Adoption and identity formation. In D. M. Brodzinsky & M. D. Schechter (Eds.), *The psychology of adoption,* (pp. 144–166). New York: Oxford University Press.

Howard, J. (1978). The influence of children's developmental dysfunctions on marital quality and family interaction. In R. Lerner & G. Spanier (Eds.), *Child influences on marital and family interaction: A life-span perspective* (pp. 275–298). New York: Academic Press.

Hudson, P., & Glomb, N. (1997). If it takes two to tango, then why not teach both partners to dance? Collaboration instruction for all educators. *Journal of Learning Disabilities, 30,* 442–448.

Hughes, S. F., Berger, M., & Wright, L. (1978, October). The family life cycle and clinical intervention. *Journal of Marriage and Family Counseling,* pp. 33–40.

Hurtig, A. L. (1994). Chronic illness and developmental family psychology. In L. L'Abate (Ed.), *Handbook of developmental family psychology and psychopathology* (pp. 265–283). New York: Wiley.

Individuals with Disabilities Education Act of 1997, Pub. L. No. 105-17 (1997).

Idol, L. (1997). Key questions related to building collaborative and inclusive schools. *Journal of Learning Disabilities, 30,* 384–394.

Idol, L., Nevin, A., & Paolucci-Whitcomb, P. (1994). *Collaborative consultation* (2nd ed.). Austin, TX: PRO-ED.

I'm not going to be John's babysitter forever: Siblings, planning and the disabled child. (1987). *The Exceptional Parent, 17*(8), 60–68.

Imber-Black, E. (1986). Toward a resource model in systemic family therapy. In M. Karpel (Ed.), *Family resources: The hidden partner in family therapy* (pp. 148–174). New York: Guilford Press.

Imber-Black, E. (1989). Idiosyncratic life cycle transitions and therapeutic rituals. In B. Carter & M. McGoldrick (Eds.), *The changing family life cycle: A framework for family therapy* (pp. 149–163). Boston: Allyn & Bacon.

Intagliata, J., & Doyle, N. (1984). Enhancing social support for parents of developmentally disabled children: Training in interpersonal problem solving skills. *Mental Retardation, 22*(1), 4–11.

Isaacs, M. L., & Duffus, L. R. (1995). Scholars' club: A culture of achievement among minority students. *The School Counselor, 42,* 204–210.

Jacob, T. J., & Tennenbaum, D. L. (1988). *Family assessment: Rationale, methods, and future directions.* New York: Plenum Press.

Jacobson, N. S., & Gurman, A. S. (Eds.). (1995). *Clinical handbook of couple therapy.* New York: Guilford Press.

Jalali, B. (1996). Iranian families. In M. McGoldrick, J. Giordano, & J. Pearce (Eds.), *Ethnicity and family therapy* (2nd ed., pp. 347–363). New York: Guilford Press.

James, S. H., & DeVaney, S. B. (1994). Reporting suspected sexual abuse: a study of counselor and counselor trainee responses. *Elementary School Guidance and Counseling, 28,* 257–263.

Jameson, P. B., & Alexander, J. F. (1994). Implications of a developmental family systems model for clinical practice. In L. L'Abate (Ed.), *Handbook of developmental family psychology and psychopathology* (pp. 392–412). New York: Wiley.

Jenkins, J., & Heinen, A. (1989). Students' preferences for service delivery: Pull-out, in-class, or integrated models. *Exceptional Children, 55,* 516–523.

Jens, K. G., & Gordon, B. N. (1991). Understanding risk: Implications for tracking high-risk infants and making early service decisions. *International Journal of Disability, 38,* 211–224.

Jenson, W. R., Sheridan, S. M., Olympia, D., & Andrews, D. (1994). Homework and students with learning disabilities and behavior disorders: A practical, parent-based approach. *Journal of Learning Disabilities, 27,* 538–548.

Johnson, C. L. (1982). Sibling solidarity: Its origin and functioning in Italian-American families. *Journal of Marriage and the Family, 44,* 155–167.

Johnson, D. (1997). *Reaching out: Interpersonal effectiveness and self-actualization* (6th ed.). Boston: Allyn & Bacon.

Johnson, D., & Johnson, R. (1994). *Learning together and alone: Cooperative, competitive, and individualistic learning.* Needham Heights, MA: Allyn & Bacon.

Johnston, J. C., & Zemitzsch, A. (1988). Family power: An intervention beyond the classroom. *Behavioral Disorders, 14,* 69–79.

Joseph, J. M. (1994). *The resilient child: Preparing today's youth for tomorrow's world.* New York: Insight Books, Plenum.

Justice, B., & Justice, R. (1990). *The abusing family* (rev. ed.). New York: Plenum Press.

Kahn, M. D. (1986). The sibling system: Bonds of intensity, loyalty, and endurance. In M. Karpel (Ed.), *Family resources: The hidden partner in family therapy* (pp. 235–258). New York: Guilford Press.

Kahn, M. D., & Lewis, K. G. (Eds.). (1988). *Siblings in therapy: Life span and clinical issues.* New York: Norton.

Kamps, D. M., & Tankersley, M. (1996). Prevention of behavioral and conduct disorders: Trends and research issues. *Behavioral Disorders, 22,* 41–48.

Kanter, R. M. (1995). Managing the human side of change. In D. A. Kolb, J. S. Osland, & I. M. Rubin (Eds.), *The organizational behavior reader* (6th ed., pp. 676–682). Englewood Cliffs, NJ: Prentice-Hall.

Kantor, D., & Lehr, W. (1975). *Inside the family.* San Francisco: Jossey-Bass.

Kantor, D. (1983). The structural-analytic approach to the treatment of family developmental crisis. In J. Hansen & H. Liddle (Eds.), *Clinical implications of the family life cycle* (pp. 12–34). Rockville, MD: Aspen.

Kaplan, C. P., Turner, S., Norman, E., & Stillson, K. (1996). Promoting resilience strategies: A modified consultation model. *Social Work in Education, 18*(3), 158–168.

Kaplan, R. M., & Toshima, M. T. (1990). The functional effects of social relationships on chronic illness and disability. In B. R. Sarason, I. G. Sarason, & G. R. Pierce (Eds.), *Social support: An interactional view* (pp. 427–453). New York: Wiley.

Karp, S. (1997). Educating for a civil society: The core issue is inequality. *Educational Leadership, 54*(4), 40–43.

Karpel, M. (Ed.). (1986a). *Family resources: The hidden partner in family therapy.* New York: Guilford Press.

Karpel, M. (1986b). Testing, promoting, and preserving family resources: Beyond pathology and power. In M. Karpel (Ed.), *Family resources: The hidden partner in family therapy* (pp. 174–234). New York: Guilford Press.

Kaufman, E., & Kaufmann, P. (Eds.). (1992). *Family therapy of drug and alcohol abuse* (2nd ed.). Boston: Allyn & Bacon.

Kaufman, J., & Zigler, E. (1993). The intergenerational transmission of abuse is overstated. In R. J. Gelles & D. R. Loseke (Eds.), *Current controversies on family violence* (pp. 209–221). Newbury Park, CA: Sage.

Kaufmann, P. (1992). Family therapy with adolescent substance abusers. In E. Kaufman & P. Kaufmann (Eds.), *Family therapy of drug and alcohol abuse* (2nd ed., pp. 63–71). Boston: Allyn & Bacon.

Kay, P. J., Fitzgerald, M., Paradee, C., & Mellencamp, A. (1994). Making homework work at home: The parent's perspective. *Journal of Learning Disabilities, 27,* 550–561.

Kazak, A. E. (1987). Families with disabled children: Stress and social networks in three samples. *Journal of Abnormal Child Psychology, 15,* 137–146.

Kazak, A. E., & Marvin, R. S. (1984). Differences, difficulties and adaptation: Stress and social networks in families with a handicapped child. *Family Relations, 33,* 66–77.

Kazak, A. E., & Wilcox, B. (1984). The structure and function of social support networks in families with handicapped children. *American Journal of Community Psychology, 12,* 645–661.

Keith, N. Z. (1997). Doing service projects in urban settings. In A. S. Waterman (Ed.), *Service-learning: Applications from the research.* Mahwah, NJ: Lawrence Erlbaum Associates.

Keith, V. M., & Finlay, B. (1988). The impact of parental divorce on children's educational attainment, marital timing, and probability of divorce. *Journal of Marriage and the Family, 50,* 797–809.

Kelso, D. R., & Attneave, C. L. (1981). *Bibliography of North American Indian mental health.* Westport, CT: Greenwood Press.

Kennedy, S., Kiecolt-Glaser, J. K., & Glaser, R. (1990). Social support, stress and the immune system. In B. R. Sarason, I. G. Sarason, & G. R. Pierce (Eds.), *Social support: An interactional view* (pp. 253–266). New York: Wiley.

Kerr, M. (1981). Family systems theory and therapy. In A. S. Gurman & D. P. Kniskern (Eds.), *Handbook of family therapy* (Vol. I, pp. 226–264). New York: Brunner/Mazel.

Kerr, M. (1988, September). Chronic anxiety and defining a self. *Atlantic Monthly,* pp. 35–58.

Kerr, M., & Bowen, M. (1988). *Family evaluation: An approach based on Bowen theory.* New York: Norton.

Kew, S. (1975). *Handicap and family crisis: A study of the siblings of handicapped children.* London: Pitman.

Keys, S. G., Bemak, F., Carpenter, S. L., & King-Sears, M. (1998). Collaborative consultant: A new role for counselors serving at-risk youths. *Journal of Counseling & Development, 76,* 123–133.

King-Sears, M. E. (1997). Disability: Legalities and labels. In D. F. Bradley, M. E. King-Sears, & D. M. Tessier-Switlick (Eds.), *Teaching students in inclusive settings: From theory to practice* (pp. 21–55). Boston: Allyn & Bacon.

Kleinbard, P. (1997). Youth participation: Integrating youth into communities. In J. Schine, (Ed.), *Youth participation: Integrating youth into communities,* (pp. 1–18). Chicago: University of Chicago.

Knight, S. M. (1994). Elementary-age children of substance abusers: issues associated with identification and labeling. *Elementary School Guidance and Counseling, 28,* 274–284.

Knoll, J. (1992). Being a family: The experience of raising a child with a disability or chronic illness. In V. J. Bradley, J. Knoll, & J. M. Agosta (Eds.), *Emerging issues in family support* (pp. 9–56). Washington, DC: American Association on Mental Retardation.

Koch, A. (1985). "If only it could be me": The families of pediatric cancer patients. *Family Relations, 34,* 63–70.

Koegel, L. K., Koegel, R. L., & Dunlap, G. (1996). *Positive behavioral support: Including people with difficult behavior in the community.* Baltimore, MD: Paul H. Brookes.

Kolko, D. J., & Stauffer, J. (1991). Child sexual abuse. In R. T. Ammerman & M. Hersen (Eds.), *Case studies in family violence* (pp. 153–186). New York: Plenum Press.

Komoski, P. K. (1990). Needed: A whole-curriculum approach. *Educational Leadership, 47*(5), 72–78.

Kottman, T., Robert, R., & Baker, D. (1995). Parental perspectives on attention-deficit/hyperactivity disorder: How school counselors can help. *The School Counselor, 43*(2), 142–150.

Kreppner, K., & Lerner, R. M. (Eds.) (1989). *Family systems and life span development.* Hillsdale, NJ: Erlbaum.

Kroth, R., & Edge, D. (1997). *Strategies for communicating with parents and families of exceptional children.* Denver, CO: Love Publishing Company.

Kuo, W. (1984). Prevalence of depression among Asian Americans. *Journal of Nervous and Mental Diseases, 172,* 449–457.

L'Abate, L. (1992). Family psychology and family therapy: Comparisons and contrasts. *American Journal of Family Therapy, 20,* 3–12.

L'Abate, L. (Ed.). (1994a). *Handbook of developmental family psychology and psychopathology.* New York: Wiley.

L'Abate, L. (1994b). What is developmental family psychology? In L. L'Abate (Ed.), *Handbook of developmental family psychology and psychopathology* (pp. 3–23). New York: Wiley.

L'Abate, L., & Bagarozzi, D. A. (1993). *Sourcebook of marriage and family evaluation.* New York: Brunner/Mazel.

Laborde, P. R., & Seligman, M. (1991). Counseling parents with children with disabilities. In M. Seligman (Ed.), *The family with a handicapped child* (2nd ed., pp. 337–368). Boston: Allyn & Bacon.

Lambert, N. (1988). Perspectives on eligibility for and placement in special education programs. *Exceptional Children, 54,* 297–301.

Larson, C. E., & LaFasto, F. M. (1989). *Teamwork: What must go right—what can go wrong.* Newbury Park, CA: Sage.

Larson, J. H., Anderson, J. O., & Morgan, A. (1984). *Workshop models for family life education: Effective stepparenting.* New York: Family Service America.

Lawler, S. D. (1991). *Parent-teacher conferencing in early childhood education.* Washington, DC: National Education Association.

Lawson, D. M., & Gaushell, H. (1991). Intergenerational family characteristics of counselor trainees. *Counselor Education and Supervision, 30,* 309–321.

LeClere, F. B., & Kowalewski, B. M. (1994). Disability in the family: The effects on children's well-being. *Journal of Marriage and the Family, 56,* 457–468.

Lee, E. (1996). Asian American families: An overview. In M. McGoldrick, J. Giordano, & J. Pearce (Eds.), *Ethnicity and family therapy* (2nd ed., pp. 227–248). New York: Guilford Press.

Leigh, I. W. (1987). Parenting and the hearing impaired: Attachment and coping. *Volta Review, 89*(5), 11–21.

Leithwood, K. (1997). Presentation made at Virginia Commonwealth University School of Education annual Scholar in Residence seminar.

LePere, D. W. (1988). Vulnerability to crises during the life cycle of the adoptive family. In D. Valentine (Ed.), *Infertility and adoption: A guide for social work practice* (pp. 73–85). New York: Haworth Press.

Levine, M. (1982). The child with school problems: An analysis of physician participation. *Exceptional Children, 48,* 296–304.

Levy, J. C., & Lagos, V. K. (1994). Children with disabilities. In L. D. Eron, J. H. Gentry, & P. Schlegel (Eds.), *Reason to hope: A psychosocial perspective on violence and youth* (pp. 197–213). Washington, DC: American Psychological Association.

Lewis, C. C., Schaps, R., & Watson, M. (1995). Beyond the pendulum: Creating challenging and caring schools. *Phi Delta Kappan, 76,* 547–554.

Lidz, T., Cornelison, A., Fleck, S., & Terry, D. (1957a). The intrafamilial environment of the schizophrenic patient: I. The Father. *Psychiatry, 20,* 329–342.

Lidz, T., Cornelison, A., Fleck, S., and Terry, D. (1957b). The intrafamilial environment of the schizophrenic patient: II. Marital schism and Marital skew. *American Journal of Psychiatry, 114,* 241–248.

Liebman, R., Minuchin, S., & Baker, L. (1974). *An integrated treatment program for anorexia nervosa.* Unpublished paper, Philadelphia Child Guidance Clinic.

Lin, K. M., Inui, T. S., Kleinman, A. M., & Womack, W. M. (1982). Sociocultural determinants of the helpseeking behavior of patients with mental illness. *Journal of Nervous and Mental Disease, 170,* 78–84.

Liontos, L.B. (1991). *Involving the families of at-risk youth in the educational process.* ERIC Document Reproduction Service No. ED 328946).

Liptak, K. (1993). *Adoption controversies.* New York: Franklin Watts.

Longo, D. C., & Bond, L. (1984). Families of the handicapped child: Research and practice. *Family Relations, 33,* 57–65.

Losen, S., & Losen, J. (1985). *The special education team.* Boston: Allyn & Bacon.

Losen, S. M., & Losen, J. G. (1994). Teamwork and the involvement of parents in special education programming. In H. G. Garner & F. P. Orelove (Eds.), *Teamwork in human services: Models and applications across the life span* (pp. 117–141). Boston: Butterworth-Heinemann.

Love, H. D. (1973). *The mentally retarded child and his family.* Springfield, IL: Charles C. Thomas.

Lowe, J. I., & Herranen, M. (1981). Understanding teamwork: Another look at the concepts. *Social Work in Health Care, 7*(2), 1–10.

Lusthaus, C., Lusthaus, E., & Gibbs, H. (1981). Parents' role in the decision process. *Exceptional Children, 48,* 256–257.

Lusthaus, E., & Lusthaus, C. (1993). A "normal" life for Hannah. In A. P. Turnbull, J. M. Patterson, S. K. Behr, D. L. Murphy, J. G. Marquis, & M. J. Blue-Banning (Eds.), *Cognitive coping, families, and disability* (pp. 43–50). Baltimore, MD: Paul H. Brookes.

Lynch, E. W., & Stein, R. C. (1987). Parent participation by ethnicity: A comparison of Hispanic, Black, and Anglo families. *Exceptional Children, 54,* 105–111.

Machotka, P., Pittman, F. S., III, & Flomenhaft, K. (1967). Incest as a family affair. *Family Process, 6,* 98–116.

Mack, C. C., Jr. (1981). Racism, educational models, and black children. In D. Claerbaut (Ed.), *New directions in ethnic studies: Minorities in America* (pp. 84–94). Saratoga, CA: Century Twenty-One.

Mack, D. (1997). *The assault on parenthood: How our culture undermines the family.* New York: Simon & Schuster.

Madanes, C., Keim, J. P., & Smelser, D. (1995). *The violence of men: New techniques for working with abusive families: A therapy of social action.* San Francisco, CA: Jossey-Bass.

Maddock, J. W., & Larson, N. R. (1995). *Incestuous families: An ecological approach to understanding and treatment.* New York: Norton.

Malatchi, A. (1997). Family partnerships, belonging, and diversity. In L. A. Power-deFur & F. P. Orelove (Eds.), *Inclusive education: Practical implementation of the least restrictive environment* (pp. 91–115). Gaithersburg, MD: Aspen.

Mannarino, A. P., & Cohen, J. A. (1990). Treating the abused child. In R. T. Ammerman & M. Hersen (Eds.), *Children at risk: An evaluation of factors contributing to child abuse and neglect* (pp. 249–268). New York: Plenum Press.

Margalit, M., & Raviv, A. (1983). Mothers' perceptions of family climate in families with a retarded child. *The Exceptional Child, 30,* 163–169.

Margolis, H., & Brannigan, G. G. (1986). Relating to angry parents. *Academic Therapy, 21,* 343–346.

Marion, R. L. (1992). The mentally retarded child in the family. In M. J. Fine & C. Carlson (Eds.), *The handbook of family-school intervention: A systems perspective* (pp. 134–156). Boston: Allyn & Bacon.

Marshak, L. E., & Seligman, M. (1993). *Counseling persons with physical disabilities: Theoretical and clinical perspectives.* Austin, TX: PRO-ED.

Marshall, S. (1992). *Teenage addicts can recover: Treating the addict, not the age.* Littleton, CO: Gylantic.

Martin, H. P. (1980). Working with parents of abused and neglected children. In R. R. Abidin (Ed.), *Parent education and intervention handbook* (pp. 252–271). Springfield, IL: Charles C. Thomas.

Maslow, A. (1970). *Motivation and personality.* New York: Harper & Row.

Masten, A. S. (1994). Resilience in individual development: Successful adaptation despite risk and adversity. In M. C. Wang & E. W. Gordon, *Educational resilience in inner-city America* (pp. 3–25). Mahwah, NJ: Lawrence Erlbaum Associates.

Masten, A. S., Best, K. M., & Garmezy, N. (1990). Resilience and development: Contributions from the study of children who overcome adversity. *Development and Psychopathology, 2,* 425–444.

Maxwell, M. G., & Widom, C. S. (1996). The cycle of violence revisited 6 years later. *Archives of Pediatric and Adolescent Medicine, 150,* 390–395.

McCabe, M. P., & Cummins, R. A. (1996). The sexual knowledge, experience, feelings and needs of people with mild intellectual disability. *Education and Training in Mental Retardation and Developmental Disabilities, 31,* 13–21.

McCarty, H., & Chalmers, L. (1997). Bibliotherapy: Intervention and prevention. *Teaching Exceptional Children, 29*(6), 12–13, 16–17.

McCubbin, H. I., McCubbin, M. A., Thompson, A. I., & Thompson, E. A. (1995). Resiliency in ethnic families: A conceptual model for predicting family adjustment and adaptation. In H. I. McCubbin, E. A. Thompson, A. I. Thompson, & J. E. Fromer (Eds.), *Resiliency in ethnic minority families, Vol. 1: Native and immigrant American families* (pp. 3–48). Madison, WI: University of Wisconsin System, Center for Excellence in Family Studies.

McCubbin, H. I., & Patterson, J. (1982). Family adaptation to crises. In H. McCubbin, A. Cauble, & J. Patterson (Eds.), *Family stress, coping and social support* (pp. 26–47). Springfield, IL: Charles C. Thomas.

McCubbin, H. I., Thompson, A. I., & McCubbin, M. A. (1996). *Family assessment: Resiliency, coping, and adaptation.* Madison, WI: University of Wisconsin Publishers.

McFadden, V. M., & Doub, G. (1983). The therapist's new role: Training families for healthy survival. In J. Hansen & H. Liddle (Eds.), *Clinical implications of the family life cycle* (pp. 134–160). Rockville, MD: Aspen.

McGill, D., & Pearce, J. (1996). British American families. In M. McGoldrick, J. Giordano, & J. Pearce (Eds.), *Ethnicity and family therapy* (2nd ed., pp. 451–466). New York: Guilford Press.

McGoldrick, M. (1995). *You can go home again: Reconnecting with your family.* New York: Norton.

McGoldrick, M., & Carter, B. (1989). Forming a remarried family. In B. Carter & M. McGoldrick (Eds.), *The changing family life cycle: A framework for family therapy* (2nd ed., pp. 399–429). Boston: Allyn & Bacon.

McGoldrick, M., & Gerson, R. (1985). *Genograms in family assessment.* New York: Norton.

McGoldrick, M., & Gerson, R. (1989). Genograms in the family life cycle. In B. Carter & M. McGoldrick (Eds.), *The changing family life cycle: A framework for family therapy* (2nd ed., pp. 164–189). Boston, Allyn & Bacon.

McGoldrick, M., & Giordano, J. (1996). Overview: Ethnicity and family therapy. In M. McGoldrick, J. Giordano, & J. Pearce (Eds.), *Ethnicity and family therapy* (2nd ed., pp. 1–27). New York: Guilford Press.

McGoldrick, M., Giordano, J., & Pearce, J. (Eds.). (1996). *Ethnicity and family therapy* (2nd ed.). New York: Guilford Press.

McGoldrick, M., Pearce, J. K., & Giordano, J. (Eds.). (1982). *Ethnicity and family therapy.* New York: Guilford Press.

McGrath, M., & Grant, G. (1993). The life cycle and support networks of families with a person with a learning difficulty. *Disability, Handicap & Society, 8*(1), 25–41.

McHale, S. M., Sloan, J., & Simeonsson, R. J. (1986). Sibling relationships of children with autistic, mentally retarded, and nonhandicapped brothers and sisters. *Journal of Autism and Developmental Disorders, 16,* 399–413.

McIntyre, T. (1996). Guidelines for providing appropriate services to culturally diverse students with emotional and/or behavioral disorders. *Behavioral Disorders, 21,* 137–144.

McLanahan, S., & Sandefur, G. (1994). *Growing up with a single parent: What hurts, what helps.* Cambridge, MA: Harvard University Press.

McLoughlin, J. A. (1981). Training together to work together. *Teacher Education and Special Education, 4*(4), 45–54.

McLuhan, M. (1967). *The medium is the message.* New York: Touchstone.

McMillan, D. L., & Turnbull, A. P. (1983). Parent involvement with special education. *Education and Training of the Mentally Retarded, 18,* 5–9.

McMillan, J., & Reed, D. (1993). At-risk students and resiliency: Factors contributing to academic success. *The Clearing House, 67*(3), 137–140.

McMillan, J., & Reed, D. (1994). *Defying the odds: A study of resilient at-risk students*. Richmond: Virginia Commonwealth University.

McNamee, S., & Gergen, K. J. (1992). *Therapy as social construction*. Newbury Park, CA: Sage.

McWilliam, P. J. (1996). Family-centered practices in early intervention. In P. J. McWilliam, P. J. Winton, & E. R. Crais (Eds.), *Practical strategies for family-centered early intervention* (pp. 1–13). San Diego, CA: Singular Publishing Group.

McWilliam, P. J., & Bailey, D. B., Jr. (1993). *Working together with children and families: Case studies in early intervention*. Baltimore, MD: Paul H. Brookes.

Meadow-Orlans, K. P. (1994). Stress, support, and deafness: Perceptions of infants' mothers and fathers. *Journal of Early Intervention, 18*(1), 91–102.

Meier, J. H., & Sloan, M. P. (1984). The severely handicapped and child abuse. In J. Blacher (Ed.), *Severely handicapped young children and their families* (pp. 247–274). New York: Academic Press.

Meyer, D. J., & Vadasy, P. F. (1994). *Sibshops: Workshops for siblings of children with special needs*. Baltimore, MD: Paul H. Brookes.

Miller, R. (1996). *The developmentally appropriate inclusive classroom in early education*. Albany, NY: Delmar.

Mills, J., & Crowley, R. (1986). *Therapeutic metaphors for children and the child within*. New York: Brunner/Mazel.

Mink, I. T., Meyers, C. E., & Nihira, K. (1984). Taxonomy of family life styles: II. Homes with slow-learning children. *American Journal of Mental Deficiency, 89,* 111–123.

Minshew, D. H., & Hooper, C. (1990). *The adoptive family as a healing resource for the sexually abused child: A training manual*. Washington, DC: Child Welfare League of America.

Minuchin, S. (1974). *Families and family therapy*. Cambridge, MA: Harvard University Press.

Minuchin, S. (1992). Constructing a therapeutic reality. In E. Kaufman & P. Kaufman (Eds.), *Family therapy of drug and alcohol abuse* (2nd ed., pp. 1–14). Boston: Allyn & Bacon.

Minuchin, S., & Fishman, H. (1981). *Family therapy techniques*. Cambridge, MA: Harvard University Press.

Minuchin, S., Montalvo, B., Guerney, B. G., Jr., Rosman, B. L., & Schumer, F. (1967). *Families of the slums: An exploration of their structure and treatment*. New York: Basic Books.

Minuchin, S., & Nichols, M. P. (1993). *Family healing: Tales of hope and renewal from family therapy*. New York: Free Press.

Minuchin, S., Rosman, B., & Baker, L. (1978). *Psychosomatic families: Anorexia nervosa in context*. Cambridge, MA: Harvard University Press.

Moles, O. C. (1993). Collaboration between schools and disadvantaged parents: Obstacles and openings. In N. F. Chavkin (Ed.), *Families and schools in a pluralistic society* (pp. 1–49). Albany: State University of New York Press.

Momeni, J. A. (Ed.). (1984). *Demography of racial and ethnic minorities in the United States*. Westport, CT: Greenwood Press.

Montalvo, B., & Guitierrez, M. (1983). A perspective for the use of the cultural dimension in family therapy. In J. C. Hansen & C. J. Falicov (Eds.), *Cultural perspectives in family therapy* (pp. 15–32). Rockville, MD: Aspen.

Montgomery, R., Gonyea, J., & Hooyman, N. (1985). Caregiving and the experience of subjective and objective burden. *Family Relations, 34,* 19–26.

Moody, E. E. (1991). *Personality characteristics of adolescent sexual offenders compared to conduct-disorder adolescents*. Unpublished master's thesis, Middle Tennessee State University, Murfreesboro.

Moody, E. E. (1994). Current trends and issues in childhood sexual abuse prevention programs. *Elementary School Guidance and Counseling, 28,* 251–256.

Moore, M., & Gergen, P. (1989). *Managing risk taking during organizational change*. King of Prussia, PA: Organizational Design and Development.

Moos, R. H. (1974). *Family environment scale: Preliminary manual*. Palo Alto: Consulting Psychologists Press.

Moran, M. (1978). *Assessment of the exceptional learner in the regular classroom*. Denver, CO: Love Publishing Company.

Morsink, C. V., Thomas, C. C., & Correa, V. I. (1991). *Interactive teaming: Consultation and collaboration in special programs*. New York: Macmillan.

Mullins, J. B. (1983). The uses of bibliotherapy in counseling families confronted with handicaps. In M. Seligman (Ed.), *The family with a handicapped child: Understanding and treatment* (pp. 235–260). New York: Grune & Stratton.

Mullis, F., & Fincher, S. F. (1996). Using rituals to define the school community. *Elementary School Guidance and Counseling, 30,* 243–251.

Nardone, G., & Watzlawick, P. (1993). *The art of change: Strategic therapy and hypnotherapy without trance.* San Francisco: Jossey-Bass.

Nastasi, B. K., & DeZolt, D. M. (1994). *School interventions for children of alcoholics.* New York: Guilford Press.

National Adoption Information Clearinghouse (1996). *Factsheet.* [www.calib.com/halc]

National Committee for the Prevention of Child Abuse, NCPCA. (1998). Twelve alternatives to lashing out at your child. [www.childabuse.org/alterntv.html]

Nazzaro, J. N. (Ed.). (1981). *Culturally diverse exceptional children in school.* Washington, DC: National Institute of Education.

Neff, P. (1996). *Tough love: How parents can deal with drug abuse* (rev. ed.). Nashville, TN: Abingdon Press.

National Institute on Alcohol Abuse and Alcoholism, NIAAA. (1994). *Alcohol Health and Research World, 18,* 243–245. See Internet web site for NCADD (National Council on Alcoholism and Drug Dependency) Alcoholism and Alcohol-Related Problems: A Sobering Look.

Nichols, M. P., & Schwartz, R. C. (1995). *Family therapy: Concepts and methods* (3rd ed.). Boston: Allyn & Bacon.

Nichols, W. C. (1996). *Treating people in families: An integrative framework.* New York: Guilford Press.

Niels, J. B. (1980). *A study of birth order and family constellation among high school and delinquent students.* Ann Arbor, MI: Xerox University Microfilms.

Nihira, K., Meyers, C. E., & Mink, I. T. (1983). Reciprocal relationship between home environment and development of TMR adolescents. *American Journal of Mental Deficiency, 88,* 139–149.

Nihira, K., Mink, I. T., & Meyers, C. E. (1981). Relationship between home environment and school adjustment of TMR children. *American Journal of Mental Deficiency, 86,* 8–15.

Nihira, K., Mink, I. T., & Meyers, C. E. (1985). Home environment and development of slow-learning adolescents: Reciprocal relations. *Developmental Psychology, 21,* 784–794.

Noddings, N. (1984). *Caring: A feminine approach to ethics and moral education.* Berkeley: University of California Press.

Noddings, N. (1995). Teaching themes of care. *Phi Delta Kappan, 76*(9), 675–679.

Notari-Syverson, A. R., & Shuster, S. L. (1995). Putting real-life skills into IEP/IFSPs for infants and young children. *Teaching Exceptional Children, 27*(2), 29–32.

Oates, R. K. (1991). Child physical abuse. In R. T. Ammerman & M. Hersen (Eds.), *Case studies in family violence* (pp. 113–134). New York: Plenum Press.

Olson, D. H. (1988). Family types, family stress, and family satisfaction: A family developmental perspective. In C. J. Falicov (Ed.), *Family transitions: Continuity and change over the life cycle* (pp. 55–79). New York: Guilford Press.

Olson, D., McCubbin, H., Barnes, H., Larsen, A., Muxen, M., & Wilson, M. (1983). *Families: What makes them work.* Beverly Hills, CA: Sage.

Olson, D. H., McCubbin, H. I., Barnes, H., Larsen, A., Muxen, M., & Wilson, M. (1984). *One thousand families: A national survey.* Beverly Hills, CA: Sage.

Orelove, F. P. (1995). The transdisciplinary model in educational programs for students with severe disabilities. In H. G. Garner (Ed.), *Teamwork models and experience in education* (pp. 31–42). Boston: Allyn & Bacon.

Orelove, F. P., & Malatchi, A. (1996). Curriculum and instruction. In F. P. Orelove & D. Sobsey, *Educating children with multiple disabilities: A transdisciplinary approach* (3rd ed., pp. 377–409). Baltimore, MD: Paul H. Brookes.

Orelove, F., & Sobsey, D. (1991). *Educating children with multiple disabilities: A transdisciplinary approach* (2nd ed.). Baltimore, MD: Paul H. Brookes.

Orelove, F. P., & Sobsey, D. (Eds.). (1996). *Educating children with multiple disabilities: A transdisciplinary approach* (3rd ed.). Baltimore, MD: Paul H. Brookes.

Orr, L., Craig, G., Best, J., Borland, A., Holland, D., Knodel, H., Lehman, A., Matthewson, C., Miller, M., & Pequignot, M. (1997). Exploring developmental disabilities through literature: An annotated bibliography. *Teaching Exceptional Children, 29*(6), 14–15.

O'Toole, T. J., & Switlick, D. M. (1997). Integrated therapies. In D. F. Bradley, M. E. King-Sears, & D. M. Tessier-Switlick (Eds.), *Teaching students in inclusive settings: From theory to practice* (pp. 202–224). Boston: Allyn & Bacon.

Otto, M. L., & Smith, D. G. (1980). Child abuse: A cognitive behavioral intervention model. *Journal of Marital and Family Therapy, 6,* 425–430.

Palazzoli, S. M., Boscolo, L., Cecchin, G. F., & Prata, G. (1980). The problem of the referring person. *Journal of Marital and Family Therapy, 6,* 3–9.

Parker, R. J. (1994). Helping children cope with divorce: A workshop for parents. *Elementary School Guidance and Counseling, 29,* 137–148.

Patterson, J. M. (1985). Critical factors affecting family compliance with home treatment for children with cystic fibrosis. *Family Relations, 34,* 79–89.

Patterson, J. M. (1988). Families experiencing stress. *Family Systems Medicine, 6,* 202–237.

Patterson, J. M. (1997). Promoting resilience in families. *Resiliency in Action, 2(2),* 8–16.

Patterson, J. M., & Garwick, A. W. (1994). Levels of meaning in family stress theory. *Family Process, 33,* 287–303.

Patterson, J. M., & McCubbin, H. I. (1983). Chronic illness: Family stress and coping. In C. R. Figley & H. I. McCubbin (Eds.), *Stress and the family: Vol. 2. Coping with catastrophe* (pp. 21–36). New York: Brunner/Mazel.

Patton, J. R. (1994). Practical recommendations for using homework with students with learning disabilities. *Journal of Learning Disabilities, 27,* 570–578.

Pearpoint, J., O'Brien, J., & Forest, M. (1995). *Planning alternative tomorrows with hope* (2nd ed.). Toronto, Ontario, Canada: Inclusion Press.

Peck, J. S., & Manocherian, J. (1989). Divorce in the changing family life cycle. In B. Carter & M. McGoldrick (Eds.), *The changing family life cycle: A framework for family therapy* (2nd ed., pp. 335–369). Boston: Allyn & Bacon.

Peck, M. S. (1978). *The road less traveled.* New York: Simon & Schuster.

Pedersen, F. A. (1983). Differentiation of the father's role in the infancy period. In J. Vincent (Ed.), *Advances in family intervention, assessment, and theory* (Vol. 3, pp. 185–208). New York: JAI Press.

Pedro-Carroll, J. L., & Cowen, E. L. (1987). The children of divorce intervention program: An investigation of the efficacy of a school-based prevention program. *Journal of Consulting and Clinical Psychology, 53,* 603–611.

Peeks, B. (1997). Revolutions in counseling and education: A systems perspective in the schools. In W. M. Walsh & G. R. Williams (Eds.), *Schools and family therapy: Using systems theory and family therapy in the resolution of school problems* (pp. 5–12). Springfield, IL: Charles C. Thomas.

Peeks, B. (1993). Revolutions in counseling and education: A systems perspective in the schools. *Elementary School Guidance and Counseling, 27,* 245–251.

Peled, E., Jaffe, P. G., & Edleson, J. (Eds.). (1995). *Ending the cycle of violence: Community responses to children of battered women.* Thousand Oaks, CA: Sage.

Pell, E. C., & Cohen, E. P. (1995). Parents and advocacy systems: A family systems approach. In M. C. Wang, M. C. Reynolds, & H. J. Walberg (Eds.), *Handbook of special and remedial education: Research and Practice* (2nd ed., pp. 371–392). New York: Elsevier Science.

Peng, S. S., Wang, M. C., & Walberg, H. J. (1992, April). *Resilient students in urban settings.* Paper presented at the annual meeting of the American Educational Research Association, San Francisco, CA.

Perosa, L. M., & Perosa, S. L. (1981). The school counselor's use of structural family therapy with learning disabled students. *The School Counselor, 29,* 152–155.

Peschley, D. J. (1988). Minority MMR overrepresentation and special education reform. *Exceptional Children, 54,* 316–323.

Peterson, E. T., & Kunz, P. R. (1975). Parental control over adolescents according to family size. *Adolescence, 10,* 419–427.

Pfeiffer, S. (1980). The school-based interprofessional team: Recurring problems and some possible solutions. *Journal of School Psychology, 18,* 388–394.

Pfeiffer, S. I., & Tittler, B. I. (1983). Utilizing the multidisciplinary team to facilitate a school family systems orientation. *School Psychology Review, 12,* 169–173.

Phillips, V., & McCullough, L. (1990). Consultation-based programming: Instituting the collaborative ethic in schools. *Exceptional Children, 56,* 291–304.

Phillips-Hershey, E. H., & Ridley, L. L. (1996). Strategies for acceptance of diversity of students with mental retardation. *Elementary School Guidance & Counseling, 30,* 282–291.

Piaget, J. (1952). *The origins of intelligence in children.* New York: International Universities Press.

Piaget, J., & Inhelder, B. (1958). *The growth of logical thinking from childhood to adolescence* (A. Parsons & S. Milgram, Trans.). New York: Basic Books.

Piaget, J., & Inhelder, B. (1969). *The psychology of the child.* New York: Basic Books.

Piercy, F. P., & Wetchler, J. L. (1996). Structural, strategic, and systemic family therapies. In F. P. Piercy, D. H. Sprenkle, J. L. Wetchler, & Associates (Eds.), *Family therapy sourcebook* (2nd ed., pp. 50–78). New York: Guilford Press.

Pinkney, A. (1975). *Black Americans.* Englewood Cliffs, NJ: Prentice-Hall.

Plummer, C. A. (1993). Prevention is appropriate, prevention is successful. In R. J. Gelles & D. R. Loseke (Eds.), *Current controversies on family violence* (pp. 288–305). Newbury Park, CA: Sage.

Pollner, M., & Wikler, L. (1985). The social construction of unreality. *Family Process, 24,* 241–259.

Popenoe, D. (1994). The evolution of marriage and the problem of stepfamilies: A biosocial perspective. In A. Booth & J. Dunn (Eds.), *Stepfamilies: Who benefits? Who does not?* (pp. 3–27). Hillsdale, NJ: Erlbaum.

Powell, T. H., & Gallagher, P. A. (1993). *Brothers and sisters: A special part of exceptional families* (2nd ed.). Baltimore, MD: Paul H. Brookes.

Power-deFur, L. A., & Orelove, F. P. (Eds.). (1997). *Inclusive education: Practical implementation of the least restrictive environment.* Gaithersburg, MD: Aspen.

Poyadue, F. S. (1993). Cognitive coping at parents helping parents. In A. P. Turnbull, J. M. Patterson, S. K. Behr, D. L. Murphy, J. G. Marquis, & M. J. Blue-Banning (Eds.), *Cognitive coping, families, and disability* (pp. 95–109). Baltimore, MD: Paul H. Brookes.

Price, M., & Goodman, L. (1980). Individualized Education Programs: A cost study. *Exceptional Children, 46,* 446–458.

Prosen, H., Toews, J., & Martin, R. (1981). The life cycle of the family: I. Parental midlife crisis and adolescent rebellion. *Adolescent Psychiatry, 9,* 170–179.

Pugach, M. C., & Seidl, B. L. (1995). From exclusion to inclusion in urban schools: A new case for teacher education reform. *Education and Urban Society, 27,* 379–395.

Pugach, M. C., & Wesson, C. L. (1995). Teachers' and students' views of team teaching general education and learning-disabled students in two fifth-grade classes. *Elementary School Journal, 95*(3), 279–295.

Putnam, J. W., Spiegel, A. N., & Bruininks, R. H. (1995). Future directions in education and inclusion of students with disabilities: A Delphi investigation. *Exceptional Children, 61,* 553–576.

Quinn, W. H., Newfield, N. A., & Protinsky, H. O. (1985). Rites of passage in families with adolescents. *Family Process, 24,* 101–111.

Rainforth, B., York, J., & Macdonald, C. (1992). *Collaborative teams for students with severe disabilities: Integrating therapy and educational services.* Baltimore, MD: Paul H. Brookes.

Rak, C. F., & Patterson, L. W. (1996). Promoting resilience in at-risk children. *Journal of Counseling & Development, 74*(4), 368–373.

Ralph, J. (1989). Improving education for the disadvantaged: Do we know whom to help? *Phi Delta Kappan, 70,* 385–401.

Ramey, S. L., & Ramey, C. T. (1992). Early educational intervention with disadvantaged children to what effect? *Applied and Preventive Psychology, 1*(3), 131–140.

Rasku-Puttonen, H., Lyytinen, P., Poikkeus, A., Laakso, J., & Ahonen, T. (1994). Communication deviances and clarity among the mothers of normally achieving and learning-disabled boys. *Family Process, 33,* 71–80.

Raynor, L. (1980). *The adopted child comes of age.* London: Allen & Unwin.

Reece, B. L., & Brandt, R. (1987). *Effective human relations in organizations* (3rd ed.). Boston: Houghton Mifflin.

Reed, D. F. (1993). Culturally diverse students. In J. Wood (Ed.), *Mainstreaming: A practical approach for teachers* (pp. 122–154). Columbus, OH: Merrill.

Register, C. (1991). *"Are those kids yours?": American families with children adopted from other countries.* New York: Free Press.

Reimers, S., & Street, E. (1993). Using family therapy in child and adolescent services. In J. Carpenter & A. Treacher (Eds.), *Using family therapy in the 90s* (pp. 32–56). Cambridge, MA: Blackwell.

Reinsmith, W. A. (1989). The whole in every part: Steiner and Waldorf schooling. *Educational Forum, 54,* 79–91.

Reiss, D., & Oliveri, M. E. (1980). Family paradigm and family coping: A proposal for linking the family's intrinsic adaptive capacities to its responses to stress. *Family Relations, 29,* 431–444.

Reiss, D., Steinglass, P., & Howe, G. (1993). The family's organization around the illness. In R. Cole & D. Reiss (Eds.), *How do families cope with chronic illness?* (pp. 173–213). Hillsdale, NJ: Lawrence Ferlbaum Associates.

Reitz, M., & Watson, K. W. (1992). *Adoption and the family system: Strategies for treatment.* New York: Guilford Press.

Reppucci, N. D., & Haugaard, J. J. (1993). Problems with child sexual abuse prevention programs. In R. J. Gelles & D. R. Loseke (Eds.), *Current controversies on family violence* (pp. 306–322). Newbury Park, CA: Sage.

Rhodes, W. A., & Brown, W. K. (1991). *Why some children succeed despite the odds.* New York: Praeger.

Rich, C. L., Warsradt, G. M., Nemiroff, R. A., Fowler, R. C., & Young, D. (1991). Suicide, stressors, and the life cycle. *American Journal of Psychiatry, 148,* 524–527.

Rich, S. (1986, November 12). Parental fighting hurts even after divorce. *The Washington Post,* p. H–12.

Richards, L. N., & Schmiege, C. J. (1993). Problems and strengths of single-parent families: Implications for practice and policy. *Family Relations, 42,* 277–285.

Richardson, G. E., & Hawks, S. R. (1995). A practical approach for enhancing resilience within families. *Family Perspective, 29,* 235–250.

Roberto, L. G. (1992). *Transgenerational family therapies.* New York: Guilford Press.

Roit, M., & Pfohl, W. (1984). The readability of P.L. 94-142 parent materials: Are parents truly informed? *Exceptional Children, 50,* 496–505.

Rollins, B. C., & Galligan, R. (1978). The developing child and marital satisfaction of parents. In R. Lerner & G. Spanier (Eds.), *Child influences on marital and family interaction: A life-span perspective* (pp. 71–106). New York: Academic Press.

Rosenberg, E. B. (1992). *The adoption life cycle: The children and their families through the years.* New York: Free Press.

Rosenberg, M. S., & Gilberson, R. S. (1991). The child witness of family violence. In R. T. Ammerman & M. Hersen (Eds.), *Case studies in family violence* (pp. 231–253). New York: Plenum Press.

Rosenthal, R., & Jacobson, L. (1968). *Pygmalion in the classroom.* New York: Holt, Rinehart & Winston.

Rosenthal, R., & Rubin, D. B. (1978). Interpersonal expectancy effects: The first 345 studies. *The Behavioral and Brain Sciences, 3,* 377–415.

Rossi, A. S., & Rossi, P. H. (1990). *Of human bonding: Parent-child relations across the life course.* Hawthorne, NY: Aldine.

Rossiter, A. B. (1988). A model for group intervention with preschool children experiencing separation and divorce. *American Journal of Orthopsychiatry, 58,* 387–396.

Roy, S. A. (1995). The process of reorganization. In H. G. Garner (Ed.), *Teamwork models and experience in education* (pp. 85–101). Boston: Allyn & Bacon.

Rubin, K. H. (1985). Socially withdrawn children: An "at risk" population? In B. H. Schneider, K. H. Rubin, & J. E. Kedingham (Eds.), *Children's peer relations: Issues in assessment and intervention* (pp. 125–140). New York: Springer-Verlag.

Rueveni, U. (1979). *Networking families in crisis: Intervention strategies with families and social networks.* New York: Human Sciences Press.

Rutter, M. (1994). Stress research: accomplishments and tasks ahead. In R. J. Haggerty, L. R. Sherrod, N. Garmezy, & M. Rutter (Eds.), *Stress, risk, and resilience in children and adolescents: Processes, mechanisms, and interventions,* (pp. 354–385). Cambridge, UK: Cambridge University Press.

Sadowski, P. M., & Loesch, L. C. (1993). Using children's drawings to detect potential child sexual abuse. *Elementary School Guidance and Counseling, 28,* 115–123.

Safer, D. J. (1966). Family therapy for children with behavior disorders. *Family Process, 5,* 243–255.

Sagor, R. (1996). Building resiliency in students. *Educational Leadership, 54*(1), 38–43.

Saitoh, S., Steinglass, P., & Schuckit, M. A. (Eds.). (1992). *Alcoholism and the family.* New York: Brunner/Mazel.

Samuels, S. C. (1990). *Ideal adoption: A comprehensive guide to forming an adoptive family.* New York: Plenum Press.

Sarason, S. (1982). *The culture of the school and the problem of change* (2nd ed.). Boston: Allyn & Bacon.

Sarason, S. B. (1996a). *Barometers of change: Individual, educational, and social transformation.* San Francisco: Jossey-Bass.

Sarason, S. B. (1996b). *Revisiting "The culture of the school and the problem of change."* New York: Teachers College Press.

Satir, V. (1972). *Peoplemaking.* Palo Alto, CA: Science and Behavior Books.

Satir, V. (1978). *Our many faces.* Millbrae, CA: Celestial Arts.

Satir, V. (1983a). *AVANTA Process Community III. The Third International Summer Institute.* Crested Butte, CO: AVANTA Process Community.

Satir, V. (1983b). *Conjoint family therapy* (3rd ed.). Palo Alto, CA: Science and Behavior Books.

Satir, V. (1988). *The new peoplemaking.* Mountain View, CA: Science and Behavior Books.

Satir, V., & Baldwin, M. (1983). *Satir, step by step.* Palo Alto, CA: Science and Behavior Books.

Satir, V., Bitter, J. R., & Krestensen, K. K. (1988). Family reconstruction: The family within—a group experience. *The Journal for Specialists in Group Work, 13,* 200–208.

Satir, V., Stachowiak, J., & Taschman, H. (1975). *Helping families to change.* New York: Jason Aronson.

Saunders, D. (1987). Cultural conflicts: An important factor in the academic failure of American Indian students. *Journal of Multicultural Counseling & Development, 15,* 81–90.

Schaefer, C. E., Briesmeister, J. M., & Fitton, M. E. (Eds.). (1984). *Family therapy techniques for problem behaviors of children and teenagers.* San Francisco: Jossey-Bass.

Schaefer, C. E., & DiGeronimo, T. F. (1994). *How to talk to your kids about really important things: For children four to twelve.* San Francisco: Jossey-Bass.

Schell, G. (1981). The young handicapped child: A family perspective. *Topics in Early Childhood Special Education, 1*(3), 21–27.

Schibuk, M. (1989). Treating the sibling subsystem: An adjunct of divorce therapy. *American Journal of Orthopsychiatry, 59,* 226–237.

Schlesinger, S. E., & Horberg, L. K. (1988). *Taking charge: How families can climb out of the chaos of addiction and flourish.* New York: Simon & Schuster.

Schniedewind, N., & Davidson, E. (1998). *Open minds to equality: A sourcebook of learning activities to affirm diversity and promote equity.* Boston: Allyn & Bacon.

Schulman, G. L. (1984). Transitions in family structure. In C. E. Schaefer, J. M. Briesmeister, & M. E. Fitton (Eds.), *Family therapy techniques for problem behaviors of children and teenagers* (pp. 337–340). San Francisco: Jossey-Bass.

Schvaneveldt, J. D., & Ihinger, M. (1979). Sibling relationships in the family. In W. R. Burr, R. Hill, F. J. Nye, & I. L. Reiss (Eds.), *Contemporary theories about the family* (Vol. 1, pp. 96–97). New York: Free Press.

Schwab, J. (1990). *A resource handbook for Satir concepts.* Palo Alto, CA: Science and Behavior Books.

Schwartz, L. L., & Kaslow, F. W. (1997). *Painful partings: Divorce and its aftermath.* New York: Wiley.

Seligman, M. (1991a). Family systems and beyond: Conceptual issues. In M. Seligman (Ed.), *The family with a handicapped child* (2nd ed., pp. 27–53). Boston: Allyn and Bacon.

Seligman, M. (1991c). Siblings of disabled brothers and sisters. In M. Seligman (Ed.), *The family with a handicapped child* (2nd ed., pp. 181–201). Boston: Allyn & Bacon.

Senge, P. M. (1990). *The fifth discipline: The art and practice of the learning organization.* New York: Doubleday.

Serafica, F. C. (1990). Counseling Asian-American parents: A cultural-developmental approach. In F. C. Serafica, A. I. Schwebel, R. K. Russell, P. D. Isaac, & L. B. Myers (Eds.), *Mental health of ethnic minorities* (pp. 222–244). New York: Praeger.

Sergiovanni, T. J. (1995). Small schools, great expectation. *Educational Leadership, 53*(3), 48–52.

Sevcik, B., & Ysseldyke, J. (1986). An analysis of teachers' prereferral interventions for students exhibiting behavioral problems. *Behavioral Disorders, 11,* 109–117.

Sexson, S. B., & Madan-Swain, A. (1993). School reentry for the child with chronic illness. *Journal of Learning Disabilities, 26,* 115–125.

Sexton, D., Lobman, M., Constans, T., Snyder, P., & Ernest, J. (1997). Early interventionists' perspectives of multicultural practices with African-American families. *Exceptional Children, 63,* 313–328.

Shapiro, J. (1983). Family reactions and coping strategies in response to the physically ill or handicapped child: A review. *Social Science Medicine, 17,* 913–931.

Sheehy, G. (1976). *Passages: Predictable crises of adult life.* New York: Dutton.

Sheehy, G. (1995). *New passages: Mapping your life across time.* New York: Random House.

Shepard, H. A. (1995). On the realization of human potential: A path with a heart. In D. Kolb, J. Osland, & I. Rubin (Eds.), *The organizational behavior reader,* (6th ed., pp. 168–178).Englewood Cliffs, NJ: Prentice Hall.

Showers, B., Joyce, B., & Bennett, B. (1987). Synthesis of research on self-development: A framework for future study and a state-of-the-art analysis. *Educational Leadership, 45*(3), 77–87.

Shulman, B., & Mosak, H. H. (1977). Birth order and ordinal position: Two Adlerian views. *Journal of Individual Psychology, 33,* 114–121.

Silver, L. B. (1984). *The misunderstood child. A guide for parents of learning disabled children.* New York: McGraw-Hill.

Simon, R. J., & Altstein, H. (1992). *Adoption, race, and identity.* New York: Praeger.

Simpson, R. (1990). *Conferencing parents of exceptional children* (2nd ed.). Austin, TX: PRO-ED.

Simpson, R. (1996). *Working with parents and families of exceptional children and youth: Techniques for successful conferencing and collaboration* (3rd ed.). Austin, TX: PRO-ED.

Singer, G. H. S., & Nixon, C. (1996). A report on the concerns of parents of children with acquired brain injury. In G. H. S. Singer, A. Glang, & J. M. Williams (Eds.), *Children with acquired brain injury: Educating and supporting families* (pp. 23–52). Baltimore, MD: Paul H. Brookes.

Skrtic, T. (1991). *Behind special education: A critical analysis of professional culture and school organization.* Denver, CO: Love Publishing Company.

Slavin, R., & Madden, N. (1989). What works for student at risk: A research synthesis. *Educational Leadership, 46*(5), 4–13.

Slavin, R. E., Madden, N. A., Dolan, L. J., & Wasik, B. A. (1996). *Every child, every school: Success for all.* Thousand Oaks, CA: Corwin Press.

Sloman, L., & Konstantareas, M. M. (1990). Why families of children with biological deficits require a systems approach. *Family Process,* 417–432.

Sluckin, A., & Smith, P. (1977). Two approaches to the concept of dominance in preschool children. *Child Development, 48,* 911–923.

Smith, A. H. (1978). Encountering the family system in school-related behavior problems. *Psychology in the Schools, 15,* 379–386.

Smith, R. (Ed.). (1993). *Children with mental retardation: A parent's guide.* Rockville, MD: Woodbine House.

Smith, S. L. (1981). *No easy answers: The learning disabled child at home and at school.* New York: Bantam Books.

Smith, S. W. (1990). Individualized Education Programs (IEPs) in special education: From intent to acquiescence. *Exceptional Children, 57,* 6–14.

Snow, R. L. (1997). *Family abuse: Tough solutions to stop the violence.* New York: Plenum Press.

Sobsey, D. (1994). *Violence and abuse in the lives of people with disabilities: The end of silent acceptance?* Baltimore, MD: Paul H. Brookes.

Sobsey, D., Wells, D., Lucardie, R., & Mansell, S. (1995). *Violence and disability: An annotated bibliography.* Baltimore, MD: Paul H. Brookes.

Solomon, Z. P. (1991). California's policy on parent involvement: State leadership for local initiatives. *Phi Delta Kappan, 72,* 359–362.

Somers, M. N. (1987). Parenting in the 1980s: Programming perspectives and issues. *Volta Review, 89,* 68–77.

Sonnenblick, M. D. (1997). The GALSS club: Promoting belonging among at-risk adolescent girls. *The School Counselor, 44,* 243–245.

Sontag, J. C., & Schacht, R. (1994). An ethnic comparison of parent participation and information needs in early intervention. *Exceptional Children, 60,* 422–433.

Soriano, F. I. (1994). U.S. Latinos. In L. D. Eron, J. H. Gentry, & P. Schlegel (Eds.), *Reason to hope: A psychosocial perspective on violence and youth* (pp. 119–132). Washington, DC: American Psychological Association.

Spark, G. M., & Brody, E. M. (1970). The aged are family members. *Family Process, 9,* 195–210.

Sprinthall, N. A., Hall, J. S., & Gerler, E. R. (1992). Peer counseling for middle school students experiencing family divorce: A deliberate psychological education model. *Elementary School Guidance and Counseling, 26,* 279–294.

Stainback, S., Stainback, W., East, K., & Sapon-Shevin, M. (1994). A commentary on inclusion and the development of a positive self-identity by people with disabilities. *Exceptional Children, 60*(6), 486–490.

Stanton, M. D., Todd, T. C. (1982). *The family therapy of drug abuse and addiction.* New York: Guilford Press.

Staples, R. (1994). *Black family: Essays and studies* (5th ed.). New York: Van Nostrand Reinhold.

Stinson, K. M. (1991). *Adolescents, family, and friends: Social support after parents' divorce or remarriage.* New York: Praeger.

Strickland, B., & Turnbull, A. (1990). *Developing and implementing Individualized Education Programs* (3rd ed.). Columbus, OH: Merrill.

Strom, R., Rees, R., Slaughter, H., & Wurster, S. (1981). Child rearing expectations of families with atypical children. *American Journal of Orthopsychiatry, 51,* 285–296.

Stutman, S. S. (1984). *Family life cycle development: Examination of the pathway linking differentiation from the family of origin, marital adjustment, child-focused triangulation, and adolescent adjustment.* Los Angeles: California School of Professional Psychology.

Suelzle, M., & Keenan, V. (1981). Changes in family support networks over the life cycle of mentally retarded persons. *American Journal of Mental Deficiency, 86,* 267–274.

Sugai, G., & Lewis, T. J. (1996). Preferred and promising practices for social skills instruction. *Focus on Exceptional Children, 29*(4), 1–16.

Sussell, A., Carr, S., & Hartman, A. (1996). Families R Us: Building a parent/school partnership. *Teaching Exceptional Children, 28*(4), 53–57.

Sutton, C. T., & Broken Nose, M. A. (1996). American Indian families: An overview. In M. McGoldrick, J. Giordano, & J. Pearce (Eds.), *Ethnicity and family therapy* (2nd ed., pp. 31–44). New York: Guilford Press.

Suzuki, L. A., & Kugler, J. F. (1995). Intelligence and personality assessment. In J. G. Ponterotto, J. M. Casas, L. A. Suzuki, & C. M. Alexander (Eds.), *Handbook of multicultural counseling* (pp. 493–515). Thousand Oaks, CA: Sage.

Swann, W. B., Jr., & Brown, J. D. (1990). From self to health: Self verification and identity disruption. In B. R. Sarason, I. G. Sarason, & G. R. Pierce (Eds.), *Social support: An interactional view* (pp. 150–172). New York: Wiley.

Switlick, D. M. (1997a). Curriculum modifications and adaptations. In D. F. Bradley, M. E. King-Sears, & D. M. Tessier-Switlick (Eds.), *Teaching students in inclusive settings: From theory to practice* (pp. 225–251). Boston: Allyn & Bacon.

Switlick, D. M. (1997b). Integrating specialized curricula. In D. F., Bradley, M. E. King-Sears, & D. M. Terrier-Switlick (Eds.), *Teaching students in inclusive setting: From theory to practice* (pp. 252–282). Boston: Allyn & Bacon.

Switlick, D. M., & Bradley, D. F. (1997). Collaborative team building. In D. F. Bradley, M. E. King-Sears, & D. M. Tessier-Switlick (Eds.), *Teaching students in inclusive settings: From theory to practice* (pp. 83–108). Boston: Allyn & Bacon.

Szapocznik, J., & Kurtines, W. M. (1989). *Breakthroughs in family therapy with drug abusing and problem youth.* New York: Springer.

Tashima, N. (1981). Asian Americans in psychiatric systems. In D. Claerbaut (Ed.), *New directions in ethnic studies: Minorities in America* (pp. 95–106). Saratoga, CA: Century Twenty One.

Tavormina, J. B., Boll, T. J., Dunn, N. J., Luscomb, R. L., & Taylor, J. R. (1981). Psychosocial effects on parents of raising a physically handicapped child. *Journal of Abnormal Child Psychology, 9,* 121–131.

Taylor, B. R. (1994). Inclusion: Time for a change—a response to Margaret N. Carr. *Journal of Learning Disabilities, 27,* 579–580.

Tew, B. J., Lawrence, K. M., Payne, H., & Rawnsley, K. (1977). Marital stability following the birth of a child with spina bifida. *British Journal of Psychiatry, 131,* 79–82.

Teyber, E. (1994). *Helping children cope with divorce.* New York: Lexington Books.

Thaxton, L. (1985). Wife abuse. In L. L'Abate (Ed.), *The handbook of family psychology and therapy* (Vol. 2, pp. 876–899). Homewood, IL: Dorsey Press.

Thompson, S. C. (1993). Individual and interpersonal influences on the use of cognitive coping. In A. P. Turnbull, J. M. Patterson, S. K. Behr, D. L. Murphy, J. G. Marquis, & M. J. Blue-Banning (Eds.), *Cognitive coping, families, and disability* (pp.165–172). Baltimore, MD: Paul H. Brookes.

Thorin, E. J., & Irvin, L. K. (1992). Family stress associated with transition to adulthood of young people with severe disabilities. *Journal for Association of Severe Handicaps, 17,* 31–39.

Thousand, J. S., Villa, R. A., & Nevin, A. I. (1994). *Creativity and collaborative learning: A practical guide to empowering students and teachers.* Baltimore, MD: Paul H. Brookes.

Tindal, G., Shinn, M., & Rodden-Nord, K. (1990). Contextually based school consultation: Influential variables. *Exceptional Children, 56,* 324–336.

Tittler, B., Friedman, S., Blotcky, A., & Stedrak, J. (1982). The influence of family variables on an ecologically-based treatment program for emotionally disturbed children. *American Journal of Orthopsychiatry, 52,* 123–130.

Todd, T. C., & Selekman, M. D. (Eds.). (1990). *Family therapy approaches with adolescent substance abusers.* Boston: Allyn & Bacon.

Toman, W. (1969). *Family constellation: Its effect on personality and social behavior.* (2nd ed.). New York: Springer.

Toman, W. (1976). *Family constellation: Its effect on personality and social behavior.* (3rd ed.). New York: Springer.

Toman, W. (1993). *Family constellation: Its effect on personality and social behavior* (4th ed.). New York: Springer.

Topper, M. D. (1992). Multidimensional therapy: A case study of a Navajo adolescent with multiple problems. In L. A. Vargas & J. D. Koss-Chioino (Eds.), *Working with culture: Psychotherapeutic interventions with ethnic minority children and adolescents* (pp. 225–245). San Francisco: Jossey-Bass.

Trachtman, R. (1991). Early childhood education and child care: Issues of at-risk children and families. *Urban Education, 26*(1), 25–42.

Trailor, C. B. (1982). Role clarification and participation in child study teams. *Exceptional Children, 48,* 529–530.

Treadway, D. (1987, July/August). The ties that bind: Both alcoholics and their families are bound to the bottle. *Family Networker,* pp. 17–23.

Trimble, J. E. (1992). A cognitive-behavioral approach to drug abuse prevention and intervention with American Indian youth. In L. A. Vargas & J. D. Koss-Chioino (Eds.), *Working with culture: Psychotherapeutic interventions with ethnic minority children and adolescents* (pp. 246–275). San Francisco: Jossey-Bass.

Trout, M. D. (1983). Birth of a sick or handicapped infant: Impact on the family. *Child Welfare, 62,* 337–347.

Trute, B., Adkins, E., MacDonald, G., McCannel, K., & Herbert, C. (1994). *Coordinating child sexual abuse services in rural communities.* Buffalo, NY: University of Toronto Press.

Tseng, W., & McDermott, J. (1979). Triaxial family classification. *Journal of the American Academy of Child Psychiatry, 18,* 22–43.

Tuckman, B. W. (1965). Developmental sequences in small groups. *Psychological Bulletin, 63,* 384–399.

Turnbull, A. P., Patterson, J. M., Behr, S. K., Murphy, D. L., Marquis, J. G., & Blue-Banning, M. J. (Eds.). (1993). *Cognitive coping, families, and disability.* Baltimore, MD: Paul H. Brookes.

Turnbull, A. P., & Turnbull, H. R. (1982). Parent involvement in the education of handicapped children: A critique. *Mental Retardation, 20,* 115–122.

Turnbull, A. P., & Turnbull, H. R. (1986). *Families, professionals, and exceptionality: A special partnership.* Columbus, OH: Merrill.

Turnbull, A. P., & Turnbull, H. R. (1990). *Families, professionals, and exceptionality: A special partnership* (2nd ed.). Columbus, OH: Merrill.

Turnbull, A. P., & Turnbull, H. R. (1996). *Families, professionals, and exceptionality: A special partnership* (3rd ed.). Upper Saddle River, NJ: Prentice-Hall.

Turner, A. L. (1980). Therapy with families of a mentally retarded child. *Journal of Marital and Family Therapy,* 167–170.

Turner, R. (1981). Social support as a contingency in psychological well-being. *Journal of Health and Social Behavior, 22,* 357–367.

U.S. Bureau of the Census (1993, September). *We, the first Americans.* Washington DC: U.S. Department of Commerce, Economics and Statistics Administration.

Upshur, C. C. (1991). Families and the community service maze. In M. Seligman (Ed.), *The family with a handicapped child* (2nd ed., pp. 91–118). Boston: Allyn & Bacon.

Vadasy, P. F., Fewell, R. R., Meyer, D. J., & Schell, G. (1984). Siblings of handicapped children: A developmental perspective on family interactions. *Family Relations, 33,* 155–167.

Vaillant, G. E. (1995). *The natural history of alcoholism revisited.* Cambridge, MA: Harvard University Press.

Vail-Smith, K., Knight, S. M., & White, D. M. (1995). Children of substance abusers in the elementary school: A survey of counselor perceptions. *Elementary School Guidance and Counseling, 29,* 163–176.

Vetere, A. (1994). Using family therapy in services for people with learning disabilities. In J. Carpenter & A. Treacher (Eds.), *Using family therapy in the 90s* (pp. 111–130). Cambridge, MA: Blackwell.

Villa, R. A., Thousand, J. S., Stainback, W., & Stainback, S. (Eds.). (1992). *Restructuring for caring and effective education: An administrative guide to creating heterogeneous schools.* Baltimore, MD: Paul H. Brookes.

Visher, E. B., & Visher, J. S. (1979). *Stepfamilies: A guide to working with stepparents and stepchildren.* New York: Brunner/Mazel.

Visher, E. B., & Visher, J. S. (1990). Dynamics of successful stepfamilies. *Journal of Divorce and Remarriage, 14,* 3–12.

Visher, E. B., & Visher, J. S. (1991). *How to win as a stepfamily* (2nd ed.). New York: Brunner/Mazel.

Visher, E. B., & Visher, J. S. (1996). *Therapy with stepfamilies.* New York: Brunner/Mazel.

Vondra, J. I. (1990). Sociological and ecological factors. In R. T. Ammerman & M. Hersen (Eds.), *Children at risk: An evaluation of factors contributing to child abuse and neglect* (pp. 149–170). New York: Plenum Press.

Waddock, S. A. (1993). The spider's web: Influences on school performance. *Business Horizons, 36*(5), 39–48.

Waddock, S. A. (1995). *Not by schools alone: Sharing responsibility for America's education reform.* Westport, CN: Praeger.

Wagner, P. J. (1992). *Building support networks for schools.* Santa Barbara, CA: ABC-Clio.

Wahler, R. G. (1980). The insular mother: Her problems in parent-child treatment. *Journal of Applied Behavior Analysis, 13,* 207–219.

Wahler, R. G., & Sansbury, L. E. (1990). The monitoring skills of troubled mothers: Their problems in defining child deviance. *Journal of Abnormal Child Psychology, 18,* 577–589.

Wallerstein, J. S. (1983). Children of divorce: The psychological tasks of the child. *American Journal of Orthopsychiatry, 53,* 230–243.

Wallerstein, J. S., & Blakeslee, S. (1989). *Second chances: Men, women, and children a decade after divorce.* New York: Ticknor & Fields.

Wallerstein, J. S., & Kelly, J. B. (1980). Divorce counseling: A community service for families in the midst of divorce. In R. R. Abidin (Ed.), *Parent education and intervention handbook* (pp. 272–298). Springfield, IL: Charles C. Thomas.

Walsh, F. (1982). *Normal family processes.* New York: Guilford Press.

Walsh, F. (1983). The timing of symptoms and critical events in the family life cycle. In J.

Hansen & H. Liddle (Eds.), *Clinical implications of the family life cycle* (pp. 120–132). Rockville, MD: Aspen.

Walsh, F. (1996). The concept of family resilience: Crisis and challenge. *Family Process, 35,* 261–280.

Walsh, F., & McGoldrick, M. (Eds.). (1991). *Living beyond loss: Death in the family.* New York: Norton.

Walsh, M. E., & Buckley, M. A. (1994). Children's experiences of homelessness: Implications for school counselors. *Elementary School Guidance & Counseling, 29,* 4–15.

Walsh, W. M., & Williams, G. R. (1997). *Schools and family therapy: Using systems theory and family therapy in the resolution of school problems.* Springfield, IL: Charles C. Thomas.

Walters, M. (1972). We became family therapists. In A. Ferber, M. Mendelsohn, & A. Napier (Eds.), *Book of family therapy* (pp. 118–120). New York: Science House.

Wang, M., & Birch, J. (1984). Effective special education in regular classes. *Exceptional Children, 50,* 391–397.

Wang, M. C., & Gordon, E. W. (Eds.). (1994). *Educational resilience in inner-city America: Challenges and prospects.* Hillsdale, NJ: Lawrence Erlbaum.

Wang, M. C., & Haertel, G. D. (1995). Educational resilience. In M. C. Wang, M. C. Reynolds, & H. J. Walberg (Eds.), *Handbook of special and remedial education: Research and practice* (2nd ed., pp. 159–200). New York: Elsevier Science.

Wang, M. C., Haertel, G. D., & Walberg, H. J. (1994). Educational resilience in inner cities. In M. C. Wang & E. W. Gordon (Eds.), *Educational resilience in inner-city America: Challenges and prospects* (pp. 45–72). Hillsdale, NJ: Erlbaum.

Watzlawick, P., Weakland, J. H., & Fisch, R. (1974). *Change: Principles of problem formation and problem resolution.* New York: Norton.

Weber, J. L., & Stoneman, Z. (1986). Parental nonparticipation in program planning for mentally retarded children. An empirical investigation. *Applied Research in Mental Retardation, 7,* 359–369.

Wegscheider-Cruse, S. (1985). *Choicemaking.* Pompano Beach, FL: Health Communications.

Weinberg, R. B., & Mauksch, L. B. (1991). Examining family-of-origin influences in life at work. *Journal of Marital and Family Therapy, 17,* 233–242.

Weisner, T. S. (1982). Sibling interdependence and child caretaking: A cross-cultural view. In M. E. Lamb & B. Sutton-Smith (Eds.), *Sibling relationships* (pp. 305–328). Hillsdale, NJ: Erlbaum.

Weissbourd, R. (1996). *The vulnerable child: What really hurts America's children and what we can do about it.* Reading, MA: Addison-Wesley.

Wendell, H. V., & Leoni, D. (1986). *Multiethnic/multicultural materials.* Richmond: Virginia State Department of Education.

Wendt, R. N., & Ellenwood, A. E. (1994). From impotence to activation: Conjoint systemic change in the family and school. In M. Andolfi & R. Haber (Eds.), *Please help me with this family: Using consultants as resources in family therapy* (pp. 219–233). New York: Brunner/Mazel.

Werner, E. E. (1984). Resilient children. *Young Children, 40*(1), 68–72.

Werner, E. E. (1986). Resilient offspring of alcoholics: A longitudinal study from birth to age 18. *Journal of Studies on Alcohol, 47,* 34–40.

Werner, E. E. (1989). High risk children in young adulthood: A longitudinal study from birth to 32 years. *American Journal of Orthopsychiatry, 59,* 72–81.

Werner, E. E. (1993). The children of Kauai: Resiliency and recovery in adolescence and adulthood. *Journal of Adolescent Health, 13,* 262–268.

Werner, E. E. (1994). Overcoming the odds. *Journal of Developmental and Behavioral Pediatrics, 15,* 131–136.

Werner, E. E. (1995). Resilience in development. *Current Directions in Psychological Science, 4,* 81–85.

Werner, E. E. (1997). *Conceptual and methodological issues in studying minority children: An international perspective.* Paper presented at the Biennial Meeting of the Society for Research in Child Development (62nd, Washington, DC, April 3–6, 1997). (ERIC Document Reproduction Service No. ED 414 010)

Werner, E. E., & Smith, R. S. (1992). *Overcoming the odds: High risk children from birth to adulthood.* Ithaca, NY: Cornell University Press.

Werner, E. E., & Smith, R. S. (1998). *Vulnerable but invincible: A longitudinal study of resilient children and youth.* New York: Adams, Bannister, Cox.

West, J. (1990). Educational collaboration in the restructuring of schools. *Journal of Educational and Psychological Consultation, 1,* 23–40.

West, M. (1991). Peoplemaking: Self esteem or shame? In B. J. Brothers (Ed.), *Virginia Satir: Foundational ideas* (pp. 143–154). New York: Haworth Press.

Westfall, A., & Pisapia, J. (1994). *Students who defy the odds: A study of resilient at-risk students* (Research Brief No. 18). Richmond, VA: VCU Metropolitan Education Research Consortium.

Whetsell-Mitchell, J. (1995). *Rape of the innocent: Understanding and preventing child sexual abuse.* Washington, DC: Accelerated Development.

White, J. M. (1991). *Dynamics of family development.* New York: Guilford Press.

Whiteside, M. F. (1983). Families of remarriage: The weaving of many life cycle threads. In J. Hansen & H. Liddle (Eds.), *Clinical implications of the family life cycle* (pp. 100–119). Rockville, MD: Aspen.

Wickham-Searl, P. (1991). Mothers with a mission. In P. M. Ferguson, D. L. Ferguson, & S. J. Taylor (Eds.), *Interpreting disability: A qualitative reader* (pp. 251–274). New York: Teachers College Press.

Wikler, L. (1981). Chronic stresses of families of mentally retarded children. *Family Relations, 30,* 281–288.

Wikler, L., Wasow, M., & Hatfield, E. (1981). Chronic sorrow revisited: Parent vs. professional depiction of the adjustment of parents of mentally retarded children. *American Journal of Orthopsychiatry, 51,* 63–70.

Wilchesky, M., & Reynolds, T. (1986). The socially deficient LD child in context: A systems approach to assessment and treatment. *Journal of Learning Disabilities, 19,* 411–415.

Will, M. (1986). Educating children with learning problems: A shared responsibility. *Exceptional Children, 52,* 411–415.

Willie, C. V. (1991). *A new look at black families.* (4th ed.). Bayside, NY: General Hall.

Willis, D. J., Dobrec, A., & Sipes, D. S. B. (1992). Treating American Indian victims of abuse and neglect. In L. A. Vargas & J. D. Koss-Chioino (Eds.), *Working with culture: Psychotherapeutic interventions with ethnic minority children and adolescents* (pp. 276–299). San Francisco: Jossey-Bass.

Willis, D. J., Holden, E. W., & Rosenberg, M. (Eds.). (1992). *Prevention of child maltreatment: Developmental and ecological perspectives.* New York: Wiley.

Wilson, W. J. (1982). The declining significance of race. In N. R. Yetman & C. H. Steele (Eds.), *Majority and minority: The dynamics of race and ethnicity in American life* (3rd ed., pp. 385–392). Boston: Allyn & Bacon.

Winfield, L. F. (1991). Resilience, schooling and development in African-American youth. *Education and Urban Society, 24*(1), 53–63.

Winton, P. J. (1996). Understanding family concerns, priorities, and resources. In P. J. McWilliam, P. J. Winton, & E. R. Crais (Eds.), *Practical strategies for family-centered early intervention* (pp. 31–53). San Diego, CA: Singular Publishing Group.

Winton, P. J., & Turnbull, A. P. (1981). Parent involvement as viewed by parents of preschool handicapped children. *Topics in Early Childhood Special Education, 1,* 11–19.

Wlodkowski, R. J., & Ginsberg, M. B. (1995). A framework for culturally responsive teaching. *Educational Leadership, 53*(1), 17–21.

Wolfe, D. A., Wekerle, C., Gough, R., Reitzel-Jaffe, D., Grasley, C., Pittman, A., Lefebvre, L., & Stumpf, J. (1996). *The youth relationships manual: A group approach with adolescents for the prevention of woman abuse and the promotion of healthy relationships.* Thousand Oaks, CA: Sage.

Wolfe, D. A., Wekerle, C., Reitzel, D., & Gough, R. (1995). Strategies to address violence in the lives of high-risk youth. In E. Peled, P. G. Jaffe, & J. Edleson (Eds.), *Ending the cycle of violence: Community responses to children of battered women* (pp. 255–274). Thousand Oaks, CA: Sage.

Wolfe, D. A., Wekerle, C., & Scott, K. (1997). *Alternatives to violence: Empowering youth to develop healthy relationships.* Thousand Oaks, CA: Sage.

Wolin, S. J., & Wolin, S. (1993). *The resilient self: How survivors of troubled families rise above adversity.* New York: Villard.

Wolin, S., & Wolin, S. J. (1996). Beating the odds: Some kids who have been dealt a losing hand end up winning the game. What can we learn from them? *Learning, 25,*(1), 66–68.

Wynne, E. A., & Walberg, H. J. (1995). The virtues of intimacy in education. *Educational Leadership, 53*(3), 53–54.

Yoder, D. I., Retish, E., & Wade, R. (1996). Service learning: Meeting student and community needs. *Teaching Exceptional Children, 28*(4), 14–18.

York-Barr, J. (1996). *Creating inclusive school communities: Module 4 collaboration—Redefining roles, practices, and structures.* Baltimore, MD: Paul H. Brookes.

Yoshida, P. K., Fenton, K. S., Kaufman, M. J., & Maxwell, J. P. (1978). Parental involvement in the special education pupil planning process: The school's perspective. *Exceptional Children, 44,* 531–534.

Yoshida, R., Fenton, K., Maxwell, J., & Kaufman, M. (1978). Group decision making in the planning team process: Myth or reality? *Journal of School Psychology, 16,* 237–244.

Youngblade, L. M., & Belsky, J. (1990). Social and emotional consequences of child maltreatment. In R. T. Ammerman & M. Hersen (Eds.), *Children at risk: An evaluation of factors contributing to child abuse and neglect* (pp. 109–146). New York: Plenum Press.

Young-Eisendrath, P. (1996). *The gifts of suffering: Finding insight, compassion, and renewal.* Reading, MA: Addison-Wesley.

Youngstrom, N. (1990, October). Therapy in the schools aids children of divorce. *APA Monitor,* p. 22.

Ysseldyke, J., Algozzine, B., & Allen, D. (1982). Participation of regular education teachers in special education team decision making. *Exceptional Children, 48,* 365–367.

Ysseldyke, J. E., Christenson, S., & Kovaleski, J. F. (1994). Identifying students' instructional needs in the context of classroom and home environments. *Teaching Exceptional Children, 26*(3), 37–41.

Yung, B. R., & Hammond, W. R. (1994). Native Americans. In L. D. Eron, J. H. Gentry, & P. Schlegel (Eds.), *Reason to hope: A psychosocial perspective on violence and youth* (pp. 133–144). Washington, DC: American Psychological Association.

Zetlin, A. G. (1985). Mentally retarded teenagers: Adolescent behavior disturbance and its relation to family environment. *Child Psychiatry and Human Development, 15,* 243–254.

Zill, N., & Nord, C. W. (1994). *Running in place: How American families are faring in a changing economy and an individualistic society.* Washington, DC: Child Trends.

Zuvarin, S. J., & Starr, R. H. (1991). Psychosocial characteristics of mothers of physically abused and neglected children: Do they differ by race? In R. L. Hampton (Ed.), *Black family violence: Current research and theory* (pp. 35–70). Lexington, MA: D.C. Heath.

Author Index

Subject Index

Note: Page references followed by *f* indicate
    figures. Those followed by *t* indicate
    tables.

A

Abusive families, at-risk students from.
    See Incestuous/sexual abuse families,
    at-risk students from; Neglectful, abusive,
    and violent families, at-risk students from
Addictive families, at-risk students from
    behavioral patterns of, 156-157
    characteristics of, 154
    child concerns in, 155-156
    parental impact in, 154-155
    support, prevention, and intervention,
        157-158
Adolescents, family life cycle and families with,
    25, 27, 34-36
Adoption life cycle, 19. *See also* Family life
    cycle
Adoptive families, at-risk students from,
    141-146
    adoption adjustment for, 143-145
    special-needs adoptions and, 142
    support and intervention for, 145-146
African Americans, and cultural values of at-risk
    students, 105-106
Alcoholic families, at-risk students from. *See*
    Addictive families, at-risk students from

Asian (Pacific) Americans, and cultural values of
    at-risk students, 106-108
Assessment, of family systems, 413-414
At-risk students
    from dysfunctional families
        (*See* Dysfunctional families, at-risk
        students from)
    and environmental factors (*See* Ethnic
        differences, of at-risk students;
        Socioeconomic differences, of at-risk
        students)
    from nontraditional families
        (*See* Nontraditional families, at-risk
        students from)
    resilience in (*See* Resilience, in at-risk
        students)
    school-home interactions for (*See* Family-
        school interactions, at-risk and special-
        needs students and)
    team functioning for (*See* Team functioning,
        for at-risk students and their families;
        Team functioning, for special-needs
        students)
AVANTA Network, 384

B

Bateson, Gregory. *See* Strategic family therapy
    model